ACCOUNTING, ORGANIZATIONS, AND
INSTITUTIONS

Accounting, Organizations, and Institutions

Essays in Honour of Anthony Hopwood

Edited by

CHRISTOPHER S. CHAPMAN,

DAVID J. COOPER, AND PETER B. MILLER

OXFORD
UNIVERSITY PRESS

OXFORD

UNIVERSITY PRESS

Great Clarendon Street, Oxford OX2 6DP

Oxford University Press is a department of the University of Oxford.
It furthers the University's objective of excellence in research, scholarship,
and education by publishing worldwide in

Oxford New York

Auckland Cape Town Dar es Salaam Hong Kong Karachi
Kuala Lumpur Madrid Melbourne Mexico City Nairobi
New Delhi Shanghai Taipei Toronto

With offices in

Argentina Austria Brazil Chile Czech Republic France Greece
Guatemala Hungary Italy Japan Poland Portugal Singapore
South Korea Switzerland Thailand Turkey Ukraine Vietnam

Oxford is a registered trade mark of Oxford University Press
in the UK and in certain other countries

Published in the United States
by Oxford University Press Inc., New York

© Oxford University Press, 2009

The moral rights of the authors have been asserted
Database right Oxford University Press (maker)

First published 2009

British Library Cataloguing in Publication Data

Data available

Library of Congress Cataloging in Publication Data

Data available

Typeset by SPI Publisher Services, Pondicherry, India
Printed in Great Britain
on acid-free paper by
CPI Antony Rowe, Chippenham, Wiltshire

ISBN 978–0–19–954635–0 (Hbk.)

3 5 7 9 10 8 6 4 2

This book is dedicated to the long-standing and ongoing foresight, energy, intellectual curiosity, institution building, and insight of Anthony G. Hopwood, without whom accounting as a discipline would not be the creative and respected social science that it is today.

Contents

List of Figures

List of Tables

Preface and Acknowledgement

This book is dedicated to Anthony Hopwood who continues to make a major contribution to accounting and social science generally.

In most academic circles, Anthony is best known for his founding and continuing position as Editor in Chief of *Accounting, Organizations and Society*. It is perhaps difficult in retrospect to appreciate the innovative intellectual position adopted for the journal at its inception. At the time of its founding in 1975, accounting journals were largely wedded to professional concerns and understandings, and a rather crude positivism, typically dependent on simple-minded economics and statistics. *Accounting, Organizations and Society* both carved out and helped constitute a new body of research. Of course, new intellectual developments have important antecedents, and in our introductory essay we indicate some of these. But this in no way diminishes Anthony's profound and continuing contribution; instead, it highlights the wide-ranging and extensive scholarship that was required to produce a new vision for accounting research.

The journal is now ranked among the top four accounting journals in the world. This is due in large part to Anthony's careful editorial guidance, and to the vigorous and rigorous intellectual community that it has engendered. He has taken an active editorial role, through promoting specialized and innovative conferences and editorial statements that help to identify emerging and potential areas of research. In so doing, he has also encouraged and advised many academics in their research, demanding the highest levels of scholarship, while stimulating them with his pithy and probing questions, encouraging that difficult mixture of creativity and detail that comprises real scholarship. In many respects, this collection is a testimony to his intellectual influence and widespread respect throughout the social sciences.

His own research has been enormously influential, stimulating the creation of a major body of interdisciplinary research investigating the roles of accounting in organizations and society. His Ph.D. at the University of Chicago was a detailed empirical examination of the use of accounting information in performance evaluation, informed by a mix of social psychology and the sociology of groups. That study stimulated a body of research on the reliance on accounting in performance measurement, work that continues today. On returning to the United Kingdom at the beginning of the 1970s, Anthony extended his interest in sociological, institutional, and philosophical analyses, but with a very firm grounding in the overall project of explaining the roles of accounting in organizations and society. His project with several colleagues on social accounting leads to the conceptualization of accounting as constitutive, not simply representational (Burchell et al. 1980). This understanding was substantially elaborated and illustrated through an examination of the intersections between accounting change and wider social developments (Burchell et al. 1985). The success of *Accounting, Organizations and Society* and his efforts at institution building, which we discuss below, meant that he had less time for major empirical projects but this did not stop him reflecting in insightful ways about the complexities of accounting change through his informal interactions with senior managers (Hopwood 1987) and regulators (Hopwood 1994). These, and several of his other academic publications, are amongst the most widely cited academic accounting articles in the world.

As well as his own prolific and influential research and publications, Anthony has made an outstanding contribution to building accounting and management academic institutions in Europe and in the United Kingdom. He has played a major role at a number of prestigious British universities, most notably the Manchester Business School, London Business School, the London School of Economics and Political Science, and the Saïd Business School (Oxford University). His achievements at Oxford culminated in a very successful period as Dean, building the School into a leading business school. Recognizing the importance of a European forum for accounting research (again at a time when such a concept was a radical idea) from the 1970s he actively participated in the European Institute for Advanced Studies in Management and for a number of years served as its President. He was a founder of the European Accounting Association, and has played a major role (including President) throughout its nearly thirty-year history, helping it to achieve its status as a major, professional academic body with over 2,000 members. He was very active in the formation and management of *European Accounting Review*.

One of the problems of accounting in academia has been the education of young scholars. Anthony has taken on a consistent and influential role in doctoral education. His own doctoral students have authored several of the chapters in this collection and many of those who learned their craft under Anthony are now active researchers and hold senior appointments in Universities in Sweden, the United Kingdom, Italy, the United States, and Australia. He has encouraged networks of junior researchers, especially in Europe, most notably through the European Institute for Advanced Studies in Management and his creation of, and subsequent active participation in, the doctoral colloquium for the European Accounting Association.

In recent years, Anthony has become more and more concerned about the careerism, specialization, and introverted nature of accounting and management education and research. He has lobbied and written passionately about the dangers of the increasing preoccupation with research rankings in Universities, and the crude quantification that this typically depends on. Like so much else, he writes about such matters with concern, insight, and an appreciation of the difficulty of finding solutions. His suspicion of quick fixes and simple solutions reinforce his long-standing commitment to mutual tolerance and a respect for intellectual diversity. These values permeate this volume and we trust they will continue to illuminate the paths of future research on accounting.

Acknowledgement

David Cooper is pleased to acknowledge the financial support of the Certified General Accountants of Alberta and the Social Sciences and Humanities Research Council. A volume such as this could not be constructed without a network of colleagues and assistants. All the chapters were subject to review and we thank the anonymous reviewers for their willingness to provide careful and supportive reviews under considerable time pressure. We are pleased to acknowledge the help of Sherry Wang and Dwayne Loewen (University of Alberta). Sammye Haigh at Elsevier has been a source of moral and financial support. Finally, we appreciate the editorial dedication and thoughtfulness of David Musson at Oxford University Press.

Imperial College Business School,   Christopher S. Chapman
Imperial College London

School of Business, University of Alberta   David J. Cooper

Department of Accounting,   Peter B. Miller
London School of Economic and Political Science

List of Abbreviations

ABC	Activity Based Costing
AICPA	American Institute of Certified Public Accountants
ANT	Actor network theory
AOS	*Accounting, Organizations and Society*
APB	Accounting Principles Board
BCBS	Basle Committee on Banking Supervision
BI	Business Intelligence
BIS	Bank of International Settlements
BRS	Business Risk Audit
CAS	Contribution Accounting System
CDO	Collateralized debt obligation
CDS	Credit Default Swaps
CGP	Capital guarantee products
CR	Collaborative relationship
EC	European Commission
ECG	European Contact Group
ERP	Enterprise Resources Planning
EU	European Union
FASB	Financial Accounting Standards Board
FDA	Food and Drug Administration
FEE	Fédération des Experts Compables Européens
FoF	Forum of Firms
FSD	Financial Services Department
FSF	Financial Stability Forum
GAA	Global Accounting Alliance
GDP	Gross Domestic Product
GPPC	Global Public Policy Committee
GPPS	Global Public Policy Symposium
GSC	Global Steering Committee
IAASB	International Auditing and Assurance Standards Board
IAIS	International Association of Insurance Supervisors

IAPC	International Auditing Practices Committee
IAS	International Auditing Standard
IASC	International Accounting Standards Committee
IASB	International Accounting Standards Board
ICAEW	Institute of Chartered Accountants in England and Wales
IFAC	International Federation of Accountants
IFAD	International Forum on Accountancy Development
IFIAR	International Forum of Independent Audit Regulators
IFRS	International Financial Reporting Standards
ILG	IFAC Leadership Group
IMF	International Monetary Fund
IOSCO	International Organization of Securities Commissions
ISA	International Standard on Auditing
JFSD	Jersey's Financial Services Department
LLP	Limited Liability Partnership
MD&A	Management's Discussion and Analysis
NIFA	New international financial architecture
OEM	Original Equipment Manufacturer
OFC	Offshore Financial Centre
PCAOB	Public Company Accounting Oversight Board
POB	Public oversight board
PIOB	Public Interest Oversight Board
ROSC	Reports on Standards and Codes
SAB	Staff Accounting Bulletin
SAS	Statement on Auditing Standards
SEC	Securities and Exchange Commission
SMA	Strategic Management Accounting
SSA	Social Studies of Accounting
SSAP	Statements of Standard Accounting Practice
STS	Studies of science and technology
TAC	Transnational Auditors Committee
UBS	Union des Banques Suisses
US GAAP	US Generally Accepted Accounting Principles
VA	Value Added

1

Linking Accounting, Organizations, and Institutions

Christopher S. Chapman, David J. Cooper, and Peter B. Miller

A simple proposition underpins the title of this volume and the papers collected here: that there is much to be gained by looking at the relations among accounting, organizations, and institutions. This of course begs many questions, not least what is meant by each of the three nouns that make up the title. For the moment, we shall adopt some rudimentary definitions without being too sensitive to nomenclature and the intellectual traditions that are attached to certain words. By accounting, we mean all those spatially and historically varying calculative practices—ranging from budgeting to fair value accounting—that allow accountants and others to describe and act on entities, processes, and persons. By organizations, we mean not only those formally constituted and bounded entities—such as firms, not-for-profit, and government organizations responsible for providing services—but the plethora of less formal and less bounded associations of actors and activities, such as industry associations, inter-firm alliances, and even ad hoc advisory groups. And, by institutions, we mean those stabilized and legitimized ideas and groupings, together with their attendant bodies of knowledge and ways of classifying, that are taken for granted and accorded authority (more or less) by common assent.

This tripartite schema leaves out much of course, and it also risks overstating the boundaries between each component and the solidity of each.[1] For instance, at what point does an organization become an institution (and vice

David Cooper is pleased to acknowledge the financial support of the Certified General Accountants of Alberta and the Social Sciences and Humanities Research Council.

[1] We also limit our focus largely to the field of accounting research that is represented and constituted by a number of journals, most notably *Accounting, Organizations and Society, Critical Perspectives on Accounting* and *Accounting, Auditing and Accountability Journal*. That means that this chapter and volume tend to underplay the substantial contributions from research inspired by conventional economics and psychology.

versa), how can we understand accounting practices without recourse to the languages and rationales that mobilize them as practices, and to what extent is accounting itself an 'institution'? These are no doubt important questions, but we think for the time being that a highly simplified schema helps us to at least pose some questions that are generic to the contributions to this volume and the research tradition they exemplify.

Many before us have adopted similar terminology and addressed similar issues. Anthony Hopwood, in particular, has argued for at least three decades that we should pay attention to the organizational and social contexts in which accounting operates (Hopwood 1978).[2] He has also argued that we should attend to the 'external' origins of 'internal' accounts, that we should not see 'context' as something external to organizations, but as something that passes through them, and that we should see accounting as both shaped by, and shaping, wider social processes (Hopwood 1983; Burchell et al. 1985).

Our arguments here are very much in line with this way of thinking, as are the contributions to this volume. We suggest that accounting, organizations, and institutions should be viewed as fundamentally interrelated and interdependent, that the links among them should be viewed as mutually constitutive. Accounting, one might say, is simultaneously social and technical. Put differently, the roles of accounting co-emerge with the social relations that it helps make possible. To paraphrase and adapt Hacking (1992): if our accounts of the world fit reasonably snugly with the world we observe, this is less because we have found out how the world is, than because we have tailored each to fit the other. The calculative practices of accounting here are primary, but understood in a specific sense: the objects upon which they act are the correlates and constructs of its practices, rather than something pre-existing or given. As Hopwood (2007) has recently re-emphasized, those who claim to know what accounting *is* are simply wrong. Accounting changes, and those changes are part and parcel of changing social and economic relations. Accounting is a craft without an essence. It has changed significantly across time, adopting new forms, devices, and roles. We need to study those changes, rather than treat the present forms of accounting as immutable.

This broad sensitivity to the nature of accounting and its implications for the ways of studying, understanding, and intervening in accounting can be found in all the chapters of this volume. Of course, they individually approach these wider questions in different ways and with different emphases. Some focus more on the development of particular themes, whereas others focus more on emergent and future research themes. Some focus on methodology while others stress modes of intervention or understanding. Both

---

[2] Lowe and Tinker (1977) is another early (albeit less influential) example of these arguments.

individually and collectively, however, they demonstrate the interest and relevance of a concern with the links between accounting, organizations, and institutions.

In framing the writings brought together within this volume in this way, we mean to address not only accounting researchers, many of whom may view these general arguments as well established. We also mean to address a wider social science audience that is now paying increasing attention to the ways in which social and economic life is constituted to an important extent through the calculative practices that give it visibility. This is perhaps one of the greatest achievements of the research that is gathered here, and the much wider set of writings that it draws upon and connects with: to have contributed to the creation of a distinctive field of research within the social sciences; to have borrowed concepts and categories from elsewhere and adapted them; but, equally, to have given something back to social science, having engaged with a phenomenon—accounting—that seems to be of ever-increasing significance in contemporary society. Somewhat belatedly, social scientists are beginning to pay attention to the important roles that accounting plays in so many aspects of social and economic life. Accounting is no longer perceived as 'mere' bookkeeping, as a set of records that neutrally records the facts of economic life. Accounting has finally arrived, or, to be precise, arrived *back* on the social science agenda.

A quarter of a century ago, such claims for accounting research could not have been voiced, even if 'behavioural accounting' was in full swing by then. And, a quarter of a century before that, even behavioural accounting—the idea that accounting should be studied in terms of social psychological dynamics—was novel. This is a remarkable transformation of a discipline that increasingly is seen as a legitimate social scientific endeavour. The contributors to this volume, along with many others, have brought this about. The purpose of this introduction is to step back a little, to reflect on how far the social scientific understanding of accounting has developed in the past half century.[3] Our reflections on developments in the areas of accounting research that we examine lead us to ask two basic questions. First, what are the historical and emerging relations between an important subset of the social sciences and accounting research, and what implications do these interrelations have for the future. Second, what interesting questions are raised by stressing the links between accounting, organizations, and institutions; for example, whether conventional boundaries within accounting (such as the

---

[3] This opportunity to reflect on the history of the discipline is also combined with a desire to remember and build on some of the classical founders. As Adler (2009) argues, 'a social science that forgets its founders is lost' (2009: 3).

distinction between financial and management accounting) are helpful in understanding the effects of accounting on organizations and institutions. Finally, in the conclusion we consider some challenges currently facing accounting, both as an academic discipline and as a practice.

CLASSICAL CONCEPTIONS OF ACCOUNTING AS A SOCIAL SCIENCE

Max Weber, writing in the first two decades of the twentieth century, considered accounting to be at the heart of the rationalization of society under capitalism. Weber argued that capitalism should be understood as the continuous pursuit of profit by means of 'rational, capitalistic enterprise' (Weber 1930: 17). This 'rational' pursuit of profit required as its counterpart calculations in terms of capital. The modern, rational organization of capitalistic enterprise would not have been possible, Weber argued, without the calculative practice of book-keeping. Weber was concerned with the conditions which gave rise to and enabled the spread of the 'specifically modern calculating attitude' (Weber 1956: 86). Accounting, in the sense of both budgetary management and capital accounting, was central to his analysis of the sociological conditions of economic activity. Calculation was the mechanism by which rational economic provision could be conducted, and capital accounting was the form of monetary accounting peculiar to rational economic profit-making.

Weber defined an economic enterprise as 'autonomous action capable of orientation to capital accounting' (Weber 1956: 91), and stated that 'this orientation takes place by means of "calculation"' (Weber 1956: 91). To this extent, he placed a concern with calculation at the heart of a sociological analysis of economic activity. Calculation was located mid-way between rational profit-making enterprises and the opportunities available to them, and helped mediate between them. Double-entry bookkeeping, according to Weber (1956: 92), was 'the most highly developed' form of bookkeeping, in so far as it permits 'a check in the technically most perfect manner on the profitability of each individual step or measure' (p. 93). Sombart (1902) put forward an even stronger argument concerning the links between double-entry bookkeeping and capitalism, speculating whether it was double-entry bookkeeping that had enabled the rise to capitalism.

Prior to Weber, Marx had also signalled the importance of the relationship between accounting or bookkeeping and capitalism. Marx remarked in Volume I of *Capital* that one of the first tasks of an aspiring capitalist is to keep a set of books (Marx 1974*a*: 81). In Volume II of *Capital*, where Marx deals with the transformations of the forms of capital from commodities into money, and from money into commodities, he addresses the issue of the labour-time expended in bookkeeping, which is depicted as a deduction from the productive process, albeit an essential part of the circulation process (Marx 1974*b*: 136). In so far as capital seeks its own reproduction, this deduction from what Marx regarded as the real process of production is an essential part of the capitalistic process. And as the production process becomes ever more social in character, and loses its individual character, bookkeeping becomes ever more necessary.

Marx did not accord accounting as central a role as did Weber. Nonetheless, when placed in the context of a theory of value and the concept of mode of production, Marx gave accounting an important place alongside other political interventions in the relations of production. In Marx's writings, accounting is accorded a macro-structural role, both shaping and reproducing the nature of capitalist relations of production. To this extent, Marx and Weber occupy a similar terrain. For both, accounting helps shape the social and economic relations that define a society, although these classical social scientists tended to equate accounting with book keeping.

But, following these bold pronouncements concerning the link between accounting and societal development, accounting was more or less ignored by social scientists for almost half a century. It was not until the 1950s that the interest of social scientists in accounting resurfaced. And, when it did, the large economic and sociological questions about accounting that Weber, Marx, and Sombart had posed were replaced by more micro-level concerns with the role of accounting in organizational design and the operation of groups.[4]

The role of accounting in organizational design is signalled by a study by the influential US Controllership Foundation, which commissioned a leading group of management theorists from Carnegie Mellon University (Simon et al. 1954) to study the organizational location of controllers. The study was grounded in the emerging theories of the bounded rationality of organizational decision-making and the importance of intra-organizational politics and the local allegiances of managers in large dispersed organizations. These theories connect strongly with concerns about the functioning (and dysfunctions) of bureaucracy, exploring the limits of Weberian conceptions of instrumental rationality and the limits of viewing organizations as well-functioning

---

[4] There are some prominent antecedents to the developments discussed in this chapter. In the English language tradition, authors such as Scott, Devine, and Chambers are worth mentioning as accountants who took social sciences seriously. Similar examples can no doubt be found in the non-English literature.

machines. It examined whether controllers should be part of the centralized management of the organization, reporting on the actions of local management teams, or should be part of the decision-making group of local management teams, providing specific information for local decisions.[5] That study also identified different purposes of accounting, emphasizing its multiple roles, for example in decision-making for the future as well as providing a scorecard of the past.

The role of accounting in the operation of groups is signalled by Chris Argyris's (1952) influential study on the impact of budgets on people (also commissioned by the Controllership Foundation). Argyris examined what 'budget people' think of budgets, and how factory supervisors think very differently about budgets. He combined a study of accounting practices with a sociological concern with groups. Rather than taking groups as given and self-evident, he described the interaction between people and budgets as one of the *creation* of groups. If management puts increased pressure on individuals via budgets, he argued, groups are likely to form. These groups can in turn help absorb the increased pressures placed by management on individuals. Once formed, such groups can persist even after the initial pressure to produce them has disappeared. In proposing that the interaction of people and accounting practices be understood in this way, Argyris was drawing on research that emphasized groups and their dynamics.

'Behavioural accounting' is a common label for describing the wave of studies that appeared from the late 1950s onwards, and which built on these developments in the analysis of groups and organizational design. It examined in differing ways the interrelations between accounting, organizational design, and group relations. For example, Dalton (1959) showed how pressure to meet cost targets, when combined with reward schemes based on success in meeting such targets, can result in the distortion of records. Historians of business such as Chandler and Litterer pointed out the crucial role of accounting calculations in developments in organizational design, particularly the creation of multidivisional enterprises. Wildavsky (1964) examined the interaction between calculations and politics in his study of budget processes, particularly in government organizations. Ridgway (1956) offered analysis of different types of performance measurement systems, pointing out, many decades before it became a common observation, that single, accounting-based measures often had undesirable performance effects. While these examples involve researchers who would not define themselves as

---

[5] This is an issue that has resurfaced in post-SOX debates about corporate governance and the role of controllers in recent corporate scandals.

accountants, increasing numbers of accounting researchers began to develop 'behavioural accounting'.

Within accounting, Shillinglaw (1964) and Gordon (1964) explored the accounting implications of developments in operational research and economics on the optimal design of organizations and management control systems (Bonini et al. 1964). They discussed the interrelations between responsibility accounting, internal performance reporting, transfer pricing, and organizational design. The organizational and behavioural aspects of budgeting became a central preoccupation for many researchers in the 1960s and early 1970s, partly stimulated by the behavioural theory of the firm (Cyert and March 1963), which offered insightful comments about the role of routines and standard operating procedures in organizational resource allocation (e.g. Lowe and Shaw 1968). Increasingly, accounting research traditions emphasized positivist approaches to research, particularly the value of laboratory experiments. In the area of management accounting, Becker and Green (1962) used laboratory settings to examine the interrelations between the cohesiveness of work groups and the acceptance of budget goals, and the impact of this interrelation on outcomes. A series of influential experiments was published under the editorship of Tom Burns (1972, 1979) at Ohio State. However, the use of a wider range of research methods and approaches to epistemology was also sustained. Hofstede (1968) depicted the budgetary process as a game which people play for its own sake, the key ingredient of which, he argued, was the 'game spirit' with which managers entered the 'budget game'. And this line of reasoning was extended significantly by Hopwood (1974), who identified three distinct ways of using budgetary information, styles he called 'budget constrained', 'profit conscious', and 'non-accounting'. Only the 'profit conscious' style succeeded in producing an intelligent concern with costs, one that went without the manipulation of accounting reports and general deterioration in relationships between managers and those to whom they reported.

Two decades of research into the behavioural aspects of budgeting and related evaluation mechanisms transformed the discipline of accounting and placed it firmly within the social sciences. Accounting was no longer to be perceived as a purely technical process, but was to be viewed as organizational and behavioural. But, despite the advance this represented, this was a highly constrained view of the roles of accounting, one that was limited to studying accounting *within* organizations only, and often at the micro level of groups and group dynamics. Across these two decades, the links between accounting and organizations became less prominent and institutions were simply absent. From the mid-1970 onwards, however, things began to change in line with wider developments in the social sciences.

MAKING ORGANIZATIONS MORE COMPLEX

Accounting researchers enthusiastically adopted an approach to behavioural accounting that emphasized the psychological rather than the sociological and political basis of behaviour. Some, however, continued to be inspired by the earlier focus on organizational design, and looked to sociology and political science to understand how and in what ways accounting was implicated in wider organizational processes. In so doing, they opened up analysis that stressed the complex nature both of organizations and accounting. Particularly influential were those social scientists that empirically examined the operation of bureaucracies, and applied ideas from systems thinking and from theories of bounded rationality to organizational decision-making.

At a time when large organizations were increasingly dominating economic and social life, empirical studies conducted by Woodward, Burns and Stalker, and the 'Aston Group' in the United Kingdom, Crozier in France, and Lawrence and Lorsch and Perrow in the United States drew on systems thinking and the idea that organizations have environments that can affect organizational functioning. They pointed out that contingencies, such as technology and environmental change, could impact the optimal design of organizations. This gave rise to what came to be called the 'contingency' approach, which investigated the impact of a range of environmental factors on organizational design and ultimately organizational performance. Galbraith (1973) offered a synthesis of the various factors identified (such as production technology, size, strategy, and various conceptualizations of an organization's environment) that placed accounting at the centre of organizational design, positing that these environmental factors all reflected aspects of uncertainty and that the effectiveness of an organization to manage uncertainty was dependent on its ability to handle information.

The contingency approach was enthusiastically applied by those seeking to both understand and prescribe accounting system design. Early empirical applications include Khandwalla (1971); Bruns and Waterhouse (1975); and Hayes (1977); and the innovative essay by Gordon and Miller (1976). These studies demonstrated that simple prescriptions for the design of organizations were unlikely to be universally valid. They also emphasized the importance of fitting the internal accounting systems, whether we are referring to cost, responsibility, budgeting, or performance evaluation and incentive systems, to the overall logic of organizational design. Although these studies were subsequently the subject of criticism (Cooper 1981), they demonstrate a commitment to studying the overall package of accounting technologies (Otley 1980) in its organizational context. This project continued in the

1980s with studies such as Merchant (1981) and Chenhall and Morris (1986) further developing our understanding of the contingent nature of accounting. Developments in this literature offer increasingly complex views of accounting and organizations, aided by further theorization of the role of accounting coupled with new statistical techniques such as structural equation modelling.

One of the most influential developments was inspired by Simons (1987), who sought a more detailed understanding of organizations and accounting after being puzzled by his own quantitative results on the relation between strategy, innovation and design, and use of accounting systems. He carried out further research, combining qualitative, quantitative, and theoretical analysis, which resulted in his levers of control framework (Simons 1995). Just as Miles and Snow (1978) had previously triggered a stream of studies in the contingency literature by making the concept of strategy measurable, so the multiple and ever more complex measures of different types of control offered ways to move beyond limited notions of the role of accounting (Chapman 1997). More recent studies have become increasingly sensitive to the significance of the nature of communication patterns surrounding accounting systems and information. This has led to questioning of the continued fruitfulness of simple oppositions between stylizations of mechanistic and organic organization (e.g. Chenhall and Morris 1995) that had dominated contingency modelling in accounting.

Reviewing these developments, Ahrens and Chapman (2004) suggest the notion of enabling control to overcome some of the challenges to be faced in researching complex organizations and complex accounting systems and calculations. Widener (2007) demonstrates the continuing value of the levers of control framework, particularly when it incorporates the costs and benefits of management control activities. Together with the 'business systems' approach of Whitley (1999), all these developments point to the importance of detailed understandings of organizations and accounting and the associated role of careful field studies that capture the complexities of organizations and internal accounting systems and practices.

ACCOUNTING AS AN ORGANIZATIONAL
AND INSTITUTIONAL PRACTICE

Periodizing is a risky business, but it has benefits. For the case in hand, it helps identify turning-points in research agendas, highlights the limits of previous ways of posing questions, and allows the scale and potential of a new research

agenda to gain sharper relief. If 'behavioural accounting' helped place accounting research within the social sciences for about two decades until the mid-
1970s, it was also constraining as a paradigm. In focusing almost exclusively on
things that happened within organizations, it left out much. The need to alter
this was firmly and unambiguously stated by Hopwood (1978). This was a call
to arms to address the interrelations between accounting change and large-
scale social change. Hopwood had been a strong advocate of the importance of
studying the uses of accounting within organizations. But, he suggested, this
needed to be matched by attending to the pressures arising in the wider
social and economic environment, and how they impacted on accounting
(Hopwood 1974). In so far as much contemporary accounting reflects the
ethos of capitalism, so too would one expect the forms and philosophies of
accounting to change in line with changes in the social and political environment. The initial editorial of *Accounting, Organizations and Society* referred to
an 'urgent need for research which can provide a basis for seeing accounting as
both a social and organizational phenomenon' (Hopwood 1976: 3), arguing
that studies of power, influence, and control should complement studies of the
behavioural aspects of accounting within organizations.

Research traditions do not change overnight, however. Indeed, it was to be
a few more years before things began to alter noticeably and Hopwood (1978)
could still comment that there was little research that addressed the wider
social and political influences on accounting. The more social—psychological
focus that was characteristic of the North American research tradition continued to dominate, in contrast to European approaches that drew increasingly on research traditions that emphasized broader influences that went
beyond the boundaries of groups and organizations. Even as late as 1980,
Hopwood argued, along with others, that a sociological analysis of accounting
that could blend successfully micro-level and macro-level concerns remained
largely an aspiration. Indeed, it was not even clear what concepts and issues
would guide such a research agenda.

Some suggestions, however, were put forward in an influential paper that
sought to identify the roles of accounting in organizations and society (Burchell et al. 1980). A wide range of hitherto neglected issues should, it was argued,
be brought within the purview of accounting researchers, and the basic
premise on which accounting was analysed should change. Rather than seeing
the technical dimensions of accounting as independent of social dynamics,
they should be seen as interrelated. Just as Argyris had argued nearly three
decades earlier that accounting practices can create groups, so too, it was
argued, can accounting create other social forms. The role of accounting in
creating particular organizational visibilities, in impacting particular patterns
of organizational and social management, and in affecting structures of power

needed to be addressed. The analysis of accounting within organizations should be connected explicitly with the analysis of more general forms of economic and social management. Accounting should, that is to say, no longer be conceived as a purely organizational phenomenon. Particular emphasis was placed on the institutional nature of accounting. The earlier tradition of sociological enquiry concerning accounting, as embodied in the writings of Marx and Weber, was appealed to as having identified issues worthy of systematic study. Processes of rationalization should be addressed, as should the mythical, symbolic, and ritualistic roles of accounting (Cooper 1983). Studies of the organizational roles of accounting should, it was argued, be complemented by studies of the societal and institutional roles of accounting.

A MULTIPLICATION OF METHODOLOGIES

From 1980 onwards, the range of methodologies drawn upon by researchers broadened, as did the focus. Institutional structures and processes, and their interrelations with accounting practices, were given increasing attention. A concern with organizations remained, but this was now paired with an interest in the social and institutional aspects of accounting (Hopwood and Miller 1994). In part this reflects the increasing attention to the power of institutions such as the modern state, accounting standard setting and other regulatory bodies, professional associations and, more recently, multinational accounting firms and transnational organizations (Cooper and Robson 2006; Suddaby et al. 2007).

A diverse range of researchers began to focus increasingly on examining the interplay between accounting, organizations, and institutions, partly as these institutions were seen by a range of social scientists as prominent actors in society. In the process, the discipline of accounting was reshaped, as it became more reflective both of the methodologies to be used and the objects to which they should be applied. Of course, researchers did this in very different ways. There was a multiplication or proliferation of methodologies used, in line with what was happening in the social sciences more generally. But there was more. For, along with this multiplication of methodologies, the domain of accounting research itself broadened. If the pressures on accounting were now seen to extend beyond the enterprise, things worked in the other direction too—accounting itself came to be seen as contributing to the shaping of those social and economic relations themselves. The distinction between management accounting as a matter of 'internal' reporting, and financial accounting as a matter of 'external' reporting, no longer worked so neatly, if it ever did. External accounts, and requirements for them, were seen to influence internal accounts (Miller and O'Leary 1994, 2007). Reciprocally, internal accounts could influence wider social relations (Miller and O'Leary 1987). Finally, this was to have profound effects for accounting research.

To characterize this pluralization of approaches to the analysis of accounting from 1980 onwards again requires that we simplify drastically. But, hopefully, this simplification allows us to appreciate not only methodological diversity but also the diversification of substantive analyses of accounting. Once opened up to a wider social science agenda, accounting turned out to be more interesting and significant than many had previously realized. It is a much larger endeavour, and one that has a far-reaching role in shaping social and economic life. We identify four strands of research that contributed to this expansion of the domain of accounting research from 1980 onwards: first, a concern with the *institutional environments* of accounting; second, a *political economy* of accounting; third, an *ethnography* of accounting; and fourth, a concern with the roles of accounting in *governing economic life*.

The Institutional Environments of Accounting

The ground was already laid within organization theory and sociology for the analysis of the institutional environments of accounting. In the late 1970s, the study of the institutionalized 'myth structure' (Meyer and Rowan 1977) of rationalized societies had emerged. Meyer and Rowan argued that prevailing theories neglected a concern with the legitimacy of rationalized formal structures, as distinct from day-to-day work activities. In so far as rationalized and impersonal prescriptions attribute a social purpose to technical activity, and specify the appropriate manner in which to pursue this activity, these rationalized prescriptions were worthy of study in their own right. Terming such prescriptions 'myths', their importance stems from the extent to which they become institutionalized, that is to say taken-for-granted ways of achieving organizational ends. Such myths, Meyer and Rowan argued, become binding on particular organizations, and shape the development of organizations and societies.

The myths of the accountant thus took their place alongside those of doctors, management thinkers, lawyers, and others. Whether it was a matter of a particular category of cost, or the broader ceremonial role attributed to financial values in a rationalized society, myths, rationalization, and organizations were to be linked, with accounting playing a key role. Echoing some of Max Weber's formulations, formal organizations were depicted as being driven to adopt practices and procedures defined as rational. The conventions of modern accounting were central here, key mechanisms by which organizations come to be linked to their institutional environments. To the extent that organizations incorporate practices defined as rational within their institutional environment, it was argued that they increase their legitimacy and survival prospects. The rules embodied in such practices then become binding on the organization. The formal structures of organizations thus come to reflect the myths of the institutional environment, as well as the demands of the work activities of the organization.

Viewed in institutional terms, accounting is understood as one of the mechanisms through which organizations come to incorporate rational conceptions of ways of organizing. Accounting is one of many such practices in contemporary societies, albeit a highly significant one in a number of contemporary societies. It provides a set of techniques for organizing and monitoring activities, and a language with which to define and delineate organizational goals, procedures, and policies. Accounting performs a ceremonial function that helps legitimate an organization among its 'users', whether these are participants within the organization, stockholders, the public, or regulatory bodies such as the Securities Exchange Commission. Instead of presuming only efficiency effects, the adoption and diffusion of particular accounting practices can be studied with regard to their roles as rational institutional myths. At a societal level, one can study how the amount of accounting performed in a particular society or organization is influenced by its environment, rather than by the intrinsically necessary technical work processes.

An important new research agenda within accounting was opened up by this focus on institutional environments. Researchers within accounting were encouraged to look beyond the organization, to see changes within the organization as dynamically linked with changes in the wider environment. Accounting lost some of its apparent uniqueness in this view, and became part of the cultural apparatus of a society. Budgetary and performance measurement practices within an organization could be viewed in terms of the articulation, enforcement, and modification of societal expectations of acceptable budgetary practices during a period of organizational decline (Covaleski and Dirsmith 1988; Oakes et al. 1998). Questions such as how this occurred, to what purpose, and from whom and where such expectations arose, could be directed to a range of actors beyond the organization. The increasing dominance of finance personnel in the control of large corporations could be explained by pointing to national cultures and traditions (Armstrong 1987), changes in the strategy and structure of organizations (Berry et al. 1985), changes in anti-trust laws, and the mimicking of firms in similar environments (Fligstein 1990). A shift in intra-organizational power relations is viewed as a result of events within the organizational environment, and as a result of the way in which key actors within organizations define their problems. A range of further studies drew more loosely on the institutional perspective (Ansari and Euske 1987; Espeland and Hirsch 1990; Bealing et al. 1996), and demonstrated the importance of linking changes in accounting and auditing practices within an organization to the demands and expectations of the institutional environment.

An appreciation of institutional environments also stimulated research on accounting institutions, such as the accounting profession and the regulatory bodies that produce and legitimize accounting rules. Initially, such studies were conducted within the relatively untheorized traditions of conventional histories (Zeff 1972). Yet, new forms of historical accounting scholarship, influenced by theoretical developments in sociology and political science that drew on Weber, began to emerge. Studies of the emergence and elaboration of professional fields were sensitized to the social relations between producers and consumers of accounting and audit services by sociologists of professions (Johnson 1972) and studies of accounting standard setting were influenced by developments in political science that emphasized legitimacy, ideology, and power (Lukes 1974). Accounting institutions and traditions were linked to other social institutions such as the modern state (Puxty et al. 1987; Miller 1990); educational practices (Hoskin and Macve 1986); stock market regulators (Miranti 1988); and more general ideological and discursive developments (Montagna 1986). A concern with accounting institutions thereby began to interconnect with studies that took a more explicitly political economy approach.

A Political Economy of Accounting

Other researchers also drew attention to the importance of addressing the macro-environment within which accounting operates, but borrowed their theoretical coordinates instead from Marx and later writers in the political economy tradition. Here, the emphasis was on the conflicting political and economic interests at stake in accounting, both within and beyond organizations. Political economy writers placed particular emphasis on the ways in which historically specific power relations are shaped by and in turn shape accounting practices. The image of accounting as a technically neutral and objective practice was rebutted sharply by political economy writers. Accounting was viewed instead as a partial and interested language and practice, one that represents and reinforces the interests of particular occupational groups and classes.

Political economy is used here in a broad sense. We refer not only to those writers who drew their inspiration more or less directly from the writings of Marx (Tinker 1980; Bryer 1999), but also to those who drew on the writings of those such as Braverman and Gramsci who did much to demonstrate the need to extend and develop political economy analyses. *Labor and Monopoly Capital* (Braverman 1974) was an intellectual call to arms to those who are interested in understanding changes in the productive process and in the occupational structure of the workforce that had occurred across the century following Marx's writings. He examined the ways that the knowledge and expertise of workers was appropriated by management, and stressed the enduring exploitation and alienation of work in capitalist enterprises. Braverman inspired many accounting researchers to explore the role of accounting in the accumulation of wealth through large organizations. For instance, Hopper and Armstrong (1991) and Armstrong (2002) analyse the role of costing systems in such processes, while Hopper and his associates (e.g. Uddin and Hopper 2001; Wickramasinghe and Hopper 2005) have extended this form of analysis to developing countries.

Braverman further argued that monopoly capitalism devotes ever more resources to accounting for value, to the point at which the labour expended on such processes begins to approach or even exceed the labour used in producing the underlying commodity or service. The growth in the amount of accounting carried out in monopoly capitalism, according to Braverman, is not just a function of increasing complexity. It is a matter also of trust, or the lack of it. Indeed, the first principle of modern accounting, Braverman argued, is the presumption of dishonesty. And, if distrust is the norm, then auditing has an important role as a means of certifying—or at least aspiring to reassure—outside parties about the truth of the financial records. Cast in these terms, monopoly capitalism is characterized by a vast paper empire which appears as real as the physical world, and which comes increasingly to dominate it.

Within accounting, a number of writers developed and extended the political economy approach, albeit with differing emphases. The changing form and content of *Annual Reports* were linked to changing strategies of capital accumulation (Neimark and Tinker 1986; Neimark 1992). A 'social critique of accounting' based on marginalist economics was proposed (Tinker 1980), together with an historical analysis of the material basis of accounting ideas about the nature of value (Tinker et al. 1982). Such critiques were coupled with a proposal for an 'emancipatory accounting' (Tinker 1985: 201). With a somewhat different emphasis, Bryer (1993, 2005, 2006) has embarked on an extensive series of historical analysis of accounting, arguing that shifting calculations of accounting returns reflect the dominant mode of capital appropriation in different historical eras. A particular strength of such analyses is their focus on the roles of accounting in shifting forms of capitalist economic organization, whether they be historical analyses of the forms studied by Bryer or more current forms, such as privatizations (Arnold and Cooper 1999) or the international division of labour (Hanlon 1994).

Other writers in the same tradition drew less directly from the writings of Marx, and more from recent political economy approaches. Drawing on more cultural forms of Marxist analysis, influenced by writers as diverse as Gramsci and Habermas, accounting researchers have studied representations of accounting in various media (Lehman and Tinker 1987), accountability practices in public sector organizations (Broadbent et al. 1991; Townley et al. 2003), as well as returning to the question raised by Sombart concerning the necessity of accounting for the development of capitalism (Chiapello 2007). Variations in modes of regulation of accounting practices (e.g. between state, market, and professional) were linked to variation in the institutional and political structures between capitalist economies (Puxty et al. 1987). The roles of accounting in industrial relations and wage determination negotiations were addressed (Bougen 1989; Bougen et al. 1990). The dominance of accounting controls over the labour process in the United Kingdom were explained by reference to the 'collective mobility project' of the accounting profession in the United Kingdom, and the dominant position it has achieved within the 'economic functions' of the global function of capital (Armstrong 1985, 1987). And the differential spread in the United States and the United Kingdom of practices such as standard costing, budgeting, and performance reports were examined using a historical-comparative method. A number of further studies were conducted drawing broadly on the principles and concepts of political economy. The interaction between state actions and the distributional consequences of accounting policies were examined (Arnold 1991), as were the links between cost accounting techniques and attempts to control the labour process. More recently, the importance of using concepts of class, ideology, and social structure in analysing labour relations, and a factory reorganization programme in particular, has been reaffirmed (Arnold 1998; Froud et al. 1998).

Ethnographies of Accounting

A different agenda, one that can be labelled approximately an *ethnography* of accounting, also emerged in the early 1980s. The concern here was with the meanings and perceptions of the actors who develop and use accounting practices in highly localized settings. An ethnography of accounting sought to understand what was said, done, and understood by the actors involved in a particular situation. While loosely influenced by anthropological and sociological methods of field research (notably Glaser and Strauss 1967), the study of the meaning of accounting calculations drew on a variety of theoretical positions, from the dramaturgical approach of Goffman, the phenomenology of Schutz, the symbolic interactionism of Mead and Blumer, the social constructivism of Berger and Luckmann, and the ethnomethodolgy of Garfinkel. Sense-making, understood as the conditions and consequences of accounting in specific organizations, provided a popular focus here (Weick 1979).

The 'lived experience' of individual actors was addressed through case analyses that emphasized the symbolic use and interpretation of budgets (Boland and Pondy 1983). An understanding of how practices of accountability contributed to the production and reproduction of organizational life was the aim of such research (Roberts and Scapens 1985). Based on participant observation, Preston (1986) uses symbolic interaction and sense-making theories to analyse the multiple and often informal ways that managers inform themselves. Pentland (1993) alerts us to the emotional dimensions of auditing, stressing the central role of comfort-producing practices in the production of a credible account. A focus on the changing relations between volumes and costs in advanced manufacturing (Jonsson and Gronlund 1988) allowed one to understand how practices and procedures are worked out in local settings. In so far as new ways of accounting have to be understood and made sense of, an understanding of accounting change in a particular organization could be enhanced by referring to the meanings people attach to the social world (Nahapiet 1988). The emergence of a new accounting-based organizational culture could be analysed using an interpretive or ethnographic frame (Dent 1991), as can the different uses of accounting calculations in different countries (Ahrens 1996). Meanwhile, the process of 'becoming' a professional accountant (Power 1991) could be viewed as analogous to that of the 'moral career' of the mental patient (Goffman 1961).

The constructivism of Berger and Luckmann was augmented by an increasing use of the actor network theory of Callon and Latour. Thus Preston et al. (1992) examine the fabricating of hospital budgets, identifying the processes by which an accounting innovation becomes taken for granted. Changes in accounting practices and systems within hospitals (Chua 1995; Kurunmäki 2004) and manufacturing (Briers and Chua 2001) were studied in terms of changing understandings of how and why the new accounting numbers were produced, and how the social linkages among a relatively small group of people enabled this to occur. More recently, this set of sensitivities to the situated functionality of accounting has drawn on a growing range of theorizations of practice (e.g. Ahrens and Chapman 2007; Lounsbury 2007).

Accounting and Governing Economic Life

By the mid-1980s, there was an increasing acceptance that accounting did more than mirror economic reality, and that its sphere of influence extended beyond the boundaries of organizations and firms. But the notion that accounting could shape and create social relations, that it could influence the way we live our lives, that it could alter the ways in which individuals and organizations understand the choices open to them, remained to be demonstrated. A set of diverse yet loosely connected bodies of work made this possible, and in the process broadened the terrain of accounting research significantly.

A concern with enterprise calculation in the concrete conditions of specific capitalist economies had directed attention to the forms of organization and conditions of operation of enterprises (Cutler et al. 1977, 1978). The criteria of calculation and the forms they took were seen to be shaped within particular institutional and social arenas. The calculation of profit was viewed as an outcome of particular norms of measurement, and those norms of measurement were themselves held to be understandable in terms of the particular national context in which they gained acceptance and significance. Economic policy, taken to include the objectives and practices of any agent in the economic sphere, similarly directed attention at both the means and instruments through which particular calculative techniques were accorded significance (Tomlinson 1994). In a manner that prefigured some of the arguments of Callon (1998), economic calculation was seen to require some agent or agency that calculates, and that in turn was seen to be explicable in terms of a dispersed organizational and institutional matrix (Thompson 1986).

Within accounting, Hopwood and others pointed to the importance of studying historically specific 'constellations' (Burchell et al. 1985). This referred to the particular social space where a set of diverse practices, processes, and institutions intersected. A proposed accounting innovation (the 'value added' event) was analysed as a field comprised of a very particular set of relations established between calculative practices and norms, bodies of knowledge, economic and administrative processes, and institutions. In a related manner, although drawing on distinct reference points, Robson (1991) set out explicitly to apply and extend this approach in a study of accounting standard setting in the United Kingdom. Accounting practices change, Robson argued, when a particular group or institution is able successfully to enrol other actors in their proposals by incorporating and translating the interests of others into the solutions proposed. In this process, problems are defined as shared, alliances formed, arguments mobilized, and the interests of other groups, parties, and institutions enrolled towards a common interest.

At the margins of the discipline, the issue of calculation as a complex calculative practice was placed centre stage by the writings of Miller and Rose (1990) and Callon (1998). These gave pride of place to the material reality of calculation, the figures, mechanisms, and inscriptions that are decisive in performing calculations. For Miller and Rose the emphasis was how the technologies of calculation and management gave shape to the rationalities of administrative and political programmes. Calculation and agency are two sides of the same coin, according to this view, and the existence of calculative agencies correlates closely according to Callon with that of calculative tools. These tools, viewed as 'performative', mutually define the nature and content of the calculations made by calculative agencies, and the tools themselves are open, plastic, and reconfigurable. These ideas, along with others coming from science studies,[6] gave renewed impetus across the social sciences to a concern with the tools of economic calculation. Out of this concern emerged what has since come to be termed the sociology of finance (Mackenzie and Millo 2003; Beunza and Stark 2004; Kalthoff 2005; MacKenzie 2006).

Viewed in terms of governing economic life, the emphasis was not only on the tools of economic calculation. Of equal interest was the language or vocabulary in terms of which particular forms of accounting were articulated and called for. As Hopwood had put it some years earlier, the spread of costing is typically linked to the spread of a language of costliness. Likewise with tools for assessing investment opportunities and divisional performance, which are typically framed in terms of managerial decision-making (Miller 1998). If the single financial figure is a potent tool for intervening—in so far as it appears to confer objectivity and neutrality—then its deployment is always in relation to a particular object and objective, whether that be improving efficiency, reducing waste, or transforming individuals into calculating selves (Miller 1994). The same holds for audit, as Power (1997) convincingly demonstrated. For audit is made up not only of samples, checklists, and analytic methods. Equally important is that audit is an idea, a generalized aspiration that is shared by a wide range of regulatory agencies and policy designers. Auditing is more than a collection of tests and an evidence gathering task, it is also an assemblage of values and goals that are inscribed in the official programmes that demand and desire it.

By the late 1990s, the constitutive or inventive capacities of accounting had been firmly demonstrated in a number of studies. The importance of attending

[6] The humanities are similarly interested in calculative practices, particularly in the rhetoric of economic calculation and valuation, literary understandings of the relation between individuals, capital and markets, and the power of objectivity and facts in modernity (MacIntyre 1984; Zelizer 1994; Porter 1995; Poovey 1998).

to the links between what happens *within* organizations, and what happens *beyond* them had been widely accepted. The basic premise set out at the beginning of this introduction was established by this point. Accounting practices were seen as inextricably linked not only to what took place within firms and other organizations, but were also viewed as similarly linked to what happened beyond their boundaries. Accounting was a legitimate object of social scientific enquiry.

ACCOUNTING FOR THE FUTURE

Disciplines can be discomforted by reflections on their past, just as they can be by analyses of their current practice. We have seen this, for instance, with disciplines that seem distant from accounting, such as anthropology, psychiatry, and medicine. Commentary can appear as critique, and critique can in turn be viewed as outright opposition. An implicit belief in progress can be unsettled by a demonstration that things could have turned out differently, and the present can be made to seem at least a little less secure and stable. Our aim here has been neither critique nor opposition, but we have sought to disturb the self-evidence that can be attached to the present state of accounting and accounting research. We have drawn attention to the curiously punctuated history of a social science concern with accounting. Initially, central to social science at the start of the twentieth century, accounting more or less disappeared from the social sciences for approximately half a century. And, when it was 'rediscovered' by social scientists in the 1950s and 1960s, this was in terms of a rather constrained social—psychological and rationalistic framework. It was not until the mid-1970s that a broader concern with the links between accounting, organizations, and institutions began to emerge, and it was not until the last two decades of the twentieth century that this research tradition began to flourish.

But a social scientific concern with accounting as an organizational and institutional phenomenon is still very much in its early stages. For too long, the economy has been left to the economists, and other social scientists have failed to address this immensely important phenomenon. If we learn only one thing from recurrent financial crises, it should be that a fuller understanding of all those calculative practices that underpin the modern economy is urgently needed. And this understanding should not be viewed as a narrow technical understanding, but it should be viewed as including the ideas and aspirations that are so intimately attached to the roles of accounting in organizations and institutions. If we neglect the latter, then our understanding of the former is seriously diminished. Accounting is too important to be studied only by accountants! But, even today, the growing interest in accounting by those such as economic sociologists is partial and geographically differentiated. While European economic sociologists are paying increasing attention to accounting, mainstream North American economic sociology has barely registered it as a topic worthy of attention (Mennicken et al. 2008). Organization theorists outside accounting, including 'critical' management studies writers, have been similarly neglectful of accounting. The chapters in this volume, which come from both 'within' and 'beyond' the discipline of accounting, seek to redress this neglect, and hopefully they indicate the scale of the research agenda that lies ahead.

This research agenda also entails an engagement with practice and methodology. Engagement with practice could include, but should also extend beyond, managerialist improvements in the service of those in positions of authority and influence (Sikka et al. 1995). Critical financial analysis (Shaoul 1998) and policy advice in the public interest, however difficult that term is to operationalize, need to be encouraged (Sikka and Willmott 1997; Neu et al. 2001). Practice also refers to academic institutions and practices and we can elaborate our argument and the rationale for this book by turning our gaze inwards and encourage critical reflexivity.

There is little point in suggesting that 'others' should take note of accounting, if we fail to take note ourselves of the ways in which particular forms of economic calculation are shaping and reshaping professional and academic life. Academic practice includes recognizing the increasing schism between teaching and research and the impact of performance measurement regimes on academic life and student experience. We know already how audit and performance assessment, when deployed more or less indiscriminately to evaluate such entities as schools, hospitals, and universities, can transform accountability into a simplified and standardized set of metrics (Power 1994; Strathern 2000). Inspired at least in part by desires to increase accountability and transparency, such measures can result in a focus on the indicators themselves, rather than the qualities the measures were supposed to evaluate. Likewise, rankings and reactivity to rankings can become difficult to differentiate, with consequent effects on the distribution of resources, definitions of work, and the extent of gaming strategies (Espeland and Sauder 2007). Investment in metrics and rankings of academic performance seems to reinforce some of the very trends—writing only for prestigious journals, teaching that becomes separate from research, and narrow, mono-method, and managerialist research—that the investments are purportedly trying to combat.

One possible implication of these developments, which may be more severe in accounting and other business disciplines than in the social sciences more generally—and possibly even more severe in the United States than else-where—is the decoupling of research from the institutional and philosophical traditions that gave rise to it (Hopwood 2007). This can result in a situation where the only consumers of accounting research are other accounting researchers. In such circumstances, institutional careerism can produce intel-lectually constrained and conformist research agendas, whose incremental contribution to knowledge is minimal and where only elite researchers have the authority to innovate. The risks of careerism also include intolerance of intellectual and methodological diversity. We can only speculate on solutions to such problems, although an appreciation of what is already known about the linkages between accounting, organizations, and institutions suggests change will be difficult. It can, however, be fostered through increased reflex-ivity and dialogue with respect to the multiple roles of accounting in organ-izations and institutions, whether those reside within academia or beyond.

The chapters in this volume are, we hope, a testament to intellectual diversity, experiment, and how far we have travelled, even though reading them makes one appreciate how much further we need to travel in under-standing and intervening in the interrelations among accounting, organiza-tions, and institutions. Appreciating their collective contribution requires a serious commitment to understanding multiple methodologies and a respect for different research traditions. By commissioning chapters from a diverse set of researchers from inside and outside accounting, we trust this volume demonstrates the value of such an endeavour.

REFERENCES

Adler, P.S. (ed.) (2009). *The Oxford Handbook of Sociology and Organization Studies: Classical Foundations.* Oxford: Oxford University Press.

Ahrens, T. (1996). Styles of accountability. *Accounting, Organizations and Society,* 21 (2–3), 139–73.

——and Chapman, C.S. (2004). Accounting for flexibility and efficiency: A field study of management control systems in a restaurant chain. *Contemporary Account-ing Research,* 21, 271–301.

————(2007). Management accounting as practice. *Accounting, Organizations and Society,* 32, 1–27.

Ansari, S., and Euske, K. (1987). Rational, rationalizing and reifying uses of account-ing data in organizations. *Accounting, Organizations and Society,* 12(6), 549–70.

Argyris, C. (1952). *The Impact of Budgets on People.* New York: Controllership Foundation.

Armstrong, P. (1985). Changing management control strategies: The role of competition between accountancy and other organizational professions. *Accounting, Organizations and Society*, 10, 129–48.

—— (1987). The rise of accounting controls in British capitalist enterprises. *Accounting, Organizations and Society*, 12(5), 415–36.

—— (2002). The costs of activity based management. *Accounting, Organizations and Society*, 27(1–2), 99–120.

Arnold, P. (1991). Accounting and the state: Consequences of erger and acquisition accounting in the US hospital industry. *Accounting, Organizations and Society*, 16(2), 121–40.

—— (1998). The limits of postmodernism in accounting history: The decatur experience. *Accounting, Organizations and Society*, 23(7), 665–84.

—— and Cooper, C. (1999). A tale of two classes: The privatization of Medway Ports. *Critical Perspectives on Accounting*, 10(2), 127–52.

Bealing, W., Dirsmith, M., and Fogarty, T. (1996). Early regulatory action by the SEC: An institutional theory perspective on the dramaturgy of exchange relations. *Accounting, Organizations and Society*, 21, 317–38.

Becker, S., and Green, D. (1962). Budgeting and employee behavior. *The Journal of Business*, 35(4), 392–402.

Berry, A.J., Capps, T., Cooper, D.J., Ferguson, P., Hopper, T., and Lowe, E.A. (1985). Management accounting in an area of the NCB: Rationales of accounting practices in a public enterprise. *Accounting, Organizations and Society*, 10(1), 3–28.

Beunza, D., and Stark, D. (2004). Tools of the trade: The socio-technology of arbitrage in a Wall Street trading room. *Industrial and Corporate Change*, 13(2), 369–400.

Boland, R.J., and Pondy, L.R. (1983). Accounting in organizations: A union of natural and rational perspectives. *Accounting, Organizations and Society*, 8(2–3), 223–34.

Bonini, C.P., Jaedicke, R.K., and Wagner, H.M. (eds.) (1964). *Management Controls: New Directions in Basic Research*. New York: McGraw Hill.

Bougen, P. (1989). The emergence, roles and consequences of an accounting-industrial relations interaction. *Accounting, Organizations and Society*, 14(3), 203–34.

—— Ogden, S.G., and Outram, Q. (1990). The appearance and disappearance of accounting: Wage determination in the UK coal industry. *Accounting, Organizations and Society*, 15(3), 149–70.

Braverman, H. (1974). *Labor and Monopoly Capital: The Degradation of Work in the Twentieth Century*. New York: Monthly Review Press.

Briers, M., and Chua, W.F. (2001). The role of actor-networks and boundary objects in management accounting change: A field study of an implementation of activity-based costing. *Accounting, Organizations and Society*, 26(3), 237–69.

Broadbent, J., Laughlin, R., and Read, S. (1991). Recent financial and administrative changes in the NHS: A critical theory analysis. *Critical Perspectives on Accounting*. 2(1), 1–29.

Bruns, W., and Waterhouse, J. (1975). Budgetary control and organization structure. *Journal of Accounting Research*, 13(2), 177–203.

Bryer, R.A. (1993). The late nineteenth-century revolution in financial reporting: Accounting for the rise of investor or managerial capitalism? *Accounting, Organizations and Society*, 18(7–8), 649–90.

—— (1999). Marx and accounting. *Critical Perspectives on Accounting*, 10(5), 683–709.

—— (2005). A Marxist accounting history of the British industrial revolution: A review of evidence and suggestions for research. *Accounting, Organizations and Society*, 31(1), 25–65.

—— (2006). The genesis of the capitalist farmer: Towards a Marxist accounting history of the origins of the English agricultural revolution. *Critical Perspectives on Accounting*, 17(4), 367–97.

Burchell, S., Clubb, C., Hopwood, A., Hughes, J., and Nahapiet, J. (1980). The roles of accounting in organizations and society. *Accounting, Organizations and Society*, 5(1), 5–27.

——————— (1985). Accounting in its social context: Towards a history of value added in the United Kingdom. *Accounting, Organizations and Society*, 10(4), 381–413.

Burns, T.J. (ed.) (1972). *Behavioral Experiments in Accounting*. Columbus, Ohio: Ohio University Press.

—— (ed.) (1979). *Behavioral Experiments in Accounting II*. Columbus, Ohio: Ohio University Press.

Callon, M. (ed.) (1998). *The Laws of the Markets*. Oxford: Blackwell.

Chapman, C.S. (1997). Reflections on a contingent view of accounting. *Accounting, Organizations and Society*, 22, 189–205.

Chenhall, R.H., and Morris, D. (1986). The impact of structure, environment and interdependence on the perceived usefulness of management accounting systems. *The Accounting Review*, 61, 16–35.

—————— (1995). Organic decision and communication processes and management accounting systems in entrepreneurial and conservative business organizations. *Omega, International Journal of Management Science*, 23, 485–97.

Chiapello, E. (2007). Accounting and the birth of the notion of capitalism. *Critical Perspectives on Accounting*, 18(3), 263–96.

Chua, W.F. (1995). Experts, networks and inscriptions in the fabrication of accounting images: A story of the representation of three public hospitals. *Accounting, Organizations and Society*, 20(2–3), 111–45.

Cooper, D.J. (1981). A social and organizational view of management accounting. In M. Bromwich and A.G. Hopwood (eds.), *Essays in British Accounting Research*. London: Pitman Publishing.

—— (1983). Tidiness, muddle and things: Commonalities and divergencies in two approaches to management accounting research. *Accounting, Organizations and Society*, 8(2–3), 269–86.

—— and Robson, K. (2006). Accounting, professions and regulation: Locating the sites of professionalization. *Accounting, Organizations and Society*, 31(4–5), 415–44.

Covaleski, M.A., and Dirsmith, M.W. (1988). The use of budgetary symbols in the political arena: An historically informed field study. *Accounting, Organizations and Society*, 13(1), 1–24.

Cutler, A., Hindess, B., Hirst, P., and Hussain, A. (1977). *Marx's 'Capital' and Capitalism Today: Volume One.* London: Routledge & Kegan Paul.

———— Cutler, A., Hindess, B., Hirst, P., and Hussain, A. (1978). *Marx's 'Capital' and Capitalism Today: Volume Two.* London: Routledge & Kegan Paul.

Cyert, R., and March, J.G. (1963). *A Behavioural Theory of the Firm.* Englewood Cliffs: Prentice Hall.

Dalton, M. (1959). *Men Who Manage: Fusions of Feeling and Theory in Administration.* New York: John Wiley & Sons.

Dent, J. (1991). Accounting and organizational cultures: A field study of the emergence of a new organizational reality. *Accounting, Organizations and Society,* 16(8), 705–32.

Espeland, W.N., and Hirsch, P.M. (1990). Ownership changes, accounting practice and the redefinition of the corporation. *Accounting, Organizations and Society,* 15 (1–2), 77–96.

Fligstein, N. (1990). *The Transformation of Corporate Control.* Cambridge, Mass: Harvard University Press.

Froud J., Williams, K., Haslam, C., Johal, S., and Williams J. (1998). Caterpillar: Two stories and an argument. *Accounting, Organizations and Society,* 23(7), 685–708.

Galbraith, J. (1973). *Designing Complex Organizations.* Reading, Mass: Addison Wesley.

Glaser, B., and Strauss, A. (1967). *The Discovery of Grounded Theory: Strategies for Qualitative Research.* New York: Aldine de Gruyter.

Goffman, E. (1961). *Asylums: Essays on the Social Situation of Mental Patients and Other Inmates.* New York: Doubleday & Co.

Gordon, M.J. (1964). The use of administered price systems to control large organizations. In C.P. Bonini, R.K. Jaedicke, and H.M. Wagner (eds.), *Management Controls: New Directions in Basic Research.* New York: McGraw Hill, 1–26.

Gordon, L.A., and Miller, D. (1976). A contingency framework for the design of accounting information systems. *Accounting, Organizations and Society,* 1(1), 59–69.

———— (1992). The Self-vindication of the laboratory sciences. In A. Pickering (ed.), *Science as Practice and Culture.* Chicago: University of Chicago Press.

Hanlon, G. (1994). *The Commercialization of Accountancy.* London: St. Martin Press.

Hayes, D.C. (1977). The contingency theory of management accounting. *The Accounting Review,* LII, 22–39.

Hofstede, G. (1968). *The Game of Budget Control.* London: Tavistock.

Hopper, T.M., and Armstrong, P. (1991). Cost accounting, controlling labour and the rise of conglomerates. *Accounting, Organizations and Society,* 16(5–6), 405–38.

Hopwood, A.G. (1974*a*). *Accounting and Human Behaviour.* London: Haymarket Publishing.

———— (1974*b*). Leadership climate and the use of accounting data in performance evaluation. *The Accounting Review,* 49, 485–95.

———— (1976). Editorial: The path ahead. *Accounting, Organizations and* Society, 1(1), 1–4.

———— (1978). Towards an organizational perspective for the study of accounting and information systems. *Accounting, Organizations and Society,* 3(1), 3–13.

Hopwood, A.G. (1983). On trying to study accounting in the contexts in which it operates. *Accounting, Organizations and Society*, 8(2–3), 287–305.

—— (2007). Whither accounting research? *The Accounting Review*, 82(5), 1365–74.

—— and Miller, P. (eds.) (1994). *Accounting as Social and Institutional Practice.* Cambridge: Cambridge University Press.

Hoskin, K.W., and Macve, R.H. (1986). Accounting and the examination: A genealogy of disciplinary power. *Accounting, Organizations and Society*, 11(2), 105–36.

Johnson, T.J. (1972). *Professions and Power.* London: Macmillan Press.

Jonsson, S., and Gronlund, A. (1988). Life with a sub-contractor: New technology and management accounting. *Accounting, Organizations and Society*, 13(5), 512–32.

Kalthoff, H. (2005). Practices of calculation: Economic representations and risk management. *Theory, Culture and Society*, 22(2), 69–97.

Khandwalla, P.N. (1971). The effects of different types of competition on the use of management controls. *Journal of Accounting Research*, 275–285.

Kurunmäki, L. (2004). A hybrid profession: The acquisition of management accounting expertise by medical professionals. *Accounting, Organizations and Society*, 29(3–4), 327–47.

Lehman, C., and Tinker, T. (1987). The 'real' cultural significance of accounting. *Accounting, Organizations and Society*, 12(5), 503–22.

Lounsburg, M. (2008). Institutional rationality and practice variation: New directions in the institutional analysis of practice. *Accounting, Organizations and Society*, 33(4–5), 349–61.

Lowe, E.A., and Shaw, R.W. (1968). An analysis of management biasing: Evidence from a company's budgeting process. *Journal of Management Studies*, 5(3), 305–15.

—— and Tinker, A.M. (1977). Sighting the accounting problematic: Towards an intellectual emancipation of accounting. *Journal of Business Finance and Accounting*, 4(3), 263–76.

Lukes, S. (1974). *Power: A radical View.* London: Macmillan.

—— (2006). *An Engine Not a Camera: How Financial Models Shape Markets.* Cambridge, Mass.: MIT press.

—— and Millo, Y. (2003). Constructing a market, performing theory: The historical sociology of a financial derivatives exchange. *American Journal of Sociology*, 109(1), 107–45.

MacIntyre, A. (1984). *After Virtue: A Study in Moral Theory.* Notre Dame, Ind.: University of Notre Dame Press.

Marx, K. (1974*a*). *Capital Volume I* (1887). London: Lawrence & Wishart.

—— (1974*b*). *Capital Volume II* (1893). London: Lawrence & Wishart.

Mennicken, A., Miller, P., and Samiolo, R. (2008). Accounting for economic sociology. *Economic Sociology*, 10(1), 3–6.

Merchant, K.A. (1981). The design of the corporate budgeting system: Influences on managerial behavior and performance. *The Accounting Review*, 56, 813–29.

Meyer, J.W., and Rowan, B. (1977). Institutionalized organizations: Formal structure as myth and ceremony. *American Journal of Sociology*, 83(2), 340–63.

Miles, R.E., and Snow, C.C. (1978). *Organizational Strategy, Structure and Process*. New York: McGraw Hill.

Miller, P. (1990). On the interrelations between accounting and the state. *Accounting, Organizations and Society*, 15, 315–38.

——(1994). Accounting and objectivity: The invention of calculating selves and calculable spaces. In A. Megill (ed.), *Rethinking Objectivity*. Durham: Duke University Press.

——(1998). The margins of accounting. In M. Callon (ed.), *The Laws of the Markets*. Oxford: Blackwell.

——and O'Leary, T. (1987). Accounting and the construction of the governable person. *Accounting, Organizations and Society*, 12(3), 235–65.

————(1994). Accounting, 'economic citizenship' and the spatial reordering of manufacture. *Accounting, Organizations and Society*, 19(1), 15–43.

————(2007). Mediating instruments and making markets: Capital budgeting, science and the economy. *Accounting, Organizations and Society*, 32(7/8), 701–34.

——and Rose, N. (1990). Governing economic life. *Economy and Society*, 19(1), 1–31.

Miranti, P.J. (1988). Professionalism and nativism: The competition in securing public accountancy legislation in NY during the 1890s. *Social Science Quarterly*, June, 361–80.

Montagna, P. (1986). Accounting rationality and financial legitimation. *Theory and Society*, 103–38.

Nahapiet, J. (1988). The rhetoric and reality of an accounting change: A study of resource allocation. *Accounting, Organizations and Society*, 13(4), 333–58.

Neimark, M.K., and Tinker, T. (1986). The social construction of management control systems. *Accounting, Organizations and Society*, 11(4–5), 369–95.

——(1992). *The Hidden Dimensions of Annual Reports: Sixty Years of Social Conflict at General Motors*. New York: Markus Wiener.

Neu, D., Cooper, D.J., and Everett, J. (2001). Critical accounting interventions. *Critical Perspectives on Accounting*, 12(6), 735–62.

Oakes, L., Townley, B., and Cooper, D.J. (1998). Business planning as pedagogy: Language and control in a changing institutional field. *Administrative Science Quarterly*, 43(2), 257–92.

Otley, D. T. (1980). The contingency theory of management accounting: Achievement and prognosis. *Accounting, Organizations and Society*, 5(4), 413–28.

Pentland, B. (1993). Getting comfortable with the numbers: Auditing and the micro-production of macro-order. *Accounting, Organizations and Society*, 18(7–8), 605–20.

Poovey, M. (1998). *A History of the Modern Fact: Problems of Knowledge in the Sciences of Wealth and Society*. Chicago: University of Chicago Press.

Porter, T (1995). *Trust in Numbers: The Pursuit of Objectivity in Science and Public Life*. Princeton, NJ: Princeton University Press.

Power, M. (1991). Educating accountants: Towards a critical ethnography. *Accounting, Organizations and Society*, 16(4), 333–53.

——(1997). *The Audit Society: Rituals of Verification*. Oxford: Oxford University Press.

Power, M. (2004). *The Audit Explosion.* London: Demos.

—— Espeland, W. and Sauder, M. (2007). The reactivity of rankings: How public measures recreate social worlds. *American Journal of Sociology,* 113, 1–4.

Preston, A.M. (1986). Interactions and arrangements in the process of informing *Accounting, Organizations and Society,* 11(6), 521–40.

—— Cooper, D.J., and Coombs, R.W. (1992). Fabricating budgets: A study of the production of management budgeting in the national health service. *Accounting, Organizations and Society,* 17(6), 561–93.

Puxty, A.G., Willmott, H.C., Cooper, D.J., and Lowe, T. (1987). Modes of regulation in advanced capitalism: Locating accountancy in four countries. *Accounting, Organizations and Society,* 12(3), 273–91.

Ridgway, V. (1956). Dysfunctional consequences of performance measurement. *Administrative Science Quarterly,* 1, 240–47.

Roberts, J., and Scapens, R. (1985). Accounting systems and systems of accountability: Understanding accounting practices in their organizational contexts. *Accounting, Organizations and Society,* 10(4), 443–56.

Robson, K. (1991). On the arenas of accounting change: the process of translation. *Accounting, Organizations and Society,* 16(5–6), 547–70.

Shaoul, J. (1998). Critical financial analysis and accounting for stakeholders. *Critical Perspectives on Accounting,* 9(2), 235–49.

Shillinglaw, G. (1964). Divisional performance review: An extension of budgetary control. In C.P. Bonini, R.K. Jaedicke, and H.M. Wagner (eds.), *Management Controls: New Directions in Basic Research.* New York: McGraw Hill, 149–63.

Sikka, P., Willmott, H., and Puxty, T. (1995). The mountains are still there: Accounting academics and the bearings of intellectuals. *Accounting, Auditing & Accountability,* 8(3), 113–40.

—— —— (1997). Practising critical accounting. *Critical Perspectives on Accounting,* 8(1/2), 149–65.

Simon, H.A., Guetzkow, H., Kozmetsky, G., and Tyndall, G. (1954). *Centralization Vs. Decentralization in Organizing the Controller's Department: A Research Study and Report.* New York: Controllership Foundation.

Simons, R. (1987). Accounting control systems and business strategy: An empirical analysis. *Accounting, Organizations and Society,* 12, 357–74.

Sombart, W. (1902). *Der Moderne Capitalismus.* Leipzig: Duncker & Humblot.

Suddaby, R., Cooper, D.J., and Greenwood, R. (2007). Transnational regulation of professional services: Governance dynamics of field level organizational change. *Accounting, Organizations and Society,* 32(4/5), 333–62.

Thompson, G. (1986). *Economic Calculation and Policy Formation.* London: Routledge.

Tinker, A.M. (1980). Towards a political economy of accounting. *Accounting, Organizations and Society,* 5(1), 147–60.

Tinker, T. (1985). *Paper Prophets: A Social Critique of Accounting.* New York: Praeger.

—— Merino, B., and Neimark, M. (1982). The normative origins of positive theories: Ideology and accounting thought. *Accounting, Organizations and Society,* 7(2), 167–200.

Tomlinson, J. (1994). The politics of economic measurement: The rise of the 'productivity problem' in the 1940s. In A.G. Hopwood and P. Miller (eds.), *Accounting as Social and Institutional Practice*. Cambridge: Cambridge University Press.

Townley, B., Cooper, D.J., and Oakes, L. (2003) Performance Measurement and the rationalization of organizations. *Organization Studies*, 24(7), 1045–67.

Uddin, S., and Hopper, T. (2001). A Bangladesh soap opera: Privatisation, accounting, and regimes of control in a less developed country. *Accounting, Organizations and Society*, 26(7–8), 643–72.

Weber, M. (1978). *Economy and Society*. Berkeley, Calif.: University of California Press (first published 1956).

—— (1992). *The Protestant Ethic and the Spirit of Capitalism*. London: Routledge (first published 1930).

Weick, K.E. (1979). *The Social Psychology of Organising*, 2nd edn. Reading, Mass.: Addison Wesley.

Whitley, R. (1999). *Divergent Capitalisms*. Oxford: Oxford University Press.

Wickramasinghe, D., and Hopper. T. (2005). A cultural political economy of management accounting controls: A case study of a textile mill in a traditional *Sinhalese* village. *Critical Perspectives on Accounting*, 16(4), 473–503.

Widener, S. (2007). An empirical analysis of the levers of control framework. *Accounting, Organizations and Society*, 32, 757–88.

Wildavsky, A. (1964). *The Politics of the Budgetary Process*. Boston, Mass.: Little Brown.

Zeff, S. (1972). *Forging Accounting Principles in Five Countries*. London: Stipes.

Zelizer, V. (1994). *The Social Meaning of Money*. New York: Basic Books.

2

Everyday Accounting Practices and Intentionality

Thomas Ahrens

INTRODUCTION

There is now an urgent need for research which can provide a basis for seeing accounting as both a social and organisational phenomenon. More explicit consideration needs to be given to questions of power, influence and control. Even what might be the quite significant ritualistic role of many accounting systems needs to be recognised. And every opportunity should be taken to move beyond static forms of analysis to study the complexities of the evolving dynamic processes of accounting in action. (Hopwood 1976: 3)

Throughout his distinguished career, Anthony Hopwood has made the context of accounting an important theme of his scholarship. In his first editorial for *Accounting, Organizations and Society* he emphasized the dynamic character of accounting and the limitations of our understanding of the design and use of accounting systems and their actual functioning. Associated with *Accounting, Organizations and Society*, and the like-minded journals that were established subsequently, has become a series of inquiries into the social and organizational influences on accounting as well as the ways in which accounting itself influences organizations and societies and, in important ways, constitutes aspects of their functioning.

Central to those inquiries have been efforts at understanding accounting practices. Such research has mainly drawn on what Tomkins and Groves (1983) called 'naturalistic' approaches. An important promise of such approaches has lain in understanding the specificity of the social and organizational contexts as part of which accounting functions. Tomkins and Groves called specifically for research into the everyday accountant's reality, high-lighting our lack of understanding of the complex ways in which accounting is interwoven with the fabric of day-to-day organizational activity (see also Baxter and Chua's [this volume] discussion of Hopwood's contribution to naturalistic research into everyday accounting).

In this chapter I want to explore further the significance of everyday accounting practices for accounting scholarship and especially the ways in which accounting can be mobilized for the pursuit of organizational and social objectives. What do we know about the intentions that practitioners of the craft pursue through accounting? From a practice perspective accounting is an array of activities that is ordered by practical understandings, rules, and objectives and projects (Schatzki 2002), and that forms a nexus of practices together with management and control practices, commercial prac-tices, reporting practices, bookkeeping practices and suchlike. By analysing the key components and influences on practices and the various ways in which they interact with other practices, a practice lens emphasizes the complexity of seemingly mundane everyday accounting. It also underlines the variability of accounting and, thereby, the highly specific ways in which accounting can be practised in different places and times.

From a practice perspective everyday accounting is therefore not a syno-nym for routine, humdrum accounting. Unlike some interpretations of institutional theory it does not conceptualize the embedding of accounting in its context as routine in the sense of (unthinking) repetition. Practice theorists recognize repetition and its potential to order activities but they conceive of practices as much wider 'tangle[s] of samenesses and similarities' (Schatzki 2001: 42). A break in a series of repetitions may mean that a routine was interrupted or that it ceased to exist. For a practice, by contrast, a break in a series of repetitions may constitute an integral element, a demonstration that the practice is changing with the times and maintaining its relevance. Practices are ongoing achievements. They are the result of skilful accomplish-ment. To contribute to a practice it may be useful to imitate activity but it is essential to want to contribute. Mindless repetition is a sign that a practice is in the process of disintegration or, perhaps, has not formed yet because practices are meaningful.

Intention is a key element of practice theories. It enables the theorist to describe social orderings that are inhabited and sustained by purposeful people whose actions are not determined by the social orderings. Rather, their desire to be and act as practitioners defines the rules and objectives of their activities *qua* practitioner, and their experience is the store from which they develop their practical understandings, the cognitive, bodily, emotional, interpersonal, etc., abilities to practise. Practitioners are thus capable of deliberation on all aspects of practice. They can blend repetition and innovation in their practice in seeking to preserve it, tweak it, or change it radically.

By locating intention in the everyday practice a site is defined for the study of how a phenomenon as ancient and complex as accounting can be harnessed in the pursuit of particular individual, organizational, and social objectives, without having to rely on spectacular accounting changes, be they conceptual or technical. Rather, the explanation resides in how accounting is understood and used every day, as a matter of course. For those everyday understandings and uses already bear the experience, skills, and judgements of skilful practitioners who, all things considered, find their activities practical on that day.

Practice theory is neither interested in the 'hero sociology' (Law 1991) of practitioner management journals nor in social determinism. To understand practices like accounting through a practice lens it is not enough to focus on this one practice. Individual practices may be defined by specific histories of objectives, rules, and technologies, but the social world is constituted by meshes of different practices, more or less densely interwoven. This creates opportunities for practitioners to highlight their membership of some and not other practices, and mobilize different kinds of rules and objectives. Experienced practitioners are well aware that their intentions can influence practices in their organizations, and sometimes beyond. They also know that the pursuit of intentions that do not map onto well known and relevant practices can be costly for them (Vaivio 1999; Ahrens and Chapman 2000; Baxter and Chua 2008). Over time they can establish a relationship between the specific context of their practices and the nature of their intentions and how they are perceived by other practitioners.

THE ROLE OF INTENTION IN DIFFERENT STRANDS OF PRACTICE THEORIZING

The accounting literature offers several points of contact for the study of everyday accounting practices beyond field studies of accounting practitioners and their practices. Conceptually and practically, accounting history has played a prominent role in supporting insights into the everyday reality of accounting by developing distinctive notions of accounting change. Contemporary everyday accountings have become what they are through complex historical processes because they are socially embedded. The New Accounting History has outlined a vision of history that rejects the abstract imperatives of orderly progress and evolution as explanations of accounting change and acknowledges the serendipity of the everyday.

One aspect of the distinctiveness of the new accounting history is its focus on shifts in the forms of knowledge or expertise that typifies accounting at a particular moment in time and in a certain social context, whether this be a particular national or a more local cultural setting. (Miller et al. 1991: 399)

With this goes a widening of the area of inquiry for accounting history from one traditionally concerned with a preconceived notion of accounting to one oriented towards a more general interest in genealogies of calculation (Miller and Napier 1993). Rather than search for the origins of an empirically ill-defined accounting, they suggest that we attend to the diversity of historically specific practices and discourses which can be related to the emergence of the present,

... to think in terms of multiple and dispersed surfaces of emergence of disparate and often humble practices, rather than in terms of present accountings as those to which all preceding practices have necessarily and inexorably been headed, and to attend to specific 'localized conditions out of which [practices] emerge[]'. (Ibid.)

They see the 'surfaces of emergence' on which '*ensembles* of practices and rationales' (ibid.; emphasis in original) gain shape, as temporary social constructs arising from everyday accounting practices without claims towards profounder historical inevitability. Emphasizing the ensembles of practices and rationales of which accounting can become part (cf. Schatzki's [2002] 'meshes' of practices), they highlight the potential of calculative practices to engage with other forms of organizational expertise as well as institutions beyond the organization.

The principles of the New Accounting History resonate with diverse practice theories, all of which have sought to conceptualize the emergence of accountings in their various contexts, referring variously to the connections between change and the everyday. Four strands of practice theories of accounting can be distinguished (Ahrens and Chapman 2007*b*). Common to all of them is a concern with accounting in action in everyday organizational and social life.

Governmentality uses a practice notion that emphasizes the disciplinary powers of accounting (e.g. Hoskin and Macve 1988; Miller and O'Leary 1987; Ogden 1997; Radcliffe 1998). Studies of governmentality show accounting practices as fusions of programmes of government with specific technologies. The technologies, such as accounting, have historically specific programmatic ambitions imprinted on them. They are essential for the pursuit of those ambitions by mobilizing large numbers of disciplined actors who can be distributed across organizations or even societies. Those actors have choices that are conditioned but not determined by the programmes and technologies described by governmentality studies (Miller 2001). Its concern with the diffusion of power through (what come to be) the 'normal' activities of people gives it great potential for the study of everyday accounting practice.

A second strand of practice studies is actor network theory (ANT). Like governmentality ANT has sought to trace the generative paths of programmes of organizing and the ways in which such programmes come to fruition through networks of human and non-human actors such as machines, software, materials, etc. (e.g. Law and Hassard 1999; Latour 2005). Often the tracing of those networks seeks to deconstruct particular events, for example, the introduction of management budgets in the National Health Service (Preston et al. 1992) or the assembly of a new costing system and it subsequent demise (Briers and Chua 2001). Yet the deconstruction of notable events often emphasizes their everyday qualities, the difficulties of articulating programmes of change, assembling coalitions of support, defining appropriate technologies, overcoming hurdles of technical implementation and social acceptance, etc. What the actors want to achieve through accounting, is, like the actors themselves, a series of network effects. ANT studies tend not to start out as studies of everyday accounting practice but their style of narration often highlights the everyday nature of momentous change, for example, by showing the micro activities of macro actors.

A third strand might be labelled accountability. It has principally been concerned with the systems of accountability to which accounting systems can give rise, '... analysed as institutionalized forms of interdependent social practices' (Roberts and Scapens 1985: 446). Its potential to shed light on everyday accounting practices stems from its interest in the disembedding of personal and face-to-face notions of accountability through accounting based systems of accountability that privilege the reality of financial performance measurement over other organizational concerns (e.g. Roberts 1990; Ahrens 1996; Seal et al. 2004). Accountability studies have thereby shown some of the ways in which such performance measurement can be taken for granted in everyday organizational action and decision-making. Accountability studies have tended not to deconstruct the origins of the profit motives that are pursued through accounting.

A fourth group of practice papers shares an interest in the situated functionality of accounting. It has sought to specifically articulate some of the ways in which accounting can function as a management tool for the ordering of organizational activities and the setting and development of organizational agendas and priorities (e.g. Bower 1970; Hopwood 1987; Ahrens and Chapman 2007a). Accounting systems are designed and used in the pursuit of objectives which themselves are conditioned by existing accounting and other organizational practices and the visibilities, projects, normative ends, and emotions which constitute them. Focusing on the meaningful ordering thus afforded to organizational and social practices through accounting, situated functionality studies have sought to give somewhat greater prominence to the role of objectives and managerial agency. By studying everyday accounting they seek to shed light on the ways in which accounting and control practices are embedded in dense meshes of other organizational practices and arrangements.

Even though everyday accounting is in various ways relevant for all of those strands of accounting practice scholarship it has hardly been the focus of research. If anything it served as a backdrop for accounting change, because the majority of practice studies have been concerned with change (Ahrens and Mollona 2007). Governmentality studies have tended to trace the emergence and spread of novel disciplinary techniques and powers (e.g. Radcliffe 1998), ANT studies have often reported on the construction (and demise) of accounting systems (e.g. Preston et al. 1992), accountability studies have frequently been concerned with new regimes of accountability (e.g. Roberts 1990), and situated functionality studies have, for example, investigated long-term organizational change (Hopwood 1987) and investment decision-making (Bower 1970). Change has tended to provide the occasion for scholarly work and been the catalyst for developing insights into the accounting phenomenon.

Tomkins and Groves' call (1983) for research into the everyday has therefore met with a less enthusiastic response than a glance at the considerable volume of field research in accounting might suggest. The volume of studies concerned with 'the everyday accountant and researching his [sic] reality' (Tomkins and Groves 1983) has remained modest even though it showed recent growth (e.g. Hopwood 1972, 1989; Preston 1986; Jonsson 1998, this volume; Ahrens and Chapman 2005, 2007*a*; Baxter and Chua 2008, this volume). Their concern has been to understand better the practices of accounting, their uses and effects in day-to-day organizational and social life, as well as key influences that have shaped the accounting phenomenon.

KNOWLEDGE OF EVERYDAY ACCOUNTING HELPS UNDERSTAND, CONTEXTUALIZE, AND ANTICIPATE ACCOUNTING CHANGE

This is not to downplay the significance of accounting change or disregard the achievements of studies which have overtly addressed change. The theme of accounting change has been useful for defining a broad research interest across many different accounting techniques and contexts of use (see, e.g., Burns and Vaivio 2001).

Even though the accounting practices observable during times of organizational change differ in many respects from those of everyday business-as-usual, the two are also in important ways connected. For example, a focus on changing practices may bring to light everyday assumptions and convictions that are so fundamental to the functioning of an organization that they are not normally articulated. It is not unlikely, for example, that prior to a series of measures to improve European Railways' financial performance (Dent 1991) many of its managers were not fully aware of the operations and engineering principles which, up to then, had ordered the organization's everyday managerial practices. Also, series of small changes may, without drawing much attention, adapt everyday practices.

Some of the most vivid and best-illustrated studies of accounting change are grounded in a deep understanding of the everyday accounting practices that made up the context of change. From the point of view of practice theory everyday accounting is not clearly distinct from accounting change. Accounting practices as meaningfully ordered arrays of activity are never entirely free from change (Schatzki 2001; Busco et al. 2007). The intensity and speed of change may change over time but it never stops.

Often one can only tell retrospectively if the overall effect of many small changes was to give rise to sustained change of everyday practices or amounted to ensuring overall continuity of practices, perhaps in the face of changing circumstances. For example, in the first case of their study, Quattrone and Hopper (2005) illustrated how a significant change of accounting systems, a new enterprise resource planning system, could serve to reinforce and, in some ways, make more effective the functioning of existing everyday organizational relationships.

Rather than re-defining relations between hierarchical levels, functional areas, and operational activities, ERP reinforced the status quo. Its configuration created a unitary notion of space and time enabling action at a distance (Latour 1987) to continue. (Quattrone and Hopper 2005: 738)

This point is pertinent for a practice perspective because practices are not about the formulaic repetition of activities. Practice reckons with the agency of practitioners to experiment and adapt in pursuit of achieving the best practical results (Barnes 2001). As change becomes endemic to the functioning of accounting (Ahrens and Chapman 2002: 156–7) everyday accounting practices rely for their continuity on different kinds of change.

An example of small changes in simple, everyday accounting practices that support continuity in organization-wide accounting and management practices is found in the case of a UK brewing company (Ahrens 1997: 630). Its management put great emphasis on meeting financial objectives yet the practices that characterized the overall organizational role of the finance function were much more complex than this objective may suggest. The management accountants prided themselves in their insights into the functioning of line management and their ability to 'challenge' the plans for revenues, costs, and investment of the managers responsible for sales, production, logistics, etc. But the management accountants also saw themselves as line management's 'business partners', supporting their planning and achievement of targets. The specific example concerns a review of departmental budgets half way through the financial year in order to ensure that the company met its overall profit target.

Asked by the finance director to suggest savings of £1.2 m, two experienced management accountants analysed the departmental forecasts to date and formulated a series of questions to departments, using the phrase, 'What would be the pain of not spending X?' Through the day-long review meeting the two management accountants initially sought to use their commercial acumen to identify budget cuts that entailed little business risk. 'I guess we should be careful. We're not going to use all the good news and fire at it, and ignore all the risks' (Ahrens 1997: 631). But when a fellow management accountant joined them briefly they joked with her that the true nature of finance's 'partnership' with line management was deeply antagonistic: 'Yeah, stuff them' (ibid.). Yet later, when a financial accountant, who did not work closely with line managers, joined them they reverted to emphasizing the close working relationship that they had with line managers and that the financial accountant lacked. Then, after a few more hours of reviewing they grew impatient with 'sloppy' forecasts and emphasized again their antagonism with line management:

'That is just hideous, that forecast.'
'It's not a forecast at all.'
'We could tell them, give us a forecast or give us 300 grand.' (Ibid.)

The management accountants' attitude towards the review and the ways in which they reviewed the forecasts changed several times during this day-long meeting, depending, for instance, on which of the two management accountants took the lead in any one of the reviewed forecasts, how much time they had already spent on previous reports, and who else was present in their meeting. Throughout the review meeting the two management accountants expressed much criticism of the finance function's partnership practices with line management. They did not, however, change the array of activities that constituted those practices. Rather their activities formed part of that array, making it more thoughtful and adding a measure of reflectiveness. In that sense their criticism served to strengthen the partnership practices because it provided an occasion to think through their advantages and disadvantages and to strengthen the management accountants' independence of judgement whilst conducting the review. This example therefore suggests that the continuity of complex practices, such as the overall organizational role of the finance function, can draw support from small variations and changes in the activities that make up simple everyday practices, such as budget review practices.

Compared to such ruminations of colleagues who work in the same function organizations often exhibit more public and forceful occasions of discussion and criticism. Contests of accountability, for example from challenges to hierarchical power, can similarly allow organizational members to test the assumptions underlying pervasive organizational practices (Ahrens and Chapman 2002: 168). Such contests can become integral to everyday organizational life and an important source of flexibility for organizational practices. Close observation of the small variations of practices to which contests of accountability give rise can help anticipate emerging sources of disagreement over the usefulness of certain organizational practices and, thereby, potentially larger organizational change. Practices are essentially unpredictable (Schatzki 2001), but emerging changes may announce themselves in the variability of mundane everyday practices.

This insight underlies many studies of changing accounting practices. Changes in key organizational performance metrics and performance measurement practices can be brought about in regular question and answer sessions in management meetings and they can be reversed with reference to their effects on the everyday handling of operational priorities (Vaivio 1999). The effects of large-scale accounting change can be gauged through a closer examination of their reception in everyday meetings that may be seriously focused on recasting organizational activity in the language of accounting or ridicule the accounting language by making reference to 'Donald Duck-money' (Kurunmaki 1999: 114). Often an in-depth study of the managerial everyday tensions generated by macro organizational change agendas can illuminate the conflict-ridden rationales of emerging accounting and other performance metrics (Andon et al. 2007).

WHY THE FUNCTIONING OF EVERYDAY ACCOUNTING PRACTICES MAY HAVE TO REMAIN OBSCURE

Everyday accounting, therefore, holds in many ways the key to understanding accounting change. But this is not to overstate the visibility of everyday practices and the intelligibility of their rationales. Privileged sites of explanation are rarely found in the field. Discourses that seek to encapsulate the functioning of practices offer only ever partial renditions (Block 1991; Archer 2000). The multiplicity of meaning in practices cannot be exhausted in texts. Moreover, in politically charged contexts, discourses that purport to characterize practices need to conceal the real functioning of practices as a condition of the continued functioning of those practices (Bourdieu 1992). At the level of individual interactions, where certain practices involve the pursuit of political advantage it can be essential that the selfish motives underlying those practices remain concealed for them to remain intact. Bourdieu pursued the duplicity of action and discourse to the general social level. He regarded the public account of the workings of practice—folk wisdom, proverbs, etc.—as deeply ideological because they reify culture. In those accounts, culture exists as *opus operatum*, as product. Bourdieu distinguished it from the *modus operandi*, the way culture operates.

In Bourdieu's ethnography, the function of the *opus operatum* was to hide the *modus operandi* from the members of the society he studied. For the culture portrayed in his ethnography to appear as a coherent system its members must not know how it actually operates, for else they might exploit this knowledge to their advantage in the concrete ways in which they operate amidst the often conflicting rules of polite behaviour and good manners. For example, social rules exist for offering and returning gifts, or for proposing and accepting marriages. But the various rules that may apply are complex and often contradictory. To offer a small gift is mean. Too great a gift is arrogant and tactless because it can never be returned. To return a gift too hastily is to reject the social bond that the gift was to strengthen. To return it too late can damage social relations. The application of marriage rules to a concrete situation is equally difficult. Through which channels, with what kinds of inducements, and with reference to which of the possible kin relationships should a marriage be proposed?

Bourdieu's practice theory offers a highly particular explanation of social order. It assumes that people's acquisition of knowledge makes them act in accordance with social structures. Actors' public references to ideologically accepted rules of behaviour as well as the ways in which they go about their private calculations of the costs and benefits of different courses of action (with respect to money, reputation, honour, security, and so forth) are subject to the workings of the *habitus*. The *habitus*, as the unverifiable kernel of his theory, defines the mode of social action and defines the achievements of the members of a culture as members. Their specific calculations are made not as a matter of unbounded choice. Instead, individual deliberation mirrors the objective and defining feature of specific cultures, the public and private

spaces and modes they assign to the pursuit of appropriate behaviours and
desired advantages. Bourdieu's concept of the *habitus* offers a powerful
argument for studying everyday practices. They hold the key for understanding the deep orderings of cultural systems, the code, if you want, for practitioners' interpretations and uses of the elements of their practices.

Bourdieu's emphasis on the complexity of the practical, real time uses of
cultural templates has had many parallels in the anthropological literature.
His theorizing gives rise to an important problem, however. His theory is
remarkable for its totalization of practice in the *habitus*, through which he
sought to establish for himself a powerful argumentative strategy for organizing the diverse tactics of the natives on whose everyday lives his ethnography and theorizing rest. If practices are acknowledged to be subject to
spontaneous agency (besides being structured by routines and traditions)
how can they, in the next theoretical move, be subjected to a meta-discourse
that seeks to reinsert this agency into its 'proper' theoretical slot? Discourse
cannot, after all, encapsulate action. De Certeau (1988) suggests that the
concept of the *habitus* is itself an ideological construct born of the desire to
subsume Bourdieu's subtle observations of natives' everyday life in Algeria or
provincial France under the dogma of his particular practice theory in order
to make it palatable for the Parisian audience as scientific sociological
discourse.

De Certeau made the autonomy of action from strategic discourse, the
capacity of actors to break out of institutionalized, traditional, or otherwise
expected behaviour the focus of his own practice theory. He did this primarily
through studies of the responses of consumers to advertising and purchased
products and services, consumers' actual uses of representations that may have
been intended for quite different uses. This led de Certeau to a more general
distinction between the practices of the powerful and the disenfranchised.

The powerful develop what de Certeau called strategies.

I call a strategy the calculus of force-relationships which becomes possible when a
subject of will and power (a proprietor, an enterprise, a city, a scientific institution)
can be isolated from an 'environment.' A strategy assumes a place that can ... serve as
the basis for generating relations with an exterior distinct from it (competitors,
adversaries, 'clienteles,' 'targets,' or 'objects' of research). Political, economic, and
scientific rationality has been constructed on this strategic model.

But consumers seek to resist producers' strategies.

I call a 'tactic,' on the other hand, a calculus which cannot count on a 'proper' (a
spatial or institutional localization), nor thus on a borderline distinguishing the other
as a visible totality. ... A tactic insinuates itself into the other's place, fragmentarily,
without taking it over in its entirety, without being able to keep it at a distance. (Ibid.)

Through tactics, consumers can ignore or subvert carefully designed advertising messages and put products to unintended uses.

The weak must continually turn to their own ends forces alien to them. This is achieved in the propitious moments when they are able to combine heterogeneous elements (thus, in the supermarket, the housewife confronts heterogeneous and mobile data—what she has in the refrigerator, the tastes, appetites, and moods of her guests, the best buys and their possible combinations with what she already has on hand at home, etc.); the intellectual synthesis of these given elements takes the form, however, not of a discourse, but of the decision itself, the act and manner in which the opportunity is 'seized'. (Ibid.)

De Certeau's notion of 'seizing opportunities' is a humanistic perspective on everyday practices. In contrast with Foucault's insistence on the power that enmeshes society through the spread of mundane and minute disciplinary practices, de Certeau emphasizes the evasive '... procedures and ruses of consumers [that] compose the network of an anti-discipline ...'. His is a reminder of the creativity of individuals and their possibilities of resistance to power, suppressive or disciplinary. Crucially, the cognitive work of those engaged in 'tactics' relies on the spur of the moment. Their performance depends not on carefully articulated cognitive procedures because they need to work with what they find in the concrete situation. Cognition in practice is thus dependent on the elements of its context.

DEFINING EVERYDAY ACCOUNTING

De Certeau offers a notion of the everyday that competes with Bourdieu's. His notion of the everyday does not contain the code for deep structures of meaning but the resources, through unpredictable opportunities of make-do assemblages, for the disenfranchised to subvert the challenges of the powerful. He remains vague on the nature of the resources of the disenfranchised and does not discuss the extent to which they can learn over time the principles of successful assemblies. But his suggestion of an everyday that retains a measure of independence from carefully planned strategies is a useful antidote to the notion that critique of practices simply serves to refine and strengthen them, such as Ahrens and Chapman's (2002) suggestion that hierarchical contests of accountability can remind organizational members of shared commercial objectives and serve to articulate acceptable ways of achieving them. This may have worked in the organization which they studied but it cannot be assumed to hold generally. Preston (1986), for example, notes how a clique of production managers maintained an informal network of information exchange separate from the formal management reporting. This parallel reporting practice protected the clique from hierarchical interventions. It meant that the formal reporting lagged updates and senior management did not obtain information as fast as might have been possible.

This raises the question of the definition of accounting practices and the membership of practitioners. Practices are arrays of purposeful activity whose ordering is brought about by the practitioners' attempts at meaningful practice. Depending on whether one focuses on the practice of factory reporting or informal networking—and, therefore, defines the practitioners as all factory managers or just the members of the clique—the act of, say, selectively passing on information gleaned from an ad hoc inventory count can advance one practice (informal networking) and harm another (factory reporting). Therefore, the question of whether hierarchical contests of accountability ultimately strengthen accounting and other organizational practices depends on how widely one draws the envelope of the practices under discussion. They might be confined to subsets of organizational members, or they might be extended to the whole division, perhaps the corporate group, or even accounting as such.

In organizations with distinctive organizational subcultures notions of company-wide practices may remain weak (Ahrens and Mollona 2007). Such subcultures may even give rise to highly specific notions of profitability and capital that remain indigenous to members of the subculture. From a practice perspective such organizations can be dysfunctional in the sense that they do not exhibit practices in which all members of the organization are strongly invested. Ahrens and Mollona showed how all members of their case organization were members of practices of production that were ordered such that raw materials and intermediate products could be passed from department to department and become finished goods. In that sense organizational members were members of organizational practices that formed functioning chains of action. The production of meaning and identity, however, was invested in those aspects of the productive process which were specific to individual departments. Pride in production and efforts at improving production practices were tied up with discourses and practices of demarcating membership of subcultures, not membership of the company.

A focus on the everyday accounting practices of an organization, to the level of detail of individual shop floors and shifts, can offer valuable insights into the functioning of accounting by exploring its embeddedness in specific cultural, social, economic, and technical contexts. For this, culture should be conceived as '... practical and ideational at the same time because meanings do not exist independent of practices' (Ahrens and Mollona 2007: 309). In Ahrens and Mollona's study distinctive subcultures:

... arose from the workers' tasks and shop floor practices, skills and occupational histories, the technologies they used, their broader outlooks on work and organisational membership, and, significantly, those aspects of their social backgrounds that clarified their reasons for seeking out, and acquiescing to, particular organisational subcultures. (2007: 328)

In this manner a cultural perspective on accounting and other everyday practices of calculation can shed light on potential alternative uses of accounting, and future options for managerial and organizational activity and the practices which they constitute more generally.

CONCLUSIONS

An aspect of accounting practices that holds much fascination for accounting scholars is the sheer variety and malleability of the forms of accounting and their uses and effects. The literature is filled with examples of how accounting can become a resource for change or an obstacle to it; how it can be used to exercise tight control or support debate and innovation; how it can be combined with other forms of expertise or remain isolated; and how it can dominate social and organizational debates or be consigned to the realm of the technical and ignored.

An important difficulty for the study of everyday accounting lies in its definition. Accounting is a heterogeneous phenomenon. It combines with other forms of expertise; it manifests itself in diverse technologies. It is not static but changes in response to organizational circumstances and external influences. The specific ways in which accounting is practised and comes to affect organizations, institutions, and societies is not a matter of abstract imperatives but ongoing, everyday practices.

Both a fluidity and a specificity have been introduced into our understanding of accounting in action. The significances attached to accounting have been shown in the process of their reformulation. The craft has been seen as becoming embedded in different organisational configurations and serving very different organisational functions in the process of its change. The mobilising vehicles for these changes have been seen as residing in a very diverse number of organisational processes and practices and, not least, in accounting itself. (Hopwood 1987: 231)

Practice studies of accounting have emphasized accounting's specificity by developing frames of intelligibility for accounting in action. They offer schemes with which to locate specific accountings in particular contexts such that activities particular to a time and a place can shed light on the orderings of and through accounting found in other times and places. Through engaging diverse conceptual framings of practice with the empirical detail of everyday accounting rich accounts have been produced of the ways in which the everyday can anchor and support grand schemes and ambitions for change and, in the process, yield to such change. The practice literature has demonstrated the usefulness of encompassing categories, such as change, by connecting them with attention to the detail of organizational activity. In the case of change much has been learned by showing its relationship with everyday accounting, for it is made up of activities that potentially constitute change, as well as activities that are intended to comment on change or thwart it.

But the potential of everyday accounting for accounting scholarship extends beyond concerns with change. Greater attention to the everyday can help shed light on questions such as, in what ways does accounting become related with social, economic, cultural, and technical aspects of organizations and society for it to become practical? When is action part of practices and of which practices does it become part? What counts as everyday normal and desirable accounting and under what circumstances does it change? How resilient might the everyday accounting practices portrayed in studies of organizational subcultures be to the reassemblages of the actor networks described in ANT studies?

The uses of accounting for the pursuit of practitioners' specific intentions is an important theme for the study of accounting in action but one from which accounting scholars have often shied away. After all, the intentions of individual practitioners are not the concern of scholars. Consultants are paid to help managers achieve what they want. And yet such intentions are crucial for scholarly insight into the accounting phenomenon. Jönsson (this volume) outlines his suggestions for studying some of the different logics of interaction within management accounting practices in order to better understand 'the full complexity of controller work' (p. 1 of his script). And Baxter and Chua (this volume) remind us of the practitioners' work of ordering heterogeneous practices and the scholars' work of sorting the accounts of such practices, privileging some over others.

Action is simply a series of doings that are sometimes set in counterpoint to structure. Practical action, by contrast, forms part of arrays of activity that are ordered and reordered in pursuit of practical ends. It is through attention to the everyday resources and effects of those accounting practices that accounting scholarship can heed Hopwood's call to study:

... accounting elaboration and change as attempts are made to ensure the continued integrity, legitimacy, effectiveness and power of the craft.   (1987: 212)

REFERENCES

Ahrens, T. (1996). Styles of accountability. *Accounting, Organizations and Society*, 21 (2/3), 139–73.

——(1997). Talking accounting: An ethnography of management knowledge in British and German brewers. *Accounting, Organizations and Society*, 22(7), 617–37.

—— and Chapman, C.S. (2000). Occupational identity of management accountants in Britain and Germany. *European Accounting Review*, 9(4), 477–98.

———(2002). The structuration of legitimate performance measures and management: Day-to-day contests of accountability in a U.K. restaurant chain. *Management Accounting Research*, 13(2), 151–71.

———(2005). Accounting and the crafting of strategy: A practice-based view. In C.S. Chapman (ed.), *Management Accounting and Strategy*. Oxford: Oxford University Press, 106–24.

———(2007*a*). Management accounting as practice. *Accounting, Organizations and Society*, 32(1–2), 1–27.

———(2007*b*). Theorizing practice in management accounting research. In C.S. Chapman, A.G. Hopwood, and M.D. Shields (eds.), *Handbook of Management Accounting Research*, Vol. 1. Oxford: Elsevier Publishing, 299–318.

—— and Mollona, M. (2007). Organisational control as cultural practice: A shop floor ethnography of a Sheffield steel mill. *Accounting, Organizations and Society*, 32 (4–5), 305–31.

Andon, P., Baxter, J., and Chua, W.F. (2007). Accounting change as relational drifting: A field study of experiments with performance measurement. *Management Accounting Research*, 18, 273–308.

Archer, M.S. (2000). *Being Human: The Problem of Agency*. Cambridge: Cambridge University Press.

Barnes, B. (2001). Practice as collective action. In T.R. Schatzki, K. Knorr Cetina, and E. von Savigny (eds.), *The Practice Turn in Contemporary Theory*. London: Routledge, 17–28.

Baxter, J. and Chua, W.F. (2008). Be(com)ing the chief financial officer of an organisation: experimenting with Bourdieu's practice theory. *Management Accounting Research*, 19(2), 212–30.

Bloch, M. (1991). Language, anthropology and cognitive science. *Man*, 26(2), 183–98.

Bourdieu, P. (1977). *Outline of a Theory of Practice.* Cambridge: Cambridge University Press.

—— (1992). *The Logic of Practice.* Cambridge: Polity Press.

Bower, J. (1970). *Managing the Resource Allocation Process.* Boston, Mass.: Harvard Business School Press.

Briers, M. and Chua, W.F. (2001). The role of actor networks and boundary objects in management accounting change: A field study of an implementation of activity-based costing. *Accounting, Organizations and Society,* 26(3), 237–69.

Burns, J. and Vaivio, J. (2001). Management accounting change. *Management Accounting Research,* 12, 389–402.

Busco, C., Quattrone, P., and Riccaboni, A. (2007). Management accounting issues in interpreting its nature and change. *Management Accounting Research,* 18(2), 125–49.

De Certeau, M. (1988). *The Practice of Everyday Life.* Berkeley: University of California Press.

Dent, J.F. (1991). Accounting and organizational cultures: A field study of the emergence of a new organizational reality. *Accounting, Organizations and Society,* 16, 705–32.

Hopwood, A.G. (1972). An empirical study of the role of accounting data in performance evaluation. *Empirical Research in Accounting: Selected Studies,* Supplement to *Journal of Accounting Research,* 156–82.

—— (1976). Editorial. *Accounting, Organizations and Society,* 1(1).

—— (1987). The archaeology of accounting systems. *Accounting, Organizations and Society,* 12(3), 207–34.

Hoskin, K. and Macve, R. (1988). The genesis of accountability: The West Point connections. *Accounting, Organizations and Society,* 13(1), 37–73.

Jonsson, S. (1998). Relate management accounting research to managerial work! *Accounting, Organizations and Society,* 23(4), 411–34.

Kurunmaki, L. (1999). Professional vs financial capital in the field of health care: Struggles for the redistribution of power and control. *Accounting, Organizations and Society,* 24(2), 95–124.

Latour, B. (2005). *Reassembling the Social: An Introduction to Actor-Network-Theory.* Oxford: Oxford University Press.

Law, J. (1991). Introduction: Monsters, machines and sociotechnical relations. In J. Law (ed.), *A Sociology of Monsters: Essays on Power, Technology and Domination.* London: Routledge, 1–25.

—— and Hassard, J. (eds.) (1999). *Actor Network Theory and After.* Oxford: Blackwell Publishers.

Miller, P. (2001). Governing by numbers: Why calculative practices matter. *Social Research,* 68(2), 379–96.

—— and Napier, C. (1993). Genealogies of calculation. *Accounting, Organizations and Society,* 18, 631–47.

—— and O'Leary, T. (1987). Accounting and the construction of the governable person. *Accounting, Organizations and Society,* 12, 235–65.

——Hopper, T., and Laughlin, R. (1991). The new accounting history: An introduction. *Accounting, Organizations and Society*, 16, 395–403.

——(1976). Editorial. *Accounting Organization and Society*, 1(1).

Ogden, S.G. (1997). Accounting for organizational performance: The construction of the customer in the privatized water industry. *Accounting, Organizations and Society*, 22(6), 529–56.

Preston, A. (1986). Interactions and arrangements in the process of informing. *Accounting, Organizations and Society*, 11(6), 521–40.

——Cooper, D., and Coombs, R.W. (1992). Fabricating budgets: A study of the production of management budgeting in the National Health Service. *Accounting, Organizations and Society*, 17(6), 561–93.

Quattrone, P. and Hopper, T. (2005). A 'time–space odyssey': Management control systems in two multinational organisations. *Accounting, Organizations and Society*, 30(7–8), 735–64.

Radcliffe, V.S. (1998). Efficiency audit: An assembly of rationalities and programmes. *Accounting, Organizations and Society*, 23(4), 377–410.

Roberts, J. (1990). Strategy and accounting in a UK conglomerate. *Accounting, Organizations and Society*, 15(1–2), 107–26.

——and Scapens, R. (1985). Accounting systems and systems of accountability: Understanding accounting practices in their organizational contexts. *Accounting, Organizations and Society*, 10, 443–56.

Schatzki, T.R. (2001). Practice theory: An introduction. In T.R. Schatzki, K. Knorr Cetina, and E. von Savigny (eds.), *The Practice Turn in Contemporary Theory*. London: Routledge, 1–14.

——(2002). *The Site of the Social*. University Park, PA: Pennsylvania State University Press.

Seal, W., Berry, A., and Cullen, J. (2004). Disembedding the supply chain: Institutionalized reflexivity and inter-firm accounting. *Accounting, Organizations and Society*, 29(1), 73–92.

Tomkins, C. and Groves, R. (1983). The everyday accountant and researching his reality. *Accounting, Organizations and Society*, 8(4), 361–74.

Vaivio, J. (1999). Examining 'the quantified customer'. *Accounting, Organizations and Society*, 24(8), 689–715.

3

Institutional Perspectives on the Internationalization of Accounting

Patricia J. Arnold

*Accounting research is not keeping pace with the growing international-
ization of the world of accounting practice. While accounting in action is
now embedded in multi-national enterprises and multi-national audit
firms, and subject to emerging forms of supranational regulation, accounting research still tends to focus on national contexts and thereby remains
largely influenced by national traditions and national schools of thought.
One result is that we still have a rather crude notion of accounting
diversity and the reasons for it, and rather minimal understandings of
the nature and forms of international pressure for change.*

(Anthony Hopwood 1997)

Over the past decade, the world of financial accounting practice, which was
traditionally governed by national states, has internationalized at a surprisingly
rapid pace. International Financial Reporting Standards (IFRS) are now widely
accepted and international harmonization of auditing, educational, ethics,
and professional licensing standards are on the horizon. These developments
together with pressures for mutual recognition of professional credentials
obtained in other jurisdictions are eliminating what representatives of the
accounting and financial services industry refer to as 'national regulatory
barriers' to the creation of a global market in accounting services and a global
professional workforce. The consequences of this transformation in the
accounting world are non-trivial. For the United States and Europe, the
prospects of a global professional workforce foreshadow a trend towards
the offshoring of accounting and auditing work and a downward pressure on
white-collar wages. For emerging economies, harmonization and the dismantling of national regulation threaten domestic accounting industries by enabling
a small cartel of multinational accounting firms, based within Western
nations, to consolidate power and control over their international affiliates.

And, in rich and poor nations, alike, entire economies face the threat of systemic instability within an international financial system that is very loosely governed by a 'standards–surveillance–compliance' system (Wade 2007) in which the newly internationalized world of financial accounting and auditing plays a key quasi-regulatory role. Given these consequences, Hopwood's (1997) call for research to enhance our understanding of the forces driving the internationalization of financial accounting remains an important challenge for contemporary accounting research.

The brand of orthodox economic thinking that has long dominated accounting research is ill equipped to explain the dynamics of transformation within the field of financial accounting. According to the neoclassical paradigm, the emergence of multinational audit firms and the international harmonization of financial reporting and auditing standards is a response to investors' need for transparency in a rapidly globalizing capital market (Dye and Sunder 2001). Implicit in this functionalist interpretation of accounting's role in the global financial marketplace is an unexamined assumption that markets exist in a social vacuum: international capital markets and accounting's quasi-regulatory role within them are treated as seemingly natural phenomena, akin to the weather, that have emerged devoid of history or the influence of social, economic, and political power. At most orthodox theory posits that an exogenous force, namely technological innovation, is the driving force behind the growth of global financial markets and associated changes within the accounting and financial services markets (Friedman 2000). While advances in telecommunications technology have undoubtedly accelerated the pace of global financial market integration, orthodox theory's tendency towards technological determinism, like its functionalism, obscures the ways in which historically developed institutional forms and political actions have shaped the evolution of capitalist economies, financial markets, and financial accounting practice.

In response to the limitations of the market paradigm, many scholars have turned to institutional theories as an alternative framework for understanding the dynamics underlying the internationalization of accounting practice. Unlike orthodox economic approaches, institutional analysis recognizes that economies and economic actions are embedded in societies (Granovetter 1985) and that economic outcomes are often shaped by non-market institutions in processes that are often politically saturated (Zukin and DiMaggio 1990). In place of economic determinism, institutional approaches offer a method for systematically examining the development of historically determined institutional arrangements for governing capitalist economies, and for understanding in a non-deterministic way how the internationalization of accounting practice has both shaped and been shaped by the contemporary world political economy where financial speculation plays an increasingly central role in capitalist accumulation. This chapter provides a synopsis of the contributions that institutional analysis has made to our understanding of the internationalization of financial accounting practices and outlines directions for further research. In the processes, I argue in favour of a broad view of institutional analysis as a multidisciplinary field that is capable of interrogating not only the social and cultural underpinnings of accounting practice, but also the political and economic forces that underlie the internationalization of financial accounting practice.

DEFINING INSTITUTIONS

While institutional analysis has gained prominence within the social sciences as an alternative to economic determinism, there is a lack of consensus within the field regarding the basic question of what is meant by institutions and institutional analysis (Hollingsworth 2003). These terms have been conceptualized differently by scholars from diverse intellectual traditions who sometimes differ radically in their assumptions and research questions. On one extreme are institutional economists (Williamson 1985) who remain closely bound to the neoclassical economic paradigm; their aim is to expand, rather than supplant, the market paradigm by introducing concepts such as bounded rationality, transaction costs, and path dependency. On the other extreme are scholars, such as the regulation theorists (Aglietta 1976; Boyer 1990), who come to institutional analysis from the tradition of Marxism. In attempting to explain how capitalism has survived over the long term despite its internal contradictions, regulation theorists point to the various institutional arrangements that have been developed historically to mitigate capitalism's tendencies towards economic crisis and social instability. Beyond neoclassical and neo-Marxian economists lay a broad spectrum of sociologists, economic sociologists, historians, and political scientists who share interests in institutions (Campbell et al. 1991; Hirst and Zeitlin 1991; Streeck 1992; Hollingsworth and Boyer 1997). Among these are organizational sociologists (DiMaggio and Powell 1983; Greenwood and Hinings 1996; Greenwood et al. 2002) whose embrace of institutional analysis has demonstrated that organizational behaviour is not only driven by economic motivations, but also by socially embedded norms, values, and shared meanings. While organizational sociology has had the most direct influence on accounting scholarship to date, the field of institutional studies is actually much broader. It encompasses a rich diversity of intellectual traditions which at times share little common ground beyond the general consensus that institutions matter to their respective pursuits.

In order to advance interdisciplinary research among these diverse traditions, Hollingsworth (2003) has developed a map of the field of institutional research to enable scholars to position their work in relation to the wider domain of institutional studies. His typology identifies no less than five distinct domains of institutional analysis. They are studies of (*a*) institutions defined as norms, rules, conventions, habits, and values; (*b*) institutional arrangements involving markets, states, corporate hierarchies, networks, associations, and communities; (*c*) institutional sectors such as the financial system, the education system, or the accounting and auditing field; (*d*) institutions defined as organizations themselves; and (*e*) institutions defined as societal or organizational outputs such as laws or administrative rules.

For purposes of this analysis, I have condensed Hollingsworth's map to specify three levels of institutional analysis: micro-, mezzo-, and macro-analysis. Microanalysis is the form of institutional analysis that examines how economies and economic decisions are embedded in norms, values, shared meanings, habits, and behavioural templates. Mezzo-level analysis refers to studies that examine economic activity within sectors of the economy, such as accounting and financial sectors. This level of analysis aims to understand how economic activity is embedded in institutional arrangements such as legal and regulatory regimes, and to explore the dynamics of change within these institutional fields. Marco-level analysis is defined as the study of institutional arrangements governing economies as a whole. Research at this level examines the long-term historical processes whereby the institutional arrangements governing capitalist economies have come into being and changed in response to economic crisis, political mobilization, and social struggle. The following sections examine each of these three levels of institutional analysis and their respective contributions—actual and potential—to our understanding of the internationalization of financial accounting practice.

MICRO-LEVEL INSTITUTIONAL ANALYSIS

Within the financial accounting literature, Young's study (1996) of 'institutional thinking' (Douglas 1986) by accounting policy-makers offers a prime example of a micro-level institutional analysis of how norms, conventions, and cognitive scripts influence economic decisions and actions. Based on an analysis of the deliberations leading to the Financial Accounting Standard

Board's (FASB) adoption of the financial reporting standard that specifies the rules for accounting for complex financial instruments on corporate balances sheets, Young contends that rule-makers were guided by taken-for-granted assumptions and conventional ways of thinking. US standard setters followed established norms of action based on the unexamined belief that financial market innovations such as complex derivative securities were efficient, and the presupposition that accounting's purpose was to provide investors with decision-relevant information on these exotic new financial products. Such institutional thinking, Young (1996) argues, explains why accounting policy-makers did not ask more fundamental questions about the risks these financial innovations posed to financial stability or the need for stronger regulatory oversight. Notwithstanding the emergence of an increasingly risky international 'casino economy' (Strange 1986), the creation of exotic and opaque derivative products, and the difficult, if not intractable, problem of assigning values to thinly traded securities, accounting standard setters followed old scripts and conventions, characteristic of narrow institutional thinking, when they adopted fair value accounting for financial instruments. By purporting to provide information to investors and creditors about the value of complex derivatives, financial accounting gave the appearance of normality and legitimacy to high-risk securitization and international financial speculation.

By showing how financial accounting is embedded in cognitive scripts and normative templates, Young's work, like other micro-level institutional analyses, serve as an important reminder of the continuities that persist in the midst of change. Continuities between past and present are also evident in the realm of international harmonization (Hopwood 2000). Although nominal adoption of international financial reporting and auditing standards has been widespread, field studies conducted by the World Bank in developing market economies show that non-compliance is rampant in practice (Hegarty et al. 2004). The World Bank's Report on the Observance of Standards and Codes (ROSC) programme found that although many governments have adopted legislation mandating or allowing international standards, the standards are often not applied in practice. Barriers to the implementation include misunderstandings about the nature of international standards, lack of enabling legislation needed to implement and enforce them, and mismatches between accounting and auditing requirements and countries' capacity to comply with and enforce mandated standards. In some cases, misunderstandings are fundamental: the ROSC report cites the example of a country which claims that it requires all listed companies to use international reporting standards even though the country's law actually mandates use of an outdated translation of standards that were effective in 1999 (Hegarty et al. 2004: 3). Further research at the mezzo level is needed to enhance our understanding of this observed discrepancy between the abstract notion of international harmonization and the actual practice of financial reporting as it operates in concrete social contexts (Hopwood 2000).

Micro-level institutional analysis is often considered more adept at explaining continuities with the past than the dynamics of change (Hollingsworth 2003). Institutional theory's focus on deeply embedded social norms, values, and cognitive schemes, however, does not preclude an analysis of change. To the contrary, the study of how the norms and values that rationalize economic behaviours shift over time represents an important new area of institutional study. In their expansive study of *The New Spirit of Capitalism,* Boltanski and Chiapello (2005), show how the normative justifications and rationalizing ethos that both legitimate and constrain capitalist accumulation have changed throughout history. Similarly, the accounting literature has begun to examine how the socialization process within international accounting firms (Hanlon 1994) and the 'institutional logics' governing the accounting field (Suddaby et al. 2007) have shifted in recent decades away from reliance on disinterested professionalism as a rationalizing narrative. Today international accounting firms openly embrace commercialism as they appeal to consumer (rather than public) interests and the supposed benefits of market competition and free trade as a rationale for harmonization and a justification for the expansion of global trade in financial and accounting services. At its best, micro institutional analysis can provide a basis for social critique and political action by identifying the tensions and contradictions within such rationalizing logics, and by revealing the social divisions that underpin cultural changes and shifting normative justifications for capital accumulation (Oakes et al. 1998; Boltanski and Chiapello 2005).

MEZZO-LEVEL INSTITUIONAL ANALYSIS

At the mezzo level, accounting research has begun to analyse the transformations in the institutional arrangements governing the accounting field that gave rise to the development of an international market for accounting and auditing services. These include the obvious shift in governance arrangements from national to international sites as evidenced by international harmonization of standards and emergence of supranational regulatory bodies. It also includes a more subtle accompanying shift away from what institutional theorists (Streeck and Schmitter 1985; Campbell et al. 1991) call associational governance and towards a hierarchical corporate form of governance. This shift is evidenced by the declining relevance of national professional accounting associations and the increasing dominance of a few powerful international firms (the Big 4 or Big 5 depending on the time frame) over the accounting field (Cooper and Robson 2006; Suddaby et al. 2007). Whereas in the past professional associations negotiated with nation states to secure privileged status and monopoly power for the accounting profession (Willmott 1986; Willmott et al. 1993), the increasing size and scope of the major firms, their consolidation of economic power and political influence, and their ability to shape interpretations of accounting rules and standards as they translate them into practice have transformed the major firms into sites, rather than subjects, of regulation (Cooper and Robson 2006).

Mezzo-level institutional analysis has demonstrated that the internationalization of accounting has not been an adaptive response to the demands of global financial markets. To the contrary, the accounting literature shows that the large international accounting firms, acting with and through states and international economic institutions, have worked proactively to create a global market for accounting and auditing services. Anglo-American and European-based firms played a pivotal political role in opening international professional service and labour markets by lobbying for preferential rules in international trade agreements designed to encourage harmonization, promote mutual recognition of professional credentials, and dismantle national regulatory barriers to trade in services (Arnold 2005; Suddaby et al. 2007). When necessary, international firms have also enlisted the aid of powerful state sponsors and international agencies to stymie protectionist efforts by domestic accountancy industries (Caramanis 2002). In short, mezzo-level institutional analysis of the accounting sector has revealed how the visible hand of corporate power has shaped the contours of the global market for financial and professional services.

In mezzo-level research, the unit of analysis is the economic sector or 'institutional field'. The 'field' has been defined as the 'communities of organizations or clusters of actors that, in the aggregate, constitute a recognized area of institutional life: key suppliers, resource and product consumers, regulatory agencies and other organizations that produce similar services or products' (DiMaggio and Powell 1983). In practice, the concept of the institutional field has proven to be highly flexible. Early institutional studies of the financial accounting field focused mainly on the relationships between professional associations and nation states (Willmott 1986; Willmott et al. 1993). Recent research has broadened the concept of the field to examine the interplay between international accounting firms and international regulatory regimes (Arnold 2005; Suddaby et al. 2007). In both cases, mezzo-level institutional analysis has proven adept at exploring the political struggles within and between international accounting firms, professional bodies, and regulatory authorities that shape the field of accountancy.

Institutional theorists have also employed the concept of the field to encompass not only the accounting sector, but the professions as a whole. Institutional sociologists, for example, have shown how jurisdictional disputes between professional associations and professional service firms shape the field of professional knowledge (Abbott 1988; Suddaby and Greenwood 2001, 2005). A promising area for future research lies in expanding the concept of the institutional field beyond accounting to encompass the financial sector as a whole. Since their origin is in the US 1929 stock market crash and subsequent securities legislation mandating independent audits, financial reporting requirements have always been deeply embedded in the broader financial sector. Over the past three decades, coincident with the internationalization of financial accounting, finance capital has come to play an increasingly important role in capital accumulation. Further in-depth research at the mezzo level promises to contribute to our understanding of the role that the financial sector as a whole, including banks and other financial intermediaries, national regulators and central banks, and international regulatory authorities such as the IMF and World Bank, has played in shaping the institutional arrangements that underpin the internationalization of the world of finance and financial accounting's role within it.

MACRO-LEVEL INSTITUTIONAL ANALYSIS

Macro-level analysis examines the institutional arrangements governing economies as a whole and the changes in those arrangements over the long term. It often takes the form of comparative national studies examining the various ways that national economies are embedded in historically determined institutional, legal, and regulatory forms and/or in particular cultural contexts (Campbell et al. 1991). International accounting research is no exception: comparative national studies have emphasized the ways in which financial reporting requirements are embedded in national societies, institutions, and cultures. For example, prior to the adoption of international financial reporting standards, the relative conservatism of German financial reporting practices was attributed to institutional factors such as a legal regime that linked corporate taxes to financial reporting numbers, the importance of banks rather than stock markets to capital financing which reduced the need for German firms to report short term profits, and the strength of the German labour unions which demanded to share in reported corporate profits (Nobes and Parker 1995).

The view that financial accounting is entrenched in national institutions or in national cultural forms such as American individualism, French statism, or German corporatism, however, rests uneasily with the fact that financial accounting has rapidly become internationalized. In his assessment of comparative international accounting research, Hopwood (2000) observes that the expectation that deeply embedded accounting practices would be slow to change has not been confirmed by developments in the financial accounting sector. He suggests that one reason for comparative international accounting research's inability to explain the rapid pace at which accounting has been internationalized may lie in its focus on national determinants of financial accounting practices. A narrow focus on national contexts underestimates the way in which accounting practices have historically followed the path of trade routes, colonial conquests, and imperialist ambitions (Hopwood 2000). World systems analysis, similarly, recognizes the limits of comparative studies of nation states and national cultures and proposes instead an approach to social analysis that views nation states as political units of modern society's interstate system and economy (Wallerstein 2004).

Although macro-level institutional analysis at the world system, rather than national, level is yet to emerge as a major paradigm in international accounting research, its parameters can be identified. Rather than focusing on how accounting is embedded in national cultures or national legal and institutional forms, it would focus on how accounting is embedded in world society and/or the world interstate system. Two distinct branches of macro-level analysis can be envisioned; one focused on world society and its culture, and another focused on the interstate world system and its political economy.

The first branch draws its theoretical foundations from the view advanced by Meyer et al. (1997) that widely shared cognitive and ontological models of reality constitute the cultural dimension of world society. These universalizing and rationalizing world models, in turn, account for the surprising degree of isomorphism that can be observed between modern nation states despite their vastly different histories and traditions (Meyer et al. 1997). From this perspective, the internationalization of financial accounting can be understood as a product of the ascendancy of neoliberalism as a hegemonic world model that legitimates a particular form of economic development based on open financial markets, transparency, and good accounting practice as the path to economic growth and development.

The second branch of macro-level analysis takes a world systems approach to social analysis (Wallerstein 2004; Amin 2006; Arrighi 2007), and emphasizes the influence of geopolitical and economic power on the diffusion of world culture. From a world systems perspective, macro-level institutional research could examine the ways in which financial accounting is embedded not only in ruling ideologies, but also in the institutional arrangements that govern the interstate political economy in different historical periods. As capitalism has evolved it has adopted different institutional forms in response to economic crises, class struggles, and political mobilizations. The evolution of financial markets and financial accounting, in turn, has taken place within the framework of macro-level transformations in the international political economy. International financial markets flourished during the Golden Age of liberalism in the late nineteenth century (Polanyi 1944), contracted after the Great Depression of the 1930s, and re-emerged in the final decades of the twentieth century. This pattern of development occurred not merely in reaction to economic imperatives, but as a result of social struggles, class mobilizations, and political pressures (Schor 1992; Kapstein 1994). By grounding our understanding of the evolution of contemporary financial accounting—from its origins in the aftermath of the Great Depression to its internationalization in the current day—within the context of transformations in world political economy, macro-institutional analysis offers a method for identifying the social relations of power that underlie the internationalization of financial accounting.

TOWARDS A NEW INTERNATIONAL ACCOUNTING RESEARCH AGENDA

Giovanni Arrighi's work (1994, 2007) can be used to illustrate how a world systems approach to social analysis could inform macro-level research and contribute to our understanding of the forces driving the internationalization of financial accounting. Taking an historical perspective, Arrighi (2007: 93), observes that over successive epochs, the centre of capital accumulation shifted from the Italian city states in the sixteenth century, to Holland in the eighteenth century, to Britain in the nineteenth century and most recently to the United States in the twentieth century. The emergence and decline of each of these centres of accumulation followed a pattern that began with a period of productive growth, followed by an economic downturn, and culminating in a period of financial expansion that foreshadowed a decline in power and transition to the next regime. In his comparison of Britain in the nineteenth century and the United States in the twentieth century, Arrighi

(2007: 118) shows that each epoch underwent similar periods of growth, stagnation, and financial resurgence. In the twentieth century, the United States experienced a period of rapid growth in the post-Second World War years, followed by decline and stagnation in 1973–93, and a return to economic prosperity in the 1990s based on the expansion of the financial sector and an equity boom. Arrighi (2007) refers to the final stage as 'financialization', which is characterized by financial expansion, the ascendancy of finance capital over industrial capital, and a return to profitability based on financial returns from credit markets and speculation.

Financial expansions occurred in Britain and Europe in the 'belle époque' at the close of the nineteenth century, and again in the US-led global financial boom that occurred at the close of the twentieth century. In both cases 'financialization' served as a mechanism to restore profitability—albeit profitability based on financial dealings rather than trade and production. Financial expansions, however, have an inherent tendency towards systemic instability. The 'belle époque' ended dramatically with the Great Depression in the 1930s. The contemporary period has been marked by a succession of financial crises including the Mexican peso devaluation of 1994, the Asian financial crisis in 1997, the collapse of Long Term Capital Management in 1998, and the 2008 global financial crisis. Arrighi (2007) argues that this tendency towards instability and crisis makes financialization a temporary fix to the problem of declining profitability. Periods of financial expansion characteristically mark the end of their respective epochs, and prefigure a transition to a new centre of capital accumulation. In the twenty-first century, China has emerged as the new centre of productivity and economic growth as US hegemony has waned.

This historical analysis has significant implications for understanding the rapid internationalization of financial accounting that occurred in conjunction with the financialization of economic life in the final decades of the twentieth century. It suggests that a fundamental reorientation is needed in international accounting research away from a focus on globalization, and towards a focus on financialization. The force driving the internationalization of accounting may not be the globalization of national economies and national financial markets as is so often assumed, but rather the financialization of the international economic system. From a world systems perspective, the fundamental question is not how has globalization influenced financial accounting, but rather how has accounting shaped and been shaped by the financialization of the world interstate economy at the end of the twentieth century.

A refocus of financialization, rather than globalization, opens new lines of inquiry and poses several new research questions for international accounting. First, what is the relationship between financialization and the expansion in size, scope, and power of the major international accounting firms? The financialization of the world economy in the closing decades of the twentieth century began with Reagan/Thatcher monetarist counter-revolution in the 1980s. It was marked by macroeconomic policies supporting tight money and a strong dollar, the dismantling of the welfare state and privatization of state enterprises, IMF imposed structural adjustment programs, and the elimination of national capital controls. These measures prompted the ascendance of finance capital and created profitable niches not only for financial intermediaries, but also for international accounting firms as they expanded into financial advisory services and recast themselves as specialists in mergers and acquisitions, corporate reorganization, offshore tax shelters, and privatization consulting (Arnold and Cooper 1999). Further research is needed to examine the linkages between macro-level transformation in the economy and mezzo-level institutional transformations within the accounting sector. This research could examine the hypothesis that financialization created the conditions that enabled international accounting firms to expand in size and scope, consolidate power over the accounting sector, and play a more proactive role at the mezzo level in shaping the international accounting field.

Second, what is the relationship between financialization and the international accounting standard setting process? As Arrighi (2007: 230) describes it, financialization is characterized by the 'capacity of finance capital to take over and dominate for a while at least all the activities of the business world'. The financial euphoria of the 1990s affected non-financial enterprises as well as the financial sector. As profitability declined, non-operating income became an increasing vital component of corporate income as corporations of all types turned towards investments, reorganization, and merger and acquisition strategies to supplement declining operating profits with financial gains. To what extent has financialization and the ascendance of finance capital over industrial capital influenced the International Accounting Standards Board's (IASB) agenda? Does financialization explain financial accounting policy-makers' leap to fair value accounting, or their turn away from a traditional income measurement accounting model towards a balance sheet valuation approach to financial reporting? And, if financialization is a temporary phenomenon, as Arrighi (2007) argues it is, have accounting policy-makers acted too hastily in making theoretical concessions to the dominance of financial over industrial capital?

Finally, to what extent has concern over systemic financial instability contributed to the internationalization of accounting? The Asian financial crisis of 1997 highlighted the need for an international regulatory architecture capable of reducing systemic instability within the international financial system. In the aftermath of the crisis, the IMF and other regulatory authorities considered proposals for creating a much stronger international regulatory regime to govern global financial markets. These included proposals for a global financial regulator, an international bankruptcy court, an international deposit-insurance corporation, and even a global central bank (Wade 2007: 117). Wade (2007: 119) argues that none of these proposals came to fruition primarily because of the 'unwillingness of private financial markets to accept greater international authority'. Instead of a substantive overhaul of the international financial architecture, Western governments settled on a regulatory regime that Wade (2007: 115) calls the 'standards–surveillance–compliance' system. This regime relies on less forceful measures, namely transparency and compliance with international financial standards, including international financial accounting and auditing standards, to reduce systemic risk in the international financial system.

In 1999, on the initiative of G7 finance ministers and central bank governors, the Financial Stability Forum (FSF) was convened to implement the 'standards–surveillance–compliance' system. The establishment of the Forum brought the full backing and authority of the World Bank, IMF, OECD, and authorities responsible for financial stability in major international financial centres to the task of promoting adoption of and compliance with international financial reporting and auditing standards. Accounting research has yet to appreciate the role that this institutional response to financial instability played in speeding the internationalization of financial accounting. Further macro- and mezzo-level research is needed in order to evaluate the 'standards–surveillance–compliance' system, and to understand the political processes and power relationships that precluded the development of stronger institutional arrangements for governing the international financial system.

BRINGING POLITICS AND ECONOMICS BACK IN

This chapter defines institutional analysis broadly—so broadly as to include unlikely bedfellows from diverse disciplines and intellectual traditions. The objective of this exercise is not to attempt to achieve unity or consensus where there is none, but rather to provide a typology that identifies the range of diversity that exists within the multidisciplinary field of institutional studies. In summarizing contributions that institutional analysis at the micro-, mezzo-, and macro-level have made to our understanding of the internationalization of financial accounting practices and in sketching an agenda for further research, I have also made two implicit arguments. The first is that institutional analysis can embrace the study of power at all levels; the second is that institutional perspectives can be enriched by the study of economic history and political economy. Since both these arguments are rather unconventional, they merit further discussion.

The first argument is that institutional perspectives need not ignore power. Institutional analysis has often been criticized for ignoring politics and the role of social, economic, and political power (Khan et al. 2007). While this criticism has some validity, institutional analysis need not be apolitical. In sketching the diversity within institutional perspectives, I have argued for an institutional analysis capable of examining power at all levels. At the micro level, the institutional logics that provide the normative rationale for capital accumulation are not static; dominate cultural myths shift over time in response to social critique, political mobilization, class power, and social movements. Power becomes visible at the mezzo level in the turf battles within and between international accounting firms, professional associations, financial regulators, and states that give shape to the institutional arrangements governing the accounting sector. This visibility makes mezzo-level analysis well suited to grappling with the question of agency by showing how power is expressed concretely in the process of institution building. Finally, macro-level institutional analysis can examine the roles that class relations, social struggles, and geopolitics play in shaping the institutional arrangements governing the world interstate system and its economy.

The second argument is that an institutional perspective is not the antithesis of an economic perspective. Institutionalism's tendency to shun economic explanations in favour of cultural ones is understandable given its origins as a reaction to the economic determinism found in both neoclassical and Marxist economics. But, institutional analysis has reached a stage of maturity in the accounting literature where it is possible to reintegrate political economy and economic history in order to understand the interplay between economics, politics, and culture that is expressed in the institutional arrangements that govern the economy. In outlining an agenda for international accounting research, I have proposed an approach to institutional analysis that draws heavily from political economy and economic history. While this approach may appear alien to accounting scholars whose approach to institutional analysis is drawn mainly from organizational sociology, it is consistent with the work of economic historians, economic sociologists, and regulation theorists who embrace the study of institutions in order to understand capitalism in all its various historically specific institutional forms. These include the institutional forms that capitalism has taken in response to social movements and shifts in the balance of class power, as well as its expression in varied cultural contexts.

What distinguishes institutional perspectives on political economy from orthodoxy economics is a commitment to be non-deterministic which is expressed in the conviction that institutions matter. To say that institutions matter is to say that history is not the outcome of immutable economic laws; but rather that the course of history is shaped by institutional forms that are brought into being by political and social struggles. In the context of inter- national finance and accounting, it matters whether we develop strong inter- national financial institutions capable of governing international financial markets and protecting populations from the consequences of systemic instability, or rely on the weaker 'standards-surveillance-compliance' system favoured by the financial markets. It also matters whether financial account- ing policy-makers and academics engage in institutional thinking by follow- ing old scripts and the taken-for-granted assumption that accounting's function is to provide transparency to the market, or engage in a critique of an international regulatory system that relies chiefly on transparency as a mechanism for governing risky and crisis prone global financial markets.

Institutions matter because they have distributional consequences. The distributional consequences of international financial institutions designed to protect society from the ravages of financial crises, such as international deposi- tory insurance, a Tobin tax on international financial transactions, or an inter- national pension system (Blackburn 2007), are far different from the consequences of the incumbent regulatory system based on transparency and compliance with international financial standards. The intersection between institutional analysis and political economy offers a promising framework for future accounting research aimed not only at enhancing our understanding of the forces driving the internationalization of the accounting world, but also at developing a vision of alternative institutional arrangements for governing the international financial system that are more equitable and responsive to the social needs.

REFERENCES

Abbott, A. (1988). *The System of Professions*. Chicago: University of Chicago Press.
Aglietta, M. (1976). *A Theory of Capitalist Regulation: The US Experience*. London: New Left Books.
Amin, S. (2006). *Beyond U.S. Hegemony? Assessing the Prospects for a Multipolar World*. London: Zed Books.
Arnold, P.J. (2005). Disciplining domestic regulation: The World Trade Organization and the market for professional services. *Accounting, Organizations and Society*, 30(4), 299–330.
—— and Cooper, C. (1999). A tale of two classes: The privatization of Medway Ports. *Critical Perspectives on Accounting*, 10(2), 127–52.
Arrighi, G. (1994). *The Long Twentieth Century: Money, Power and the Origins of Our Times*. London: Verso.

—— (2007). *Adam Smith in Beijing: Lineages of the Twenty-First Century.* London: Verso.

Blackburn, R. (2007). A global pension plan. *New Left Review*, 47, 71–92.

Boltanski, L., and Chiapello, E. (2005). *The New Spirit of Capitalism.* London: Verso.

Boyer, R. (1990). *The Regulation School: A Critical Introduction.* New York: Columbia University Press.

Campbell, J., Hollingsworth, J.R., and Lindberg, L.N. (eds.) (1991). *Governance of the American Economy.* Cambridge: Cambridge University Press.

Caramanis, C. (2002). The interplay between professional groups, the State and supranational agents: Pax Americana in the age of 'globalization'. *Accounting, Organizations and Society*, 27(4–5), 379–408.

Cooper, D.J., and Robson, K. (2006). Accounting, professions and regulation: Locating the sites of professionalization. *Accounting, Organizations and Society*, 31(4–5), 415–44.

DiMaggio, P.J., and Powell, W. (1982). The Iron Cage revisited: Institutional isomorphism and collective rationality in organizational fields. *American Sociological Review*, 32(3), 147–160.

Douglas, M. (1986). *How Institutions Think.* Syracuse, N.Y.: Syracuse University Press.

Dye, R.A., and Sunder, S. (2001). Why not allow FASB and IASB standards to compete in the U.S.? *Accounting Horizons*, 15(3), 257–71.

Friedman, T.L. (2000). *The Lexus and the Olive Tree.* New York: Anchor Books.

Granovetter, M. (1985). Economic action and social structure: The problem of embeddedness. *American Journal of Sociology*, 91(3), 481–510.

Greenwood, R., and Hinings, C.R. (1996). Understanding radical organizational change: Bringing together the old and new institutionalism. *Academy of Management Review*, 21(4), 1022–54.

—— Suddaby, R., and Hinings, C.R. (2002). Theorizing change: The role of professional associations in the transformation of institutional fields. *Academy of Management Journal*, 45(1), 58–80.

Hanlon, G. (1994). *The Commercialization of Accountancy.* London: St. Martin Press.

Hegarty, J., Gielen, F., and Barros, A.C.H. (2004). Implementation of International Accounting and Auditing Standards: Lessons learned from the World Bank's Accounting and Auditing ROSC Program. Available online at http://www.worldbank.org/ifa/LessonsLearned_ROSC_AA.pdf

Hirst, P., and Zeitlin, J. (1991). Flexible Specialization versus Post-Fordism: Theory, evidence and policy implications. *Economy and Society*, 20(1), 1–56.

Hollingsworth, J.R. (2003). Advancing the socio-economic paradigm with institutional analysis. *Socio-Economic Review*, 1(1), 130–4.

—— and Boyer, R. (eds.) (1997). *Contemporary Capitalism: The Embeddedness of Institutions.* Cambridge: Cambridge University Press.

Hopwood, A.G. (1997). Internationalizing international accounting research. *Accounting, Organizations and Society*, 22(8), 3–4.

Hopwood, A.G. (2000). Understanding financial accounting practice. *Accounting, Organizations and Society*, 25(8), 763–6.

Kahn, F.R., Munir, K.A., and Willmott, H. (2007). A dark side of institutional entrepreneurship: Soccer balls, child labor and post colonial impoverishment. *Organization Studies*, 28(7), 1055–77.

Kapstein, E.B. (1994). *Governing the Global Economy: International Finance and the State*. Cambridge, Mass.: Harvard University Press.

Meyer, J.W., Boli, J., Thomas, G.M., and Ramirez, F.O. (1997). World society and the nation state. *American Journal of Sociology*, 103(1), 144–81.

Nobes, C., and Parker, R. (1995). *Comparative International Accounting*. New York: Prentice Hall.

Oakes, L., Townley, B., and Cooper, D.J. (1998). Business planning as pedagogy: Language and control in a changing institutional field. *Administrative Science Quarterly*, 43(2), 257–92.

Polanyi, K. (1944). *The Great Transformation*. Boston: Beacon Press.

Schor, J.B. (1992). Introduction. In T. Banuri and J.B. Schor (eds.), *Financial Openness and National Autonomy*. Oxford: Claredon Press, 1–14.

Strange, S. (1986). *Casino Capitalism*. Cambridge, Mass.: Basil Blackwell.

Streeck, W. (1992). *Social Institutions and Economic Performance: Studies in Industrial Relations in Advanced Capitalist Economies*. London: Sage Publications.

——and Schmitter, P. (1985). Community, markets, state—and associations? The prospective contribution of interest governance to social order. *European Sociological Review*, 1(2), 119–38.

Suddaby, R., and Greenwood, R. (2001). Colonized knowledge: Commodification as a dynamic of jurisdictional expansion in professional firms. *Human Relations*, 54(7), 933–53.

————(2005). Rhetorical strategies of legitimacy. *Administrative Science Quarterly*, 50(1), 35–67.

————(2007). Transnational regulation of professional services: Governance dynamics of field level organizational change. *Accounting, Organizations and Society*, 32(4–5), 333–62.

Wade, R. (2007). A new global financial architecture? *New Left Review*, 46, 113–29.

Wallerstein, I.M. (2004). *World-Systems Analysis: An introduction*. Durham, N.C.: Duke University Press.

Williamson, O.E. (1985). *The Economic Institutions of Capitalism*. New York: The Free Press.

Willmott, H. (1986). Organising the profession: A theoretical and historical examination of the development of major accountancy bodies in the UK. *Accounting, Organizations and Society*, 11(6), 555–80.

——Cooper, D.J., and Puxty, T. (1993). Maintaining self-regulation: making 'interests' collide in discourses of governance of the ICAEW. *Accounting, Auditing and Accountability Journal*, 6(4), 68–93.

Young, J.J. (1996). Institutional thinking: Financial instruments. *Accounting, Organizations and Society*, 21(5), 487–512.

Zukin, S., and DiMaggio, P. (1990). *Structures of Capital: The Social Organization of the Economy*. Cambridge: Cambridge University Press.

4

Studying Accounting in Action: The Challenge of Engaging with Management Accounting Practice

Jane Baxter and Wai Fong Chua

INTRODUCTION

This collection of essays celebrates and reflects on the scholarly contributions of Professor Anthony Hopwood. There would be little argument that his contributions to the field of accounting have been both significant and extensive. Even a volume of this size, encompassing the range of issues under consideration, is unable to fully document and evaluate all the nuances of his work. As such, we can only be highly selective and partial in terms of the ambit of our essay. Given this, we have chosen to concentrate on one particular aspect of Hopwood's work. We focus on the substantive nature and effects of his influential call, published in *Accounting, Organizations and Society* (1983), encouraging us to pay greater attention to studying accounting practice—and to conduct such research in the context in which various accounting practices are located. We do so because, although this paper was written over 25 years ago, its central arguments have stood the test of time and continue to resonate within the academic community today, conveying possibilities for contemporary developments in the conduct of management accounting research. But wherein lays the enduring quality of this particular publication?

In the pages that follow, we revisit the basic thrust of Hopwood's (1983) paper with the aim of more generally exploring the challenges that this has created in relation to engaging with accounting practice. We commence our exploration by reiterating the relevant and significant insights contained in the 1983 paper, focusing on claims regarding the heterogeneous and shifting nature of management accounting practices. We then outline broadly how these insights have informed the shape of management accounting research to date. This encompasses a broad consideration of ensuing methodological debate, as well as a consideration and illustration of the influence of Hopwood's argument in terms of extant management accounting field research. After this, we indicate how his call for more practice-based accounting research continues to engage with and inform developments in current management accounting research, raising both interesting and significant issues concerning the nature of accounting practice and how we may seek to comprehend it. This is addressed by outlining the ways in which contemporary scholars critically engage with and seek to influence the emerging trajectory of practice-based management accounting research. Further, it is contended that the research agenda proposed by Hopwood is both consistent with and capable of being regenerated by current debates within the social sciences regarding the nature of practices and their contexts. This creates interesting areas for exploration, especially in relation to the ways in which we problematize, deconstruct and attempt to understand the sites of various management accounting practices and their accomplishment.

CONSTITUTING THE CHALLENGE

The following quotation is taken from Hopwood's (1983: 297) seminal publication which underpins this chapter:

Similar discussions also focused on the diverse nature of the accounting craft, particularly in respect of the practice of management accounting. Not only was there an awareness of the enormous range of technical practices in use (summarised by one participant in the terms of 'you name it; somebody is using it!') but also consideration was given to the diversity of those organizational linkages which ground accounting and other information and control systems into the ongoing processes of organizational life. Accounting and control systems are variously organized. Planning, budgeting and performance monitoring procedures operate at different organizational levels, are subject to different degrees of participation, have different expectations and practices for their revision, and even can consider very different time periods. Accounting systems also serve to establish very different patterns of organizational segmentation and relate to the practices for the management of organizational interdependence in a variety of ways. From these and many other viewpoints the accounting domain was seen to exhibit a diversity that was seemingly at odds with the myth of a more generalised phenomenon that permeates accounting texts and those manuals that seek to guide accounting change and reform. (p. 297)

As the above quotation indicates, Hopwood's (1983) paper is significant because it highlighted a lack of engagement between generalized characterizations of management accounting within academe and the richness of management accounting practices in different situations. In short, Hopwood contended that 'accounting research had tended to isolate itself from accounting in practice' (p. 302).

Reflecting on the state of management accounting research from this era, Scapens (2006) argues that this was, in part, due to its general orientation at the time, wherein precedence was given to research styled on marginal economic analyses and various forms of mathematical modelling. Such research was only loosely aligned with practice, being accompanied by a hope that improvements in the dissemination of results would bring about progression and development in those practices which it sought to typify (see Scapens 2006: 3). Hopwood's paper, however, mobilizes a lingering sentiment that neither increasing analytical elegance nor mathematical refinement and sophistication can compensate for a fundamental lack of understanding of how accounting actually operates *in situ*. The challenge, as Hopwood presented it, was (and is) 'to study, analyse and interpret accounting in the contexts in which it operates' (1983: 303). From this perspective, it is insufficient to study management accounting as a disembedded phenomenon which fails to give due recognition to the contexts which both inform and are informed by the constitution of management accounting practices. Hopwood, therefore, argued that it was important for researchers to understand the *organizational* functioning of those practices being studied. (This line of argument was augmented by other papers [e.g. Burchell et al. 1985] which further encouraged an understanding of accounting practices in their *social* contexts too.)

As such, Hopwood, and those sympathetic to his position, argued that this basic desire to re-engage with accounting practices in the context of organizational functioning was, and is, a necessary part of a shift towards more granular and situated characterizations of management accounting. Without such a commitment to practical engagement, our understandings of management accounting would remain limited to what Ahrens and Chapman (2007: 3) have described as 'generic exhortations'. Indeed, it was Hopwood's thesis that management accounting is far removed from a stable set of generic practical accomplishments. Instead Hopwood used this 1983 paper as a platform for articulating practical knowledge about the local and dynamic nature of management accounting in its organizational context, with this insight reshaping the management accounting research agenda of many scholars over the intervening years.

Hopwood's argument concerning the local and dynamic nature of management accounting practice has two main elements. First, Hopwood (1983: 297) argued that accounting is a 'heterogeneous' set of practices. This is the invariable consequence of a view in which it is recognized that accounting is practised differentially because of variations in the contexts in which it operates. It follows from this that researchers must take seriously local variations in activities constituting a particular practice, be it a balanced scorecard, activity-based costing system, or a budgeting process and so on. This acknowledges the possibility of many different forms of *accountings*. Second, he argued that accounting is not comprised by static practices; it is constantly changing and becoming what it is not (1983: 289). However, such changes remain outside the confines of the research gaze unless we undertake to engage with practice, particularly over extended periods of time. More recently, Scapens (2006) has re-emphasized the range and dynamic nature of management accounting practice.

Further to this, Hopwood's (1983) paper is also significant in that it has motivated sustained debate and reflection on how it is that we are to engage with management accounting practice in terms of its perceived range and dynamics. As such, his 1983 paper was instrumental in motivating field-based research methods as a means of appropriate practical engagement (Tomkins and Grove 1983; Chua 1986; Kaplan 1986). Nonetheless, Hopwood (1983) noted that the realization of such an ambition confronts a number of major obstacles. It was acknowledged that field research is both time consuming and resource intensive in terms of the personal demands placed on the researcher in relation to data collection and analyses. Adding to this, access is often difficult to organize, restricting opportunities for the type of detailed practical engagement required by this type of research. Even when such research is possible, it is not clear that its outputs will be acknowledged readily by peers when either promotion or good quality journal outlets are sought. Contemporary debate amongst researchers in accounting suggests that little has changed on this front (see Ahrens et al. 2008): studying accounting in the context in which it operates is difficult and not always good for one's career.

Nevertheless, a number of scholars have been motivated to study the situated accomplishment of management accounting. This has provided many unique and surprising accounts of management accounting practices (for an overview of this research, see Baxter and Chua 2003). In the following section we consider the scope of the influence of Hopwood's argument concerning the characterization of accounting in its organizational context, examining its consequences in terms of the shape of extant management accounting research.

CHARACTERIZING ACCOUNTING IN ACTION

The management accounting community's subsequent desire to study accounting in action has been premised on a realization that 'researchers' knowledge of management accounting practice was severely limited and based largely on anecdotal evidence. Few researchers had systematic or in-depth knowledge of management accounting practice' (Scapens 2006: 4). This recognition not only spawned a growing number of field-based research studies which sought to study accounting in the context in which it operates, significantly, it also acted as a springboard for debate and reconsideration of the nature of and relationship between accounting research and practice.

Various papers broached this subject of how it is that we may conceive of the relationship between accounting practice and research (see Colville 1981; Cooper 1983), but for illustrative purposes we will confine our discussion to Chua's paper (1986). In her paper, Chua provides an extended argument highlighting the misplaced conclusion that studying accounting in action will result in some 'lesser' form of research accomplishment. Rather her paper makes it clear that what a research community considers as being 'scientific' (and, by implication, 'good' research) is very much a product of the beliefs and practices prevailing within academe at a particular time and place. Therefore, Hopwood's call for research on accounting in its organizational context created unease for many because it invoked assumptions about the nature of accounting practice and research which sat uneasily in relation to the prevailing paradigm at that point in time.

As Chua's paper illustrates, a desire to study accounting in action sits uncomfortably in relation to 'mainstream' views of practice and research. The mainstream views accounting practice as being both objective and external to researchers, with research being used to test theories via mainly quantitative means. However, the kind of experience of practice which Hopwood also envisaged was coupled to a quite different view of accounting practice and research. Both 'interpretive' and 'critical' (Chua 1986) perspectives on accounting practice and research were seen as being appropriate (if not more appropriate) for studying accounting in its organizational contexts, in part, because these perspectives recognize the constitutive potential of organizational participants and the situations in which they are located in relation to the phenomenon under investigation. The interpretive perspective draws on various forms of social constructionism (Gergen 1999) which highlight the ways in which individuals interacting in particular situations constitute accounting practices, as well as the meanings afforded to these in various contexts. Within the interpretive perspective, researcher explanations of accounting practices acknowledge and draw on these so-called first-order constructions of practice (see Agar 1986; Kirk and Miller 1986) in building and assessing the adequacy of accounts of accounting in action. Further, the so-called critical perspective, drawing from Marxist, critical and labour process theories (Habermas 1968, 1976; Atkinson 1972; Braverman 1974), configures accounting practices as a means of limiting the potentialities of

Table 4.1.   Constructions of accounting practice and research

Perspective	Beliefs about research	Beliefs about practice	Relationship between research and practice
Mainstream	Research builds theories that are separate from practice and informed by the hypothetico-deductive method.	Accounting practice is objective and external to the researcher. Humans are passive and goal oriented.	Accounting research does not question the status quo or extant practices and their relationship to context.
Interpretive	Research aims to describe and characterize actors' commonsense interpretations.	Accounting practice is subjectively created, with the formation of meanings being coupled to contextual contingencies.	Accounting research both informs and is informed by accounting practices.
Critical	Research is acknowledged as being temporally and contextually located.	Accounting practice is connected to the alienation of individuals and conflict in organizations.	Accounting research aims to change practice by creating a heightened awareness of inequality between individuals and the potentiality of individuals.

Source: Based on Chua (1986).

organizational participants by contributing to their unequal access to resources and opportunities. Research of a critical nature is invariably characterized within a very strong sense of its contextual contingencies, with longitudinal studies being very important to the contribution of its aims.

As such, Table 4.1 highlights the different forms of 'science' to which the study of accounting in action has become attached. In short, what this table demonstrates is that there are various ways of engaging with accounting practice.

Whilst a small number of mainstream research studies have attempted to study management accounting in action (see, e.g., Miller and O'Leary 1997; Malina and Selto 2001), we will confine our subsequent discussion of studying accounting in the context in which it operates to non-mainstream forms of engagement. We do so because non-mainstream forms of scholarship cultivate beliefs about practice and research that are germane to future developments in management accounting research which respect the basic thrust of Hopwood's (1983) seminal call, whilst arguably possessing a capacity to reinvigorate and extend our understandings of accounting in action.

Accordingly, Hopwood's (1983) paper is central to the impetus of research seeking to provide more 'naturalistic' (Hopper et al. 1987) and 'everyday'

(Tomkins and Grove 1983) insights into management accounting in its organizational context. But, as indicated earlier, there is a certain degree of latitude in terms of how non-mainstream investigations have approached the furtherance of this research aim. A variety of data collection methods have been used to construct and comprehend accounting in action. These include interviewing, observation and supporting documentary sources (see Preston 1986; Vaivio 1999). Such data collection methods have been used in studies either seeking to compare and contrast management accounting practices in different contexts (Hansen and Mouritsen 2005) or to intensively investigate them over time in a particular organizational context (Jönsson 1982; Dent 1991). In addition to this, a diversity of theories has been adopted to inform our understandings of accounting in action. These theories have encompassed, for example, institutional theory (DiMaggio and Powell 1991); actor network theory (Latour 1987); structuration theory (Giddens 1984, 1991); and Foucauldian narrations of governance (Foucault 1977). As we have discussed the theoretical framings of non-mainstream management accounting research and its contributions elsewhere (Baxter and Chua 2003), we do not intend to dwell further on this particular contribution of extant research into management accounting in action. Rather, at this point, we plan to focus on illustrating how studies of accounting in action have contributed to our understanding of diverse and shifting forms of management accounting practices, as outlined by Hopwood (1983).

Extant studies of accounting in action have illuminated and illustrated Hopwood's (1983) claim that accounting is a heterogeneous practice. As a result of a growing group of researchers being prepared to base their studies on first-hand experiences, we have come to realize and appreciate the range of practices which may be encompassed by the seemingly singular labels used to denote various forms of accounting work. Take, for example, the work of Hansen and Mouritsen (2005) regarding the balanced scorecard. As a result of considering the performativity of the balanced scorecard in four different Danish organizations, they concluded that the balanced scorecard was constituted differently in each of the organizations under consideration. In one research site from the pharmaceutical industry, the balanced scorecard was comprised by a set of practices which enabled cross-functional integration. In another, a textile firm, the balanced scorecard became the means of building a planning culture. Further to this, the balanced scorecard emerged as a way of enacting internal benchmarking and re-engineering practices in two other research sites, an IT company and mortgage credit provider respectively. Hansen and Mouritsen's study (2005) serves to demonstrate the heterogeneity of an illustrative management accounting practice (the balanced scorecard) *across* various organizations; an insight which arguably remains beyond the scope of research approaches which disembed accounting from the context in which it operates.

Other extant studies of accounting in action convey the heterogeneity of accounting practices which may inhabit an organization. The research of Mouritsen (1999) is illustrative of this possibility. Mouritsen examined a Danish manufacturing organization with a view of better understanding the constitution of organizational flexibility. Rather than presenting a unified construction of organizational flexibility, Mouritsen characterized the heterogeneous nature of flexibility in this organization. On the one hand, the production manager narrated flexibility as a set of practices requiring co-operation between management, workers, production teams, and product-developers. On the other hand, the chief financial officer maintained a distinct and divergent view of flexibility: to him flexibility was a practice which impeded cost management via careful planning and budgeting.

Studies of accounting in action have also contributed to our understanding of Hopwood's (1983) argument that management accounting practices are constantly changing and becoming what they are not. For illustrative purposes, we will refer to our own research (Andon et al. 2007) which examined organizational practices related to the operation of a balanced scorecard in the call centre operation of a large Australasian telecommunications organization. First-hand encounters of practice provided relatively detailed insights into the ongoing processes of experimentation that resulted from various attempts to stabilize and make the balanced scorecard work in this particular context. In attempting to implement the balanced scorecard, it shifted and changed, becoming what it was not. The balanced scorecard changed from a set of practices aimed at replacing a public-service past with a commercial and contestable organizational context, to a set of practices aimed at managing the performance of staff in terms of time-based measures, to a set of practices attempting to achieve a balance between time and service quality considerations, and, finally, to a set of practices promoting the rhetoric of strategic alignment and integration. These four significant and subtle shifts in the sets of practices constituting the balanced scorecard were witnessed over an eleven-month period. This suggests that many and various translations and transformations of practices may accompany the operation of enduring management accounting technologies in their organizational context.

Overall, extant micro-studies of accounting in action have provided an invaluable sense of the constant reworkings of, and improvisations in management accounting practices that occur within and between organizations and across time. This has occasioned Scapens (2006: 10) to reflect on the 'mish-mash'-like nature of management accounting practices. Such a variegated metaphor belies the unproblematic, unitary constructions of practice inhabiting textbooks and the many research studies which do not problematize the management accounting phenomenon under investigation. Ultimately, studies of accounting in action have been central to informing our understanding of the immanent 'flexibility' and 'variability' (Ahrens and Chapman 2007: 2) of management accounting practices.

CRITIQUING AND REINVIGORATING RESEARCH ENGAGEMENT WITH ACCOUNTING PRACTICE

Without wishing to diminish the important contributions of studies such as those reported above, it is nonetheless appropriate to reflect on this research agenda, particularly as a means of refining and rejuvenating its focus in the contemporary research environment. Such a process of critique has commenced in the management accounting literature, with Ahrens and Chapman (2007) being central to the direction of this debate. Although Ahrens and Chapman's (2007) basic arguments amplify Hopwood's (1983) seminal call to concentrate on understanding accounting in its organizational context, these writers have a distinct vantage point: they are able to reflect on over two decades of such research with a view to considering its limitations and potentialities. Correspondingly, Ahrens and Chapman (2007) are critical of the ways in which particular studies of accounting in its organizational context have been undertaken in recent manifestations of this type of research. They concentrate their remarks on two genres of such research, critiquing research which has drawn on theories of governmentality (Foucault 1977) and actor network theory (Latour 1987).

In terms of research based on theories of governmentality, Ahrens and Chapman (2007) argue that this genre of accounting research has as its central emphasis the various webs of discourse making particular forms of accounting practices possible (see Miller and O'Leary 1987). They conclude that this type of research provides a keen sense of the programmatic context in which accounting practices operate, but fails to 'detail the uses and functionings of accounting in specific situations' (Ahrens and Chapman 2007: 5). They state:

For instance, Miller and O'Leary's (1994) study of a new manufacturing initiative at Caterpillar Inc. conceived of accounting practices at the level of designing accounting policies, mainly for investment decision making and building accounting information systems. The relationship between accounting and organizational processes was discussed only to the extent to which it 'rendered them operable'. How, or even whether, accounting was mobilised in any particular organizational activity was not discussed. Accounting remained a potential.

According to Ahrens and Chapman's argument, such research is wanting because the notion of practice is not deconstructed into the specific routines and meanings characteristic of the site of their operation.

Likewise, actor network theories of management accounting practice, whilst shifting the focus of accounting in its organizational context from 'a potential' to specific, local forms of practices (see Preston et al. 1992; Mouritsen 1999), also attract criticism from Ahrens and Chapman (2007). Ahrens and Chapman are critical primarily of this corpus of research because it aims to configure networks of organizational practices in terms of 'flat surfaces' that eschew privilege and priority. They argue that this methodological presumption results in a lack of alignment between actor network theory and the object of its study—that is, management accounting practice. In contradistinction, Ahrens and Chapman (2007: 7) argue that managers (one element in the networks of practices being studied) are '*a priori* privileged' and have a marked influence on the organizational functioning of management accounting through their ability to influence its design and uses. They mount an argument that the anti-managerialist sentiment of actor network theory has produced distorted accounts of practices. However, this criticism stops short of recognizing that in seeking to characterize management accounting practices it is insufficient to consider only the minutiae of accounting in action. It is necessary also to appreciate, configure, and critique the enduring webs of practices constituting and perpetuating privilege in particular fields, as well as the differential allocation of various forms of power enabling such privileging and ordering of practices.

Subsequent to this, Chua's (2007) review essay adds further weight to Ahrens and Chapman's (2007) desire to encourage reflection on the state of research seeking to engage with management accounting practice. In her essay she adopts a line of argument consistent with Ahrens and Chapman's; there is a need for a renewed 'interest in the intricacies and complexities of accounting practice' (Chua 2007: 487). However, the particular turn in the debate offered by Chua revolves around a reorientation of such research in terms of understanding practice as a way of *doing* accounting. Whilst this represents a re-expression of Hopwood's (1983) argument for studying accounting in action, and is premised on the type of detailed engagement which both Hopwood (1983) and Ahrens and Chapman (2007) have advocated, Chua's (2007) essay is marked by its implications in terms of how we construct and narrate management accounting practices. She argues that we must understand management accounting as and through verb forms (Chua 2007: 487), that is, as practices that are ongoing, emerging, and shifting.

Despite differences at the margins between these reflective essays, both Ahrens and Chapman (2007) and Chua (2007) agree that a research agenda focusing on accounting in its organizational context retains great pertinence for contemporary scholars in the field of management accounting. These authors agree that there is a need for more sustained research focusing on the *detailed* accomplishment of particular practices. Chua describes this as a need to focus on the 'situated accomplishment' (2007: 492) of management accounting practices, entailing an understanding of how 'skilful' and 'effective' practices are constituted locally and in response to global systems of management accounting (2007: 488). Ahrens and Chapman accordingly call for greater understanding of the 'situated functionality' (2007: 23) of management accounting practices.

As the above discussion indicates, there is a growing momentum for the development of a 'practice' view of management accounting (Ahrens and Chapman 2005). This is not to suggest, however, that management accounting research is to descend into a morass of highly specific empirical detail that gains salience only from its local context. Rather there is a desire to experiment with theories that are able to couple accounts of management accounting practices to concepts enabling their analytical framing. More specifically, there is an interest in applying 'practice theories' of social action to management accounting situations.

An example of such an analytical frame may be found in the practice theory of Bourdieu (see Bourdieu 1977, 1990, 1998, 2000; Baxter and Chua [2008a] provide a more extended discussion of this form of practice theory). Bourdieu argues that the performance of everyday practices, such as basic management accounting functions (e.g. interpreting financial reports, compiling product costs, forecasting cash flows, and evaluating investment proposals), involves a high degree of situated accomplishment. That is, skilful social actors embody a significant amount of practical knowledge concerning the range of practices which are possible and appropriate in a given situation. Bourdieu encourages us therefore to seek the type of engagement with practice which Hopwood (1983) extolled, but provides a sensitizing frame for doing this: his concepts of habitus and habitat. Bourdieu (1977) uses the notion of habitus to refer to the predictable ways in which the incumbents of various positions (such as a cost accountant, CFO, or budget accountant) enter into a relationship with practice. As researchers it is of interest to understand and convey the range of practices that accounting practitioners invoke (in different positions and stages of their career) to establish their accomplishment in particular fields or 'social worlds' (Bourdieu 1998: 138), taking into account the ways in which possible practices are enabled and constrained by habitat (the institutionalized expectations embedded in the history of the position) and also the capacity of actors to accumulate and mobilize various forms of capital conferring prestige, opportunity, and influence in a field. Accordingly, the configuration of skilful practices is highly informed by the situation in which practical accomplishments occur. In short, practice theories (such as that found in the writings of Bourdieu) provide a frame that accounting researchers may find useful in reinvigorating and complementing investigations into management accounting practice, doing so in such a way that maintains debates about the diverse and shifting nature of accountings in their organizational contexts.

Overall, the possibilities afforded by contemporary emphases within the social sciences concerning the nature of practice provide challenging opportunities for management accounting researchers to characterize their engagement with accounting in the context in which it operates. This emerging shift in theoretical emphasis also arguably reflects and extends the natural progression and subtle changes that attend the ways in which researchers make sense of accounting in action (Scapens 2006).

The following section outlines some of the challenges we perceive as being connected to this renewed interest in studying situated management accounting practices, given the contemporary theoretical milieu informing this research.

CONTEMPORARY CHALLENGES IN ENGAGING WITH ACCOUNTING PRACTICE

It is the basic contention of this section that current developments and emphases in social science research offer interesting possibilities for a distinctive shift in, and extension to, the ongoing research agenda outlined above. Contemporary research more broadly concerned with the nature of practice provides opportunities for a return to and reconsideration of the basic concepts on which Hopwood's (1983) ground-breaking work resided, enabling further possibilities in terms of how we conceive of both management accounting practice and the context in which it is practised. The following discussion outlines some of these possibilities. The discussion turns first to recent debate informing our understanding of the heterogeneous nature of practices and the challenges that this possesses for researchers in the area of management accounting. This is then followed by an appreciation of arguments pertaining to the nature of context and its implications for understanding practice and, by extension, management accounting in its situation.

In relation to the issue of accounting practice, the following discussion should acknowledge the prescience of Hopwood's (1983) original remarks in the context of the ensuing discussion. As was stated earlier, Hopwood was struck by local variations which distinguished management accounting practice in action, highlighting the heterogeneity of the practices which mingle under the seemingly unified banner of various forms of management accounting. This is echoed in contemporaneous discussions within the social sciences which similarly contemplate the nature of practice (Law 2004; Law and Singleton 2005).

Basically, the heterogeneity of accounting practice which Hopwood outlined over 25 years ago is encompassed and elaborated in current debates about the import of so-called 'messy' objects in day-to-day social life (Law and Singleton 2005: 332). Both Law (2004) and Law and Singleton (2005), for example, use the notion of messy objects to convey local variations in practice across time and space. The 'practise of practice' (be it in the field of medicine in relation to the diagnosis and treatment of particular diseases or in the field of accounting in relation to the design and implementation of various management control systems) is not clean-cut and invariant from one site of action to another; rather objects such as diseases of a human body or management accounting control systems in particular organizations are messy because they are fluid. This fluidity manifests itself in the shifting nature of objects. Objects created through the practices of human agents are not 'immutable' (Law and Singleton 2005: 325). Objects, such as various forms of management accounting practice, possess a capacity for both 'shape' and 'name' shifting (Law and Singleton 2005: 340). Objects change their shape as a result of local practices involving tinkering, improvisation, and experimentation (see Ciborra 2002). Objects can also change their names as different titles are adopted to denote local appropriations of generic technologies and/or the concurrent emergence and recognition of 'home-grown' practices solving site-specific problems.

And there has been some implicit recognition of this capacity for messiness in recent research engaging with management accounting practice. For example, Andon et al. (2007) (discussed earlier) narrate the shape-shifting which occurred in relation to the balanced scorecard in an Australasian organization. The balanced scorecard in question underwent a number of shifts in its shape in a relatively short period of time, that is, about one year. First, the balanced scorecard shifted from being a control technology designed to contain costs (through the management of time-based measures) to a balanced scorecard which aimed at striking a balance between a need for efficiency and the delivery of customer satisfaction. A subsequent shift was also narrated as the balanced scorecard assumed the form of a strategic planning and control methodology which had as its aim the promotion of 'alignment' and 'integration' within the business unit fostering its implementation.

Recognition of the local name-shifting capabilities of management accounting technologies may also be construed in recent research, with studies investigating intellectual capital reporting practices providing a particularly fecund example of this form of messiness. By way of illustration, the research of Larsen et al. (1999) contains five brief case studies which indicate the different labels under which intellectual capital reporting may be constituted in different organizations. Larsen et al. outline this name shifting by outlining Skandia's 'system of capitals'; Ramboll's 'holistic accounting statements'; Sparnord's 'Ethical Accounting Statements'; Sparbanken's 'Tools for the Future'; and ABB's 'EVITA'.

Nonetheless, whilst narrations of such forms of heterogeneity are emerging from contemporary engagements with management accounting practices, it remains that there has been little elaboration and exploration of the challenges that this presents. How do we typify and make sense of this heterogeneity or messiness assuming that, like Law and Singleton (2004), we do not believe this to be an artefact that can be overcome by the technical refinement of our research methods?

Rather the challenge that we confront is to embrace and work through the epistemological and ontological implications of this heterogeneity inherent in management accounting practices. From an epistemological stance, such messiness is a result of the different perspectives (see Law and Singleton 2004) which organizational participants adopt when constructing and making sense of particular management accounting technologies-in-action. Indeed, characterizing various management accounting practices as boundary objects which can at least temporarily bind together different perspectives (Bowker and Star 1999) is consistent with an epistemological reconciliation of messiness, with the work of Briers and Chua (2001) on activity-based costing being indicative of this approach. But what if such heterogeneity is considered as ontological in nature (Law and Singleton 2004)? What if multiple objects are brought into being because of differential practices in and between organizations? For example, Sandhu et al. (2008) raise this possibility in the context of their study of the initial stages of the implementation of a balanced scorecard in a Singaporean firm. The finance manager considered the balanced scorecard to be a means of improving capital appropriation procedures. Operations personnel constituted the balanced scorecard as a solution for a 'free-riding' problem within the organization. Human resources characterized the balanced scorecard as a way of developing a learning organization. Senior managers enacted the balanced scorecard as a technology for improving service levels to key customers in a competitive marketplace. The balanced scorecard was constituted differently by various organizational participants connected to the implementation process. But as Sandhu et al. (2008: 22) stated, 'if we admit that a BSC [balanced scorecard] has multiple identities in practice, is there a point at which these different and multiple local transla-tions cease to be a BSC and become something else?'. When do shifting and changing practices transform into different objects?

Correspondingly, these multiplicities comprise a number of challenges in terms of our engagements with management practice. For instance, we need to give due consideration to the ways in which actors in organizations—and also research into these local forms of accountings—accommodate heterogeneous constitutions of practices. What kinds of ontological strategies are being used? Law (2004) provides us with a starting point for thinking about this in relation to the ordering practices of organizational participants. Are heterogeneous realities 'kept apart' (Law 2004: 75) or partitioned in day-to-day activities? If so, how are they separated by actors and what are the consequences of such discontinuities in management accounting practices in terms of organiza-tional functioning? Furthermore, how do practitioners shift from one hetero-geneous frame to another in accomplishing their organizational work? Alternatively, are messy practices integrated in some way by organizational participants? How and in what ways do they undertake such integrations?

Likewise, how do we as members of a research community order and sort the inevitable and varied accounts of these heterogeneous practices which are constructed by and through our engagements with management accounting in its organizational context? As researchers (and readers of research) we chronically engage in analytical reordering of practices and, arguably, central to these reordering processes are the writing strategies used to narrate man-agement accounting in action. As such, much turns on the 'convincingness' (Golden-Biddle and Locke 1993, 2007) of textualizations of first-hand experiences of practices, especially in terms of the capacity of these narrations to facilitate our perception, appreciation, and consensual validation of various possibilities surrounding the characterization of management accounting practices. One challenge that accompanies this recognition, therefore, is a need to better understand how and why it is that we privilege some accounts of practice over others. How is the convincingness of research constituted, particularly in relation to the field-based research methods which are com-monly used in conjunction with the furtherance of this research agenda? There is a corresponding need to understand the institutionalized academic norms which are perpetuated and developed through the writing of practice-based forms of management accounting research (see Baxter and Chua 2008*b*).

Moreover a further challenge that we confront in understanding the first-order and researcher-constructed reorderings of heterogeneous management accounting practices resides in a desire to also understand the network of interactions that inform and yet limit the emergence of possible multiplicities in particular situations. Also, if some framings of practice are afforded more importance than others (e.g. as was argued by Ahrens and Chapman [2007] in relation to managerial constructions of practice), then we need both to investigate and theorize the strength and durability of the meshes of activities informing the privileging of specific practices.

Similarly, there are also many ongoing challenges in terms of refining and redefining our understanding of the context in which management accounting practices operate. Evoking Hopwood's insistence on a fundamental entanglement between management accounting practices and their organizational settings (see 1983: 287) is Law's more recent reference (2004) to the situated nature of the heterogeneous practices outlined above: 'the new "is" is one that is situated' (Mol 2002: 53–4 cited in Law 2004: 59). Accordingly, we would argue that it is fitting that management accounting researchers place a greater emphasis on understanding the nature of context coupled to situated practices, as well as considering the ramifications of this. The writings of Schatzki (2000*a*, 2000*b*, 2000*c*), a practice theorist, are helpful and stimulating in this regard.

Schatzki (2000*a*) argues that these 'perpetually metamorphosing' practices which we find in social life, such as the doing of management accounting in different organizations, are highly 'contingent' on their situation (p. 103). Schatzki uses the term 'site' (2000*b*: 22) to describe the particular context informing specific practices. He states, 'A site is a kind of context. To analyse sociality via a site is to hold, *inter alia*, that the nature and transformation of social life are inherently, as well as decisively, tied to the context in which it takes place' (2000*b*: 22). Schatzki further develops the notion of site in his essays, outlining various 'genres' (p. 23) of site. He argues that we need to mobilize multiple senses of site. Researchers must attend to where practices take place—in terms of their particular location in space, time, teleology, or in terms of the layout of their local performance. Schatzki also encourages researchers to gain an awareness of the more general sites in which practices are embedded, for instance, in terms of various fields of activities (such as within a particular industry or profession). By implication, a challenge confronting researchers working in this area involves a careful mapping of the various constitutions of site which are integrally connected to the accomplishment of specific management accounting practices.

Yet an acknowledgement of the site-specific nature of management accounting practice creates other challenges in relation to studying accounting in the context in which it occurs. Acknowledging the highly contingent and situated functioning of management accounting presses us to consider the limits of management accounting practices. To what extent and in what ways do local management accounting practices interconnect? How might we configure larger 'confederations' (Schatzki 2000c: 195) or fields (Bourdieu 1998) of practices, whilst recognizing the situatedness of practices? What role and relevance do societist institutions have in practice-based theories? Additionally, how can we reconfigure notions of generalizability given the highly situated origins of practice-based constructions of management accounting, particularly as such research is not adverse to the general notion of providing constructive insights which may be of benefit to those practitioners with whom we seek to engage (Scapens 2006)? As such, it remains for researchers active in this area to grapple with the challenges of providing more nuanced and detailed accounts of management accounting practices which highlight the multiplicities of practices and their sites, as well as apprehending and configuring the types of more durable and broad-scale interconnections which have made the pursuit of a set of practices called management accounting possible to date.

CONCLUSION

It has been the purpose of this essay to return to Hopwood's influential 1983 paper in which he urges us to study accounting in its organizational context. We have noted the influence of this particular research paper on our discipline—motivating a corpus of research seeking first-hand engagement with management accounting practices. We have also outlined and illustrated how Hopwood's claims regarding the heterogeneous and situated nature of management accounting practice have spawned a vital research agenda with a capacity to maintain its saliency in the current intellectual clime, articulating with more general and emerging debates within the social sciences concerning multiple and site-specific ontologies of practices. It is our contention that recourse to such contemporary debates provides areas of considerable challenge in terms of how we may approach the study of management accounting in action, furthering the momentum and sustainability of this influential and telling research agenda.

REFERENCES

Agar, M.H. (1986). *Speaking of Ethnography* (Sage University Paper series on Qualitative Research Methods 2). Newbury Park, Calif.: Sage Publications.
Ahrens, T., and Chapman, C. (2005). Management control systems and the crafting of strategy: A practice-based view. In Chapman, C. (ed.), *Controlling Strategy: Management,*

Accounting, and Performance Measurement. Oxford: Oxford University Press, ch. 6.

Ahrens, T., and Chapman, C. (2007). Management accounting as practice. *Accounting, Organizations and Society,* 32, 1–27.

—— Becker, A., Burns, J. et al. (2008). The future of interpretive accounting research: A polyphonic debate. *Critical Perspectives on Accounting,* 19, 840–66.

Andon. P., Baxter, J., and Chua, W.F. (2007). Change or 'relational drifting?' A field study of accounting experimentation, *Management Accounting Research,* 18, 273–308.

Atkinson, D. (1972). *Orthodox Consensus and Radical Alternative.* London: Heinemann Educational Books.

Baxter, J.A., and Chua, W.F. (2003). Alternative management accounting research: Whence and whither. *Accounting, Organizations and Society,* 28, 97–126.

—— —— (2008*a*). Be(com)ing the chief financial officer of an organization: Experimenting with Bourdieu's practice theory. *Management Accounting Research,* 19, 212–30.

—— —— (2008*b*). The field researcher as author-writer. *Qualitative Research in Accounting & Management,* 5, 101–21.

Bourdieu, P. (1977). *Outline of a Theory of Practice* (translated by Richard Nice). Cambridge: Cambridge University Press.

—— (1990). *The Logic of Practice* (translated by Richard Nice). Cambridge: Polity Press.

—— (1998). *Practical Reason.* Cambridge: Polity Press.

—— (2000). *Pascalian Meditations* (translated by Richard Nice). Cambridge: Polity Press.

Bowker, G., and Star, S. (1999). *Sorting Things Out.* Cambridge, Mass.: MIT Press.

Braverman, H. (1974). *Labor and Monopoly Capital.* New York: Monthly Review Press.

Briers, M., and Chua, W.F. (2001). The rogle of actor-networks and boundary objects in management accounting change: A field study of an implementation of activity-based costing. *Accounting Organizations and Society,* 26, 237–69.

Burchell, S., Clubb, C., and Hopwood, A. (1985). Accounting in its social context: Towards a history of value added in the United Kingdom. *Accounting, Organizations and Society,* 10, 381–413.

Chua, W.F. (1986). Radical developments in accounting thought. *Accounting Review,* LXI, 601–32.

—— (2007). Accounting, measuring, reporting and strategizing—re-using verbs: A review essay. *Accounting, Organizations and Society,* 32, 487–94.

Ciborra, C. (2002). *The Labyrinths of Information: Challenging the Wisdom of Systems.* Oxford: Oxford University Press.

Colville, I. (1981). Reconstructing 'behavioural accounting'. *Accounting, Organizations and Society,* 6, 119–32.

Cooper, D. (1983). Tidiness, muddle and things: Commonalities and divergencies in two approaches to management accounting research. *Accounting, Organizations and Society,* 8, 269–86.

Dent, J.F. (1991). Accounting and organizational cultures: A field study of the emergence of a new organizational reality. *Accounting Organizations and Society,* 16, 705–32.

DiMaggio, W., and Powell, P. (eds.) (1991). *The New Institutionalism in Organizational Analysis.* Chicago: University of Chicago Press.

Foucault, M. (1977). *Discipline and Punish: The Birth of the Prison.* Middlesex: Peregrine Books.

Gergen, K.J. (1999). *An Invitation to Social Construction.* London: Sage Publications.

Giddens, A. (1984). *The Constitution of Society.* Cambridge: Polity Press.

—— (1991). *Modernity and Self-identity: Self and Society in the Late Modern Age.* Cambridge: Polity Press.

Golden-Biddle, K., and Locke, K. (1993). Appealing works: An investigation of how ethnographic texts convince. *Organization Science,* 4, 595–616.

———— (2007). *Composing Qualitative Research.* Thousand Oaks, Calif.: Sage Publications.

Habermas, J. (1968). *Toward a Rational Society.* London: Heinemann Educational Books.

—— (1976). *Communication and the Evolution of Society.* London: Heinemann Educational Books.

Hansen, A., and Mouritsen, J. (2005). Strategies and organizational problems: Constructing corporate value and coherence in balanced scorecards processes. In Chapman, C. (ed.), *Controlling Strategy: Management, Accounting, and Performance Measurement.* Oxford: Oxford University Press, ch. 7.

Hopper, T., Storey, J., and Willmott, H. (1987). Accounting for accounting: Towards the development of a dialectical view. *Accounting, Organizations and Society,* 12, 437–56.

Hopwood, A. (1983). On trying to study accounting in the contexts in which it operates. *Accounting, Organizations and Society,* 8, 287–305.

Jönsson, S. (1982). Budgeting behavior in local government: A case study over 3 years. *Accounting, Organizations and Society,* 3, 287–304.

Kaplan, R. (1986). The role for empirical research in management accounting. *Accounting, Organizations and Society,* 11, 429–52.

Kirk, J., and Miller, M.L. (1986). *Reliability and Validity in Qualitative Research* (Sage University Paper series on Qualitative Research Methods 1). Newbury Park, Calif.: Sage Publications.

Larsen, H., Bukh, P., and Mouritsen, J. (1999). Intellectual capital statements and knowledge management: 'Measuring', 'reporting', 'acting', *Australian Accounting Review,* 9, 15–26.

Latour, B. (1987). *Science in Action.* Cambridge, Mass.: Harvard University Press.

Law, J. (2004). *After Method: Mess in Social Science Research,* London: Routledge.

—— and Singleton, V. (2005). Object Lessons. *Organization,* 12, 331–55.

Malina, M.A., and Selto, F.H. (2001). Communicating and controlling strategy: An empirical study of the effectiveness of the balanced scorecard. *Journal of Management Accounting Research,* 13, 47–90.

Miller, P., and O'Leary, T. (1987) Accounting and the construction of the governable person. *Accounting, Organizations and Society*, 12, 235–65.

—— —— (1997). Capital budgeting practices and complementarity relations in the transition to modern manufacture: A field-based analysis. *Journal of Accounting Research*, 35, 257–72.

Mol, A. (2002). *The Body Multiple: Ontology in Medical Practice*. Durham, N.C.: Duke University Press.

Mouritsen, J. (1999). The flexible firm: Strategies for a subcontractor's management control. *Accounting, Organizations and Society*, 24, 31–55.

Preston, A. (1986). Interactions and arrangements in the process of informing. *Accounting, Organizations and Society*, 11, 521–40.

—— Cooper, D., and Coombs, R. (1992). Fabricating budgets: A study of the production of management budgeting in the National Health Service. *Accounting, Organizations and Society*, 17, 561–93.

Sandhu, R., Baxter, J., and Emsley, D. (2008). The balanced scorecard and its possibilities: The initial experiences of a Singaporean firm. *Australian Accounting Review*, 18, 16–24.

Scapens, R. (2006). Understanding management accounting practices: A personal journey. *The British Accounting Review*, 38, 1–30.

Schatzki, T. (2000*a*). Wittgenstein and the social context of an individual. *History of the Human Sciences*, 13, 93–107.

—— (2000*b*). The social being of nature. *Inquiry*, 43, 21–38.

—— (2000*c*). A new societist social ontology. *Philosophy of the social sciences*, 33, 174–202,

Tomkins, C., and Groves, R. (1983). The everyday accountant and researching his reality. *Accounting, Organizations and Society*, 8, 361–74.

Vaivio, J. (1999). Examining 'the quantified customer'. *Accounting, Organizations and Society*, 24, 689–715.

5

Management Accounting in a Digital and Global Economy: The Interface of Strategy, Technology, and Cost Information

Alnoor Bhimani and Michael Bromwich

INTRODUCTION

This chapter discusses aspects of the digital economy and globalization and their influence on management accounting. Strategy, technology, and costs, it is argued, are increasingly co-mingled in globalized and digitized organizational contexts. Conceiving ways of doing things has traditionally been regarded as a necessarily distinct process from the actual execution of activities. This notion is embedded across the majority of established enterprise management approaches. But managerial intentions and actions are becoming intertwined in many enterprises. Decision-based thinking does not necessarily always precede managerial action. The chapter discusses how digitization and globalization are altering decision-making processes and organizational action. It does so by considering collaborative alliances and virtual organization-based issues and explores some wider possible implications for strategic management accounting. A case study of a firm tackling digitization and globalization issues is discussed before presenting some brief conclusions.

THE DIGITAL AND GLOBAL ECONOMY

Gutenberg's printing press was, in the fifteenth century, an information technology (IT) revolution. In this past century, this revolution has continued— IT has become faster, cheaper, easier to use, more versatile, and more extensively impacts enterprise processes. Today IT is effectively ubiquitous across organizations and it is central to economic activities. So much so that many regard modern times as being a 'digital economy' represented by:

... the pervasive use of IT (hardware, software, application and telecommunication) in all aspects of the economy, including internal operations of organizations (business, government and non-profit); and transactions between individuals, acting both as consumers and citizens, and organizations. (Atkinson and McKay 2007: 7)

Communication technologies including telephony, radio, and television have over much of the past century evolved very rapidly in terms of functionality, capacity, and features but have only partially engaged computer technologies in doing so. Some of the most important developments in telephony have been the introduction of optic fibre networks in the late 1980s, greatly increasing storage and processing capacity, the enormous growth in mobile phones providing much flexibility in communication and the introduction of broadband in the early 1990s.

Since their invention in the 1940s, computers have developed at an extremely rapid pace. The vast majority of managers and administrative employees today access or influence others through a desktop or mainframe computer. Another industry which has seen extensive continuous improvement over the twentieth century is that of media and entertainment. As distinct industries, what has been achieved by computer technologies alongside the transformation of telephony, media, and entertainment as well as the software industry during the twentieth century has been wide-reaching and transformational. But the digital economy could only emerge from the convergence of these different industries.

It is now incongruous to think of these industries outside the context of their merged potential. The Internet achieved its large-scale impact given the wide-level availability of computers and network technologies. This then paved the way for media and commerce to become electronically interconnected. The ready availability of software applications and content was in turn enabled by connectivity. The large-scale availability and effective commoditization of digital cameras, handsets, mobile telephones, flat-screen high definition TVs, and MP3s has been fuelled by networked IT systems enabling greater coordination. In other words, digital convergence is at the heart of creating an irreversibly connected environment which has brought previously distinct industries together. The result is that it is rapidly becoming inconceivable for traditionally independent machines, software systems, PCs, and communication products to be regarded as not networkable. The digital age is an enmeshed world of interpenetrating digital devices affecting very many areas of social and economic activity.

This chapter argues that the convergence of the technologies described above and their economic, managerial, and social impacts raise important issues for the premise upon which management accounting is now founded. Financial control and management accounting activities as part of the digital economy are at a turning point facing the likelihood of extensive alterations. They are having to confront a much closer integration of decision-making and action in supporting the co-mingling of strategy, technology, and cost information.

GLOBALIZATION

The challenge to accountants to respond to the digital economy arises not just given the above-discussed shift, but also in terms of other dimensions of globalization. There are many definitions of globalization. One is:

Globalisation is about the changing influence of space and time in our lives. With the advent of the communications revolution distance has a different relationship to self-immediacy and experience than it used to have. Distance isn't simply wiped out, but when you have a world where the value of the money in your pocket is affected immediately by ongoing electronic transactions happening many miles away, it's simply a different situation from how the world was in the past. (Giddens 1999)

Another:

Almost all contemporary social theorists endorse the view that globalization refers to fundamental changes in the spatial and temporal contours of social existence, according to which the significance of space or territory undergoes shifts in the face of a no less dramatic acceleration in the temporal structure of crucial forms of human activity. (*Stanford Encyclopedia of Philosophy* 2002)

Globalization in everyday language refers to the diminished distance and time between countries, organizations, and people. In industry and services, firms are seeking to supply globally, they are establishing a presence across the globe and are outsourcing throughout the world. The digital economy and globalization are leading organizations to base their strategies on the opportunities and challenges of these environmental influences.

Figure 5.1 shows some of the areas held to be highly important in globalization for a manufacturing or service organization. The broad arrows indicate that organizations can establish strategies in these areas. Thus, strategy identification is seen as fundamental to effective globalization. The thin arrows indicate that the digital economy is viewed as enabling or facilitating

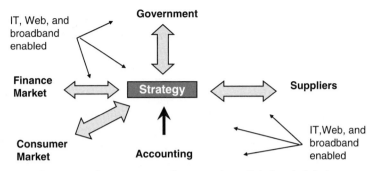

Figure 5.1. Strategy and corporate performance in a digital and global economy

globalization in each of these areas. The arrow from accounting indicates that accounting is seen as having a role in strategic choice. The globalization opportunities in most of the areas listed are well known. Thus, in seeking to raise capital, the choice is to fund locally or from international markets. The latter opportunity is becoming extensively dependent on the digital economy. Similarly, consumer-supply choices reflect whether to supply locally, to a number of countries or for some product or services, to supply globally. These choices also require decisions on the mode of supply including between joint ventures and direct investment overseas. Again, the digital economy facilitates such endeavours, not just with regard to initial set up but also in reporting and monitoring progress.

Similar considerations apply to the supply chain. Here, accountants in addition to reporting and monitoring may be involved in investment appraisal and in making and/or buying decisions and performance measurement. In some firms, planning departments may be closer to strategy than accounting departments and may play the lead role in appraising investments and analysing outsourcing decisions. All these roles reflect aspects of the digital economy. The broad arrow to government in Figure 5.1 reflects the ability of governments to inhibit or encourage globalization and to facilitate or hinder the adoption of elements of the digital economy.

To bring out some of the cost and learning relationships in a digital economy allowing cross-organizational and global exchanges, the next part of the chapter discusses changing enterprise structures. Collaborative firm linkages and pure trading relationships are explained and how pure trading links between firms can be restructured by virtual enterprise forms enabled by IT innovations is explored. Associated cost and strategic issues are subsequently identified. The possible implications of this shift for management accounting are carved out drawing on the above arguments.

EMERGING ENTERPRISE STRUCTURES

From Collaborative Alliances to Virtual Linkages

The 'make-or-buy' option for a firm requiring subcomponents or input material has been extensively discussed in the management accounting literature. Conceptually, the costs and benefits accruing to a firm producing required parts or subcomponents internally are weighed against the financial and managerial consequences of outsourcing via competitive bidding by suppliers of the products (Meer-Kooistra 1994; Quinn and Hilmer 1994; Vining and Globerman 1999; Groot and Merchant 2000; Speklé 2001; Dekker 2004; Callioni et al. 2005). Economic theorizing on transaction costs has shaped accounting thought on firm structure over a long period. Incremental cost analysis has been advocated as an appropriate approach to assessing the financial consequences of buy/make managerial decisions.

The virtual firm enabled by digitization can be regarded as an agglomeration of multiple 'buy' transactions weaved together by extensively structured coordination. Cost analyses are likely to entail a variety of factors reflective of the complexities of such an agglomeration. Ultimately, the 'make-or-buy' decision can in some virtual contexts become a 'make-and/or-buy' series of decisions. These decisions may themselves be grounded in the implementation of the decisions.

Over the past two decades, much has been written about alterations to buyer–supplier links enabling firms to consider an alternative to the make or buy option: the collaborative relationship (CR) which is in effect a 'quasi-vertical' form of integration (Richardson 1993; Das and Teng 2000; Tomkins 2001). CRs play an increasingly prevalent role among many enterprises today (Helper and Sako 1995; Trent and Monczka 1998; Handfield et al. 2000; Lambert and Cooper 2000; Leiblein and Miller 2003; Liker and Choi 2004; Sako 2008). Sheth and Sharma note that: '... organizational buying is dramatically shifting from the transaction oriented to the relational oriented philosophy and will shift from a buying process to a supplier relationship process' (1997: 91). Management accounting scholars have commented on the control implications of this shift (Anderson and Sedatole 2003; Dekker 2004; Hakansson and Lind 2007; Kamminga and Van der Meer-Kooistra 2007; Kraus and Lind 2007) but have not formally addressed its implications for cost management processes. These relate to product development input, price rebates, after sales warranties, supplier inspection policies, and information systems integration. Many scholars recognize that strategic and contractual issues between buyers and sellers are gaining relevance, particularly in new product development contexts (Reyniers and Tapiero 1995; Cousins 1999; Arnold 2000; Axelsson et al. 2000; Gadde and Snehota 2000; Narayanan and Raman 2004).

The development of relationships-based or collaboration-oriented purchasing behaviour is influenced by many factors including similarities between the industry and technologies of buyers and suppliers (Buvik and Halskan 2001; Gadde and Håkansson 2001; Dalmin and Mininno 2003); prior experiences of change among suppliers (Hahn et al. 1990; Frey and Schlosser 1993); effective communications between buyer and suppliers (Lascelles and Dale 1989; Hoberman and Mailick 1992; Mohrman and Mohrman 1993; Van Weele 2000); the creation of cost information exchange relationships (Ellram 1996); and the consideration of purchase leverage factors and volume of initial business (Billington and Ellram 2001; Kulmala 2004). The importance of experiential learning is a major characteristic of customer supplier links and of living in a digital and global economy (Krapfel et al. 1991; Dyer and Singh 1998; Langfield-Smith and Greenwood 1998; Bessant et al. 2003; Stjernstrom and Bengtsson 2004).

In practice, two options generally exist for a company wishing to purchase a subcomponent or a service-based product from an external supplier. On the one hand, the buyer can put out a bid tender and choose the most competitive quote for a certain number of parts over a period of time. Benefits from past performance are limited; exchanges tend to be at arm's length and product specifications; and prices are well defined. In contrast to this transaction-based competitive bidding approach, the buyer can establish a collaborative relationship with a supplier. Such a relationship would entail sharing of technical and financial information, managerial interaction and liaison, and a more flexible buyer–supplier link as to time/volume variables and product specification. The costs involved in identifying the right supplier for a collaborative relationship and operationalizing such a link differ from those in a bidding situation. Firms regard one or the other approach as a strategic issue.

Traditional competitive purchasing entails the assessment of certain economic transactions whose terms are made explicit prior to the commencement of trading. Agreements (contracts) with recourse options for faltering on the terms of the contract and the buyer–supplier link is designed within attempts to minimize each party's dependence on the other. In contrast, collaborative subcontracting relationships are founded on trust and transactional dependence with specific supply undertakings (often made orally) extending over only part of the overall trading relationship. The obligations of such long-term relationships are diffuse and guide the resolution of specific transaction problems on a case-by-case basis usually through informal channels. The collaborative link exhibits mutual indebtedness that can extend over long periods of time with a loose principle of give and take. The usual pure buy situation is characterized by narrow and formal channels of communication between the buyer's purchasing department and the supplier's sales department whereas a CR tends to have extensive and multiple channels of communication between a variety of functional managers and departments within the two companies.

The most significant difference between a pure purchase and a collaborative linkage is that the latter establishes non-specific terms of trade as to supply quantity, timing of supply, product specifications, and product price at the time of establishing the trading relationship. In contrast, in pure purchase contexts, the economic exposure can be calculated with a high degree of accuracy prior to the commencement of trading. Table 5.1 identifies some contrasting characteristics of collaborative alliances and pure trading.

The absence of a contractual predetermination of quantity, price, and timing of supply makes it difficult to assess the financial consequences of creating a CR trading link. The buyer's ability to alter quantities purchased from the supplier and the buyer's, and sometimes the supplier's, power to change product specifications confers operational flexibility. There may be a variety of product life cycle considerations that affect strategically desirable

Table 5.1. Contrasting characteristics of pure trading versus collaborative relationships

Buyer–supplier link characteristics	Pure trading	Collaborative relationship
Knowledge	Proprietary	Operational knowledge flows between each party and there is sharing of information between competing suppliers
Price	Lowest bidder usually obtains contract	Immediate price competitiveness is often secondary
Timing terms	Strictly stipulated penalties for deviations from contractual terms. Commitments tend to be short term	Option exists to delay and even abandon purchases either temporarily or permanently without relinquishing buyer–supplier link over long term
Contract specificity	Product specifications usually predetermined	Limitless product specification changes may be made
Communication channels	Narrow and formal	Multiple channels, information exchange is less formal and more frequent

time frames relating to market entry (Dunk 2004). Additionally, both parties learn from producing, transacting, and cooperating with one another which brings about cost consequences and interdependencies. An alliance creates the possibility of rapid expansion and growth in ways not anticipated at the outset (Child 2005).

The initial subcomponent cost or service offering cost of a supplier able to engage in a CR may be greater than that in a pure trade with a supplier but this needs to be evaluated in terms of foregoing the pay-offs from a CR. In particular, the transfer of knowledge and the availability of flexibilities say between a supplier and assembler may over time contribute to value advantages exceeding those of pure initial subcomponent price differentials between a competitive bid purchase based on a contract and a CR (Gietzmann and Larsen 1998).

Some firms will opt for both CR and pure trades depending on their purchasing portfolio mix (Axelsson et al. 2000). If there are learning effects, costs will possibly decrease with output. Process improvement, product standardization, economies of scale, and other elements can all offer learning. The extent to which economies and opportunities emerge out of learning varies across and within industries and is conditioned by differences in R&D expenditure and capital intensity as well as team effects (Dutton and Thomas 1984; Lieberman 1984; Gruber 1992; Dyer 1997). In practice, learning effects are higher under CR links than in trading links.

In broad terms, the decision to enter into a collaborative relationship with a supplier as opposed to engaging in transaction focused pure purchase for required products entails a variety of organizational consequences with cost–benefit implications that stem from the various options affordable by the alliance. Learning and knowledge transfer play a key role. This is so for collaborative alliances where the nature of interactions facilitates information exchange both formal and informal as well leaving loose certain terms of trade including the length of the relationship. Conversely, pure purchase situations and particularly those enabled electronically within virtual firms, allow little room for collaboration or for learning which is not a primary objective of the virtual firm set-up.

The features of CRs have control issues relating to the flexibilities offered vis-à-vis the resource implications of establishing CRs. Creating an alliance can be time-consuming with resources being required to set up a workable trading infrastructure. There has to be an infrastructure and a willingness to share operational information including accounting information between the trading entities (Dyer and Singh 1998; Vining and Globerman 1999; Handfield et al. 2000).

Learning effects affect the economic viability of engaging in a supplier alliance. Cost reductions can flow from a subcomponent supplier to the partner firm as part of a CR. It may be possible for the firm to earn superior returns through learning rate differentials from a CR which may not be acceptable via virtually structured coordination. As elaborated below, virtual firms are not designed to tap into organizational learning. Whilst the accounting literature recognizes learning-related cost effects, the strategic implications of establishing both collaborative and virtual relationships are complex and have not been investigated to any great degree. The next part of the chapter considers the virtual organization as a rapidly emerging form.

The Virtual Enterprise

This section explains the basis upon which 'virtual' enterprises operate and provides an illustration of the governance and control mechanisms in place which, to a degree, pre-empt the dissociation between thinking and acting and planning and controlling.

A virtual enterprise has been considered to be: '... A temporary network of independent companies-suppliers, customers and even rivals-linked by information technology to share skills, costs and access to one another's markets. This corporate model is fluid and flexible' (Byrne et al. 1993: 36). Stress has been placed on bringing together resources and goal achievements via the view of a virtual enterprise being a goal-orientated arrangement between several firms or a unit within a firm which temporarily assembles dispersed competencies and capabilities. Virtuality has been taken to suggest transient connections between otherwise independent entities via appropriate IT structures: 'A virtual company is created by selecting organizational resources from different companies and synthesizing them into a single electronic business entity' (Nagel and Dove 1991). Of particular note is that the creation of this organizational form raises the question of the goal realization path:

> The essence of the virtual organization is the management of goal-orientated activity in a way that is independent of the means for its realization. This implies a logical separation between the conception and planning of an activity on the one hand, and its implementation on the other. (Mowshowitz 1994: 279).

Implementation necessitates the planning of certain decisions to be achieved during implementation action rather than a priori. One characterizing feature of virtual organizations is the commoditization of information to enhance flexibility and 'infinite switching capacity' so that 'by reducing dependency on the human being as the bearer of knowledge and skill, it is possible to increase the flexibility of decision-making and control to unprecedented levels' (Mowshowitz 1994: 281). A second feature is the standardization of interaction whereby enterprises can be readily coupled and decoupled as the need for altered supply arises. This is enabled by the codification of information (Boisot 1998) which provides a basis for enhancing information's control potential.

A virtual enterprise is likely to have overhead costs largely tied to running its information systems infrastructures and carrying out coordination processes. Additionally, overhead costs will reflect personnel costs with employees likely being rewarded on some measure of coordination effectiveness. Virtual corporations may find the achievement of scale and scope economies difficult and will have to seek value creation through coordination structures and flow mechanisms rather than by reducing costs of material input, processing, or packaging for physical products. This is because virtual flows are set up with quite specific predetermined objectives for suppliers followed by disengagement. Proprietary information leakage can be a risk with precaution against opportunistic behaviour also being essential.

Within virtual corporations, little room exists for tapping into organizational learning. A virtual organization is effectively 'a repertoire of variable connectable modules built on an electronic information network' (Child et al. 2005: 168) with each linked firm's function being to deliver a specific standardization output before decoupling. The intent is to create a flexible organization of companies whereby each undertakes one or more functions rather than to provide a structure for enabling information exchange with a view to learning.

Managerial emphasis within virtual enterprises is placed on sound information processing as well as on the coordination of individuals and connecting firms, and on guidance via the clear articulation of the organization's vision. Managerial focus is on the management of people, coordination activities, and technology. If carried out effectively, the benefits to the corporation will be the sound management of integral supply chains, desired response to competitors' actions, and shorter time to market. Such consequences can come about in the face of very low face-to-face contacts.

Significantly, virtual organizations are less focused on controlling how work is undertaken and more on outcomes of work. A firm which has its own hierarchy to carry out activities will be highly integrated. Its insourcing activities will need close operational controls. It will retain high involvement with physical processes. At an opposite extreme, an organization may structure itself as a virtual trading firm with arm's length transactions enabling short-term exchange between electronically linked organizations. The focus here will be on coordination rather than ownership of physical assets and on operating as an 'intellectual holding company' (Straub 2004: 300).

Traditionally, individual firms carrying out operational activities will invest in process controls via standard costing analysis and budgetary controls based on operating plans and activities. They will be aware of and be able to act on performance monitors of their output. Conversely, the virtual trading firm will focus on outcome controls. In virtualizing, firms become less operationally management control orientated and instead, evaluate performance by monitoring outcomes. The ability to monitor outsourced processes via outcome controls becomes a relevant core competency for virtual corporations. Where a firm has integrated activities, it will control its processes via some equity in production activities providing legitimacy for monitoring those processes. A virtual firm by contrast will likely not hold an equity position vis-à-vis the purchase or trading partners it engages with and its core resource for effective coordination and service delivery will lean towards outcome-based performance controls.

Focusing on the control of outcomes without an equity stake engages a shift in the balance and focus of costs for an enterprise. Typically, disengagement from owning resources and emphasizing coordination can be accompanied by a tilt towards variable costs and a lesser fixed cost base. However, if the scope and scale economies hurdle which virtual firms typically face can be overcome, reduction in both fixed and variable costs can accrue. Such a position gives rise to network effect like benefits. Larger virtual firms become bigger because of their ability to tap into scale benefits as they enlarge. The chapter next discusses some of the possible accounting effects of these influences and, more generally, those arising from globalization.

THE END OF LINEARITY

In a digitized and globalized complex enterprise, people can act whilst thinking about desirable actions. Actions subsume or include objectives. That is, objectives become defined simultaneously with actions and are embedded in actions. Processes therefore become concomitant with intentions. However, management thinkers in the past have mostly regarded decision-making activities and managerial action as being sequential. The notion that some organizational actors think whilst others engage in action became a characterizing feature of industrial management at the turn of the last century. Management accounting is archetypical of this approach when historically characterized as providing only information for decision-making. Conceiving ways of doing things is mostly still regarded as an activity that is distinct from the actual execution of desired activities. This is embedded across the majority of prescribed approaches to enterprise management. Managers however often think of strategic processes and related organizational activities as being closely intertwined.

Given the extent to which professional management accountancy bodies are embracing a more strategic posture for the field, strategic thinking in the practice of financial and cost management is an increasingly important issue. Financial managers and accountants are encouraged to be more strategic (Nyamori et al. 2001: 65). Strategic control and cost management frameworks define approaches to strategic decisions as distinct from their implementation and from operationalizing separately derived intentions. Retaining the traditional staff instead of line role for accountants in organizations makes it difficult for strategic thinking not to be viewed as dissociated from operational action. Many cost management approaches, including activity-based management, product life cycle costing, target cost management, customer profitability analyses, and strategic investment appraisal among others, have been predicated on the idea that strategic thinking should guide managerial action (see Langfield-Smith 2008). Essentially, it is still believed that conceptions of intent should be formulated prior to the implementation of decisions.

Within emerging organisational structures, the notion that strategic decisions should uniformly be dissociated from action may be a partial view. In the digital economy, businesses cannot separate all technological or operational activities from their strategic decision-making processes. The meshing of strategic, technological, and operational factors suggests a need to reformulate management accounting precepts across at least some areas whereby reported management accounting information is used within emerging organizational forms.

Industrial enterprises may have been regarded as being able to predefine a strategy in order to modernize production processes. Decision-makers would then have been presented with technological improvement investment options. Supporting accounting and financial information on the likely economic implications would subsequently have been collated and supplied to the decision-makers so that managerial action would rest on financial analyses of possible technological options stemming from the strategy being pursued.

But the co-mingling of strategic, technological, and operational decisions within many new organizations implies that managerially useful information can no longer be purely financial whereby strategic intent and technological options are regarded as distinct elements that are separable from one another and which follow a sequential path. What comprises relevant information and the presumed sequence of its deployment vis-à-vis management accounting action in the organizationally networked world has to be reconsidered.

Just as convergence among previously distinct and independent industries has integrated desire and action, so is management becoming integrated in terms of decision-making and action. Consider for instance emerging enterprise software applications. A leading player in the Enterprise Resources Planning (ERP) market is SAP. SAP is seeking to link Business Intelligence (BI) solutions to its existing ERP-based approaches. This is being undertaken on the argument that the distance between analysis and execution is being eliminated in enterprises—to create a 'closed loop' of performance management. The Strategic Marketing Director for Business Objects at SAP notes that: '... when BI and ERP are integrated, business processes can automatically be redirected on the basis of analytics, removing the need for explicit decision making' (T. Elliott in *Information Age*, June 2008: 41). Separating thinking from action is not seen as an essential step for some organizational systems designers and decision-makers. Coca-Cola's Innovation Specialist in the German Customer and Business Strategy Department notes that there is a potential within enterprises to 'close the gap between modeling and executing and so the gap between IT and business' (A. Grobe in ibid.). Management accounting information systems may follow suit.

Without being partners in the strategic integration of decisions and actions, management accountants are limited in the roles they can play in helping firms to adjust to the digital economy and to globalization. In contemporary organizations, accountants are not seen as 'owning' either the foundational disciplines of the digital economy or being responsible for the major elements that underlie globalization. Taken to an extreme, this view would restrict management accountants to their traditional roles of aiding investment and other management decisions and reporting on and monitoring the plans of others. Admittedly, these are more difficult tasks in digitized and global organizations, especially in devising appropriate reporting platforms and performance measurement systems.

Financial information relevance is increasingly about the effective representation of strategic and technological interdependencies enabling managerial decisions to align with present day organizational action. In some situations, the coupling of strategy, technology, and process are coordinated by informational intensity. Enterprises which depart from the industrial structural model couple strategic and financial considerations. The interrelationships make it difficult for management accounting activities as they exist to rest within specific predefined entry points. Financial information is potentially becoming integral to and immanent within assessments of operational, strategic, and cost considerations.

Identifying how new organizational forms bring about new informational dimensions that can impact organizational action with consequences for costs is relevant to consider. In particular, although accepted technical wisdom proposes that traditional incremental cost analysis can be applied to internal production versus outsourcing decisions, modern enterprises operating in digitized and globalized environments indicate the need to problematize this notion. The structure within which organizational transactions take place have altered the extent and consequences of strategic thinking as well as associated cost/revenue impacts.

MANAGEMENT ACCOUNTING AND STRATEGY

The above perspective on the digital economy suggests that management accounting thinking may likely witness changes given the interdependencies between strategy, technology, and financial control. Similarly, the effects of globalization highlight altered conceptions of strategy's role in relation to the finance function. Strategic decisions as has been argued are co-mingled with technical and control issues (Bromwich 1990; Rayport and Jaworski 2003; Bhimani 2008). Historically, management accountants have played a relatively indirect role in strategy determination-providing information seen as having strategic implications (Bhimani and Keshvarz 1999). Anecdotal evidence suggests that many managers either have or would welcome accountants taking a more proactive role in strategy formulation if not also implementation. This is to possibly avert those involved in strategic decisions entirely favouring strategies reflecting their own personal and professional interests with a lesser concern for the cost-based aspects of accepted strategies. This points to the need for accountants to understand the organization's changing nature and its dependence on the technologies underlying the digital economy and the globalization process. But there is evidence that the management accounting discipline including more recent and avant guarde ideas related to strategic management accounting are slow to change.

There is very scant empirical literature concerning the accountant's role in strategy except a few studies concerning the applications of what is sometimes called Strategic Management Accounting (SMA) which is briefly discussed below (see also Bhimani 2009; and LangWeld-Smith 2007). Two recent UK studies of what management accountants do are Burns et al. (2003) and Burns and Yazdifar (2001) which both surveyed a small sample of UK members of the Chartered Institute of Management Accountants, the first in 1997 and the second in 2000. These studies focused on why management accounting systems seem to be slow to change. The 1997 study suggested the then new techniques were taken up by accountants but in a relatively moderate way, but the 2000 sample expected their usage to grow substantially. New methods of aiding strategy were used by 27 per cent of the sample in 1997 but the 2000 sample, perhaps, optimistically, expected the take up rate to be 65 percent by 2005. More studies are needed to monitor these developments. A recent study of 41 UK manufacturing companies (Dugdale et al. 2006) suggests that management accounting systems were basically traditional, featuring budgeting, standard costing, and incentive systems based on accounting numbers. An interview-based survey of 16 manufacturing companies in Ireland found that accountants in the early and mid-2000s in their decision-making role were seen by other managers not as decision partners but as information providers and that in the main modern accounting techniques were not implemented (Byrne and Pierce 2007). However, the strong emphasis on contribution reporting and reporting non-financial performance measures found by Dugdale et al. (2006) suggests some response to strategy matters. There is also evidence from case studies of the emergence of what are called hybrid accountants who combine the skills of business managers and accountants working very closely with process managers (Burns et al. 2003). Such accountants may be more willing to reshape management accounting design and processes around the digital economy and globalization issues.

STRATEGIC MANAGEMENT ACCOUNTING

Rather than accountants getting fully involved in strategy formulation, some commentators have suggested they should seek to provide more information specifically tailored to strategy (Simmonds 1981; Shank 2006). What has often been called SMA refers to a variable portfolio of financial techniques geared towards aiding strategic decision-making rather than dealing with the tactical and operational issues which are focused on in traditional management accounting. SMA usually encompasses two types of information (Langfield-Smith 2008). The first concerns providing information and future estimates concerning consumer markets, especially customer characteristics, and competitors, especially their cost structure, both currently and in the future (Bromwich 1990). The second type focuses on the industry value chain and the company's position in this chain leading to reconfiguring the enterprise's value chain (Shank and Govindarajan 1993). This information would seem to help in those strategic decisions prevalent in a digital and global environment. Both field studies of SMA and the survey literature on SMA are sparse. Generally, SMA adopts prescriptive rather than descriptive views of strategy (Bhimani 2008). Two field studies are Lord (1996) and Dixon (1998) which both suggest that SMA practices are used in highly specific ways and that accountants were not involved in these implementations of SMA. A more recent study of a large multinational German company did find evidence of the use of SMA and the strong involvement of controllers using and developing SMA ideas (Tillmann and Goddard 2008).

Although the term SMA seems only to be recognized sporadically in practice, many of the techniques that are generally recognized as elements of SMA are found to be used in practice. However, these may be performed either entirely by non-accountants or in combination with hybrid accountants even though SMA implicitly claims these techniques for management accounting.

Researchers especially those undertaking surveys include different techniques as comprising SMA. Such lists include the costing of product attributes, brand value accounting, competitive positioning, pricing relative to competitors, life cycle costing, quality costing, strategic costing relative rivals, target costing, and value chain costing (Guilding et al. 2000). Other techniques that could be added are activity-based costing geared towards costing strategies, benchmarking, and accounting for servicing groups of similar customers (Cinquini and Tenucci 2007).

A leading survey article in this area is Guilding et al. (2000), which surveyed the use of what are usually called SMA techniques in the largest companies in New Zealand, the United Kingdom, and the United States. The response rates were 51 per cent, 38 per cent, and 13 per cent, respectively. The study asked about the usage of 12 SMA practices measured on a 7 point Likert scale with 7 indicating use to a great extent.[1] The usage of only two practices in the set of techniques labeled costing and pricing scored above the mid-point on the scale or around the mid-point in both the full sample and for individual countries samples. The rankings for the perceived merit of these practices yielded much higher scores on a scale: not at all helpful or to a large extent helpful. All but one of the practices scored at mid-point or better in the full sample with strategic pricing and costing getting scores of well over 5 and nearly 5, respectively. This does suggest that further development of these techniques which may be deemed germane to decision-making in the digital and global economy are likely.

---

[1] These 12 practices were classified into three groups: those concerned with strategic costing and pricing made up of attribute, life cycle, quality, target, value chain costing, and strategic costing and strategic pricing, the second comprised of competitive accounting made up of competitive position monitoring and cost assessment and competitor performance based on published financial statements, and the third was a group of two measures relative to brand values.

The second set of techniques were concerned with competitive position and performance and competitor cost assessment generally scored between 4 and 5 for usage and nearly 6 on their merit. This is encouraging as these practices seem very relevant to assessing the organization's competitive adaption to the digital economy and globalization.

The results of this study with regard to the first set of techniques have been used to suggest that SMA has not really shown the promise its advocates have claimed. The sample included companies likely to exhibit very different characteristics not captured by adjusting for company size. Possibly, the usage of SMA techniques may depend on organizational characteristics. For instance, a cost leader organization may use different SMA practices to those used by a differentiator company or, differ in the intensity to which they are used. Using average scores over the samples may not capture this.

A more recent study of the largest Italian manufacturing firms attempted to incorporate the contingent factors likely to affect the usage of SMA techniques (Cinquini and Tenucci 2007). The final sample was 93 organizations and 14 SMA techniques were employed in the questionnaire. These practices built on Guilding et al. (2000; see also Guilding and McManus 2002), with activity costing, customer accounting, integrative performance measurement (balanced scorecard) and benchmarking added and brand value measures deleted. The respondents were asked to rank these practices on a 5 point Likert scale related to usage where 1 equals 'never' and 5 'always'. Here the scores were substantially higher than in the Guilding study. Attribute costing ranked the highest and the scores for only two measures fell below the mid-point of the scale. It is shown that relatively few organizations use all the techniques but that most use up to 10 of these practices. Most of the contingency variables investigated did not explain organizational use of SMA measures except for partial support being found for differentiators using SMA techniques more than cost leaders, though as might be suspected cost leaders do use the relevant cost measures. Firm size was not found to be important but this may reflect the narrow base of the sample. Given the earlier suggestion that an important role for accountants in the global and digital economy was project appraisal, it is surprising that neither of the surveys considered this from a strategic perspective in terms of, at least, asking about the use of what has come to be called strategic investment appraisal (Bromwich and Bhimani 1994; Shank 1996).

Even given the concerns that have expressed about SMA, the arguments here suggest that organizations seeking to adapt to the digital and global economy should consider experimentation with and the use of these techniques where appropriate. The next section considers a brief case study of a firm experimenting with collaborative alliances to bring out some of the accounting implications. It points to the co-mingling of strategy, technology, and cost management as well as to the impact of globalization and digitization on possible organizational processes and opportunities.

LI & FUNG: A VIRTUAL ENTERPRISE WITH COLLABORATIVE ALLIANCES

The Li & Fung group was founded in Guangzhou, China, in 1906. Li & Fung was one of the first companies financed solely by Chinese capital to engage directly in exports from China. It initially traded largely in porcelain and silk before diversifying into bamboo and rattan ware, jade, ivory, handicrafts, and fireworks. From 1996 to 2007, Li & Fung's annual turnover rose nearly seven fold and its profits grew nearly six fold (McFarlan and Young 2000).

The group has today activities in export sourcing, distribution, and retailing with 26,000 employees across 40 countries and with revenues of almost $14 billion in 2007 (Liandfung.com). It is the world's largest outsourcer (supplier) in the garment industry. Li & Fung is now a virtual company with collaborative links, acting as a value chain coordinator. It does not own any manufacturing capability but rather, coordinates a network of over 10,000 suppliers. Li & Fung 'does not own a stitch when it comes to making garments. No factories, no machines, no fabrics. Instead, Li & Fung deal only with information' (Lee-Young and Barnett 2001: 77).

The core business of the firm is to serve as a 'one-stop shop' for Western retailers by delivering a 'global value-added package', including 'product design and development, raw material and factory sourcing, production planning and management, quality assurance, shipping consolidation' (ibid.). Li & Fung illustrates a key present trend of the textile and garment industry which is that processes and exchanges have become increasingly fast and globalized while remaining embedded in local milieus from the viewpoint of customers.

The company is organized across over 90 autonomous subsidiaries, located close to major markets, which is considered critical in a fashion-orientated industry. The Hong Kong-based headquarters provides the centralized IT system and financial and administrative support (McFarlan and Young 2000). An important factor in the company's success is that it allows small and medium-sized manufacturers in developing countries, to meet together for doing business, while benefiting from scale economies which derive from its large purchasing and sales volume.

Li & Fung has offices in nearly all the global regions significant in textile and apparel manufacturing. The company's philosophy rests on a continuous search for low costs and utmost flexibility. Li & Fung-led manufacturing operations illustrate relevant aspects of the much finer spatial division of labour that characterizes the digital economy (Bhimani 2003). The dispersion, density, and diversity of the network of suppliers allow Li & Fung to switch easily from one manufacturer to another. If a part of the supply chain manufacturing or shipping collapses for technical, social, or political reasons, Li & Fung can readily switch to another supplier elsewhere in the world. The profit possibilities of electronic operations in terms of flexibility and time-to-market capabilities are extensive. Prior to the fabric being dyed, the client can alter the colour and size prior to cutting (McFarlan and Young 2000). This level of agility has been referred to as the 'power of postponement' harnessable for mass customization requirements (Feitzinger and Lee 1997).

The tradition of retail stores was in the past to rotate their inventory through the four primary seasons, so that goods where shipped four times a year. Currently, the trend has moved to getting fashions in and out more quickly with shorter life cycles and a greater variety to customers on a more regular basis. Zara uses a similar strategy in its retail operations (Ghemawat and Nueno 2003).

Li & Fung's investments in information technology help it manage the logistics of the supply chain process similar to Zara. Li & Fung focuses on connecting and sharing information across the customers, sourcing, offices, and factories. Its operating groups adopt each specific customer's in-house system software systems from logistics to billing. In this manner, collaborative relationship potential is created. Victor Fung, the company's Chairman, explains:

Say we get an order from a European retailer to produce 10,000 garments. We determine that, because of quotas and labor conditions, the best place to make the garments is Thailand. So we ship everything from there. And because the customer needs quick delivery, we may divide the order across five factories in Thailand. Effectively we are customizing the value chain to best meet the customer's needs. Five weeks after we received the order, 10,000 garments arrive on the shelves in Europe, all looking like they came from one factory. (Victor Fung cited in Magreta 1998)

Li & Fung clients benefit in several ways: supply chain customization shortens order fulfillment to weeks instead of months. This faster turnaround allows clients to reduce inventory costs. But also, main customers create longer term collaborative relationships with Li & Fung whereas the suppliers are coordinated virtually. According to Victor Fung, 'Li & Fung manage and orchestrate it from above. The creation of value is based on a holistic conception of the value chain'.

William Fung, the company's Managing Director, points out that:

Because of our old-economy history and our network, we can inspect suppliers' goods much easier. Buyers don't have confidence to buy from anonymous suppliers that they don't know. We think we can bring the two together within the Li & Fung network, we can build a business using the Internet to aggregate suppliers on their stock positions. (William Fung cited in Lee-Young and Barnett 2001: 77)

Opportunities to learn from agglomerating with both pure trading firms as well as collaborative partners have important consequences:

If you can shorten your buying cycle from three months to five weeks, for example, what you are gaining is eight weeks to develop a better sense of where the market is heading. And so you will end with a substantial savings in inventory markdowns at the end of the selling season. (Ibid.)

Strategy, IT-based links, and cost information are integrated in the company to achieve this balance. The value of an organizational design which brings together firms for the provision of standardized inputs over time phases and from which learning benefits are minimal alongside longer term collaborations on the design side is extensive and an aid to competitiveness tied to organizational structure, technology, strategy and cost information thus:

Our customers have become more fashion driven, working six or seven seasons a year instead of just two or three. Once you move to shorter product cycles, the problem of obsolete inventory increases dramatically. Other businesses are facing the same kind of pressure. With customer tastes changing rapidly and markets segmenting into narrower niches, it's not just fashion products that are becoming increasingly time sensitive... We need flexibility... And we also benefit from their exposure to their customers. (Victor Fung cited in Magreta 1998)

Li & Fung is an example of a new organizational firm poised to couple both traditional trading links and collaborative relationships. The cost effects of such structuring allows the firm to minimize fixed cost investments via extensive outsourcing and to minimize variable costs by having standardized products and using its IT-based infrastructure to render visible minimum cost providers. Cost management acquires new meaning in such contexts because it integrates strategic choices, technological input, and cost control (Bhimani 2008). The process of identifying one or more of many suppliers for satisfying the needs of a specific customer with a defined strategy-technology-cost balance subsumes the firm's operational premise. Thus, Li & Fung's enterprise processes focus on a highly rationalized cost management philosophy of tight cost management and revenue generation via a total focus on customer needs. This also illustrates a turning point in the visualization of strategic input within the firm's *modus operandi*.

The management accounting implications of such highly refined organizational structuring and activities are extensive. Here, form subsumes strategy which co-integrates both IT inputs and cost control. Organizational action simultaneously creates and implements strategy. A transaction dictates thinking about and operationalizing in a specific way via both traditional trading processes and collaborations. Each transaction may differ in the mix of pure trade and collaboration deployed. Each transaction thereby creates high strategy-technology-cost control specificity. Management accounting in such contexts may serve to facilitate the enabling of such organizational potential by focusing on the exclusive information needs of that specificity.

CONCLUSIONS

Whilst traditional management accounting techniques continue to play a role in terms of cost–benefit and incremental costing-based impact, the complexities of fast-changing markets point to the managerial adaptation of coupled decision-making thinking and action. Standardized and electronic-enabled transactions embed both decisions and actions and globalization underscores this type of combined decision-making and action. But a wide set of organizational activities still presume action consequent to decision-making. Yet such decisions are themselves only partially formalized and partly loose and flexible and collaboratively grounded. Moreover, managers increasingly take action when planning and deciding on organizational action rather than after formal strategic plans are settled. Thus, organizational complexities do not allow clear distinctions between decisions and actions and the formalized and informal control of operations.

The traditional duality of decisions such as make or buy or insource/outsource is not clearly distinguishable in a globalizing and digitizing environment. There is increased ambiguity of organizational engagement where both competitive bidding and collaborative relationships coexist and operations are coupled together. Information systems themselves do not have clear boundaries coinciding with rigid organizational structures or precepts especially where the boundaries themselves are becoming blurred between organizations. Systems have to span enterprises with information being accessible to competing and cooperating partners, suppliers, assemblers, designers and developers, and other organizational players as well as customers.

Organizations are increasingly adopting 'fluid' structures. Globalization and the digital economy mean that industrial value chains have altered in structure over the past decade. Convergence across industries has created new organizational missions and novel business models. Products are often now co-conceived and co-produced by enterprises, their suppliers, and their customers. Customer groups themselves have altered products, enhanced features, and deleted functions. Indeed, customers determine prices and costs, in vogue and out of style product content and create the nature of business platforms for trading (Bhimani 2008).

In a digitized, global, and fluid economic environment within which firms must compete, financial management and cost control face important challenges. This applies to both large and small enterprises with the presumed conceptual linkage between firm size and control no longer remaining unproblematic. Management accounting has always encountered calls for change. Sometimes these have often been premature and at times reflective of consultancy linked interests. This essay is not intended to be a forecast of doom for management accounting. Rather, the concerns presented here are meant to be indicative of some of the pressures which the field and organizations will have to tackle progressively on a scale not, perhaps, previously witnessed. Management accountants themselves may wish to question whether in the face of these pressures, they should either retain or retreat to their familiar character of costing the firm's existing operational activities, reporting on past managerial performance, acting as the organization's financial police force and running what other managers see as a separate, independent, and expertise focused functions.

As has been noted here the digital and global economy compress together strategy formulation and actions. To help in such a combined generation of objectives and actions, accountants may become more part of the decision-making process both by becoming hybrid accountants and becoming more grounded members of management teams. Digital and global influences are bringing to bear within firms both consumer and supply markets characteristics and wider strategic concerns.

A number of approaches have been discussed in the management accounting literature. In accounting, portfolios of these techniques have sometimes been called SMA. At least, for some of these practices, management accountants have comparative advantages. However, the danger for accountants is that organizations in the midst of a global and digital environmental change will use these techniques whether accountants are involved or not. Further, the possibility exists that SMA, as it has been conceived, may not continue to address emerging organizational challenges if it retains a static form. Management accounting is not immune to continuous reinvention and interpretation. Thus, like organizations, the management accounting field itself must address issues raised by modern day globalization and digitization forces.

REFERENCES

Anderson, S.W. and Sedatole, K.L. (2003). Management accounting for the extended enterprise: Performance management for strategic alliances and networked partners. In A. Bhimani (ed.), *Management Accounting in the Digital Economy.* Oxford: Oxford University Press, 36–73.

Arnold, N. (2000). New dimensions of outsourcing: A combination of transaction cost economics and the core competencies concept. *European Journal of Purchasing and Supply Management*, 6, 23–9.

Atkinson, R., and McKay, A. (2007). *Digital Prosperity: Understanding the Economic Benefits of the IT Revolution.* Washington, D.C.: ITI Foundation.

Axelsson, B., Van Weele, A., and Wynstra, F. (2000). Driving and enabling factors for purchasing involvement in product development. *European Journal of Purchasing and Supply Management*, 6, 129–41.

Bessant, J., Kaplinsky, R., and Lamming, R. (2003). Putting supply chain learning into practice. *International Journal of Operations and Production Management*, 23(2), 167–84.

Bhimani, A. (2003). *Management Accounting in the Digital Economy.* Oxford: Oxford University Press, 36–73.

—— (2008). *Strategic Finance.* London: Strategy Press.

—— and Keshvarz, H. (1999). British management accountants: Strategically oriented? *Journal of Cost Management*, 13(2), 25–31.

—— and Langfield-Smith, K. (2007). Structure, formality and the importance of financial and non-financial information in strategy development and implementation. *Management Accounting Research*, 18(1), 3–31.

Billington, C., and Ellram, L. (2001). Purchasing leverage considerations in the outsourcing decision. *European Journal of Purchasing and Supply Management*, 7, 15–27.

Boisot, M. (1998). *Knowledge Assets.* Oxford: Oxford University Press.

Bromwich, M. (1990). The case for strategic management accounting: The role of accounting information for strategy in competitive markets. *Accounting, Organizations and Society*, 15(1/2), 27–46.

—— and Bhimani, A. (1994) *Management Accounting: Pathways to Progress.* London: CIMA.

Burns, J., and Yazdifar, H. (2001). Tricks, or treats? The role of management accounting is changing. *Financial Management*, March, 33–5.

—— Ezzamel, M., and Scapens, R. (2003). *The Challenge of Management Accounting Change: Behavioural and Cultural Aspects of Change Management.* Oxford: Elsevier/CIMA.

Buvik, A., and Halskan, Ø. (2001). Relationship duration and buyer influence in just-in-time relationship. *European Journal of Purchasing and Supply Management*, 7, 111–19.

Byrne, S.M., and Pierce, B. (Forthcoming). Towards a more comprehensive understanding of the roles of management accountants. *European Accounting Review.*

Callioni, G., Montgros, X., Slagmulder, R., Wassenhowe, L., and Wright, L. (2005). Inventory-driven costs. *Harvard Business Review*, March, 271–82.

Child, J. (2005). *Cooperative Strategy.* Oxford: University Press.

Cinquini, L., and Tenucci, A. (2007). Is the adoption of strategic management accounting techniques really strategy driven? Evidence from a survey. *Mar. 2007—Cost and Performance in Services and Operations.* Trento, Italy, June 18–20.

Cousins, P.D.(1999). Supplier base rationalisation: Myths or reality? *European Journal of Purchasing and Supply Management*, 5, 143–55.

Dalmin, R., and Mininno, V. (2003). Supplier selection using a multi–criteria decision aid method. *Journal of Purchasing and Supply Management*, 9, 177–87.

Das, T.K., and Teng, B. (2000). Instabilities of strategic alliances: An internal tensions perspective. *Organization Science*, 11(1), 77–101.

Dekker, H.C. (2004). Control of inter-organizational relationships: Evidence on appropriate concerns and coordination requirements. *Accounting, Organizations and Society*, 29(1), 27–49.

Dixon, R. (1998). Accounting for strategic management: A practical application. *Long Range Planning*, 31(2), 272–9.

Dugdale, D., Jones, T.C., and Green, S. (2006). *Contemporary Management Accounting Practices in UK Manufacturing.* Oxford: Elsevier/CIMA.

Dunk, A. (2004). Product cost life cycle analysis: The impact of customer profiling, competitive advantage and quality of IS information. *Management Accounting Research*, 15(4), 379–410.

Dutton, J., and Thomas, A. (1984). Treating progress functions as a managerial opportunity. *Academy of Management Review*, 9, 235–48.

Dyer, J.H. (1997). Effective interfirm collaboration: How firms minimize transaction costs and maximize transaction value. *Strategic Management Journal*, 18(7), 535–56.

—— and Singh, J.H. (1998). The relational view: Cooperative strategy and sources of inter-organizational competitive advantage. *The Academy of Management Review*, 23(4), 660–79.

Ellram, L.M. (1996). A structured method for applying purchasing cost management tools. *International Journal of Purchasing and Materials Management*, 32, 11–19.

Feitzinger, E., and Lee, H. (1997). Mass customization at HP. *Harvard Business Review*, 71(1), 116–21.

Frey, S.C., and Schlosser, M.M. (1993). ABB and Ford, creating value through cooperation. *Sloan Management Review*, 35, Fall, 65–72.

Gadde, L-E., and Hakansson, H. (2001). *Supply Network Strategies.* Chichester: Wiley.

—— and Suehota, I. (2000). Making the most of supplier relationships. *Industrial Marketing Management*, 29, 305–16.

Giddens, A. (1999). The director's lectures: Runaway world. The Reith Lectures, Revised. London School of Economics, 10 November.

Gietzmann, M.B., and Larsen, J. (1998). Motivating subcontractors to perform development and design tasks. *Management Accounting Research*, 9(3), 285–309.

Ghemawat, P., and Nueno, J.L. (2003). Zara: Fast fashion. Harvard Business School, case no. 9703497.

Groot, T.L.C.M., and Merchant, K.A. (2000). Control of international joint ventures. *Accounting, Organizations and Society*, 25(6), 579–607.

Guilding, C., and McManus, L. (2002). The incidence, perceived merit and antecedents of customer accounting: An exploratory note. *Accounting, Organizations and Society*, 27, 45–59.

——Cravens, K.S., and Tayles, M. (2000). An international comparison of strategic management accounting practices. *Management Accounting Research*, 11(1), 113–35.

Gruber, H. (1992). The learning curve in the production of semiconductor memory chips. *Applied Economics*, 24, 885–95.

Hahn, C.K., Watts, C.A., and Kim, K.Y. (1990). The supplier development program: A conceptual model. *Journal of Purchasing and Materials Management*, 26, Spring, 2–7.

Hakansson, H., and Lind, J. (2007). Accounting in an interorganizational setting. In C. Chapman, A. Hopwood, and M. Shields (eds.), *Handbook of Management Accounting Research*. Oxford: Elsevier, 885–902.

Handfield, R.B., Krause, D.R., Scannel, T.V., and Monczka, R.M. (2000). Avoid the pitfalls in supplier development. *Sloan Management Review*, 42(2), 37–49.

Helper, S.R., and Sako, M. (1995). Supplier relations in Japan and the United States: Are they converging? *Sloan Management Review*, 36, Spring, 77–84.

Hoberman, S., and Mailick, S. (1992). *Experiential Management Development—From Learning to Practice*. New York: Quorum Books.

Kamminga, P.E., and Van der Meer-Kooistra, J. (2007). Management control patterns in joint venture relationships: A model and an exploratory study. *Accounting, Organizations and Society*, 32, 131–54.

Krapfel, R.E. Jr., Salmond, D., and Spekman, R. (1991). A strategic approach to managing buyer–seller relationships. *European Journal of Marketing*, 25(9), 22–37.

Kraus, K., and Lind, J. (2007). Management control in interorganzational relationships. In T. Hopper, D. Northcott, and R. Scapens (eds.), *Issues in Management Accounting*. London: FT Prentice Hall, 269–96.

Kulmala, H.I. (2004). Developing cost management in customer supplier relationships: Three case studies. *Journal of Purchasing and Supply Management*, 10, 65–77.

Lambert, D.M., and Cooper, M.C. (2000). Issues in supply chain management. *Industrial Marketing Management*, 29(1), 65–83.

Langfield-Smith, K. (2008). Strategic management accounting: How far have we come in 25 years? *Accounting, Auditing and Accountability Journal*, 21(2), 204–18.

——and Greenwood, M. (1998). Developing cooperative buyer–supplier relationships: A case study of Toyota. *Journal of Management Studies*, 35, 331–54.

Lascelles, D.M., and Dale, B.G. (1989). The buyer–supplier relationship in total quality management. *Journal of Purchasing and Materials Management*, 25, Summer, 10–19.

Lee-Young, J., and Barnett, M. (2001). Furiously fast fashions. *The Industry Standard*, 7, 3–9.

Lieberman, M. (1984). The learning curve and pricing in the chemical processing industries. *Rand Journal of Economics*, 15, 216–29.

Leiblein, M.J., and Miller, D.J. (2003). An empirical examination of transaction and firm level influences on the vertical boundaries of the firm. *Strategic Management Journal*, 24, 839.

Liker, J.K., and Choi, T.Y. (2004). Building deep supplier relationships. *Harvard Business Review*, 82, December, 29–38.

Lord, B.R. (1996). Strategic management accounting: The emperor's new clothes? *Management Accounting Research*, 7(3), 347–66.

McFarlan, F., and Young, F. (2000). Li and Fung (A): Internet issues. *Harvard Business Review*, case study no. 9, 301–9.

Magreta, J. (1998). Fast, global and entrepreneurial: An interview with Victor Fung. *Harvard Business Review*, September/October, 103–7.

Mohrman, S.A., and Mohrman, A.M. (1993). Organizational change and learning. In J.R. Galbraith, and E.E. Lawler (eds.), *Organizing for the Future*. San Francisco: Josey Bass, 87–108.

Mowshowitz, A. (1999). Virtual organization: A vision of management in the information age. *The Information Society*, 10, 267–88.

Narayanan, V.G., and Raman, A. (2004). Aligning incentives in supply chains, *Harvard Business Review*, November, 42–51.

Nyamori, R.O., Perera, M., and Lawrence, S. (2001). The Concept of strategic change for management accounting research. *Journal of Accounting Literature*, 62–83.

Quinn, J.B., and Hilmer, F.G. (1994). Strategic outsourcing. *Sloan Management Review*, 35, Summer, 43–55.

Rayport, J., and Jaworski, B. (2003). *Introduction to E-commerce*. New York: McGraw Hill.

Reyniers, D., and Tapiero, C. (1995). The delivery and control of quality in supplier-product contracts. *Management Science*, 41, 1581–9.

Richardson, J. (1993). Parallel sourcing and supplier performance in the Japanese automobile industry. *Strategic Management Journal*, 14, 339–50.

Sako, M. (2008). *Shifting Boundaries of the Firm*. Oxford: Oxford University Press.

Shank, J.K. (1996). Analysing technological investments—From NPV to strategic cost management. *Management Accounting Research*, 7, 185–97.

—— (2006). Strategic cost management: Upsizing, downsizing and right-sizing. In A. Bhimani (ed.), *Contemporary Issues in Management Accounting*. Oxford: Oxford University Press, 355–79.

—— and Govindarajan, V. (1993). *Strategic Cost Management*. New York: The Free Press.

Sheth, J.N., and Sharma, A. (1997). Supplier relationships—Emerging issues and challenges. *Industrial Marketing and Management*, 26(2), 91–100.

Simmonds, K. (1981). Strategic management accounting. *Management Accounting*, 59, April, 26–9.

Speklé, R.F. (2001). Explaining management control structure variety: A transaction cost economics perspective. *Accounting, Organizations and Society*, 3(4), 141–67.

Stanford Encyclopedia of Philosophy. (2002). Globalisation. Substantive revision, 2006. Available online at www.seop.leeds.ac.uk/entries

Stjernstrom, S., and Bengtsson, L. (2004). Supplier perspective on business relationships: Experiences from six small suppliers. *Journal of Purchasing and Supply Management*, 10, 137–46.

Straub, D. (2004). *Foundations of Net-enhanced Organizations.* New Jersey: John Wiley.

Tillmann, K., and Goddard, A. (2008). Strategic management accounting and sense making in a multinational company. *Management Accounting Research*, 19 (1), 80–102.

Tomkins, C. (2001). Interdependencies, trust and information in relationships, alliances and networks. *Accounting, Organizations and Society*, 26, 161–91.

Trent, R.J., and Monczka, R.M. (1998). Purchasing and supply management: Trends and changes throughout the 1990s. *Journal of Supply Chain Management*, 34(4), 7–21.

Van der Meer-Kooistra, J. (1994). The coordination of internal transactions: The functioning of transfer pricing systems in the organizational context. *Management Accounting Research*, 5, 123–52.

Van Weele, A.J. (2000). *Purchasing and Supply Management: Analysis, Planning and Practice.* London: Business Press.

Vining, A., and Globerman, S. (1999). A conceptual framework for understanding the outsourcing decision. *European Management Journal*, 17, 645–54.

6

Organizationally Oriented Management Accounting Research in the United States: A Case Study of the Diffusion of a Radical Research Innovation

Jacob G. Birnberg and Michael D. Shields

Management accounting research in the US has changed over time in terms of the management accounting practices investigated as well as the theoretical perspectives and research methods used in those investigations. Reviews of the historical development of this research are in American Accounting Association (1976); Johnson and Kaplan (1987); Klemstine and Maher (1984); and Maher (2001). The question arises as to what causes change in management accounting research. Change in management accounting research can arise from environmental forces, such as when the Ford Foundation in the 1950s called from reform in business schools, including doing more scientific research (Maher 2001). Change can also arise from the enthusiastic efforts of individuals to create and diffuse radical innovations (Sandberg 2007).

The purpose of our chapter is to provide theory and evidence on how an innovator's enthusiasm for a radical innovation—a change in the orientation and location of management accounting research—influences its diffusion. In particular, we analyse the impact in the United States of Anthony Hopwood's idea that research on management accounting practice should be informed by organizational and social theories and use field research methods to investigate management accounting in its natural contexts. Our chapter is a case study that examines Anthony as an innovator, his innovation, and strategy for diffusing his innovation to US researchers, as well as early adopters of his innovation, and factors that influenced the diffusion of his innovation in the United States.

We thank Shannon Anderson, Michael Bromwich, Mark Covaleski, Mark Dirsmith, Ken Merchant, and Mark Young for their comments on an earlier version of our chapter.

We limit the geographical scope of our chapter to the United States for three reasons. First, the publisher's chapter page limit constrains our scope. Second, we are much more aware of the development of management accounting research in the United States than in other locations. Third, almost all management accounting research in the United States was and is based on two orientations, which can broadly be labelled analytical and behavioural/experimental, that are in conflict with the research orientation proposed by Anthony. Thus, investigating the diffusion of Anthony's innovation in the United States is an interesting context in which to study how a conflicting research orientation is diffused and factors that affect this diffusion.

Our chapter begins with a selective review of literature on the diffusion of innovations and 'gaps' that can limit the diffusion of radical innovations. This review identifies concepts that we will use to describe actors and events in our case study. Next, we report our case study of Anthony's enthusiasm and diffusion strategy for changing research on management accounting practice, focusing specifically on how his diffusion strategy played out in the United States and the factors that influenced this innovation diffusion process. Our chapter concludes with a discussion of the diffusion of Anthony's innovation in the United States.

LITERATURE REVIEW

We selectively review literature on the diffusion of innovation and 'gaps' that limit diffusion of radical innovations in order to provide the concepts used to structure and interpret our case study.

The process of diffusing an innovation can be considered to have four parts:[1] (*a*) An innovation is (*b*) communicated through channels (*c*) over time (*d*) among units in a social system (e.g. individuals, groups, organizations, and cultures) (Rogers 2003). An innovation is 'an idea, practice, or object that is perceived as new by an individual or other unit of adoption' (Rogers 2003: 12). Communication about an innovation occurs in channels (e.g. mass media and interpersonal networks) in which people inform others about the innovation. Diffusion occurs over time, and is usually represented as an S-shaped logistics curve in which the percentage of units in a social system who have adopted an innovation is a function of the length of time since an innovation is introduced to the social system. Finally, a social system is a set of interrelated units who work together to accomplish a common goal. Social systems have a structure

---

[1] The review of diffusion analysis in this section is limited to what is used in this chapter. For extended discussions, see Rogers (2003) and Wejnert (2002).

(e.g. organizational hierarchy and American Accounting Association) and norms of behaviour (e.g. normal science), and the units in a social system have interpersonal networks of units with whom they communicate.

Social systems can be viewed as having five types of adopters who have different roles in the diffusion process. They are innovators, early adopters, early majority, late majority, and laggards (Rogers 2003). For the purposes of our case study, we will focus on the innovator and early adopters. Innovators are the people who initially develop an innovation. Innovators possess 'venturesomeness'—they have a 'desire for the rash, the daring, and the risky'—and 'may not be respected by other members of a local system, [but] the innovator plays an important role in the diffusion process: that of launching the idea in the system by importing the innovation from outside the system's boundaries' (Rogers 2003: 283). Innovators of radical ideas are enthusiastic about their innovations, where enthusiastic means having a 'great eagerness to be involved in a particular activity, because it is something you like and enjoy or that you think is important' (Sandberg 2007: 265).

Early adopters play a key role in the diffusion of innovations because of their characteristics and temporal location in the diffusion process. Compared to others in a social system, they tend to have more education, intelligence, rationality, and cosmopolitanism, and less dogmatism. They are likely to exhibit more social participation and be more interconnected through their interpersonal networks, to possess higher aspirations and social status, and to have greater empathy and ability to deal with abstraction, change, and uncertainty. Many early adopters are elites, who are a relatively small dominant group within a social system. For example, academic elites are graduates of and/or faculty at key research-intensive universities who publish heavily cited articles in top-quality journals and who are editors and review board members of these journals.[2] These characteristics of early adopters result in their having the highest opinion leadership. Because of early adopters' characteristics and the fact that they are believed by potential adopters to carefully study new innovations and make well-informed adoption decisions, potential adopters observe their behaviour or seek their advice before adopting innovations. Thus, early adopters play a key role in linking innovators and their innovations to others in a social system. Adoption by early adopters is followed by adoption by early-majority adopters, which in turn leads to a rapid increase in adoption in a social system.

Communication channels for diffusing innovations include mass media (e.g. journals) in which a person's message can be communicated to many

---

[2] For definitions of elites and analysis of elites in accounting research, particularly behavioural accounting research, see Williams et al. (2006).

people and interpersonal channels which involve face-to-face exchange between two or more people (Rogers 2003). Interpersonal network channels are more effective than mass media at persuading people to adopt innovations, particularly when the people are similar in status, education, or other important characteristics.

Diffusion of innovation is more effective in homophilous social systems (i.e. systems whose members are similar in their beliefs, education, and socio-economic status) than in heterophilous social systems (i.e. systems whose members differ in their beliefs, education, and socioeconomic status). This is because communication in homophilous systems occurs more frequently and easily among like-minded individuals, which speeds diffusion of an innovation. In contrast, heterophilous communication occurs less frequently and is more difficult because it involves individuals communicating who are different in their beliefs, education, competence, and language. However, it can potentially diffuse an innovation across a wider interpersonal network because it transmits information to members of different cliques in the total social system.

Communication issues are important for understanding innovators in both types of social systems because innovators differ in important ways from non-innovators (e.g. risk taking, values, research orientation, social network status). These differences can make it difficult for innovators to communicate their innovations effectively to others, potentially inhibiting diffusion of their innovation. In heterophilous systems, innovators should target the most elite opinion leaders to facilitate dissemination of innovations to others in the social system. If elite opinion leaders are convinced to adopt innovations, then others are more likely to exhibit enthusiasm for and readiness to learn about the innovation and thus to adopt them. This 'domino effect' will, in turn, reduce others' resistance to adopting innovations.

In contrast, in homophilous systems facilitating diffusion of innovations to entire social systems is more difficult. Opinion leaders in homophilous systems may avoid promoting or adopting innovations to protect their opinion leadership. For example, if opinion leaders become advocates for a radical innovation that is inconsistent with their social system's norms, their status may be threatened or diminished if others do not agree to adopt the innovation. Because opinion leaders may resist promoting or adopting innovations, a wider group of opinion leaders, including some of the less elite members of a social system, should be targeted to assure the diffusion of an innovation. When opinion leaders do want to promote a radical innovation, they need to communicate a persuasive rational argument favouring the innovation in order to increase the compatibility of the innovation with their social system's norms.

The diffusion of innovations has been found to be influenced by several factors related to innovations: innovators, adopters, and social systems (Wejnert 2002).

An innovation's diffusion is more likely as its potential benefits to adopters increase (e.g. research success) and costs to adopters decrease, such as the cost of being able to implement the innovation (e.g. education and training) and the potential social conflict arising between adopters and non-adopters (e.g. professors in a department). Diffusion increases when potential adopters are more familiar with an innovation, early adopters have higher status in the interpersonal network (e.g. management accounting research community), members of a social system are more open to innovation, and individuals' interpersonal networks are more interconnected. The social system in which an innovation and its diffusion occurs (e.g. the culture and strategy of US management accounting researchers) also influences diffusion.

Developing and diffusing radical innovations can depend on minimizing 'gaps' that diminish the willingness of individuals to adopt them (Sandberg 2007). In the context of Anthony's innovation, important gaps can be an *engagement gap* (people adopting an innovation feel isolated from non-adopters, which can lead to interpersonal conflict), a *help gap* (people worry if they will have sufficient help to become proficient in using an innovation), an *openness gap* (people feel it is not safe to discuss an innovation), a *results gap* (people are concerned that the result of using an innovation will not be as good as expected), and a *time gap* (people believe they do not have enough time to learn about and how to use an innovation).

CASE STUDY

Our case study has three parts. The first part describes the two most common orientations to management accounting research in the United States circa the 1960s. The second describes Anthony as innovator and his radical innovation. The last section describes the four communication channels Anthony used to diffuse his innovation.

Management Accounting Research in the United States Circa the 1960s

Management accounting research in the United States circa the 1960s had two orientations, broadly labelled analytical and behavioural/experimental.[3]

---

[3] Many key articles using these two approaches to management accounting research in the US published circa the 1960s are in Anton and Firmin (1972); Benston (1970); Rappaport (1970); Bruns and DeCoster (1969); and DeCoster et al. (1974).

Analytical research used quantitative models from economics, operations research, and statistics to deductively develop models for optimizing management accounting, decisions, and performance (see Anthony 1973; and Kaplan 1977). Behavioural/experimental used psychology and other behavioural theories and quantitative research methods (e.g. experiments and surveys) to investigate effects of management accounting on individuals' (or dyads' or small groups') decisions, judgements, motivation, and social interaction (see Bruns and DeCoster 1969; Schiff and Lewin 1974; and Birnberg et al. 2007). Both research orientations were located largely at 'arms length' from management accounting practice because the research occurred at a researcher's desk (armchair research) as the researcher read, thought, and wrote about management accounting or conducted a mail survey, or in a laboratory to conduct an experiment.

ANTHONY HOPWOOD: INNOVATOR AND HIS INNOVATION

Anthony Hopwood began his graduate study at the University of Chicago in 1965 as an MBA student after receiving a B.Sc. (Econ) degree specializing in accounting from the London School of Economics. The reference disciplines at Chicago for management accounting (as well as the other functional areas in the business school) were economics and psychology. With the development of the CRSP database, financial accounting at the University of Chicago had come under the sway of archival finance research (e.g. Ball and Brown 1968). Archival financial accounting research was quickly to become the most active and dominant type of accounting research at Chicago. Indeed, when Anthony arrived at Chicago he intended to study accounting, industrial economics, and finance (Hopwood 1988). His intent, however, changed when he took a required course in organization theory taught by Paul Goodman. He provided Anthony with a new idea of how to research management accounting. He received the support for changing his doctoral study from George Sorter, then professor of accounting and director of the doctoral programme, and Dick Hoffman, a professor of social psychology on the University of Chicago's organizational behaviour faculty, which facilitated his pursuit of the relationship between management accounting and its organizational context.

As a result of this new orientation to research, Anthony found the two then existing orientations to management accounting research in the United States to be in conflict with the orientation in which he had come to believe management accounting research should go. He believed that management accounting research should study management accounting in its natural context, which required field research. This belief was reflected in his disser-tation research which was conducted on the shop floor of a steel company. His idea also required using organizational and social theories as opposed to using only economics and psychology theories.

Anthony depicted his idea about the role and context of management accounting as a set of concentric circles with the individual at the centre, groups next, followed by organizational structure, and then the social and economic environment (Hopwood 1976: 5). He summarized his idea in the introduction to his collected papers (Hopwood 1988: xxi), saying he had come to understand 'how organizational cultures and managerial philoso-phies might shape the significance attached to accounting systems and play some role in influencing their effects'.[4] His innovative idea was at odds with the popular idea in the United States that management accounting was independent of its organizational and social contexts.

On returning to the United Kingdom after finishing his doctoral degree, Anthony found a scholarly environment quite different than that in the United States. The interests of some accounting researchers in the United Kingdom and on the continent, especially in Scandinavia, were similar to his idea. They not only were active as behavioural managerial accounting researchers, but also were interacting with organizational researchers, and researchers at some universities were open to experimenting with new orien-tation to researching management accounting. Given the contrast between Anthony's idea and the current orientation of management accounting research in the United States, he could have directed his attention exclusively to European accounting research and researchers. Whether consciously or simply because of the depth of his commitment to his belief in the value of more organizationally oriented accounting research, Anthony proceeded to diffuse his innovation to US management accounting researchers.

Anthony's idea that management accounting research should study manage-ment accounting in its organizational and social contexts using field research methods was inconsistent with the two existing orientations to management accounting research in the United States. In short, what Anthony proposed was a radical innovation in the orientation of management accounting research in the United States. An important challenge for Anthony in diffusing his idea to the United States would be effective heterophilous communication because, at the beginning of his diffusion process, there were at best only a few management accounting researchers in the United States who held similar views. Effective heterophilous communication to diffuse his innovation required Anthony to get

---

[4] This also applies to other areas in accounting. However, that is beyond the scope of our chapter.

his innovation to the most elite innovative opinion leaders in the United States, who, if they adopted it, would diffuse it to others in the United States.

Communication Channels Anthony Used to Diffuse his Radical Innovation

In this section we will describe Anthony's strategy to diffuse his radical innovation to the United States and enthusiasm for his innovation by using four communication channels—his research publications, personal network with US researchers, founding and editing *Accounting, Organizations and Society* (*AOS*), and research conferences associated with *AOS*.

Anthony Hopwood's Research Publications

Anthony's research publications have influenced US-based management accounting researchers to a greater extent than might be suggested by the relatively low number of their citations to his publications.[5] We use ISI and Google Scholar to identify citations (up to 18 August 2008) to Anthony's publications in management accounting articles published by US-based researchers. Combining the results from ISI and Google Scholar, we find that Anthony has four management accounting publications with over 100 citations from authors around the world.

Anthony's most cited publication is Hopwood (1987) in which he introduces Foucault's perspective to the management accounting literature in his study of the development of management accounting at Wedgwood. Of the 328 citations to this article, there are 12 citations by US-based researchers. His second most cited publication, *Accounting and Human Behaviour* (Hopwood 1976),[6] with a total of 267 citations, is cited ten times by US-based accounting researchers in accounting journals. Anthony's third most cited publication is an article published in *AOS* in 1983 in which he argues for researching management accounting in its organizational context. This article has been cited a total of 232 times, with a total of ten citations in articles published by US-based researchers in accounting and non-accounting journals. While

---

[5] We include as US-based researchers people who have doctoral degrees from US universities and conducted research in the US even though they are not from the US. The most prominent such person is Peter Brownell, an Australian who received a doctoral degree at U.C. Berkeley and then remained in the US for a few years before returning to Australia. We include his articles that have US data.

[6] An earlier version was published in 1974 in the United Kingdom by Haymarket Publishing Limited.

Anthony earlier (e.g. Hopwood 1976) had articulated his idea about the role of accounting in organizations, his 1983 article in *AOS* (as well as Hopwood 1978, 1980) represented a formal presentation of his idea of how research should study management accounting. In some ways, Hopwood (1978, 1980, 1983) provided the rationalization for his choice of the name for *AOS*. The fourth most cited publication is Hopwood (1972), the primary article published from his dissertation. This article has been cited a total of 201 times, 20 times by US-based researchers in accounting journals. We did not detect an increasing or decreasing trend in the rate of citations that would indicate that the influence of Anthony's most cited articles is changing over time.

Anthony's initial attempt to influence US-based management accounting research was his dissertation-based article published in the *Journal of Accounting Research* (Hopwood 1972). This article has been important in diffusing Anthony's innovation in two ways: it introduced the idea that accounting is not only a technical practice but also has a behavioural context, and it introduced field-based research. In this article Anthony critiques prior research and offers a vision for future research. In particular, he argues that prior research has focused on accounting as a technical discipline instead of a behavioural (in particular, psychology, organizational, and sociology) discipline. For example, upon finding that accounting information can have negative effects on employees (e.g. myopic goal-incongruent decisions, poor interpersonal relations, stress), prior research had proposed technical (i.e. accounting) fixes to these problems such as changing the information content of a performance measure.

In contrast, Anthony proposed that these negative effects are also caused by how accounting information is used (e.g. in performance evaluation which is the focus of his article) and that eliminating these negative effects requires changing how accounting information is used, not necessarily changing the information per se. That is, many negative effects of accounting can be reduced or eliminated by changing the way in which people use accounting information without necessarily changing the information (technical fixes). Hopwood (1972) uses literature from organizational behaviour, psychology, and sociology to hypothesize and provide survey evidence that a subordinate manager's dysfunctional behaviour (stress, poor relations with other employees, falsification of accounting data, dysfunctional decisions) is a response to the style in which his or her superior uses accounting information for performance evaluation (budget constrained, profit conscious, or non-accounting), holding constant the accounting information.

Hopwood (1972) is important because it is cited by several elite authors or in influential articles. These authors and/or articles include two that were published in the 1970s: Demski and Feltham (1978), which was the first article in management accounting to use agency theory, and Kenis (1979), which provided a broad empirical survey of how budget characteristics are related to individual behaviour. In the first half of the 1980s, the nascent influence of Hopwood (1972) on US-based management accounting researchers became more visible. Now-elite researchers and their articles that cited Hopwood (1972) in the early 1980s include Merchant (1981); Birnberg et al. (1983); Brownell (1983); Chow (1983); Govindarajan (1984); and Waller and Chow (1985). Of these articles, Merchant (1981); Birnberg et al. (1983); and Brownell (1983) helped change the orientation of behaviourally oriented US-based management accounting research. Merchant (1981) has influenced many studies that investigate how organizational characteristics influence the role and use of budgets and how budgets affect managerial behaviour and performance. Birnberg et al. (1983) analyse literature to further develop how various dysfunctional behaviours can be caused by the psychological and organizational context in which accounting information is used. Brownell (1983) is one of several publications by Peter Brownell in which he uses organizational behaviour and psychology theories to explain how the effects of accounting information on individuals' motivation, performance, satisfaction, stress, and social behaviour (e.g. relations with their supervisor, peers, and subordinates) is conditional on a variety of factors.

Hopwood (1972) also introduced a new research method to management accounting, which is now called field-based research (Young 1999; Anderson and Widener 2007). Hopwood (1972) combines two research methods. Its primary research method is a quantitative survey of cost centre managers in one firm that measures their supervisors' style of using accounting information for performance evaluation and the effects of their style on several behavioural variables such as stress that are used to test the hypotheses. An important feature of his survey is that it is tailored to the organizational context of management accounting in one firm as opposed to being a general survey that could be administered in any organization. Its secondary research method is interviews of selected cost centre managers to study the dysfunctional behaviour of managers who responded differently to the survey to provide more detailed insight into his hypotheses.

Over time, field-based research has become more popular in the United States. As Anderson and Widener (2007) note, Hopwood (1983) had a big influence on encouraging researchers to do field research in order to study management accounting in its organizational context. Shannon Anderson (personal communication) provided insight into how Anthony influenced individual researchers. When, through a fellow Harvard doctoral student, she first encountered the work of Anthony (and others doing field studies in management accounting), she initially found the style of analysis and writing difficult to understand. However, she 'also knew from my brief experience in practice that the fields of economics and engineering did not provide a fully satisfying account of business. . . . I was personally very attracted to the need for grounded study of accounting in the natural world and to consider a broader range of social science theories than economics alone' (Shannon Anderson personal communication).

While several US researchers have engaged in field-based research (see Anderson and Widener 2007), the field-based research of Shannon Anderson, Ken Merchant, and Mark Young probably is closest to that in Hopwood (1972). Their approach is to conduct interviews of key employees in an organization(s) in order to ground their study of management accounting in the organizational context of the organization(s) under investigation and then to tailor quantitative surveys to certain characteristics of the organization(s) based on information obtained during the interviews (e.g. Merchant 1981, 1985, 1989, 1990; Selto et al. 1995; Anderson and Young 1999; Anderson et al. 2002). Relatedly, Anderson (1995*a*) used interviews and quantitative archival data from one firm. Besides using quantitative evidence from field-based research, US researchers were also inspired by Anthony to conduct qualitative field studies (e.g. interviews and analysis of archival information) to study management accounting in its organizational context. Notable early examples of this research are Anderson (1995*b*) which used archival documents and interviews of employees from one firm to study the implementation of activity-based costing and Covaleski and Dirsmith's (1983, 1986, 1988*a*, 1988*b*) use of institutional theories to interpret qualitative field study evidence about budgeting in hospitals and universities.

Anthony published *Accounting and Human Behavior* in 1976. While it is his second most cited publication, it has been cited infrequently in the United States. However, many of those citations are in articles that have been influential in management accounting research. The first two articles by US-based authors to cite this book are important in the development of management accounting research. They were published in the same issue of *The Accounting Review*, used the same quote from that book to motivate their research, and used the same causal model form (interaction) albeit at different levels of analysis (individual vs. organization). The quote is (Hopwood 1976: 79):

While it appears that an increase in participation in decision making can often improve morale, its effect on productivity is equivocal at the best, increasing it under some circumstances but possibly even decreasing it under other circumstances. The practical problem is in trying to identify which conditional factors determine the wider impact of a particular type of participative management programme.

In retrospect, Anthony's statement started the search for moderator variables[7] that lasted for about the next ten years. Related, this statement provided support and encouragement for researchers to use a 'contingency theory' approach to management accounting research that was intended to explain how organizational (and individual) characteristics influenced the design of management accounting practices. The issue centered on the mixed findings of studies on participative decision-making and budgeting in which various studies found participation to have positive, negative, or no direct effects on individuals such as their motivation, morale, and performance (see Shields and Shields 1998). Anthony in his book cautioned researchers not to expect management accounting practices like participative budgeting and supervisory style in using accounting information for performance evaluation to have direct additive effects. Rather, we should expect their effects to be interactive (conditional was his term) and part of a complex web of relations (i.e. causal chains with mediating variables). The immediate interpretation of action stemming from Anthony's caution was to initiate the search for moderator variables that would explain these conditional effects. Anthony provided some clues by suggesting that the moderator variables can be classified into four groups or levels of analysis—individual, organizational, social (interpersonal), and societal (cultural).

Merchant (1981) used the quote above as a basis to justify investigating how organizational-level variables (e.g. decentralization and organizational size) can influence how participative budgeting affects organizational performance. In contrast, Brownell (1981) used the same quote to justify investigating how individual-level variables (locus of control in this study) can affect how participative budgeting influences individual performance. Subsequently, Brownell (1982) reviewed literature to identify many variables at the individual, interpersonal, organizational, and cultural levels that might moderate the effects of participative budgeting. Brownell (1981) and Merchant (1981) are the first of many studies to investigate how a variety of individual-, interpersonal-, organizational-, and societal-level variables moderate the effects of management accounting practices. For example, Merchant in several articles (see Luft and Shields 2003) investigates how organizational- and subunit-level variables (e.g. environmental uncertainty, subunit differentiation, size of department, product standardization, and technology automation) influence management accounting (e.g. supervisory style in using budget and accounting information for performance evaluation, participative

---

[7] Hopwood (1976) called moderator variables conditional factors. Moderator variables affect the relation between the dependent and independent variables but not the dependent or independent variables (see Luft and Shields 2003).

budgeting, flexible budgets, control system tightness, short-term managerial orientation (myopia), and long-term incentives) or how they affect the effects of management accounting. At the individual level, Brownell in several articles (see Luft and Shields 2003) studies how variables at the individual level (e.g. task uncertainty, superior's leadership style, and internal locus of control) influence management accounting (e.g. participative budgeting, supervisory style in using budget and accounting information for performance evaluation, and management by exception).

In summary, our review of Anthony's published research identifies a pattern we will observe in his other communication channels. His publications strongly influenced a small set of now-elite US-based management accounting researchers. Viewed in terms of the diffusion process, these researchers are the early adopters of organizationally oriented management accounting research who would serve as opinion leaders during the diffusion process. These publications provide an important communication channel for diffusing Anthony's ideas because they have the potential to expose a large portion of the US management accounting research community to his ideas. However, publications are most likely only to be read by and to have influence on people who are ready and willing to learn about the ideas because they share a common interest in the management accounting topic, theoretical perspective, or research method. Given the two dominant orientations to researching management accounting in the United States, Anthony's publications had much more influence and were more widely diffused outside the United States. It is important to note, however, that while Anthony in diffusing his ideas through his publications faced issues related to heterophilous communication, he was fortunate to have his early publications influence the publications (as represented by their citations) of what are now elite, innovative, and opinion leaders in management accounting research in the United States.

Anthony's Interpersonal Network with US Researchers

A second communication channel that Anthony used was his interpersonal network, which enabled him to reach albeit a much smaller portion of the US management accounting research community more intensely than did his research publications. While Anthony's interpersonal network is smaller and more focused than is the publication of his research in journals (mass media channel), it could potentially be more influential in persuading elites and opinion leaders to consider adopting his innovation. Beyond persuading others that an idea is good, personal interaction can facilitate learning about the innovation and how to implement it. Anthony used his personal interactions with selected US accounting researchers—management accounting researchers and elite opinion leaders in other areas of accounting, in particular financial accounting—for both of these purposes. He did this by attending conferences in the United States (see below), as a visiting professor at Penn State during the summers of 1983–88 (where he offered a seminar in 1987) and the University of Rhode Island in the summer of 1989, and presenting papers at workshops at other universities in the United States.

Anthony's interactions provided him with the opportunity to meet informally with the then young faculty (e.g. Mark Covaleski, Mark Dirsmith, Steve Jablonsky, and C.J. McNair) and doctoral students (e.g. Bill Bealing, Brian Carpenter, Tim Fogarty, and Patrick Keating) who were in the process of developing their research ideas. The opportunity to have discussions in informal settings, as Mark Covaleski noted (private communication), provided Anthony with the opportunity to suggest research he believed would interest and expose them to the broader view of management accounting. This broader view included research perspectives (e.g. organizational and social theories and field research methods) and researchers (e.g. Michel Foucault) that were within the range of awareness and interests of many European management accounting researchers, but resided outside the awareness and interest of almost all US-based management accounting researchers and doctoral seminars. Several of the people with whom Anthony met became early adopters of his innovation.

Anthony's interpersonal network provided him with a communication channel through which he could discuss the importance of organizational and social theories and field research. At this time when economics and psychology theories and analytic modelling, experiments, and surveys dominated management accounting research in the United States, persuading US researchers to learn and then to use these theories and research methods was difficult. For Anthony it involved heterophilous communication, which required finding some common ground as a basis for discussion and persuasion.

Founding and Editing *Accounting, Organizations and Society*

Probably the biggest impact Anthony Hopwood has had on management accounting research in the United States is through his role as the founding and only editor of *AOS*. *AOS* was first published in 1976 as an international journal devoted to the behavioural, organizational, and social aspects of accounting. *AOS* is intended to be more than a forum for Anthony's views.

Rather, Anthony intended for *AOS* to provide a forum for sharing new ideas about accounting from a *variety* of theoretical and research-method perspectives and across national boundaries.

AOS provides a home for behavioural management accounting research of all types by US-based researchers. All of the elite US-based organizationally oriented researchers in management accounting have published articles in *AOS*. It has been a key communication channel for US management accounting researchers, especially among the elite. For example, consider the 25 management accounting researchers in the world who have the highest 'network centrality', defined as the number of times a researcher's publications cite another researcher's publications from 1981 to 2000 in ten top-quality scholarly journals that publish management accounting research (*AOS*, *Behavioral Research in Accounting*, *Contemporary Accounting Research*, *Journal of Accounting and Economics*, *Journal of Accounting Literature*, *Journal of Accounting Research*, *Journal of Management Accounting Research*, *Management Accounting Research*, *Review of Accounting Studies*, and *The Accounting Review*; Hesford et al. 2007). Eighteen of these 25 researchers are US-based and 15 of the 18 have published in *AOS*.

Hesford et al. (2007) also identify what they call 'central authors', those authors with at least eight citations to their publications in these ten journals from another author and in total have at least three authors who cite their publications. Of the six central authors (Baiman, Brownell, Chow, Merchant, Shields, and Waller), all are US-based and have published in *AOS* and only one, Baiman, does not do behaviourally oriented organizational research. Considering the eight of the ten journals that are edited in North America, of the nine central authors (defined as having at least five citations by another author)—Baiman, Banker, Brownell, Chow, Gupta, Richelstein, Shields, Waller, and Young—all are US-based and only Gupta and Richelstein have not published in *AOS*. Four of these nine (Chow, Shields, Waller, and Young) have published a large portion of their management accounting articles in *AOS*. Six elite US-based management accounting researchers have seven or more management accounting articles in *AOS* (Birnberg, Chow, Covaleski, Merchant, Shields, and Young) and other elite US-based management accounting researchers who have multiple articles in *AOS* include Anderson, Baiman, Ittner, Larcker, Selto, and Waller.

This pattern of publishing by many of the elite US-based management accounting researchers indicates that *AOS* serves as a popular and valuable journal for *them* to diffuse *their* research. As such, *AOS* has provided them with an opportunity to influence others. One could conclude from this that Anthony has succeeded in providing a good, but limited, communication channel where elite US-based management accounting researchers publish their research. This does not mean that they or all those who read their work in *AOS* subscribe to Anthony's innovative idea about management accounting research. However, it does reflect positively on the status of *AOS* among elite US-based management accounting researchers. *AOS* provided early adopters of Anthony's idea with a respected journal in which to publish their research. As Ken Merchant (personal correspondence) noted:

But Anthony had perhaps an even greater positive influence on management accounting research through his creation of *Accounting, Organizations and Society*. This journal has become immensely important as a publication outlet for empirical management accounting research [especially because] the *Journal of Accounting Research* has narrowed its focus .... [and if researchers] don't share the religion of the editors of *Journal of Accounting & Economics*, that left only *The Accounting Review*...But the *TAR* editors' taste for management accounting research has not been consistent over the years. So *AOS* became my preferred publication outlet...If *AOS* had not existed, I probably would have diverted my attention to other topic areas...or left academia. Since *AOS* exists, I feel empowered to study the issues that I think are most interesting, relevant and important and to do so using the research methods that are most informative. I know that if I conduct the study well, I will have an excellent publication outlet for my work.

Absent a journal like *AOS*, it would have been much riskier to undertake such research if accounting researchers were the target audience. In a related vein, Mark Dirsmith (personal conversation) noted that the composition of *AOS*'s editorial board has been important. The presence of important researchers in sociology and political science as well as psychology gave *AOS* great face validity among non-accounting researchers. This could be a significant factor in the tenure and promotion decision process as it moved *outside* the accounting department.

Research Conferences Associated with AOS

Another important communication channel Anthony used to diffuse his innovation was research conferences associated with *AOS* (Hopwood 2008*a*). These conferences provided a forum to present and discuss research that identified and elaborated on management accounting practices using organizational and societal theories, with some papers using field research methods. Many of the papers presented at these conferences were later published in *AOS*, which helped Anthony to diffuse his idea to readers of *AOS* in the United States and elsewhere. The early conferences were the most important in highlighting Anthony's idea about management accounting research. They all revolved primarily around the organizational aspects of accounting, although the social aspects also were included. The papers presented were prominently displayed when they were later published in *AOS*. The conference themes were 'Studies of the Organizational Aspects of Information and Accounting Systems' (1978);[8] 'The Role of Accounting in Organizations and Society' (1980); 'Accounting in Its Organizational Context' (1983); and 'Towards Appreciating Accounting in its Organizational and Social Context' (1986).

These conferences had an important role in Anthony's strategy for diffusing his innovation. Many conferences were attended by like-minded people, with the result that there was a lot of homophilous communication, which diffuses ideas among that social clique. However, to diffuse his idea more broadly Anthony promoted heterophilous communication between management accounting researchers and both non-accounting researchers who use organizational and social theories and do field research and accounting researchers using the existing orientations to accounting research in the United States. Heterophilous communication is most effective when the communicators are elite innovative opinion leaders. Their ideas later will be communicated to non-elites. Consistent with this, Anthony invited elite opinion leaders who do either behaviorally oriented management accounting research such as Jake Birnberg, Dick Boland, David Cooper, Peter Miller, and John Waterhouse or elites who do other types of (management) accounting research including Michael Bromwich, Ray Chambers, Bill Cooper, Yuji Irjri, Bob Kaplan, and Shyam Sunder. Anthony also was able to attract a diverse set of elite social scientists to these conferences, including Michael Aiken, Bill Starbuck, Steve Kerr, Ed Lawler, Lynn Markus, John Meyer, William Nord, Jeff Pfeffer, Lou Pondy, Aaron Wildavsky, and Mayer Zald.

The diversity of researchers at these conferences set the stage for many long discussions (some very heated) about the benefits and costs of various orientations to research. As Mark Covaleski noted (personal correspondence), the 1984 *AOS* conference at the University of Wisconsin-Madison was particularly successful in achieving Anthony's goal. The diverse set of accounting and social science researchers led to wide ranging discussions as the various participants saw the same issues through different lenses. The exchange among accounting and non-accounting researchers served to highlight questions of mutual interest at the intersection of the disciplines. These were and are issues that in the absence of the conference would not have been identified. They also served to validate the range of research methods and theories that was appropriate to study these issues.

[8] The year shown is the year in which the papers appeared in *AOS*. The conferences were held in 1976, 1979, 1981, and 1984, respectively.

To US management accounting researchers, the message from these conferences was clear: Management accounting should not be viewed as if it exists in a vacuum unaffected by the organizational and social contexts within which it exists—the context in which management accounting is located is relevant to their research. These conferences also had the reverse effect. Many of the social scientists who attended found that their views about organizations and accounting changed as a result of the presentations and discussions. For example, John Meyer, an elite sociologist, reflected (personal communication) that the flow of knowledge went in both directions. Since the potential impact of accounting on organizations was not frequently discussed by sociologists, the presentations and discussions with accounting researchers at the conferences provided insights that influenced his subsequent work. He noted that a recent volume he co-edited (Drori et al. 2006) on the internationalization of organizations contains a chapter on the role of accounting in facilitating this change.

The direct effects that publicizing and publication of these conferences had on management accounting research are difficult to measure. They clearly reinforced Anthony's enthusiasm for diffusing his idea. One measure is a citation analysis of the papers presented. A random sample of the papers presented showed a pattern of citations similar to Anthony's own research publications—citations to these papers by US-based researchers tend to be small in number but occur frequently by elite US-based researchers.

DISCUSSION

Anthony's radical innovation is his idea that the appropriate way to conduct management accounting research is to study management accounting in its natural contexts using organizational and social theories and field research methods. Anthony displayed great enthusiasm for his innovation and its diffusion to and into the United States by four communication channels—his own research, his interpersonal network with US researchers, founding and editing *AOS*, and research conferences associated with *AOS*. Each of these four communication channels has had a significant influence on management accounting research in the United States.

His own research, in particular three publications (Hopwood 1972, 1976, 1983), has influenced the orientation of research and researchers' thinking about management accounting research in the United States. However, the low level of citations to his research by US researchers, both the absolute number of citations and the percentage of total citations to his research, is evidence that diffusion of Anthony's innovation to and into the United States is limited. While several elite organizational-oriented management accounting researchers in the United States cite these publications, the vast majority of management accounting researchers in the United States has not.

His interpersonal network has enabled him to encourage and assist early adopters of his innovation. Several of these early adopters are now elites in organizationally oriented research in management accounting who have had a tremendous influence on the management accounting literature that is read by US researchers.

Founding and editing *AOS* probably is the communication channel that has provided Anthony the widest and most continuous opportunity to diffuse his innovation in the United States. In particular, *AOS* has provided a high-quality journal that encouraged early adopters to use a broader set of social science theories and research methods than those that constituted the then current research orientations in the United States.

Finally, the conferences associated with *AOS* provided Anthony with important opportunities to diffuse his idea to a broad group of US researchers: the then-elites in accounting as well as junior faculty in management accounting who have become the elite organizational management accounting researchers in the United States, as well as elite non-accounting researchers.

While these communication channels have provided Anthony with much success in diffusing his radical innovation to and into the United States, overall his diffusion strategy has not (so far) resulted in a major change in the orientation of management accounting research in the mainstream of the United States. The success that Anthony has realized in the United States is almost totally related to diffusing organizationally, but not socially, oriented management accounting research. The two dominant orientations to management accounting research in the United States still are analytical and behavioural/experimental (Shields 1997). We believe that the success that Anthony has realized in diffusing his radical innovation is due to his enthusiastic efforts and his diffusion strategy. We also believe that the lack of greater diffusion of his innovation in the United States. is due to organizational and social forces led by some elites in accounting research in the United States[9] who promote the accepted orientations to (management) accounting research in the United States. These forces are related to five diffusion gaps, which are discussed below.

---

[9] Our estimate is that the vast majority of these people are not engaged in management accounting research.

The lack of diffusion of Anthony's radical innovation and hence the lack of change in the orientation towards management accounting research in the United States can be explained by US researchers who did adopt or attempted to adopt Anthony's innovation of having to deal with and worry about five gaps (Sandberg 2007). These gaps are not indicative of a diffusion failure by Anthony. Rather, they are potentially present in any diffusion process. They are an indication of the organizational and social context of the diffusion in the United States and thus are beyond the control of Anthony (or anyone else). These gaps reduce people's willingness to adopt radical innovations and can help to explain the factors limiting Anthony's influence on management accounting research in the United States. In particular, the gaps related to engagement, help, openness, results, and time inhibited the diffusion of Anthony's innovation. These gaps can cause people to have organizational and social worries or beliefs that they may have problems if they consider adopting or do adopt Anthony's innovation.

Doctoral students and faculty may worry that adopting Anthony's innovation will create an engagement gap in which they feel isolated from non-adopters. This can create conflict with other doctoral students and/or faculty. An openness gap arises when researchers worry about whether it is safe to talk to mainstream researchers about adopting a non-mainstream research orientation. Researchers may also be concerned about whether adopting this innovation in their research will cause a results gap (i.e. their research will not be successful in terms of journal acceptance or publications). These gaps all raise issues related to promotion, tenure, compensation, and reputation.

Anthony has recognized the problems created by these three gaps. In his 2006 presidential address at the annual meeting of the AAA he noted:

The very strong career emphasis in research planning encourages conservatism and conformity—doing the next safe thing and staying within recognized intellectual parameters. Only the minority cast their aspirations at a much higher level, consciously striving to develop a reputation for innovation.   (Hopwood 2007: 1371)

He returned to this point with specific reference to management accounting in accepting the AAA's Management Accounting Section 2008 Lifetime Contribution Award:

My concern is therefore future oriented. It is in this context that I am troubled by what I see as an increasing narrowness of outlook, the careerist rather than the curiosity oriented nature of an increasing amount of research, the increasing domination of what I see as the domination of 'mainstream' tendencies that prioritise particular conceptual and methodological approaches to the research task, and an associated growth in intolerance towards different equally valid and equally rigorous approaches.
(Hopwood 2008*b*: 4)

If doctoral students and faculty get past these gaps and decide to adopt, then they still may encounter time and help gaps. For example, undertaking this type of research can take time, which can create stress for doctoral students expected to learn the existing research orientations and for faculty under publish-or-perish pressure. For example, Mark Young (personal communication) indicated that Anthony's breadth of knowledge and insights were quite persuasive in motivating him to change his use of research methods. Given Mark's doctoral training in the traditional US research methods, it took him about a decade to shift from laboratory research (e.g. Young 1985) to field-based research (e.g. Selto et al. 1995). Shannon Anderson (personal communication) indicated a similar transition path from a traditional doctorate in business economics (archival econometrics) to field research. Finally, besides the time gap, people can worry about the help gap, which is whether they can get sufficient help to help them learn about this new type of research from seminars, other people, and reading.

In looking to the future, while Anthony's radical innovation has been diffused to and into the United States, further diffusion may be more difficult. As Hopwood (2007, 2008*a*, 2008*b*) worries, accounting research in the United States is increasingly dominated by economics-based research while behavioural research is increasingly marginalized and field research is almost non-existent (also see Williams et al. 2006; and Oler et al. 2008). Moreover, he worries about the decrease in management accounting research *of any kind* in the United States (also see Tuttle and Dillard 2007; and Oler et al. 2008).

Anthony (Hopwood 2008*b*) attributes these trends to several related factors, corresponding to the five gaps discussed above. These include the idea that in the current organizational and social context of accounting research in the United States, economics and finance knowledge are believed to be more relevant and thus of higher status, which has tended to focus journals on such research, thus making publication of other types of research more difficult. Related, most doctoral seminars in the United States only focus on what is currently being published in these journals. This reinforces the status quo as well as limiting the opportunities for doctoral students to even be aware of other types of research, let alone become proficient in doing it. Anthony speculates that factors related to hiring, tenure, promotion, and performance evaluation are also motivating many accounting departments to encourage only research that uses the existing orientations to research. As Shannon Anderson (personal communication) laments, 'With the decline of accounting as a career that an MBA would aspire to, and the concurrent ascent of finance and financial markets as a career of choice, perhaps there was no real chance of success for Hopwood's advocacy of research that is grounded in understanding how accounting is used to manage companies'.

In concluding, we believe that Anthony developed an important radical innovation and has had an excellent strategy for diffusing it using four communication channels. Overall, Anthony has realized much success in diffusing his innovation, and his diffusion strategy and early adopters will continue to increase his diffusion success. The big challenge for the continued success of the diffusion of Anthony's radical innovation in the United States will be to overcome organizational and social forces that can create gaps which limit the diffusion of his radical innovation to and into the United States and elsewhere (Hopwood 2008*a*).

REFERENCES

American Accounting Association. (1976). *Management Accounting Literature Abstracts*. Sarasota, Fl.: American Accounting Association.

Anderson, S. (1995*a*). Measuring the impact of product mix heterogeneity on manufacturing overhead cost. *The Accounting Review*, 70(3), 363–87.

—— (1995*b*). A framework for assessing cost management system changes: The case of activity based costing implementation at General Motors, 1986–1993. *Journal of Management Accounting Research*, 7, 1–51.

—— and Widener, S. (2007). Doing quantitative field research in management accounting. In C. Chapman, A. Hopwood, and M. Shields (eds.), *Handbook of Management Accounting Research, vol. 1*. Oxford: Elsevier, 319–41.

—— and Young, S.M. (1999). The impact of contextual and process factors on the evaluation of activity-based costing systems. *Accounting, Organizations and Society*, 24(7), 525–60.

—— Hesford, J., and Young, S.M. (2002). Factors influencing the performance of activity-based costing teams: A field study of ABC model development time in the automobile industry. *Accounting, Organizations and Society*, 27(3), 195–211.

Anthony, R. (1973). Some fruitful directions for research on management accounting. In N. Dopuch and L. Revsine (eds.), *Accounting Research 1960–1970: A Critical Evaluation*. Urbana, IL.: University of Illinois.

Anton, H., and Firmin, P. (eds.) (1972). *Contemporary Issues in Cost Accounting*, 2nd edn. Boston: Houghton Mifflin.

Ball, R., and Brown, P. (1968). An empirical evaluation of accounting income numbers. *Journal of Accounting Research*, 6(2), 159–78.

Benston, G. (eds.) (1970). *Contemporary Cost Accounting and Control*. Belmont, CA: Dickenson Publishing Co.

Birnberg, J., Turopolec, L., and Young, S.M. (1983). The organizational context of accounting. *Accounting, Organizations and Society*, 8(2/3), 111–29.

Birnberg, J., Luft, J., and Shields, M. (2007). Psychology theory in management accounting research. In C. Chapman, A. Hopwood, and M. Shields (eds.), *Handbook of Management Accounting Research, vol. 1*. Oxford: Elsevier, 27–95.

Brownell, P. (1981). Participation in budgeting, locus of control and organizational effectiveness. *The Accounting Review*, 56(4), 844–60.

—— (1982). Participation in the budgeting process: When it works and when it doesn't. *Journal of Accounting Literature*, 20, 124–50.

—— (1983). The motivational impact of management-by-exception in a budgetary context. *Journal of Accounting Research*, 21(2), 456–72.

Bruns, W., and DeCoster, D. (eds.) (1969). *Accounting and Its Behavioral Implications*. New York: McGraw-Hill.

Chow, C. (1983). The effects of job standard tightness and compensation scheme on performance: An exploration of linkages. *The Accounting Review*, 58(4), 667–85.

Covaleski, M., and Dirsmith, M. (1983). Budgeting as a means for control and loose coupling. *Accounting, Organizations and Society*, 8(4), 323–40.

—————— (1986). The budgeting process of power and politics. *Accounting, Organizations and Society*, 11(3), 193–214.

—————— (1988a). The use of budgetary symbols in the political arena: An historically informed field study. *Accounting, Organizations and Society*, 13(1), 1–24.

—————— (1988b). An institutional perspective on the rise, social transformation, and fall of a university department budget category. *Administrative Science Quarterly*, 33(4), 562–87.

DeCoster, D., Ramanathan, K., and Sundem, G. (eds.) (1974). *Accounting for Managerial Decision Making*. Los Angeles: Melville Publishing Co.

Demski, J., and Feltham, G. (1978). Economic incentives in budgetary control systems. *The Accounting Review*, 53(2), 336–59.

Drori, G., Meyer, J., and Hwang, H. (eds.) (2006). *Globalization and Organization: World Society and Organizational Change*. Oxford: Oxford University Press.

Govindarajan, V. (1984). Appropriateness of accounting data in performance evaluation: An empirical examination of environmental uncertainty as an intervening variable. *Accounting, Organizations and Society*, 9(2), 125–36.

Hesford, J., Lee, S.-H., Van der Stede, W., and Young, S.M. (2007). Management accounting: A bibliographic study. In C. Chapman, A. Hopwood, and M. Shields (eds.), *Handbook of Management Accounting Research, vol. 1*. Oxford: Elsevier, 3–26.

Hopwood, A. (1972). An empirical study of the role of accounting data in performance evaluation. *Journal of Accounting Research (Supplement)*, 10, 156–82.

—— (1976). *Accounting and Human Behaviour*. Englewood Cliffs, N.J.: Prentice-Hall.

—— (1978). Towards an organizational perspective for the study of accounting and information systems. *Accounting, Organizations and Society*, 3(1), 3–13.

—— (1980). Editorial. *Accounting, Organizations and Society*, 5(1), 1.

—— (1983). On trying to study accounting in the contexts in which it operates. *Accounting, Organizations and Society*, 8(2/3), 287–305.

—— (1987). The archaeology of accounting systems. *Accounting, Organizations and Society*, 12(3), 207–34.

—— (1988). *Accounting from the Outside: The Collected Papers of Anthony G. Hopwood*. New York: Garland.

—— (2007). Whither accounting research? *The Accounting Review*, 82(5), 1365–74.

—— (2008*a*). Changing pressures on the research process: On trying to research in an age when curiosity is not enough. *European Accounting Review*, 17(1), 87–96.

—— (2008*b*). Management accounting research in a changing world. *Journal of Management Accounting Research*, 20, 3–13.

Johnson, H., and Kaplan, R. (1987). *Relevance Lost: The Rise and Fall of Management Accounting*. Boston, Mass.: Harvard University Press.

Kaplan, R. (1977). Application of quantitative methods in managerial accounting: A state of the art survey. *Management Accounting—State of the Art*, Buyer lecture series 1977. Madison: University of Wisconsin.

Kenis, I. (1979). Effects of budgetary goal characteristics on managerial attitudes and performance. *The Accounting Review*, 54(4), 707–21.

Klemstine, C., and Maher, M. (1984). *Management Accounting Research: A Review and Annotated Bibliography*. New York: Garland.

Luft, J., and Shields, M. (2003). Mapping management accounting: Graphics and guidelines for theory-consistent empirical research. *Accounting, Organizations and Society*, 28(2/3), 169–249.

Maher, M. (2001). The evolution of management accounting research in the United States. *British Accounting Review*, 33(3), 293–305.

Merchant, K. (1981). The design of the corporate budgeting system: Influences on managerial behavior and performance. *The Accounting Review* 56(4), 813–29.

—— (1985). Budgeting and the propensity to create budgetary slack. *Accounting, Organizations and Society*, 10(2), 201–10.

—— (1989). *Rewarding Results: Motivating Profit Center Managers*. Boston, Mass.: Harvard Business School Press.

—— (1990). The effects of financial controls on data manipulation and management myopia. *Accounting, Organizations and Society*, 15(4), 297–313.

Oler, D., Oler, M., and Skousen, C. (2008). Characterizing accounting research. Working Paper. Indiana University.

Rappaport, A. (eds.) (1970). *Information for Decision Making: Quantitative and Behavioral Dimensions*. Englewood Cliffs, N.J.: Prentice-Hall.

Rogers, E. (2003). *Diffusion of Innovations*, 5th edn. New York: The Free Press.

Sandberg, B. (2007). Enthusiasm in the development of radical innovations. *Creativity and Innovation Management*, 16(3), 265–73.

Schiff, M., and Lewin, A. (eds.) (1974). *Behavioral Aspects of Accounting*. Englewood Cliffs, N.J.: Prentice-Hall.

Selto, F., Renner, C., and Young, S.M. (1995). Assessing the organizational fit of a just-in-time manufacturing system: Testing selection, interaction and systems models of contingency theory. *Accounting, Organizations and Society*, 20(7/8), 665–84.

Shields, M. (1997). Research in management accounting by North Americans in the 1990s. *Journal of Management Accounting Research*, 9, 3–61.

Shields, J., and Shields, M. (1998). Antecedents of participative budgeting. *Accounting, Organizations and Society*, 23(1), 49–76.

Tuttle, B., and Dillard, J. (2007). Beyond competition: Institutional isomorphism in U.S. accounting research. *Accounting Horizons*, 21(4), 387–409.

Waller, W., and Chow, C. (1985). The self-selection and effort effects of standard-based employment contracts: A framework and some empirical evidence. *The Accounting Review*, 60(3), 458–76.

Wejnert, B. (2002). Integrating models of diffusion of innovations: A conceptual framework. *Annual Review of Psychology*, 28, 297–326.

Williams, P., Jenkins, J.G., and Ingraham, L. (2006). The winnowing away of behavioral accounting research in the US: The process for anointing academic elites. *Accounting, Organizations and Society*, 31(8), 783–818.

Young, S.M. (1985). Participative budgeting: the effects of risk aversion and asymmetric information on budgetary slack. *Journal of Accounting Research*, 23(2), 829–42.

—— (1999). Field research methods in management accounting. *Accounting Horizons*, 13(1), 76–84.

7

On the Relationship between Accounting and Social Space

Salvador Carmona and Mahmoud Ezzamel

INTRODUCTION

The last few decades have witnessed an increased interest in theorizing space in the social sciences, particularly in postmodern geography (e.g. Soja 1989, 1996; Gregory 1994; Harvey 1990); social theory (e.g. Foucault 1977; Giddens 1984, 1991; Lefebvre 1991; Hillier and Hanson 1984; Bauman 1993); and colonial studies (Said 1993). Moreover, many researchers interested in globalization have given some attention to the conceptualization, configuration, and partitioning of space (e.g. Robertson 1993). Much more recently, there has been a growing concern to examine the implications of these efforts to theorize space in organization theory, with a special issue of *Organization* in 2004 devoted to this topic (Jones et al. 2004), a book entitled *Space, Organization and Management Theory*, edited by Clegg and Kornberger in 2006, and a number of journal articles (e.g. Spicer 2006). These more recent contributions in organization theory add to previous literature in the area, for example research on workplace (e.g. Becker and Steele 1995); corporate landscape (e.g. Rapoport 1980; Gagliardi 1990); and aesthetics (e.g. Strati 1999). Yet, despite this significant attention to space in the social sciences, there appears to be remarkably little interest in exploring the relationship between accounting and space. With a few exceptions, notably Miller and O'Leary (1994), Carmona et al. (2002), Quattrone and Hopper (2005) and some of the literature on accounting and globalization (Cooper et al. 2005), accounting

This project is partially funded by the Spanish Ministry of Education's research grant # SEJ2007-67582-C02-01. We are grateful to David Cooper and an anonymous referee for their helpful comments on previous drafts of this chapter.

researchers have shown little interest in theorizing the relationship between accounting and space or in exploring their interconnection at the level of practice. Even those accounting studies that purport to examine the role of accounting technologies in monitoring work organization hardly explore issues of space reconfiguration and reallocation, let alone aspire to theorize the relationship between accounting and space. In view of the potentials of accounting and architecture to enable control at a distance, this lack of theorization on the relationship between accounting and space constitutes a significant omission. Therefore, we believe that an overview of the literature is timely, with the aim of seeking to identify the achievements, limitations, and potential for future research in this field.

The aim of this chapter is to argue the case for studying the relationship between accounting and social space, which has held considerable promise as a theoretical framing and a heuristic for studying the differentiation of groups in the social world; in some formulations, it postulates certain connections between the internal subjective order and the external spatial order. It has been utilized to explain, for example, occupational residence patterns that may be traced to differences in resources and/or life styles (Feldman and Tilly 1960), and the emergence of coalitions or competitions between individuals sharing social space (Rauterberg et al. 1995). The notion of social space has been regarded as a key concept that could underpin promising interdisciplinary research agendas. As noted by Buttimer (1969: 425), 'The notion of social space has thus served as a heuristic and seminal concept, producing a number of distinct research orientations, each of which could be analyzed more incisively by specialists in different disciplines. It may serve in the future as a coordinating framework for interdisciplinary research on the subjective dimensions of human behavior in space'.

In this chapter, we seek to explore the implications of some of the above ideas concerning social space and their relationship to accounting in the hope that this might help stimulate further research. In the next section, we briefly review the literature on social space. This is followed by an exploration of the relationship between accounting and space, first by providing a brief review of the sparse accounting literature before we identify areas of potential research interest. The final section summarizes our main arguments and their implications for future research and the final section contains a conclusion.

SOCIAL SPACE

The term 'social space' has its genesis in the work of Durkheim (1926) as he conceived social differentiation independently of the physical setting and, hence, in its pure social sense. In other words, Durkheim perceived social space as mere cognitive mapping. The notion of social space was developed further by a geographer, Sorre, and a sociologist, Chombart de Lauwe (1960, cited in Buttimer 1969: 420). Sorre lamented the narrowness of Durkheim's understanding of social space and sought to broaden it by adding the physical dimension to the social dimension. He saw each group of people as tending to have their own specific social space, reflecting particular values, preferences and aspirations, and viewed the density of social space as mirroring the complimentarity and degree of interaction between groups. Chombart de Lauwe (ibid.: 419–20) emphasized two dimensions of social space: the objective (the spatial framework in which people live) and the subjective (space perceived by members of a group).

Subsequently, there is increasing attention to the notion of social space. Lefebvre (1991), for example, draws a distinction between lived space (representational space), perceived space (spatial practice), and conceived space (representations of space). Lived space is directly experienced through its associated images and symbols and, hence, is the space that agents have in their minds. Spatial practice is empirically observable and is lived before it can be conceptualized; it is the practice of oppressive and repressive space. Finally, despite the abstract nature of representations of space, it plays a definite role in social and political practice. In particular, conceived space is linked to the relations of production and to the order imposed by such relations. Throughout, Lefebvre underscores the importance of the relational notion of space. Space constitutes a set of relations between objects, artefacts, and humans. As such, relational space is a social space, a relation to the Other that occupies some location in social space (see also Dobers and Strannegård 2004). Similarly, Foucault's notions (1977, 1997) of gaze, discourse, and heteropia share some similarities with Lefebvre's concepts of perceived space, conceived space, and lived space, respectively. According to Foucault, the notion of gaze refers to the process through which space is measured and labelled; discourse concerns the constitution of objects and subjects in space to determine which objects exist. Finally, heteropia focuses on individuals who live and act in space.

In a number of influential works, Bourdieu (1984, 1985, 1989) develops further the notion of social space. For Bourdieu (1985: 723–4), 'the social world can be represented as a space (with several dimensions) constructed on the basis of principles of differentiation or distribution constituted by the set of properties active within the social universe in question, i.e., capable of conferring strength, power within that universe, on their holder'. Bourdieu therefore elevates the concept of social space to one that is equivalent to the social world. In this respect, he emphasizes the importance of the principles that act to differentiate or distribute groups as reflected in power conferring *active* properties; active in the sense that they represent a 'field of forces' or a 'set of objective power relations' that are irreducible to the intentions of, or the interactions among, individual agents. Each individual agent is distributed, or more precisely assigned, a position or a region in social space. A position is defined by the distribution of the powers that are active in each of the fields that an individual can occupy. Such powers, Bourdieu (ibid.: 724) argues, are 'principally economic capital (in its different kinds), cultural capital and social capital, as well as symbolic capital, commonly called prestige, reputation, renown, etc., which is the form in which the different forms of capital are perceived and recognized as legitimate'. Social space, Bourdieu contends (ibid.: 730; original emphasis) 'tends to function symbolically as a *space of life-styles*'.

Knowledge makes possible the classification of agents into groups, or *classes* (Bourdieu 1985: 725). Therefore, it is feasible to create a space of positions on the basis of agents sharing similar conditions, dispositions, interests, and engaging in similar practices. This is because social space is so constructed that the closer the agents are situated in a particular space, the more common properties they have and the more distant they are the fewer properties they have: 'Spatial distances-on paper-coincide with social distances...In effect, social distances are inscribed in bodies, more precisely, into the relation to the body, to language and to time' (Bourdieu 1989: 16–17). Theoretically, this 'class on paper' 'makes it possible to *explain* and predict the practices and properties of the things classified—including their group forming practices' (Bourdieu 1985: 725; original emphasis). The distribution of agents into social space depends upon two factors; first, the overall volume of capital, of whatever type, they possess, and second, the structure of their capital, the relative weight of the differing types of capital in the total aggregation of their assets.

Symbolic relations of power play a key role in the construction of social space: 'Owing to the fact that symbolic capital is nothing other than economic or cultural capital when it is known and recognized, when it is known through the categories of perception that it imposes, symbolic relations of power tend to reproduce and to reinforce power relations that constitute the structure of social space' (Bourdieu 1989: 21). Bauman (1993: 144) articulates different types of social space by conceiving of it as a complex interaction of three distinct, but interconnected, processes: cognitive, aesthetic, and moral 'spacings'. Each of these processes draws upon the notions of proximity and distance, but they are different in pragmatics and outcomes. Cognitive spacing is constituted through the acquisition and distribution of knowledge. The cognitive element refers to knowing the Other; some of this is background knowledge that is taken-for-granted, for example that the Other exists, or that we live with the Other, without looking for evidence to support such knowledge. This condition is a 'with-relation' that is reciprocated by the Other; it is based on understanding, and thus any misunderstanding that may occur introduces asymmetry in knowledge and thus frustrates this reciprocated 'with-relation'. Moral spacing is the effect of an individual who feels appealed to respond to another individual. For Bauman this is driven by the idea of 'for relation' assuming that one lives *for* the Other rather than *with* the Other. Finally, aesthetic spacing assumes that agents are aware of social distances and social rules of behaviour. However, aesthetic spacing refers to the shocking value of the novelty and surprise. Therefore, it is related to curiosity about new impressions, which Bauman (1993: 168) refers to as *proteophilia*: 'The strangers, with their unknown, unpredictable ways, with their kaleidoscopic variety of appearances and actions, with their capacity to surprise, are a particularly rich source of spectator's pleasure. Aesthetically, the city space is a spectacle in which the amusement value overrides all other considerations'. Table 7.1 summarizes the above-mentioned approaches to social space.

ACCOUNTING AND SOCIAL SPACE: RESEARCH IMPLICATIONS

Several themes could form the object of future investigation concerning the relationship between accounting and social space. We group these issues under four categories: accounting inscriptions and social space; accounting for individual capital; accounting and the objectification and domination of space; and accounting and spacings. These categories should not be taken as distinctly separate from each other; rather they are interconnected but their separate treatment below is used as a heuristic for convenience of presentation.

Accounting Inscriptions and Social Space

The above discussion of social space points to the importance of forms of inscribed social distances, or 'class on paper' (Bourdieau 1989), as well as the interactions between groups occupying specific places in social space. Our concern here is to examine the possible role that accounting, as a form of inscription, can play in this context. From a theoretical perspective, we can identify a number of scenarios where the intervention of accounting

Table 7.1. The concept of social space: antecedents, notions, and processes

Antecedents	
Durkheim (1926)	Unidimensional understanding of social space: it is perceived in its pure social sense.
Chombart de Lauwe (1960)	Social space comprises two dimensions: (*a*) objective space, the spatial framework in which people live; and (*b*) subjective space, space perceived by members of a group.
Notions of social space	
Foucault (1977)	- Heteropia: Individuals who live and act in space. - Gaze: Process through which space is measured and labelled. - Discourse: The constitution of objects and subjects in space to determine which objects exist.
Lefebvre (1991)	- Lived space (representational space): Space as directly lived and experienced through its associated images and symbols. The representational space is the space that the inhabitants have in their minds. - Perceived space (spatial practice): Spatial practice is the terrain of a repressive and oppressive space and becomes directly observable. - Conceived space (representations of space): Although representations of space are abstract, they are linked to the relations of production and to the 'order' which those relations impose.
Bourdieu (1985)	- The notion of social space is equivalent to the concept of social world. - The social world can be represented as a space with several dimensions constructed on the principles of differentiation and distribution. - Agents are assigned a position on social space that depends on the powers (economic capital, cultural capital, and symbolic capital) that an individual occupy.
Processes of social space	
Bauman (1993)	- Social space is the outcome of three complex, interconnected processes: cognitive, moral, and aesthetic spacing. - Cognitive spacing: The acquisition and distribution of knowledge; it refers to knowing the Other. - Moral spacing is the effect of an individual who feels appealed to respond to another individual. For Bauman, moral spacing is driven by the idea of 'for relation' assuming that one lives *for* the Other rather than *with* the Other. - Aesthetic spacing: Although it depends on the existence of a rational social order, it seeks fuzziness and movable partitions and the shocking value of novelty, of surprising.

inscriptions can be seen to play a major role in social space. We may conceptualize an organization, for example, as a grid of social space with individuals/groups placed onto specific locations both horizontally and vertically. The invocation of accounting numbers as forms of enumeration or valuation, accounting descriptors (e.g. cost centre, loss maker, and value adding), and the designation of specific temporal and spatial locations to the activities of these groups as means of describing them, evaluating their work, and specifying their location in social space. The frequency of accounting reports on performance designate the location of a group within social space; the more frequent they are the lower the group is located within the hierarchy. Similarly, the more detailed are accounting reports the more we may assume that they relate to groups located at lower hierarchical levels.

Accounting inscriptions designate specific spatial locations to groups. Research in this area relates to the constitutive capability of accounting to reconfigure resource use and relationships among different parties (Chua 1995). In her investigation of three Australian hospitals, Chua shows that accounting numbers became 'facts' as a consequence of their ability to connect diverse interests in the health sector about resource management, which in turn represented different hierarchical levels and sundry spatial locations (e.g. federal government, state government, hospital administration, clinicians, and academics). These relationships, constituted via the accounting logic, effectively became a 'class on paper', with each group separated and distinguished from other horizontal groups that have different functional designations and from vertical groups that have different hierarchical attribution.

As groups are converted via accounting inscriptions into a 'class on paper', they feature combinability and mobility (Robson 1991). Groups can travel across space and time; their reported performance may travel from a local unit to international headquarters whilst one groups' performance in one period is contrasted against that of another period. Furthermore, the intervention of accounting into the social space in an organization converts human bodies into fragments of space (Foucault 1977). With accounting numbers being articulations of measures inscribed onto human bodies, the body is objectified and rendered amenable to discipline and monitoring. Carmona et al. (1997) have extended these ideas to the organization, differentiation, hierarchization, inclusion, and exclusion of the labour force. In their study of the Spanish Royal Tobacco Factory, a manufactory that moved operations in the 1750s from scattered buildings in downtown Seville to the purpose built New Factories outside the city walls, Carmona et al. (1997) showed how the architects of the New Factories designed spaces that rendered enclosure and partitioning more disciplinary. Furthermore, accounting data reconfigured the factory space by setting up a complex web of cost centres. In turn, accounting data quantified the activities of such centres and rendered spaces visible and subjects accountable.

Accounting for Individual Capital

As noted above, Bourdieu (1984, 1985, 1989) comprises economic capital, cultural/social capital, and symbolic/prestige capital as manifestations of the power that defines the position of an individual in social space. Accounting can play a key role in the visualization and valuation of such human capital individually as well as in terms of their overall interactions. Economic capital reflects in the human capital of an individual in terms of education, training, work experience, ability, and so on, is rewarded through salary and bonuses that are assessed to be commensurate with these attributes of capital as visualized by accounting entries. Such valuation of human economic capital also serves as the basis of future promotion as well as the determination of the value of individuals in labour markets. The literature on accounting for human assets that emerged in the 1970s is one example of how accounting discourse (e.g. treating employees as part of the assets of an organization) and metrics (placing a value on human capital) intervene in calculating and visualizing economic capital (Flamholtz 1972, 2005). Similarly, much of the literature on executive pay seeks to uncover the link between some proxy of human capital and pay (Gomez-Mejia and Balkin 1992).

Accounting can also connect to an individual's symbolic capital or prestige. For example payments to individuals that far exceed what may be calculated as their human capital or their assessed contribution to the financial performance of an organization are typically explained as a reflection of the symbolic value of an individual to an organization. In this respect, some of the corporate governance literature seeks to explain pay for CEOs that is perceived to be too high, given firm performance, by suggesting that high pay awards are consistent with rewarding CEOs for being key strategists, spokespersons, or 'father figures' for the corporation (Gomez-Mejia and Balkin 1992). Further, accounting calculations can serve to underpin the esteem of certain members of the household (Ezzamel 2002). In his investigation of accounting for private estates and the household in ancient Egypt, Ezzamel (2002) reports the case of a landowner who allocated small plots of land to farmers on the basis of calculations that measured the capacity of each individual for cultivation, the rent to be delivered to the landlord in return for the privilege, and the timing of such delivery. In a related vein, Ezzamel (2004) explores how accounting mediated the organization of work and labour discipline in state projects in ancient Egypt. In this respect, Ezzamel suggests that accounting data monitored spatial locations to set work targets and establish regular reporting on performance and, ultimately, support for the application of sanctions to recalcitrant individuals as well as to determine and distribute differential wages. In short, extant research in historical and contemporary organizations shows that accounting establishes strong links to the human capital of individuals and reinforces patterns of location, differentiation, and distribution of such individuals within social space.

Accounting and the Objectification and Domination of Space

Earlier, we emphasized the objectification of the structures of social space, the role of schemes of classification, their power and the struggles over them, the domination of space, and resistance against such domination. In this respect, accounting technologies are a means of sorting, partitioning, and classifying organizational social space. Accounting terminology, such as profit centre or cost centre, is a way of designating and attaching a particular group of individuals to specific functional locations in social space. Thus, the intervention of accounting calculation and terminology into the domain of social space converts such space into an objectified notion that is re-presented as a number or a set of positions occupied by individuals or groups commanding specific, precisely calculated, personal capital (Miller and O'Leary 1994; Carmona et al. 2002).

Miller and O'Leary (1994) examined the spatial reordering of a manufactory and the contribution of diverse bodies of expertise within the corporation. In particular, they focused on the linkages between the spatial reordering of production processes and the claim that the design of advanced manufacturing facilities offers a key opportunity to give shape and form to a 'new economic citizenship'. They argued that discourse concerning simplification, automation, and integration of operations was central to the notion of governmentality. This discourse intertwined with the new spatial reordering of machines and individuals at the manufactory with the aim of maximizing the innovative capacity of the system as a whole, with accounting playing a central role in this context. Accounting deployed new forms of calculation (e.g. investment bundles), which segmented the shop floor into physical zones or areas along four axes: cluster of machines, velocity of materials, the physical inputs of materials to an area or zone, and the costs and benefits of work done in the areas as well as the return on investment on the assets bundled with it. This, in turn, enabled the identification of calculable spaces as ways of accounting for them have been invented and that rendered possible 'not just a cost reduction ... [but] a revolution in [the plant's] ways of doing things'.

Accounting calculations, thus, provide a basis for the eventual inclusion, or exclusion, of particular individuals into specific social groups placed at clearly identifiable locations in organizational social space. Such ways of classifying the organizational social world are imbued with power relations; the power of the classificatory schemes in terms of their ability to produce performative effects, by excluding, including, homogenizing, normalizing, and hierarchizing individuals/groups by virtue of the locations designated for them in social space. In this manner, social space is rendered a malleable object via the intervention of the accounting technology. Objectified as such, social space becomes an arena susceptible to the intervention of management via measurement, reporting, analysis, reconfiguration, and reproduction.

Schemes of classification, such as those developed within the accounting craft, are amenable to contestation by virtue of their power effects (Foucault 1977, 1980). Those who produce, sustain, and operationalize the classification schemes, in particular the artisans of the accounting craft as well as other senior managers in an organization, may have vested interest in promoting such schemes as a way of rendering the organizational social world susceptible to domination and management. Yet, domination generates dynamics of resistance to the precise classification schemes used, to the meaning of the different categories they enshrine, and to the technologies of their operationalization. Drawing on evidence gathered from a division of a UK subsidiary of a motor vehicle manufacturing multinational, Knights and Collinson (1987) focused on the shop floor conditions and consequences of management accounting. In their study, Knights and Collinson (1987) found that despite a routine and continuous discounting of psychological forms of discipline, the shop floor did not develop a collective solidarity that could challenge the power/knowledge regime of accounting. Consequently, what scope there may emerge for resistance depended on the configuration of power/knowledge relations, knowledge of the accounting classificatory schemes, terminology, and valuation, as well as power invested in social relations at work. Thus, individuals with a limited knowledge of accounting found it difficult to mount resistance to practices of domination. Conversely, those equipped with good knowledge of accounting may feel in a better position to challenge its classifications and calculations. These findings were supported by Ezzamel's (1994) investigation of the relationship between the budgeting system and organizational change in a UK university. In particular, Ezzamel's results suggested that groups opposed to the proposed changes relied on their technical knowledge of accounting to successfully deploy arguments that made accounting calculations 'incorrect' or at best debatable.

ACCOUNTING AND PROCESSES OF SOCIAL SPACE

In this section, we explore the connections between accounting and three processes of social space: cognitive spacing, moral spacing, and aesthetic spacing (Bauman 1993).

Accounting and Cognitive Spacing

Cognitive spacing refers to the acquisition and distribution of knowledge. The cognitive element involves knowledge of the Other, which is a 'with-relation' reciprocated by the Other. Yet, as Bauman (1993: 158) notes, 'Defence of social space boils down to the struggle for the right to mobility for oneself and for the limitations of such rights of others'. Social space is therefore an object to be apprehended, it is an arena that is forever contested by oneself and the Other. Precisely, how such social space is partitioned depends largely upon the cognitive mapping of social space constructed by oneself and by the Other. A power relation is at play in which knowledge and power both interact to produce a particular configuration and partition of social space, a dynamic process that ebbs and flows over time. Knowledge produced to manage such space serves to apprehend as much of that space as possible, whilst acknowledging that the Other exists. But to totally exclude the Other from social space, if successful, is to result in the elimination of the right of the Other with all the attendant ethical implications and, further, rendering social space meaningless. Relevant issues for accounting researchers to consider include: How can accounting help in identifying the attributes of the Other that should be admitted to social space and those Others who are to be excluded? What are the ethical implications of exclusions? How can the accounting technology be employed by oneself or the Other to carve out more social space for self while leaving sufficient space for a reciprocal 'with-relation' to exist? How might accounting be used to impact cognition and construct such social space, expand it to admit a greater range of 'with-relations', render it visible through calculations, and apprehend as much of it as possible whilst maintaining a form of reciprocity? Importantly, examination of these issues should be contextually embedded because the institutional conditions of these settings may advance understanding about the intertwinement of accounting and social space.

Accounting can help visualize the attributes of the Other and, hence, reduce misunderstandings arising from information asymmetry. Accounting can produce a reduction in the cognitive distance that brings about greater symmetry, and hence reciprocation. An example is open-book account, a practice that is becoming increasingly popular in managing supply chain relations. Mouritsen (1999) addresses the case of Business Print, a firm committed to flexibility that focused on customers, new technology, lateral organizational arrangements, and innovation. In the focal firm of Mouritsen's study, understandings of flexibility resulted in empowered employees and customer-driven management. In turn, the notion of flexibility produced a debate around two modes of management control, the 'paper' and the 'hands-on' versions. The 'paper' version attempted to control production at a distance. In this manner, spaces became part of informational representations that enabled monitoring of production networks beyond the firm's boundaries. In contrast, the 'hands-on' version emphasized differences between spaces with respect to people, technology, and politics. Consequently, the 'hands-on' version stressed the local conditions of production. Van der Meer-Kooistra and Vosselman (2000) also examined how interfirm relations can be framed and controlled. By adopting the perspective of the outsourcer, they built a model of the management control structure of interfirm relationships that comprised how contractual relationships can be established between the outsourcing party and the supplier. Furthermore, they addressed how the parties can cooperate with each other to handle the risk inherent to the contracting out of some activities.

Overall, these investigations suggest that open-book practices feature the supplier informing the buyer of the former's activities and the open-book account process helps in visualizing these activities. By revealing the supplier's activities and any exchange that ensues in response to queries raised by the buyer, the open-book account becomes a medium through which both parties appreciate the position of the Other in social space. Similarly, reports on performance evaluation and the exchange that takes place in the appraisal process between superior and subordinate (Townley 1993) is another example of the role of accounting in facilitating recognition of the position of the Other in social space. Therefore, accounting is a key technology of managing cognitive distance by constituting knowledge about the Other.

Accounting and Moral Spacing

In considering moral spacing, our preference is to promote a notion of postmodern ethics or morality. In contrast to cognitive spacing, moral spacing is not guided by previous knowledge, nor by taken-for-granted assumptions about oneself and the Other. Neither it is dependent on notions of distance and proximity. Rather than being underpinned by a concept of 'with-relation', moral spacing is driven by the ideal of 'for-relation', that is instead of acknowledging that one lives *with* the Other, moral spacing assumes that one lives *for* the Other (Bauman 1993). Yet, cognitive and moral spacings overlap and interact in important ways. Whilst moral spacing is not predicated upon previous knowledge, deep knowledge of the Other creates the scope for better awareness and intimacy of the Other, so that the moral cause is better served. But the two processes of spacing can also clash, given their differing underlying underpinnings, to the detriment of either or both.

It is with respect to moral spacing that accounting faces its greatest challenge, which is related to how accounting can build trust within organizations. According to Rousseau et al. (1998), trust is a psychological state comprising the intention to accept vulnerability based upon positive expectations of the intentions and behaviour of another. Therefore, vulnerability constitutes a central element to the notion of trust and this implies mutual confidence that no party to an exchange will exploit another's vulnerabilities (Barney and Hansen 1994). Davis et al. (1997: 712) point out, 'being vulnerable implies that there is something of importance to be lost ... trust is not taking risk per se but rather it is a willingness to take risk'. The risk of experiencing a loss is higher than the risk of benefiting from such exchange and, hence, trust is only required if a bad outcome would make you regret your action (Luhmann 1988: 98). Despite the inherent importance of risk in trust relationships, firms might wish to enforce procedures leading to mutual trust between the agents involved in the trust dyadic: the trusting and the trusted. In situations of mistrust, organizational processes can only be monitored at very high costs (Seal and Vincent-Jones 1997: 405), given that moral spacing does not involve previous knowledge of the Other.

Accounting is implicated in the enactment of trust and moral spacing. In this spacing self and the Other live for each other, since moral concern covers each and everyone. Moral space is not predicated upon social space being a contested arena for domination and power relations; nor is it driven by self-interest, reason, or calculation. As Bauman (1993: 181) states, 'The moral act is endemically ambivalent, forever threading precariously the thin lines dividing care from domination and tolerance from indifference'. Given such conceptualization, it would be easier to suggest that this is an area characterized by accounting lack, for the intervention of accounting may annul moral spacing. This, however, would be a misleading argument for accounting can play an important role in moral spacing. Indeed, there have been several studies exploring the role of accounting in facilitating or inhibiting moral thought and practice (e.g. Noreen 1988; Arrington and Puxty 1991; Arrington and Francis 1993; Schweiker 1993; Lehman 1995; Reiter 1997; Shearer 2002). An exploration of accounting and morality inescapably connects with issues of moral spacings. To illustrate, we engage with two examples of this literature.

Schweiker (1993: 232) argues that the accounting profession has a moral responsibility in enabling 'claims about how identifiable agents can and must live together in relation to others and themselves'. By emphasizing relations with others, social as an ethical arena is implicitly invoked. Giving an account discursively provides justifications for character and conduct in relation to others in social space, thereby rendering life intelligible and meaningful. Thus, giving an account is an activity in which moral agency is realized because one has to present one's identity in relation to others and to the context within which individual action takes place. In such a process, an individual's efforts are transformed into a power that is subjected to ethical appraisal. Accountability concerning one's conduct and actions to self could also act as an ethical incentive that might promote concern for others, that is living *for* the Other. Schweiker (1993: 243–4; original emphasis) further notes

giving an account is the linguistic act of rendering time morally significant through its mutually infused dimensions of past, present, and future. Even more pointedly, we can say that persons and communities live in relations to others and self [and we may add *for* others], act as causal forces within a world of power, and have some understandable being *within* the activity of giving an account.

This rendering of account is both identity forming and morally incentivizing in relation to others in social space. Thus 'in the act of giving an account there is a temporalizing of identity through a fiduciary relation which constitutes that identity as a moral character' (ibid.: 246) that has the potential not only to live *with* others but to live *for* others as well.

The relationship between accounting and moral spacing relates to the extent to which accounting can be perceived as a moralizing technology. In this respect, Shearer (2002) takes a different view of the relationship between accounting and morality, and hence moral spacings, to that of Schweiker's. Shearer's view of accounting and morality is underpinned by the view that the identities portrayed in the accounts rendered by economic entities of their activities are dependent upon the particular conceptions of subjectivity and intersubjectivity that are instantiated by economic discourse. Thus, Shearer argues 'the good of the moral community always reduces to the good of the individual economic entity. The result is that the discourse in terms of which the account is rendered serves to negate the very obligation from which accountability to broader "human and environmental purposes" derives' (ibid.: 544). In this view, therefore, rendering an account of economic activities neither promotes the moral ideal of living *for* others nor even living *with* others. Accounting for economic activities, typically informed by neoclassical economic principles, is thus rendered a technology that under-mines the process of moral spacings. To correct for this deficiency, Shearer suggests that we draw upon the work of Levinas to broaden the concept of accountability embraced by economic entities in order to underscore the importance of answerability to the Other.

Accounting and Aesthetic Spacing

As Bauman (1993: 179) suggests:

While social [cognitive] spacing aims at (without necessarily achieving it) "structur-ing", clarity of divisions, stability of categories, monotony and repetitiveness, predict-ability, foolproof guarantees that the expectations will be fulfilled—aesthetic spacing seeks fuzziness and movable partitions, the shocking value of novelty, of surprising and the unexpected, expectations that always move faster and stay ahead of fulfillment.

Therefore, the physical space of a company or a factory, just like that of a city (Bauman 1993: 168; see also Carmona et al. 2002) is a territory of aesthetic spacing: 'the uneven distribution of interest, curiosity, capacity to arouse amusement and enjoyment'. Such aesthetic aspects are not only restricted to the physical attributes of a place, but also extend to the Other as an object of aesthetic expression. Cognitive and aesthetic spacings are distinct, yet inter-related. Thus, while the cognitive seeks to construct an identity of the Other as someone whose relationship with oneself can be managed through differen-tiation and subsequent typification, the aesthetic focuses upon identifying and enjoying the aesthetic attributes of all Others. Calculation, such as that produced by accounting systems, is not an intended motivation for the aesthetic, and neither is individualization intended as a means towards categorization, but rather as an end in itself; an end that commands enjoy-ment of what the Other is perceived to be about. Similarly, physical space in a factory is not here constructed and partitioned according to the dictates of the cognitive; rather, physical space is the object of aesthetic appreciation, although at times the configuration of cognitive spacing can delimit the arena through which the aesthetic can be enjoyed. Equally, however, aesthetic spacing can transgress the boundaries drawn by cognitive spacing, since the real limit of aesthetic spacing is the imagination of the mind.

Aesthetic spacing is inspired by novelty rather than familiarity, and by trials, tribulations, and mobility instead of immobility and lack of drift. In moral spacing 'responsibility is a lasting sediment, the consequence of attention; but attention has the capacity for aesthetic spacing only as long as it wanders freely and scans the canvas of possibilities unworried by consequences of its past stop-overs' (Bauman 1993: 180). But the two conceptions of spacings can overlap if the seeker of aesthetic enjoyment is a moral person, who accepts the conditions and constraints imposed by moral spacing.

These ideas can be connected to the accounting research agenda. To use but one example, research on actor network theory (ANT) and accounting have significantly contributed to understand the role of accounting in actor networks by exploring three key themes: inscriptions, translations, and networks, but without explicitly addressing issues of aesthetic spacing (Quattrone 2004; Mouritsen and Thrane 2006). In particular, Briers and Chua's field study (2001) field study drew on ANT to illustrate how networks of heterogeneous objects, local actors, and cosmopolitans can change an organization's accounting and productive activities. In this respect, Briers and Chua (2001) focused on the role of boundary, which enabled to stabilize and mediate diverse interests, and identified five types of boundary objects: data repositories, visionary objects ideal, ideal type objects, coincident boundaries, and standardized protocols. In this context, accounting technologies adopted a cyclical pattern; after being adopted on faith and succeeding on a temporary basis new accounting techniques were finally abandoned.

These areas also hold potentially interesting research possibilities. For example, if viewed as ordering devices, accounting may order the positions of individuals onto social space. A challenge is for accounting researchers to explore the connections that might exist between this ordering and the aesthetics of spacing. Similarly, future accounting research could explore the extent to which aesthetic spacing underpins how translation serves to position self in relation to the Other. Finally, accounting studies that have focused upon the trials and tribulations exercised in the formation of networks tend to emphasize how networks are given the appearance of stability even if they were highly unstable. Future research in ANT and accounting could emphasize mobility rather than stability in the construction of networks and how actors might appreciate the Other as an object of aesthetic expression. Rather than seeking to render relations and performance in actor networks as objects malleable to accounting quantification and categorization, a new form of accounting could promote a distancing from quantification and a greater emphasis upon appreciating and enjoying the Other as an end in itself.

CONCLUSION

In a seminal paper published nearly thirty years ago, Anthony Hopwood and his co-authors radically extended our understanding of the roles that accounting play in organizations and society (Burchell et al. 1980). Our aim of writing this piece is to provide a modest response to this challenge by pointing to a number of research possibilities concerning the connections between accounting and social space. Drawing on extant theorization of space in the social sciences, we have pointed out a number of research implications in relation to accounting inscriptions and social space, accounting for individual capital, and accounting and the objectification and domination of space. We have also explored some possible future research opportunities concerning the processes of social space: the roles that accounting can play in underpinning cognitive spacing, the connection between accounting and moral spacing, and the extent to which accounting can underpin aesthetic spacing. Wherever possible, we have connected briefly with the extant accounting literature that either explicitly or implicitly related to the relationship between accounting and specific dimensions or processes of social space. We have noted that few studies have explicitly addressed the relationship between accounting and space, and although these studies have been illuminating, much more remains to be done. We have therefore sought to move beyond the extant literature and identify a number of possible areas that future researchers could explore in order to enhance our understanding of the roles of accounting in organizations and society.

We have been selective in our choice of research themes. Our purpose has not been to provide a comprehensive coverage of all the extant literature that can connect with issues of social space. To cite just one example of areas we have excluded, the field of globalization clearly offers much potential to explore other themes of the relationship between accounting and social space. A number of commentators have linked contemporary developments in globalization, whatever these may be, with 'a tendency towards deterritorialization, so that social space can no longer be wholly mapped in terms of territorial places, territorial distances and territorial borders' (Scholte 2005: 17). Such an interpretation of globalization creates more scope for research connecting accounting for globalization and social space than has been considered here. However, despite such omissions, we hope we have done enough to bring to the attention of accounting academics the largely neglected area of social space and the importance of studying roles of accounting therein.

REFERENCES

Arrington, C.E., and Francis, J.R. (1993). Giving economic accounts: Accounting as a cultural practice. *Accounting, Organizations and Society*, 18(2/3), 107–24.
—— and Puxty, A.G. (1991). Accounting interests and rationality: A communicative relation. *Critical Perspectives on Accounting*, 2(1), 31–58.

Barney, J., and Hansen, M. (1994). Trustworthiness as a source of competitive advantage. *Strategic Management Journal*, special issue: Competitive Organizational Behavior, 15, 175–90.

Bauman, Z. (1993). *Postmodern Ethics*. Oxford: Blackwell.

Becker, F.D., and Steele, F. (1995). *Workplace by Design: Mapping the High-Performance Workspace*. San Francisco, Calif.: Jossey-Bass.

Bourdieu, P. (1984). *Distinction: A Social Critique of the Judgment of Taste*. Cambridge, Mass.: Harvard University Press.

—— (1985). The social space and the genesis of groups. *Theory and Society*, 14(6), 723–44.

—— (1989). Social space and symbolic power. *Sociological Theory*, 7(1), 14–25.

Briers, M., and Chua, W.F. (2001). The role of actor-networks and boundary objects in management accounting change: A field study of an implementation of activity-based costing. *Accounting, Organizations and Society*, 26(3), 237–69.

Burchell, S., Club, C., Hopwood, A.G., Hughes, J., and Nahapiet, J. (1980). The roles of accounting in organizations and society. *Accounting, Organizations and Society*, 5(1), 5–27.

Buttimer, A. (1969). Social space in interdisciplinary perspective. *Geographical Review*, 59(3), 417–26.

Carmona, S., Ezzamel, M., and Gutiérrez, F. (1997). Control and cost accounting practices in the Royal Tobacco Factory of Sevilla. *Accounting, Organizations and Society*, 22(5), 411–46.

—— —— —— (2002). The relationship between accounting and spatial practices in the factory. *Accounting, Organizations and Society*, 27(3), 239–74.

Chua, W.F. (1995). Experts, networks and inscriptions in the fabrication of accounting images: A story of the representation of three public hospitals. *Accounting Organizations and Society*, 20(2), 111–45.

Clegg, S., and Kornberger, M. (2006). *Space, Organization and Management Theory*. Copenhagen: CBS Press and Liber.

Cooper, D., Barrett, M., and Jamal, K. (2005). Globalization and the coordinating of work in multinational audits. *Accounting Organizations and Society*, 30(1), 1–24.

Davis, J., Schoorman, D., Mayer, R., and Hwee Hoon, T. (1997). The trusted general manager and business unit performance: Empirical evidence of a competitive advantage. *Strategic Management Journal*, 25(5), 563–76.

Dobers, P., and Strannegård, L. (2004). The cocoon—A traveling space. *Organization*, 11(6), 825–48.

Durkheim, E. (1926). *De la Division du Travail* (reprinted in 1978). Paris: PUF.

Ezzamel, M. (1994). Organizational change and accounting: Understanding the budgeting system in its organizational context. *Organization Studies*, 15(2), 213–40.

—— (2002). Accounting for private estates and the household in the twentieth-century BC Middle Kingdom, Ancient Egypt. *Abacus*, 38(2), 235–62.

—— (2004). Work organization in the Middle Kingdom, Ancient Egypt. *Organization*, 11(4), 497–537.

Feldman, A.S., and Tilly, C. (1960). The interaction of social and physical space. *American Sociological Review*, 25(6), 877–84.

Flamholtz, E.G. (1972). Towards a theory of human resource value in formal organizations. *The Accounting Review*, 47(4), 666–78.

—— (2005). Conceptualizing and measuring the economic value of human capital of the third kind. *Journal of Human Resource Costing and Accounting*, 9(2), 78–93.

Foucault, M. (1977). *Discipline and Punish: the Birth of the Prison*. London: Allen Lane.

—— (1997). *The Birth of the Clinic: An Archaeology of Medical Perception*. London: Routledge.

—— (1980). *Power/Knowledge*. Brighton: Harvester.

Gagliardi, P., Delacroix, J., and Goodstein, J. (1988). Political environment of organizations: An ecological view. *Research in Organizational Behaviour*, 10, 359–92.

Giddens, A. (1984). *The Constitution of Society*. Cambridge: Polity Press.

—— (1991). *The Consequences of Modernity*. Cambridge: Polity Press.

Gómez-Mejía, L., and Balkin, D. (1992). Determinants of faculty pay: An agency theory perspective. *Academy of Management Journal*, 35(5), 921–55.

Gregory, D. (1994). *Geographical Imagination*. Oxford: Blackwell.

Harvey, D. (1990). *The Condition of Postmodernity*. Oxford: Blackwell.

Hillier, B., and Hanson, J. (1984). *The Social Logic of Space*. Cambridge: Cambridge University Press.

Jones, G., McLean, C., and Quattrone, P. (2004). Spacing and timing. *Organization*, 11(6), 723–41.

Knights, D., and Collinson, D. (1987). Disciplining the shopfloor: A comparison of the disciplinary effects of managerial psychology and financial accounting. *Accounting, Organizations and Society*, 12(5), 457–77.

Lefebvre, H. (1991). *The Production of Space*. Oxford: Blackwell.

Lehman, C. (1995). A legitimate concern for environmental accounting. *Critical Perspectives on Accounting*, 6(5), 393–412.

Luhmann, N. (1988). Familiarity, confidence, trust: Problems and alternatives. In D. Gambetta (ed.), *Trust: Making and Breaking Cooperative Relations*. Cambridge, Mass.: Basil Blackwell, 94–107.

Miller, P., and O'Leary, T. (1994). Accounting, 'economic citizenship', and the spatial reordering of manufacture. *Accounting, Organizations and Society*, 19(1), 15–43.

Mouritsen, J. (1999). The flexible firm: Strategies for a subcontractor's management control. *Accounting, Organizations and Society*, 24(1), 31–55.

—— and Thrane, S. (2006). Accounting, network, complementarities and the development of inter-organisational relations. *Accounting, Organizations and Society*, 31(3), 241–75.

Noreen, E. (1988). The economics of ethics: A new perspective on agency theory. *Accounting, Organizations and Society*, 13(4), 359–69.

Quattrone, P. (2004). Accounting for god: Accounting and accountability practices in the Society of Jesus (Italy, XVI-XVII centuries). *Accounting, Organizations and Society*, 29(7), 647–83.

Quattrone, P., and Hopper, T. (2005). A 'time space odyssey': Management control systems in two multinational organizations. *Accounting, Organizations and Society*, 30(7/8), 735–64.

Rapoport, A. (1980). Cross-cultural aspects of environmental design. In I. Altman, A. Rapoport, and J.F. Wohlwill (eds.), *Human Behavior and Environment*. New York: Plenum, 7–46.

Rauterberg, M., Sperisen, M., and Dätwyler, M. (1995). *Human–Computer Interaction*. Proceedings of the 5th East-West International Conference, EWHCI'95, Moscow, Russia, 4–7 July, Volume II, II-94-II-101.

Reiter, S.A. (1997). Storytelling and ethics in financial economics. *Critical Perspectives on Accounting*, 8(6), 605–32.

Robertson, R. (1992). *Globalization: Social Theory and Global Culture*. London: Sage.

Robson, K. (1991). On the arenas of the accounting change: The process of translation. *Accounting Organizations and Society*, 16(5/6), 547–70.

Rousseau, D., Sitkin, S., Burt, R., and Camerer, C. (1998). Not so different after all: A cross-discipline view of trust. *Academy of Management Review*, 23(3), 393–404.

Said, E. (1993). *Culture and Imperialism*. New York: Vintage Books.

Scholte, J.A. (2005). *Globalization: A Critical Introduction*. Basingstoke: Palgrave Macmillan.

Schweiker, W. (1993). Accounting for ourselves: Accounting practice and the discourse of ethics. *Accounting, Organizations and Society*, 18(2/3), 231–52.

Seal, W., and Vincent-Jones, P. (1997). Accounting and trust in the enabling of long-term relations. *Accountability Journal*, 10(3), 406–31.

Shearer, T. (2002). Ethics and accountability: From the for-self to the for-the-other. *Accounting, Organizations and Society*, 27(6), 541–73.

Soja, E.W. (1989). *Postmodern Geographies*. London: Verso.

—— (1996). *Third Space*. Oxford: Blackwell.

Spicer, A. (2006). Beyond the convergence–divergence debate: The role of spatial scales in transforming organizational logic. *Organization Studies*, 27(10), 1467–83.

Strati, A. (1999). *Aesthetics and Organization*. London: Sage.

Townley, B. (1993). Performance appraisal and the emergence of management. *Journal of Management Studies*, 30(2), 221–38.

Van der Meer-Kooistra, J., and Vosselman, G.J. (2000). Management control of interfirm transactional relationships: The case of industrial renovation and maintenance. *Accounting Organizations and Society*, 25(1), 51–77.

8

What is the Object of Management? How Management Technologies Help to Create Manageable Objects

Barbara Czarniawska and Jan Mouritsen

TECHNOLOGY—INDIFFERENT ORGANIZATIONS

In the recent decade, many students of management—students of accounting, marketing, and organization theory at least—have turned their interest to studies of science and technology (STS; see, e.g., Czarniawska and Hernes 2005). One of the reasons is that this trans-disciplinary endeavour produces fascinating insights into the contemporary world, joining the forces of traditional disciplines such as sociology, philosophy, anthropology, and political science in an inquiry of phenomena at the centre of present-day world. Modern science belongs, no doubt, to phenomena that are central today, but so does the economy, which has been left too long to economists (see McKenzie et al. 2007). The other reason was that the STS's interests in calculation centres corresponded with the emerging perspective, which suggests that such managerial practices as accounting should be seen as social and institutional practices, rather than neutral technical procedures (Hopwood and Miller 1994). Yet another reason is that many STS scholars have unwittingly undertaken studies of management and organizing (see, e.g., Latour and Woolgar 1979; Knorr Cetina 1981). STS has therefore become an important source of inspiration, not the least to the present authors, but also a basis for an analogy between science studies and management studies, which may help to make both more nuanced and informative.

As Czarniawska (2004) has pointed out, laboratories are technology-focused sites, whereas many other economic organizations are not. This is not to claim that technology-barren organizations exist. All organizations are extremely dependent on technology, and computer technology is the most commonly spread of all technologies. Yet, in many organizations or parts of organizations, or, even more correctly, segments of organizing, technology, and material objects are rarely at the centre of attention. One can speak of 'technology-indifferent organizations' in which technological artefacts and material objects in general remain at a (safe!) distance.

Curiously, one technology-indifferent practice is the segment of organizing called management. Practitioners of management, even in technology-obsessed organizations, often have an ambiguous stance to things in general and to technological artefacts in particular. This stance is characterized by, on the one hand, a tendency to push material technology away, and on the other hand to introduce more of it in a form of various mediators.[1] Even more peculiar is the attempt to keep technological artefacts and material objects at bay as a way of making them more manageable. As we will show, managers are rarely interested in technology. They are, however, interested in management technologies, which allow them to stay distanced from technology.

Before we embark on a tour of our examples, we need to add that the difference between technology-focused sites and other sites of organizing has been addressed earlier on. The new institutionalists (see, e.g., Meyer and Scott 1983), who distinguished between 'institutional' and 'technical' environments, made one attempt. This distinction, however, created more problems that it resolved. Granted, there are sites of organizing and types of organizing in which the role of technology can be greater or smaller, or at least given more or less attention, as mentioned previously. However, all environments are institutionalized, and all environments use and are held together by artefacts and technology. Artefacts and technologies are suitable and durable carriers of institutions (Joerges and Czarniawska 1998).

Thus, *all* organizing is related to social institutions and to technology. Yet the relationship is ambiguous, because managers try to avoid direct contact with material objects, inserting instead a set of mediators that act on material technology. Up close, material objects are frightening; their solid shape impresses but also inhibits management—they are too concrete and firm. Managers want things to be mouldable, so that they can be reformed and transformed to new uses. Therefore managers tend to avoid direct contact

---

[1] Latour (1993) introduced a distinction between an 'intermediary' and 'a mediator'. An intermediary merely carries or transports; a mediator actively constitutes, creates, and modifies. According to him, things are most often treated as intermediaries, whereas in fact they always act as mediators translating that which is transported into something else.

with technological things and material objects, and concentrate on quasi-objects such as accounting reports and management technologies that work primarily as mediators.

This puzzling observation made us ask, in the first place: 'What is management?' The simplest answer is that it is a linguistic synonym of administration, which only recently has acquired a different, and almost opposing meaning. Originally, it meant leading horses by hand. Even if the element of leadership is maintained in the present day definitions, it is certainly not horses that are being led. This led us to the second question: 'What or who is being managed?' Again, a commonsensical answer would have it that it is things, people, money, and actions. Which leads us to a third question: 'How is management performed?' The answer is again, with the aid of things, people, money, and actions. Yet some things seem to be preferable to others, both as the objects to manage with and the objects to be managed, as we shall try to demonstrate in the examples that follow. In the four next sections we present examples of managerial concerns and associated concerns with management technology—city-planning, venture capital, human resources, and firm performance. Then we discuss our thesis that technology is dismissed by managers and only embraced when mediated by management technology. Fighting against the insubordination of things, managers construct new objects to be managed. Successful management is enabled by turning complex things and people into separate objects, with help of quasi-objects such as managerial technologies.

KEEPING THE MD'S OFFICE MANAGEABLE

When Czarniawska (1985) conducted a study of US executives in the early 1980s, one of the surprising observations was that computers were kept out of executive offices. Computers stopped at the threshold of a CEO's office: they belonged with secretaries. In the late 1990s, computers made it inside, yet many city managers in Warsaw and Rome did not have computers in their offices, although secretaries did (Czarniawska 2002). Almost all Stockholm city managers and even politicians had computers in their offices, but all Swedes use computers—period—so this is no surprise. Still, they did not spend most of their time at their computers, as their subordinates did. They checked their e-mails, wrote letters, and surfed the Internet when in need of data, although this latter activity was typical for managers with a proclaimed interest in information technology. Otherwise, their subordinates or secretaries did the surfing and printed the results.

Such a situation is so pervasive, that it has been immortalized in fiction. In Donna Leon's detective stories from Venice, the inspector goes to the secretary of his boss, Signorina Elettra, with all problems that can be solved by a computer, and Signorina Elettra and her network of hacker friends are capable of almost anything. Similarly, in Andrea Camilleri's Montalbano stories, it is Catarella, the person lowest in the police hierarchy, who turns out to be a computer genius. This situation is not limited to Italy.

Does that mean that management can be accomplished without things, as many of our idealist colleagues seem to maintain? No! There are at least three typical management artefacts. One is, obviously, the Phone, which nowadays tends to be a cellular phone. Another is the Dictaphone, which, although not as popular, is quite ubiquitous (medical consultants, who at least attempt to manage nurses, tend to dictate their notes, to be typed by one of the nurses). Yet another is a Talking Table, artefact that requires more attention than it is usually spared.

A Talking Table is not a table that talks, but a table at which talks are held. It varies in size from a relatively small coffee table to a relatively large conference table. If, in the United States, managerial status can be guessed from the make of car a person was driving, in Europe a Talking Table reveals that the person is a manager (a professional may have a reading chair, but the presence of a Talking Table indicates that the professional is at least a project manager). Talking to other people takes the majority of a manager's time, as observed in systematic studies by Mintzberg (1973) and corroborated more recently by Tengblad (2003).

Tables are silent artefacts: they rarely talk back, seldom break and are useful for delivering bottom-line reality arguments; they can be banged upon when an argument about the bottom line is involved (Edwards et al. 1995). Telephones and Dictaphones are more fragile, but not much. Telephones constitute staple technology nowadays, whereas Dictaphones are simple and cheap. If they break, they can be easily replaced—everyone who uses them has at least two, and the secretary (the one womanning the computer) has another. But not all artefacts are that docile: computers reveal the distancing tendency showed by managers in relation to things that are too big, too solid, or too unruly.

Computers, as all professionals know, talk back aplenty. They are capable of malice and erratic behaviour; not even computer specialists who have a tendency to sneer at the average user can claim to know *why* certain things happen or fail to happen. The ways professionals deal with recalcitrant computers are many and variegated: obsessively trying to deal with them far into the night, asking around, reading complete manuals, or abandoning oneself to the insults of the computer specialist.

Managers, even middle managers, cannot afford this type of encounter. After the first signal, they step back and distance themselves from the rebelling thing by inserting a mediator. The most usual approach is to call the computer specialist—or to call the secretary and ask her to call a computer specialist (with the exception of the IT fanatics; yet even they will step back much quicker than any professional).

Sometimes, in order to avoid direct contact with unruly artefacts, the executives are put in contact with them when they are not working. This was the case when the Mayor of Paris visited Aramis, the automated train system was safely stationary and a few months away from its demise, as shown by Bruno Latour (1996). Similarly, they visit new plants before they are put to work, and admire big machines at a safe distance.

However, as mentioned, the relationship between managers and the objects is highly ambiguous. They use some objects to manage others, and they use them to separate themselves from the objects to be managed. When things to be managed are not objects or are complex objects, the managers turn them into new types of objects in order to make them manageable. The next sections offer two such examples.

CONSTRUCTING OBJECTS OF INVESTMENT

Sometimes, it is necessary to develop a large detour, which in effect transforms a material object, in order to understand it. Consider, for example, the work of financial analysts aimed at deciding if a particular project or start-up company deserves venture capital financing (Mouritsen et al. 2001, 2002). The artefact on which a venture is to be based has no strong history; it may, at best, have some physical form, such as a prototype or a preliminary product, which can be shown and presented to an inquisitive investor. However, it is still primarily a technology, and not yet a product that can be produced and sold. Even if the project-maker may be able to show how the technology works in an artificially created environment or in a limited market, this does not tell how it may 'really' work when challenged by the real, large markets the investor envisages. So, even if the technology appears to work at the stage at which investors make decisions, it does not really do so. The working technology is not a good performer because, as any investor will claim, it must not only demonstrate the ability to begin and to end an operation, but must also demonstrate the ability to work *for* something or somebody else—for a company, for example. And it is a long way from a technology to a (possible) company.

The investor, therefore, has no interest in the technology, merely in the conditions that will favour its translation[2] into something that 'really works'. Such a translation takes place in a voyage around the technology rather than in the voyage of technology itself. However, after this travel has ended, the technology appears in a completely new form. It becomes another object.

1. The first step on this voyage is taken when the investor meets the project in paper form. Accounting report forms are often inadequate for this purpose, as there is no strong history of the project in question. Business plans are more interesting, because they set the technology in relation to uses, users, production facilities, and distribution mechanisms. These are the first proofs of existence of the technology, but the proofs are frail and typically hold only briefly—the project can be terminated at this point. The analysts do not have time to look into all proposed projects for more than a minute or two.

2. If the project passed the first trial, the analysts may spend some time visiting the investors to learn more about them: their interests, their family conditions and their capacity to produce results. Is the workshop dirty? Is the investor prepared to put his or her house up as collateral? The visit translates the technology by setting it in the context of a person and a family, and by calibrating it by such factors as the dust on the workshop windows.

3. If successful, the third trial may send the project into orbit. The analysts parcel out various aspects of the technology's problems and assess them one by one, by harvesting expert advice pertaining to two questions: 'Will this technology work in a manufacturing setting? Will customers want to buy it?' These yes/no answers are then consolidated in a decision about the viability of the venture.

4. If this decision is made, the analysts will propose conditional financing programmes (size and timing of cash flows, interest, and ownership) in which subsequent finance allocation must be accompanied by results.

5. If this programme is acceptable to the project-maker, then the analyst/ investor proposes changes to management principles. The preliminary workshop, or in some cases a small factory, has to be transformed to make a product out of the technology, and the technology in turn is translated in a company. To make the company viable, the investor adds a board of directors, an accounting system, and a social network that will help the project-maker to learn what it means to be a true business manager.

[2] We use here the concept of translation in its non-linguistic sense introduced by STS; for its use in organization theory, see Czarniawska and Sevón (1996, 2005).

This sequence of activities demonstrates the process whereby the material technology is assessed as an object of investment but is never taken literally as the object it is. It may work for itself, but it has not demonstrated that it can work for—or as—a company. Therefore, the technology-as-thing must be translated and become a proper object of investment, a thing that will permit the development of a company.

Analysts and investors work on the context of the technology rather than work only on its actual operation and performance. This widening of a context is a voyage around the technology because through this procedure the technological project is understood less and less as a 'technology to be adopted' and more and more as a 'technology to be adapted'—a technology to be continuously reframed. This does not happen by gauging the power of the technology-as-is, but by gauging the power of its context and thus by creating the conditions that may make the project-maker into a manager and transform the technology gradually into a company. The company is the goal; the technology follows as an afterthought.

Thus the company is a pre-thought and the technology an afterthought, but neither the pre- nor the after-thought is closed. The analysts/investors continuously attempt to equip the company with new capabilities. One such additional equipment is translation of the identity of the project-maker into that of a business-manager-to-be: a person who believes in markets more than in technology. Technology may be great, but its greatness is no longer assessed in technical terms, but in terms of marketability and growth. Technology can easily be compromised in such an assessment, and the adequate technology wins over a wonderful one.

This last movement has two parts. One consists of consulting advice from the analyst/investor on how to become a professional business manager; another is the imitation and social reinforcement, which follows from the analyst/investor placing the project-maker in a network of other project-makers who share experiences of their transformation into business managers. By creating social networks around project-makers, analysts/investors give them identity and ambition as managers.

Another additional equipment is management technologies. A business plan is translated into a strategy plan though the intervention of the analyst/investors; accounting systems are added by the same analyst/investors; and product development principles are developed in cooperation, so that technology becomes manufacturable and affordable—which means that it becomes simpler. These new objects—strategies, accounting systems, and operations principles—are added to the original object, technology. The original object gradually changes form, so that it has a market, so that is affordable, and so it can be produced. In short, at the end of the translation chain it becomes *an object of investment*: It permits the construction of a company, which acts upon it and makes its performance yield more than its technical capability stands for.

There are good grounds for claiming that the constructors of objects of investment are largely disinterested in the actual technology proposed by the project-maker. The technology rests aside; it is not the centre of things, but occupies a space on the margins of the process. Surely it must be there, but not as a centre of value but as a thing most likely to become different in the end. It will not work as it is and there is, therefore, a limit to how seriously it will be taken. It certainly will not be taken literally. The analysts/investors do not assume that technology is powerful as it is and do not subordinate themselves to it. On the contrary, they require the technology to be subordinate. The analysts/investor constructs something quite different: a company, which *in turn* will take care of technology by giving it new properties. Not only the technology, but also the project-makers, must be translated into persons who can understand the requirements of markets, impose them on technology, and redesign the technology accordingly.

In effect, the chain of translations thus accomplished does not only make technology manageable; the project-makers must also become manageable. And in return for this, they acquire a new identity—that of business managers. Thus management quasi-objects help to turn other things and people into manageable objects.

HUMAN RESOURCE MANAGEMENT IS NOT ABOUT TRANSPLANTATION

How, when, and why did it happen that a term used previously to denote keeping human organs to be transplanted in proper conditions replaced an organizational function known as 'personnel administration' and later as 'personnel management'? A search among HRM's websites was not particularly helpful:

Key principles and practices associated with HRM date back to the beginning of mankind. Mechanisms were developed for the selection of tribal leaders, for example, and knowledge was recorded and passed on to youth about safety, health, hunting, and gathering. More advanced HRM functions were developed as early as 1000 and 2000 B.C. Employee screening tests have been traced back to 1115 B.C. in China, for instance. And the earliest form of industrial education, the apprentice system, was started in ancient Greek and Babylonian civilizations before gaining prominence during medieval times. (http://www.referenceforbusiness.com/encyclopedia/Gov-Inc/Human-Resource-Managememt-HRM.html accessed 08–04–19)

Although this retroactive inclusion is fascinating, we choose to rely on that of Karen Legge (1989, 2005), who suggested a more modest version of events. She traced the emergence of HRM back to the writings of US academics and managers in the 1980s (Tichy et al. [1982] is the earliest example).[3] From there, it travelled to the repertoire of management consultants, and soon after to the United Kingdom and to managers and academics in other countries. UK surveys of 1990 and 1992 noted few personnel specialists with the title of HR-manager, but the professional journals and the popular media had already focused themselves on the new term, and the practice followed suit (Legge 2005: 101). At present, there is no business school without courses or Masters in HRM, our schools included.

Legge mapped the consequent translation of 'the problem of employees' from 'labour relations' to 'industrial relations' and then to 'employee relations'. She rightly related the latest version of the term to recent changes in global economies. During the 1980s a distinct move occurred: away from traditional manufacturing industries to process, hi-tech, and service industries, none of which were strongly unionized, even in Scandinavian countries. Legge emphasized the dramatic shift from a collection of employees to the individual conception that followed suit. However, the movement may be even more dramatic than that, as there was a further translation: from the individual (the term which means something indivisible) to elements or aspects of a person (those that can be counted as 'resources').

What is HRM, then? Legge (2005) distinguished between a hard and a soft version of it, but, as she herself noticed, the soft version is used primarily 'to reassure and secure "core" employees whose resourcefulness is deemed essential for the achievement of competitive advantage' (Legge 2005: 126). In short, the soft version evokes the old vocabulary of Human Relations and Organization Development, softening the more brutal language of the hard version (in practice, the two are combined).

The hard model postulates a crucial importance of the integration of human resources policies, systems, and activities with business strategy. People are social capital, capable of development (Beer and Spector 1985).[4] Observe the ambiguity—is it people or capital that can be developed? And, further in the same tune: 'Human resources management is directed mainly at management needs for human resources (not necessarily employees) to be provided and deployed.' (Torrington and Hall 1987, quoted after Legge 2005: 104). Another ambiguity: they may be speaking of outsourcing, or perhaps of

---

[3] Although Roy Jacques (1999) noted that Mason Haire used the expression as early as 1970.
[4] For a study in which the consequent refinement, 'intellectual capital', is discussed, see Mouritsen and Flagstad (2005).

quasi-human resources—machines that can replace humans, for examples. Human resources are the object of formal planning, and are a factor of production as much as land and capital, a variable cost.

Many advocates and critics of HRM have noted its many similarities (if not identicalness) to personnel management. And while the friends and foes agree that the change is mostly in terminology, there is no doubt that consequences of a change in rhetoric can be profound. As Karen Legge said in her analysis:

> The importance of HRM lies not in the objective reality of its normative models and their implementation, but in the phenomenological reality of its rhetoric … It should be understood as a cultural construction comprising a series of metaphors redefining the meaning of work and the way individual employees relate to their employers. Just as a metaphor gives new meaning to the familiar by relating it to the unfamiliar (and vice versa), so those that comprise HRM can give a new, managerially prescribed meaning to employment experiences that, within a pluralist perspective, might be considered unpalatable. (2005: 123)

This example helps us to disentangle the ambiguous relationships between managers and objects further. Perhaps the most important trait of a (proper) object of management is its simplicity. The more complex things are, the more difficult they are to manage. Natural events, material technology and especially their combination provide insurmountable challenges; thus distance-producing objects are developed and mobilized to retrieve manageability. Actual plants and companies are far too complex; they must be simplified to become objects of intervention. Also people, and especially collectives of people are far too complex to manage: to make them manageable, they need to be divided first into individuals or groups of individuals, which can be separated from other people and organized from the vantage point of the external markers that make them homogeneous such as role, background, gender or age.

But individuals are also difficult because of their complex social and psychological make-up, and are therefore taken into account not as whole persons, but as specific skills and qualities that can be seen as resources. Individual competencies and capabilities such as project management experience, language capabilities, customer-interaction abilities, and commitment to the firm are such resources.[5] Not all skills and qualities are relevant, however—only those that link the person to the firm, to its customers, to technologies, to its modes of operation, and to its strategies.

The chain of translations—from a collective to individuals and to bundles of competencies—corresponds to a gradual simplification. More and more

---

[5] Townley (1994) arrived at a similar conclusion after having applied a Foucauldian perspective on HRM.

social and individual characteristics of the employee are stripped away, and only those traits are left that can be related to other things. The relationship to these other things makes a person an appendix to them; a complex person in a complex social setting is gradually translated into a skill–technology relationship, combining two resources. This makes a person even more manageable, as these other objects have already been made manageable. Thus being capable of providing consumer satisfaction is a resource, as is the capacity of learning new information systems, or even creativity (the creation of new objects or practices). The person has been largely displaced, often through the application of various quasi-objects such as intellectual capital statements (Mouritsen and Larsen 2005). At all stages of turning complex objects into simple ones and managing them afterwards, management technologies—in the form of accounting calculations, for example—are used to mediate between the actual personhood of employees and the management.

INSCRIPTIONS, VISIBILITY, AND INTERVENTION

Accounting systems assemble inscriptions of profits, assets and liabilities which occur at the end of a process of organizing, thus reducing and/or amplifying its traces. Inscriptions develop knowledge about phenomena as they mark some of their traces, summarize them and transport them to a centre from which they can be acted on. This produces the potential of a managerial action at a distance.

Inscriptions, however, constitute knowledge that managers have little choice but to attend to. They are a sizeable part of a manager's knowledge about the world. Accounting inscriptions in particular are related to concerns about profitability. These concerns may seem obvious, but on inspection, profitability is ambiguous. There may be competing inscriptions, each of which favours or motivates radically different processes of strategizing and organising. Such inscriptions compete in creating visibility and thus *compete* in deciding the future of the firm.

Mouritsen (1999) described a production manager who was particularly adept at instituting a flexible mode of managing. Capable of negotiating with unions and workers, he was able to develop a highly flexible manufacturing system based on local knowledge. In terms of timetables and throughput, the factory was highly effective in meeting customer orders. The company also sought to meet all customer requirements, even to the point where finished goods were taken out of inventory, disassembled and reassembled into a new product if there was a rush order. New technologies were constantly incorporated, not only in new products but also into the existing product lines. The focus was on non-financial performance, which was firmly based in the production manager's interaction with the workers.

Such a personalized form of management, and the complexities of the factory organization were increasingly questioned by higher-level management, however (especially by the Managing Director [MD]) on the grounds of lack of transparency. Even though the production manager was acknowledged an able factory manager, lack of insight was a concern for the MD to whom the factory was simply a black box. The contribution margins did not help much, because even if they were substantial, the company's profitability was meagre, the difference being the pool of fixed costs. The MD thus suggested that the firm should be constructed so that it fitted the contribution margin calculation, a translation that created visibility for the direct gross profit of a product, but which paid little attention to the pool of fixed costs in the factory.

Drawing on the Contribution Accounting System (CAS), the MD proposed to translate fixed overhead costs into variable costs, which CAS can easily monitor. Through a movement towards outsourcing of intermediate products and services that were previously produced within the factory, their costs would be counted only as variable cost. The fixed element would be extracted, and services and intermediary products would be variable costs monitored by CAS. There would be another implication: less factory capacity would be needed and the fixed costs would consequently be reduced. A central effect of outsourcing would be the translation of fixed overhead costs into variable costs, which would change the production process to fit a CAS image of the world.

The factory manager fought back. However, he did not do it by marketing his abilities to manage the shop floor, which would have been reasonable given his historical success. Rather, he developed (the contours of) a new accounting model: an Activity Based Costing (ABC) system, which would account in greater detail for the consumption of resources in the factory. Via ABC, he suggested, it would be possible to make use of the indirect resources which made fixed overhead costs visible. This could be information about resources needed to plan, to coordinate, to adapt products to customer wishes, to monitor and control quality, and to develop rush-orders. The ABC information would make the economics of flexibility visible.

In this way, the factory manager was not only bringing the resources behind the fixed costs to light, he was also proposing a completely new problematization of the boundaries of the firm. The ABC system permitted an integration of even more shop-floor operations into the factory because it promised detailed insight and thus more effective management activity. It could help to decrease outsourcing and increase insourcing. Instead of making the factory smaller, the ABC system could make it larger. The manager justified this suggestion by saying that if all production activities were located in a geographical proximity, bottlenecks would be less troublesome and the factory system would become faster and more responsive.

This story shows that accounting inscriptions lead towards large questions that extend far beyond the set of traces that comprise the inscriptions. They allow managers to account for many more things than are counted. Both CAS and ABC calculations alluded to the boundaries of the company and its relations to subcontractors. While CAS extended environmental relations and minimized in-house production, the ABC modelled largely in the opposite direction, with the suggestion that the factory should grow in size and that subcontractors ought to be avoided. At stake was the boundary of the company, which would become an effect of the work of the accounting inscription.

It is noteworthy that the factory manager needed another accounting inscription to resist or problematize CAS. Merely to dislike an accounting inscription was not enough; even a past record of results generally defined as successful was not enough. In order to challenge one accounting inscription, one must produce an alternative (see also Mouritsen et al. 2009). This new accounting inscription was not predicated on its being a superior descriptive account of the company; it was justified by its ability to make the company visible in a new way which requires the strategies of the company to be reassessed. In other words, each accounting inscription makes the company a different object of investment, and a different object of management, by moulding the firm via its construction of visibility.

THE OBJECT OF MANAGEMENT

The examples we have presented illustrate the ambiguous relationships between managers and objects material things, machines, and technologies. Solid and complex objects often appear too strong for managers, who, for purposes of intervention and control must translate them into something malleable, mouldable, and simple. In order to make complex and hard things simple and soft, managers need another type of object—management technologies—which are mediators allowing them to operate on the material world from a distance.

These vignettes helped us to explore insights developed earlier by Anthony Hopwood. He pointed out that accounting systems act as mediators and change organizations rather than mirror them:

> The particular visibilities created by accounting systems and the means by which they, in turn, shifted perceptions of organizational functioning, mediated the recognition of problems and the options available for their resolution, and infused the patterns of language, meaning and significance within the organization. (1987: 228)

Our examples illustrate this point and extend it to other type of objects and quasi-objects, among which the accounting inscription plays a central role in contemporary management.

Protection from the Insubordination of Things

Managers have two strategies for defending themselves from the insubordination of material things and technologies. One is to make material objects and technologies that offer resistance malleable. They cannot do this directly, but must insert mediators, which help to translate the material technology into something else. The MD who mobilized a CAS attempted to change the factory's organization, its inter-organizational supply chain and its relationship with customers. Without CAS, the MD would hardly be able to problematize current production affairs, which appeared to be successful by standards of responsiveness and flexibility. The CAS would allow the MD to transform the factory from a large black box to a small link in a large supply chain. Suddenly, production matters and organizational arrangements were not solid and concrete, but mouldable objects.

Another strategy used in this situation is to extend the chain of mediators between the object and managers. If material objects cannot be made malleable, at least they can be kept at bay. Telephones, secretaries, and technicians protect managers from large machines and unrulable computers. A technology in operation is daunting, and getting as far away from it as possible appeals to managers; in its proximity they are pushed or pulled by its work.

Managers Construct New Objects to Manage

So, instead of managing objects directly, managers manage indirectly through mediators. These are often new objects, which create new contexts for new actions. When analysts and investors look at an investment possibility, they not only try to avoid any direct contact with the technology; they also develop new mediators which define the contexts for technology anew. The model pursued by analysts and investors is used to gauge the context into which they seek to push the material technology. They seek assurance in the ambitions of the entrepreneur who applied for their financial resources; they strive to understand the market of a potentially reformed technology; they attempt to assess the manufacturability with a view to new reformations of technology; and they try to develop a phased model of finance. Much of this happens through mediators such as business plans, accounting statements and budgets, as well as more particular mediators such as feedback in yes/no statements from experts, each of whom has scrutinized part of the technology or of the market.

Analysts and investors draw on mediators in order to develop and gauge the context for the technology—yet not for the technology in its present form, but in its potential form. Such an activity will translate the technology into a quasi-object: a company that can develop, manufacture, and sell it. The technology undergoes change via its mediation through management technologies that guide its transformation into a company. The mediator makes the technology malleable.

The object to manage, then, is no longer the material technology, but its various inscriptions such as business plans, budgets, market reports, and technical feasibility studies. In sum, these diverse yet paper-based inscriptions comprise managerial objects—the objects that interest analysts and investors.

This is, in many ways, similar to managers' mobilization of HRM techniques, through which managers attempt to escape from having to account for the complexities of actual human beings. Instead, they identify only those aspects that allow new connections to be established—the connections among people and the connections between people and technology. Modern HRM approaches inscribe people not as persons but as resources and capabilities. This movement singles out and preserves only some aspects of the person and omits other, more difficult psychological and social ones. This is in itself a simplification of the management task. In addition, people redefined as resources and capabilities can be appended to other organizational objects and quasi-objects such as machines and business strategies. The unruliness of people is contained by making them objects that are fit to be related to other manageable objects.

Whereas people as complex persons offer resistance to management, the inscriptions of people offer only little complexity and therefore less resistance. Put on the table—in particular on the Talking Table—they can always be renegotiated, re-framed and inserted into new contexts. It is suddenly easy to manage people, because the friction of the complexity of the person evaporates.

Turning Complex Things and People into Separate Objects

Inscriptions help to simplify complex objects such as people, technologies, and organizations. Simplicity is gained by separating traits of the object and making them visible as separate entities. This separation enables a further recombination of elements into new ventures.

Separation allows control, because it simplifies. Even if things and people are connected in actual functioning, their separation into distinct objects is necessary in order for intervention to happen. Intervention occurs when something can be increased or decreased, when something can be added or subtracted, when something can be equipped with new properties, or when something can be inserted into new relationships. The process of separation was clearly visible in analysts' and investors' work to make a technology into a company, where the technology can be evaluated separately, for instance, as entrepreneurs' ambitions, as a stream of cash flows, as a possible market, and in terms of manufacturability. These separate evaluations provide cues for a possible future company.

Likewise, in HRM practices, separating the individual from the collective, and then separating the resources from the complex psychological and social dimensions of motivation and identity, allows a purified object to emerge which is easily combinable with other entities.

In all these cases, simplification happens through separation. Things, persons, skills, and actions, however, are not discrete in action. The inscriptions may separate and individualize so as to make objects of intervention, but this simplification comes at a cost. Managers have one more daunting task: to account for much more than accountants count for them! They must add things to the inscriptions and reintroduce new context to fit the inscriptions to the world. The MD who preferred a CAS to a responsive factory added many factors not directly inscribed in the accounting system. It did encourage making costs variable, but it did not show how customers were to be incorporated, how to select suppliers, and how to make new targets and contracts. There was a huge set of complexities that was absent from the inscription and which returned as the chain of translations began.

Such an *excess of reality* (Baudrillard 2003; Klein 2007)[6] is in tension with apparent stability and durability of management technologies. Objects and people will not go away, and the process of turning them into manageable objects may continue endlessly. Managers who believe that things are simple intermediaries that can be settled once and for all may do better to understand

---

[6] Baudrillard and Klein after him, use the term to denote that what is happening but cannot be accounted for within the existing frames of reference.

that they are mediators that translate and in translation often distort, which is why they not only help, but also lure and betray.

REFERENCES

Baudrillard, J. (2003). *The Spirit of Terrorism.* London: Verso.

Beer, M., and Spector, B. (1985). Corporate wide transformations in human resource management. In R.E. Walton and P.R. Lawrence (eds.), *Human Resource Management, Trends and Challenge.* Boston, Mass.: Harvard Business School Press, 219–53.

Czarniawska, B. (1985). *Controlling Top Management in Large Organisations: Poland and USA.* Aldershot: Gower.

—— (2002). *A Tale of Three Cities, or The Globalization of City Management.* Oxford: Oxford University Press.

—— (2004). On time, space and action nets. *Organization,* 11(6): 773–91.

—— and Hernes, T. (eds.) (2005). *ANT and Organizing.* Malmö/Copenhagen: Liber/CBS.

—— and Sevón, G. (eds.) (1996). *Translating Organizational Change.* Berlin: de Gruyter.

—— —— (eds.) (2005). *Global Ideas.* Malmö/Copenhagen: Liber/CBS.

Edwards, D., Ashmore, M., and Potter, J. (1995). Death and furniture: The rhetoric, politics and theology of bottom line arguments against relativism. *History of Human Sciences,* 8(2), 25–49.

Hopwood, A.G. (1987). The archaeology of accounting systems. *Accounting, Organizations and Society,* 12(3), 207–34.

—— and Miller, P. (eds.) (1994). *Accounting as Social and Institutional Practice.* Cambridge: Cambridge University Press.

Jacques, R. (1999). Developing a tactical approach to engaging with 'strategic' HRM. *Organization,* 6(2), 199–222.

Joerges, B., and Czarniawska, B. (1998). The question of technology, or how organizations inscribe the world. *Organization Studies,* 19(3), 363–85.

Klein, N. (2007). *The Shock Doctrine.* London: Allen Lane.

Knorr Cetina, K. (1981). *The Manufacture of Knowledge.* Oxford: Pergamon Press.

Latour, B. (1993). *We Have Never Been Modern.* Cambridge, Mass.: Harvard University press.

—— (1996). *Aramis, or the Love of Technology.* Cambridge, Mass.: Harvard University Press.

—— and Woolgar, S. (1979/1986). *Laboratory Life.* Princeton, N.J.: Princeton University Press.

Legge, K. (1989). Human resource management—A critical analysis. In J. Storey (ed.), *New Perspectives on Human Resource Management.* London: Routledge, 19–40.

Legge, K. (2005). *Human Resource Management: Rhetorics and Realities.* London: Palgrave Macmillan.

McKenzie, D., Muniesa, F., and Siu, L. (2007). *Do Economists Make Markets? On the Performativity of Economics*. Princeton, N.J.: Princeton University Press.

Meyer, J.W., and Scott, W.R. (1983). *Organizational Environments: Ritual and Rationality*. Beverly Hills, Calif.: Sage.

Mintzberg, H. (1973). *The Nature of Managerial Work*. Englewood Cliffs, N.J.: Prentice Hall.

Mouritsen, J. (1999). The flexible firm: Strategies for a subcontractor's management control. *Accounting, Organizations and Society*, 24(1), 31–55.

—— and Flagstad, K. (2005). The making of knowledge society: Intellectual capital and paradoxes of managing knowledge. In B. Czarniawska, and T. Hernes (eds.), *ANT and Organizing*. Malmö/Copenhagen: Liber/CBS, 208–29.

—— and Larsen, H.T. (2005). The 2nd wave of knowledge management: Re-centring knowledge management through intellectual capital information. *Management Accounting Research*, 16(3), 371–94.

—— Munk, N.J., Lindhart, J., and Stakemann, B. (2001). Klog kapital, social kapital og finansiel kapital: Episoder i formidlingen af kapital i videnøkonomien. *Ledelse and Erhvervsøkonomi*, 65(4), 199–215.

—— —— —— (2002). Kapitalmarkedet og videnøkonomien: Analytikernes repræsentationer og den videnbaserede virksomhed. *Finans/Invest*.

—— Hansen, A., and Hansen, Ø. (2009 forthcoming). Short and long translations: Management accounting calculations and innovation management. *Accounting, Organizations and Society*.

Tengblad, S. (2003). Classic, but not seminal: Revisiting the pioneering study of managerial work. *Organization Studies*, 25(4), 583–606.

Tichy, N., Fombrun, C., and Devanna, M.A. (1982). Strategic human resource management. *Sloan Management Review*, 23(2), 47–61.

Torrington, D., and Hall, L. (1987). *Personnel Management: A New Approach*. London: Hyperion Books.

Townley, B. (1994). *Reframing Human Rresource Management: Power, Ethics and the Subject at Work*. London: Sage.

9

Governance and Its Transnational Dynamics: Towards a Reordering of our World?

Marie-Laure Djelic and Kerstin Sahlin

INTRODUCTION

The transnationalization of our world, sometimes hastily labelled 'globalization', is not only—and far from it—about flows of goods, capital, or people. Nor is transnationalization simply a discourse even though it does have important discursive dimensions. Together with others, we suggest that our transnationalizing world is also defined by powerful dynamics of reordering. Some contributions point to the emergence of an 'audit society' where accounting and control become powerful social and institutional practices with an increasingly transnational scope (Hopwood and Miller 1994; Power 1997). Other contributions document the emergence and increasing density of a 'world of standards' (Brunsson and Jacobsson 2000; Tamm Hallström 2004). Others still provide evidence of a 'golden era of regulation' and regulatory activities (Levi-Faur and Jordana 2005; Djelic and Sahlin-Andersson 2006; Graz and Nölke 2008). All in all, what we witness is a profound redefinition of structuring frames for action and of normative and cognitive reference sets. Our transnationalizing world is a world where institutional rules of the game are in serious transition.

This chapter proposes an analytic reading of this powerful contemporary trend. We do emphasize the complex, progressive, and historical nature of this reordering process—a process still very much in the making. Our objective in this chapter, though, is to suggest that there are identifiable and shared mechanisms underlying transnational regulatory and governance dynamics— over and beyond the specifics of each regulatory story. The following two sections explore some of the existing literature and draw from there important theoretical insights. The next section suggests, in particular, the consequential impact on regulatory and governance dynamics of three related self-reinforcing spirals. In the second section of the chapter, we propose to re-appropriate the concept of field as a useful tool to capture the multi-level nature of regulatory and governance dynamics. Then we apply those structuring concepts to the phenomenon of transnational regulation and governance. This allows us to bring forward and describe some of the key and shared mechanisms characteristic of transnational regulatory dynamics. We end, in the conclusion, with a foray into notions of power and interest as we see them playing out in our reordering world.

REGULATORY ACTIVISM

Our reordering world is marked by more—not less—rule-making activity. The intensity of the latter is such, in fact, that it would probably be more accurate to talk of regulatory 'activism'. The proliferation of regulatory activities, actors, networks, or constellations leads to an explosion of rules and to the profound reordering of our world. An increasing share of this intense governance activity takes place between and across nations. Regulatory boundaries do not necessarily coincide anymore with national boundaries.

Regulatory activism with a transnational scope can go in at least two main directions. First, it can go towards the re-regulation of spheres of human action and interaction that had been regulated before at the national level. Second, it can mean the regulation of previously virgin territories.

The emergence and development of global standards for accounting and financial reporting is an interesting illustration of the first direction.[1] At the end of the Second World War, accounting standards were national sets of hard rules (and quite often in fact part of the formal code law system). In this sense they were important dimensions of national business systems and varied across states and regions of the world (Whitley 1999; Botzem and Quack 2006). There had already been some discussion around the harmonization of accounting standards in the early part of the twentieth century but with little result on the whole. After the Second World War, those discussions intensified and the next sixty years tell the story of the progressive and complex emergence and structuration of a transnational field of governance around

---

[1] This account is a brief summary of a long and complicated history. We build primarily on the empirical work done by Tamm Hallström (2004) and Botzem and Quack (2006) to structure this account.

accounting standards. This field proved multi-nodal and extremely fluid through time. Professional bodies and associations played an important role. But so did key private actors and accounting firms. Regulatory agencies, such as the Securities and Exchange Commission (SEC), international organizations like the OECD, or a supranational construction like the European Union (EU) were all also closely involved (Hopwood 1994; Botzem and Quack 2006). Throughout this period, multi-level interaction—where national regulators and actors met an emerging transnational body and logic—was a defining feature of the process (Botzem and Quack 2006, Loft et al. 2006). Ultimately, by the early years of the new millennium, new international accounting standards had been constructed and agreed upon—the International Financial Reporting Standards (IFRS). A few years later, those standards had spread throughout Europe and were poised to profoundly transform and even possibly displace national standards and codes of law (Botzem and Quack 2006). The main regulator today for accounting standards is transnational. The International Accounting Standards Board (IASB) is a London-based organization. It is privately funded and committed to developing, in the interest of the public, a set of high-quality, understandable and enforceable global accounting standards. The story is not over, though, and the main focus of a still fluid and multi-nodal field of governance has moved to the complex questions of implementation, interpretation, homogenization, community building, and the management of conflicts. National laws are being transformed to reflect those standards. And as national laws are being transformed, transnational standards may be adapted and hence in part translated and reworked to fit local specificities and contextualities. Hence, the current situation is one in which complex nets of regulators and regulations evolve in response and reactions to each other. This pattern of transnational regulatory formation is far from being specific to the accounting field. Rather, the emergence and development of transnational accounting standards is a typical illustration of contemporary regulatory dynamics. Parallel processes are at work in many other spheres of human action and interaction—such as education (Morgan and Engwall 1999; Hedmo and Wedlin 2008); health (Blomgren 2007); labour markets (Jacobsson 2004); or competition (Djelic and Kleiner 2006).

Regulatory activism could go in a second direction. It might mean an expansion into virgin territories—towards spheres of social life that were not regulated before. This is the case, for example, with environmental and pollution issues (Frank et al. 2000; McNichol and Bensedrine 2003; Power 2003; Engels 2006); ethical, social, and environmental aspects of corporate activities (e.g. Cutler et al. 1999; Kirton and Trebilcock 2004); the life and rights of animals (Forbes and Jermier 2002); administrative procedures

(Brunsson and Jacobsson 2000; Beck and Walgenbach 2002), or with the structuring of love and intimate relationships (Franck and McEneaney 1999).

Soft Regulation with Potentially Hard Consequences

Contemporary regulatory activism with a transnational scope is associated with a profound transformation of the nature of rule-making (Braithwaite and Drahos 2000). In a number of areas, the decline of state-centred control has tended to combine with the rise of an 'age of legalism' (Schmidt 2004). New regulatory modes—such as contractual arrangements, standards, rankings, and monitoring frames—are taking over and are increasingly being used by states themselves (Hood et al. 1999). In order to characterize more precisely this transformation, we can distinguish between four dimensions of regulatory developments: who is regulating, the mode of regulation, the nature of rules, and the nature of compliance mechanisms (cf. Baldwin et al. 1998). There have been developments and transformations along all four dimensions.

First, we note the multiplication of regulatory actors. Many new regulations are issued by states and intergovernmental bodies but there is an unmistakable expansion of regulatory constellations that transcend the state/non-state divide. This development cannot be described as a simple move from state to non-state regulation—but it is a development where state regulators are increasingly embedded in and interplay with many other regulatory actors. If we go back to the illustrative example of accounting standards, developments there clearly show the complexity of the regulatory constellation. The list of groups and organizations that have been involved through time is quite long! What is more the process itself led to the transformation of groups and organizations and even to the formation and structuration of new groups, committees, and organizations that then became actively involved. Amongst those 'new' actors, we naturally find the International Accounting Standards Committee (IASC; later IASB) but also the OECD Working Group on Accounting Standards, the UN Intergovernmental Working Group of Experts on International Standards of Accounting and Reporting, the EU's Accounting Advisory Forum, the International Federation of Accountants (IFAC), the International Organization of Securities Commissions (IOSCO), or the Fédération des Experts Comptables Européens (FEE) (Hopwood 1994).

With this development come changes in modes of regulation, in the nature of rules and also in the nature of compliance mechanisms. Regulation and rule-making in their contemporary form tend to emerge from complex and multi-nodal processes, where competition combines with collaboration and where negotiation plays an important role. The consequence is an explosion of 'soft rules' and 'soft law' (Mörth 2004). 'Soft law' does not displace 'hard law'—rather it adds on, complements, modifies, or reinforces it. Contemporary rule-making comes together with intense organizing and monitoring activities that sustain and reproduce emerging rules but also target adoption and implementation.

Many new rules are voluntary (Brunsson and Jacobsson 2000; Mörth 2004). This implies that those who are to comply should be attracted to following the rules rather than forced to do so. Some of the new regulatory regimes are constituted as 'markets' where the incentives for following rules are essentially financial. The new market for CO_2 emission rights is a good illustration (Engels 2006). Other rule systems are also structured as markets but with reputation, trust, and legitimacy as a combined set of incentives. This is the case with accreditation and rankings in management education (Hedmo et al. 2006), forestry certification schemes (McNichol 2006), or the UN global compact for corporate social responsibility (Sahlin-Andersson 2004). Compliance can also be obtained as new rules are presented as progressive and contributing to prosperity broadly understood—usually with reference to science and expertise—rather than as controlling tools. Quite often, compliance will also rest on socialization, acculturation, or normative pressures (cf. Scott 2004).

Even though soft rules are often voluntary, we still find in the background to their explosion the potential threat that states would come to issue harder rules—both more restrictive and less open to interpretation and adjustment by those following rules. In fact soft rules can be either a way to buffer the field from harder forms of regulation or a first step towards harder forms of regulation. This suggests important dynamics where regulations develop and expand in response and reaction to each other. These dynamics clearly involve power relations and structures of authority, including when the latter are hidden under the apparent neutrality of references to science and expertise.

Even when they lean on the shoulders of potentially harder modes of controlling, soft rules are typically formed in general terms. They are open, as a consequence, to negotiations and translations by those who are regulated. In fact, this form of regulation requires the active participation of those being regulated during the phase of interpretation but also at the moment of elaboration and during monitoring. Soft rules are generally associated with complex procedures of self-presentation, self-reporting, and self-monitoring.

A direct consequence of extended soft regulation is therefore a multiplication of resources put on formalized systems of self-presentation and monitoring in many organizations. This had been identified by Power (1997) in his studies of the audit society, as well as in recent writings on the US Sarbanes-Oxley Act and its impact (e.g. Power 2004, 2007). So, what could appear to be at first sight a 'softening' of the rule system in fact fosters most of the time extended re-regulation and increased organizing and formalization.

Governance with Governments

There is often an assumption that transnationalization and the opening of the world mean drastic reduction of rules everywhere—competition should favour the weakest governance orders. Evidence, though, does not confirm this (Brunsson and Jacobsson 2000; Levi-Faur and Jordana 2005; Djelic and Sahlin-Andersson 2006; Graz and Nölke 2008). Instead, as described above, the intensity of rule-making activity is high and if anything only increasing with an impressive overall progress of soft regulation, particularly with a transnational scope. We have moved well beyond a Westphalian world, where sovereign isolates (nation states) confront each other in an essentially anomic international arena. States, however, do not 'withdraw' but remain very much involved in what appears to be a profoundly changing regulatory game. The transnational world is characterized by increasing and intense 'governance with government'. Naturally, the recent financial crisis is likely to intensify this trend. Everywhere, the crisis is generating calls for even more regulation—and if possible regulation with more 'bite'. These calls are being heard within nation states but also in regional and transnational settings. They are being heard within both private and public spheres.

As they interact, the various kinds of actors involved in processes of rule-making tend to develop common forms and common identities. In the process, states are going through significant transformation. They become more business-like as they incorporate management tools and modes of organizing (e.g. Hood 1991). Non-profit and non-governmental organizations are also restructuring to become more business-like (e.g. Powell et al. 2006). Corporations, on the other hand, are expected to act as 'citizens' of global society (e.g. Zadek 2001). They are expected to claim and assume a degree of political power and responsibility. In general, the distinction between public and private (actors or sectors) is getting blurred and a clear tendency is for all actors involved to be increasingly defined, controlled, and governed as 'organizations' (Brunsson and Sahlin-Andersson 2000).

With this degree of multipolarity, expanded regulation reflects coordination and ordering ambitions. This is not a world where some units are assumed to have authority over others; instead relations among organizations are increasingly shaped in market terms (Djelic 2006). Monitoring tends to be done through mechanisms of socialization and on the basis of an increasingly rationalized global moral order (Boli 2006). This soft path to regulation should, however and as noted above, not always be taken at face value. Control remains an objective but is often hidden behind references to science and expertise (Drori and Meyer 2006). There are clear power games and power stakes in transnational governance fields. We certainly should neither miss nor neglect those. A seemingly paradoxical illustration is that states may in fact be increasing their power and influence, rather than 'withering away' as the literature often assumes. Indeed, as states form coalitions and constellations beyond their own borders; as they increasingly rely on neutralized discursive references to expertise and science, they can gain leverage both over local constituencies and in transnational arenas.

Consequential Incrementalism and Regulatory Spirals

This expanding regulatory activity with a transnational scope develops along a road that is both progressive and bumpy—with long moments of standstill, periods of backlash and an undeniable role for historical opportunities and chance. Institutional rules of the game do not change according to a pattern of punctuated equilibrium and radical ruptures. Instead this institutional change is often step-by-step, inscribed in long historical developments and generally associated with resistance, struggles, conflicts, negotiation, and cooperation. Institutional change is, in other words, an incremental process. However, incrementalism does not imply that the transformations generated would be only minor adaptations. Institutional change as it characterizes our contemporary transnationalizing world is both incremental and highly consequential, with a profound transformative impact (see also Djelic and Quack 2003; Streeck and Thelen 2005).

Transnational rule-making expands in part through self-reinforcing spirals. Regulation and the monitoring, evaluating, and auditing activities that come together with it only seem to breed greater needs and calls for still further rules and regulation. We identify three main associated spirals that altogether contribute to and feed the explosion of regulatory activity and activism. These three spirals are moved respectively by distrust, the question of responsibility and the associated search for control.

In line with previous research (Power 1997, 2004) we find that the movement towards expanded regulation is driven in part by a lack of trust. A diffuse distrust generates the need for activities that reveal, make transparent, and set rules, with a view to building more trust. Those activities, however, may in fact not only solve problems but also reveal and suggest new problems and new questions (Shapiro 1987). In the process, rather than building trust, they could be undermining it further, leading to still more requests for auditing, monitoring, and regulation. We suggest that this could be particularly true in the case of transnational governance as it is characterized by three specific features. First, the absence of a formal and sovereign holder of legitimacy in the transnational arena makes for the relative fragility of rules and monitoring activities. There is competition out there for claims to authority and the regulatory arena can be described as a regulatory market—where demand and offer stimulate and reinforce each other. Some of it may even have the feel of a market (regulatory) bubble! Second, in the absence of other legitimacy holders, science and expertise tend to impose themselves. There is quite an ambivalent relationship to science, however, in our societies. While science in general is legitimate and legitimating, individual experts and individual expressions of expertise are often contested. Third, this contestation is reinforced by the trend towards deliberative and participative democracy, so characteristic of our transnationalizing world. Deliberative democracy means expanded claims to be involved and contribute in rule-making and rule-monitoring. Ultimately, this is bound to generate regulatory or governance 'inflation'—where 'your' regulation fosters 'my' monitoring or counter-regulation, and so forth.

Hence, behind exploding regulatory and governance activities, one finds a distrust spiral (Power 1997, 2004). Partially connected, we also find a 'responsibility spiral'. Governance and regulation are in part about allocation of responsibility. When rules are precise and focused, responsibilities are relatively clear. With the multiplication of regulatory and governance activities, responsibilities get diffused and dispersed. The movement towards soft regulation has a tendency to reroute, furthermore, responsibility away from rule-setters and towards rule-followers. Voluntary rules that are open to translation mean that those who choose to follow the rules and to follow them in certain ways are held responsible. This double blurring of responsibilities may drive the need for regulation and governance still further and at the local level expanded soft regulation may foster a culture of defensiveness (see Power 2008). Organizational representatives then have to allocate extended resources not only to follow rules but also to explain why they choose to follow certain rules in particular ways or why they should not be held responsible.

A third mechanism feeding the spiral has to do with the search for control. The transnational world is a world in motion, with unclear and shifting boundaries and organizations in flux. On the regulatory market, the way to reach control or to react to regulations that are not favourable to one's position and strategy is essentially to organize and drive a competing regulatory set-up. We find examples of this in the field of management education (Hedmo et al. 2006). When European business schools realized that US accreditation and ranking systems increasingly shaped the norms for what counted as good management education, they reacted. Feeling marginalized within the existing governance frame, they structured and defined competing and complementary ranking and accreditation systems. Similar control spirals have emerged in many areas, particularly with the development of the EU and of a European identity. In a world where transnational regulation is expanding, the way to seek control is not by avoiding regulation. A more promising strategy is active involvement to issue and support an alternative and more satisfactory regulatory scheme!

CAPTURING MULTI-LEVEL DYNAMICS—THE FIELD CONCEPT

The expansive and self-reinforcing spirals identified above are fed by a number of mechanisms that reflect at one extreme individual, localized action and at another broad macro-institutional pressure. To go further in our understanding of those mechanisms, we therefore need a conceptual framework that can capture the multi-level dynamics of transnational rule-making. We suggest that the concept of field, if properly used, can be a useful theoretical tool allowing us indeed to capture interplays across levels.

Although the concept of field has become immensely popular in social sciences, it is rarely scrutinized in details (but see Martin 2003, Mohr 2005). In practice, many studies tend to reduce fields to networks of actors and interactions. This, we argue, is neither enough nor satisfying. We need to find ways to combine and integrate studies of individual behaviours, studies of interactions and processes, together with studies of institutional and cultural forces—the latter shaping and structuring both patterns of behaviours and patterns of interactions. We find guidance and insight in the exploration of different but complementary meanings of the field concept that have been developed and used in social sciences.

Fields as Spatial and Relational Topographies

Variants of the field concept reveal inspiration from different disciplines. Kurt Lewin (1936, 1951) was a pioneer of the introduction of the field concept into the social sciences. His socio-psychological conceptualization built upon a combination of insights drawn from *gestalt* theory and theoretical physics. Striving to embrace the complexity of the world, he defined fields as the 'totality of coexisting facts which are conceived of as mutually interdependent' (Lewin 1951: 240). Physics inspired him to develop a topological model—a spatial view—that could depict this mutual interdependence and enable him to identify 'everything that affects behaviour at a given time' (1951: 241).

From there, one line of development has been towards the modellization of topographies understood essentially as relational fields. While we certainly acknowledge the methodological contribution of complex mathematical modellization (see also Martin 2003; and Mohr 2005), we argue that it is important not to close the conceptual black box too early. A formalization that comes too early may lead us to disregard rather than embrace complexity, all the more if that complexity is dynamic.

The introduction of the notion of organization has been another way to go. A topography populated by organizations is—to use a concept developed by Emery and Trist (1965)—a 'ground in motion' and should not be reduced to a mere geographical and relational space. Warren (1967), following upon Emery and Trist (1965), coined the concept of interorganizational field and outlined the complex texture of interactions and relations in fields where organizations shape and structure individual decisions and behaviours. With a focus on community-level planning organizations in three cities, however, his field concept became closely associated with the notion of territory and geographical space. His topography remained mostly a relational one. Furthermore, Warren's perspective on the interorganizational field still started from a focus on organizations and their importance. Studies of fields have in fact only rarely considered the organizing aspects of fields—over and beyond organizations and their interactions (cf. Greenwood et al. 2008). Hence, we still need to know more about field-level organizing processes, how they develop and how they come to have an impact on fields and their members.

Bringing in the Missing Dimension—the Notion of Force

On the whole, this limited understanding of topography—in its spatial and relational dimensions—has had a tendency to prevail in social scientific uses of the concept of field. However, if we take the notion of field seriously, then this limited understanding is not satisfying. We need to develop a theoretical toolbox allowing us to find how spatial and relational dimensions in field topography relate to the other key notion running through field theories in physics—the notion of force. In physics, the notion of force goes back to Newton's work on gravity and Maxwell's formalization of the electromagnetic field (Pire 2000; Martin 2003). In social sciences, this notion was creatively blended with a focus on cultural and meaning aspects—first by Kurt Lewin and Pierre Bourdieu, soon relayed by certain strands of neo-institutional theory.

Bourdieu (1977, 1984) argued that fields were held together by common beliefs in the importance of certain activities. Coherent patterns of action and meaning thus developed, even without any single actor or group of actors intentionally striving for coherence or conformity. Fields, however, are also systems of relationships and resources where dominant actors occupy central positions whilst peripheral actors continuously seek greater influence and a more central position. The struggle is in great part about and around what are and/or what will be the structuring patterns of meaning and action, the dominant frames and understandings in the field. Peripheral actors challenge dominant understandings, which they try to modify and/or displace. Central actors have a tendency to protect and defend the status quo. They may envision to bend and adapt dominant understandings somewhat, if only to anchor and stabilize them further.

When the notion of force was brought into the neo-institutional theoretical fold, it was often in association with Weberian ideas of rationalization, 'iron cage' and spheres of value. Meyer and Rowan (1977) and DiMaggio and Powell (1983), the latter explicitly using the terminology of iron cage and field, emphasized the fact that organizations may have a great deal in common and develop in similar ways without ever being in direct contact with one another. Thus, the analysis of organizational and institutional change should not focus only on interactions between organizations but also on those cultural and normative forces that foster homogenization in a more indirect and diffuse manner. Scott and Meyer (1983) revisited and recombined Warren's (1967, 1972) work on interorganizational fields to talk about the duality of space and meaning associated with the organization and development of societal sectors.

The neo-institutionalist project has from there evolved essentially in two directions. On the one hand, in a significant number of studies, the focus on meaning has been lost. As Mohr (2005: 22) puts it, commenting on this evolution:

While the project as a whole is conditioned on the assumption that it is the meaningfulness of space that matters, in its implementation it is the space itself (seen now as system of communicative structures) which is actually revealed through empirical analysis. Demonstrations of the homogenization of organizational structure are used again and again as a way to prove the existence and efficacy of these communicative pathways. The meanings embedded inside these institutional objects are left unexamined.

A partial explanation to this evolution is probably a methodological one. Territories, interactions and relationships are (relatively) easy to observe and measure while cultural frames and patterns of meaning are more complex to capture. As a consequence, there is a distinct tendency in neo-institutional literature to 'create a spatial metaphor that privileges the structures of communication over the actual meanings that flow through these structures. As a result, the communicative channels in an organizational field are not analysed in a way that enables these meanings to be treated as constitutive of the field itself' (Mohr 2005: 22).

While this has clearly been the dominant trend, there is nevertheless another path—and this is to focus on meanings. Certain institutionalists have tried, in particular, to understand how cultural frames, ideas, or patterns of meaning shape and constitute new structures and new modes of action and interaction across the world (e.g. Meyer and Scott 1983; Thomas et al. 1987; Meyer et al. 1997). The risk there, as Mohr also notes, is for spatial and relational dimensions to disappear and be evacuated. The very existence of a spatial field and the role of networks and relational patterns are in a sense wiped out by the strength and power of diffuse cultural and meaning templates.

Ultimately, it seems that we still lack the conceptual tools to investigate the duality and interplay of meaning and space as constitutive of fields. There is a need to revive the institutionalist focus on this duality. In fact, we propose to go one step further. We understand fields as complex combinations of spatial and relational topographies with powerful structuring forces in the form of cultural frames or patterns of meaning. Hence, we see the need to integrate and combine three (and not two) dimensions as constitutive of fields—the spatial, the relational, and the meaning dimensions.

INSTITUTIONAL DYNAMICS IN FIELDS OF TRANSNATIONAL GOVERNANCE

We propose to look at transnational regulation and governance in the making through a revisited field perspective. Fields do have spatial dimensions. However, in fields of transnational regulation and governance, spatial topographies are both complex and fluid. Spatial topographies in this context cross over traditional territorial boundaries, rendering obsolete older lines of demarcation in particular between local, national, and transnational spaces. Spatial topographies in fields of transnational governance look like patch-works, or even better, kaleidoscopes. They are fragmented rather than unified; a juxtaposition of multiple sub-topographies that collide and sometimes overlap. They are also highly fluid and constantly evolving. Furthermore, those spatial dimensions are not necessarily territorial. There is, for example, a spatial dimension to negotiations structured by international organizations that is by nature extraterritorial.

Fields of transnational governance are also relational topographies. They imply, reflect and are partly constituted by and through networks. In that context the meanings of 'networks' and 'relational topographies' are broad and highly encompassing. First, networks do not connect only individuals, but also organizations, groups, or even networks. While we should not disregard the importance of interpersonal networks, including in a trans-national world, we should also wonder how those interpersonal networks articulate with other types of networks (connecting organizations, groups, or networks)—the result being complex and multidimensional relational top-ographies. Moreover, relational topographies can imply varying degrees of direct contact and interaction. In fields of transnational governance, rela-tional topographies could be combinations of tightly knit kin or family clans with virtual networks where members may never meet or exchange and are only indirectly connected.

Finally, fields of transnational governance are fields of forces. Those fields are crossed and structured by powerful institutional forces that altogether constitute, we propose, a transnational culture or meaning system.

Just like any other, fields of transnational governance are naturally also battlefields. Building upon Bourdieu, we want to move away from the idea of benign cooperation generally associated with the concept of networks. Instead, we underscore the power and struggle dimensions of relational topographies where dominant actors occupy central positions and peripheral actors constantly struggle for greater influence and power. At the same time, these power struggles are framed by institutional forces and dynamics that can reflect hegemonic logics (Gramsci 1971; Foucault 1991). Hence, relational power games need to be looked at in the context of structuring fights for hegemony building.

Institutional Forces or the Meaning Dimension

The regularities of transnational regulatory dynamics stem in great part from a set of institutional forces that increasingly and progressively structure fields of transnational governance. Those institutional forces are powerful, and in a sense paradigmatic, rules of the game for contemporary regulatory and associated organizing and monitoring activities.

The first such institutional force is scientization—the 'extraordinary and expansive authority of modern scientific rationalization' as revealed in the overwhelming role and presence in our contemporary world of scientific agencies, scientists, scientific products, and argumentation (Drori and Meyer 2006). A sub-dimension of scientization is the strong drive towards measurement and quantification. Expertise and the legitimacy of science have a tendency to express themselves in figures, measurement, and statistical relations. The ontology, methods and models characteristic of mathematics, physics, and natural sciences have all but triumphed. They have a tendency to be purely and simply conflated with 'science', marginalizing as it were alternative understandings of scientific endeavor.

A second institutional force, increasingly shaping fields of transnational governance and transnational regulatory dynamics, is marketization (Djelic 2006). The powerful contemporary marketization drive reflects a belief that markets are superior arrangements for the allocation of goods and resources and this in every sphere of economic, social, or even cultural and moral life. This 'belief' in markets is itself institutionalizing fast and, as a consequence, markets are increasingly defined and perceived as the 'natural' way to organize and structure human interactions. The recent financial and economic crisis certainly represents a challenge to this marketization trend. It might altogether, and quite radically, lead to a reorientation towards alternative forms of economic organization and coordination. More likely, though, markets are there to stay but they will have to combine with, and accept, to a greater extent, external forms of regulation and control.

Organizing is a third institutional force highly structuring of fields of transnational governance and of regulatory dynamics. Organizing is a way to create order transnationally in the absence of a world state and of a world culture (Ahrne and Brunsson 2006). In our transnational world, it often takes the particular form of 'meta-organizing', where organizations are structured, coordinated, and controlled largely through 'soft' kinds of rules and regulatory processes.

A fourth institutional force we term moral rationalization. Rationalized and scientized assessment and celebration of virtue and virtuosity become increasingly prominent in the transnational public realm and act as a powerful sustaining and structuring force of transnational governance and regulatory dynamics (Boli 2006).

Deliberative democracy is a fifth institutional force shaping the context of transnational governance and regulatory dynamics. The transnational world is increasingly permeated by a view of democracy that emphasizes dialogue and deliberation and the autonomy of participating actors (Mörth 2006). A sub-dimension associated with deliberative and participative democracy is the explosion and expansion of soft forms of governance.

Reinforcing Interplays

Those five institutional forces and the two associated sub-dimensions are closely intertwined; in fact they nurture and foster each other. Scientization, for example, is often an important background to the contemporary elaboration of soft regulation or the rationalized celebration of virtue and virtuosity (Boli 2006). Meta-organizations rely on soft regulation—standardization in particular, often quite closely coupled with measurement and quantified objectives. Deliberative democracy and discussions around soft regulation generate 'markets' for rules—and therefore reinforce the marketization trend. The progress of marketization has, in turn, a tendency to rely on both formal organizing and scientized expertise as a two-dimensional backbone. The spread of markets and marketization in many different spheres of social life also suggests open participation and 'free' or competitive involvement, pushing even further the trend towards deliberative democracy and soft regulation. The disclosure and transparency associated with deliberative democracy and soft regulation are often further rationalized and can even be articulated with formal celebrations of virtue and virtuosity. As to moral rationalization, it is generally revealed and expressed through sustained organizing efforts.

The close and mutually reinforcing interplay between those institutional forces generate, we propose, a highly structured and ordered world. Despite the absence of a world culture and political order, we find in fact a tight and constraining frame. Institutional forces should not be treated as external to the actors—as representing an environment to which actors are merely adapting. Rather, they are constitutive of the actors. Institutional forces frame and constitute organizations and individuals—their interests, values, structures, contents and meaning, activities, and the nature and form of their interactions. There is another sense in which institutional forces are not external to actors and activities. If one adopts a long-term perspective, they reflect and express the aggregation of strategies, interests, and activities of multiple individuals and groups through time. They have been historically and progressively constructed, even if they tend today to function as an external and progressively hardening 'iron cage' (Weber 1978).

From Battlefields to Stabilization?

The five institutional forces identified above and their two associated sub-dimensions are sometimes colliding and conflicting with other institutional sets—generally structured at a national level. Those national institutional systems are still powerful systems of constraints—localized ones for the most part but with a potential reach, at least for some, in other geographical spaces (Westney 1987; Djelic 1998). Building again on the physics metaphor, we view this as the confrontation of different fields of forces. In some cases, forces will work in parallel or similar directions. In other cases, they will counter each other and there will be powerful resistance. Altogether, though, we identify three broad tendencies in the dynamics of institutional forces today. First, the progress of the five institutional forces identified above is quite fast on the whole and probably only accelerating because of the mutually reinforcing interplays described before. Second, this institutional frame is not potent and powerful only in fields of transnational governance and in the context of transnational regulatory dynamics. Its impact is progressively being felt, in both direct and indirect ways, in governance processes that remain for various reasons still strongly national or local. Third, behind those institutional forces, their competition and their struggles, there are individuals, groups, organizations, or networks; sets of colliding and conflicting interests; and interactions and power plays.

When considered together and in their interaction, these institutional forces are increasingly turning into meta-rules of the game for governance and rule-making in our world. The structuring we are talking about is essentially of a normative and cognitive kind. This meta-institutional frame sets and defines a 'meaning' or 'cultural' system that constrains the way we think and talk about governance, the way we undertake, negotiate, and structure it, the way we sustain and reproduce it—across, between, but also, increasingly, within national boundaries. Thus, these institutional forces and dynamics also frame and shape the more visible power struggles that we can identify and document as we study interactions among people, organizations, and nations. This institutional frame, this meaning or cultural system and its components follow the route of all institutional sets. They progressively become taken for granted and as it were fade in the background and become 'invisible'.[2] This transnational culture increasingly sets and defines the 'natural' way of doing, acting and being—and even resistance, reaction, and

---

[2] Robert K. Merton (1957) talked about 'obliteration by incorporation' to describe very similar dynamics of knowledge appropriation and assimilation.

protest activities tend to express and inscribe themselves within rather than outside the institutional frame.

It is interesting, in that respect, to consider the anti-globalization movements that define themselves as strong critiques of the logics of transnationalization. Many features of anti-globalization movements in reality reinforce, rather than question, the advancing transnational meaning and cultural system presented here (see, e.g., Keraghel and Sen 2004). Anti-globalization movements are highly organized, very much along meta-organization principles. Anti-globalization movements have appropriated, for themselves and their own functioning, claims to deliberative democracy and soft regulation and they even refer to expertise and science. Finally, they also make use of the tools associated with moral rationalization to build and diffuse their critique.

Topography or the Spatial Dimension

Fields of transnational governance are undeniably fields of forces—and, as we discussed above, highly structured ones. Those fields, however, also have a spatial dimension.

The Notion of Space and its Evolution

The notion of 'governance space' could have two main dimensions. First, the term could refer to the space where governance is being constructed. Second, the term could refer to the space where governance applies. A clear analytical and empirical differentiation between those two dimensions would point towards a sharp separation between rule-makers and rule-followers. In a Westphalian world, this separation would tend to be particularly marked. In a Westphalian world, furthermore, the horizon would remain essentially national. The space where governance was constructed would broadly follow the contours of the nation state and political administration. The space where governance applied would be tightly congruent with a particular national territory or subparts thereof.

In a transnationalizing world, the spatial dimension of governance and regulatory dynamics appears to be much more complex, fluid, and multidimensional. First, the notion of space is not always or systematically associated with a political and geographical territory. Governance spaces can range all the way from referring to a geographical and political territory, to an organizationally structured arena marked by a degree of physical reality (i.e. buildings) or, finally, to virtual spaces structured through a combination of technology and cognitive frames. Second, governance spaces are neither unitary nor centralized as this would be the case in a Westphalian scenario where the nation state would essentially represent the governance kernel. Rather governance spaces in a transnational world are decentred and multi-centred, or even fragmented. A multiplicity of governance and regulatory initiatives are often going on in parallel—in complex patterns of cooperation, competition, or simple juxtaposition. Third, governance spaces have a horizon that is not, by far, simply national. The boundaries of governance are increasingly porous and blurred. Governance spaces span multiple levels—the subnational, the national, and the transnational—and a sharp differentiation between those levels becomes in fact increasingly less meaningful and useful. Fourth, and finally, the analytical separation between a space where governance is constructed and a space where governance applies becomes less relevant in a transnational world. There is, here also, a blurring of categories and boundaries. Rules are increasingly being constructed, at least in part, by those who will then have to follow them. The active involvement, if not dominance, of large accounting firms in developing and harmonizing accounting standards may be the clearest example of this (Hopwood 1994; Botzem and Quack 2006).

At the same time, however, even if boundaries are blurring and easily crossed, those different levels remain a reality of sort. They are always present—to be used and brought up when necessary in the interest of actors seeking influence, as tools to allocate blame and responsibility or as excuses to avoid difficulties and liabilities. Sub-national, national, and international levels in other words largely become discursive categories at the disposal of actors, to be used as they take part in transnational, national, or local governance games.

Who are the Actors?

Transnational governance spaces are densely populated. There is a large and in appearance always increasing number of actors involved in regulation and associated organizing and monitoring activities. Regulation and governance breed even more regulation and governance. This in itself explains in part the explosion in the sheer numbers of actors involved. We have seen, though, that the evolution of regulatory modes, leading to the widespread diffusion of softer types of rules, fosters regulatory competition—and as such is also a factor explaining the multiplicity of actors involved.

Out of this diversity and multiplicity, we can still differentiate between four broad categories. The first category contains those actors that are parts of or directly associated with nation states and political administrations. States and administrative units have undeniably lost their monopoly position over regulation (Knill and Lemkuhl 2002; Jacobsson and Sahlin-Andersson 2006). Nevertheless, they remain powerfully involved in regulatory and governance processes. We even find two particular and quite consequential roles for those types of actors. First, in many governance stories, an endorsement by states and/or administrative units gives much greater clout and strength to a set of rules, particularly when it comes to local and national adoption and implementation. In the story of accounting standards recounted above, what was originally soft-rule was hardened when the EU rendered compliance mandatory (for January 2005). Then, the relay at the level of nation states was undeniably important and increased the legitimacy of this major regulatory revolution. Second, the threat of coercion undeniably remains a resource in the hands of states even in times so clearly characterized by soft and interactive forms of regulation and governance.

In the second category of actors, we can put international organizations of a public nature and transnational political constructions—the IMF, the World Bank, the GATT, and later the WTO, the OECD, or the various avatars of the EU amongst others. It is undeniable that the role, place, and clout of this second category of actors have increased powerfully and significantly, particularly since the end of the Second World War. Those international or transnational arenas and organizations have fostered and stimulated the generation of transnational governance. The explosion of transnational governance has in turn stabilized and reinforced those actors, their power, and their reach.

A third category brings together what we call here 'reinvented old actors'. A general trend is for former 'rule-takers' and 'rule-followers' to increasingly be involved in governance processes. A consequence is that many economic and societal actors have to reinvent themselves as active participants in transnational governance. Universities, corporations, the media, or professions are striking exemplars of those actors who reinvent themselves. From rule-takers and rule-followers, who sometimes tried to bypass and go around externally imposed regulation and constraints—those actors have to turn into governance co-constructors in spaces that span multiple levels. This, of course, has profound implications for the features and competences that those actors need to develop (e.g. Botzem and Quack 2006; Morgan 2006).

The fourth category contains what we broadly call 'new' actors. By 'new' we essentially mean two things. Those actors—organizations, networks, or entities—can be 'new' in terms of their structures, features, and qualities. They can also be 'new' in the sense of having stood until then quite far away from regulatory and governance activities. They could as well naturally be 'new' on both counts. Non-governmental organizations, whether national or international, enter into this category. They are becoming increasingly important and powerful actors of transnational governance (Boli and Thomas 1999; Cutler et al. 1999; Mörth 2004). Standards or experts organizations, here again with a national and/or a transnational dimension, have also exploded (Brunsson and Jacobsson 2000), following upon and reinforcing at the same time the scientization trend identified above. We would also like to point to another type of 'new' actors that we propose to call 'transnational communities of interest'. The IASC—later Board, IASB (Bozem and Quack 2006) is one such actor that played a crucial if not dominant role in developing and spreading global accounting standards. We find similar transnational communities of interest in other areas of transnational governance—the community of central banks and central bankers (Marcussen 2006), the International Competition Network (Djelic and Kleiner 2006), the AACSB or efmd (Hedmo et al. 2006) or the Forest Stewardship Council (McNichol 2006). This type of entity is somewhere in between an epistemic and expert community, a profession and a meta-organization and a combination of all those. It has a transnational nature and dimension by construction and it spans and bridges national boundaries.

We propose that this type of actor is an important element of contemporary regulatory dynamics. Transnational communities of interest can bridge the boundaries between public and private spheres and actors—as the cases of the International Competition Network, the IASC, and the efmd all illustrate. Those transnational communities of interest tend to be expansive and missionary in the sense that their *raison d'être* is to rally around a project not only their members but also potentially well beyond. Interestingly, the expansive and sometimes highly inclusive nature of those 'actors' means that they can turn, from regulatory actors, into regulatory spaces.

The Relational Dimension

Transnational regulatory dynamics are hence highly structured by institutional forces. But they also reflect a richly populated spatial topography. This combination generates a partly paradoxical situation—where activities, interplays, and interactions are extremely intense in what is ultimately a fairly constrained and rigid landscape.

Paradoxical Dynamics...

Governance and rule-making are characterized in our transnational world by intense activity and activism, by dense and multidirectional interplays and interactions. We have seen above some of the main mechanisms behind that level of activity. At the very same time, though, it appears that the more intense and dense activities and interplays become, the more they are working towards the strengthening and stabilization of those structuring institutional forces identified above.

There is, in fact, a paradoxical loop here. Meta-rules of the game, as they progressively stabilize foster the development of regulatory activities and the intensification of interplays. This happens through the diffusion of market-ization, organizing, and deliberative democracy principles that justify and call for multiple and multidirectional involvements and initiatives. The move-ments thus generated can appear at first sight relatively chaotic. Steps are taken in many different directions and the rhythm seems to be constantly accelerating. However, the combination of different transnational regulatory stories points to an emergent and stabilizing order. The intensity of activities and the density of interplays reinforce, in the end, the meta-rules of the game and the institutional 'cage' in which transnational governance appears to be set. This means that a lot of what, at first sight, seems to be regulatory competition should ultimately be reinterpreted as many steps pushing in a parallel, if not the same, direction. Competition in the short term contributes, in other words, to the emergence of collective stabilization in the longer term.

We therefore propose a reading of transnational regulatory arenas as highly constrained and constraining fields—if not monolithic ones—with an intense surface activity that tends to generate and reproduce order behind an appear-ance of complexity and competition. The longitudinal study of the reordering of the accounting standards field provides a vivid illustration of this. At a first level, Botzem and Quack (2006) document a multiplicity of initiatives, competing actors and efforts, a lot of back and forth movement, resistance, conflicts, and give and take. At the same time, they also point to standard-ization in the long term—accounting rules and standards progressively become more homogeneous, more similar, and compatible across and between national boundaries. This process of standardization both emerges through and reinforces further the intensity of activity.

... Often Unrecognized

A further finding is that this collective stabilizing tends not to be noticed by the actors involved while competitive pressures are being acutely perceived.

In fact, we would propose that intense competition at an apparent and superficial level tends to blind both actors themselves and most observers to the profound ordering and stabilization associated with meta-rules of the game. If we look at it this way, differences tend to become limited variations around a common theme. This is true of apparent conflict and competition of standards in a number of different fields—the case of accounting standards (Botzem and Quack 2006) or that of competition regulation (Djelic and Kleiner 2006) are two clear illustrations of this.

The literature on 'globalization' has had a tendency to picture our world as being highly complex and unpredictable, if not on the verge of 'chaos'. The emphasis on complexity and unpredictability appear, in fact, both in pros-elytizing accounts and in more critical analyses of 'globalization'. What we find is different. We find a world which is much more simple and orderly than it superficially appears. This order and simplicity stem from, and reflect, meta-rules of the game, a set of structuring institutional forces. Surface interactions and chaos are in fact deeply framed and tamed by those institutional forces. Complexity remains possible but it should be associated rather with developments that do not seem to be in focus with the structuring frame—and hence have the potential to question and disturb its progress. Unpredictability and chaos are also possibilities. As we understand it, though, they would seem to follow from radical contradiction and undermining of structuring forces rather than from visible power games in relational battlefields. It is still to be seen whether the recent crisis generates indeed such a radical rupture.

The same applies, we propose, to the notion of diversity. At a first level the topography of transnational governance suggests a rich pool of actors concerned with and to a greater or lesser degree involved in governance. Behind multiplicity, however, we also find significant progressive convergence. A central bank is much more like another central bank today than twenty years ago (Marcussen 2006). NGOs increasingly look alike—including when some work for and others against the same project. Hence, multiplicity is not necessarily synonymous with diversity and we argue that our transnationalizing world is characterized by a double and partly contradictory trend. The number of actors involved in and concerned by regulation and governance has increased. However, each 'species' or category of actors has had a tendency to become increasingly homogeneous, leaving less and less space to variation inside a given category. Even more, homogenization happens also across categories. Actors all tend to become rationalized organizations with a will and an identity of their own (Brunsson and Sahlin-Andersson 2000; Meyer and Jepperson 2000).

A Representation of Institutional Dynamics

To get at a real understanding of transnational regulatory dynamics, a challenge undeniably is to grasp how surface activity or activism generates background stability and how the progress of background stability fosters surface activity—in a self-reinforcing loop. This finding is represented visually in Figure 9.1, where we get a three strata cut on transnational governance fields. Those fields have a 'dark side'—the set of increasingly powerful institutional forces. Those forces are active and generate dense activity at the surface of the field but with ultimately a stabilizing and reinforcing impact for themselves. The 'dark side' or to use Merton's words (1957) the 'obliterated side' is thus labelled because it has a tendency to be invisible, undetected, and taken for granted.

Transnational governance fields have on the other hand a highly dynamic 'bright side', bright in the sense here of visible—that can be mapped and described. This bright side is made up of dynamic topographies of actors that negotiate, enact, transform, resist, translate, or embrace evolving rules of the game. The activity at that surface level is dense but increasingly powerfully set and embedded in, constrained and directed by, homogenizing meta-rules of the game. Institutional forces shape, constrain, and embed both dynamic topographies of actors and surface regulation. In their rule-setting and governance activities, dynamic topographies of actors express and enact, spread, further, stabilize and reproduce but also try to resist and potentially bend the

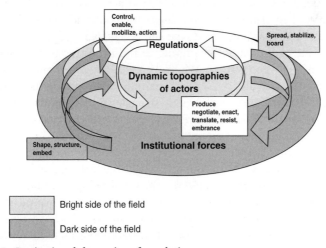

Figure 9.1. Institutional dynamics of regulations

institutional 'cage' in which they are more or less comfortably set and inscribed.

The struggle is increasingly unfair, though, we argue. On the bright side of the field, a lot of energy is spent on what are, ultimately, battles around minor variations. On the whole, the impact of activities that run parallel to and follow the structuring logic of meta-institutional forces can be quite real. Headlong battles against the increasingly stabilized meta-institutional forces are getting increasingly difficult, on the other hand, if not doomed from the start.

CONCLUDING REMARKS: POWER, INFLUENCE, AND HEGEMONY IN TRANSNATIONAL GOVERNANCE

As a last word, it seems important to go back and draw attention to issues of power, interests, and influence. Fields of transnational governance and transnational regulatory dynamics tend to wrap themselves in discursive references to efficiency and best practices—legitimized by science and measurement or market mechanisms and validated through rational benchmarks and scales. The discourse and self-presentation of actors involved in transnational governance processes is often highly neutralized—void of references to issues of power and interests.

We have emphasized, throughout this chapter, however, that the transnational dynamics of regulation include in fact contestation, struggle, and power plays. The elaboration and deployment of new types of regulatory frames are in great part interest-driven and reflect logics of power and control. Actors use the neutral language of science and expertise; they invoke coordination and a common good. When we consider governance processes in more detail, however, and take in the longitudinal dimension in particular, we find that those processes evolve with struggles and conflicts between self-interested actors and through the formation of coalitions and counter movements. Such processual studies also provide evidence that interests are not stable but that they are shaped and reshaped over time and across situations. The institutional embeddedness of actors—or the 'softness' of actors to use a term coined by John Meyer (1996)—does not mean in other words that interests are absent. Rather, what this suggests is that the shaping of interests and their evolution through time should also be subject to scrutiny and analysis. The background to relational forms of power itself reveals other forms of power and control, more indirect ones with a hegemonic potential. What is interesting and necessary in that context is to be able to combine a focus on power in its relational dimension with an interest for background hegemonic forms of control. Power relations are multilayered and we need to understand how those different layers of power—at the relational and institutional level—contradict or reinforce, mutually shape, and transform each other.

It is clear from our empirical evidence that the complexity of the transnational world does not always, far from it, block individual interests and activities. We often find the opposite—organizations or networks and even individual persons can become extremely powerful and influential as they navigate through the densely organized transnational world and gain significant leverage in the process. There can be different explanations to the strength of particular actors—size, network centrality, resources are all possibilities. As a concluding remark, though, we focus only on one other possible explanation that we label here the 'first mover advantage'.

This notion of 'first mover advantage' can be declined at many levels. Those who set and define the rules early on—or at least are involved at an early stage—are more likely to be able to influence the emergent regulation to their advantage, to fit and serve their own interests and to increase their position of power and capacity to control. There is another way in which the first mover advantage plays itself out. Those participating in the definition of the rules of the game are more likely to better understand the rules and to be able to manoeuvre within and around them. Knowledge means control and power and an understanding of the rules of the game gives a head start to those actors that were involved early on in rule-setting.

At the macro- and meta-level this takes on a particular dimension, we argue. There is a fair amount of evidence pointing to a 'first mover advantage' for the United States and for American actors in many fields of transnational governance. Detailed regulatory stories document a unique and often powerful role and place of American actors and blueprints in regulatory processes—both at the origins and at critical and key moments. Those stories also tell of reinforcing mechanisms whereby non-US actors often construe American blueprints as 'models' of development or modernization, or see those blueprints as a path towards and a 'promise of' international legitimacy and recognition.

Hence, the transnational regulatory explosion is, already at this level, an 'Americanization'. There is another sense, even more significant, in which the contemporary regulatory and governance explosion is a form of 'Americanization'. The institutional forces, the fundamental rules of the game of the rule-making process in our world have developed originally from within North-American society and system and thus their transnational diffusion also reflects the power and influence of American actors, groups, networks, organizations, and cultural and cognitive blueprints. This power and influence is particularly linked historically to the post-Second World War period and is associated in part with the threading of an international organizational net—key nodes being the World Bank, the IMF, the OECD, the United Nations and its satellites, the GATT, or the WTO.

The important consequence, naturally, is that American actors, organizations, and networks often have a head start in transnational governance fields that are shaped according to institutional principles with which they are in a sense 'genetically' familiar. The concept of hegemony (Gramsci 1971) is applicable here or as Foucault would put it 'power is everywhere; not because it embraces everything, but because it comes from everywhere' (Foucault [1978]1990: 93). These concluding reflections should encourage us to go beyond simple conceptions of power and/or hegemony. We should be looking further into the complex interplay of hegemonic logics and more classical and 'visible' resource and interest-based power games. There lays, we suggest, an important dimension of the institutional dynamics of contemporary regulation and governance.

REFERENCES

Ahrne, G., and Brunsson, N. (2006). Organizing the world. In M.L. Djelic and K. Sahlin-Andersson (eds.), *Transnational Governance: Institutional Dynamics of Regulation*. Cambridge: Cambridge University Press.

Baldwin, R., Scott, C., and Hood, C. (eds.) (1998). *A Reader on Regulation*. Oxford: Oxford University Press.

Beck, N., and Walgenbach, P. (2002). The institutionalization of the quality management approach in Germany. In K. Sahlin-Andersson and Engwall (eds.), *The Expansion of Management Knowledge: Carriers, Flows and Sources*. Stanford: Stanford University Press, 145–74.

Blomgren, M. (2007). The drive for transparency: Organizational field transformations in Swedish healthcare. *Public Administration*, 85(1), 67–82.

Boli, J. (2006). The rationalization of virtue and virtuosity in world society. In M.L. Djelic and K. Sahlin-Andersson (eds.), *Transnational Governance: Institutional Dynamics of Regulation*. Cambridge: Cambridge University Press.

——and Thomas, G. (eds.) (1999). *Constructing World Culture*. Stanford: Stanford University Press.

Botzem, S., and Quack, S. (2006). Contested rules and shifting boundaries: International standard setting in accounting. In M.L. Djelic and K. Sahlin-Andersson (eds.), *Transnational Governance: Institutional Dynamics of regulation*. Cambridge: Cambridge University Press.

Bourdieu, P. (1977). *Outline of a Theory of Practice.* Cambridge: Cambridge University Press.

—— (1984). *Distinction: A Social Critique of the Judgment of Taste.* Cambridg, Mass.: Harvard University Press.

Braithwaite, J., and Drahos, P. (2000). *Global Business Regulation.* Cambridge: Cambridge University Press.

Brunsson, N., and Jacobsson, B. (eds.) (2000). *A World of Standards.* Oxford: Oxford University Press.

—— and Sahlin-Andersson, K. (2000). Constructing organizations: The example of public sector reform. *Organization Studies*, 21, 721–46.

Cutler, A.C., Haufler, V., and Porter, T. (eds.) (1999). *Private Authority and International Affairs.* Albany: State University of New York Press.

DiMaggio, P., and Powell, W.W. (1983). The Iron Cage revisited: Institutional isomorphism and collective rationality in organizational fields. *American Sociological Review*, 48, 147–60.

Djelic, M.L. (1998). *Exporting the American Model.* Oxford: Oxford University Press.

—— (2006). Marketization: From intellectual agenda to global policy making. In M.L. Djelic and K. Sahlin-Andersson (eds.), *Transnational Governament: Institutional Dynamics of Regulation.* Cambridge: Cambridge University Press.

—— and Kleiner, T. (2006). The international competition network—Moving towards transnational governance. In M.L. Djelic, and K. Sahlin-Andersson (eds.), *Transnational Government: Institutional Dynamics of Regulation.* Cambridge: Cambridge University Press.

—— and Quack, S. (eds.) (2003). *Globalization and Institutions.* Cheltenham: Edward Elgar.

—— and Sahlin-Andersson, K. (eds.) (2006). *Transnational Governance: Institutional Dynamics of Regulation.* Cambridge: Cambridge University Press.

Drori, G., and Meyer, J. (2006). Scientization: Making a world safe for organizing. In M.L. Djelic, and K. Sahlin-Andersson (eds.), *Transnational Government: Institutional Dynamics of Regulation.* Cambridge: Cambridge University Press.

Emery, F., and Trist, E. (1965). The causal texture of organizational environments. *Human Relations*, 18(1), 21–32.

Engels, A. (2006). Market creation and transnational rule-making: the case of CO_2 emissions trading. In M.L. Djelic, and K. Sahlin-Andersson (eds.), *Transnational Government: Institutional Dynamics of Regulation.* Cambridge: Cambridge University Press.

Forbes, L., and Jermier, J. (2002). The institutionalization of bird protection: Mabel Osgood Wright and the Early Audobon Movement. *Organization* and *Environment*, 15, 458–74.

Foucault, M. (1991). Governmentality. In G. Burchell, C. Gordon, and P. Miller (eds.), *The Foucault Effect: Studies in Governmentality.* London: Harvester Wheatsheaf, 87–104.

—— ([1978] 1990). *The History of Sexuality: An Introduction, Vol. 1.* Translation by Hurley, R. New York: Vintage Books.

Frank, D., and McEneaney, E. (1999). The individualization of society and the liberalization of state policies on same-sex sexual relations, 1984–1995. *Social Forces*, 77, 911–44.

—— Hironaka, A., and Schofer, E. (2000). The nation-state and the natural environment over the twentieth century. *American Sociological Review*, 65, 96–116.

Gramsci, A. (1971). *Selections from the Prison Notebook*. Edited and translated by H. Quintin, and N.S. Goffrey. London: Lawrence and Wishart.

Graz, J.C., and Nölke, A. (eds.) (2008). *Transnational Private Governance and Its Limits*. London: Routledge.

Greenwood, R., Oliver, C., Sahlin, K., and Suddaby, R. (2008). Introduction. In R. Greenwood, C. Oliver, K. Sahlin, and R. Suddaby (eds.), *The Sage Handbook of Organizational Institutionalism*. London: Sage.

Hedmo, T. and Wedlin, L. (2008). New modes of governance: The re-regulation of European higher education and research. In C. Mazza, P. Quattrone, and A. Riccaboni (eds.), *European Universities in Transition: Issues, Models and Cases*. Cheltenham: Edward Elgar.

—— Sahlin-Andersson, K., and Wedlin, L. (2006). The emergence of a European regulatory field of management education. In M.L. Djelic and K. Sahlin-Andersson (eds.), *Transnational Government: Institutional Dynamics of Regulation*. Cambridge: Cambridge University Press.

Hood, C. (1991). A public management for all seasons? *Public Administration*, 69, 3–19.

—— Scott, C., James, O., Jones, G., and Travers, T. (1999). *Regulation Inside Government*. Oxford: Oxford University Press.

Hopwood, A. (1994). Reflections on the harmonization of accounting in the European Union. *European Accounting Review*.

Jacobsson, K. (2004). Between the deliberation and discipline: Soft governance in EU Employment Policy. In U. Mörth (ed.), *Soft law in Governance and Regulation: An Interdisciplinary Analysis*. Cheltenham: Edward Elgar., pp. 81–102.

—— and Miller, P. (eds.) (1994). *Accounting as Social and Institutional Practices*. Cambridge: Cambridge Universtiy Press.

Jacobsson, B. (2006). Regulated regulators: Global trends of state transformation. In M.L. Djelic and K. Sahlin-Andersson (eds.), *Transnational Government: Institutional Dynamics of Regulation*. Cambridge: Cambridge University Press.

—— and Sahlin-Andersson, K. (2006). Dynamics of soft regulation. In M.L. Djelic and K. Sahlin-Andersson (eds.), *Transnational Government: Institutional Dynamics of Regulation*. Cambridge: Cambridge University Press.

Keraghel, C., and Sen, J. (2004). Explorations in open space: The World Social Forum and cultures of politics. *International Social Science Journal*, 56(182), 483–93.

Kirton, J.J., and Trebilcock, M.J. (2004). *Hard Choices, Soft Law*. Aldershot: Ashgate.

Knill, C., and Lehmkuhl, D. (2002). Private actors and the State: Internationalization and changing patterns of governance. *Governance*, 15(1), 41–63.

Levi-Faur, D., and Jordana, J. (eds.) (2005). The rise of regulatory capitalism: The global diffusion of a new regulatory order. *The Annals of the Americal Academy of Political and Social Science, Vol. 598*. London: Sage.

Lewin, K. (1936). *Principles of Topological Psychology.* New York: McGraw Hill.

—— (1951). *Field Theory in Social Science: Selected Theoretical Papers,* ed. D. Cartwright. New York: Harper & Row.

Loft, A., Humphrey, C., and Turley, S. (2006). In pursuit of global regulation: Changing governance and accountability structures at the International Federation of Accountants (IFAC). *Accounting, Auditing and Accountability Journal,* 19 (3), 428–51.

Marcussen, M. (2006). The transnational governance network of central bankers. In M.L. Djelic and K. Sahlin-Andersson (eds.), *Transnational Government: Institutional Dynamics of Regulation.* Cambridge: Cambridge University Press.

Martin, J.L. (2003). What is Field Theory? *American Journal of Sociology,* 109(1), 1–49.

McNichol, J. (2006). Transnational NGO certification programs as new regulatory forms: Lessons from the forestry sector. In M.L. Djelic and K. Sahlin-Andersson (eds.), *Transnational Government: Institutional Dynamics of Regulation.* Cambridge: University Press.

—— and Bensedrine, J. (2003). Multilateral rulemaking: Transatlantic struggles around genetically modified food. In M.L. Djelic and S. Quack (eds.) (2003). *Globalization and Institutions.* Cheltenham: Edward Elgar, pp. 220–44.

Merton, R.K. (1957). *Social Theory and Social Structure, Revised.* Glencoe, IU: The Free Press.

Meyer, J., and Jepperson, R. (2000). The actors of modern society. The cultural construction of social agency. *Sociological Theory,* 18(1), 100–20.

—— and Rowan, B. (1977). Institutionalized organizations: Formal structure as myth and ceremony. *American Journal of Sociology,* 83, 340–63.

—— and Scott, W.R. (1983). *Organizational Environments.* Beverly Hills, Calif.: Sage.

—— Boli, J., Thomas, G., and Ramirez, R. (1997). World society and the nation-state. *American Journal of Sociology,* 103(1), 144–81.

Mohr, J. (2005). Implicit terrains: Meaning, measurement, and spatial metaphors in Organizational Theory. In M.J. Ventresca and J. Porac (eds.), *Constructing Industries and Markets.* New York: Elsevier.

Morgan, G. (2006). Transnational actors, transnational institutions, transnational spaces: The role of law firms in the internationalization of competition regulation. In M.L. Djelic and K. Sahlin-Andersson (eds.), *Transnational Government: Institutional Dynamics of Regulation.* Cambridge: Cambridge University Press.

—— and Engwall L. (1999). *Regulation and Organisations: International Perspectives.* London: Routledge.

Mörth, U. (ed.) (2004). *Soft Law in Governance and Regulation: An Interdisciplinary Analysis.* Cheltenham: Edward Elgar.

—— (2006). Soft regulation and global democracy. In M.L. Djelic and K. Sahlin-Andersson (eds.), *Transnational Government: Institutional Dynamics of Regulation.* Cambridge: Cambridge University Press.

Pire, B. (ed.) (2000). *Dictionnaire de la physique.* Paris: Encyclopaedia Universalis/ Albin Michel.

Powell, W.W., Gammal, D.L., and Simmard, C. (2006). Close encounters: The circulation and reception of managerial practices in the San Francisco Bay Area nonprofit community. In B. Czarniawska and G. Sevón (eds.), *Global Ideas: How Ideas, Objects and Practices Travel in the Global Economy.* Lund, Sweden: Liber.

Power, M. (1997). *The Audit Society.* Oxford: Oxford University Press.

—— (2003). Evaluating the audit explosion. *Law & Policy,* 25(3), 115–202.

—— (2004). *The Risk Management of Everything: Rethinking the Politics of Uncertainty.* London: Demos.

—— (2007). *Organized Uncertainty.* Oxford: Oxford University Press.

Sahlin-Andersson, K. (2004). Emergent cross-sectional soft regulations: Dynamics at play in the Global Compact Initiative. In U. Mörth (ed.), *Soft law in Governance and Regulation. An Interdisciplinary Analysis.* Cheltenham: Edward Elgar. pp. 129–54.

Schmidt, P. (2004). Law in the age of governance: Regulation, networks and lawyers. In J. Jordana and D. Levi-Faur (ed.), *The Politics of Regulation: Institutions and Regulatory Reforms for the Age of Goverance.* London: Edward Elgar.

Scott, C. (2004). Regulation in the age of governance: The rise of the Post-Regulatory State. In J. Jordana and D. Levi-Faur (ed.), *The Politics of Regulation: Institutions and Regulatory Reforms for the Age of Goverance.* London: Edward Elgar.

Scott, W.R., and Meyer, J. (1983). The organization of societal sectors. In J. Meyer and W.R. Scott (1983). *Organizational Environments.* Beverly Hills, Calif.: Sage.

Shapiro, S. (1987). The social control of impersonal trust. *American Journal of Sociology,* 93(3), 623–58.

Streeck, W., and Thelen, K. (eds.) (2005). *Beyond Continuity.* Oxford: Oxford University Press.

Tamm Hallström, K. (2004). *Organizing International Standardization.* Cheltenham: Edward Elgar.

Thomas, G., Meyer, J.W., Ramirez, F., and Boli, J. (1987). *Institutional Structure.* Newbury Park, Calif.: Sage.

Warren, R.L. (1967). The interorganizational field as a focus for investigation. *Administrative Science Quarterly,* 12, 396–419.

—— (1972). *The Community in America.* Chicago, ILL.: Rand McNally.

Weber, M. (1978). *Economy and Society.* Berkeley, Calif.: University of California Press.

Westney, E. (1987). *Imitation and Innovation.* Cambridge, Mass.: Harvard University Press.

Whitley, R. (1999). *Divergent Capitalism.* Oxford: Oxford University Press.

Zadek, S. (2001). *The Civil Corporation: The New Economy of Corporate Citizenship.* London: Earthscan Publications.

10

Governing Audit Globally: IFAC, the
New International Financial Architecture
and the Auditing Profession

Christopher Humphrey and Anne Loft

[M]any key aspects of accounting action in the European and international spheres are poorly documented and indeed little known.

(Hopwood 1994: 242)

INTRODUCTION

In providing a critical commentary on Thorell and Whittington's analysis
(1994) of the pursuit of international accounting harmonization in the European
Union (EU), Anthony Hopwood essentially laid down a research agenda
emphasizing the need to improve knowledge of the 'complex and shifting
interrelationships between the different bodies that make up the international
accounting institutional arena' (p. 245). Hopwood saw enhanced understanding of the political dynamics of the European and international accounting
arena as vital to the appreciation of the processes through which policy
options emerge, choices delineated, and decision processes orchestrated.
One of his primary concerns was the influential roles played in such contexts
by the audit industry (referring to the accounting profession) and its agents—
roles that research to date had ignored, or at best, underestimated in assuming
that international accounting issues were primarily technical rather than
political. He also highlighted the role played by bodies he regarded as 'agents
of the audit industry', such as the International Federation of Accountants
(IFAC), which seemed to be exerting a significant influence over the forms in
which options and debates concerning international accounting policy were
being cast; and of particular importance was their growing interface with a

variety of supranational regulatory authorities (p. 247). In considering how 'amazingly little' (p. 247) was known of such policy making activities and arenas, Hopwood speculated on the constraining influence of there being relatively few people involved with the global world of accounting, and that in such a 'small world' (Lodge 1984) there could be little concern with openness (Hopwood 1994: 242). Nevertheless, he saw this as a huge knowledge gap and highlighted the urgent need for research investigation (p. 247).

At the time that Hopwood was developing such arguments and claims, the expectations for international accounting were not high, with Sutton (1993) observing that: '[g]lobal agreement on harmonization may eventually be reached, but for now, it remains a distant and elusive goal' (p. 183). In the fifteen years from 1994 to 2009, however, much has happened in the international accounting arena. International Financial Reporting Standards (IFRS) produced by the International Accounting Standards Board (IASB)[1] are rapidly becoming world standards. The EU has required listed companies to prepare their consolidated accounts in accordance with IFRS since 2005, and 114 countries now accept or require IFRS. In 2007 the Securities and Exchange Commission (SEC) abolished the need for non-US companies to reconcile their accounts to US Generally Accepted Accounting Principles (US GAAP) and just a year later, in November 2008, this was followed by the publication of a roadmap proposing IFRS as the primary reporting standards for US listed companies by 2014. This plan was reinforced by the leaders of the G20 at their meeting, 'Financial Markets and the World Economy', the same month, where it was declared that '[T]he key global accounting standards bodies should work intensively toward the objective of creating a single high-quality global standard'.[2] With the International Standards on Auditing (ISAs) produced by IFAC's International Auditing and Assurance Standards Board (IAASB) appearing to follow a similar path to becoming world standards, there is a clear expectation that accounting and auditing standards, as used by the world's listed companies, will converge quickly. Whilst many issues concerning national variants of standards remain as well as issues of interpretation and compliance in practice, the speed of change would surely have surprised those who, fifteen years ago, saw global convergence in accounting and auditing practices in such 'distant and elusive' terms.

The research ideas and agendas laid down in Hopwood's paper (1994) have been re-emphasized in a number of relatively recent accounting research papers. Lehman (2005), for instance, uses a critical accountability framework

---

[1] The IASB, formed in 2001, is the successor organisation to the International Accounting Standards Committee (IASC).

[2] See http://www.whitehouse.gov/news/releases/2008/11/20081115–1.html

to reinforce Hopwood's observation (1994: 251) that new vocabularies and perspectives may help other voices to enter the international accounting/harmonization arena, whilst Gallhofer and Haslam (2007) provide a critical analysis of the IASB's public interest commitments. Parker (2007) has criticized a perceived continuing narrowness of much financial and external reporting research and the lack of emphasis on the social, institutional and political world within which such accounting practices are constructed (also see Baker and Barbu 2007; Rodrigues and Craig 2007). Cooper and Robson (2006) highlight the continuing limited understanding of the involvement of the big audit firms in international regulatory processes and the importance of focusing explicitly on the interactions between bodies active on the global regulatory stage, noting that it is

scarcely possible to discuss seriously ... the work of the IASB, IFAC, ASB, FASB, IOSCO or the EU ... without considering the complex of alliances, agreements and accords that now exists between these agencies on various accounting and auditing matters, and how these agreements and alliances affect implementation in specific jurisdictions (Robson et al. 2005). (Cooper and Robson 2006: 431).

Overall, while research is developing on the global auditing arena (e.g., see, Ball 2004; Dewing and Russell 2004; Loft et al. 2006; Suddaby et al. 2007), it is probably fair to say that Hopwood's agenda (1994) has not produced the response it deserves in terms of the study of global audit regulatory institutions. This chapter seeks to contribute in this regard by considering the developments in the global governance of auditing that have taken place since the mid-1990s, specifically analysing: (*a*) the developing role of IFAC in the context of what is commonly referred to as the new international financial architecture (NIFA); and (*b*) the growing interest and involvement of the 'Big Four' audit firms in global regulatory processes.

The analytical spirit informing our work derives from the equally developing field of global governance research. This has, as its basic assumption, a sense that nation states are surrendering authority in many areas to regional and global institutions. It is concerned directly with the emergence of regulatory and governing institutions, whose connections 'back' to the traditional authority of nation states established through democratic processes, appear rather distant. The usage of the term 'global governance' to describe the growing importance of 'governance beyond government' by international organizations is now quite widespread (Held and McGrew 2002). One of the arenas most affected by such developments is the financial arena, with the massive global growth in the number and type of financial transactions and their potential to affect, in varying ways, most of the world's citizens (Scholte

2002, 2004). In this context, global financial governance research involves studying issues relating to the legitimacy and accountability of transnational governmental organizations in the financial sphere, as well as specific governance processes and regulatory practices.

Here global financial governance will be defined following Germain (2007: 73) as:

[T]he contested interplay between market actors, private authorities and public authorities (state and international) that establishes the rules or boundaries within which global financial resources are mobilised and channelled towards economic, social and political activity.[3]

An important element of the growing global governance of finance appears to be the presence of private (non-state) as well as public governance processes. The IASB has been used by a number of writers in this field as an example of a non-state organization involved in global governance (although IFAC has notably been ignored). Examples include Woods (2002, 2006); Slaughter (2004*a*, 2004*b*); Mattli and Büthe (2005); Perry and Nölke (2006); Botzem and Quack (2006); and Black (2008). Black, for instance, includes the IASB in a list of organizations whose activities 'are not based on or mandated by national, supranational, or international law" and which have no existing structures ... to which recourse can be made to render them accountable' (p. 2) and IFAC clearly falls into this category although it is not mentioned.

The above writers come from a variety of academic disciplines, including international relations, political science, and international law; and use differing theoretical approaches in their work as well as a variety of methods and types of data. Rather than generating or relying on a single theory the field, of global financial governance is suitably characterized as comprising a wide variety of attempts to analyse and theorize the existence and operation of global governance systems and practices. An attractive feature of a good part of this literature is the adoption of analytical perspectives sensitive both to the larger picture of global governance and to the practical details through which governance systems operate. Writers coming from a political science perspective can be quite explicit in their discussions of interests served. Wade (2007), for example, claims that the promotion of global economic standards of best practice across areas such as 'data dissemination, bank supervision, corporate governance and financial accounting' (p. 120) have furthered the interests of the West in the pursuit of financial liberalization. However, in emphasizing the way in which such

---

[3] Our definition adds 'private authorities' to Germain's original, we do this because such authorities are playing an increasingly significant role in NIFA. They have tended to be underestimated by political scientists working in the field—although this is changing (see, e.g., Perry and Nölke 2006).

reforms have been undertaken in the name of 'financial transparency', Wade and others (e.g., see, Hale 2008) also illustrate the importance of studying the structures, mechanisms, and processes through which notions of transparency are constructed. In so doing, such work is suggestive not just of the potentially significant role of global auditing and other verification functions but also the competitive advantage that auditing researchers have in studying such activity given their familiarity with the work and operations of the institutions setting and implementing international auditing standards.

We believe that auditing regulatory structures and systems in the broader field of global financial governance are worthy of more research attention. Collectively, this chapter assesses the contemporary strength of Hopwood's (1994) reflections on global audit regulation and also provides a response to more recent calls for more research in this area (see Cooper and Robson 2006; Loft et al. 2006). A key finding from the chapter is that the global regulatory arena governing auditing is certainly more multifaceted, complex, and dynamic than that represented in Hopwood's writing—with a developing form of network governance that raises important policy questions both for regulatory institutions and the polity on whose behalf such regulatory systems are supposed to operate. The chapter is divided into four subsequent sections. The first section discusses the development of NIFA and the developing structures and perspectives associated with the global governance of audit. The next section of the chapter then focuses on IFAC itself, including changes in its organizational structure and financing. The third section considers the developing global activities and strategies of the big audit firms[4] while the final section provides concluding reflections.

THE DEVELOPMENT OF NIFA: DEVELOPING A REGULATORY REGIME OF STANDARDS AND CODES

Known as 'NIFA', the new international financial architecture had its origins in the questions raised in the wake of the financial chaos resulting from Mexico's devaluation of the peso in 1994 (Woods 2006). Mexico was supposed to have been a star pupil of the 'Washington Consensus' policies.[5]

---

[4] The 'Big 4' are Deloitte, Ernst and Young, KPMG, and PricewaterhouseCoopers; there are other large firms, but they are relatively much smaller.

[5] This was the name given to policy advice for developing/emerging economies developed by Washington-based institutions, in particular the IMF, World Bank, and US Treasury Department—policy recommendations that included trade liberalization, privatization, deregulation, and strict fiscal policies.

Whilst solutions were being debated, the Asian financial crisis of 1997/8 struck, placing the economies of whole countries in serious difficulty. With 'contagion' spreading the crisis, global economic prosperity appeared threatened (e.g. see Clinton 1998). Huge resources were put into trying to find out what went wrong, with the source of problems significantly being connected to the nature of global policies (see Davies 2003; Germain 2001). Suggested solutions even included that of a global financial regulator, but the idea of new regulation was unpopular, particularly because it would also amount to an admission that the deregulation and liberalization characterizing the Washington Consensus was not working.

As the causes were analysed in depth, domestic weaknesses in accounting and auditing were also identified as a significant problem. A study prepared for United Nations Conference on Trade and Development (UNCTAD) sharply criticized the (then) Big 6 audit firms in countries struck by the crisis for following inadequate national auditing standards rather than international ones (Rahman 1998). World Bank Economists later reinforced this critique, writing that '(u)sers of the accounting information were misled and were not able to take precautions in a timely fashion' (Vishwanath and Kaufman 2001: 119). The President of the World Bank made his poor opinion of accountants known to the World Congress of Accountants in Paris in the autumn of 1997 (Wolfensohn 1997). Such criticisms came on top of a growing concern among stock market regulators with the apparently declining status of the audit in the large multinational accounting firms and threats to auditor independence from a growing business orientation. IFAC was criticized for having 'little clout and little influence' and encouraged to take a more active role in establishing accounting professions in developing nations.[6]

The internationally agreed 'solution' lay in the promotion of and commitment to 'standards and codes' of behaviour and practice. Gordon Brown, the then British Chancellor, was a strong promoter. In his role as chair of the G7 Finance Ministers, he issued a press release outlining three general codes (Brown 1998)—first, a 'code of fiscal transparency'; second, 'a code of monetary and financial policy'; and a third a 'code of corporate behaviour'. Brown described the latter as something new and would include: principles for auditing, accounting, and disclosure in the corporate sector and standards of corporate government (ibid.). Crucially, this gave accounting and auditing standards a new significance as an important contributor to global financial stability.

On the same theme, later in 1998, the G22 Report of the Working Group on Transparency and Accountability produced recommendations stressing the

---

[6] Robert Bruce in *The Times*, 30 October 1997.

importance of **transparency**, emphasizing that this meant the provision of more financial information not just at the macroeconomic level (e.g. levels of public debt) but also better information at the micro, corporate level. Generally transparency was seen as enabling capital markets to operate better. Camdessus, the then Managing Director of the International Monetary Fund (IMF), wrote that 'there is a strong consensus for making transparency the "golden rule" of the new international financial system … it is absolutely central to the task of civilizing globalisation' (Camdessus 1999: unpaginated). Or as King (1999: 6) emphasized, transparency 'is not simply a question of making available certain data, it is an approach to economic policy, almost a way of life'.[7]

In considerable contrast to the talk of a global financial regulator, which most thought problematic, the pursuit of transparency was a unifying factor—'everyone could agree on the need for more transparency and more standards' (Wade 2007: 119). Accounting and auditing were the 'Columbus Egg' here—a genial idea—for accurate financial reporting made using agreed upon accounting and auditing standards would seemingly provide the transparency necessary for investors to make the economically correct decisions, and this would in turn lead to enhanced global financial stability! Significantly, the concept of a company's accounts as being something 'just' useful for investors was being reconfigured—with accounting and auditing standards becoming an essential building block in NIFA.

Institutional initiatives were needed to realize the vision of the G7, and in February 1999 at their meeting in Bonn, the G7 established the Financial Stability Forum (FSF). Its membership included representatives from finance ministries, central banks, international financial institutions, and other relevant experts' groupings. It had no legal powers, but was set up to promote information exchange and coordination between financial regulators in the interest of financial stability. Part of the aim was to work towards realizing the ideas concerning standards and codes in the framework of transparency. Andrew Crockett, the General Manager of the Bank for International Settlements (BIS) became the first chairperson (FSF 1999). He supported strongly the important role of accounting and auditing in financial stability, arguing that providing 'high-quality information is essential for proper market functioning, and will not come about spontaneously' (Crockett 2002*a*: 4). 'Ultimately, better financial reporting holds the promise of a more efficient allocation of financial capital in our global economy and a sounder and more stable financial system' (2002*b*: unpaginated).

---

[7] This emphasis on transparency was linked to a transformation in the language of global public policy—which according to Lawrence Summers, the deputy secretary of the US Treasury, was increasingly becoming the 'language of economics' (Summers 1999: unpaginated).

In a related initiative, a Reports on Standards and Codes (ROSC) pro-gramme at the IMF and World Bank was set up, the idea being to examine the extent to which emerging and developing countries were using key standards and codes (IMF and World Bank 2005). This commenced in 1999, and International Standards on Accounting (ISAs) and International Auditing Standards (IASs)became benchmark standards for the country reports on accounting and auditing, the remit being to: 'analyze comparability of na-tional accounting and auditing standards with international standards' and 'assist the country in developing and implementing a country action plan for improving institutional capacity with a view to strengthening the country's corporate financial reporting regime' (www.worldbank.org/ifa/rosc_aa.html).

In 2000, the FSF formally listed ISAs and IASs as part of the list of 12 key standards for financial stability (FSF 2000). This was an important develop-ment in that it placed public authority behind these private standards, and it is notable that the list of key standards formally notes that the IASs/IFRSs and ISAs are produced by private organizations, unlike the other standards that were produced by bodies with public authority, that is, bodies backed by some kind of trans-governmental authority. More important than this, the whole set of ideas behind NIFA heralded a 'Post Washington Consensus' which spread the idea of a 'standards-surveillance-compliance' system (Wade 2007), in which accounting and auditing played a prominent part.

PRIVATE STANDARD SETTERS IN THE PUBLIC SPHERE: THE DEVELOPMENT OF MONITORING AND OVERSIGHT OF IFAC—AND THE INFLUENCE OF THE INTERNATIONAL REGULATORS

The formal acceptance of international auditing standards in this new regime, occurred despite concerns on the part of regulators, first, about the organ-ization and status of IFAC as a private standard setter and second, the capabilities of the big audit firms to ensure that audits in developing and emerging economies were of the same standard as in developed economies. In response to the World Bank's criticisms, IFAC acknowledged that more needed to be done to enhance accounting capacity and capabilities in such countries and meetings were held with the World Bank concerning the need to work jointly on this issue (GCPAS 2001). A collective body, the International Forum on Accountancy Development (IFAD) was established in 1999, bringing together representatives from IFAC and a range of international bodies including the big audit firms, securities regulators, and the World Bank. IFAD started the process of researching the usage of international standards and the capacity for accountancy and educational development. However, it appeared ultimately to be hindered by the scale of its ambition—with the big audit firms feeling that they were being asked by international regulators to help developing countries in ways which were beyond their jurisdiction (see Street and Needles 2002). Despite its limited success it represents a significant development as it provides evidence of the way in which the agendas of IFAC, international regulators, and the big firms were starting to intertwine. This was further illustrated in IFAC's four point strategic plan, presented to the IFAC Board in Edinburgh in May, 2000, and committing IFAC to:

1. Putting additional resources into audit standard setting and revising the membership, operational and governance procedures of the international audit standard-setting body.[8]
2. Tightening compliance procedures to ensure that member bodies are following IFAC best practice as to how to run a professional body.
3. Improving the quality and consistency of work on transnational audits, through the establishment of the Forum of Firms (FoF) and its associated operational committee, the Transnational Auditors Committee (TAC).
4. Establishing a public oversight body. (See IFAC 2003a: 51–2)

IFAC continued to receive criticisms that it needed to do more in terms of its public interest commitments. The O'Malley Panel on Audit Effectiveness (POB 2000) emphasized that the international auditing profession must have a global oversight body serving the public interest as its centerpiece. In December 2000, John M. Morrissey, Deputy Chief Accountant of the SEC encouraged IFAC to work vigorously to create a set of globally acceptable auditing standards of high quality, emphasizing that it was important that the standard-setting procedures were transparent, and that there should be a public oversight board (POB) staffed by 'public interest representatives without ties to the accounting profession' (Morrissey 2000: 6). In response, IFAC stressed that it was 'fully committed to the establishment of a truly independent, credible, and respected POB as a critical part of its transformation into the global self-regulatory body for the accounting and auditing professions... *it must be truly independent—of the profession, the regulators and other interested parties*—if it is to provide a

---

[8] The existing International Auditing Practices Committee (IAPC) was restructured and re-launched as the IAASB in January 2002.

credible public interest perspective' (Fujinuma 2000: 3; emphasis added). The press release accompanying this statement emphasized that 'POB members shall also be independent of the securities and banking regulators and should not currently be regulators or otherwise be directly associated with regulators' (section 4).

The public oversight reform proposals made by IFAC in 2001 were never implemented. Shortly after the ending of the IFAC POB consultation process the Enron scandal broke, and this brought the value of self-regulation, of the form exercised by the US POB over the US accounting profession, into question. In early 2002 the POB disbanded itself and following the passing of the Sarbanes-Oxley Act later in the year, the Public Company Accounting Oversight Board (PCAOB) was established under the supervision of the SEC. It was a body with a far more wide-ranging remit and power than the old US POB. Inevitably, in this atmosphere, it was necessary for IFAC to reconsider the whole public oversight issue, and this was reinforced by statements made by the International Organisation of Securities Commissions (IOSCO) in October 2002 in response to Enron and other high-profile corporate failures. The three 'statements of principles' IOSCO issued (IOSCO 2002*b*, 2002*c*, 2002*d*),[9] described: first, the 'essential features of regulatory systems requiring transparency and disclosure by listed entities; second, the independence of external auditors; and, third, the need for public oversight of the audit function' (IOSCO, Press Release, 18 October 2002).[10] In the context of the third statement, IOSCO's Technical Committee remarked on a growing consensus internationally as to the benefits of independent auditor oversight systems working in the public interest—as opposed to systems based mainly or totally on self-regulation.

In a speech at the 16th World Congress of Accountants in Hong Kong in November 2002, the new IFAC President, René Ricol acknowledged that the international regulatory environment for the accounting profession had changed and that there was a need for more external oversight.[11] It was evident that a form of regulatory renaissance was in progress, reflected in the informal discussions that took place during congress between IFAC and the international regulatory community. In January 2003, IFAC organized a meeting, primarily with the chief executives of various IFAC member bodies, to discuss the strategic direction to be taken. Here it was agreed that the objectives of high-quality standard setting and obtaining international

---

[9] These followed on from earlier papers considering the effectiveness of self-regulatory regimes and the nature of regulatory oversight (see IOSCO 2000, 2002).

[10] See http://www.iosco.org/news/pdf/IOSCONEWS2.pdf

[11] See http://www.ifac.org/Library/ArticleFiles/WorldCongress-ReneRicolClose.doc

regulatory endorsement of ISAs should have the highest priority for IFAC. IFAC followed up this meeting with one the following month with representatives of the international regulatory community. These were drawn from IOSCO, the Basle Committee on Banking Supervision (BCBS), the International Association of Insurance Supervisors (IAIS), the FSF, the European Commission (EC), and the World Bank. According to Susan Koski-Grafer, Senior Associate Chief Accountant of the SEC, this group, which was soon to become known as the 'Monitoring Group', exerted pressure on IFAC for improvements to be made in international audits. In a press release[12] dated 25 March 2003, the FSF noted that it wanted to see developments in the public oversight of international audit standard setting. It 'urged that an independent, external body acting in the public interest be established to oversee the work of the IAASB' (p. 2). In May, the European Commission (2003) also made similar demands and even contemplated the IAASB being transformed into a standard-setting body independent of IFAC (see Section 3.1: 7).[13]

An IFAC Leadership Group (ILG) was set up by the IFAC Board; it was tasked with formulating proposals and managing the public oversight reform process (see IFAC 2003*b*: para. 1.3). The ILG met with the newly established Monitoring Group of international regulators at a meeting in Washington, D.C., in June, 2003. At the meeting IFAC put forward the ILG's proposals, which were apparently received very positively by the regulatory organizations in attendance. These proposals were also effectively endorsed in August 2003 by the final report of an independent task force set up by IFAC in the wake of the Enron scandal to consider ways of rebuilding public confidence in financial reporting. In the wake of the positive responses, plans were made for the establishment of a Public Interest Oversight Board (PIOB) to oversee international audit standard setting and other IFAC public interest activities (Koski-Grafer 2005). A revised set of proposals for reform were unanimously approved by the IFAC Board and IFAC Council, respectively in September and November 2003.

IFAC stated that the approved PIOB reforms were intended to ensure that IFAC's standard-setting processes met the public interest expectations of the regulatory community (IFAC 2003*b*: 2, 6). Public support was expressed by the FSF and the Basel Committee, while IOSCO was said to be strongly supportive. René Ricol, spoke of the reforms as representing:

... the most significant changes in IFAC's standard setting since its inception over 25 years ago ... (providing) for public interest oversight of IFAC's standard-setting and compliance activities, greater public input into the process, and increased

---

[12] See http://www.fsforum.org/press/press_releases_56.html
[13] For more discussion, see Humphrey et al. (2006).

transparency. Additionally and equally significant, *they provide for ongoing collabor-*
ation between regulators and the profession, formalizing the collaborative process estab-
lished in 2003. (Ricol 2004: 3; emphasis added)

After some delays the PIOB was formally established in February 2005, with
its members drawn from nominees provided by the Monitoring Group and
the majority having held senior regulatory posts in the financial sphere.
Stavros Thomadakis, the new chair of the PIOB stated that: 'the creation of
the PIOB is a landmark in the **cooperation of world regulatory organizations**
for the oversight of international standard-setting for auditors … and a
novelty for world-level public oversight'.[14]

Significantly, the impact of IFAC's 'regulatory bargain' (Loft et al. 2006)
with international regulators had seen the membership of IFAC's oversight
board shift dramatically. Originally in 2001 the desire was to have a POB
membership completely independent of regulators (and virtually everything
else!), but the PIOB which came into operation in 2005 was mostly staffed by
ex-regulators nominated by international regulatory bodies. The Monitoring
Group formalized its role, meeting with the IFAC Regulatory Liaison Group
approximately twice a year. Arguably, the establishment of the Monitoring
Group and the PIOB can be seen as a structural development that centrally
positions regulatory influence within IFAC. It also raises the question as
to whether IFAC's structural reforms more accurately resemble a form of
'embedded' oversight, wherein IFAC stands as an organizational site in which
compatible and potentially competing interests and strategies of influence of
the international regulatory community and others are pursued. Such interactions become more evident when consideration is given to the developing
position and involvement of the big audit firms in IFAC.

Central to IFAC's reform agenda was the concept of transparency, this
being clearly influenced by the general idea associated with NIFA discussed
earlier, that transparency was a good idea, especially for a private based
standard setter. The goal of transparency has been substantially helped in
recent years by the capacities and possibilities made available by the Internet
and IFAC's own web site (www.ifac.org). IFAC has in fact been classified as a
highly transparent non-governmental body in the financial services arena (see
Delonis 2004) and this is evident in the considerable amount of information
that is now freely available on IFAC's web site—including complete sets of all
the standards, extensive background papers for standard-setting board meetings, exposure drafts of these standards, and the comments made on them.
There are even downloadable sound recordings of the meetings of the IAASB.
This makes it possible for anyone with access to the Internet to follow what is

[14] http://www.iosco.org/news/pdf/IOSCONEWS83.pdf (emphasis added).

going on at IFAC. Seen in historical terms, this high level of transparency was a bold and innovative move for IFAC. Going further, public participation has also been enabled in that, it is also possible for members of the public to register to observe meetings, to send in comments on exposure drafts and to nominate persons for membership of the standard-setting committees. In the case of observations of meetings, it is clear that obvious cost constraints for unfunded observers act to limit any consistent and long-term presence at meetings that are routinely scheduled to take place in different parts of the world (see Loft and Humphrey 2006).

In general, the whole due-process around standard setting has been carefully structured to allow IFAC to meet its transparency goals at the same time as operating on a global basis. The affordances provided by the Internet are crucial to this.[15] This level of openness and the ability of interested individuals to comment on standards, adds legitimacy to the standard-setting process and the standards themselves. It is especially important given IFAC's potential vulnerability in being a private standard setter in an arena where most standards and rules are set by public authorities. In fact IFAC makes far more information publicly available than a number of other organizations in this global regulatory sphere with a closer link to public authorities, such as IOSCO and BCBS.

However, it is important not to regard transparency through the Internet as a panacea for all regulatory ills. There are certainly practical limits as to what the Internet can deliver in terms of enhancing dialogue between key stakeholder groups (see Unerman and Bennett 2004). In addition, IFAC's standard-setting processes, in what are often complex technical areas, are arguably destined to remain substantially in the hands of a limited number of active experts with time and resources to devote to the task (see Loft et al. 2006). Despite IFAC's high level of transparency, some important forums for discussion remain private, for instance task-force meetings and the day-to-day activities of IFAC officers. Whilst public comments on draft standards appear on the web, the possibility of private lobbying and other activities seeking to push the decisions of standard setters in particular directions, remains a live consideration.[16] In the case of ISAs, the potential for such behind-the-scenes, non-transparent activities is evident, not least because the various constituencies involved in the standard setting may have different interests. For example, small audit firms for a variety of operational reasons may not have the same

---

[15] See Hutchby (2001) on Internet affordances.

[16] For instance, Zeff's work on the development of the American Accounting profession demonstrates clearly that, in the case of certain standards, the FASB was extensively lobbied by the preparers of financial reports (2003: 273–4).

perspective on ISAs as the Big 4 firms. Similarly, different national professional accountancy bodies may have different viewpoints on the prescriptions required in international standards on auditor education and ethics. An important issue concerning transparency is that it is sometimes seen as a substitute for regulation (Fung et al. 2003). There is an argument grounded in neo-liberal economics that once things are made transparent, the market will do the rest. This point of view seems to have been quite important when transparency/disclosure was chosen in 1997/8 as a central concept in NIFA. The problem, though, is that transparency is not the same as compliance— and this has become evidently clear in the current, global financial crisis of 2008. Ultimately, transparency cannot simply be assumed to exist or to be guaranteed by the existence of formal governance structures. Rather, it is something that has to be kept under empirical review, with questions needing to be asked in each particular case as to what exactly is being made transparent and what interests are being served, or best served, by 'enhanced' levels of transparency (Hale 2008).

THE BIG FIRMS—FROM LOBBYING TO DIRECT FUNDING AND PARTICIPATION?

Hopwood saw the big audit firms as investing heavily in processes of institutional elaboration and political mobilization—and, at the time he was writing in 1993, the big audit firms began to set up a European Contact Group' (ECG). This consisted of the then Big Six, plus BDO and Grant Thornton (Manardo 1996). It was formed to coordinate the views of the big audit firms[17] in Europe in order to present a single view to the EC on various proposed audit regulatory initiatives (Røder 2001: 9; Manardo 1996: 40).[18] In early 1999, a new global organization was formed (modelled on the ECG and its US counterpart) called the Big 5 Global Steering Committee (GSC),[19] with Jacques Manardo as chairperson, a position subsequently

[17] When the profession writes 'large firms' in this context it generally means the Big 4 firms (or Big 5, pre-Enron) plus the two next largest, Grant Thornton and BDO (who are much smaller than the Big 4 firms).

[18] Jacques Manardo, a Deloitte's partner chaired it from 1996–9. The ECG carried on with Jens Røder, from PricewaterhouseCoopers, taking over as chairman.

[19] The GSC was set up with a full time Secretary, Brian Smith, a retired partner from Arthur Andersen, who supplied him with an office to undertake this work. The GSC was referred to by several names, including the 'Large Firms Steering Committee'. When Morris took the chairmanship in 2001 it comprised representatives of each of the seven largest audit firms—the Big 5 plus BDO and Grant Thornton.

assumed by David Morris (of PricewaterhouseCoopers) in 2001. According to Morris (2001), the creation of the GSC was to some extent a response to the criticism coming from the World Bank in the wake of the Asian Crisis of 1997/8 but essentially reflected that the big firms 'needed a body that could deal on a global basis with issues of common professional and regulatory concern ... to lead the effort and interact with "outside" partners' (p. 14).

A major aim of the GSC was '[s]trengthening IFAC as the global audit standard setter and self-regulatory body for the international profession' (Morris 2001: 15; Turley 2001), a project which was seen as closely related to the strengthening and restructuring of the IASC which was completed with the formation of the IASB in April 2001. The GSC under the chairmanship of Manardo had been active in the IASC reform (see Camfferman and Zeff 2007: 478) and became perhaps even more so in the establishment of the IAASB, with Morris (2001) claiming that the reform plan had originated from the suggestions of a GSC subcommittee.

According to Morris, IFAC was now in the process of creating, through the FoF and its executive arm, the TAC, 'structures that better reflect the modern reality of the profession—that the large firms play a key role in driving consistent standards of audit methodology, training and performance across borders' (2001: 15). The FoF, with its plans for global peer reviews of firms doing transnational audits, was hailed as 'a "major step" forward in the programme to strengthen the global financial architecture' (*Accountancy*, 1 February 2001: 10). The growing involvement of the big audit firms in IFAC was reflected in the membership of the new IAASB (which started work on 1st January 2002)—its 18 members included 5 designated representatives from the big audit firms (as proposed by the new TAC), 10 from IFAC member bodies, and 3 public members. Significantly, the 10 IAASB members from IFAC member bodies could (and did) also include individuals who came from the big firms.[20]

With the demise of Enron, in 2002, the FoF's peer review agenda lost momentum amidst the Sarbanes–Oxley Act and the move to extra-territorial inspection by the PCAOB. In 2004, the big firms held a Global Public Policy Symposium (GPPS) in Brussels. This was linked to the successor of the GSC, namely, the Global Public Policy Committee (GPPC), which currently describes itself in the following way: 'The GPPC of the six largest international accounting networks comprises representatives of BDO International, Deloitte, Ernst and Young, Grant Thornton International, KPMG

[20] One of the aims of the PIOB has been to reduce the number of members from the profession on the IAASB (both firms and professional associations) to less than 50 per cent of the Board's membership—a goal achieved for the first time in 2007.

and PricewaterhouseCoopers, and focuses on public policy issues for the Profession' (GPPC 2007). The GPPC has a Regulatory Working Group and a Standards Working Group. While their work is undertaken out of the public eye, it has published a number of policy papers. A GPPS has been held every year since 2004, most recently in New York in January 2008, and it now has a minimal web site.[21] The GPPS is attended by the top partners of the large firms and the world's top regulators in the field are also present. Although focusing on public policy issues for the profession, the GPPC seeks legitimation through a stated commitment to acting in the public interest and enabling the world economy to operate successfully—a viewpoint presented very clearly in the GPPC (2006) document entitled, 'Global Capital Markets and the Global Economy: A Vision from the CEO's of the International Audit Networks'.

This collaboration between firms[22] has clear consequences for the global governance of audit as it represents a stronger, more interlocking relationship than depicted by Hopwood's notion (1994) of the firms 'interfacing' with supranational regulatory authorities (p. 247). In a reconfiguration of the old regulatory bargain between the profession and the state, the international regulators very much need the large audit firms to ensure, within NIFA, that there is 'economic truth' (Volcker 2002) and stability in financial markets—while the audit firms need a monopoly over the service of auditing and limited levels of liability for their own financial security. With evident recent indications that neither party wants to see the collapse of another large audit firm, this is a developing relationship that looks set to flourish—as evidenced recently in the current credit crisis where the GPPC (2007) issued a paper with the title 'Determining the fair value of financial instruments under IFRS in current market conditions'. Significantly, this paper noted that:

The G7 Finance Ministers and Central Bank Governors have requested the Financial Stability Forum to review and report on certain aspects of the recent market turbulence, including valuation issues. As a result, the paper issued today by the accounting networks was shared in draft form with the Financial Stability Forum, some Board members and staff of the International Accounting Standards Board, the Standing Committee No.1 of the International Organisation of Securities Commissions (IOSCO) and the Accounting Task Force of the Basel Committee on Banking Supervision.[23]

---

[21] http://www.globalpublicpolicysymposium.com

[22] This collaboration does not include economic matters to do with the pricing of audit services. It is said by members of the GPPC committees that lawyers are present at meetings to ensure that does not happen.

[23] Source: http://www.pwc.com/servlet/pwcPrintPreview?LNLoc = /extweb/ncpressrelease. nsf/docid/00B25E49FECD10A2852573AD006E8C84

While the paper emphasizes at the outset that its role is to enhance awareness of the requirements of IFRS; that developing and interpreting IFRS is the responsibility of the IASB; and that the paper does not seek to amend or interpret IFRS, its production reflects a desire on the part of the GPPC to be seen as an authoritative actor in the global regulatory arena.

IFAC has certainly been able to expand the nature and scale of its standard-setting activities[24] through being in receipt of substantial direct funding from the large audit firms, which started in 1994 and now amounts to approximately one-third of IFAC's total revenues.[25] Indeed, it now has, what Graham Ward, the then President of IFAC, described in February 2006, when speaking at a global network firms' conference in London, as a close relationship:

The firms are part of our Regulatory Liaison Group, as I have mentioned; we meet regularly with the firms; the Transnational Auditors Committee and the Forum of Firms provide a formal relationship with international accounting firms; the firms are represented on IFAC's Planning and Finance Committee; nominees of the Transnational Auditors Committee serve on IFAC standard-setting bodies, providing immensely valuable practical expertise; in addition, many of the individual members of our member bodies are partners in, or employed by, the firms which, facilitate their participation in IFAC's standard setting and other activities. (Ward 2006: 11)

Accordingly, just as the international regulators are embedded within IFAC, so it appears are the big audit firms. Such potentially competing interests and influences represent a challenge to IFAC's perceived independence as a global audit standard setter, but something that it has to manage on an active basis, not least by seeking to enhance the transparency of its standard-setting processes as was discussed in the previous section.

CONCLUSION

When writing in 1994 about the 'very active politics' in the emergent international arena in accounting and auditing, Hopwood touched on a set of relationships and arrangements between international financial, regulatory and governmental organizations that over the subsequent 15 years have

---

[24] We do not have the space in this chapter to discuss the detail of IFAC's historical development, but it is important not to assume that this pattern has been one of automatic growth. The pursuit of global influence is very much an ongoing activity—in which battles can be won and lost, with a notable example of the latter being the AICPA's failed attempt to establish an interdisciplinary global credential (see Covaleski et al. 2003).

[25] Prior to this, IFAC was funded solely from the subscriptions of its member bodies—the national professional accounting institutes around the world.

developed into what is now widely recognized as the new international financial architecture' (NIFA). In terms of global accounting and auditing regulation, however, while the IASB has increasingly attracted research attention, little attention has been paid to the regulatory activities of IFAC or the audit arena more generally.

This chapter stands as a direct response to such a research gap, using the empirical lens of the global governance of auditing to assess the contemporary pertinence of Hopwood's (1994) observations and reflections on what was then probably best described as an emerging problematic—and one that still remains so! One of the residing strengths of Hopwood's paper is the sensitizing qualities of the writing. It has certainly helped to frame our discussions of developments on the positioning of IFAC and the big audit firms within NIFA. It says much of Hopwood's foresight that many of the research questions and challenges presented have been repeated and reaffirmed over intervening years.

Global governance emerges from this chapter as a contested interplay between a range of market actors and private and public (regulatory) authorities. Such a perspective usefully brings to the fore the issue of how governance gets done, by whom and to whom—in effect, it represents global governance as a moving puzzle. The global audit regulatory arena is one that clearly demands continuing analysis, review, and explanation. It is certainly a more complicated arena than when Hopwood was framing his arguments, with regulatory processes standing as an interwoven network of national, regional, and global systems and responsibilities.

Hopwood depicts 'small world' standard-setting processes, undertaken in a spirit of considerable complexity, limited openness and with international professional accounting and auditing bodies acting on behalf of (or as agents for) the audit industry and its dominant large, international firms. However, as our analysis has demonstrated, such assessments are not capable of being applied in a single, across-the-board fashion to today's global audit regulatory arena. While Hopwood mentions the need for more 'openness', he could not imagine the enormous impact of the Internet in facilitating this. Ironically though, it is private organizations in the auditing arena, in particular IFAC, which have sought to grasp the mantle of 'transparency': being persuaded to do so in order to legitimize their continued presence on a scene dominated by organizations with governmental connections.

The combination of IFAC's 'public interest' regulatory arrangements and its commitments to a publicly visible standard-setting process does not sit comfortably with Hopwood's claim: that bodies like IFAC routinely serve as agents for the audit industry and its powerful global players and work in ways that are hidden from public view. Indeed, there are grounds to suggest that enhanced transparency on the part of IFAC's standard-setting processes has developed side-by-side with the establishment of a less visible, but potentially more significant and fast moving field of influence in the form of the global policy work of the big audit firms. Intriguingly, while Hopwood wrote of the 'interface' between international regulators and organizations like IFAC, under today's NIFA, both international regulators and the big audit firms are structurally embedded within IFAC—such that IFAC has become not just a player in the global regulatory community but also an institutional site on which regulatory interactions are played out. In moving from just **interfaces** between organizations to **interlocking** relationships, what has resulted is a form of global governance which can be characterized as coordinated network governance where the international regulators and the international profession are bound together in a project of global governance in the audit arena—one characterized by cooperation and by 'moral suasion' rather than international law. IFAC has become a worldwide regulatory body seeking to enhance global standards of auditing (see IFAC 2007) and not just an association tasked solely with 'representing' and 'promoting' the interests of the international accounting profession; a body with strong ties to the big audit firms, but a consequent need to remain distinct from them and their developing global organization, the GPPC.

The multi-layered and network oriented mode of governance in the audit arena depends on specified notions of due process—with claims of applying technical expertise in a transparent and consultative fashion, underpinned by explicit commitments to serve in the public interest. Nevertheless, the regime adopted by the global institutions that make up the NIFA is one that has been constantly criticized for being dominated by the United States and a few other developed countries, allowing developing nations very little influence. Wade (2007) describes this post-Washington consensus as representing a narrowing of policy space pushing one particular kind of capitalism—the Anglo-American type. Regardless of whether one accepts such analysis, it is of value in the context of this chapter as it emphasizes the importance of devoting sufficient attention to the way in which competing interests are both represented and served by emerging institutional structures, arrangements, and policy declarations regarding the global governance of audit.

In this 'moving puzzle' what confronts IFAC is a conflicting set of organizational objectives and stakeholder expectations and a global regulatory arena inhabited by other regulatory bodies and professional associations/alliances. IFAC both cooperates and competes with these. The active nature of this arena is illustrated by recent organizational initiatives at the global level; these include the establishment of the Global Accounting Alliance (GAA) and the International Forum of Independent Audit Regulators (IFIAR), bringing together a host of national, independent audit oversight boards. We have already seen how the GPPC has been working closely with international regulatory organizations such as the FSF and providing interpretative guidance to the global profession when the circumstances (namely, the global credit crunch) demanded speedy, authoritative action. It is also noteworthy in this respect to see that at its most recent meetings in Norway and South Africa, IFIAR held individual sessions with the chief executives of the big audit firms.

Today, at the close of 2008, there is concern over the spreading financial crisis and more general recession, which has followed from the credit crisis. There is a feeling of unease, a concern that there is still no resolution of the crisis, and continuing comparisons to the 1929 Wall Street Crash, and its ruinous consequences. All of which somewhat weakens the achievements that were being claimed by the proponents of NIFA in the period up to the current credit crisis. More countries are now being involved in the formulation of a global regulatory response to the crisis as compared to when the FSF was established in 1999—and the G20 has replaced the G7 on the global scene. There are certainly some notable similarities in the current appeals to financial transparency and stability to regulatory policy discussions of a decade ago. However, a more diverse and radical range of solutions is starting to emerge—usefully illustrated in claims by BBC's influential business editor, Robert Peston, that 'we are a million miles from having created the political and regulatory institutions to help us to contain the risks of globalisation' and by Robert Wade, a prominent economist from London School of Economics, that '[g]lobal economic regimes need above all to be rethought to allow a diversity of rules and standards, instead of imposing ever more uniformity than there were then' (2008: 16). So, whilst there are some notable similarities in the current appeal to financial transparency and stability to that of a decade ago, it seems that a more diverse and radical range of solutions are appearing.

In what direction these developments will take regulation auditing is a moot question. Will it result in a fully functioning global governance system for audit or a rather uncoordinated group of organizations whose activities overlap in an unhelpful way? Such a contrast surely reminds us of the importance of researchers and other interested parties maintaining a watchful, critical eye over the values and practices embodied within any regulatory system.

APPENDIX A: TIMELINE

1973	- International Accounting Standards Committee (IASC) formed.
1974	- Basle Committee on Banking Supervision (BCBS) formed.
1977	- International Federation of Accountants (IFAC) formed.
1983	- International Organisation of Securities Commissions (IOSCO) formed.
1994	- **Anthony Hopwood's article published in European Accounting Review.** - Financial crisis in Mexico. - IFAC codifies standards on auditing (ISA). IOSCO decides not to endorse them. - International Association of Insurance Supervisors (IAIS) founded.
1995	- Regulators work on development of international financial regulation to prevent another crisis like that in Mexico.
1996	- European Commission Green Paper suggests possibility of ISA as EU standards.
1997	- Financial crisis in Asia begins. - President of World Bank heavily criticizes the accounting profession at their World Congress.
1998	- Financial Crisis continues, appears in other countries, for example, Russia. - G7 finance ministers, under chairmanship of George Brown, develop proposed solution to financial instability; it relies on the introduction of standards and codes for financial stability and transparency (idea of a global financial regulator dismissed). International accounting and auditing standards expected to play an important role.
1999	- Financial Stability Forum (FSF) formed by the G7. - World Bank begins Reports on Standards and Codes (ROSC) programme. - Big audit firms meet with each other, Global Steering Committee (GSC) formed. - International Forum on Accountancy Development (IFAD) established; bringing together IFAC, regulators, and the big audit firms.
2000	- Pressure on IFAC (particularly from US) to establish a global oversight board and work in the public interest for global auditing standards. - FSF includes ISA (and IAS) in its list of 12 key standards for financial stability.
2001	- IASC reconstituted as an independent standard setter, the International Accounting Standards Board (IASB) begins work. - IFAC makes first proposal for an independent public oversight board (POB), it includes the provision that its members should neither be regulators nor members of the accountancy profession. - Negotiations concerning the future of the IAPC begin, decision made to reorganize as the International Auditing and Assurance Standards Board (IAASB), big audit firms begin to contribute directly to IFAC's funding. - IFAD holds last meeting.
2002	- IAASB starts work. - Enron scandal reveals poor work by Big 5 audit firm, Andersen. Andersen collapses. - Sarbanes-Oxley Act passed, Public Company Accounting Oversight Board (PCAOB) to set standards for auditing.

(cont.)

- World Congress of Accountants held in Hong Kong, negotiations for restructuring IFAC begin.

2003
- IFAC's Monitoring Group is formalized (IOSCO, BCBS, IAIS, World Bank, and EC).
- IFAC's new structure is developed and agreed with Monitoring Group and member bodies. Proposals agreed include an independent Public Interest Oversight Board (PIOB).

2004
- Throughout the year IFAC negotiates with the EC as to what its position is re.PIOB.
- First Global Public Policy Symposium (GPPS) of the large audit firms is held. This becomes an annual event bringing together large firms and regulators. A Global Public Policy Committee (GPPC) of the large firms establishes working parties on regulation and standards.

2005
- PIOB membership finally agreed; European Commission takes observer status.

2006
- European Commission adopts Statutory Audit Directive proposing use of ISA for statutory audits in Europe.
- International Forum of Independent Audit Regulators (IFIAR) formed.

2007
- Credit Crisis in US begins – first signs of new financial crisis.
- IASB institutes constitution review, a monitoring group of senior world regulators proposed.

2008
- European Commission observers on the PIOB become full members.
- SEC agree roadmap to converge US GAAP and IFRS, discussion of possible convergence of ISA and PCAOB's auditing standards.
- Global Financial Crisis brings reconsideration of the international financial architecture developed a decade ago, G20 meets in Washington to consider the way forward.

APPENDIX B: ABBREVIATIONS

AICPA   American Institute of Certified Public Accountants
BCBS   Basle Committee on Banking Supervision
BIS   Bank of International Settlements
EC   European Commission
ECG   European Contact Group
EU   European Union
FoF   Forum of Firms
FSF   Financial Stability Forum
GAA   Global Accounting Alliance
GPPC   Global Public Policy Committee
GPPS   Global Public Policy Symposium
GSC   Global Steering Committee

IAASB	International Auditing and Assurance Standards Board
IAIS	International Association of Insurance Supervisors
IAPC	International Auditing Practices Committee
IAS	International Accounting Standard
IASB	International Accounting Standards Board
IASC	International Accounting Standards Committee
IFAC	International Federation of Accountants
IFAD	International Forum on Accountancy Development
IFIAR	International Forum of Independent Audit Regulators
IFRS	International Financial Reporting Standard
ILG	IFAC Leadership Group
IMF	International Monetary Fund
IOSCO	International Organisation of Securities Commissions
ISA	International Standard on Auditing
NIFA	New International Financial Architecture
PCAOB	Public Company Accounting Oversight Board
POB	Public Oversight Board
PIOB	Public Interest Oversight Board
ROSC	Reports on Standards and Codes
SEC	Securities and Exchange Commission
TAC	Transnational Audit Committee
UNCTAD	United Nations Conference on Trade and Development
US GAAP	US Generally Accepted Accounting Principles

REFERENCES

Baker, C.R., and Barbu, E.M. (2007). Evolution of research on international accounting harmonization: A historical and institutional perspective. *Socio-Economic Review*, 5, 603–32.

Ball, I. (2004). IFAC, IAASB, IASB, IOSCO, the FSF and the world regulatory environment. In G. Ward (ed.), *A Practitioner's Guide to Audit Regulation in the UK*. London: City and Financial Publishing. Available online at http://www.cityandfinancial.com/assets/documents/20051124110112aud1sample_WEB.pdf

Black, J. (2008). Constructing and contesting legitimacy and accountability in poly-centric regulatory regimes. *Regulation* and *Governance*, 2, 137–64.

Botzem, S., and Quack, S. (2006). Contested rules and shifting boundaries: International standard setting in accounting. In M-L. Djelic, and K. Sahlin-Andersson, *Transnational Governance: Institutional Dynamics of Regulation*. Cambridge: Cambridge University Press.

Brown, G. (1998). Press conference: Gordon Brown, Chancellor of the Exchequer, London, 9 May. Available online at http://www.g8.utoronto.ca/summit/1998birmingham/brown.html

Camdessus, M. (1999). Stable and efficient financial systems for the 21st century: A quest for transparency and standards. Address to the XXIVth Annual Conference of the International Organisation of Securities Commissions (IOSCO) Lisbon, Portugal, 25 May.

Camfferman, K., and Zeff, S.A. (2007). *Financial Reporting and Global Capital Markets: A History of the International Accounting Standards Committee, 1973–2000*. Oxford: Oxford University Press.

Clinton, W.J. (1998). Global economy. Speech to the Council on Foreign Relations, 14 September. Available online at http://www.cfr.org/publication/9349/ (as on 16 August 2008).

Cooper, D., and Robson, K. (2006). Accounting, professions and regulation: Locating the sites of professionalization. *Accounting, Organizations and Society*, 31, 415–44.

Covaleski, M.A., Dirsmith, M.W., and Rittenberg, L. (2003). Jurisdictional disputes over professional work: The institutionalisation of the global knowledge expert. *Accounting, Organizations and Society*, 28, 328–55.

Crockett, A. (2002*a*). Towards global financial reporting standards: A critical pillar in the international financial architecture. Speech held at the US–Europe Symposium, Rüschlikon, Switzerland, 27 February.

—— (2002*b*). Financial reporting: From shadows to limelight. Keynote speech at the conference, Risk and Stability in the Financial System: What Role for Regulators, Management and Market Discipline? Bocconi University, Milan, 13 June. Available online at http://www.bis.org/speeches/sp020613.htm

Davies, H. (2003). Is the global regulatory system fit for purpose in the 21st century. Monetary Authority of Singapore Annual Lecture, Singapore, 20 May.

Delonis, R.P. (2004). International financial standards and codes: Mandatory regulation without representation. *International Law and Politics* 36, 563–630. http://www.nyu.edu/pubs/jilp/main/issues/36/36_2_3_Delonis.pdf

Dewing, I.R., and Russell, P. (2004). Accounting, auditing and corporate governance of EU listed companies: EU policy developments before and after Enron. *Journal of Common Market Studies* 42, 289–319.

European Commission. (2003). Communication from the Commission to the Council and the European Parliament. Reinforcing the Statutory Audit in the EU. COM (2003) 286 final. Available online at http://eur-lex.europa.eu/LexUriServ/site/en/com/2003/com2003_0286en01.pdf

FSF (Financial Stability Forum). (1999). First meeting of the Financial Stability Forum. Press Release, 6 April. Available online at http://www.bis.org/press/p990406.htm (as on 24 August 2008).

—— (2000). Issues paper of the task force on implementation of standards. Paper presented at the meeting of the FSF, 25–6 March. http://www.fsforum.org/publications/r_0003.pdf?noframes=1.

Fujinuma, A. (2000). Available online at http://www.iasplus.com/pastnews/2000dec.htm (as at 31 August 2008).

Fung, A., Graham, M., and Weil, D. (2003). The political economy of transparency: What makes disclosure policies sustainable? Faculty Research Working Paper Series RWP03–039, John F. Kennedy School of Government, Harvard University.

Gallhofer, S., and Haslam, J. (2007). Exploring social, political and economic dimensions of accounting in the global context: The International Accounting Standards Board and accounting disaggregation. *Socio-Economic Review*, 5, 633–64.

GCPAS. (2001). German CPA society newsletter. Downloaded from http://www.gcpas.de in 2002, no longer available.

Germain, R.D. (2001). Reforming the international financial architecture: The new political agenda. G8 Scholarly Publications and Papers, University of Toronto. Available online at www.g8.utoronto.ca/scholar/germain2001/Germain_G20.pdf

—— (2007). Global finance, risk and governance. *Global Society*, 21, 71–93.

GPPC (Global Public Policy Committee). (2006). Global capital markets and the global economy: A vision from the CEOs of the international audit networks. Available online at http://www.globalpublicpolicysymposium.com/GPPC_Vision.pdf

—— (2007). Determining fair value of financial instruments under IFRS in current market conditions. Available online at http://www.pwc.com/extweb/ncpressrelease.nsf/docid/00B25E49FECD10A2852573AD006E8C84/$File/PwC_GPPC.pdf

Hale, T.N. (2008). Transparency, accountability and global governance. *Global Governance*, 14, 73–94.

Held, D. and McGrew, A.G. (2002). Introduction. In D. Held, and A.G. McGrew (eds.), *Governing Globalization: Power, Authority and Global Governance*. Cambridge: Polity Press.

Hopwood, A.G. (1994). Some reflections on 'the harmonization of accounting within EU'. *European Accounting Review*, 3, 241–53.

Humphrey, C. (2008). Auditing research: A review across the disciplinary divide. *Accounting, Auditing and Accountability Journal*, 21, 170–203.

—— Loft, A., Jeppesen, K.K., and Turley, S. (2006). The international federation of accountants: Private global governance in the public interest? In G.F. Schuppert (ed.), *Global Governance and the Role of Non-state Actors*. Baden-Baden: Nomos Verlag.

Hutchby, I. (2001). Technologies, texts and affordances. *Sociology*, 35(2), 441–56.

IFAC. (2003a). *Rebuilding Public Confidence in Financial Reporting*. New York: IFAC.

—— (2003b). *Reform Proposals*. New York: IFAC.

—— (2007). Regulation of the accountancy profession. Policy position, December. Available online at http://www.ifac.org/Store/Details.tmpl?SID=119681492324-5928andCart=121956834697583 (as seen on 24 August 2008).

IMF (International Monetary Fund). (1999). *International Financial and Monetary Stability: A Global Public Good*. Washington, D.C.: IMF.

IMF (International Monetary Fund) and World Bank. (2005). The standards and codes initiative—Is it effective? And how can it be improved? Available online at http://www.worldbank.org/ifa/ROSC%20review%202005.pdf. Seen (as on 31 August 2008).

IOSCO (International Organisation of Securities Commissions). (2000). *Model For Effective Regulation.* Report of the SRO Consulative Committee of the International Organization of Securities Commissions. Madrid: IOSCO.

—— (2002*a*). *Principles for Auditor Oversight.* A statement of the Technical Committee of the International Organization of Securities Commissions. Madrid: IOSCO.

—— (2002*b*). *Principles for Ongoing Disclosure and Material Development Reporting by Listed Entities.* A statement of the Technical Committee of the International Organization of Securities Commissions. Madrid: IOSCO.

IOSCO. (2002*c*). *Principles of Auditor Independence and the Role of Corporate Governance in Monitoring Auditor's Independence.* A statement of the Technical Committee of the International Organization of Securities Commissions. Madrid: IOSCO.

—— (2002*d*). *Principles for Auditor Oversight.* A statement of the Technical Committee of the International Organization of Securities Commissions. Madrid: IOSCO.

King, M. (1999). *Reforming the International Financial System: The Middle Way.* Speech by the Deputy Governor, Bank of England to a session of the Money Marketeers. Federal Reserve Bank of New York, 9 September.

Koski-Grafer, S. (2005). Remarks at the South Florida Program: Understanding the financial infrastructure for globalisation. Speech held at Tampa, Fl., 4 February. Available online at http://www.sec.gov/news/speech/spch020405skg.htm

Lehman, G. (2005). A critical perspective on the harmonisation of accounting in a globalising world. *Critical Perspectives on Accounting,* 16, 975–92.

Lodge, D. (1984). *Small World.* New York: Macmillan.

Loft, A., and Humphrey, C. (2006). IFAC.ORG—Organizing the world of auditing with the help of a website. In H.K. Hansen, and J. Hoff (eds.), *Digital Governance:// networked societies—Creating Authority, Community and Identity in a Globalised World.* Copenhagen: Samfundslitteratur Press/NORDICOM, 47–78.

—— —— and Turley, S. (2006). In pursuit of global regulation: Changing governance structures at the International Federation of Accountants (IFAC). *Accounting, Auditing and Accountability Journal,* 19, 428–51.

Manardo, J. (1996). Challenges for large audit firms in the European single market. Speech given to the Green Paper Conference on the Statutory Auditor, December.

Mattli, W., and Büthe, T. (2005). Accountability in accounting? The politics of private rule-making in the public interest. *Governance: An International Journal of Policy, Administration, and Institutions,* 18, 399–429.

Morris, D. (2001). Putting the 'vision' into practice. World Watch, Pricewaterhouse-Coopers, December, 14–16.

Morrissey, J.M. (2000). International reporting: The way forward. Speech to the 28th Annual National Conference on current SEC developments, 5 December. Available online at http://www.sec.gov/news/speech/spch443.htm

Parker, L.D. (2007). Financial and external reporting research—The broadening corporate governance challenge. *Accounting and Business Research*, 37, 39–54.

Perry, J., and Nölke, A. (2006). The political economy of international accounting standards. *Review of International Political Economy*, 13, 559–86.

Peston, R. (2008). A crash as historic as the end of communism. The Times, London, 9 December.

POB (Public Oversight Board). (2000). Report of the Panel on Audit Effectiveness. Available online at http://www.pobauditpanel.org/

Rahman, Z. (1998). The role of accounting in the East Asian financial crisis: Lessons learned. *Transnational Corporations*, 7, 1–51.

Riol, R. (2004). Choosing the right path toward credibility. President's message. *IFAC News*, 3 January.

Robson, K., Humphrey, C., and Loft, A. (2005). Globalizing technologies of performance: From national jurisdictional competition to co-ordinated network governance. Paper presented at the Government without Governance conference. Cardiff University, Cardiff, May.

Røder, J. (2001). Profile: Jens Røder. World Watch, PricewaterhouseCoopers, December, 8–9.

Rodrigues, L.L., and Craig, R. (2007). Assessing international accounting harmonization using Hegelian dialectic, isomorphism and Foucault. *Critical Perspectives on Accounting*, 18, 739–57.

Scholte, J.A. (2002). Civil society and democracy in global governance. *Global Governance*, 8, 281–304.

——(2004). Civil society and democratically accountable global governance. *Government and Opposition*, 39, 336–63.

Slaughter, A-M. (2004a). *A New World Order*. Princeton: Princeton University Press.

——(2004b). Disaggregated sovereignty: Towards the public accountability of global government networks. *Government and Opposition*, 39, 159–90.

Street, D.L., and Needles, B.E. (2002). An interview with Brian Smith of the International Forum on Accountancy Development (IFAD). *Journal of International Financial Management and Accounting*, 13, 254–73.

Suddaby, R., Cooper, D., and Greenwood, R. (2007). Transnational regulation of professional services: Governance dynamics of field level organizational change. *Accounting, Organizations and Society*, 32, 333–62.

Summers, L.H. (1999). Reflections on managing global integration. Speech to the annual meeting of the Association of Government Economists, New York City, 4 January.

Sutton, V. (1993). Harmonization of international accounting standards: Is it possible? *Journal of Accounting Education*, 11, 177–84.

Thorell, P., and Whittington, G. (1994). The harmonization of accounting within the EU: Problems, perspectives and strategies. *European Accounting Review*, 3, 215–39.

Turley, J. (2001). Comments at the US SEC Major Issues Conference: Securities regulation in the global internet economy. Washington, D.C., November 15.

Unerman, J., and Bennett, M. (2004). Increased stakeholder dialogue and the internet: Towards greater corporate accountability or reinforcing capitalist hegemony. *Accounting, Organizations and Society*, 29, 685–707.

Vishwanath, T., and Kaufman, D. (2001). Towards transparency: New approaches and their application to financial markets. *The World Bank Research Observer*, 16, 41–57.

Volcker, P.A. (2002). Accounting, accountants and accountability in an integrated world economy. Remarks made to the opening session of the World Congress of Accountants, Hong Kong, November.

Wade, R. (2007). A new global financial architecture? *New Left Review*, 46, 113–29.

Wade, R. (2008). Financial regime change? *New Left Review*, 53, 5–21.

Ward, G. (2006). Progress on the road to quality: Ethics, standards and regulation. Speech given at the ICAEW International Firms Networks Conference, London, 9 February.

Wolpensohn, J. (1997). Accountants and Society: Serving the public interest. Remarks to the World Congress of Accountants. Speech made to World Congress of Accountants, Paris, 26 October. Available online at http://web.worldbank.org/WBSITE/EXTERNAL/NEWS/0, content MDK: 20025564~menuPK: 34472~page PK: 34370~piPK: 34424~the Site PK: 4607,00.html

Woods, N. (2002). Global governance and the role of institutions. In D. Held, and A. G. McGrew (eds.), *Governing globalization: Power, Authority and Global Governance*. Cambridge: Polity Press.

—— (2006). Understanding pathways through financial crises and the impact of the IMF: An introduction. *Global Governance*, 12, 373–93.

Zeff, S.A. (2003). How the US profession got where it is today: Part II. *Accounting Horizons*, 17(4), 267–86.

11

The Study of Controller Agency

Sten Jönsson

INTRODUCTION

It seems to me that research in management control and especially the work
role of controllers therein has not made as much progress as it could have
done over the last few decades. Writers have applied different approaches
inside a system perspective, seeing management accounting more or less like a
technology. Some valuable insight have been presented, for example, about
integrated information systems to support management control (Dechow
and Mouritsen 2005; Quattrone and Hopper 2005); different roles for the
controller deduced from emphasis on different tasks (Sathe 1983); or the use
of different parts of the systems for different purposes (Simons 1991); and the
variety of tasks for an accounting department (Mouritsen 1996). However my
concern here is that there remain root (ontological) assumptions of management control systems—modelled, as they are, on a cybernetic conception of
information about outcomes in relation to a target value, negative feedback,
and the consequent idea about equilibrium maintenance—which prevent us
from seeing the full complexity of controller work. One could, of course,
claim that we are only interested in controller work when they do what we
(academics) define as controller work. But then we would condemn (in the
accounting literature) the controller to eternal hard reporting and analysing
labour and a boring identity as appendix to accounting machinery. Unproblematic for the academic discipline perhaps, but in the field we observe
controllers in much more challenging and complex situations. They have
more fun than that! It is time to re-conceptualize the controller as agent in
a structured context. To do that we need more direct observation of controllers at work. Tomkins and Groves (1983) suggested that the everyday work of
controllers should be studied as Hopwood has also, repeatedly, encouraged us

to do (1983, 1994). Jönsson (2001) argued that management accounting research should be aligned with managerial work.

There is Variety Within

Simon et al. (1954) found the three classical functions of accounting in their study of the controller's department and recommended that specialists should be responsible for each type, but few further studies followed. Hopper (1980) found that although decentralization of the management accounting function was associated with greater interaction between accountants and managers the most problematic aspect seemed to be that the accounting workflows pushed accountants toward passivity. Hofstede (1967) pointed at the fact that other units could do things more effectively (benchmarking) was a valid budget argument that had effects on behaviour, but only after consultants introduced benchmarking as a method much later did it become a fashion. Chapman (1998) demonstrated how accountants were part of differing managerial networks within the company as the task (budgeting, monthly reports etc) in focus shifted.

In the meantime there have been some efforts to relate controllership in practice to its environment. Kaplan and Johnson (1986) argued that the relevance of the numbers was lost (due to excessive 'systems thinking'?) and Kaplan was also party to influential efforts toward remedy in the ABC (Cooper and Kaplan 1991) and BSC (Kaplan and Norton 2001) concepts. But, looked upon with a critical eye, heroic and admirable as these efforts are in a practice sense, they must be considered as aiming at best at restoring a cybernetic sense to controllership.

The interesting aspect of these efforts is their starting point in the need to relate controller work to the strategic decisions by management. This means that the traditional conception of controllership (as defined by cybernetic budget control) is rendered obsolete. Simons (1991: 49), to take an example, found that control systems are not always used to 'manage by exception' but managers also use them interactively (note: rich communication required), if only during short periods, to promote innovation, change, and learning. Tomkins (2001), exploring the interaction between trust and information in alliances and networks, indicates that we need to develop theory to eliminate the current gap in our knowledge. He points to the social bonds, and as a consequence, obligations, between parties that emerge with regular patterns of transaction.

Obligations develop through mutual trust and fulfilment of positive expectations between managers, but they need also, increasingly, to be upheld 'at a distance' since managers do a lot of their managing somewhere else than in their home office (Strannegård and Friberg 2001; Tengblad 2002). The fragmentation in time of managerial work, highlighted by Mintzberg (1973), is now complemented by fragmentation in space, meaning not only global dimensions for networks but also that the structures of organizations and their very borders are fuzzy. Managers (including controllers) need, consequently, to visit sites inside these patterns of transactions to create structure, rules, and some measure of order by rich (face-to-face) communication. This is because rule making requires rich communication, and the use of a several types of controls. Hopwood (1974) argues that organizational control can be seen as the somewhat unpredictable outcome of the interaction between three modes of control, namely 'self-controls' (the individual controlling her/his own behavior), 'social controls' (mutual and informal control of each others' behaviour among members of a team), and 'administrative controls' (intentional and formal control by managers of subordinates' behaviour). It is therefore reasonable to expect that the controller's ordinary, everyday work will include building context for and exploiting this whole cocktail of controls. The more unstructured situations are this work will be more complex and demanding. In alliances and other kinds of hybrid organizations (Granovetter 1985; Heckscher and Donellon 1994; Grandori and Soda 1995; Ménard 1995, 2002; Lane and Bachmann 1998; Hodgson 2004) part of the complexity will stem from the need for the controller to work across hierarchical structures and reach understandings valid in more than one regime.

... And the Context is Changing

One further reason why the work of the controller is seriously put to the test is that the incidence of hybrid organizations is growing in frequency as well as variety. Few organizations, especially manufacturing ones, have 'clean' market relations for inputs and outputs. There is by definition, a legitimate variety in priorities and interests at the centres of deliberation. Members of an alliance between firms in the car industry, to take an example, compete and cooperate at the same time; members of industrial networks, like those related to aircraft production, may see opportunities to improve their position as the whole network adapts to external shocks, like September 11. In such cases structures crumble and new ones need to be erected, and the controller is implicated. Also in the management of product development projects of some size—the project management team being constituted of experts in different functional areas (like electronics, transmission, styling, etc.)—the controller needs to work creatively to build and maintain responsibility structures in the face of conflicting values. This, again, requires activity to establish and uphold structures for reporting to be aligned with. And it is not only structures of responsibility, but of accountability in the wider sense of appropriateness also need attention. As managers negotiate structures of appropriateness, within which trust and expediency can be built, emerging/contemplated activities need to be made accountable in the sense of Garfinkel (1967) in order to become accountable in the sense of management accounting. We need details of controller activity at the frontier as accounting emerges out of narratives of possibilities.

Scientific progress concerning studies of controlling and controllers in these, increasingly 'post-modern' situations, will probably benefit from being based in more descriptive assumptions (ontology) about the nature of controller work under such circumstances—keeping in mind that there is a limit to the usefulness of complex models—the ultimate version being the situation itself. As we know since our 101 in scientific method (and from Popper 1959), scientific progress happens through elimination of error. Therefore Popper encourages us to be bold in our conjectures, but strict in our refutations. The demarcation criterion, separating scientific approaches from other ones, is the fact that scientific hypotheses are refutable. With this criterion it is not a good idea to start from an ontology that is axiomatic in nature, that is its statements about the nature of the object under study are assumed to be inherently true and in need of no further proof. Starbuck (2006) argues referring to Hedges (1987) that one explanation to the slow progress of social sciences in comparison with sciences like physics, is that theories have a more stabilizing role in the latter type. When there is a deviation from expected results physics does not seek new theories on every occasion. Instead reasons for the inconsistency are sought in the methodology. Only an extended series of inconsistencies will force a major re-conceptualization.

In this way general theoretical propositions may serve as heuristics (even if they are so general that they convey little or no information). Starbuck (2006) gives an account of how theoretical frames in industrial psychology have replaced each other over the last decades and blames the lack of progress, largely, on the dominance of null hypothesis testing and the use of 'statistical significance' as scientific argument (rather than contribution to knowledge). The explanation seems to be that there is some basic confusion in social sciences about the difference between ontology and epistemology. The remedy may be, besides de-confusing the difference between the two concepts, to seek ontologies that make theories more robust. After all the challenge to formulate hypotheses and measures will be more rewarding without the over-simplistic basic assumptions about men and organizations we struggle with today. I make this claim in all modesty. I certainly do not wish to poke (too much) into the hornets' nest of the Pfeffer (1993)—van Maanen (1995) controversy over the need for theoretical unification/diversity in organizational scholarship. My suggestion is to focus on, as a start, what ontology-in-use one could identify in situated controller work. I have no quarrel with the use of statistical methods in testing hypotheses, but it should be recognized that such testing falls in the realm of epistemology. This discussion concerns whether scientific progress in this area can be furthered by a conscious development of an adequate ontology suitable for such progress. To illustrate the plausibility of this proposition I will first present and discuss three selected sequences of managerial deliberation taken from a large material of video taped management team meetings (with controllers present) collected over the last 10–15 years. Second, I will use the theory of practice discourse, represented by Bourdieu and Schtzki, to sketch a conception of good controller work in such structuring situations. Finally there will be occasion to mention the possibility of generalizing from single cases, an activity we engage (successfully) in every day.

ACTION IN THE FIELD—HERE AND NOW

We want to catch data on how competent managers (including the controller) go about doing their job. Managers work with words (Jönsson 1998*a*), and words are used in meetings where problems are solved and decisions made. Words bind subordinates and managers alike to tasks and commitments. Communication has organizing effects (Cooren 2000). Interviews with participants in meetings can give some information, but interview statements have already been subject to interpretation by the respondent. Furthermore they are cast in a form that the respondent believes is suitable for the outsider interviewer. So data will be at least twice codified when the researcher takes them down. Different informers will give different accounts of the same situation since they view it from different perspectives. Therefore direct observation is required in order to have a referent in interpretation and coding. This argument has been put forward by ethnomethodologists like Garfinkel (1967), Sacks (1992), and Silverman (1993). First, we have video recorded meetings, and then edited short sequences from the tapes. These sequences have been played back to participants individually with the question 'What is going on here?' The comments have been audio recorded and transcribed. Furthermore a number of background interviews with the participants giving reason to claim that the situations have been interpreted from a position of familiarity with the setting.

MORPHOGENESIS AND RULE SENSE MAKING

Acting appropriately means applying prudence in the classical sense.[1] To be able to take rational decision one needs access to relevant information. The controller may be instrumental in helping to design structures of information flows that match responsibilities (it is a firmly held belief in most organizations that you can only be held responsible for things you can influence and if you have the relevant information—but these conditions are often not met). The illustration shows how a controller may evoke rules to win time to re-design work at the interface between hierarchy and project. The opportunity to do some 'plumbing' at the interface between a development project and a production control department arises in a meeting, and would probably go away if the controller does not intervene with the appropriate argument.

CASE A: THE WINDOW PERSON SOLUTION—DESIGNING STRUCTURE

In the car industry product development is big business. Even a modest model year change is a major event. Project members can further their career by being brilliant, and by keeping within time schedules and target costs, while controllers are usually at a loss in doing something about overruns and delays. In mass production firms discipline is often quite strong; you are supposed to design to specification (pre-study), while in the premium segment design changes often come late because improvements stemming from R&D need to be introduced as soon as possible. Controllers may see the benefits of improving the value of the new model, but Production Control will have a hard time seeing the point in replanning the logistics up to the assembly line.

In this case we are observing a project management meeting for a year-model change project. The year is late 1997 and the work on the design of the 1999 year model is halfway through and as Production Control (Albert, a Dutchman) has its usual presentation of complaints about the projects lack of order in the project (like confirmed delivery dates for about 30 suppliers

---

[1] McCloskey (1998), has given an account of how the conception of prudence has changed over time, since Bentham, to assume a very limited meaning (efficiency) among today's economists.

missing). As Albert is about to leave the front of the room after his report Charles (Chassi) takes the opportunity to ask a question about the situation concerning information that he would have needed at a recent Cost Review Meeting (CRM is the target costing arena).

NedCar is the production company's name. Cost Review Meetings occur at each project gate—at this time a project had 10 gates. The project is divided into STs (System Tasks, like Chassi, Engine, etc.), which are, in turn, divided into DTs (Design Tasks, like Brakes). A PEC is a document that confirms a Product Engineering Change. Attached to a PEC is a 'yellow sheet' that details investment in production or tools due to that change. Activity teams are joint ad hoc teams set up to solve implementation problems when a model is prepared for production start. The 'basic plan' is the budget for the production of the new model based on the pre-study's Design Concept Sheets (i.e. exclusive of late design changes, PECs).

Background

In 1994, Mitsubishi Motor and Volvo Car formed an alliance to build the Carisma and the Volvo S/V 40, on the same assembly line, in a jointly owned assembly plant in Born, Holland, for both car models. Production was streamlined into a lean mode, which makes Production Control very sensitive to late design changes. The Volvo project for the 1998 model was located in Born (even if many of the lead engineers [ST managers, e.g. Engine, Electronics, Chassi] travelled to the meetings from Gothenburg) and held PMG (Project Management Group) meetings every two weeks, to report progress and solve problems. The agenda is similar each time with the different lead engineers having a few minutes each in the beginning to report on the status of their part of the project and then more detailed reports on selected areas. The following exchange takes place fairly late in the meeting; Production Control (represented by Albert) could not (as usual) participate in the whole meeting (reduced personnel at his department) so he had to report as he arrived. Charles takes the opportunity to complain about the lack of information on cost effects in production due to design changes:

Sequence Begins

Charles:
During the CRMs we had the cost engineering guys from NedCar here coming in saying that this is going to cost you this and this is going to cost

you that and my DTs and myself have not heard about these costs. And while you are here Albert, I sent you a memo on this.

< lower voice >

I don't know whether you agree.

< normal voice >

But I don't know where all these costs come from. We can't find them in PECs, we can't find any memos and some of them have not even been discussed properly in activity teams.

< Body trying to break in >

Albert:

Costs come from the basic plan and from issues. Yeah I suppose now they are updated and in those ... that document you find the investments.

Adam:

But isn't it normal that you have it also in PECs?

Albert:

Initially that is not needed!

Electricity:

But if the investment is dependent upon the technical design that we do? But if you don't get the feedback that this will cost you that much!?

Albert:

But, listen! We have sheets for design, design concept sheets. That is correct! So we know the design. We report that in the cost integrated plan. So you can discuss with these departments about the cost, of course. No problem, if you are okay on that then you know that this will be the cost for this project. If you change the design then you have a problem!

Quality:

Then you will see it on the PECs.

Electricity:

I had the same experience as Charles! The first time I saw these costs was when I got a thick booklet,

< showing with the fingers how thick a pile of paper it was >

and when I read it through it said 'investment in final assembly'! I never heard of it! It had never been reported to me nor my DTs! It is not implemented in yellow forms, I don't have a budget for it! I don't know what it is!

Albert:

I don't report to DTs not even to STs.

Electricity:

Then it is not my problem, because I don't take the cost!

Controller:

But Albert! If we do not have corresponding figures between the sum of the yellow sheets and the basic plan we cannot sign the basic plan. We don't have those costs in the PECs therefore we do not have them in the yellow sheets. So we need to have the PECs updated, and the costs are split (sic!) up per DT!

Albert:

No need. There is no need to have that additional investment on the PECs.

Controller:

Yes.

Albert:

Why?

Controller:

Because we need to penetrate those costs as well as all other costs per DT, and it is the STs' responsibility to say if these figures are correct or not. The basic plan is just the sum of all costs and when that sum fits with the sum of our yellow forms then the basic plan is okay. If it is not the same sum then it is not okay!

Sequence Ends

In the project each lead engineer (ST) is responsible for all cost effects that his/ her design changes cause (also in production). The owners, Mitsubishi and Volvo, sign the production budget (basic plan) for their part and additions to that budget (e.g. due to PECs) have to be decided by the Board of the production company. The controller in this project is also the assistant to the NedCar board member representing Volvo. All Volvo additions to the budget go through him for checking before the decision by the NedCar board. In a sense he is therefore Albert's principal. Albert is a man of hierarchical control and the Controller can use the rules of the hierarchy to have the last word. Not that Albert would change his ways, but, with the help of the project leader, a process could be started that provided Production Control with a Window Person through which all communication should flow and who was also the NedCar representative on the PMGs. This person had experience from both organizations and was a flexible solution that satisfied project engineers. The opportunity to set up a better flow of formal information emerged out of this situation and the controller caught it—both sides expressed a need for order—and gave both parties a good reason to be more disciplined in the future.

This project controller was well regarded by project members, partly for his competence and partly for his ability to design solutions at the interface between project and production, solutions that made it easier (and therefore more compelling) for design engineers to live up to their target cost responsibilities. The more experienced engineers would, of course, continue to use informal channels of information to win time. Still, there would be a structure and a formal, traceable path for inquiries and answers concerning important cost effects.

MORPHOSTASIS: HELPING OR REMINDING

Every day the structure of responsibilities need to be confirmed and re-confirmed because practices tend to drift and emergencies may be at odds with current practices, or somebody forgot what is required. There are numerous opportunities for the controller to remind managers of their duties to mind cost effects. In development projects like the one used in the illustration above such opportunities emerge at an astounding frequency. We calculated an average of 20 such incidents in 4-hour project management meetings in car projects. Another type of process where stereotyping and narrativising future structures tend to have its own dynamic is in the integration of former independent organizations. All right, the managers of the acquired company tend to say, we have a new owner, but we know how to run this company, and if the new owner has any suggestions he could take them up in board meetings and we will judge them on their merits. Soon, however, the managers will know that an important motif in acquisitions is to achieve synergy effects. This will certainly include rationalizing purchasing, which means that two fairly well functioning and inherently rational operations need to find new ways of working. Even if there is a new organizational design in place a large number of practices need to be abandoned and invented. The controller's point of view may be forgotten in struggles for turf.

CASE B: SEEK THE RATIONAL SOLUTION!

As mentioned a difficult part concerning acquisitions is the integration of the acquired company to achieve the expected synergies that justified the deal. A Norwegian company had been acquired (friendly takeover) by a Swedish one. It had been owned by the state before, was used to a passive owner and expected the new owner to continue the same way. The acquiring company saw integration of the purchasing departments as one of the first, easy, steps to collect synergy effects. For the Norwegian side it was of strategic importance to remain a 'complete' company, with all the functional departments, to be able to compete for the best young engineers in southern Norway. In this perspective a move of purchasing to the Swedish headquarters was seen as a first step in the reduction of their company to a mere production facility. The Business Area Head had tried to run 'soft' merger process in a matrix form (integration by function and country), but the crisis following September 11 made it necessary to press on and run a more centralized regime.

At this time there were three divisions (Norway, Aero, and Space) with staff for policy, strategy and integration on the Business Area level. The BA management team had 9 members (two Norwegians) and met every third week. On the agenda at this time (Spring 2002) were the integration of the Norwegian company and handling the devastating effects on the air transport industry of September 11 and the new low price competition in combination with rising fuel prices. Usually the atmosphere is friendly and informal. There are frequent jokes. Adam, the business area manager leads the meetings in a relaxed manner. But sometimes the conversation becomes highly argumentative, and that is usually when David (the head of division Norway) feels that integration threatens to reduce the Norwegian division to a mere production plant. David is sensitive to such issues.

In the situation shown below Charlie, from Purchasing, is reporting in the meeting early in 2002 on action to gain synergy by coordinating purchasing. For a certain category of material he proposes a package where about 15 suppliers will be deleted. Charlie is presenting and has got to a problematic supplier when David (head of the Norwegian division) sees a problem:

Legend

Adam: Business Area Head
Charlie: Project leader Purchasing
David: Norwegian Division Head
Erik: Aero Division Head
Fiona: Business Area Controller

Sequence Begins

Charlie:

< pointing to the OH picture >

Alfa Steel, as you know, we have production stoppages among other things, blanks that are hard to process, and so on. You all know about Chapter 11 and in this situation you in [Norway] had not made a decision... *[inaudible]* ... on how to proceed... *[inaudible]* ... so we could sign... *[inaudible]* ... this is a bit...

David:

< *breaks in* >

Here I really have... this is... < *David stands up and starts to move towards the projector* >... I brought some papers with me... < *while walking* > ... this is... as we have said before... here is a... on this issue we have diverging opinions about what the problem is < *he has reached his position, placed the transparency* > As I said to XX just before this meeting, and as we have seen in this meeting < *looks pointedly at Charlie* > ... Alfa Steel is our, by far, cheapest and best supplier < *turns back towards the screen* > And we would lose million by dropping Alfa Steel < *turning to Adam* > AND WE HAVE A PROBLEM! < *looks at Adam* > WE HAVE DIVERGING OPINIONS IN [Swedish company] AND [Norwegian company] < *starts walking back to his seat* > about several of the purchasing issues... this is a problem...

Erik:

Is it... is it...

Adam:

< *breaks in* >

But that is... that is why we will have a Purchasing Council [which David is heading].

David:

Yes, but... OK... but we haven't come very far on this... because now the (purchasing) delegation has gone to the USA... on their own anyway... WE DO HAVE DIVERGING OPINIONS AND INTERESTS HERE!

Charlie:

[inaudible] But our conclusion was that in the final analysis it is no great problem for you to stay on with Alfa Steel.

Erik:

If you put that diagram with Alfa Steel back < *points at Charlie to get his attention, Charlie does as he suggests* >... because is there something that is wrong in this picture? It would be a good thing if we could agree about what it says... < *pointing to the screen* > ... is there anything in this picture that is not correct?

David:

No, no... YOU HAVE A PROBLEM, and we do NOT have a problem with this!

Erik:

No... but Alfa Steel is sliding towards... has been under bankruptcy threat and we cannot live with them considering the quality they deliver and late deliveries...

David:

...BUT WE CAN...

Erik:

We can't afford to go on with them, so you have to weigh... how hard does it hit you and how hard does it hit us. And then we must see that it does not work if we break with them and you continue with Alfa Steel...

Charlie:

[Yes, we can].

David:

[Yes, we can]. < *Charlie nods towards Erik to confirm the correctness of David's statement* >

Adam:

Yes, well, of course... I agree about that... that it can be done... but should one REALLY do it eyes open... I mean this is a company that has been in Chapter 11... BEFORE the slump hit us... HOW!... could they MAKE IT over the next three years? We have to be pretty sure that they are not doomed.

Erik:

Yes! Yes! They couldn't even pay their electricity bill last fall! That's how bad it was!

Fiona:

Have you checked < *turns to David* > what it is that differs? Why [Norway] has a different opinion on this than [Sweden]?

Adam:

No...

Fiona:

You HAVE to do that!

Sequence Ends

In this exchange David uses the rhetorical device to cast the exchange as a difference of opinion (not as differing calculations). Asking for a factual basis for the different opinions the controller (Fiona) upholds a practice/ structure of decision-making, and defuses a conflict situation where arguments start to repeat themselves and might escalate. Furthermore Charlie had discussed this issue with his colleagues in Norway and they agreed that if the Swedish company were to drop this supplier it would not push Alfa

Steel over the edge toward bankruptcy. So there was time to find a joint solution. (This information was not included in the discussion.) This was what the delegation to the USA David mentions was working on. Unfortunately the Norwegian company had no representative to send on this trip (another cause for David's concern). Fiona calls for rationality, and a factual basis for discussions on structural change, and that goes down well with the members who are mostly engineers. In a follow-up interview Fiona showed how the difference of opinion was explained by the fact that the Norwegian company bought simpler components and the Swedish one bought more complex ones. The matter was soon defused and purchasing integration could continue. The opportunity to defuse an emotional situation was generated by the emotional charge used by David to protect his division. Fiona's timing was good. One can read embarrassment in the faces of some of the managers.

MORPHOLOGY: TALK ABOUT A POSSIBLE FUTURE REDESIGN OF AN INDUSTRIAL NET

In industrial networks one of the strategic issues is how to improve your position. If you can get recognition as party to product development or as an integrator of components to sub-assemblies you can add value to your output. The best option, if you are not already an OEM (Original Equipment Manufacturer), is to become a Centre-of-Excellence meaning that the OEM hands over responsibility for development, production, spare parts etc. for a part of the final product, that is places trust in you and closes down its own capacity in that area. The problem here is that the decision rests with the OEM—we have to persuade the other to take a strategic decision on our behalf. If we could do that it would change the structure of the net and our own way of doing business. But it would be a structural change based in operational excellence rather than in excellent controlling. So the controller is well advised to keep quiet while the future Centre-of-Excellence is narrativized collectively by the division heads (mainly).

CASE C: THE CENTER-OF-EXCELLENCE INITIATIVE

In this case a group of senior managers at a first-tier supplier of components for aircraft engines (AERO) to a handful of OEMs discuss and gives a go-ahead to a new strategic initiative. The time is April 2002 when the air transport industry faced a crisis after September 11 and there was a virtual stop in new orders for aeroplanes. Several nodes in the network that makes up the aerospace industry were in trouble. An opportunity was at hand for strong actors to take initiatives to improve their position. We observed the management team meetings of AERO over several months and interviewed members several times on their understanding of what was going on in the deliberations. The incident constituting this case became significant to us when we, more than 5 years later, read in the press that the initiative seemed to have become a success (at last).

In the autumn 2007 AERO issued a number of press releases announcing a success in its cooperation with a large customer (OEM1): It was awarded 'best partner' status to OEM1, this customer had also accepted an application of lightweight technology developed by AERO in one of its components (production start 2010), and, finally, pursuing world leadership in this light weight technology an important acquisition of a research-based company in composite materials was announced. Reading about this in the press our observations of the top management team some 5 years earlier took on a new significance. We had the discussion that started it all on videotape! How could such a vague discussion yield such path breaking results? There was reason to revisit the decision event. Here with a view to the role of the controller in that situation.[2]

The issue at stake in that discussion was how to persuade OEM1 to afford AERO a 'Centre-of-Excellence' status for a group of components that goes into a specific engine, which was currently (i.e. in 2002) developed by OEM1. This would add value by including more design work and it would also provide some shelter from price competition. If granted CoE status AERO must assume life-cycle responsibility for the design, production, and spare part provision of a group of components for current and future versions of a type of engines, which would require recruiting more engineering staff. It would also mean that OEM1 would place their trust in AERO and reduce or even eliminate a whole department of engineers. This might be an attractive offer for OEM1 since the whole aircraft industry was in cutback crisis after the terrorist attack. The strategy of AERO in this situation was to add R&D resources, which had generated the lightweight technology mentioned, but there was no breakthrough yet. The prevailing manufacturing principle was

---

[2] For the record it should be noted that when we approached two members of the management team (separately) with congratulations on the successful completion of the initiative we had videofilmed five years earlier, both of them responded by claiming not to remember that they had discussed this issue so long ago.

still 'make-to-print' albeit in very difficult and expensive alloys. The management team at AERO was running a major cost improvement project as well, but an improvement of the strategic position was required. The department for Business Development had sensed that OEM1 might be interested to discuss an upgrading of the relation with AERO and had charged Charlie with working out a 'script' for how the Center-of-Excellence prospect could be put on the agenda in an upcoming lower level meeting with OEM1 in a few weeks. He and a colleague will represent AERO in that meeting. The management team of AERO had invited Charlie to present his approach when bringing the initiative up. The 9 members of the group listen to Charlie and then deliberate on the pros and cons of the prospect (seen from OEM1's perspective as well as for us).

The transcribed text from this 29 minute discussion consists of 630 numbered lines of dialogue and 53 inserted lines of text describing body language, simultaneous talk, laughter, etc.[3]

Charlie's presentation takes about 250 lines (including inserted questions of clarification). His claim is that AERO will offer OEM1:

o The benefits of not keeping people employed in this section of their technical office.
o They will avoid spending R&D money in this area.
o They may free people and capital for application in other areas where they can do more good.

These are all sound economic arguments. He also comments on how he will go about getting to the point in the upcoming meeting (starting with concrete engineering discussion of the design of a specific part of an engine (highlighted on his first slide) and then move into more strategic issues).

The bulk of the deliberation that follows concerns what an acceptance of the prospect would mean for AERO and of how significant other actors might influence the outcome. The discussion is driven by questions posed from different perspectives. Most of the questions are for clarification and as such easy enough for Charlie or other members to answer (we could identify 21 such questions), but some are of a more probing nature and as such they constitute/identify a distinct perspective on the prospect under construction.

One such probe concerns how the design of the compressor in the X-engine of OEM1 will affect the design of 'our' component Y. The answer constructed

---

[3] It is impractical to present the entire exchange (30 pages of text) in its details in a short text like this. I have chosen to refer to the numbered lines to indicate where in the conversation a quote or statement is located.

in concert by several speakers is that the current compressor version is not competitive so OEM1 has a number of options including 'outsourcing' the compressor to a German firm, which has a 7-step compressor under development, which, in turn, will have an effect on 'our' design should it be chosen. This leads to a discussion of the design philosophy of the German firm (scientific and not enough concern for manufacturability), which in turn, gives the boss reason to a value statement that stresses 'our' concern for manufacturability (which is an argument that the OEM1 people like). The discussion ends with a somewhat vague endorsement of Charlie's presentation. The decision comes at the prodding of Charlie (he seems to think that the group has wandered into trivialities) as he says: 'Well... eeh... I don't hear a no here... we do see eye to eye on this don't we... I mean that this is an extremely good step to take?' (line 558). The business area head, responds: 'No, you hear a resounding Yes!' Charlie: 'Yes < *laughs* > all right!' The head: 'Isn't that so?' < *looks around the room while pounding, in a slow motion, the back of the chair next to him* > Space division head cuts in: 'It sounds like a great opportunity' (line 563).

Charlie's point is rounded off with a formal decision on a budget allocation for the study to determine the production cost of the new lightweight design. Only in this latter part does the controller take active part in the discussion, and then only to confirm that she will take care of the budget allocation formalities.

In this case the vagueness of the decision was striking, the utterances of members seemed to indicate that they were including this emerging possibility in their own narratives for the future of the company and their own area of responsibility. The endorsement was more of Charlie's approach than of a strategic plan. The controller, wisely, was quiet throughout the discussion of the prospect of Centre-of-Excellence status, even if the arguments to be aimed at OEM1 had to do with cost savings. However the discourse is solidly engineering talk and the basis for calculating any financial of cost implication is too vague for a controllers' competence to have any bearing. The rules of the game of the relations within this industrial network are based in trust in engineering competence, certifications, and quality assessment.

This strategic decision is based in value judgements by a group of experienced managers on the basis of a middle manager's loosely stitched synopsis for pending negotiations, rumours, and opinions about the situation of relevant actors in the network. This is no basis for calculation of financial consequences. Members agree that, should the project succeed, the future prospects of the company would be rosy, and the business situation would be fundamentally altered. The decision situation should be seen as pre-rational in the sense that it concerns a prospective change in the industrial network.

Only much later will there be room for rational calculation. Then the controller will have a role to play. Had she demanded facts in this situation she would have generated uncertainty. Her judgement of the ontology of this situation helped her refrain from interference.

DISCUSSION

Theorizing Situated Management

After decades of suffering of an inferiority complex, because of the sense of being at a pre-paradigmatic stage (Kuhn 1962) for most social sciences, there seems to be a stabilizing development toward an ontological basis for some of the social sciences (Bourdieu 1998, 2000; Schatzki 2000, 2002, 2005), particularly for those who deal with management, i.e., intentional efforts to influence and direct activities in and between organizations. Schatzki (2000, 2005) introduces the notion of 'site ontology'. He argues that the site of the social is a complex 'mesh' (not just a network of nodes and links) of practices and material arrangements. Every practice is constituted by a set of (possible) acts linked together by:

- o Understandings (related to these acts).
- o Rules (explicit prescriptions).
- o Teleoaffective structures (appropriate ends and uses of resources, and 'even' emotions that are acceptable).

Ahrens and Chapman (2007) are of the opinion that Schatzki's site ontology offers advantages in the study of management control practice because it is more (than Latour's notion of actor network theory) accepting of structures of intentionality—I agree. The point, and difficulty, of the site ontology conception is that it 'situates' the ontology of the actor (not only that of the researcher observing the actor) in the mind *and* context of the actor. An actor who wants to do a good job of whatever she is doing needs to demonstrate skill in context. Much like Smith ([1759]1997) argued that the actor in seeking the sympathy of others—that this was the right thing to do given the circumstances and the intentions of the actor—must perform the impartial spectator procedure. In such a procedure the actor contemplating action considers what an impartial spectator would think about the action and acts accordingly. Sympathy, according to Smith, is a parallel emotion of approval (Ottesen 2002). It is not the same emotion as the actor's (you do not feel the same sorrow as I do when my father dies, but you have sympathy) but a similar one. The civil society that emerges when people act in a sympathy seeking way á la Smith ([1759] 1997) is an unintended consequence. This happens because members decentre their selfish utility and argue on a community level. It should be noted that Smith ([1776]1997) developed a further version of structures as unintended consequences when he discussed how people can improve their lot by specializing in action they are good at and 'truck and barter' for goods they do not produce themselves. Markets emerge. Competition will award those who are more skilful. Darwin (1859) applied this idea (referring to Smith) as he presented his theory of evolution where individuals struggle for survival in context and those with viable strategies (in that context) start to form species (as an unintended consequence) through selection and retention.

The difficulty with site ontology is that the context is patterned by structures of intentionality—it is a 'mesh' of practices—and this means that the actor will need to diagnose the situation in order to be able to act appropriately. Skill will be demonstrated in diagnosis and design of action; the decision to go ahead with action will come as a reasoned output of such deliberation, and will include its own success criteria in the form of a script for successful action (in that context). Skilful action will be rewarded by others in the form of recognition of identity and reputation for skilfulness (Wenger 1998). Membership work is constituted by identity and alignment (Munro 1996). Its script (narrative form; cf. Cooren 2000) may be retained as exemplar of skilful action by the actor and by observers. Together with other (possible) scripts it may form a (malleable) practice. Observers judging skilful action must be acquainted with the appropriate practice for judgement to be competent. This means to take an interest in the site ontology emerging as a management team constructs a collective understanding of a situation and its implications.

From early on, Bourdieu (1977, 1990) has argued for the study of practical knowledge and its situational logic. Understanding such logic requires a study of action to map 'repertoires' that accomplish everyday management through various situations. The 'stylistic unity' of a practice, its operating principles, Bourdieu (1977, 1990) name its habitus. This allows habitual performance of an expected function under normal circumstances, giving us dispositions that help us avoid considering 'unthinkable' practices. Habitus adapts to habitat (Jönsson 1998b). However, contextual change as well as a gap between expectations and experiences may engage actors in re-constitutive conversation (Bourdieu 1990).[4] The illustrations in this chapter have been selected to give varieties of such managerial re-constitution and the controller's possible roles in them. He/she needs to do the appropriate thing in site at the time.

---

[4] A more extensive discussion of Bourdieu applied to management accounting may be found in Baxter and Chua 2008).

The Logic of Appropriateness

In a logic of consequentiality (i.e. rational choice, March and Olsen 1976; March 1994) it is the consequences for the agent (or the principal of the agent) that count and are the object of calculation. This simplifies things for the rational agent since the goal set by the principal identifies what is relevant (and what is not), even if the situation is complex. In situations where there are several legitimate agents (with principals) the perspective of the other and the conventions of proper behaviour have to be considered. Even if the agent is determined to act in self-interest the fact that the other agents may apply counter-strategies generates an uncertainty that will, at least, require monitoring and a readiness to reconsider. This does not mean that the situation is readily described as a game since the rules are not clear enough to constitute a game. Even if they were (partly) the outcome over time will be genuinely uncertain (look what activity over decades the announcement by Axelrod (1984) of a competition between strategies in the simple game Prisoner's dilemma generated!). This leaves the agent with the question: 'What should a person like me do in a situation like this?' This implies consideration of:

o What situation (diagnosis)?
o Who am I (or want to become)?
o What to do (what rules guide legitimate action)?

A logic of appropriateness will bring the person and her/his identity, skills, and experience into play in context. This particular situation may offer an opportunity for the actor to enhance his/her competence and standing, i.e. identity, if action is constructed appropriately, i.e. in concert with other actors. Dominance strategies may work temporarily, but the long term argues for community concerning action in and by organizations.

Diagnosing a complex situation may be thought of in terms of what doctors do when they link symptoms—diagnosis—therapy. Even in a field like medicine where this linkage is well backed up by scientific knowledge (remember evidence based medicine) there is controversy over therapies as individual patients differ. The practitioner of management may be well advised to do like good doctors do Starbuck (2006: 108 ff.), act and watch how patients respond to treatment. In an organizational setting this would correspond to calling a meeting of people with different skills to discuss the situation and arrive at what is appropriate therapy. Managers spend a lot of their time in meetings, listening, and discussing. We should pay more attention to what goes on in those meetings.

Implications for Method

I claim that what goes on in those meetings is a joint construction of order, and the controller's specific task there is to safe guard the structures that uphold/underpin this order. The controller, working on the crumbling or emerging structures, needs to seize the opportunities as they emerge and therefore must be expected to apply a logic of appropriateness. Baxter and Chua (2008) report on a case where a controller (CFO) uses different methods to take charge in a turn-around situation, but most of the time the situations have a less dramatic character. What is implied here is that controller action should be expected to be contingent upon the site ontology as judged by controller and other management members.

It seems obvious that action by those participants in meetings, here and now, cannot be adequately captured in ex post interviews since respondents will give interpretations in the light of hindsight (making sense of the current situation by re-interpreting history). What is required to capture the moment is some kind of concurrent recording. Notes by an experienced field worker might do, but the opportunity to come back and apply different interpretations to the same material is secured with a recording. Video makes the researcher aware of the importance of body language in communication. A further advantage is that clips from a recording can be replayed to participants with the question: 'What is going on here?' The differences among members in their interpretation of the same sequence are surprising every time. How can a joint decision be understood so differently? And how can a decision, understood so differently, serve a coordinating purpose? We have a long way to go before we have theorized 'site ontology' well enough to have an instrument for understanding controller work. There is no time to lose.

It is true that this type of data collection (direct observing video recording) runs the risk of infringing on personal integrity of those observed and that there is (in most countries) a procedure for informing the participants about the conditions that apply. Written consent explicit enough to cover all contingencies will probably dissuade prospective subjects from giving such consent. The regulation of proper behaviour by researchers may prevent them from even trying to set up a study of this kind. This would be a pity. The researcher needs to gain the trust of the subjects and behave responsibly harvesting the insights that multifaceted and multiple analyses of the same discourse may offer.

As industrial networks grow more complex, globalization pit ways of working against each other in close encounters, and life cycles of product offers grow shorter, organizations need to be manoeuvrable. This calls for compact organizations able to manage rich communication (in meetings). To study 'control at a distance' is not enough. We need to study control at close range as well.

It is at this close range that prospects find their form. Hopefully the three illustrations above, short as they are, have demonstrated that vast amounts of information are needed to diagnose a managerial situation. Also, the same situation will be understood differently from different perspectives. The prospect, that is the view from a perspective, will be different for different perspectives. Assume that people start their sense making, or prospect building, from islands of order they detect in an initially chaotic situation. Such islands (chaos theory's 'attractor') may differ when they are seen from the professional perspective of the controller versus the perspective of operational managers. It is reasonable to assume that a collective prospect developed by operational managers will have narrative form (and then, and then, and then), while the controller frame will be systemic, or, to use the Bruner (1990) term, paradigmatic. It is in this field that the active controller is charged to create stabilizing structures, and it is more like a plumbing job at the interface between the driving narratives of operations and the paradigmatic structures of accounting.

At this fuzzy border between narrative and paradigm the controller needs to grasp the unfolding situation ('ontically') to see an opportunity to further good resource use. Part of the making sense of that situation is to assess the bases for arguments ('ontology') used by interlocutors. Only when a statement can be understood as a 'fact' ('epistemology') inside the frame used by the other can the controller establish a 'boundary object' (Star 1989; Bowker and Star 1999) that may serve as a link between the relevant frames (or communities of practice). Moscovici (and Doise 1994) has shown in a large number of experiments that collectives exhibit 'group polarisation', that is members tend to seek agreement in the direction of extreme opinions. Management teams are consensus seeking collectives and are thus likely to arrive at extreme opinion (for instance, the boss is always right). In our study of the practitioner achieving 'artful integration' (Suchman and Trigg 1993) in complexity it seems necessary to work sense making on all these three levels of abstraction (ontic, ontology, epistemology).

The not so desirable aspect of this approach is that the knowledge gained will not be of a general nature, as we normally understand it, that is applicable to a whole class of phenomena. Possibly it is time to recognize a new form of generalization, extracting principles from sequences of cases, that is by shifting the level of analysis. This is done as we learn to discern critical aspects of the learning object (in our case managerial situations; Marton and Pang 2006). We (children) learn to discern the dog-ness of dogs by being exposed to many instances of the object of learning (small dog, big dog, black dog, and dead dog) but also by contrasts (a cat is not a dog), which help us identify the critical aspects. Furthermore these contrasts generate a need for concepts for that which is similar between contrasting instances (the 'dog' and the 'cat' will require an 'animal' concept). In this sense a vocabulary, useful in diagnosing managerial situations, will be generated as a generalization, over time, with the appended recipes for appropriate action. In parallel the community (Wenger 1998) of controller scholars may develop a generalizing vocabulary over a growing number of observed instances.

We need to pay attention to the details (even if the Devil is in there)! The resulting theories are not likely to be simple (cf. Thorngate's [1976] 'impostulate of theoretical simplicity'; Weick [1999]). And we need time to do the necessary observations. Management situations should be the unit of analysis and strict observation of what went on (at least audio recorded) the data set. The constellation of participants and the matrices of arguments will explain outcomes. References to earlier studies and relevant philosophical discourse (e.g. virtue ethics) will guide us in building, accumulatively, a sound empirical basis (continuously renewed). 'Statistical significance' (Starbuck 2009) will not save us!

REFERENCES

Ahrens, T., and Chapman, C.S. (2007). Management accounting as practice. *Accounting, Organizations and Society*, 32, 1–27.

Baxter, J., and Chua, W.F. (2008). Be(com)ing the chief financial officer of an organization: experimenting with Bourdieu's Practice Theory. *Management Accounting Research*, 19, 3, 212–30.

Bourdieu, P. (1977). *Outline of a Theory of Practice*. Cambridge: Cambridge University Press.

——— (1990). *The Logic of Practice*. Cambridge: Cambridge University Press.

Bowker, G., and Star, S.L. (1999). *Sorting Things Out—Classification and Its Consequences*. Cambridge, Mass.: MIT Press.

Bruner, J. (1990). *Acts of Meaning*. Cambridge, Mass.: Harvard University Press.

Chapman, C.S. (1998). Accountants in organizational networks. *Accounting, Organizations and Society*, 23(8), 737–66.

Cooper, R., and Kaplan, R.S. (1991). *The Design of Cost Management Systems*. Englewood Cliffs: Prentice Hall.

Cooren, F. (2000). *The Organizing Property of Communication*. Amsterdam: Benjamins.

Darwin, C.R. (1859). *The Origin of Species*. London: John Murray.

Dechow, N., and Mouritsen, J. (2005). Enterprise resource planning systems, management control and the quest for integration. *Accounting, Organizations and Society*, 30, 691–733.

Garfinkel, H. (1967). *Studies in Ethnomethodology*. Englewood Cliffs: Prentice-Hall.

Grandori, A., and Soda, G. (1995). Inter-firm networks: Antecedents, mechanisms and forms. *Organization Studies*, 16(2), 183–214.

Granovetter, M. (1985). Economic action and social structure: The problem of embeddedness. *American Journal of Sociology*, 91(3), 481–510.

Heckscher, C., and Donellon, A. (eds.) (1994). *The Post-bureaucratic Organization: New Perspectives on Organizational Change*. London: Sage.

Hedges, L.V. (1987). How hard is hard science, how soft is soft science? *American Psychologist*, (42), 443–55.

Hodgeson, D. (2004). Project work: The legacy of bureaucratic control in the post-bureaucratic organization. *Organization*, 11(1), 81–100.

Hofstede, G.H. (1967). *The Game of Budget Control*. Assen: Koninklijke van Gorcum.

—— (1980). *Culture's Consequences: International Differences in Work-related Values*. Beverly Hills: Sage.

Hopper, T.M. (1980). Role conflicts of management accountants and their position within organization structures. *Accounting, Organizations and Society*, 5(4), 401–11.

Hopwood, A.G. (1974). *Accounting and Human Behaviour*. London: Haymarket Publishing.

—— (1983). On trying to study accounting in the context in which it operates. *Accounting, Organizations and Society*, 8(2/3), 287–305.

—— (1994). Accounting and everyday life. *Accounting, Organizations and Society*, 19(3), 299–301.

Johnson, H.T., and Kaplan, R.S. (1987). *Relevance Lost: The Rise and Fall of Management Accounting*. Boston: Harvard Business School Press.

Jönsson, S. (1998a). Relate management accounting research to managerial work! *Accounting Organizations and Society*, 23(4), 411–34.

—— (1998b). *Accounting for Improvement*. Chichester: Wiley.

—— Nilsson, L., Rubenowitz, S., and Westerståhl, J. (1999). *The Decentralized City: Democracy, Efficiency, Service*. Gothenburg: BAS.

Kaplan, R.S., and Norton, D. (2001). *The Strategy Focused Organization: How Balanced Scorecard Companies Thrive in New Business Environment*. Boston: Harvard Business School Press.

Kuhn, T.S. (1962). *The Structure of Scientific Revolutions*. Chicago: Chicago University Press.

Lane, C., and Bachmann, R. (1998). *Trust Within and Between Organizations: Conceptual Issues and Empirical Implications*. New York: Oxford University Press.

March, J.G. (1994). *A Primer on Decision Making*. New York: Free Press.

—— and Olsen, J.P. (eds.) (1976). *Ambiguity and Choice in Organizations*. Bergen: Universitetsforlaget.

Ménard, C. (1995). Markets as institutions versus organizations as markets? Disentangling some fundamental concepts. *Journal of Economic Behaviour and Organization*, 28(2), 161–82.

——(2002). The economics of hybrid organization. Presidential address, International Society for New Institutional Economics, MIT, September 29.

Mintzberg, H. (1973). *The Nature of Managerial Work.* New York: Harper and Row.

Mouritsen, J. (1996). Five aspects of accounting departments' work. *Management Accounting Research,* 7, 283–303.

Munro, R. (1996). Alignment and identity work: The study of accounts and accountability. In R. Munro, and J. Mouritsen (eds.), *Accountability, Power, Ethos* and *the Technologies of Managing.* London: Thompson.

Ottesen, J.R. (2002). *Adam Smith's Marketplace of Life.* Cambridge: Cambridge University Press.

Pfeffer, J. (1993). Barriers to the advance of organizational science: Paradigm development as a dependent variable. *Academy of Management Review,* 18, 599–620.

Popper, K.R. (1959). *The Logic of Scientific Discovery.* London: Hutchinson.

Quattrone, P., and Hopper, T. (2005). A 'time odyssey': Management control systems in two mutinational organizations. *Accounting, Organizations and Society,* 30, 735–64.

Sacks, H. (1992). *Lectures on Conversation, vol. I–II,* G. Jefferson ed. Oxford: Blackwell.

Sathe, V. (1983). The controller's role in management. *Organizational Dynamics,* Winter, 31–48.

Schatzki, T.R. (2000). A new societist social ontology. *Philosophy of the Social Sciences,* 33, 174–202.

——(2003). *The Site of the Social: A Philosophical Account of the Constitution of Social Life and Change.* University Park, PA: Pennsylvania State University Press.

——(2005). The sites of organizations. *Organization Studies,* 26(3), 465–84.

Silverman, D. (1993). *Interpreting Qualitative Data: Methods for Analysing Talk, Text, and Interaction.* London: Sage.

Simon, H.A., Guetzkow, H., Kozonetsky, G., and Tyndall, G. (1954). *Centralization vs Decentralization in Organizing the Controller's Department.* New York: The Controllership Foundation.

Simons, R. (1991). Strategic orientation and top management attention to control systems. *Strategic Management Journal,* 12(1), 49–62.

Smith, A. ([1759] 1997). *The Theory of Moral Sentiments.* Washington: Regenery.

——([1776]1981). *An Inquiry into the Nature and Causes of the Wealth of Nations.* Indianapolis: Liberty Classics.

Star, S.L. (1989). The structure of ill-structured solutions: Heterogeneous problem-solving, boundary objects and distributed artificial intelligence. In M. Huhns, and L. Gasser (eds.), *Distributed Artificial Intelligence.* Menlo Park, Calif.: Morgan Kaufmann, 37–54.

Starbuck, W.H. (2006). *The Production of Knowledge—The Challenge of Social Science Research.* Oxford: Oxford University Press.

——(2009). The constant causes of never-ending faddishness in the behavioural and social sciences. *Scandinavian Journal of Management,* 25(1), 108–16.

Strannegård, L., and Friberg, M. (2001). *Already Elsewhere. Play, Identity and Speed in the Business World*. Stockholm: Raster Förlag.

Suchman, L., and Trigg, R. (1993). Artificial intelligence as craftwork. In S. Chaiklin, and J. Lave (eds.), *Understanding Practice: Perspectives on Activity and Context*. New York: Cambridge University Press.

Tengblad, S. (2002). Time and space in managerial work. *Scandinavian Journal of Management*, 18(4), 543–66.

Thorngate, W. (1976). Possible limits on a science of social behaviour. In J.H. Strickland, F.E. Aboud, and K.J. Gergen (eds.), *Social Psychology in Transition*. London: Wiley, 121–39.

Tomkins, C. (1983), and Groves, R. The everyday accountant and researching his reality. *Accounting, Organisations and Society*, 8(4), 361–74.

—— (2001). Interdependencies, trust and information in relationships, alliances and networks. *Accounting, Organizations and Society*, 26, 161–91.

Van Maanen, J. (1995). Style as theory. *Organization Science*, 6, 133–43.

Weber, M. (1976). *Wirtschaft und Gesellschaft. Grundriss der verstehenden Soziologie*, 5th edn. Tübingen: Mohr.

Weick, K.E. (1999). Conclusion—Theory construction as disciplined reflexivity: Tradeoffs in the 90s. *Journal of Management Review*, 24, 797–806.

Wenger, E. (1998). *Communities of Practice—Learning, Meaning, and Identity*. Cambridge: Cambridge University Press.

12

Sketch of Derivations in Wall Street and Atlantic Africa

Vincent-Antonin Lepinay and Michel Callon

INTRODUCTION

With the first issue of *Accounting, Organization and Society* and its editorial written by Anthony Hopwood (1976), accounting re-emerged as a primary topic and one of great importance in the field of social sciences (Rose and Miller 2008). The studies that followed in the wake of Hopwood's contribution did more than repeat the lesson learned from Weber and Sombart on the central role of double entry bookkeeping in the rise of capitalism. They directed attention to the intricate relations between accounting practices on the one hand and shaping of social relations on the other. The Social Studies of Accounting (SSA) have become a crucial field of investigation where measurement technologies, calculation practices, and calculative agencies have been grasped together in their collaborative contributions to social ordering and economic structuring.

Recently, a convergence of interests and objects of study has taken place between SSA and scholars trained in Science, Technology, and Society (STS) studies: it has taken place around questions of calculation and objectivity (Latour 1987; Daston 1994; Schaffer 1994; Wise 1995; Porter 1995; Callon 1998) and also more recently around the role of economics in the formatting of economies (Guala 2001, 2007; Callon 2007; MacKenzie et al. 2007; Callon and Caliskan 2009*a*, 2009*b*; Latour and Lepinay 2009). This article dwells on the fruitful convergence of SSA and STS. Its starting point is the research of one of the authors (Lepinay 2009) dedicated to understanding the unique character of derivative products.

They have assumed a major role in the current economies. The *Credit Default Swaps (CDS)* crisis has popularized them, so much that they have become a common topic of main street conversations. Despite the considerable amount of money that they mobilize and their centrality to many industrial enterprises,[1] these products are considered peripheral to real economies. They are also quickly associated with the notion of speculation, greed, and corruption. This convergence of misunderstandings and flawed theoretical framework explains why there are few theoretical attempts at capturing the proper object of derivatives. The crux of this inability to grasp derivation in its full economic scope stems from an erroneous premise in current analyses of finance. Derivations are opposed to that which precedes them— usually production and the sound and harmonious combination of productive factors. Yet, that opposition falls short of an explanation of the mechanisms of value creation through production and derivation.

This chapter sets out to fill this gap and offer the first elements of an analysis of economic derivation. Against the common view that alternates between overlooking derivation's role and demonizing it, we posit that derivation is the central operation accounting for economic value creation and circulation. In order to demonstrate the foundational character of derivation, we bring together and compare two cases: on the one hand, financial practices in an investment bank among the most prestigious in Wall Street and, on the other hand, commercial transactions in Atlantic Africa described by Jane Guyer (2004) in an important book, *Marginal Gains*, whose title is itself a theoretical inspiration.

In the first part of this chapter we present the principles of a derivative product—the capital guarantee product—and Guyer's analysis of value conversion. Studying these two practices together indicates the strong similarities that exist between them and the fruitfulness of a frame that combines them to understand economic processes. The following sections use these notions to revisit some of the categories that are mobilized to describe and analyse the creation and measure of economic values. Derivation casts new lights on situations of innovation as well as on the distinction between production and consumption. To conduct this analysis, we have to investigate further the notion of formula as it turns out to be central in the processes of value calculation. Instructed by the centrality of formulae in value creation, it becomes possible to show how derivation/conversion depends on spaces that are disconnected, disjuncted, and fragmented: value creation takes place in these asymmetrical and non-equivalent interstices. As such, this

---

[1] Short term financing by SWAPS is definitely not the exclusive realm of speculative hedge funds. On the contrary, it is part of the usual battery of budgetary tools used by CFOs of major as well as mid-size companies.

notion forces us to rethink the old question of political and moral fairness of economic pricing. We conclude by drawing on the mathematical notion of derivation and show that the economic value of goods and their measures are nothing but the series of chains of derivations created by transactional formulae. No value without derivation! Derivation is not peripheral but central to economies.

TWO EXOTISMS: DERIVATIONS AND CONVERSIONS IN WALL STREET AND NIGERIA

With the raging financial crisis nobody can ignore that financial markets have been the sites of major economic innovations, some of which are now held responsible for the current economic upheavals. First among these innovations are derivative products. A derivative product is a contract or a security (such as a forward, future, option, or swap) whose value depends on the price of another underlying[2] asset, or on the level of an index or interest rate. Derivatives cover many different types of product but what they have in common is the process of derivation: The value of a new good is derived from values already existing and public. The dependence of a good's price upon other goods is obviously not new (economists have long played with the notion of price elasticity between goods). What is new and what finance has exploited with success stems from the way derivation is defined. The definition of a derivative is both captured and exhausted by this relationship of dependency on the primary good: nothing else interferes with the derivative, which comes down to the monetary amount produced by the derivative formula itself. Financial derivatives are the purest engineering experiment of economic derivations. They come close to the purity allowed by the crafting of the mathematical notion of derivative, itself central to the mathematical intuition used by traders who trade derivatives.

At the time when Wall Street and its engineers and traders were embracing these new products, sometimes dubbed exotic for the distance that they were creating with regard to more traditional finance, American anthropologist Jane Guyer (2004) embarked on the study of commercial transactions in Atlantic Africa. What she quickly discovered was a world starkly different

---

[2] We use underlying alternatively as an adjective and as a noun. In so doing we follow the financial operators' idiom and we emphasize the relation between the existing economic goods and the derivatives and the redefinition of the former achieved by the latter.

from the picture drawn by early Africanists. She was soon struck by the centrality of interfaces, margins and boundaries of every kind in the organization of exchanges and in the calculation of values. As Anthony Carter notes in his foreword:

Economic actors in Atlantic Africa have long sought to produce, perpetuate and profit from a ramifying network of asymmetrical exchanges. 'Difference is a resource to be cultivated'. Diverse and disjunctive currencies and other registers of value are used to create margins or frontiers across which asymmetries can be enacted and premium for access charged.   (Guyer 2004: 10)

Derivation on the one hand, margins and difference on the other: the words used to characterize the creation of value have a family resemblance. This article studies the conceptual affinity between derivation and valuation. To do so, we start from two exoticisms: Wall Street and its financial derivatives; Atlantic Africa and its marginal gains. Each situation can be characterized as an exacerbation of the role of discontinuities and engineered differences in the process of valuation. Starting from such apparently different sites helps us to dispel the exoticism of each commercial scene and to define the notions of derivation and conversion in a broader way, one that transcends the borders of Nigeria and contemporary finance. To shed light on the indigenous inventions of these two sites, a short description is appropriate here.

Financial Derivatives

In the mid-1990s, French investment bank Société Générale decided to launch a new class of products aimed at a wide range of clients. Dubbed capital guarantee products (hereafter CGP but also, in more technical terms, 'correlation products'), they had already been tested by the large international bank UBS (Union des Banques Suisses), but had been a failure.[3] The principle of correlation products was simple: the return depended on a formula linking several[4] outstanding securities (Doc1). We can not go into the details of the product's management by the bank. Suffices to know that Société Générale would invest a first portion of the capital lent by clients into a risk free bond paying no interest[5] and the rest in futures of the underlying assets present in

---

[3] The Swiss bank had miscalculated the correlation between the components of its portfolio: it ended up losing money and withdrew from the market.

[4] The number of underlying financial securities (national debts, interest rates, leading multinational companies' stocks, and national stock markets indices) could vary a lot. From 5, it could go up to 20 in some cases.

[5] In technical terms, a zero coupon. They would account for around 70 to 80 per cent of the capital received from the client.

the formula. CGPs were synthetic products engineered around existing derivative products. Their value was derived from these underlyings and along the terms of the formula.

Combining indices, stocks, and currencies from different national markets was not new when Société Générale launched the product.[6] But the real innovation came from its turning a service (like the ones provided by portfolio managers and hedge funds) into a continuously negotiable, transferable security. This was not in services provided simultaneously—as when wealthy individuals ask their fund manager to buy in different stocks to diversify the risk of their portfolio—but one service covering the exchange and representing the economy of each component.

A CGP is a wager based on the decorrelation of the underlying assets (so that upward trends of some assets are offset by downward trends of others). The absence of this decorrelation, even for a short period of time, immediately translates into capital loss, so that it is fair to expect banks to pay attention to the formula they design. As the formulae aim to build a new entity out of known and existing ones their success hinges upon the viability of the composition ventured by the new entity. New enterprises launched around smart formulae whose components turn out to be incompatible[7] are plentiful. The strength and survival of the formula depends on the composition that it tries to bring to life. Yet these components, bent by the formula, are as much 'worlds' in their own right as the formulae of which they are part. Although they are indeed starting points for the CGP formula, they are also the results of other bending processes. A formula is the tipping point of a series (or family) of existing formulae but it can be enrolled by subsequent formulae that jump onto it and derive from it. This inheritance is a curse and a blessing. It means that a past has informed these building bricks that the financial service tries to conglomerate. But this past can resist the particular bending that the formula tries to achieve; it can derail the blueprint. However, the background of these bricks is also what makes them such useful ingredients of a new recipe. They are already in shape: they carry information that is used by the derivative formula and need not be generated again.

---

[6] Portfolio managers, hedge funds, and even some services for individuals would cross the boundaries of national economies and combine securities exchanged in remote financial places.

[7] The success of this new product depends on the stability of the hosts on top of which it is built. Crucial in this respect is the continuity of price measurements. If a stock price came to be disrupted on the date and at the time of measurement, the whole architecture of derivation would be shattered and would demand sometimes complex procedures of substitution to guarantee the survival of the derivative beyond the hiccup of the underlying.

A derivative product, such as the CGP, creates value from the existing values of underlying assets. It is tied to outstanding products but simultaneously derives its specificity and its value from the lack of any prior integration between these carefully picked underlyings. Its value stems from the existence of gaps and discontinuities, and its ability to bridge these gaps while maintaining them. Derivatives stand at the fringes of existing values and only this peripheral position makes them valuable and possible candidates for becoming economic goods.

Conversions in Atlantic Africa

One might well imagine that this marginal innovation, this combining of existing values to the end of producing artificially, by sheer speculation, new values utterly disconnected from the real world and the sound economy, would be a feature of most advanced economies, breathlessly seeking to keep alive the cycle of accumulation through new sources of profit. Derivation has indeed been diagnosed the degenerative disease of capitalism.

The immense interest of Guyer's (2004) book is to point to the fact that derivation—so central to contemporary finance—is also the most widespread modality of value creation in societies that are exotic but in a more literal way. Guyer does not use the notion of derivation but the concepts that she reactivates in her study, such as conversion, disjunctures, marginal gain, and scales of valuation, are as many steps toward a better understanding of the mechanisms of derivation.

The question she raises is a very general one: What is the process through which a good is simultaneously defined and calculated in a commercial transaction? The exchange is not the resource and the starting point of the transaction; rather, it is its result. Her argument leads her to oppose the famous model of Paul Bohannan (1955) who has had so much influence on economic anthropology and sociology. Against Bohannan, she asserts that conveyance is the exception in transactions, while the rule is the conversion. Transactions take place in sites of discontinuities whereby simple quantitative calculations are ruled out. If values can be created and gains can be made, it is because exchange qua exchange[8] is problematic. If agents want to succeed in their transactions, they must first set a space of commensuration that will

---

[8] As we will see, exchange is a rare and unstable case, that economists and even anthropologists have unduly made centre stage. Michel Serres has long brought attention to the precedence of derivation processes. See in particular the bold economics embedded in The Parasite (Serres [1980] 2007).

allow monetary calculations. Guyer (2004) describes in detail the commercial circuits of Atlantic African societies, and shows that they are structured by discontinuities, disjunctures, and barriers generated by the multiplicity of currencies, ethnic groups, numeracy systems, and transportation infrastructures. Agents prefer and seek these situations of conversion, where equivalence is to be built and cannot be taken for granted, because the uncertainty carries with it the opportunity of gains. For conveyances, those transactions in which the only uncertainty regards the ratio of values and not their existence, the possibility of gains is rules out. If we simplify Guyer's message to its gist, gains take place only at the margins. In this context, the valuation of goods with a view to converting them (and it is important to use the term conversion and not exchange) becomes a central activity and the object of her book. The generality of her analysis is a rich contribution to the critical accounting research programme initiated by Hopwood and his colleagues in the 1970s.

For Guyer, the monetary valuation of a good rests on the combination of three operations that are distinct but tightly entangled. The good must first be pointed at and named. It becomes part of a network of semantic classes and categories of objects with regard to which it acquires its difference and singularity. This first operation allows for a second one whereby the good can be inserted into hierarchies. This second ranking operation makes space for the third stage: goods named and set in order can be given numbers and ratios when they are compared. Guyer singles out each stage of valuation as nominal, ordinal, and numerical. This multi-layered calculation of a good in situations of problematic conversion is what Guyer calls a scalar judgement. She insists that the three modalities of valuation take place not sequentially but simultaneously: each judgement is immediately scalar and each numerical operation entails an assessment of goods' qualities (on a similar distinction, see Power 2004).

When Guyer puts this analytical framework to use in different situations, she underlines the role of tropes. A trope is a figure of speech or a metaphor in which a word or expression is used figuratively. It authorizes shifts, displacements, and derivations; operating by relations, translations, and conversions. Each scale, whether nominal, ordinal or numerical, has its trope through which formerly incommensurable worlds can communicate, and words can pair up with figures and ranks. Tropes pave the way for conversions but maintain enough leeway so that agents can combine them; they do not force any mechanical associations. They are mobilized in situations of disjuncture and they ride on these discontinuities by limiting them, concealing them, and creating equivalence where there was nothing. They make long series of conversions possible and end up with valuations which synthesize and sum up in a unique way each initial value seized in the whirl of conversions.[9]

Just as derivative products studied by social studies of finance, the value of goods that Guyer (2004) studies depend on values and value metrics that pre-exist but are simultaneously drawn upon and defined by calculative formulae. This dual movement is crucial to derivation and conversion and the two notions are two inseparable moments in the process of economic change. Guyer shows convincingly that in order to succeed at converting a good whose value is not clear—that is, to launch it in a transaction between two parties—it is necessary to present the good as the outcome of a series of conversions—derivations of values and calculation of values already accepted.

DERIVATIONS

Financial markets with their exotic products and subtropical African markets with their marginal gains should help us to clarify the importance of phenomena of derivation in the constitution and dynamics of economic activities. What we would like to suggest in this chapter, is that the systematic study of the mechanisms of derivation and conversion, in societies both in the North and the South, could shed new light on the old question of the creation of economic values and their measurement. One of the advantages of the concept of derivation—conversion is the fact that it establishes an intelligible relationship between different critical components of markets mechanisms.

Derivation and Innovation

Market activity can be viewed from two different but complementary angles: as organized exchanges around constituted goods and services whose values have been tested and recognized; and as a source of innovations, that is, of new goods whose values are problematical and undecided. One of the characteristics of contemporary Western economies is to favour innovation which—as the numerous studies on them attest—simultaneously concern

---

[9] Guyer reports that the term *ackie* can be used to single out a good which corresponds to a weight of gold whose value is 480 cowries. At other times, *ackie* translates as *soa*, but this corresponds to a different weight of gold. 'The same goods were "differently" valued by an equation of terms from the various languages: *ackie = soa = gros = mithqal*, spanning gold values from approximately 0.06 to 0.15 ounces and 480 to 1200 *cowries*' (2004: 54).

products, processes, and forms of organization. Paradoxically, the African economies that Guyer (2004) studied are in a similar position, which is why her book is crucial to our argument. On the one hand, there is a constant inflow of goods from the West and Asia, which have to find their place and their value, for African economies are open economies. On the other, 'natives' or foreigners who travel on the African continent constantly have to cross borders and barriers, for the African market is fragmented, made up of interfaces and disjunctures whose political geography Guyer examines. In Atlantic Africa, innovation, in the strict sense of the word (introduction of a good or process that was not yet present), is constant.

The concept of innovation is central in the economic and sociological literature devoted to markets. It serves to name and to emphasize the creative dimension of economic activities and of the institutions that frame them. But it can also be misleading by suggesting that innovations are in stark opposition with situations in which goods are stabilized, their qualities established and their value simply needs to be calculated by the laws of supply and demand. When analysts study the birth and effects of innovation, they have no alternative but to find a compromise between these two antagonistic approaches. Innovation challenges existing structures, whether social, economic, or cognitive. To prevail it has to find a way of getting rid of that which already exists: for the new to happen, the old must disappear. This work of elimination is expressed superbly in the notion of creative destruction proposed by Schumpeter. Many researchers have since endeavored to describe its various modalities or, as Abernathy and Clark (1985) put it in the title of a seminal article, to map the winds of creative destruction which do not always blow in the same direction nor with the same force. Simpler classifications, such as those between incremental innovations and breakthrough innovations, adopt the same idea: an innovation is characterized as much by the intensity of the novelties that it produces as by the amplitude of the destructions that it induces (Dosi 1982). In any case, whether it is a violent storm or a gentle breeze, innovation has to destroy to succeed.

The concept of derivation that we articulate here has the advantage of not confining the analyst to this dialectic of novelty and destruction. Deriving means creating new values, making them exist and accepted, yet based on existing (economic) values which will be strengthened if the derivation is successful. The formula proposed by Société Générale, clearly a product innovation, illustrates this mechanism. The new value is created from existing share values, which it strengthens rather than eliminates. By saying that there was not a direct switch from the candle to the electric lamp, or from the stagecoach to the railway line, we emphasize the existence of a discontinuity (in this case maximum), but simultaneously affirm, as the sentence indicates, that the new value lies in the continuation of a former value. Hence, the concept of derivation—conversion accounts for both the gap and the link. The terminology that Guyer proposes for Africa is useful for measuring this relationship. In the qualification of the new link (the railway or the lamp) there is what she calls a nominal scale, that is, the constitution and mobilization of a semantic network which establishes a relationship of proximity between the two goods: the old and the new, the candle and the lamp. Admittedly, the latter is not spawned by the former, but is nonetheless connected to it, derived from it. The success of the light-bulb is based on the earlier success of the candle (the latter benefiting from the fact that its value is indexed on that of the former since, like it, although differently, it guarantees the existence of what the formula—the lamp is comparable to the candle, but different—implicitly considers as the existence of a demand for lighting). Derivation—conversion that creates a discontinuity, a disjuncture, while establishing a link does not imply the destruction of the underlying asset (as we all know from still using candles). The candle carries on living its life, in the niches that suit it, a life that has been set on a different course, altered but not destroyed by the lamp. It is this strange relationship, that the notion of derivation describes, which also applies to the situations of conversion described by Guyer (2004).

Her book teems with analyses of cases where agreement must be obtained on the qualification and mechanisms of calculation of goods, before they can be engaged in commercial transactions. These goods, seen from the West, hardly look like innovations. Yet from the point of view of the agents who are about to organize their exchange, they really are innovations. In situations of profound fuel shortages, a 35-litre can of diesel in a gas station in the Nigerian hinterland is a good whose underlying asset (the same can, but in a situation of abundance and in the city) is known, but whose value, which obviously depends on the value of its underlying, has to be recalculated in an acceptable way. In chapter 6, she shows how the owner of the gas station, who has just been resupplied, is able to satisfy all her customers at a fixed price throughout the course of the operation by skillfully playing on the combination of several scales—nominal, numeric, and ordinal—which enable her to derive the value of the can of diesel (that day, in that place, in exceptional circumstances) from a series of existing values. Neither the relationship between the supply and the demand, nor the order of arrival, nor the social hierarchy, nor the regulations in force (which put caps on prices), nor the social networks, nor the prices usually charged, are enough to explain the success of the commercial transaction. If the transaction does take place, to the satisfaction of all interested parties, it is because the owner of the filling station was able to transform the singular, new good that she was selling into a derived good which could be linked to other goods well known to all. The assets sold in these exceptional circumstances (general shortage, unexpected supply of a petrol station in the middle of nowhere) are also liters of diesel—just like diesel we fill our Paris or Cambridge car tanks with—but made into different goods because they are exchanged in other circumstances at other times and in different settings. The liter of diesel put on sale is a new good (a product innovation) and, to become an object of transaction, this innovation is linked by her to a series of goods which are also liters of diesel, but negotiated in other circumstances. The case is particularly striking, for the derived good strongly resembles the assets from which it is derived (if only in its chemical composition). Similarly, the CGP is also so much a derivation of existing shares readily available to customers on the market that people do not easily recognize its innovation and promptly criticize a sheer decal of its antecedent. But from an economic point of view it is profoundly different. Diesel liters with their rules of servicing clients in a situation of penury and bundles of shares bent by a formula have a different flavor to them than their underlying goods. It highlights the advantage of conceiving of any innovation (from a drastic innovation such as the electric light to one that could be qualified as minor and superficial since all that changes are the conditions of the supply of a good which remains materially identical to existing goods) as a derivation of pre-existing values (and therefore goods).

Derivation, Formulation, and Calculation of Economic Values

The value of goods is determined and measured during commercial transactions. Only when these goods are known, forecasts can be made. In these rare cases, the so-called law of supply and demand, complemented by price elasticity calculations, applies satisfactorily and makes it possible to anticipate price variations. When, on the other hand, the good to be valued deviates from the pool of known goods, value calculation is more difficult. The existence of these difficulties does not mean that no calculation can be made; on the contrary, they are the fuel of economic transactions and they generate new solutions to pricing issues. The agents apply a great deal of imagination and ingeniousness to design and implement tools or procedures enabling them to define, anticipate, and even enforce the value of the new goods that they propose. Here again, the notion of derivation—conversion is useful for furthering the understanding of calculative behaviors in situations of innovation and uncertainty.

The creativity of economic actors studied by Guyer (2004) resonates with the solutions devised by the financial engineers who design and negotiate derivative products in financial markets. Agents who strive to take advantage of disjunctures tap into the repertoires of available solutions tried and tested by others, in other places and at other times, and transform, combine and adjust them to suit new situations. The notion of formula explicitly used by financial markets and by designers of derivative products is similar to that of transactional forms that Guyer (2004) proposes to capture these qualculation[10] modules which are already there, and which economic agents tinker with to solve problems and value conversions. Linking these two worlds, we talk of transactional formulae, and say that the calculation of the value of a derivative good (in Wall Street or Nigeria), operates by establishing one or several transactional formulae. These usually make use of existing formulae which constitute repertoires on which the agents draw and which they combine to meet the conditions of felicity enabling them to reach an acceptable compromise between the different parties. For CGP, the two main formulae that frame the design of the product are pure insurance (nothing but the guarantee) and pure investment (nothing but the return of the underlying shares). The grammars of each of these transactional regimes are well in place: the prospectus weaves them in such a way that the notions of insurance and investment are within sight but still sufficiently bent through the formula that the product stands as unique. It is worth looking carefully at these formulae

In the simplest cases, the formulae, which are what financial derivatives are made of, explicitly and transparently calculate the economic value of these products. This calculation is 100 per cent numeric, and is generally based on purely mathematical formulae. The price of options[11] is provided by an equation with partial derivatives using observable and identifiable[12] economic (numeric) values as variables. These values exist independently of the formula defining the option. In the case of the CGP, the derivation is twofold. First, it establishes a good that, at any moment, defines the value of a sum of money that a client entrusts to his or her bank. Second—and this obviously depends on the first derivation — it defines the price of the derived product that the client will pay to obtain the sum calculated by the first formula. We know nothing about the calculation of the second derivation's value, since it is the result of a private and highly asymmetric negotiation

---

[10] We owe the notion of qualculation to Franck Cochoy's (2002) studies of consumers' strategies. It reconciles the two approaches of goods as bundles of qualities and goods as items that features in chains of calculation.

[11] See MacKenzie (2006) for its recent history.

[12] Daniel Beunza and David Stark (2008) have a nice illustration of the not-so-direct implication of the implied volatility used by pricers. Engineers can use the historical or the implied volatility to value a derivative, but the implied value is already the product of the formula. The economic data used by the model is filtered by the model.

between the clients and room operators. All we know is that it necessarily takes into account the formula of the first derivation (since the guaranteed value is more or less advantageous for the lender). The first derivation, present in the calculation of the second, takes on a classical formula from the mathematical repertoire of analysis (a weighted sum). Much like in the case of the Black and Schole's formula, which drew heavily on the heat diffusion equation, the innovation consists in tweaking this formula to transpose it and to adapt it to the world of finance. In Guyer's (2004) framework of analysis, the CGP mathematical formula has the particularity of combining numeric and ordinal scales in an original way as well as a redefinition of nominal scales: after the invention of CGP, insurance and investment are no longer the exclusive tropes available in financial conversation. Next to these two transactional formulae stands a new specie and when operators refer to it, they do not reduce it to the combination of the previous formulae. The African situations of derivation and conversion described by Guyer have similar characteristics but the variety of nominal scales is greater and the fluidity of the transactional formulae is also higher. In this case the qualculation of value involves a rich verbal elaboration and explanation. From this point of view, so-called breakthrough technological innovations in our Western societies are fairly close to African conversions. Their definition requires constant use of nominal scales and their viability depends on a continuous explication of their meaning. The political debate that they trigger accentuates the importance of the nominal components of valuation, especially when it involves deliberative and dialogical procedures. The current public discussion of mortgage-based securities and the even more abstruse credit default swaps illustrates how tensions over innovations can trigger attempts to find the proper qualification.

The study of derivation–conversion in Atlantic Africa contributes to making the material dimensions of transactional formulae visible. The station owner's qualculation of the value of diesel fuel is based on a transactional formula that, as we have seen, combines several scales and regular ways of valuing diesel. The description of the commercial transaction shows, moreover, that this formula is embodied in a material device, in what we have proposed to call a sociotechnical agencement or arrangement (Callon 2007). The distribution of customers into separate groups, their being served by an assistant who has to be paid independently, the organization of the queue, the soldiers whose mere presence is a reminder of the possibility of resorting to administered prices, and the size of the cans which allows for skilful games on the tariff thresholds: all of these are elements constituting the transactional formula. Far from only being a play on numbers and words, the definition and calculation of value are achieved through this sociotechnical arrangement.

The transactional formulae conceived of in situations of derivation show how agents play on three types of scale to calculate values. First, they account for the existence of leeway in the qualculation of values (choice and combinations of formulae), and for the necessary taking into account of existing scales and the existence of repertories: the value of a new good is related to other values from which it nevertheless differs. Second, they explicate the cross-derivation presented in the preceding section. The Nigerian filling station manager's successful performance establishes a formula that could be used again and adapted, and in turn weigh on the calculation of values in more conventional situations: the underlying assets are affected by the derivative product from which they are eventually derived. The same mechanism is found in financial markets: the calculation of the underlying assets of the CGP takes into account the fact that they are combined in a formula which creates a product that is itself calculated. When the transactional formula establishes unusual connections, it triggers the creation of other formulae which become part of the web of existing formulae. CAC 40 shares were decorrelated: the CGP derivation formula invents a product that correlates them. In Nigeria there is no relation between the social statuses of motorists, 35-litre cans, the time spent waiting in the sun, and the help of an assistant to make things easier: after the commercial transaction, the connection is made. Finally, the attention paid to transactional formulae highlights their sociotechnical dimension: their implementation cannot be abstracted from the arrangements in which they take place.

The analysis of operations of derivation and conversion illuminates the nature and scope of the calculation of economic values. Unlike prevailing conceptions rooted in the seminal analysis of Franck Knight ([1971] 1921), it is in situations of strong uncertainty that calculations are the richest, the most complex, and the most sophisticated. The analysis of economic calculation must not start with situations of stability and certainty. On the contrary, to analyse these situations which seem to be the simplest, we have to start with derivation–conversion and the notion of transactional formulae, to show the play on scales, the conditions under which the calculation can be limited to numeric operations, and the importance of sociotechnical arrangements.

Derivation and Production

By associating derivation and conversion, we not only perceive phenomena of innovation from a new angle, we are also able to reconsider the position and the meaning of production in economics.

The notion of production usually designates the set of human activities (most often highly equipped) that lead to the existence of goods or services meeting certain needs. These goods are subsequently distributed and consumed, but this process that goes from conception to consumption can take different forms. The most common form assumes that production is a distinct and separate stage, preceding distribution and consumption. In this case, production entails a precise and stable definition of goods. Following Guyers's (2004) terminology, we could call these goods 'conveyed goods'. They move about, are transferred and change hands in a space already equipped with metrological infrastructures (assessment of qualities and performances). This equipment reduces valuation to the numeric, and generally monetary, calculation of their value. This implies goods that are distinctly framed and well-positioned in relation to one another. We can call these goods definitional.[13] Drugs exemplify the standard set by definitional goods both up and downstream. Upstream: a minute variation in the quality of the components can turn out to be lethal. The supervision of these components has been one of the milestones in the regulation of this industry, for instance the role of the Food and Drug Administration (FDA) in the United States and the scandals over the lack of control of these drugs in less regulated countries. They are, similarly, definitional goods downstream. The distribution of any drug is strongly regulated in many different ways. The FDA again sets stringent limits to the populations entitled to take given drugs, and doctors and pharmacists monitor closely the renewal of prescriptions. The value of drugs is strictly framed by the matrix of inputs and uses that is allowed.[14]

Yet other configurations also proliferate, fueled by the rise of the service economy (Gallouj 2002). In these other configurations, goods are constantly being revised, from the moment of their conception to that of their final consumption. They are never stabilized and the continuous transformations that they undergo are the index of their qualities' calibration and their value fluctuation (Callon et al. 2002). These successive transformations are the conversions of Guyer. The good circulates only if it morphes. This trajectory is well captured by the notion dearest to financial operators: each new inflexion of the good's path is a new qualification that can be understood as a derivation. This new good never ceases to be a function of the previous

---

[13] A first attempt to lay the properties of definitional goods—as opposed to derivational goods—is in Lepinay (2007).

[14] Definition shares the spirit of the accounting revolution: each piece coming in and going out is a discrete and describable entity. See Mary Poovey (1998) for an elaborate analysis of the role of double-entry bookkeeping on the rise of the category of fact.

goods from which it comes. It is tied to them but it has been qualified into a different good altogether. In this new configuration, the notion of production as we understood it so far becomes irrelevant. Instead of being the generation of well-defined and stabilized goods, production is now the uninterrupted yet discontinuous series of derivations that accrue value on the economy. It picks up and enrolls an already existing set of goods and services. It adds qualities to these goods by securing them, but it does not create them from scratch. This dependence upon pre-existing goods limits the control that producers can entertain. Yet, it is also a major resource of alleged 'producers' to turn themselves into 'derivators' as they lean on a world already in place, with its routines. In this configuration the total control of the upstream and down-stream of goods is not only beyond the possibility of even the most ambitious companies, it would also be counterproductive: by making derivations and conversions unavoidable, and by blurring potential comparisons with existing definitional goods, economic agents put themselves in a position where capturing partners, and in particular clients, becomes easier.

To make justice to the variety of these configurations and show the exceptional aspect of definitional goods, Callon et al. (2002) have extended the notion of production to include situations of derivation. Such a choice followed the steps of Jean-Baptiste Say who used to define production as all the actions turning things into goods. In so defining production, Say asserts that distribution and trading are among the infinite ways of producing, on a par with industrial enterprises.[15] Extending that much the notion of produc-tion may be counterproductive and bring more confusion than analytic clarification. It is clearer to keep the notion of production for definitional goods and to see this mode of economic activities as a subset of derivation, just as Guyer (2004) sees conveyance as a particular case of conversion, one that is stabilized and successful. Derivation is the general mechanism through which goods become valuable.

Since derivation–production (conveyable goods) and derivation–conver-sion have been conflated by a long tradition dating back to Say and extending to the new Austrian economists, it is necessary to cast light on their modalities of value creation. In order to do that, we examine their two ideal-typical relations between the new good and the elements that are drawn upon to create it.

Conveyable goods are described as combinations of values—think of pro-duction functions or value chains—but this productive combination is very

---

[15] 'The various ways of producing all consist in turning a product from one state to another state, with more utility and value. As early as one creates or increases the utility of things, one increases their value, one is in the realm of the industry' (Say 1826: 15).

different from the one activated by derivations in general. The definitional process is characterized by the fact that it combines them and integrates them to the extent of making them disappear as individualized goods. The ingredients have to be consumed in order for new value to exist. This black-boxing is shrouded in industrial and commercial secrecy, making it difficult to access knowledge on what could be called the productive formula describing the combination of elements that went into making the good. Derivatives, like conveyable or definitional goods, combine existing values and goods, but the modalities of this combination are very different from those of definitional goods. This is by no means black-boxing; on the contrary, we could venture the neologism white-boxing.

The CGP formula explicitly and deliberately reveals the underlying assets of the derived product. It offers a 'package' consisting of disconnected goods (decorrelated, as financiers would say, or disjuncted, as Guyer (2004) would put it) which are reconnected, networked and (re)calculated, by means of the formula but without hiding the process of networking and qualculation. A product like CGP does not simply propose an innovation embodied in a good with interesting properties and qualities (guaranteeing capital against stock market variations); it confirms and revives the existence of the underlying assets. The notion of 'underlyings' might be misleading as it assumes a precedent and hints at a foundation. A particular index or share, chosen as underlying, when acting as a derivative carries on existing as an index or share. Derivation maintains[16] it at a distance, rather than integrating and making it disappear as such, as in the productive combination of definitional goods. It can support the existence of the goods that it draws upon or it can

---

[16] The distinction between the two combinations can be captured by the following comparison. Averaging a set of numbers, once accomplished, makes you lose sight of the originals. This is in all accounts a combination that creates a number irreducible to the initial set. The series $\{2, 4, 3, 7, 4\}$ averages at 4 if I use the arithmetic operator. From 4, I have no way of figuring out the initial set. There is actually an infinite number of possible 5-number sets $\{a, b, c, d, e\}$ averaging at 4. Critics of the all-pervasive use of statistics are eager to point to the loss of information due to the reduction performed by the average operator. Yet this widespread use also points to the political significance of taking the combination for the individuals. The figure produced by the operator empowers public agencies that try to categorize the population into sub-groups; it creates 'outliers' and 'average men and women'. Consider a set of colours that you combine to produce a new colour. It may be difficult for a non-expert to go from the result to the initial pool of colours that have been stirred together, but each combination will result in a unique new colour. Starting from the primary colour, and repeating the operation enough times, it will probably even be impossible to decipher the components. Yet the point of this comparison is to highlight the two different trajectories of numbers and colours undergone by this putting together, this bringing close and the result of it. With colours, the combination does not erase the specificity of the ingredient. The result maintains this specificity in the production of a unique new one. Derivation works only through that particular filtering.

undermine it, but in either case, it does not dissolve them into a process that consumes them. As derivative goods do not consume their underlying assets, they play a very different part than the one played by the elements constituting a conveyed-definitional good. Derivation, generally speaking, could not be decomposed into separate operations of production and consumption: such a dissociation, as said previously, is singular. In its standard form, derivation simply creates value by displacing underlyings. The risk of this economic strategy is its extreme instability.

From this point of view, the Nigerian situation is also telling. Describing the gas station owner's calculation of the price of diesel in the exceptional circumstances recounted above, Guyer (2004) insists on the transparent, visible, and public nature of this process of derivation and evaluation: everyone knows the prices applied, sees the length of the queue, knows when the customers arrived and their social status, and observes the quantity bought as well as the price agreed upon. Derivation makes transparent that which in the case of production is a commercial or manufacturing secret. It makes objective, observable, and debatable an operation which, had it been black-boxed, would be likened to gambling (for derivative financial products) or to fraud or even theft (to resell the fuel). In the latter case, as in that of financial products, the underlying assets (the different varieties of diesel fuel described in the preceding section) remain at a distance; they do not enter into a productive combination; they are not consumed. They remain what they are: liters of diesel negotiated in known circumstances, which differ from those surrounding the commercial transaction engaged in by the gas station owner.

What is striking, in the case of Nigeria, is that diesel fuel as an underlying asset remains diesel fuel with perfectly defined chemical properties. The underlying assets and derivative product are in a sense identical and yet, due to the operation of derivation, they remain distinct and cannot be reduced to one another. Without this ontological stability, conversion—and with it the marginal gains that it allows for—could not exist. Derivation–conversion, like definition–production, establishes new values based on existing ones, which in the case of derivative goods are underlying assets, and in the case of conveyed (definitional) goods are what could be called intermediary consumptions. In the former case, this distance is reflected in a 'making visible' (*mise en visibilité*)—it constitutes the initial values as underlying assets—whereas in the latter, opacity is the rule of the game—it consumes and integrates them. The derivative formula keeps the derived good distant from the goods that it derives; the productive formula eliminates this distance by organizing the consumption of the inputs that it combines.

From this perspective the notion of derivation is more fundamental than that of production which is but one specific modality of derivation. However, it does not mean that there are two distinct economic spheres, each one ruled by different mechanisms. These two forms of value creation are highly intricate. Let's take the case of a derivative like the CGP or the diesel can. It weaves together underlying assets. One of the underlying assets of the CGP may for example be a Sanofi Aventis share, which epitomizes definitional goods. As we pointed out, the CGP reinforces the definitional character of its underlying assets, and of the Sanofi Aventis share in particular. But the CGP may also be transformed into an underlying, by a derivation which chooses to strengthen its definition. Hence, there are not simply two economic poles— that of the real economy and that of the financial economy—but subtle relations of constitution and interdependence of values. Derivations create and structure conveyance; conversely, existing conveyances are the building blocks of derivation. A good defined in a stable way, like the Sanofi Aventis drug, can hardly survive and last unless it is included[17] in operations of derivation that confirm and enhance its value. A derivative good has a future[18] only if it serves as a base for new derivations. The tension between underlyings and derivatives sometimes leads to fascinating situations of overlapping dependencies as the case of commercial derivative goods suggests. Take the value of UK footballer David Beckham. It is constantly reactivated and enriched by the value attributed to the multiple derivative products of which he is the origin (e.g. the Beckham hair wax). Conversely, the value of each of the products derived from Beckham's value depends on that value. In this case, relationships of valuation reach such a high degree of symmetry that the ageing Beckham can but become the derivative of his own line of derivative products. Derivation works both ways: we clearly see that Beckham's value is defined better, and in a sense is more stable, when there are a large number of derived products whose values are based on him. Beckham can be transferred, conveyed from one club to another, without his value really being questioned or questionable: his price is the product of all his derivations. In a situation of dynamic equilibrium, each value is both operating derivations and taken as target by other derivative operators. Consequently if the derivation is the general operation through which value is

[17] Cori Hayden analyses the strategic organization of downstream derivation in the case of drugs circulating beyond their domains of regulations. See Hayden (2007, 2008).
[18] That is why many derivations do not project themselves in the future and refuse to invest, preferring instead to rip the low hanging, easily accessible fruit. Production (as defined above) qua cautious derivation injects future into this ephemeral and risky present. Derivation as degenerate production rules itself out of any future.

created, then the object to focus on is the constitution of chains of derivation, whatever their modalities.

Valuation and Space-Time

Considered from the point of view of derivation–conversion, exchange is the result of the valuation process and not its starting point. This approach leads to a new view of relationships between time and economic activity, which sheds light on financial derivatives. CGPs work and succeed in so far as they build onto existing industrial enterprises: they have to come after the fact, once the world of goods and processes is stable enough for them to be able to graft onto them without the risk of destroying or even disrupting their morphology. Derivations work when they can wait, when a time and speed differential can be constructed. Financial derivatives come after their underlying assets; they are situated downstream from the goods from which they are derived, and to ensure a clear-cut temporal and organizational disjuncture, they arrive without seeking agreement. The examples of conversion offered by Guyer (2004) have the same characteristics. The new good—the can of diesel sold in unusual conditions of shortage and economic crisis, or the brass rod used as bride wealth in an unusual place—constructs their own time, relegating to an undated past the various valuations of goods to which the agents derive when they perform their valuation. Conversion, the attempted valuation in a situation of disjuncture and non-equivalence, creates an undifferentiated 'before': the time of underlying assets is a past time now broken and interrupted. This time produced by derivation–conversion is a discontinuous time, which is the antithesis of continuous, progressive time that makes money work, gives a value to investments, and finally turns out to be an economic value. In short, time is money only in the very specific case of derivation–production and conveyed products. From this point of view the transactional formula of the CGP, like the pricing of an option, is paradoxical. It takes the underlying variables (an index, a portfolio of shares) and their value at time t, to calculate the derived product at the same time t. But the formula has a value if and only if the time of the underlying assets is frozen, disconnected from that of the transaction. Any delay in the decision-making could turn against the owner of the derivative. Time may thus work against and not for him or her. (Pure) derivation is the exact opposite of production roundaboutness. The time of derivation is not linear, productive in proportion to its course; it is a time of recycling and of loops. This is what Guyer sums up in the sentence: 'The gains embedded in conversions in Africa were dependent on time but did not, on the whole, measure it'. The fold interrupts the measurement.

Derivation folds time, breaks it, interrupts it. It also fractures space. Guyer (2004) tells us that Bohannan's main mistake was to forget that the spaces in which conveyances and exchanges take place are not immaterial fields. They consist of territories, with their perilous transport routes, their obstacles and their natural defenses, with their contrasting climates, their mutually suspicious ethnic groups, their languages, and their systems of naming things that impose hazardous translations. All these differences—those that everyone sees and those that are discovered only by the traveler seeking transactions—are disjunctures which transform journeys into odysseys and simultaneously provide opportunities for gain. The notion of circulation's space (like that of the sphere of exchange) has to be excluded, as it implies that the equivalences have been constructed; it comes after the conversions and not before. To start to understand the world in which conversions operate, it would be necessary to find an antonym for the word 'space' and another one for the word 'circulation'. The only words that are useful are those like: differences, gaps, discontinuities, and disjunctures, denoting the opposite of conversion. The space of conversion does not deserve to be called a space unless, as with time, it is said to be folded, fragmented, and broken: notions like fragmented rhizomes, gaps, interrupted trajectories, are more relevant. Financial derivatives have the same logic: they thrive nowhere better than in spatial discontinuities, those that they manage to create or that are offered to them. They play here on the assumed existence of groups of countries which, like emergent countries, afford possibilities of conversion, elsewhere in the gaps between stock markets situated in different time zones and countries with differing regulations.

The folds of time and space, the topographies of disjunctures fragmenting them, are not constituted independently of one another. They compose spacetimes which form the moving infrastructure of commercial transactions. (Marginal) gains are not simply a function of time; nor are they indexed on the distances covered. The idea that the value of a good in $t2$ and $x2$ can be obtained continuously from its value in $t1$ and $x1$, implies a continuity of spatio-temporal references that the derivation–conversion model undermines. Yes, the values do vary, but in stages, by translations and combinations of scales, and construction of thresholds. The diversity of space-times allows for sophisticated games, as Guyer shows in her analysis of the strategies enabling Africans to accumulate gains by playing on the differences between various credit offers granted in different space-times. To characterize these strategies, she uses the (financial) notion of trade-off. In situations of derivation–conversion, valuation is a trade-off between space-times that are a priori incommensurable. Guyer points out that it is consequently false to consider that the formulation of a transaction (a loan against the payment of interest, an ox against shells) is independent from its spatio-temporal frame (time and space supply fixed references). As it is derivation–conversion, the transaction constructs the equivalence, the possibility of a measured exchange, and at the same time spatio-temporal contexts and their possible transformations. The gas station owner's time is not that of the State and of its administered prices, or that of the crude oil company operating in the stock market. That of Hedge Funds, as we have seen with the sub-primes crisis, is not that of the American Texan desperately trying to sell his apartment to settle his debt. Derivation interrupts the very possibility of a continuous investment between these space-times.

The Violence of Derivation

Conversion–derivation complicates the explanation and description of exchange. A new good introduces disruptions into the state of possible interests, demands, expectations, and attachments. This disruption, irrespective of its intensity, poses the problem of the existence of values to exchange and, consequently, of the terms of their qualculation. The acceptance of the conversion depends on the formula applied and its content. This conversion can fail for many reasons: the proposed good interests no one; it is seen as an evil rather than a good, and therefore sets off resistance and controversy; or its valuation is considered unrealistic or inequitable. The extreme situations studied by Guyer (2004) have the advantage of revealing the anthropological framework that gives a common meaning to these different attitudes, and within which any attempt at innovation, at derivation—conversion, has to be situated if it is to succeed.

From this point of view chapter 6 of *Marginal Gains* is illuminating, as the conversions presented, from which the agents cannot extract themselves, could at any moment tilt over into terror. It is the diplomacy and the exceptional qualculating skills of the gas station owner that ensure that the sale of diesel does not turn into a riot. It is the moderateness of the demands expressed by the taxi drivers who, deprived of fuel, stop a bus and ask the passengers for acceptable and fair compensation—since they are able to travel—as well as the wisdom of those passengers, that avoids a bloodbath. These examples remind us that if the conversions–derivations are too distant from the underlying assets (i.e., if the chosen formulae are too distant from the existing formulae), if the translations appear to be obvious betrayals, then violence becomes the only alternative, and with it basic forms of circulation and transfer of goods: abduction and theft. Too much distance between the new derivations compared to the established values and formulae, and discontinuity becomes inevitable as the derivation turns into predation. Too much distance from the underlying assets is the first source of failure. But the derivation–conversion may fail for symmetrical reasons, due to the derived product being too close to its underlying asset. In this case the new good is reduced to nothing more than a predictable combination of existing goods. There is not strictly speaking a creation of new values: rather than shifting and broadening competition, derivation simply increases its intensity, since it offers nothing but existing goods. By insisting on repeating that which exists, it again paves the way for violence, but of another kind: mimetic violence that Girard (1979, 1989) has described so well.

We can conclude that it is in the qualculation of the new value, in the transactional formula that it proposes, that the political and moral dimension of derivation lies: the formula that stretches the bond with its underlying assets too far, that does not take into account the effects induced on their existence, that paves the way for violence and destruction; and, on the other hand, that remains too close to those same underlying assets, and fails to offer the critical examination of the values, without which competition is transformed into a general fight. A good derivation is what makes it possible to escape predation from the bottom (the prison of mimicry) and from the top (excessive innovation: hubris). In derivation there is therefore a veritable civilizing dimension. At the risk of over-simplifying, we could even venture to say that civilization is a matter of skilled derivation. Derivation is indeed one of the devices that serves to draw up an inventory of the values that we feel bound to and that bind us (the underlying assets), and to simultaneously explore the new values that we are prepared to accept (derived goods). Well qualculated, derivation re-enchants the world in which we live; badly calculated it can tilt it over into chaos. Derivation–conversion highlights the fact that, contrary to Thompson's thesis, ethics do not soften the harshness of the economic, afterwards and from the outside. It is in the technical design of the formula that moral and economic values are entangled. The search for the felicitous medium can be decided only on an ad hoc basis (even if certain tried and tested formulae allow for compromise to be reached more easily), and it is difficult to determine, a priori and in general, what a good formula is. The success of the transactional formula selected depends in particular on the reactions that it triggers, especially by the underlying assets, which are requalified, to a greater or lesser degree, by the derivations that they undergo. Let us briefly examine these possible reactions.

The financial derivatives market has been the stage of a controversy over the role played by derivatives in underlying markets. Arguing against the view that derivatives have the merit of completing markets and limiting the role of uncertainty over traded securities' future price, a few economists have pointed to their potentially destabilizing role. Instead of creating markets consistent with the price of existing securities, derivatives are said to have major feedback effects on these very prices, and to lead to their destabilization. The characteristic that economists look at is the volatility of the underlying. By measuring it before and after the launch of a derivative, it is possible to assess the impact of the derivative on the underlying asset.[19] In the cases of exchanges in which the underlying assets are traded, the risk of an increased volatility is complex. It is not entirely negative inasmuch as it attracts new investors lured by the prospect of roller coaster securities, promising risk and reward for the agile trader. Yet, it drives away those investors who seek a safe investment driven only by economic structures and not by external factors.

The concern of exchanges and companies, being the witness of the higher volatility of their shares' prices following the introduction of a derivative, is only one instance of a more general reaction of economic controls. The underlying assets may want to oppose, by all possible means, the feedback effects of the products that tend to create value by organizing their derivations. As we have said, innovation cannot be equated to an undertaking of pure and simple destruction; to extend the sphere of values, it acts on certain values already there. The prospect of this return to the debate in which the underlying assets have not been included can cause the assets to devise preventive defensive strategies. An interesting case is that of luxury goods. The notion of derivation highlights certain components usually ignored by sociological analyses obsessed with the question of the distinction of this category of goods. Luxury goods resist derivation: that is their definition and the economy they organize around their brand. Instead of agreeing to be defined downstream by derivatives embracing them and enrolling them in subsequent chains of goods, they thrive only if they succeed in remaining isolated. Luxury goods cannot suffer interferences. They make sense only in a world of unchallenged essences. Unlike goods that accept parasitical interferences from other uncontrolled goods, luxurious goods do not gain momentum from being part of chains. The economy of luxury is based on control and prestige: high prices paid by exclusive customers and fierce defence of the brand (and customers' exclusivity) by the company. Protecting one's famous brand against derivative enterprises is expensive and it is money not spent on investment, new capacities, or equipment. Only the label is at stake. Luxury and ostentation need a world where the values are set, almost frozen. All that luxury tolerates in innovation are combinations, repetitions, and self-deepening. It is narcissistic: always more of the same thing. It nourishes the struggle for distinction by protecting itself against the interferences caused by

---

[19] For a clear examination of a destabilization scenario, see Guesnerie and Rochet (1993).

derivations. With it, mimetic behaviors prevail (a good has value only because it is chosen by X). Luxury is the antithesis of the long and hazardous derivations proposed by the financial markets.

These observations are simply preliminary thoughts. The variety of the modalities of derivation and the diversity of the formulae of qualculation are echoed in the multiplicity of strategies and feelings surrounding derivations and conversions. Luxury brands ostracize derivations when they are pro-duced behind their backs, so to speak. Financial products live off them and build their prosperity on derivations that have not been agreed and which can induce resentment and a spirit of revenge. Between the two are situated the middle range of explicitly and intensely interlinking derivations, where the roles of underlying assets and derivatives are at certain times inter-changeable, as in the case of soccer players, their sponsors and their mascots. This example points towards an as yet unexplored field of analysis, that we could agree to call the strategic management of chains and spaces of inter-linking derivations, of which soccer players' jerseys and stadiums are a striking example. The strategies devised by tour operators (with their under-lying assets: hotels, airlines, car rental companies, museums, etc.), with the flat rates and packages that they invent, would be another case worth studying. The formulae of derivation–conversion, the spaces they describe, and the packages they propose, are ideal objects for analyzing economic activities.

CONCLUSION

As we write this article, Western stock markets are being shaken by a crisis that observers qualify as exceptionally serious. The unregulated proliferation of new products, and above all derived products, is pointed to as the main cause. The descriptions and explanations proposed, often rich in images and meta-phors, revolve around the idea that derivation is harmful and ends up producing uncontrollable and destructive excesses. Other voices are heard defending derivation, claiming that it increases the fluidity of economic activities, allows for a better allocation of resources, and favours change notwithstanding the associated risks. They demand only that the practices of derivation be framed better. This controversy in black and white is espe-cially violent and endless because the very concept of derivation is not questioned; in fact it is even excluded from all analysis.

This article has taken the opposite track, starting with the observation that derivation is, or may be, a source of both destructive excesses and productive detours. That is why we have posited that, to make sense of this ambivalence, it is necessary to study it as a subject in its own right. We argue that derivation closely links the dynamics of production of economic values and their measurement. Financial markets have not invented derivation; they have gradually brought it into the foreground, focusing on it in an almost exclusive and probably obsessive way. Financial markets are not however exceptions or pathological forms; they act like magnifying glasses which make all-pervading mechanisms more visible and easier to analyse. Guyer's work on Atlantic Africa offers an ideal field for investigating purified albeit different forms of derivation, which she calls operations of conversion. Atlantic Africa is a world of disjunctures, of interfaces that constitute as many obstacles to conveyances and offer the agents the opportunity to recalculate values, and thus to make marginal gains.

In Wall Street and Yoruba country alike, the agents embark on valuation processes that start with existing values and propose both new values and their qualculation. We have shown the importance of calculative formulae. The two exotisms, that of Wall Street and that of the tropics, in their extreme forms, have shed comparative and complementary light on derivation, by making possible the circulation of concepts whose general validity is thus demonstrated. We have thus played with the proximities between derivations and conversions, and between derivation–conversions and innovations, and suggested the advantages of broadening the field of application of concepts such as underlying assets, scales of qualculation (which free sterile opposition between judgement and numeric calculation of prices), and transactional formulae with their sociotechnical arrangements. As a result, we have also conceived of moderate derivation as a possible escape from the mimetic violence (or competition organized around fixed and determined values) and predatory violence (that resorts to theft, pillage, and war rather than commercial transactions). The accent has been put on the right distance that formulae have to find between simply repeating underlying assets, and complete detachment that disregards the feedback effects of value creation on existing values. Moderate derivation, in the sense of moderate action between two extremes, hubris (predation) and pusillanimity (repetition), is a derivation that chooses the right transactional formulae. Fairness, like efficiency, is at the heart of the qualculation of value—a qualculation that is itself a constituent part of new value creation. The programme initiated over thirty years ago with the publication of Hopwood's seminal article, which remained on the fringes of the sociology of economics for a long time, is now at its centre. Derivation, as a basic operation, can be analysed only if we study the formulae that it enacts. Accounting is at the centre of this political and moral economy. The idea that justice and efficiency lie in the formulae and qualculations that they operate, calls for a final comment on the mathematical notion of derivation.

What does the prime (f′) teach us that is not in the function (f)? Nothing, of course. The derivative operator adds nothing in quality to those of the function itself. The question is one of making these qualities visible in the first place, and inventing tools to do just that. Knowing the prime allows one to anticipate the function reaction itself. At each point of a continuous function, the next point is in germ. The first point precedes the next one as much as the next one attracts the first one. Observing the derivations of a process teaches us about its immediate past and its immediate future.

A reader conversant in mathematics would be right to point out the following caveat: the only unique relationship in mathematics goes from the function to its prime, not the reverse. Because deriving captures only the differential shift of a process, the location of the process itself is not captured by the operation. But more conversant readers will not be discouraged by this dissimilitude; on the contrary. They will remember the famous theorem in calculus, demonstrating that the function is nothing but the series of all its derivatives, when they can be calculated. We have seen that the object of economic derivation–conversion—and its effect, when the conditions of felicity are met—is to make formerly discontinuous and decorrelated values commensurable, continuous, and connected. In economics, deriving means constructing, point by point, the functions whose derived product seems to be a mere consequence, when it is successful. The reasoning can be taken far: it is the endless string of derivations that produces value, that of the underlying assets. In other words, to know what values are, one has to derive them as much as possible; that is, to lengthen the chain of successive derivations. The value of Beckham or of Total has been tested, performed, by the derived products that refer to them. No economic value without derivation! No analysis of value without analysis of derivations: they and they alone are observable. Would it not be justified to replace the study of systems of exchange by that of derivation, its chains, and the formulae that enact those chains?

DOCUMENT 1

The World-wide Secured Exposure 8 Year EMTN on Global Indices S&P 500, Nikkei225, Eurostoxx 50.

 – 100% Capital Guarantee at Maturity.
 – 120% Participation in the Quarterly Average Rise of the Portfolio.

– 120% Participation in the Best Performing Index in Case of Portfolio Underperformance.
– In Euro with Exchange Rate Guarantee

THE 'DOUBLE CHANCE' NOTE—HOW DOES IT WORK?

Thanks to the double chance mechanism, this Note offers two chances to make a return on the global equity market. Indeed, contrary to a classic capital-protected investment, should the final value of the portfolio be below its initial value, the Note will offer a second chance and pay the highest positive performance of the individual indices comprising the portfolio.

REDEMPTION AT MATURITY

The First Chance

On the launch date, the value of the portfolio is set at 100.

Every three months following the Start Date (each being a fixing date), the performance of the portfolio is calculated as a percentage of its initial value.

The Final Value of the portfolio will be the arithmetic average of the 32 levels recorded on each Fixing Date.

If the Final Value of the Portfolio is greater than or equal to its initial value, the investor receives 100% of his/her investment amount plus 120% of the Portfolio performance as calculated above.

The Second Chance

If the Final Value of the Basket is less than its initial value, the investor receives 100% of the nominal amount plus 120% of the average performance of the best performing index in the portfolio.

Maturity date	25 February 2008
Underlying	Equally weighted basket composed of the following indices:
	– DJ EUROSTOXX 50 (STX)
	– S&P 500 (SP)
	– NIKKEI 225 (NIX)
Issue Price	100% Nominal Amount

Reoffer Price   95% of Nominal Amount
Capital Guarantee   100% of Nominal Amount at Maturity
Redemption at Maturity   Maturity, the holder will receive the greater of
                                 the following:
                                 – Nominal × 100%
                                 – Nominal × (100% + 120% ×
                                   [Max(BKT(m) − 1; 0)])
with

$$BKT m = \frac{1}{32} \sum_{t=1}^{32} BKTt$$

$$BKT t = \left[\frac{1}{3} \times \frac{SPt}{SPi}\right] + \left[\frac{1}{3} \times \frac{STXt}{STXi}\right] + \left[\frac{1}{3} \times \frac{NIXt}{NIXi}\right]$$

where t means the 32 quarterly fixing dates taken over the life of the Note.
SPt, STXt, NIXt is the Closing Price of the fixing date 't' of the relevant index.
SPi, STXi, NIXi is the Closing Price on Start Date of the relevant index.
   BKT(i) is the Closing Value of the equally weighted basket on Start Date.
   Double Chance   If BKT(m) < BKT(i), the Note pays:

$$Nominal \times \left(100\% + 120\% \times \right.$$

$$\left. MAx \left[\frac{SPm}{SPi} - 1; \frac{STXm}{STXi} - 1; \frac{NIXm}{NIXi} - 1; 0\right] \right)$$

With

$$SPm = \frac{1}{32} \sum_{t-1}^{32} SPt; STXm$$

$$= \frac{1}{32} \sum_{t=1}^{32} STXt; NIXm = \frac{1}{32} \sum_{t=1}^{32} NIXt$$

REFERENCES

Abernathy, W., and Clark, K. (1985). Innovation: Mapping the winds of creative
   destruction. *Research Policy*, 14(1), 3–22.
Beunza, D., and Stark, D. (2008). Reflexive modeling: The social calculus of the
   arbitrageur. Working paper. Available online at http://papers.ssrn.com/sol3/papers.
   cfm?abstract_id = 1285054 (as seen December 2008).

Bohannan, P. (1955). Some principles of exchange and investment among the Tiv. *American Anthropologist,* 57(1), 60–70.

Callon, M. (1998). Introduction: The embeddedness of economic markets in economics. In M. Callon (ed.), *The Laws of the Markets.* Oxford: Blackwell, 1–57.

——Méadel, C., and Rabeharisoa, V. (2002). The economy of qualities. *Economy and Society,* 31(1), 194–217.

——(2007). What does it mean to say that economics is performative? In D. MacKenzie, F. Muniesa, and L. Siu (eds.), *Do Economists Make Markets? On the Performativity of Economics.* Princeton: Princeton University Press, 311–57.

——and Caliskan, K. (2009a forthcoming). Economization. Part I: On search of economization. *Economy and Society.*

————(2009b forthcoming). Economization. Part II: Some elements for a research program on the study of marketization. *Economy and Society.*

Cochoy, F. (2002). *Une sociologie du packaging ou l'âne de Buridan face au marché.* Paris: PUF.

Daston, L. (1994). Enlightenment calculations. *Critical Inquiry,* 21(1), 182–202.

Dosi, G. (1982). Technological paradigms and technological trajectories: A suggested interpretation of the determinants and directions of technical change. *Research Policy,* 11(3), 147–62.

Gallouj, F. (2002). *Innovation in the Service Economy.* Edward: Elgar.

Girard, R. (1979). *Violence and the Sacred.* Baltimore: The Johns Hopkins University Press.

——(1989). *The Scapegoat.* Baltimore: The Johns Hopkins University Press.

Guala, F. (2001). Building economic machines: The FCC auctions. *Study in the History and Philosophy of Science,* 32(3), 453–77.

——(2007). How to do things with experimental economics. In D. MacKenzie, F. Muniesa, and L. Siu (eds.), *Do Economists Make Markets? On the Performativity of Economics.* Princeton: Princeton University Press, 128–62.

Guesnerie, R., and Rochet, J-C. (1993). (De)Stabilizing properties of futures markets: An alternative view point. *European Economic Review,* 37(5), 1043–64.

Guyer, J. (2004). *Marginal Gains. Monetary Transactions in Atlantic Africa.* Chicago: The University of Chicago Press.

Hayden, C. (2007). A generic solution? Pharmaceuticals and the politics of the similar in Mexico. *Current Anthropology,* 48(4), 475–95.

——(2008). No patent, no generic: Pharmaceutical access and the politics of the copy. In M. Biagioli, P. Jaszi, and M. Woodmansee (eds.), *Contexts of Invention.* Chicago: University of Chicago Press.

Hopwood, A.G. (1976). Editorial: The path ahead. *Accounting, Organizations and Society,* 1(1), 1–4.

Knight, F.H. (1971/1921). *Risk, Uncertainty and Profit.* Chicago: The University of Chicago Press.

Latour, B. (1987). *Science in Action: How to Follow Scientists and Engineers Through Society.* Cambridge, Mass.: Harvard University Press.

——and Lepinay, V-A. (2009). *Economics: The Science of Passionate Interests. An Introduction to the Economic Anthropology of Gabriel Tarde*. Chicago: Prikly Press Paradigm.

Lepinay, V-A. (2007). Parasitic formulae: The case of Capital Guarantee Products. In M. Callon, Y. Milo, and F. Muniesa (eds.), *Market Devices*. Oxford: Routledge Sociology Monograph.

——(2009). *Codes of Finance*. Cambridge, Mass.: MIT Press.

MacKenzie, D. (2006). *An Engine, Not a Camera: How Financial Models Shape Markets*. Cambridge, Mass.: MIT Press.

——Muniesa, F., and Siu, L. (eds.) (2007). *Do Economists Make Markets? On the Performativity of Economics*. Princeton: Princeton University Press.

Poovey, M. (1998). *A History of the Modern Fact: Problems of Knowledge in the Sciences of Wealth and Society*. Chicago: University of Chicago Press.

Porter, T. (1995). *Trust in Numbers: The Pursuit of Objectivity in Science and Public Life*. Princeton: Princeton University Press.

Power, M. (2004). Counting, control and calculation: Reflections on measuring and management. *Human Relations*, 57(6), 765–83.

Rose, N., and Miller, P. (2008). *Governing the Present: Administering Economic, Social and Personal Life*. Cambridge: Polity Press.

Say, J-B. (1826). *Catéchismes d'économie politique*, 3ième édition. Paris.

Schaffer, S. (1994). Babbage's intelligence: Calculating engines and the factory system. *Critical Inquiry*, 21(1), 203–27.

Serres, M. (2007/1980). *The Parasite*. Minneapolis, Minn.: University of Minnesota Press.

Wise, N. (1995). *The Values of Precision*. Princeton: Princeton University Press.

13

Behavioural Studies of the Effects of Regulation on Earnings Management and Accounting Choice

Robert Libby and Nicholas Seybert

INTRODUCTION

Behavioural studies of financial reporting issues began in the 1960s, and experienced a resurgence in the last two decades. The majority of both the earlier and later research concentrates on how accounting methods and disclosure alternatives affect earnings predictions and value estimates of investors and analysts. However, a growing portion of more recent research focuses on the effects of accounting and disclosure regulation on managers', auditors', and directors' financial reporting and investment choices. These papers contribute to the broader literature on what is normally termed earnings management or accounting choice. Many of these studies were conducted since the last major review of the experimental financial reporting literature (Libby et al. 2002) and a number of major reviews of the earnings management and accounting choice literatures (e.g. Healy and Wahlen 1999; Fields et al. 2001). The purpose of this chapter is to review these more recent studies, pointing out how experiments and surveys have added unique elements to our understanding of earnings management and accounting choice. The chapter is aimed at a broad spectrum of students, researchers, and policymakers interested in learning more about earnings management and accounting choice.

The authors are deeply indebted to Anthony Hopwood for his continuing support for behavioural research in accounting settings. The authors are grateful to Robert Bloomfield, Kathryn Kadous, Lisa Koonce, and Mark Nelson for their comments on an earlier version of this chapter.

In this review, we employ an expansive definition of earnings management and accounting choice similar to that of Fields et al. (2001) and Francis (2001). This definition includes choices of accounting methods, estimates, classifications, levels of detail, and display format used in mandatory disclosures, as well as frequency, timing, and content of voluntary disclosures. It also includes 'real earnings management', or choices of the structure and amount of real production and investment activities that are aimed at achieving an accounting goal such as meeting or beating a forecast or avoiding recognizing a liability. We view these choices as the final results of interdependent decisions by managers, auditors, and directors.

Our major focus is on how these decisions are affected by financial reporting, auditing, and other corporate governance regulations. As a consequence, we limit the papers we examine to those where aspects of regulation are either manipulated or observed independent variables and accounting and disclosure choices by one or more of the three parties involved are the dependent variables of interest. Figure 13.1 represents the linkages between the three forms of regulation and the interdependent choices of the three parties which result in a final

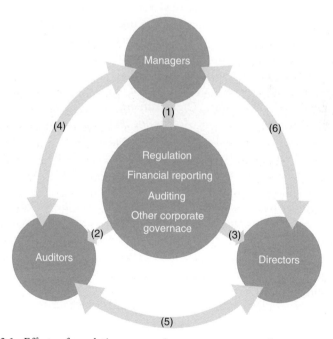

Figure 13.1. Effects of regulation on earnings management and accounting choice

Note: Links 1, 2, and 3 represent direct effects of regulations on actors; links 4, 5, and 6 represent indirect effects of regulations on actors resulting from the direct effects on another actor.

reporting or investment choice. We use this structure as a vehicle for organizing the existing literature and pointing out fruitful directions for future research.

This structure results in the omission of important areas of the behavioural literature which are relevant to understanding earnings management and accounting choice. First, we do not discuss the extensive literatures on the conduct of audit processes and negotiation processes of auditors and managers. In most cases, the omitted studies focus on independent variables other than regulation or dependent variables other than accounting and disclosure choices. We also do not provide an extensive review of studies of investor reactions to disclosure choices which provide insights related to some management motives for earnings management and accounting choice. We briefly mention these studies where they provide part of the motivation for the studies of interest.[1]

Experimental research on earnings management and accounting choice include two types of studies: (*a*) individual judgement and decision-making studies, or *behavioural research*, where the primary focus is on manipulation of the environment and observation of behaviour of experienced participants who have learnt about their incentives in the field; and (*b*) multiperson studies, or *experimental economics research*, where participants are given incentives and allowed to interact (e.g. King 2002; Bowlin et al. 2009). We are in agreement with Kachelmeier and King (2002) that many questions about the effects of regulation are best examined by a combination of studies using the two approaches. However, to meet our page constraints, we focus on behavioural experiments and survey results.

The specific papers we review are the result of a search of the 2002 through 2007 volumes of *Accounting, Organizations, and Society*; *Contemporary Accounting Research*; *Journal of Accounting Research*; and *The Accounting Review*. We also include selected working papers from SSRN and other sources, and discuss selected older papers that provide the basis for more recent work. Finally, our selections are affected by our own biases and the issues we are addressing in our current research.

The remainder of this chapter will be organized as follows. Section 2 discusses how experiments and surveys complement archival studies in developing our understanding of earnings management and accounting choice. Section 3 examines existing studies of the effects of reporting, auditing, and other corporate governance regulation on these phenomena. Section 4 discusses findings related to the choice between real and accounting-based earnings management options. Section 5 reviews studies which distinguish and rank

---

[1] These two groups of studies are reviewed in detail in the articles published in the 2005 Supplement issue of *Auditing: A Journal of Practice and Theory* and in Libby et al. (2002), respectively.

management motives for earnings management and accounting choice. Section 6 summarizes the key findings and suggests areas for future research.

ROLE OF EXPERIMENTS AND SURVEYS

A number of authors point out that archival studies of earnings management and accounting choice often suffer significant endogeneity and correlated omitted variables problems which make it difficult to draw strong causal inferences (e.g. Fields et al. 2001). They are also limited to studying the characteristics of the existing regulatory regime which makes it difficult to estimate the potential effects of proposed regulatory changes or determine the specific characteristics of accounting regulation that encourage or discourage different forms of earnings management or other accounting choices (e.g. Healy and Wahlen 1999; Libby et al. 2002). Finally, they are limited to studying dependent measures provided in existing archival records. This makes it difficult to identify the roles of specific actors (managers, auditors, and directors) in accounting decisions or the specific motivations and beliefs that underlie their behaviour (e.g. Francis 2001). Experiments and surveys have different strengths and weaknesses.

In an experiment, the decision-setting is created, so independent variables can be manipulated and other potentially influential variables can be controlled for by holding them constant or through random assignment of participants. This allows the researcher to disentangle the effects of natural confounds which leads to stronger causal inferences (Libby and Luft 1993). Furthermore, conditions that do not exist in the current regulatory environment can be created in the laboratory which allows ex ante tests of some of the effects of specific components of proposed regulatory changes. Creating the setting also involves creating the dependent measures, which allows the roles of managers, auditors, and directors to be separately identified, and intervening processes leading to financial reporting outcomes, including the participants' motives and expectations about the interaction between reporting standards and users' judgements, to be assessed. This can result in more detailed process explanations that help researchers, regulators, and financial statement users understand when and *why* earnings management is more likely and can lead to more accurate underlying assumptions for future modelling and archival studies. With these benefits come a number of costs. Experiments are usually limited in their ability to representatively sample decisions, settings, and actors. As a consequence, experiments provide less basis for judging the magnitude or pervasiveness of effects. Also, only a small number of independent variables can be manipulated in any one experiment, which makes them inappropriate for exploratory analysis.[2]

Surveys generally give up some of the control provided in experiments because independent variables are often not manipulated between participants and fewer elements of the setting are held constant. Survey responses are also valid only when the respondents have insight into the relevant components of their mental processes (see, e.g., King [2002] for a study examining unconscious bias in auditor decision processes). A strength of surveys is that they normally are able to examine a broader and more representative set of decisions, settings, and actors. To differing degrees, both surveys and experiments run the risk that participants will not respond in the same fashion they would in the natural environment as a result of various forms of response bias (desirability bias, demand effects, belief/action differences, etc.).[3]

In general, the strengths and weaknesses of archival studies, experiments, and surveys are complementary. As a consequence, a multi-method approach to examining questions about earnings management and accounting choice is generally warranted. The different methods can provide answers to different parts of our research questions, and triangulation of results across methods provides the strongest basis for valid conclusions. Experimental and survey research to date has focused mainly on three neglected areas suggested by earlier review papers. The first is the effect of different types of financial reporting, auditing, and other corporate governance regulation on earnings management and accounting choice activities of managers, auditors, and directors. These effects are represented in Figure 13.1 and are discussed in Section 3. The second area examines the determinants of managers' preferences for real versus accounting-based earnings management methods. The final area attempts to understand the role of particular motives in earnings management and accounting choice behaviour.

REGULATION EFFECTS

Prior archival research provides limited evidence on how reporting standards or regulatory interventions are likely to affect earnings management and

---

[2] Refer to Trotman (1996), Libby et al. (2002), and Bonner (2007) for more extensive discussions of experimental methods.
[3] See Groves et al. (2004) for a detailed description of survey methodology and potential response biases in behavioral research.

accounting choice (Healy and Wahlen 1999). Experimental studies are particularly well positioned to answer such questions because they can investigate
the effects of regulations that have not yet been adopted while holding
underlying macroeconomic, firm, and manager characteristics constant.
They can also vary specific components of the regulatory regime to provide
more detailed explanations of their effects. Recent studies focus on a variety of
regulations, including those governing financial reporting, auditing, and
other aspects of corporate governance. The collective evidence suggests the
manner in which specific types of regulations could affect different forms of
earnings management and accounting choice as well as the conditions under
which these effects will break down or lead to counter-intuitive outcomes.

Following Figure 13.1, we organize the discussion by the type of regulation
involved (financial reporting, auditing, and other corporate governance). Also
following Figure 13.1, each type of regulation can have direct effects on each of
the three actors in the financial reporting process (links 1, 2, and 3). Each
regulation can also have indirect effects on any of the actors resulting from its
effect on another actor (links 4, 5, and 6). As noted throughout the following
sections, each paper investigates one or more of the numbered links in the
figure. Most of the experimental studies examine direct effects of specific
regulatory elements on managers, auditors, or directors (links 1, 2, or 3).
The survey studies tend to examine broader issues, and often include effects
on more than one set of actors or examine both a direct and indirect effect.

Financial Reporting Regulation

Debates concerning financial reporting regulation often consider the potential
implications for managers' earnings management attempts. This is evident in
discussions amongst regulators, practitioners (see Bhojraj and Libby [2005] for
a discussion), and researchers (e.g. Healy et al. 2002). Understanding how
financial reporting regulations affect earnings management and accounting
choice requires consideration of managers' beliefs about how financial statement users, regulators, directors, and auditors react to different accounting
choices in different circumstances, auditors' beliefs about how managers,
financial statement users, directors, and regulators will act in different circumstances, and so on. Two areas investigated in recent experimental and survey
research are: (*a*) effects of display format and location on managers' and
auditors' beliefs and actions; and (*b*) effects of accounting method, reporting
interval, and standard precision on managers' beliefs and actions.

The prevalence of earnings management suggests that managers believe that
at least some financial statement users will be unable to easily parse out the

effects of earnings management (Fields et al. 2001). Two studies show how accounting regulations that allow choices of informationally equivalent, less-transparent presentations may unintentionally promote earnings management.[4] Hunton et al. (2006) investigate whether reporting location/transparency, which affects the proportion of users who detect earnings management (Hirst and Hopkins 1998; Maines and McDaniel 2000), will in turn affect managers' willingness to engage in related earnings management behaviour (link 1). They manipulate the transparency of comprehensive income reporting (statement of comprehensive income vs. statement of stockholders' equity) and the sign of the reporting objective (positive vs. negative) and provide managers with the option to strategically sell securities in order to meet the consensus analyst forecast. Income increasing and decreasing earnings management is in evidence, but the more transparent format significantly decreases the proportion of managers that engage in this form of strategic earnings management. The managers in the less-transparent statement of stockholders' equity conditions indicate they believe that earnings management in this case will be difficult for investors to detect, will increase company stock price, and will not significantly affect managers' reporting reputations. Those in the more transparent statement of comprehensive income condition indicate earnings management will have the opposite effects. These results suggest managers believe that the number of users that can and will parse out the effects of earnings management is an important consideration in their earnings management choices and that using a less-transparent format decreases that number. As a consequence, regulations requiring informationally equivalent more transparent reporting will likely mitigate earnings management behaviour in the area of increased transparency.

Libby et al. (2006) demonstrate how another form of reporting location/ transparency, recognition versus disclosure, can impact earnings management through its effects on auditors' beliefs and resulting actions (link 2). In two experiments involving stock compensation and leasing, audit partners require greater correction of misstatements in recognized amounts than disclosed amounts because they view equivalent misstatements in recognized amounts as more material. This occurs even though the same partners believe that sophisticated analysts treat disclosed expenses similarly to recognized expenses. As a consequence, even when the measurement rules are held constant, managers have more latitude in managing disclosed numbers simply because auditors are less likely to require adjustment. Taken together, the Hunton

---

[4] Hirshleifer and Teoh (2003) also suggest that the market will react differentially to equivalent presentations when the attentional resources necessary for information extraction are different.

et al. (2006) and Libby et al. (2006) findings suggest that reporting regulations allowing less-transparent financial reporting are likely to increase managers' earnings management attempts, and that auditors' beliefs about the effects of location on their reporting responsibilities will in some cases exacerbate this effect.

Experimental and survey research also examines the effects of reporting methods on managers' willingness to sacrifice cash flows in order to report higher short-term earnings. When managers lack alternative forms of credible communication concerning the long-term implications of their investment choices, financial reporting standards can have significant effects on these choices through their impact on the pattern of reported earnings. Two recent studies reveal how seemingly innocuous reporting methods can motivate managers to engage in real earnings management by altering their subsequent investment decisions. Jackson (2008) shows that straight-line (as opposed to accelerated) depreciation can discourage managers from replacing unproductive assets (link 1). This occurs because disposing of an asset results in a larger loss under the straight-line method, and managers are generally averse to this consequence. Managers also perceive assets with higher book value as having substantially more 'benefit' to provide in the future, which can also dissuade them from disposing of inefficient assets. Jackson's results imply that depreciation accounting affects managers' real investment decisions both through general aversion to reporting losses and also through unintentional cognitive biases. Seybert (2009) reports an experiment which shows that managers tend to abandon a failing R&D project unless two conditions are present: the manager is responsible for initiating the project and R&D expenditures are capitalized (link 1). This occurs because abandoning a capitalized project requires asset impairment and managers believe they will be held responsible for the negative reporting effects of their decisions. The results suggest that a reporting method generally believed to reduce short-term reporting concerns (R&D capitalization) can in some cases actually increase real earnings management.

An ongoing debate in many European and Asian countries focuses on financial reporting frequency, with some countries hesitant to adopt quarterly (as opposed to semi-annual) financial reporting. Quarterly reporting concerns regulators and practitioners due to the potential for increasing the focus on the short term in managerial decision-making. Bhojraj and Libby (2005) is the first paper to directly demonstrate that managers engage in real earnings management by foregoing superior projects when doing so results in higher reported earnings prior to a stock issuance (link 1). Contrary to common wisdom, the authors also demonstrate how semi-annual reporting can increase or decrease this effect. When a project has a volatile earnings stream, semi-annual reports can either postpone the reporting of unfavourable quarterly performance *or* favourable quarterly performance. As a result, managers may forego superior projects when the required quarterly or semi-annual reporting prevents them from credibly conveying that superiority to the market.

Finally, two studies examine how managers' reporting decisions are affected by standard precision and accompanying guidance. Nelson et al. (2002) examine the effect of the precision of accounting standards on auditors' encounters with various types of earnings management. Their audit partner survey respondents answer questions both about their experience with their clients' earnings management attempts as well as their responses to those attempts (direct effects in links 1 and 2 and an indirect effect in link 4). The participants indicate that managers primarily use transaction structuring (changes in the timing or nature of a contract, transaction, or activity) to manage earnings when standards are precise, and adjustments of judgements or estimates when standards are imprecise. Auditors are also less likely to require adjustments to eliminate these types of earnings management attempts. This latter finding suggests that many managers understand which types of earnings management attempts will most likely pass muster with their auditors. It also has implications for changes in management behaviour that we might expect if firms switch to less precise 'principles-based' standards. Clor-Proell and Nelson (2007) investigate whether principles-based standards accompanied by implementation guidance will bias managers' reporting judgements (link 1). The authors show that providing examples of transactions that qualify for accounting treatments can induce managers to develop unwarranted confidence that their transaction also qualifies, despite the fact that the example case may differ substantially from the manager's own. This occurs because managers focus on aspects of their situation and the example case that are similar rather than dissimilar. These results suggest that lower standard precision accompanied by implementation guidance could reduce reporting quality.

Taken together, experimental and survey studies of the effects of financial reporting regulation on earnings management suggest that reporting transparency, prior period choices of financial reporting methods, and the precision of accounting standards are likely to have effects on both the amount and form of real and accounting earnings management. Furthermore, these regulatory effects operate through their direct effects on managers' earnings management attempts, as well as through their effects on auditors' adjustment decisions (links 1, 2, and 4). The importance of financial reporting regulations are consistent with more general surveys showing that CFOs and auditors indicate that accounting and disclosure standards represent the most important input in auditor–manager accounting disputes (see Gibbins et al. [2001] for auditors; Gibbins et al. [2007] for CFOs; and Gibbins et al. [2005] for both groups). CFOs in Gibbins et al. (2007) also reveal that the bigger the role these regulations play in the dispute, the farther the final reporting outcome is from management's initial position.

The effects demonstrated in experimental and survey studies would be difficult or impossible to observe in available archival data. As a consequence, these issues were rarely discussed in the prior regulatory, practitioner, and academic literature. Experiments are able to demonstrate these effects by examining standards that are under consideration but not currently mandated, by separately examining the actions of managers and auditors, and by assessing underlying beliefs, in addition to focusing on the reporting outcomes that result from their interaction. Surveys directly ask broader samples of managers and auditors about the effects of accounting regulation on reporting choices and outcomes, providing increased confidence in the importance of these issues in the external environment.

Auditing Regulation

Financial reporting regulations directly affect managers' propensity to manage earnings and affect auditors' behaviour based on their interpretations of their responsibilities for different reporting elements, which indirectly affects managers' behaviour. As noted earlier, most experimental and survey research in auditing focuses on the effects of task properties and auditor attributes on the gathering and evaluation of audit evidence and negotiation strategies by different members of the audit team, and does not focus on effects of regulations on required adjustments (see Nelson and Tan [2005] for a recent comprehensive review). Experimental research involving audit regulations focuses on the conditions that will lead auditors to be more or less accepting of managers' earnings management attempts. Auditing regulations are intended to affect audit adjustments by directly affecting required audit procedures and/ or auditors' incentives.[5] A variety of studies show that auditors have and will act on their economic incentives to favour clients' preferred reporting methods (e.g. Hackenbrack and Nelson 1996; Beeler and Hunton 2002; Nelson et al. 2002). Consequently, audit regulations intended to increase auditor

---

[5] We consider a regulation to be an auditing regulation when it is designed to have direct effects on external auditors' actions. Regulations that affect auditors' actions through changes in directors' actions are included in the 'other corporate governance' category.

independence and objective decision-making are likely to impact earnings management.

The first two studies in this area test the direct effects of changes in auditing standards on auditor behaviour. Kadous et al. (2003) examine the effects of an Securities and Exchange Commission (SEC) mandated quality assessment of a client's preferred accounting method (link 2) on auditors' actions. This standard would require auditors to take a detailed, objective look at both a client's preferred method and alternative accounting methods. Kadous et al. (2003) find that auditors may fail to maintain objectivity during quality assessments. Specifically, auditors predisposed to accept a client's preferred method actually *increase* their commitment to this method following a mandatory quality assessment, presumably because they engage in motivated reasoning during this process. This counter-intuitive effect implies that regulations intended to increase auditor objectivity may not function properly in practice. Another regulation intended to improve auditor objectivity is mandatory audit partner rotation, as imposed by the Sarbanes–Oxley Act of 2002. Regulators believe that such rotation will increase auditor independence by reducing conflicts of interest caused by the development of close auditor–client relationships. Houston et al. (2006) investigate whether client-imposed auditor rotation will function in this manner or bring with it unintended consequences (links 2 and 4). The authors find that rotation can actually reduce auditors' required adjustments of prior period misstatements, and attribute this effect to the perceived lack of client commitment to maintaining a positive working relationship with the auditor under imposed rotation.

Two studies also examine how auditing regulation will affect reporting through its impact on auditors' interaction with other parties. Libby and Kinney (2000) investigate the effects of an auditing standard that is aimed at changing the interaction between auditors and directors and tests its effect on managers' final reporting choices (links 2, 3, and 5). Specifically, they examine whether Statement on Auditing Standards (SAS) No. 89 (AICPA 1999), a standard requiring auditors to report uncorrected misstatements to the audit committee, can reduce earnings management conducted through opportunistic correction of quantitatively immaterial errors. Auditors indicate that they expect greater earnings management when correction would result in their client missing an earnings benchmark, and that mandated audit committee communication will fail to dampen this tendency. The results suggest that auditors did not believe that audit committees of that era would act to reduce this form of earnings management. Libby and Kinney (2000) were able to examine the effectiveness of this new regulation prospectively because they utilized an experiment. Subsequently, the SEC issued Staff Accounting

Bulletin (SAB) No. 99 (Securities and Exchange Commission 1999) which was designed in part to remedy the weaknesses in SAS No. 89 by directly requiring adjustment of such errors. Portions of the Sarbanes–Oxley Act also increased the likely effectiveness of the audit committee in these matters.

Ng and Tan (2003) investigate a related scenario, asking audit managers whether they would require an adjustment that would cause their client to miss an earnings benchmark. They manipulate whether authoritative guidance exists to support the auditor's proposed adjustment and whether the client's audit committee has been effective in the past (links 2, 3, and 5). An effective audit committee increases the probability that the auditor will book the adjustment, as does the presence of authoritative guidance on the audit issue. The authoritative guidance is especially helpful when the audit committee is perceived as ineffective. Consistent with the results of Libby and Kinney (2000), auditors expect virtually no adjustment in the absence of an effective audit committee and authoritative guidance. These results again suggest that a stronger audit committee is important in reinforcing auditors' adjustment decisions.

In summary, research involving audit regulations intended to curb managers' earnings management attempts suggests that these regulations can sometimes break down in practice. The first two studies utilize the comparative advantage of experiments to show the specific psychological drivers of this breakdown (motivated reasoning and perceived client commitment). The latter two studies examine regulations and standards that are either unobservable in archival data or difficult to separate from confounding company or macro characteristics. This stream of research is relatively new and the audit regulatory environment is changing dramatically. Many regulations intended to mitigate earnings management through the auditor remain unexplored, and future experimental studies could contribute to our understanding of auditors' impact on earnings management.

Other Corporate Governance Regulation

Auditors are not the first or last line of defense against earnings management. A variety of regulations aimed at improving corporate governance could also serve this purpose. The effectiveness of the audit committee has been the focus of several studies. Since the time Libby and Kinney (2000) conducted their study, numerous corporate governance regulations have been implemented under the Sarbanes–Oxley Act, not the least of which requires increased representation of independent directors on audit committees. The emphasis of the Sarbanes–Oxley Act and other regulations on the make-up of the board has focused attention on the effects of attributes of board membership. McDaniel et al. (2002) ask audit managers and executive MBA students to assume the role of audit committee members and to review financial statements for questionable reporting items (links 1 and 2). They show that audit managers are more likely than executive MBAs to apply relevance and reliability concepts in assessing the quality of financial reporting. Executive MBAs are more likely to emphasize the importance of non-recurring, prominent accounting items such as those covered in business press, while audit managers pay more attention to less prominent items that are recurring in nature. These results suggest that financial expertise on audit committees may increase focus on reporting treatments that would otherwise be overlooked.

A number of surveys also examine the effects of Sarbanes–Oxley and audit committee characteristics on financial reporting quality. DeZoort and Salterio (2001) had conducted a survey of experienced directors to determine how experience as an independent director affects propensity to support an auditor in a dispute with management (links 3, 5, and 6). They find that directors with greater experience on corporate boards and greater audit knowledge are more likely to side with auditors, while directors who currently serve as managers in the company are less likely to do so. Similarly, DeZoort et al. (2008) surveyed audit committee members pre- and post-Sarbanes–Oxley and find that directors with Certified Public Accountant designation (CPAs) are more likely to support proposed audit adjustments after Sarbanes–Oxley (link 3). Debriefing questions indicate that audit committee members feel greater responsibility for resolving audit issues and perceive a greater need for conservative financial reporting in the post-Sarbanes–Oxley era. Beasley et al. (2009) surveyed audit committee members in the post-Sarbanes–Oxley environment and find that a majority believe that audit committees exercise significant control over managers' reporting practices. Audit committees demand financial reporting information and specifically inquire about areas such as revenue recognition, reserves, and inventory estimates. They also question auditors about financial reporting methods and potential alternatives (links 3, 5, and 6). Beasley et al. (2009) also find that audit committee members appointed post-Sarbanes–Oxley are more likely to be accounting experts and are more likely to investigate these sensitive areas (link 3), suggesting that the current regulatory environment may better facilitate detection and prevention of earnings management.

Cohen et al. (2008) provide convergent evidence on this issue by surveying audit partners and audit managers about the effectiveness of audit committees post-Sarbanes–Oxley. Auditors indicate that audit committees are more willing to confront management, ask difficult questions concerning financial reporting, and are generally more effective at monitoring in the current environment (links 3 and 6). They also believe that management certification requirements introduced by Sarbanes–Oxley will improve financial reporting integrity through direct effects on managers (link 1). On the other hand, McEnroe (2006) reports a survey of CFOs and audit partners and finds that these groups expect the new corporate governance regulations to have minimal effects on particular earnings management techniques. Both audit partners and CFOs are more likely to disagree than agree that Sarbanes–Oxley will mitigate earnings management with respect to debt securities, lease classifications, R&D capitalization, and pension estimates. However, respondents do indicate that earnings management violating Generally Accepted Accounting Principles (GAAP) (e.g. premature revenue recognition) is more likely to be mitigated as a result of Sarbanes–Oxley.[6]

While the previously discussed surveys suggest that requiring increased representation of independent directors will improve financial reporting, two studies suggest otherwise. CFO survey respondents in Gibbins et al. (2007) indicate that audit committee independence and the chair of the committee are unimportant in determining financial reporting outcomes arising from auditor–manager disputes (links 4, 5, and 6). This suggests that audit committees and independent directors may play limited roles in typical reporting issues. Hunton and Rose (2008) find that the independent director requirement could even be detrimental under certain conditions (link 3). They ask corporate directors to assume that they serve either on one board or multiple boards (as is frequently the case with independent directors) and rate the likelihood that they would require correction of an accounting misstatement related to revenue recognition. Half of the directors learn that the misstatement affects the current year, while the other half learn that correction would require a restatement of prior year earnings. Directors serving on multiple boards are less likely to require correction of the misstatement, and this is especially true when correction requires a restatement of prior year earnings. Debriefing questions demonstrate that this difference is attributable to potential reputation damage that a restatement can inflict upon directors, hindering their ability to serve on subsequent boards. In other words, independent directors may be objective when it comes to managers' incentives, but not when it comes to their own. These results suggest that this consequence of a regulation intended to strengthen corporate governance

---

[6] This is consistent with managers in Graham et al. (2005) indicating that they prefer real earnings management to accounting earnings management in the current environment compared with the extensive evidence of accounting earnings management in Nelson et al. (2002).

might actually result in fewer corrections of managers' earnings management attempts by increasing the number of 'professional' board members serving on multiple boards.

Another focus of the Sarbanes–Oxley Act is to increase the emphasis on internal controls, including the internal audit function. Internal auditing has the ability to uncover misstatements and fraud before they reach external financial statement users. Hunton et al. (2006) investigate the effects of internal audit frequency on the behaviour of middle managers (link 1). Managers are asked to assume that they are compensated based either on current year or three year average ROI, and internal audit frequency is either continuous or once every three years. Continuous internal auditing reduces managers' willingness to engage in real earnings management when they are compensated based on current year ROI, but increases this willingness when they are compensated based on three year average ROI. In other words, continuous internal auditing, which implies more frequent performance evaluation included in the operational component of internal auditing, can undo the positive effects of incentive contracts that instill a long-term focus. In debriefing questions, managers indicate that continuous internal auditing induces fear of performance evaluations, a decreased willingness to take risks, and greater focus on short-term goals. While Hunton et al. (2006) investigate a very specific internal audit and reporting context, Gibbins et al. (2007) find that CFOs do not believe the internal audit function plays an important role in typical reporting outcomes.

Much like research on financial reporting and audit regulations, experimental studies of corporate governance regulations suggest that some parts of those regulations designed to reduce earnings management will have only a minimal effect or will be accompanied by unintended consequences that increase earnings management. By manipulating the corporate governance regulation of interest, these experiments are able to control for other changes in the environment which allows for clear causal inferences. Additionally, the studies utilize incentive manipulations and insightful debriefing questions to provide greater insight into participants' earnings management motives. Surveys investigating these effects directly ask auditors, managers, and audit committee members whether new corporate governance regulations have affected financial reporting. This methodology helps to better understand the specific aspects of internal firm processes that are affected by regulation (e.g. audit committee confrontation of managers), and provides a broader picture of actors' perceptions of regulation by sampling each relevant group. However, since the surveys discussed above are general before and after questionnaires, it is more difficult to parse out which parts of a broad regulatory change such as Sarbanes–Oxley actually cause any decrease in earnings management. It is even possible that the major effect of Sarbanes–Oxley on earnings management is not through particular process changes but through an overarching increase in the penalties for all parties involved. The nature of these penalties may also have different effects on different earnings management techniques, or may lead managers to substitute one form of earnings management for another, a topic of interest to accounting researchers investigating the tradeoff between real and accounting earnings management. The next section describes behavioural findings related to the various techniques used to manage earnings and the choice between real and accounting-based earnings management.

CHOICE BETWEEN REAL VERSUS ACCOUNTING-BASED EARNINGS MANAGEMENT

Archival studies investigate managers' proclivity to manage earnings through both accounting manipulation and real activities in a variety of settings, including a recent focus on the tradeoff between real and accounting earnings management (Wang and D'Souza 2007; Zang 2007). Fields et al. (2001) and Francis (2001) note the difficulty in concluding from archival data that changes in real investment decisions are undertaken for financial reporting reasons, because there are many potential drivers of such decisions. Experiments and surveys can directly assess whether managers will engage in real and accounting earnings management. Surveys can provide a rank-ordering of the methods managers use to achieve desired earnings outcomes.

Graham et al. (2005) show that managers rank discretionary spending (R&D, advertising) and new project investment decisions as the most preferred avenues for meeting earnings benchmarks, suggesting that real earnings management may be widespread. Nelson et al. (2002) survey auditors regarding managers' earnings management attempts and find that the most common types of manipulation are accounting related and involve reserves, revenue recognition, business combinations, and intangibles. There are three important differences between the two surveys that might explain this discrepancy. First, Nelson et al. (2002) conducted their study prior to the Enron and other scandals and the implementation of Sarbanes–Oxley. Executives interviewed by Graham et al. (2005) reveal that, at least post-Sarbanes–Oxley, they prefer real earnings management to accounting-based earnings management because auditors will not challenge this form of manipulation (an outcome pertaining to links 1, 2, and 4). Second, Nelson et al. (2002) study earnings management attempts discovered by auditors. It is quite possible that many auditors do not even search for some examples of real earnings management as long as the resulting outcomes are properly accounted for. Third, it is also possible that Graham et al.'s manager participants (2005) were less willing to acknowledge accounting-based earnings management in their survey responses because it is thought to be more unethical and in fact may be illegal (a form of response bias).

Both varieties of earnings management are extensively documented in experimental studies. Experiments demonstrate that accounting earnings management can occur in the areas of revenue recognition (Kadous et al. 2003); inventory valuation (Libby and Kinney 2000; Hunton and Rose 2008); stock option and lease expense (Libby et al. 2006); and fair value estimates (Mazza et al. 2007). Real earnings management can take the form of new project selection (Bhojraj and Libby 2005); strategic security sales (Hunton et al. 2006); quality control expenditures (Hunton et al. 2006); machinery replacement decisions (Jackson 2008); and overinvestment in continuing R&D projects (Seybert 2009).

In summary, survey and experimental research investigates a variety of earnings management methods. The results contribute to our understanding of the lengths to which managers will go to achieve desired earnings outcomes, and provide triangulating evidence consistent with prior archival studies that some view as controversial (e.g. the validity of discretionary accruals models and apparent reductions in R&D spending). There is a preponderance of behavioural evidence that managers are willing to manipulate accounting numbers and sacrifice cash flows through real activities manipulation in order to boost reported earnings. However, the exact conditions under which each approach is preferred have not been documented, and specific motives on the part of managers, auditors, and directors may induce different preferences. The next section discusses how experimental and survey research has made progress in identifying the idiosyncratic effects of particular motives on earnings management behaviours.

DISTINGUISHING MANAGEMENT MOTIVES

While the existence and prevalence of earnings management is the focus of numerous archival studies, understanding the particular motives behind earnings management is fundamental to detecting and curbing this behaviour. Fields et al. (2001) describe how various motives often predict identical earnings management behaviour, making clear inferences regarding a specific motive difficult in many archival studies. Given the constraint in available proxies, it may also be difficult to isolate earnings management behaviour from other financial reporting effects. For example, Burgstahler and Dichev (1997) point towards discontinuities in the distribution of reported earnings as evidence of earnings management in order to meet earnings benchmarks, but subsequent papers demonstrate how income taxes, special items, and analyst forecast errors can also explain some of these results (Durtschi and Easton 2005; Beaver et al. 2007). Experimental studies are able to focus on one motive by randomly assigning participants to conditions and holding constant firm and manager characteristics, eliminating confounding motives. To date, motives examined include capital market pressures, individual reputation concerns, tax savings, and bonus compensation.

Given that managers behave as if earnings management will positively impact their company's stock price, it seems logical that greater incentives to boost stock price or attract additional investors will increase earnings management. Though there is considerable archival evidence consistent with this hypothesis (e.g. Teoh, Welch, and Wong 1998), Graham et al. (2005) is the first study to directly ask managers how they benefit from engaging in earnings management. Executives surveyed on this topic indicate that building market credibility and maintaining/increasing stock price are the two strongest motives behind meeting earnings benchmarks. In response to a related question, executives indicate that they would decrease discretionary spending, delay starting a new project, and book revenues early to meet these benchmarks. Bhojraj and Libby (2005) are similarly able to isolate capital market motives by manipulating the presence of an impending stock issuance, which causes managers to strategically select projects that boost reported earnings and stock price. Hunton et al. (2006) find that managers will engage in earnings management to meet the consensus analyst forecast, and believe that doing so will increase their company's stock price. Libby and Kinney (2000) show that auditors anticipate capital market pressure and expect less adjustment of earnings management targeted at meeting the consensus analyst forecast.

Whereas studies investigating capital market motives focus on external financial reporting and its effects on stock price, several studies assess whether individual reputation motives can lead to earnings management. Hunton et al. (2006) find that performance anxiety induced by frequent internal auditing can cause managers to engage in greater real earnings management. Seybert (2009) shows that R&D capitalization and impairment accounting can cause managers to overinvest in continuing R&D projects. This occurs because managers fear that their reputation will be damaged when abandoning a project results in asset impairment. Hunton and Rose (2008) find that professional directors are less likely to recommend restatement of prior years' results because doing so could damage their reputation and their chance to serve on other companies' boards. Finally, executives surveyed by Graham et al. (2005) indicate that management reputation ranks just behind capital market concerns as a reason for meeting earnings benchmarks, and CFOs surveyed by Gibbins et al. (2007) and auditors surveyed in Gibbins et al. (2005) rank management's reporting reputation as an important driver of the outcome of auditor–manager reporting disputes.

Additional earnings management motives receiving attention in archival literature include potential tax savings (e.g. Dhaliwal and Wang 1992) and managers' bonus compensation (e.g. Healy 1985). Cloyd et al. (1996) show that managers will make strategic reporting choices that reinforce their aggressive tax positions, confirming that tax motives can drive reporting manipulation. Mazza et al. (2007) find that managers will select fair value estimates that increase their bonus compensation, confirming that bonus compensation induces managers to opportunistically manage earnings. While these results demonstrate that bonus compensation motives can lead to earnings management, Graham et al. (2005) find that executives rank bonus compensation as a relatively less important reason for meeting earnings benchmarks (compared with capital market and reputation motives).

Behavioural studies of earnings management are able to isolate specific motives for earnings management and causally link them to managers' earnings management attempts. By manipulating capital market pressures, the potential for reputation damage, tax savings, and bonus compensation incentives, experiments show that each of these motives can drive real or accounting earnings management. The survey method utilized by Graham et al. (2005) provides an actual rank-ordering of executives' perceived importance of each motive. Collectively, the evidence complements that obtained in archival studies by demonstrating that managers knowingly and willingly engage in earnings management to fulfil their various objectives. Since there is presumably some degree of stigma associated with earnings management, the fact that managers reveal their propensity to engage in such behaviour provides an even greater assurance that the motives investigated would lead to earnings management in the natural environment.

DISCUSSION AND DIRECTIONS FOR FUTURE RESEARCH

Figure 13.1 provides a useful device for considering the topics that have been addressed by prior research, as well as providing suggestions for future research. The largest group of studies examines the direct effects of accounting and disclosure standards on managers' actions. Perhaps the most surprising of these results relate to the importance of display or location effects for what, on the surface, are informationally equivalent disclosures. Managers clearly believe that less-transparent disclosures that limit the number of analysts and investors that will be aware of the earnings management increases the value of these activities. Similarly, auditors believe that they have less responsibility for these more hidden, less important numbers. The view that an earnings component is more important when a greater number of market participants process it is more consistent with recent theories predicting that markets will react less to difficult to extract information (Bloomfield 2002, 2008; Hirshleifer and Teoh 2003;) than with theories dominating the literature in earlier times predicting that prices should instantaneously 'fully reflect' all information available to some market participants (Gonedes and Dopuch 1974).

Prior accounting method or reporting interval choices also affect managers' real investments in future periods. Behavioural research suggests that managers believe that they often lack credible means to signal the superiority of an investment choice, and wish to avoid reporting lower current income. The existing studies tell us less about why companies do and do not make various voluntary disclosures. Perhaps the most important finding to date is that managers believe that consistency in voluntary disclosure is important to reporting reputation, providing a disincentive for new voluntary disclosures (Graham et al. 2005). As Hirst et al. (2008) suggest, we know very little about how managers determine the characteristics of even the most common forms of voluntary disclosure. This is an area where future survey and experimental work could be useful. The conditions under which voluntary disclosures can provide credible means to signal investment superiority is also worthy of examination in future research. Finally, Gibbins and Pomeroy (2007) and Merkl-Davies and Brennan (2007) discuss how discretionary financial reporting outside of GAAP is an important area about which we know little. Such reporting includes Management's Discussion and Analysis (MD&A), earnings guidance, and environmental disclosures. Li (2008) performs an archival analysis of 10-K reports and finds that companies experiencing losses or transitory good news have longer MD&A sections that include bigger words. Li attributes this result to companies attempting to make bad news more difficult to extract from their reports. Bloomfield's (2008) discussion of the paper points out several additional explanations for this result, and it is likely that survey and experimental work could contribute to understanding how and why managers alter the language used in their annual reports by measuring intervening beliefs.

There are fewer experimental studies examining the effects of auditing and other corporate governance regulations, but surveys have helped to shed some light in these areas. Only three studies have examined the effects of auditing regulation on audit adjustment decisions. Studies such as Kadous et al. (2003) are important because they promise to highlight unexpected effects of new regulations on professionals with extensive accounting experience. Given the significant changes proposed in financial statement presentation and fair value accounting, auditors' task environment could change drastically, in turn influencing their adjustment decisions. A similar approach to studying directors' reporting decisions is utilized by Hunton and Rose (2008), and shows promise in the area of other corporate governance regulation.

Two trends are apparent from the examination of Figure 13.1 in conjunction with the reviewed papers. First, few studies have attempted to look at effects of particular regulations on multiple parties, though several surveys examine the effects of regulation on the interaction between actors in the reporting process. For example, Gibbins et al. (2007) directly ask CFOs whether the audit committee plays an important role in determining reporting outcomes in auditor–manager disputes. Nelson et al. (2002) look at three relationships in Figure 13.1 simultaneously. They jointly assess the impact of reporting regulations on managers' earnings management attempts (link 1) and auditors' adjustment decisions (links 2 and 4). Consequently, they reveal both direct effects of reporting standards on manager behaviour and indirect effects through auditor actions. Second, studies of accounting regulation gravitate towards manager participants (link 1), while studies of auditing regulation focus on auditors (link 2). Corporate governance research is less likely to rely solely on directors, presumably because this participant pool is more difficult to access. For example, Cohen et al. (2008) measure auditor beliefs about the effects of corporate governance regulation on managers and directors. Such research is also very important because beliefs about how regulations affect other actors is likely to change the nature of interaction captured by links 4, 5, and 6, and by extension the effects of links 1, 2, and 3. Future research could attempt to focus on actors and links that have been neglected in each area of regulation, determining whether actors anticipate positive or negative effects of regulation on other actors. Studies which look at multiple relationships simultaneously also promise to provide a more complete picture of the actions of managers, auditors, and directors. Such designs have been successfully utilized in the experimental economics paradigm to investigate topics including how auditor group affiliation combats self-serving biases induced by interaction with managers (King 2002), and how prior experience as an auditor influences managers' reporting decisions (Bowlin et al. 2009). While experimental economics research is likely to continue investigating these interactive settings using business students, psychology-based experiments and surveys can also contribute by examining the psychological processes and beliefs of experienced auditors, managers, and directors.

Experimental and survey research also provides a great deal of evidence on the motives leading to reporting outcomes. Considering the entirety of the results, it seems clear that both stock price and general reputation concerns are the primary motives for managers' earnings management attempts and other accounting choices. Other motives such as debt covenants, bonus compensation, and taxes also play secondary roles. Managers' actions and stated beliefs suggest that ease of detection is a prominent determinant of their choices among earnings management methods. They believe that easily detected earnings management can damage their general reporting reputation and stock price. Consequently, methods that are more difficult to detect are preferred by managers. These include alterations of estimates and allocations in areas where accounting standards are imprecise, changes in investment choices, and management of numbers that are 'hidden' in footnotes or other locations that fewer investors will access and understand. Managers believe that these types of earnings management actually benefit stock price and do not damage their reporting reputation when they help project a pattern of smoothly increasing earnings. They also believe that these methods are less likely to attract corrective action by auditors.

REFERENCES

AICPA (American Institute of Certified Public Accountants). (1999). Proposed statement on Auditing Standards Exposure Draft (22 April). *Audit Adjustments, Reporting on Consistency, and Service Organizations (Omnibus Statement on Auditing Standards – 1999)*. New York: AICPA.

Beasley, M.S., Carcello, J.V., Hermanson, D.R., and Neal, T.L. (2009). The audit committee oversight process. *Contemporary Accounting Research*, 26(1), 65–122.

Beaver, W.H., McNichols, M.F., and Nelson, K.K. (2007). An alternative interpretation of the discontinuity in earnings distributions. *Review of Accounting Studies*, 12(4), 525–56.

Beeler, J.D., and Hunton, J.E. (2002). Contingent economic rents: Insidious threats to audit independence. *Advances in Accounting Behavioral Research*, 5, 21–50.

Bhojraj, S., and Libby, R. (2005). Capital market pressure, disclosure frequency-induced earnings/cash flow conflict, and managerial myopia. *Accounting Review*, 80(1), 1–20.

Bloomfied, R.J. (2002). The incomplete revelation hypothesis: Implications for financial reporting. *Accounting Horizons*, 16(3), 233–44.

Bloomfield, R.J. (2008). Discussion of annual report readability, current earnings, and earnings persistence. *Journal of Accounting and Economics*, 45, 248–52.

Bonner, S.E. (2007). *Judgment and Decision Making in Accounting*. Upper Saddle River, N.J.: Prentice Hall.

Bowlin, K., Hales, J., and Kachelmeier, S.J. (2009). Experimental evidence of how prior experience as an auditor influences managers' strategic reporting decisions. *Review of Accounting Studies*, 14(1), 63–87.

Burgstahler, D., and Dichev, I. (1997). Earnings management to avoid earnings decreases and losses. *Journal of Accounting and Economics*, 24(1), 99–126.

Clor-Proell, S., and Nelson, M.W. (2007). Accounting standards, implementation guidance, and example-based reasoning. *Journal of Accounting Research*, 45(4), 699–730.

Cloyd, C.B., Pratt, J., and Stock, T. (1996). The use of financial accounting choice to support aggressive tax positions: Public and private firms. *Journal of Accounting Research*, 34(1), 23–43.

Cohen, J., Krishnamoorthy, G., and Wright, A. (2008). Corporate governance in the post Sarbanes-Oxley era: Auditors' experiences. Working Paper, Boston College.

DeZoort, F.T., Hermanson, D.R., and Houston, R.W. (2008). Audit committee member support for proposed audit adjustments: Pre-SOX versus post-SOX judgments. *Auditing: A Journal of Practice and Theory*, 27(1), 85–104.

——and Salterio, S.E. (2001). The effects of corporate governance experience and financial-reporting and audit knowledge on audit committee members' judgments. *Auditing: A Journal of Practice and Theory*, 20(2), 31–47.

Dhaliwal, D., and Wang, S.W. (1992). The effect of book income adjustment in the 1986 alternative minimum tax on corporate financial reporting. *Journal of Accounting and Economics*, 15, 7–26.

Durtschi, C., and Easton, P.D. (2005). Earnings management? The shapes of the frequency distributions of earnings metrics are not ipso facto evidence. *Journal of Accounting Research*, 43(4), 557–92.

Fields, T.D., Lys, T.Z., and Vincent, L. (2001). Empirical research on accounting choice. *Journal of Accounting and Economics*, 31, 255–307.

Francis, J. (2001). Discussion of empirical research on accounting choice. *Journal of Accounting and Economics*, 31, 309–19.

Gibbins, M., and Pomeroy, B. (2007). Beyond-GAAP corporate reporting: Insights for practice and opportunities for research. Working Paper, University of Alberta.

—— Salterio, S., and Webb, A. (2001). Evidence about auditor–client management negotiation concerning client's financial reporting. *Journal of Accounting Research*, 39(3), 535–63.

——McCracken, S., and Salterio, S. (2005). Negotiations over accounting issues: The congruency of audit partner and chief financial officer recalls. *Auditing: A Journal of Practice and Theory*, 24, 171–93.

—— —— —— (2007). The chief financial officer's perspective on auditor-client negotiations. *Contemporary Accounting Research*, 24(2), 387–422.

Gonedes, N., and Dopuch, N. (1974). Capital market equilibrium, information production, and selecting accounting techniques: Theoretical framework and review of empirical work. *Journal of Accounting Research*, 12, 48–129.

Graham, J.R., Harvey, C.R., and Rajgopal, S. (2005). The economics implications of corporate financial reporting. *Journal of Accounting and Economics*, 40(1–3), 3–73.

Groves, R.M., Fowler, J.F., Couper, M.P. et al. (2004). *Survey Methodology*. Hoboken, N.J.: John Wiley & Sons.

Hackenbrack, K., and Nelson, M.W. (1996). Auditors' incentives and their application of financial accounting standards. *Accounting Review*, 71(1), 43–59.

Healy, P.M. (1985). The impact of bonus schemes on the selection of accounting principles. *Journal of Accounting and Economics*, 7, 85–107.

—— and Wahlen, J.M. (1999). A review of the earnings management literature and its implications for standard setting. *Accounting Horizons*, 13(4), 365–83.

—— Myers, S.C., and Howe, C.D. (2002). R&D accounting and the tradeoff between relevance and objectivity. *Journal of Accounting Research*, 40(3), 677–710.

Hirshleifer, D., and Teoh, S.H. (2003). Limited attention, information disclosure and financial reporting. *Journal of Accounting and Economics*, 36(1–3), 337–86.

Hirst, D.E., and Hopkins, P.E. (1998). Comprehensive income reporting and analysts' valuation judgments. *Journal of Accounting Research*, 36, 47–75.

—— Koonce, L., and Venkataraman, S. (2008). Management earnings forecasts: A review and framework. *Accounting Horizons*, 22(3).

Houston, R., Peters, M., and Pratt, J. (2006). Auditor corrections of earnings overstatements and audit firm rotation. Working paper, University of Alabama.

Hunton, J. E., and Rose, J. (2008). Can directors' self-interests influence accounting choices? *Accounting, Organizations and Society*, 33, 783–800.

—— Libby, R., and Mazza, C.L. (2006). Financial reporting transparency and earnings management. *Accounting Review*, 81(1), 135–57.

—— Mauldin, E., and Wheeler, P. (2006). Intended and unintended consequences of continuous auditing and incentive compensation: Trapped between risk and reward. Working Paper, Bentley College.

Jackson, S. (2008). The effect of firms' depreciation method choice on managers' capital investment decisions. *Accounting Review*, 83(2), 351–76.

Kachelmeier, S.J., and King, R.R. (2002). Using laboratory experiments to evaluate accounting policy issues. *Accounting Horizons*, 16, 219–32.

Kadous, K., Kennedy, J.S., and Peecher, M.E. (2003). The effect of quality assessment and directional goal commitment on auditors' acceptance of client-preferred accounting methods. *Accounting Review*, 78(3), 759–78.

King, R. (2002). An experimental investigation of self-serving biases in an auditing trust game: The effect of group affiliation. *Accounting Review*, 77(2), 265–84.

Li, F. (2008). Annual report readability, current earnings, and earnings persistence. *Journal of Accounting and Economics*, 45(2–3), 221–47.

—— and Luft, J. (1993). Determinants of judgment performance in accounting settings: Ability, knowledge, motivation, and environment. *Accounting, Organizations and Society*, 18, 425–50.

Libby, R., and Kinney, W.R. (2000). Does mandated audit communication reduce opportunistic corrections to manage earnings forecasts? *Accounting Review*, 75(4), 383–404.

——Bloomfield, R., and Nelson, M.W. (2002). Experimental research in financial accounting. *Accounting, Organizations and Society*, 27, 775–810.

——Nelson, M.W., and Hunton, J.E. (2006). Recognition v. disclosure, auditor tolerance for misstatement, and the reliability of stock compensation and lease information. *Journal of Accounting Research*, 44(3), 533–60.

Maines, L.A., and McDaniel, L.S. (2000). Effects of comprehensive income characteristics on nonprofessional investors' judgments: The role of financial-statement presentation format. *Accounting Review*, 75(2), 179–207.

Mazza, C., Hunton, J.E., and McEwen, R.A. (2007). The relevance and unintended consequence of fair value measurements for asset retirement obligations: Experimental evidence from financial executives and financial analysts. Working Paper, Fordham University.

McDaniel, L., Martin, R.D., and Maines, L.A. (2002). Evaluating financial reporting quality: The effects of financial expertise vs. financial literacy. *Accounting Review*, 77, 139–67.

McEnroe, J.E. (2006). Perceptions of the effect of Sarbanes-Oxley on earnings management practices. *Research in Accounting Regulation*, 19, 141–63.

Merkl-Davies, D.M., and Brennan, N.M. (2007). Discretionary disclosure strategies in corporate narratives: Incremental information or impression management? *Journal of Accounting Literature*, 26, 116–94.

Nelson, M.W., and Tan, H-T. (2005). Judgment and decision making research in auditing: A judgment, person, and interpersonal interaction perspective. *Auditing: A Journal of Practice and Theory*, 24, 41–71.

——Elliott, J.A., and Tarpley, R.L. (2002). Evidence from auditors about managers' and auditors' earnings management decisions. *Accounting Review*, 77, 175–202.

Ng, T.B-P., and Tan, H-T. (2003). Effects of authoritative guidance availability and audit committee effectiveness on auditors' judgments in an auditor-client negotiation context. *Accounting Review*, 78(3), 801–18.

Securities and Exchange Commission (SEC), (1999). *Materiality.* SEC Staff Accounting Bulletin No. 99. Washington, D.C.: SEC.

Seybert, N. (2009). R&D capitalization and reputation-driven real earnings management. Working Paper, University of Texas at Austin.

Teoh, S.H., Welch, I., and Wong, T.J. (1998). Earnings management and the long-run market performance of initial public offerings. *Journal of Finance*, 53(6), 1935–74.

Trotman, K.T. (1996). *Research Methods for Judgment and Decision Making Studies in Auditing.* Melbourne, Australia: Coopers and Lybrand.

Wang, S., and D'Souza, J. (2007). Earnings management: The effect of accounting flexibility on R&D investment choices. Working Paper, Cornell University.

Zang, A. (2007). Evidence on the tradeoff between real manipulation and accrual manipulation. Working Paper, University of Rochester.

14

Accounts of Science

Theodore M. Porter

The president of the University of California during its years of massive post-war expansion, Clark Kerr, was moved by the heterogeneity of studies and activities there to speak of that great institution as a multiversity. It is not easy to define a standard of quality that can be brought to bear on professors engaged in such diverse activities as laboratory science, literary criticism, digging in archives, quantitative modelling, social surveys, performance arts, legal reasoning, and clinical medicine. But a 'Council on Academic Personnel' like the one on which I briefly served at UCLA needs some language to serve as a basis for promotion decisions, and official policy puts a heavy burden on the adjective 'creative'. Candidates for tenure in accounting, though they received some of the highest salaries to be found on campus among assistant professors, were often turned down for promotion, and it may be that the jarring conjunction of 'creative' and 'accounting' has something to do with the tenuous academic standing of their indispensable profession. If Albert Einstein had taken up the family electrical business, which his progenitor Einsteins had struggled (failing in the end) to keep out of the red, and endeavoured to make it flourish by applying his great brain to the accounts, could he ever have become an icon of genius? We want our accountants to be meticulous, to wear grey suits and match their socks rather than advertising flamboyantly their indifference to social conventions. Accountancy is more commonly regarded as an academic debtor than a creditor, and as properly subordinated to economics, to which accounting researchers are encouraged to look for new ideas and approaches (Miller 2003). The quantitative social disciplines, in turn, are often thought to have modelled themselves on astronomy or physics.

Modern scholars of accounting, including some in this volume, have recognized the field as creative in a specific and fundamental sense. Accountants have created many of the measures through which the world of manufacturing, commerce, and finance are governed. These have been made routine as sources of information; such quantities as 'return on investment' and the 'price/earnings ratio' provide a handy guide to investors who (may think they) need to know little else, while also being deployed in the executive offices as convenient tools of management. Corporate and national accounts define the work and the conclusions of social scientists in ways that they do not often appreciate. The methods behind such numbers are certainly creative, at least in the sense of not following in any direct way from general rules of methodology and the nature of the objects under investigation. They are, instead, concretized interpretations, snowflakes congealed into glaciers; they depend on creative work and, simultaneously, on the reining in of creativity. Accounting categories, after all, can only be regarded as *information* if they are applied as uniformly as possible. Creativity coexists uneasily with information, which in our age is idealized as not requiring wisdom or extensive experience, but as readily available for do-it-yourself use by almost anyone (Ezrahi 2004). If accounting numbers are specified only loosely, and especially if they seem to be vulnerable to self-interested manipulation, this undermines the trust they inspire. And trust, after all, is as much the currency of accounting as is money.

The significance of quantification has usually been conceived, even by researchers, as a problem of accuracy, of conveying the actual state of things by use of numbers. They construe measurement as a scientific question, a problem of true representation, and by this reasoning it makes some sense to assign logical and historical priority to the most ancient and most dignified of the sciences, perhaps beginning with mathematics itself. But if, with scholars of accounting who take institutions and culture seriously, we understand quantification as a way of acting on the world by giving solidity to new objects and by undergirding a system of incentives that regulate human action, the relations among disciplinary and professional practices may be quite different (Carruthers and Espeland 1991; MacKenzie 2006). Accounts are about accountability as well as being about the validity of financial representations, and accountability is as fundamental to the sciences as it is to economic life. Wise judgement and good character enter into accountability, but these qualities are difficult to recognize in individuals outside the space of face-to-face interactions. In the modern world, a more impersonal form is generally preferred, and the rules of legitimate financial manipulation—that is, *accounting*—provided the prototype of *accountability* in its more objective form.

It is not that accounting rules have made company balance sheets and tax forms into paragons of transparency and rectitude. Accounts have become highly regulated in an effort to close off those subtle manipulations that can bend the rules to the financial advantage of the not-too-scrupulous. But this suppleness, along with a near-universal incentive to exploit it, is precisely what has made accounting, as a social system, a model for many forms of

quantification in science. Standards in accounting have meant the specification of enforceable practices and rules to preserve them against relentless
processes of erosion. This effort is not limited to corporate balance sheets and
tax forms. Since, for example, pharmaceutical companies preside over clinical
trials whose outcomes can enrich or impoverish a company and its executives,
the research design and analysis of data have come to be seen as matters of
public accountability. The rules growing out of pharmaceutical regulation set
the standard for other sorts of medical studies as well. Similarly, official
procedures for assessing risk have helped to shape engineering, especially
engineering ethics, and rules governing rare and endangered species play a
role also in academic ecology. More generally, if a scientist should be suspected of fraud, laboratory notebooks may be inspected in much the way that
a company accused of dubious financial practices will be audited. This is
especially the case when, as happens with increasing frequency, the work of a
discipline can have financial consequences for powerful interests. Standards of
accountability have a role now throughout the sciences, as in so many other
institutions (Power 1997).

Without pretending that accounting and accountability provide a master
narrative of quantification in the sciences, we can recognize that their significance is far-reaching, and that they have helped to reshape the moral
(as well as the financial) economy of science (Daston 1995). Their pervasiveness calls attention to a different aspect of science from the quest for
objectivity in the sense of truth, as something independent of all that is
distinctively human. There is another sense of objectivity, more accessible
to our inquiries and much more commonly assessed in practice, that refers
specifically to an absence of subjectivity—to impersonality, or to independence of locality. These aspects of science are, to be sure, relevant also to the
more strenuous, ontological sense of objectivity as truth, but objectivity as
impersonality can be judged without metaphysics, and much of the time it is.
Here, independence from the ambitions and limitations of particular observers is judged not according to a transcendental standard of absolute validity,
but in relation to the actions of other observers. We may want truth, but we
can more easily identify, and indeed measure, the attainment of standardization. Often, standardization stands in for truth. Especially for accounting
purposes, it is often enough.

Standardization, to be sure, is in practice not simple at all. It is difficult
enough for a single observer or a particular laboratory to achieve consistency
in the results of an experimental measurement. The difficulties multiply when
scientists in other laboratories undertake to repeat the result, even if they use
very similar instruments and procedures. Typically, replication of this kind
depends on extensive personal communication, and almost always involves

travel by competent experimenters to acquire or to convey the techniques involved. Even when this kind of standardization is attained, constant vigilance and adaptability are required to preserve it. Wherever the precision of a result matters, researchers continually explore new methods of measurement, whose results will almost always show discrepancies from the old. One well-known episode of this kind involves estimation of the astronomical unit, the mean distance from the Earth to the Sun. The measurements have grown far more precise over the centuries, but the historical progression is not without its oddities. W.J. Youden published a graph in 1972 showing how each new method for measuring this quantity in turn produced a value that fell outside the error bars of its predecessor. Further, scientific measures made for one purpose will often be incorporated into other measurements, once more allowing discrepancies to arise. Finally, a measured value may have to be checked against a theoretical one (which will itself generally include some empirical content). If everything can be harmonized, it becomes more plausible to speak of truth. Or, leaving truth aside, the task of standardizing never ceases. In practice, precision is always in part about standardization, and in practice, objectivity is closely related to precision (see Porter 1995, 2006; Wise 1995). One influential solution in accounting was to cut through the Gordian knot of epistemological uncertainty by defining objectivity operationally in terms of the statistical variance of measurements by different practitioners (Ijiri and Jaedicke 1986; Porter 1992).

This problem of standardization ramifies also into other dimensions. Since the methods of science do not actualize themselves—since it takes skill and discernment even to perform relatively routine scientific procedures—the standardization of science depends also on the standardization of its practitioners. Such standardization is most severe, and most easily recognized, for low-level work, where very specific training and closely articulated protocols will be specified. For really creative research, the standardization is looser and more qualitative, and for that reason, it goes much deeper. A Ph.D., the most demanding and loosely defined of academic degrees, is the union card in most academic disciplines these days, and it is very difficult to work one's way up through the ranks without somehow passing through this gate. Yet researchers will sometimes overlook it in judging a piece of work if other indications of competence are sufficiently convincing, and certainly they will never assume that the conclusion of a paper is valid just because the authors have appropriate credentials. The academic degree as a standard of professional competence is not supposed to produce trained human uniformity, like automobile parts on an assembly line. The work, as everyone acknowledges, requires understanding and skill, and a person who operates with merely mechanical precision cannot contribute at a very high level. For just this

reason, the training programmes that must be followed to achieve competence are all the more demanding and rigorous. Scientists, scholars, and other
professionals must master the spirit and not only the letter of the knowledge
practices of their field, and this requires intense discipline.

Where matters of public concern are involved, as for example where state
regulation or legal vulnerability is at issue, the more subtle aspects of professional identity become harder to credit. The physician, formerly the exemplar
of the independent professional, is now subject to oversight and second-
guessing by state or private insurance bureaucracies, regulatory authorities,
and courts, and not only, as in former times, by complaisant boards of fellow
physicians. It has become necessary even for physicians in private practice to
work in a more uniform way and to make decisions more legible to outsiders
through the use of routine tests, instrument readings, photographic images of
various kinds, and official assessments of the effectiveness of drugs and
procedures. A public medical examiner, charged to determine cause of
death in suspicious cases, and always subject to courtroom interrogation,
must be still more careful about heeding protocol and keeping detailed
records (Timmermans 2006).

Objectivity, defined operationally as agreement among the relevant expert
authorities, is of course not always quantitative in character, but quantification has emerged in modern times as the preferred route to standardized
belief. Once numbers have been separated from the objects counted, there are
generally clear and explicit rules, independent of person or place, for how to
combine them; $2 + 2 = 4$ is the very model of an uncontestable proposition.
If, however, our ambition is to represent the world, we may feel some doubt
about adding two apples to two oranges, or Pippin apples to Fuji apples. What
can we learn by counting a population? Eighteenth-century political writers
were generally agreed that a census provides an excellent index of the power
and prosperity of a nation. But even an accurate census—and accuracy when
the numbers get large is not easily attained—gives no reliable prediction of
which side would win a war. It is easy enough, after the tallies are in, to add
the number of unemployed in England to those in Wales, Scotland, and
Northern Ireland. This can be performed in a windowless office in Bristol
or Bangalore by a census clerk's assistant who does not know whether these
jurisdictions are part of the same country, or even whether the unit at issue is
people, pounds, or apples. It is at once the supreme virtue of arithmetic
and the greatest source of abuse that it can be detached from all objects and
deployed mechanically to combine and analyse numbers of anything and
everything from whatever source.

Perhaps just because we are all taught to regard mathematics as rigorously
universal, disagreements about the analysis of numbers has been particularly

bitter—though in many cases, such as financial accounts and statistics, important interests are also often at stake. The transmission of mathematical skill can be intensely local (Warwick 2003), and the mathematical field of statistics was plagued from the beginning by conflict over foundations and about what form of results should be aimed at (MacKenzie 1981; Gigerenzer et al. 1989). Much of psychology and social science, and important parts of academic biology, medicine, public health, engineering, education, and business, had come by the middle of the twentieth century to depend on statistical test of significance as the standard of causal demonstration. As statistical methods acquired quasi-legal status in public decisions regarding medicine, quality control, environmental protection, and social policy, new incentives arose to preserve or to revise, to defend, to discard, or to corrupt, customary procedures of statistical design and inference, inspired sometimes by honest differences of opinion and sometimes by transparently self-interested motives (Ziliak and McCloskey 2008).

A particularly rich instance of the development of quantitative tools to standardize and mechanize decision-making is the rise of cost–benefit analysis. The authority of a cost–benefit result is like that of the accountant's bottom line, and like the bottom line these quantities depend on many assumptions and conventions that are not apparent to most observers. It is easy to forget that accountants have often rebelled against the confinement of their role to the preparation and certification of official numbers, arguing on occasion that understanding accounts is always a matter of interpretation and that their training and experience qualify them to assess what is almost never transparent from the official numbers, the financial health of the firm. In cost–benefit analysis, also, we see how an exclusive reliance on numbers can devalue or undermine expertise rather than empower it.

There are compelling reasons for trying to find out what costs and what advantages are likely to come with almost any investment under consideration. For private firms and entrepreneurs, these costs and benefits are generally limited to anticipated expenditures and receipts in money terms, the sort that are recognized in business accounts. The new cost–benefit analysis, arising from the 1930s to the 1950s, differed from such calculations first in the attempt to put a money value on 'intangible' items that are not bought and sold in a market, and second in the much greater need to defend these valuations against challenge. I should perhaps add one more difference, pertaining especially to its early history. Cost–benefit analysis was practised mainly by engineers, for whom the economic form of decision-making about their specialty, water projects, was not really how they liked to think about them (Espeland 1998). The logic of water planning they understood first of all in terms of the landforms and water flows appropriate for dams and channels

that could bring advantage to local populations. The actual process of planning, for a state engineering corps, was mainly about organizing local backers
who would benefit from a project. By identifying projects with intense local
support and little opposition, such agencies as the Army Corps of Engineers
and the Bureau of Reclamation were able to expand and to cultivate a mutually
advantageous relationship with Congressional committees. Not for nothing
were water projects practically synonymous with pork barrel politics.

The success of this strategy, in an era of vastly expanded government
domestic expenditures, increased greatly the scale of construction projects,
and led for the first time about 1940 to sustained, organized opposition from
business interests as well as fierce internecine struggle among the agencies
involved. Such challenges forced the water engineers to devote much more
effort to developing a defensible rationale for project choices. That rationale
included the quantification of benefits that were never expected to materialize
as income flows. After all, the presumed existence of such benefits was the main
reason for a state initiative, rather than leaving the work to private companies
seeking their own advantage. Thus, while accounting made up an important
element in the analysis, the general logic of decisions was more abstract and
economic. As economists and other social scientists began to supplant engineers in the conceptualization and performance of such analyses, they were
integrated more and more with national income accounting.

Still, the most immediately pressing task was to work out a form of assessment that would support an orderly process within the agencies and help them
to defend their projects in the face of challenges in committee hearings and
courts. Incomplete (or illogical) articulation of the economic rationale, especially in these early years, was much less a source of vulnerability than was
inconsistency in the application of whatever procedures the agencies had put
in place. That is, the crucial challenge was a more complete standardization,
and the really profound (and by no means unimportant) question of truth or
validity could be held for a time in abeyance. When the agencies took up such
questions as how to assign a money figure to intangibles, including recreation
benefits, lives saved and lost, or environmental values, they were sorely
tempted to prefer a convention that could be applied in a fairly uniform way
to a more logically coherent method that could not. In any case, the accounting
form persisted in cost–benefit studies, with the bottom line (here expressed as
a ratio) providing the ultimate rationale for choice.

We can understand the accounting ideal broadly as a now-ubiquitous
mode of commensuration and, still more capaciously, as exemplary of a
dynamic tension between expert judgement and more standardized forms
of knowledge and action (Espeland and Stevens 1998). The research programme initiated and supported by Anthony Hopwood and worked out,

often, in the pages of *Accounting, Organizations, and Society,* shows how accounting in all of these senses is a social activity, taking form in relation to the institutions within which it works. This work demonstrates how widely and in what diverse ways the accounting mode adapts to the bureaucratic and political cultures of government and business, and also how they are reshaped by it. The logic of accounting and the power of quantification are not remote or isolated, even when they appear most technical. Like science, which accounting practices have helped to reshape, the imperative of accountability is properly understood as acting in and on the world.

REFERENCES

Carruthers, B.G., and Espeland, W.N. (1991). Accounting for rationality: Double-entry bookkeeping and the rhetoric of economic rationality. *American Journal of Sociology,* 91, 31–96.

Daston, L. (1995). The moral economy of science. *Osiris,* 10, 2–24.

Espeland, W.N. (1998). *The Struggle for Water: Politics, Rationality and Identity in the American Southwest.* Chicago: University of Chicago Press.

—— and Stephens, L.S. (1998). Commensuration as a social process. *Annual Reviews of Sociology,* 24, 313–43.

Ezrahi, Y. (2004). Science and the political imagination in contemporary democracies. In S. Jasanoff (ed.), *States of Knowledge: The Co-production of Science and Social Order.* New York: Routledge, 254–73.

Gigerenzer, G., Swijtink, Z., Porter, T. et al. (1989). *The Empire of Chance: How Probability Changed Science and Everyday Life.* Cambridge: Cambridge University Press.

Ijiri, Y., and Jaedicke, R.K. (1986). Reliability and objectivity of accounting measurements. *Accounting Review,* 41, 474–83.

MacKenzie, D. (1981). *Statistics in Britain: 1865–1930—The Social Consruction of Scientific Knowledge.* Edinburgh: Edinburgh University Press.

—— (2006). *An Engine Not a Camera: How Financial Models Shape Markets.* Cambridge, Mass.: MIT Press.

Miller, P. (2003). Management and accounting. In T.M. Porter and D. Ross (eds.), *The Cambridge History of Science, Volume VII: Modern Social Sciences.* Cambridge: Cambridge University Press, 565–76.

Porter, T.M. (1992). Quantification and the accounting ideal in science. *Social Studies of Science,* 22, 633–52.

—— (1995). *Trust in Numbers: The Pursuit of Objectivity in Science and Public Life.* Princeton: Princeton University Press.

—— (2006). Speaking precision to power: The modern political role of social science. *Social Research,* 73, 1273–94.

Power, M. (1997). *The Audit Society: Rituals of Verification*. New York: Oxford University Press.

Timmermans, S. (2006). *Postmortem: How Medical Examiners Explain Suspicious Deaths*. Chicago: University of Chicago Press.

Warwick, A. (2003). *Masters of Theory: Cambridge and the Rise of Mathematical Physics*. Chicago: University of Chicago Press.

Wise, M.N. (ed.) (1995). *The Values of Precision*. Princeton: Princeton University Press.

Youden, W.J. (1972). Enduring Values. *Technometrics*, 14, 1–11.

Ziliak, S., and McCloskey, D. (2008). *The Cult of Statistical Significance: How the Standard Error Costs Us Jobs, Justice, and Lives*. Ann Arbor: University of Michigan Press.

15

Financial Accounting without a State

Michael Power

The analysis of accounting difference and specificity has been a guiding theme for Anthony Hopwood's many contributions to accounting scholarship, providing an influential counterpoint to pedagogic representations of accounting as a technical craft of little cultural significance. In the field of financial accounting and reporting, these insights and sensitivities have informed key debates about the changing nature of national and international accounting regulatory systems. Hopwood's subtle and sensitive understanding of the complex position and legitimacy of standard setters, and of the role of law, professional associations and interest groups in shaping accounting policy, has stimulated and inspired explorations of the politics and cultures of financial reporting (Bromwich and Hopwood 1983; Hopwood 1988a, 1988b, 1989, 1994, 1997, 2000).

Underlying this body of work is a scepticism about the prospects of accounting convergence programmes aimed at eliminating the 'constraints' of the local, and comparative analysis of cross-national differences reveals the culturally and institutionally embedded factors which are likely to restrict convergence (e.g. Puxty et al. 1987). And yet, this critical framing of a comparative financial accounting research agenda shares an epistemic commitment with the policy domain which is its target, namely that *national* financial accounting systems are the primary analytical units and starting points for comparative accounting research. Hopwood is acutely aware of these epistemic commitments rooted in simplistic notions of national difference. He calls for studies which might better explain the rapidity of the apparent internationalization of accounting in recent years (Hopwood 2000: 764), a fact which challenges 'critical orthodoxies' of accounting diversity and embeddedness.

The author is grateful for the financial support of the Institute of Chartered Accountants in England and Wales.

The rapidity of accounting internationalization becomes less puzzling if we reflect on a remarkable but considerably under-remarked fact, namely the overwhelming similarity between financial accounting statements produced in different national jurisdictions over many decades. Moreover, if we look closely at the surface level of the structure and form of financial statements it can be argued that there is much more similarity than difference. Indeed, this must be the case for philosophical reasons: Comparative studies of financial accounting only make sense because of a more fundamental resemblance, a resemblance which is the *condition of possibility* for the meaningful exploration of difference. Yet, for all the reasons Hopwood has suggested about the restricted nature of financial accounting research agendas, the sources and implications of that financial accounting *similarity* have remained relatively unexplored, until recently.

The provocation of this chapter is a simple one: The key conceptual structures of financial accounting (income, expenses, assets, and liabilities) circulated, evolved, and became more highly rationalized at a non-state and transnational level *before* they were ever an object of explicit 'national' interest. These key features give financial accounting statements in different jurisdictions their 'family resemblance' and may even be one of the major global accomplishments of the modern period grounded on centuries of diffusion, adaptation, and mobilization as part of empire building and commercial expansion. Indeed, it is this process of development at the non-nation state level which has enabled and conditioned *both* the increased formal codification of accounting norms by states *and* recent discussions about sources of national variation. In short, before formal and explicit standardization institutions for accounting took shape from the mid-twentieth century onwards, the key elements of financial accounting had been established as part of a practical and universalistic commercial culture (Meyer 1997; Arnold 2009).

The idea is an unsettling one. It demands that we cannot presume that financial accounting was ever a distinctively national affair and that we must rethink the very conception of the 'internationalization' of financial accounting. It also suggests that some of the most cherished and high profile debates in the history of accounting policy, for example about the merits of flow-through or partial provision methods for deferred taxation or about the conditions for capitalizing research and development expenditure, are for all their cultural and national variability to be regarded as skirmishes within a story of staggeringly successful global diffusion. In short, we need to redefine the starting point, not only for the political economy of financial accounting policy (see Arnold 2009; Djelic and Sahlin 2009), but also for understanding the development of financial accounting practice.

The arguments which develop these ideas are organized as follows. The first section draws on work in comparative law to suggest how the history of financial accounting might be plausibly conceptualized as a form of *Lex Mercatoria*, that is as norms of exchange formed at the level of trans-regional commercial practices. Second, it will be argued that financial accounting may be more loosely coupled to national 'culture' than is commonly imagined, and that the rise of so-called 'national' level accounting standard setters in the late twentieth century in fact marks the origin of self-validating, and increasingly autonomous, 'global actors'. Third, it will be suggested that the emergence of the International Accounting Standards Board (IASB), and its history of competition with other standard setting bodies, is largely mis-described as a conflict between 'national' and 'international' standards. It may be more fruitful to regard such conflicts and settlements as the consequence of a distinctive sub-politics involving small numbers of policy actors operating within, and constituting, a 'globalised accounting culture' characterized by competition over issue-based expertise, rather than national interest.

These three sections suggest that contemporary financial accounting policy making is not so much juxtaposed to local or cultural norms. It is, in a sense which deserves more research attention, its *own* evolving culture and locality, a regulatory field in the sense understood by institutional theorists which has progressively rationalized and self-embedded in its own norms. This is a process of self-validation for which, as Bromwich and Hopwood (1983) noted many years ago, conceptual framework projects play a fundamental role in supplying the potential conditions of communicative closure of a global accounting system. Finally, the chapter draws together these arguments, which are necessarily preliminary, to suggest a possible research programme for financial accounting informed by a new understanding of the nature of accounting embeddedness, and by a political economy less focused on the minor 'constraints' of national context and more sensitive to the dynamics of specific financial accounting norms in a system which exhibits considerable durability.

FINANCIAL ACCOUNTING AS 'GLOBAL LAW'

According to Guenther Teubner, a leading European legal scholar, comparative legal research has tended to be fixated on the nation state, an emphasis which leads to *inflated cultural and relativist claims*. He suggests that this emphasis should be supplanted by analyses more sensitive to the cross-national interrelations *between* specialized and autonomous legal sub-systems

(Teubner 1997). Such a proposed focus on discourses, and the internal dynamics of self-reproducing world systems in Wallerstein's sense (2004), suggests a contrast between nationally based politics which is weakly trans-national, and other social sub-systems, like law and financial accounting, which have forged cross-border and global knowledge and policy networks, via carriers such as the large accounting firms (Cooper et al. 1998). According to Teubner, the true source of global law is not the projection of indigenous norms onto the global level, since nation states are themselves constructs in a world system, but rather the development of a 'proto law of specialized, organizational and functional networks which are forming a global, but sharply limited identity.' From this point of view, conflict and competition must be understood in generic terms as an inter-systemic dynamic between different sources of authority, rather than between 'international' and 'na-tional' sources of standards. For Teubner, global law is not to be confused with 'international' law, which is a legal order in its own right.

The argument is illustrated by appeal to the idea of *Lex Mercatoria* as a strand of commercial law which has evolved outside and beyond states, notwithstanding varied national attempts at codification (Mertens 1997). This claim is controversial for legal scholars, not least because of the question as to whether *Lex Mercatoria*, as a set of global norms evolving beyond the nation state, is 'really' law. Whatever the answer to this question, the impli-cations for financial accounting analysis are challenging. The case of *Lex Mercatoria* as described by Teubner and others suggests that formal rules, such as accounting standards, should be understood as the product of cumu-lative transnational processes of financial accounting communication, in which categories, norms and forms of representation are stabilized at the level of practice, and form the building blocks for specific acts of expansion and codification. This picture of the growth of accounting normativity 'from below', which reaches back to ancient times (Goody 1986), is hardly surpris-ing and is consistent with broader analyses of the emergence of norms of coordination (Hechter 2008; Lounsbury 2008). However, as a more historic-ally and epistemically sensitive starting point for thinking about financial accounting, it suggests that we must presume a much looser relationship between financial accounting and the state than may have been imagined hitherto.

Of course, we know that states draw on accounting technologies for their neoliberal regulatory properties (Miller 1990) and that professional account-ing associations have, at various junctures in their development, depended closely on bargains with the state (Cooper et al. 1994). We also know that states have also appropriated financial accounting elements for the essential purposes of revenue collection, and for the design of norms of creditor protection. And it is abundantly clear that accounting and accountants have been, and are, implicated in projects of commercial and political imperialism (Carnegie and Parker 1999; Annisette and Neu 2004). Yet, in all these cases, are not the agencies of state drawing upon, and adapting, concepts, principles and technical norms which have their origins in cross-border mercantile patterns of trade and exchange at the very margins of national institutions and associated cultures (Hopwood 2000)? From this point of view, the specificities of recent norm adoption, translation, and export by states remains a most interesting research focus, but must now be recast as a feature of a larger and highly rationalized world accounting system.

This argument cannot be conclusive but is offered as an important and suggestive corrective for comparative accounting research, which might usefully redirect its attention away from the apparently contingent cultural environment of *national* accounting rule production systems towards an understanding that these systems are highly differentiated and evolving social sub-systems, or organizational fields, in their own right (Arnold 2009). Teubner's analysis (1997) suggests that 'national' systems of accounting norms are misidentified as discrete and autonomous units because they are already connected to each other, both in historical development and in the dynamics of the contemporary regulatory field. In turn, this means that we must rethink the casual juxtaposition of international accounting and national culture.

ACCOUNTING STANDARDS AND NATIONAL CULTURE

A quick look at the tangled history of relations between Germany and France immediately problematizes the 'national' nature of German and French accounting: elements of a commercial code exported by Napoleon, and adapted and reimported into France during the Second World War, suggest that 'national' financial accounting is a regional hybrid of elements, not an autonomous independent variable (Standish 1990). More generally, financial accounting as a system of evolving communicative elements is much less constrained in form and content than appeals to institutions and culture suggest (Hopwood 2000: 766). Accordingly, accounts of the history of the emergence and diffusion of financial accounting elements as a sub-system of 'world society' need to be sensitive to the contingent effects of patterns of trade, wars, and colonial influences (Hopwood 2000: 764), while also attending to the dynamics of the wider global economic system, in which the early industrializers play a leading role (Foreman-Peck 1995; Arnold 2009). The material and institutional conditions under which financial accounting becomes a stake in specific preoccupations of nation states (e.g. the depression of the 1930s and the formation of the SEC) are undoubtedly varied, but the imagery should be more that of the mobilization of highly rationalized elements for specific programmatic needs, and less that of the creation of a national form of accounting.

Strangely, the concern with the cultural and institutional embeddedness of financial accounting norms is not replicated in the *auditing* field, despite the fact that auditing practice by accountancy firms in the nineteenth and twentieth centuries has been the main source of expansion of practical financial accounting norms. These firms have been critical carriers and standardizers via guidance and implementation of 'best practice'. But in contrast to financial accounting, auditing methods have been successfully articulated as state-independent, technically neutral norms of procedure which are widely diffused by world level organizations like International Federation of Accountants (IFAC) (Mennicken 2008; Humphrey and Loft 2009). However, this close historical link between the communicative discourses of audit and financial accounting, and the norms of auditability which they share, has recently been weakened and challenged by a distinctive development within what Arnold (2009) and others call the *financialization* of the international economic system, to be discussed further below.

The close relationship between financial accounting and auditing practice suggests that the contours of a political economy of financial accounting are not primarily to be found in an opposition between the forces of international accounting standardization and national institutional and cultural constraints. Rather, they are to be found in the strategic moves of actors within an increasingly specialized global sub-system of accounting regulators, accounting firms, and world level organizations who are tightly coupled to each other in both competitive and cooperative ways (Djelic and Sahlin 2009). Regulatory tolerance for accounting difference in the past (e.g. 'mutual recognition' strategies at the European level) suggests the durability of highly specific forms of resistance within a small network of accounting policy bureaucrats, more than the intractability of something as grandiose as 'national culture'. Politics and conflict of a certain kind reflect the complex interplay between bodies such as IASB, the Financial Accounting Standards Board (FASB), The International Organization of Securities Commissions (IOSCO), and many others, as well as 'global national' actors like the US Securities and Exchange Commission (SEC) (Botzem and Quack 2006). Not only is 'international' accounting more parochial and issue-specific than is apparent from surface claims to universality, but 'national' accounting systems have also emerged more as recent constructs of a transnational system of financial accounting elements with a long history.

Given the contemporary process of global accounting convergence, it is useful for researchers to remember that financial accounting norm production has always been a communicative system at an inter-state level. The analytical problem is to understand and explain the *internal* transfers and conflicts within this system (Teubner 1997) without presuming that indigenous cultural factors are the principal axis of resistance. Such an agenda takes the study of financial accounting norm production and use much closer to the field of international political economy and international relations than hitherto, and it would be fair to say that this work has already begun (e.g. Perry and Nölke 2006). However, there are still a number of issues to digest before this agenda can acquire momentum, not least the question of labels and categories. Methodologically, we should be cautious of taking the categories of 'International' or 'British' as helpful starting points in accounting research. Indeed, while the confusion of the 'Anglo-American' label in accounting studies is well recognized, the source of the muddle is less well articulated.

There are many examples of research papers and volumes dealing with 'Accounting in X', where X is usually the country of the authors. This body of work reinforces the idea that the nation state is the appropriate starting point for analysing the trajectory of accounting norms. But, to take an arbitrary example, the 'Finnishness' of Finnish accounting, or the 'Britishness' of British Accounting are largely myths referring, at best, to minor features of accounting difference which become big stakes for some actors. In addition, the very notion of the state and its institutions is also highly stylised and needs to be understood as hybrid of standardized units (Meyer 1997; Meyer et al. 1997; Wallerstein 2004). The point is even more obvious if we consider accounting at the periphery of the developed world economies.

Teubner suggests that global law of the kind represented by *Lex Mercatoria* has an 'underdeveloped centre' and a highly developed periphery, and it is the latter which provides an important and useful methodological counterpoint to assumptions about national embeddedness. For example, in developing and transitional economies, we are much more likely to avoid the temptation to begin with a coherent view of the nation state and to presume that financial accounting was ever national or indigenous before it was affected by international trade, foreign aid, large consulting firms, and banks. Imperialism trumps culture as an explanation of accounting change—obviously true in the case of Australia and other former British colonies (Carnegie and Parker 1999). There will be exceptions of course, but it is unlikely that Icelandic or Zimbabwean financial accounting, for example, can be sensibly analysed as national and *sui generis* norms. They are more likely to be counterpoised to aboriginal culture (Annisette and Neu 2004). And as Meyer et al. (1997) have noted, the periphery is a more enthusiastic and frictionless *adopter* of formal systems than the core, something we observe in the history of the International Accounting Standards Committee (IASC) / IASB as states in transition have readily sought to align themselves with 'modern' and international accounting (Camfferman and Zeff 2007). In these settings, formalizations of the elements of financial accounting go hand in hand with state building and modernization processes. And the case of the IASB, to be discussed further below, is a perfect illustration of Teubner's (1997: 12) thesis that a new regulatory centre can emerge from key alliances with the periphery.

Even where the institutions of nationhood are well developed in many other respects, there is good reason to presume that a distinctively embedded national financial accounting system does not exist. As a system of communication, financial accounting is not uniquely connected to the totality of the social field but only to diverse fragments of it with often highly selective and contingent bonds. The lesson for the comparative accounting researcher are clear; she must proceed on a norm by norm basis to explore the nature and extent of pressures for change for there is no general cultural embeddedness of the system as such. Understood as a sub-system which tends to close itself operationally and positivistically, financial accounting is problematically coupled to cultural variables (Teubner 1997). Indeed, such variables are an explanatory last resort, not a place to begin. Before we can begin to articulate for example, the 'Britishness' of British accounting, we need to understand the history and institutional shape of a changing structural coupling between world level financial accounting elements and the preoccupations of state agencies. National cultural elements cross-cut such systems, if at all, in highly particularistic, and possibly minor, ways. Further, we may say that it is the dynamic of world-level accounting norms 'without a state' which has been a necessary condition for the creation of nationally specific centres of norm codification. While the creation of the UK Accounting Standards Committee was a response to very specific issues and events by the profession, it also contributed to the very idea of *British* financial accounting as a thinkable object of policy discourse (Hopwood 2000).

The discussion so far only addresses the development of financial accounting rules and standard setting institutions, not the complex markets for the interpretation and implementation of rules. As studies in the problematic convergence of production regimes (Hall and Soskice 2001) and quality assurance programmes (Casper and Hancke 1999) have shown, at the level of implementation and enforcement institutional difference undoubtedly persists and cultural and institutional variables have strong explanatory potential (Vogel 1986). Yet, as important as these sensitivities to locales of implementation are, there remains a fundamental, quasi-philosophical question: 'What is the *same* thing which is interpreted and implemented differently?' And this question directs us to a difficulty in recent approaches to the internationalization of accounting which emphasize institutions. While such studies rightly emphasize the variety of transnational actors competing for precedence, they may pay insufficient attention to the way in which minor accounting issues become big stakes. The problematization of accounting differences by different policy makers is also a magnification of their significance relative to a massive background consensus and family resemblance.

In conclusion, we are now in a position to offer a preliminary explanation of the rapidity of the internationalization of accounting identified by Hopwood (2000) and explained by Arnold in terms of financialization. Put very simply, the problem is perhaps a false one because the cultural embeddedness of accounting has been overstated. The internationalization of financial accounting, in the broad sense of the widespread diffusion of common norms for representing financial performance and position, has not in fact been recent. And the rapidity is somewhat illusory because the IASB has been overstated as the pre-eminent global accounting actor.

ACCOUNTING WITHOUT A STATE

The IASB, and its predecessor the IASC, has become an object of research fascination because of its highly successful project of self-legitimation over the course of three decades (Tamm Hallstroem 2004; Camfferman and Zeff 2007). This is a feature that it shares with the rise of many other non-governmental, not-state organizations at the world level, making the IASB a distinctive case study and exemplar for scholars in political science and international relations. Indeed, transnational governance is coming to be defined as the network of relations and memberships which define and span a global polity more confident of its authority to act and populated by technical experts. For many observers (e.g. Botzem and Quack 2006) the rise of the IASB, and it progressive disentanglement from its founding sponsors, shows how accounting regulation has shifted away from the nation state level, and from its dependence on professional accounting institutes, to regional and global levels, and how consensus building and national representation has given way to world-level ideas of due process.

The necessary, if not sufficient, conditions of possibility for the institution-alization of a body claiming to represent 'international' accounting were always inherent in the elements of financial accounting practice. In addition, the creation of the IASC as a new actor in the early 1970s simultaneously constructed a centre of opposition to 'national' accounting systems, an opposition which informed the early rhetoric of competition between IASC and standard setters such as the Financial Accounting Standards Board (FASB) in the United States. To understand this competition, it may be methodologically more helpful to regard all standard setting organizations as emergent generalized actors in a world system of accounting elements which has been under construction for centuries rather than decades, and which compete for priority and authority despite, and because of, the striking lack of substantive differences in the content of the rules and norms they promote. From this point of view the FASB should not even be categorized as 'American' or Anglo-American, although an institutionalized memory stretching back to the great crash has shaped its agenda, but as a significant element of a world system in which there has emerged a standardized model of what it is to be a proper accounting regulatory body. The creation of such bodies by France and Germany in the late 1990s reflects the perceived need to create recognizable 'due process' actors in the world accounting system (e.g. Volmer et al. 2007). Once created these bodies begin to have their own momentum and reference points. Axes of dispute and blame attribution are constructed in this world accounting game, such as the principles-rules debate. The surfacing of explicitly national interests, such as the French political interventions around International Accounting Standard 39, is rela-tively rare, although at the time of writing the IASB and FASB are under significant pressure from leading regulatory bodies to suspend or modify fair value accounting for the sake of global financial stability.

Accounting standards setters as generalized actors at the world level lend themselves to analysis as 'discourse coalitions' (Singer 1990) in broader fields (Arnold 2009). Rather than being ambassadors of national interest, the identity of members of standard setting bodies is increasingly determined by shared general beliefs and ideas about accounting and the definition of an accounting issue—a 'logic of appropriateness' as Young (1994) has described it. Such belief systems may still leave policy outcomes underdetermined (Singer 1990: 437), but in aggregate the policy field consists of individuals who share a belief system and display a non-trivial degree of coordinated activity over time (Singer 1990: 440). At the heart of these belief systems are the core normative elements of financial accounting around which differences of opinion may be constructed. There is a background of shared beliefs which is very great relative to the problematization of specific issues. This helps to dispel Botzem and Quack's puzzle (2006) about the stability of financial accounting despite the recent big debates; the debates are simply not that big relative to the background consensus.

From this point of view, conceptual frameworks for financial accounting have been under construction for centuries, only recently becoming formally codified, debated, and disputed. As Bromwich and Hopwood (1983) note, conceptual frameworks and due process provide a basis for the self-validating authority of accounting and a barrier to sectional efforts at influence. Since the early 1970s, the FASB conceptual framework and its successors have created a body of formalized norms which contrast with more pragmatic images of accounting as a set of 'lobbied' rules. Lobbying exists of course, but it may well become increasingly cost ineffective and voiceless without a defined institutional pathway. The recent commitment of IASB to a conceptual framework marks the creation of a kind of global law which, together with new structural and financial independencies, announces the arrival of an autonomous and confident world actor which is less responsive to sectional interests than its predecessors and more explicitly committed to its own ideas of 'good accounting'. Real users do not play much of a role in this unfolding conceptual logic of financial reporting. As Young (2006) shows, the analysis of the debate about user relevance, which reaches back to the 1930s, suggests that the 'user' has been constructed as a near mythical point of reference for actors in the financial accounting field in search of a specific kind of capital market relevance.

Arnold (2009) suggests that 'a fundamental reorientation is needed in international accounting research, away from globalization, and toward a focus on . . . how accounting has been shaped by the financialization of the world-state at the end of the 20th century'. This is important. The long history of financial accounting elements suggests how they have represented norms of financialization rooted in values of stewardship and propriety until the ideas of use value and relevance for investors came to prominence from the 1930s onwards. Indeed, it would be fair to say that the logic of financial reporting has been historically legalistic in form, creating an inherently problematic relation between accounting and capital markets. Over time accounting policy makers have found a new logic of market relevance for financial reporting in the methods and ideas of financial economics. This financialization of financial reporting developed over many years, beginning slowly with the introduction of discounting methods into specific accounting valuation issues, for example, leasing and pensions, to become a potentially dominant accounting and organizing discourse.

Recent debates about the expansion of mark to market and fair value measurement methods suggest an important axis of change within the world-level system of financial accounting, a change in logic from legalization to financialization which, as Arnold rightly notes, is misdescribed in terms of 'rapidity of internationalization'. While the variable relationship between accounting and economics has been discussed in different national settings,[1] the rise of fair value suggests a new and distinctive episode in this relationship—what might be described as the 'financialization of the accounting standard setting process'. An important factor in this process is the increasing validation of elements of financial economics both generally (Whitley 1986) and within key areas of accounting academia (Hopwood 2008), coupled to a decline of accounting pragmatism. Relatedly, the study of financial accounting has come to be defined by leading academics and journals in North America and elsewhere as a sub-branch of economics. This configuration of the academic terrain is not decoupled from the practical domain, although the relationship is a complex one (Hopwood 1988a). Despite doubt and resistance from many quarters about the practical effects of fair value accounting on the functioning of capital requirements and on the contracting process, the fair value programme had considerable momentum until the events of autumn 2008.

While many commentators on the unintended consequences of fair value accounting rightly debate its effects on capital adequacy and pension regimes, another important feature is much less discussed. If accounting is generally a cultural symbol of modernity (Hopwood 2000: 763), fair value accounting is specifically a symbol of financial market relevance and significance, something which accounting policy makers have sought for many years. In this respect, financial accounting has had a somewhat ambivalent position within the neoliberal consensus of the last twenty years. On the one hand it is central to the legitimization of neoliberal modes of discipline and governance for public and private entities (Harvey 2007). On the other hand, it has been in an almost constant state of reform and fair value measurement norms, as articulated by their proponents, represent a new and distinctive chapter in the aspiration for a market relevant accounting policy process. This process evolved from the debates about derivative accounting in the 1990s and new actors knowledgeable in financial economics were enrolled in policy and gave a distinctive flavour to ideas of 'good' accounting. Until the financial crisis of late 2008, this process seemed to be immune from the clamour of protest which surrounded it.

In conclusion, the expansion of fair value accounting suggests an intriguing hypothesis, namely that the articulation of fair value measurement norms has played a central role in defining a professional identity for standard setters

---

[1] See the special issue of the *European Accounting Review*, 1996, 5(3), on this topic.

close to the heart of the neoliberal project, contributing to the 'professional-ization' of accounting standard setters as a phenomenon distinct from that of the accountants in the accounting profession. Such a hypothesis could explain the apparent decreased responsiveness of IASB to lobbying, at least until late 2008. Fair value accounting positions accounting standards setters as mod-ernizers and as legitimate agents in a system of world neoliberal governance, a global governance club. They are less sensitive to specific private interests, and more engaged with associations and other 'organizations which organize' (e.g. G4 + 1; IOSCO; Ahrne and Brunsson 2006).

CONCLUSIONS AND IMPLICATIONS FOR RESEARCH

The arguments above suggest a potentially fruitful shift in the focus of financial accounting research and a change in the framing of comparativist agendas of analysis. This change is already happening as non-accounting scholars take an interest in accounting as an institutional field (Botzem and Quack 2006; Jang 2006; Perry and Nölke 2006). Yet even these scholars often unconsciously assume a developmental dynamic from the national to the international level, and this body of work tends to lack close attention to the way that a variety of actual accounting norms and problems are vehicles for this dynamic. For example, it is likely that the problematization of accounting for derivative financial instruments in the mid-1980s created a gateway for a distinctive financialization of financial accounting policy-making, culminat-ing in the expanded significance of fair value measurement.

The core argument of this chapter is that financial accounting has been, in a number of non-trivial respects, a highly rationalized practice at the world level before 'international accounting' and problems of diversity became an explicit research and policy theme. Financial accounting norms have emerged as a form of transnational *Lex Mercatoria,* a distinctive pre-standardization of accounting practice which *makes possible* contemporary debates. Deep and fundamental similarities across jurisdictions mean that small surface differ-ences are magnified by political processes at the world level. This conception of the space of financial accounting change and development has two poten-tial implications for research.

First, more attention needs to be given to the sources of normativity which make explicit standardization projects possible. This means that the surface features and variety of the standard setting process may be less interesting than the systemic processes which support standard setting. As Loya and Boli (1999) put it, 'varied facades attract much more attention, but underneath they are hardly distinguishable.' Rather than being normatively concerned by, for example, how to translate Italian financial reporting into, say, UK GAAP or to study the implementation of the 4th European Directive in 'country X', researchers need to explore how and why accounting in different places ever looked similar in the first place. This would require attention to the processes of institutional transfer and diffusion which must have taken place in order for the problem of differences in financial accounting systems to be thinkable at the policy level. Accordingly, 'international accounting' can no longer be discussed as if it were a self-evident category, but only in terms of the dynamics by which the globalized norms of accounting do and do not crystallize as preoccupations of states. The very notion of national difference with which many researchers operate is itself an emergent product of other forces, such as the role of European Directives in advancing broader ideas of European identity (Bromwich and Hopwood 1983). Similarly, the very idea of a national accounting system of rules is a product of communicative strategies *within* a global system of financial accounting elements, a system in which multinational organizations in general (Robe 1997) and the large firms in particular (Cooper and Robson 2006) play a critical role.

Second, it could be useful to build on analyses of the problematic accountability of bodies like IASB (Kerwer 2008) in order to develop the idea of financial accounting as a system of communicative elements which is increasingly self-referential. From this point of view, conceptual framework projects and fair value accounting suggest a distinctive vector of closure as financial accounting is framed with the tools of financial economics. Rather than seeing this as a story of functional progress towards better accounting, it could be fruitful to conceptualize fair value as a resource for standard setters engaged in a distinctive process of professionalization and construction as world actors. Such actors both depoliticize financial accounting and are emblematic of a larger political economy of transnational regulation. Interestingly, as I write in late 2008, at just the point when financial accounting has positioned itself closest to market and near market valuation processes, those processes have been largely discredited. The implications of the dependency of fair value accounting on well-functioning liquid markets have yet to be fully digested.

Finally, the arguments above are entirely consistent with Hopwood's insight (1988*b*: 215) that there is a 'complex relationship between specific practices and more generalised notions of their form and functionality, if not a more open admission of the ambiguous coupling of the two'. These generalized notions of financial accounting form have evolved over centuries as a kind of implicit 'world culture' of accounting communicative elements, only to become more explicitly juxtaposed to practice by conceptual frameworks in recent reform agendas. As Hopwood (2000: 765) puts it, there is a difference 'between accounting *in* Britain and the more abstract notions of *British* accounting' (emphasis added). So while it is true to say that the conceptual framework project is demanding that accounting become 'what it is not', it is also true that this project of reform is only possible and thinkable because of the underlying rationalization of accounting practice. All this means that studies of accounting diversity are not dead—far from it. Rather, we must be mindful of the historical and institutional conditions under which that diversity is constructed and abstracted as an issue for policy makers and scholars alike.

REFERENCES

Ahrne, G., and Brunsson, N. (2006). Organizing the world. In M-L. Djelic and K. Sahlin-Andersson (eds.), *Transnational Governance: Institutional Dynamics of Regulation.* Cambridge: Cambridge University Press, 74–94.

Annisette, M., and Neu, D. (2004). Accounting and empire: An introduction. *Critical Perspectives on Accounting,* 15, 1–4.

Arnold, P. (2009). Institutional perspectives on the internationalization of accounting. In C.Chapman, D.Cooper, and P. Miller (eds.), *Accounting, Organizations and Institutions.* Oxford: Oxford University Press.

Botzem, S., and Quack, S. (2006). Contested rules and shifting boundaries: International standard-setting in accounting. In M-L. Djelic and K. Sahlin-Andersson (eds.), *Transnational Governance: Institutional Dynamics of Regulation.* Cambridge: Cambridge University Press, 266–307.

Bromwich, M., and Hopwood, A. (1983). Some issues in accounting standard setting: An introductory essay. In M. Bromwich and A. Hopwood (eds.), *Accounting Standards Setting: An International Perspective.* London: Pitman, 5–24.

Camfferman, K., and Zeff, S. (2007). *Financial Reporting and Global Capital Markets: A History of the International Accounting Standards Committee, 1973–2000.* Oxford: Oxford University Press.

Carnegie, G., and Parker, R. (1999). Accountants and empire: The case of co-membership of Australian and British accountancy bodies, 1885–1914. *Accounting, Business and Financial History,* 9(1), 77–102.

Casper, S., and Hancke, R. (1999). Global quality norms within national production regimes: ISO 9000 standards in the French and German car industries. *Organization Studies,* 20(6), 961–86.

Cooper, D., and Robson, K. (2006). Accounting, professions and regulation: Locating the sites of professionalization. *Accounting, Organizations and Society,* 31(4/5), 415–44.

——Puxty, T., Robson, K., and Willmott, H. (1994). Regulating accounting in the UK: Episodes in a changing relationship between the state and the profession. In A.G. Hopwood and P. Miller (eds.), *Accounting as Social and Institutional Practice.* Cambridge: Cambridge University Press, 270–98

——Greenwood, R., and Hinings, R. (1998). Globalisation and nationalism in a multinational accounting firm: The case of opening new markets in eastern Europe. *Accounting, Organizations and Society*, 23, 531–48.

Djelic, M-L., and Sahlin, K. (2009). Governance and its transcendental dynamics: Towards a re-ordering of our world? In C. Chapman, D. Cooper, and P. Miller (eds.), *Accounting, Organizations and Institutions*. Oxford: Oxford University Press.

Foreman-Peck, J. (1995). Accounting in the industrialization of western Europe. In P. Walton (ed.), *European Financial Reporting*. London: Academic Press, 11–28.

Goody, J. (1986). *The Logic of Writing and the Organization of Society*. Cambridge: Cambridge University Press.

Hall, P., and Soskice, D. (2001). *Varieties of Capitalism: Institutional Foundations of Comparative Advantage*. Oxford: Oxford University Press.

Harvey, D. (2007). *A Brief History of Neoliberalism*. Oxford: Oxford University Press.

Hechter, M. (2008). The rise and fall of normative control. *Accounting, Organizations and Society*, 33, 663–76.

Hopwood, A.G. (1988a). Accounting research and accounting practice: The ambiguous relationship between the two. In A.G Hopwood (ed.), *Accounting from the Outside*. New York: Garland Publishing, 549–78.

——(1988b). The generality and specificity of the accounting craft: Some observations on grounding an understanding of accounting in the contexts in which it operates. In M. Domsch, F. Eisenfuhr, D. Ordelheide, and M. Perlitz (eds.), *Unternehmenserfolg: Planung, Ermittlung, Kontrolle*. Berlin: Gabler Verlag, 213–22.

——(ed.) (1989). *Pressures for Change in International Accounting*. London: ICAEW/ Prentice Hall.

——(1994). Some reflections on the harmonization of accounting in the EU. *European Accounting Review*, 3(2), 241–53.

——(1997). Internationalizing international accounting research. *Accounting, Organizations and Society*, 22(8), 3–4.

——(2000). Understanding financial accounting practice. *Accounting, Organizations and Society*, 25(8), 763–6.

——(2008). Changing pressures on the research process: On trying to research in an age when curiosity is not enough. *European Accounting Review*, 17(1), 87–96.

Humphrey, C., and Loft, A. (2009). IFAC global financial architecture. In C. Chapman, D.Cooper, and P. Miller (eds.), *Accounting, Organizations and Institutions*. Oxford: Oxford University Press.

Jang, S.Y. (2006). Accounting as world societal rule. In G. Drori, J. Meyer, and H. Hwang (eds.), *Globalization and Organization: World Society and Organizational Change*. Oxford: Oxford University Press, 167–95.

Kerwer, D. (2008). Watchdogs beyond control? The accountability of accounting standards organizations. In M. Boström, and C. Garsten (eds.), *Organizing Transnational Accountability*. Cheltenham: Edward Elgar, 98–113.

Lounsbury, M. (2008). Institutional rationality and practice variation: New directions in the institutional analysis of practice. *Accounting, Organizations and Society*, 33(4/5), 349–61.

Loya, T., and Boli, J. (1999). Standardization in the world polity: Technical rationality over power. In J. Boli, and G.M. Thomas (eds.), *Constructing World Culture: International Nongovernmental Organizations Since 1875*. Stanford, Calif.: Stanford University Press, 169–97.

Mennicken, A.M. (2008). Connecting worlds: The translation of international auditing standards into post-Soviet audit practice. *Accounting, Organizations and Society*, 33(4/5), 384–414.

Mertens, H-J. (1997). Lex mercatoria: A self-applying system beyond national law? In G. Teubner (ed.), *Global Law without a State*. Aldershot: Dartmouth, 31–43.

Meyer, J. (1997). Cultural conditions of standardization. Paper presented at the SCAN-CORE/SCORE seminar on standardization, Arild, Sweden, 18–20, September.

—— Boli, J., Thomas, G.M., and Ramirez F.O. (1997). World society and the nation state. *American Journal of Sociology*, 103 (1), 144–81.

Miller, P. (1990). On the interrelations between accounting and the state. *Accounting, Organizations and Society*, 15(4), 315–38.

Perry, J., and Nölke, A. (2006). The political economy of international accounting standards. *Review of International Political Economy*, 13(4), 559–86.

Puxty, A.G., Cooper, D.J., and Robson, K. (1987). Modes of regulation in advanced capitalism: Accountancy in four countries. *Accounting, Organizations and Society*, 12(3), 273–91.

Robe, J-P. (1997). Multinational enterprises: The constitution of a pluralistic legal order. In G. Teubner (ed.), *Global Law without a State*. Aldershot: Dartmouth, 45–77.

Singer, O. (1990). Policy communities and discourse coalitions. *Science Communication*, 11(4), 428–58.

Standish, P. (1990). Origins of the plan comptable general: A study in cultural intrusion and reaction. *Accounting and Business Research*, 20, 337–51.

Tamm Hallstroem, K. (2004). *Organizing International Standardization: ISO and the IASC in Quest of Authority*. Cheltenham: Edward Elgar.

Teubner, G. (1997). Global bukowina: Legal pluralism in the world society. In G. Teubner (ed.), *Global Law Without a State*. Aldershot: Dartmouth, 3–30.

Vogel, D. (1986). *National Styles of Regulation*. Cornell, N.Y.: Cornell University Press.

Volmer, P., Werner, J.R., and Zimmerman, J. (2007). New governance modes for Germany's financial reporting system: Another retreat of the nation state? *Socio-Economic Review*, 5, 437–65.

Wallerstein, I. (2004). *World Systems Analysis: An Introduction*. Durham: Duke University Press.

Whitley, R. (1986). The transformation of business finance into financial economics: The roles of academic expansion and changes in U.S. capital markets. *Accounting, Organizations and Society*, 11, 171–92.

Young, J. (1994). Outlining regulatory space: Agenda issues and the FASB. *Accounting, Organizations and Society*, 19(1), 83–109.

—— (2006). Making up users. *Accounting, Organizations and Society*, 31(6), 579–600.

16

Socio-Political Studies of Financial Reporting and Standard-Setting

Keith Robson and Joni Young

Financial accounting and reporting practices continually change. Some changes occur as corporate entities shift from one accepted accounting method or practice to another. Others occur as corporate managers, their auditors and various consultants interpret and reinterpret the requirements that comprise Generally Accepted Accounting Principles (GAAP). The formal process of standard-setting also changes the measurement, reporting, and disclosure practices of entities by bringing together diverse standard-setters, regulators, managers, auditors, and many others. In this chapter, we offer an overview of interdisciplinary research that has examined accounting change and choice within the financial reporting arena.

Our chapter places particular emphasis upon the Burchell et al. (1985) publication. This important paper offered a theoretically informed analytical method for analysing accounting change and, in so doing, stimulated new directions for research into the social, political, and institutional dimensions of such change. It helped to unpack the taken-for-granted assumptions that had been implicitly contained within much previous accounting research. In particular, accounting problems were not to be taken as given but rather regarded as contingent and constructed. The subject positions of participants in the change process were not to be seen as indicative of fixed, predictable 'interests' nor were interests to be regarded as variables adequate to explain the outcomes of regulatory processes. Finally, emphasis was explicitly placed upon the 'interventionary' and constitutive potential of accounting rather than upon its assumed representative capabilities. Subsequent interdisciplinary research in the area has further elaborated on these themes as researchers have studied accounting change by examining regulatory processes, institutional alternatives, and societal effects.

Our chapter proceeds as follows. We first briefly review research on financial accounting that preceded the publication of Burchell et al. in an effort to place the paper within its social context and thereby better understand its contribution to accounting research. This first section traces some of the shifting connections between accounting research and economics. For authors such as Paton and Littleton, Edwards and Bell, and many others, economics then served as a theoretical resource for developing a priori accounting measurement and valuation theories. Much of this research seemingly had little connection to any kind of empirical investigation. With the shift towards capital markets research, economics now served to define accounting products as information commodities. This movement facilitated interest in examining the economic consequences of regulatory and corporate accounting choices and highlighted the significance of the institutional mechanisms used to select accounting methods. While providing a useful beginning for the study of social, institutional, and political underpinnings of accounting, these studies offered little analytical insight for explaining the processes of accounting change. Within this gap appeared Burchell et al. (1985). In the second section, we describe the analytical method employed in this chapter and the key elements that it added to enrich subsequent studies of accounting change. In the third section, we describe many of these subsequent studies and their contribution to our contemporary understandings of the processes and impacts of accounting change. Particular attention is given to three areas of study—accounting problematization and the construction of accounting problems; the effect of accounting choice on other fields of action and its concomitant shaping of the environment; and examinations of various institutions association with accounting change in an effort to unpack taken-for-granted assumptions and concepts. We conclude the chapter with some suggested avenues for future research.

FROM INCOME THEORY TO ECONOMIC CONSEQUENCES: THE AWAKENING OF FINANCIAL REPORTING RESEARCH

In this section, we explore the development of studies of the financial reporting policy-making process. We follow the shift from financial accounting theories that drew upon economics to justify income measurement and asset valuation practices towards, from the late 1960s, the establishment of a new research problematic with more empirical concerns with standard-setting process and the effects of accounting information on stock prices. We outline the conditions that helped to shape this transformation as well as to change commonly accepted understandings of financial accounting regulation. In so doing we show that although accounting and economics are often assumed to share a central concern with the valuation of assets/ resources and their representation (Klamer and McCloskey 1992), this assumption has obscured the history of intellectual collaboration between accounting and economics and more importantly the ways in which the content of interdisciplinary research in accounting has also changed significantly.

The idea that accounting techniques and measurements had at their base economic principles emerged as a research problematic in the United States at the turn of the twentieth century, the same period that marginalist income theory became the dominant paradigm of economics (Ross 1991). Whilst the practice of accounting in the eighteenth and nineteenth century was viewed principally as the recording of economic 'facts', possibly the earliest academic interdisciplinary relations grew out of Fisher's concerns with business calculations of capital and income and the relationship between the real and the money rate of interest in an inflationary economy (Fisher 1906). The value of Fisher's work lay not simply in his theoretical insights into money and value but in the way that it advanced a greater degree of practical relevance than many critics of marginalism had thought possible (Ross 1991: 173). Fisher believed his work supplied: 'a link long missing between the ideas and usages underlying practical business transactions and the theories of abstract economics' (1906: vii). Although the supposition that accounting and economics were fundamentally related had already been formed, the work of Fisher demonstrated one way in which this relationship could be more closely tied by precise definitions of key accounting concepts (MacKenzie 2008). As the economist John Canning later asserted, Fisher's work helped problematize the view that: 'Accountants have no complete philosophical system of thought about income: nor is there any evidence that they have greatly felt the need for one' (Canning 1929*a*; cf. Canning 1929 *b*).

Fisher's (and Canning's) work set out to confront this absence, signalling a key moment in the changing relationship between accounting and economics: from one that was simply taken-for-granted, towards one that required clarification, enhancement, and adjustment, from the perspective of improving the accounting practice. This shift facilitated the emergence of a major research programme in accounting.

This new programme for studying and improving accounting practices on the basis of economic concepts was substantially forged in the United States— the 'business economics' tradition seems to have been less prominent in the United Kingdom (Napier 1994, 1996*a*, 1996*b*). Nevertheless, in the 1930s, Baxter, Edwards, and Coase, and their successors Edey and Solomons at the London School of Economics (LSE), helped set the agenda in the United Kingdom for applying an economics perspective to issues of income and asset measurement, particularly for inflationary economies (Gould 1974). Baxter's (1950) and Solomons' (1961) work, in particular, was indicative of the trend of researching the economic bases for accounting research and practice: developing a deductive basis for defining a 'Conceptual Framework' for financial reporting practices. Alongside the work of Hatfield (1924), Paton and Littleton (1940), Edwards and Bell (1961), and Chambers (1966), the LSE scholars' writings reflected the dominant financial accounting paradigm of the mid-twentieth century: analytical economic deductions of 'correct' accounting values—on occasion referred to as the 'Golden Age of a priori research' (Nelson 1973; Mouck 1989). This a priori research was indicative of a particular relation between accounting and economics: accounting was considered the special means through which the theories of economic value could be put into accounting practices to guide decisions and action in the firm and in the economy. Although located in a subsidiary relationship to economic income theory, accounting had the particular role of making economics 'practical' (McCloskey 1986; Klamer and McCloskey 1992).

By the end of the 1960s, however, different linkages between accounting and economics were forming. Perhaps best realized by the publication of Ball and Brown's 1968 *Journal of Accounting Research* paper 'An Empirical Evaluation of Accounting Income Numbers', a new paradigm criticized analytical (deductive) models from Canning to Chambers with the view that:

[an] analytical model does not itself assess the significance of departures from its implied measurements. Hence it is dangerous to conclude, in the absence of further empirical testing, that a lack of substantive meaning implies a lack of utility (Ball and Brown 1968: 160). At stake in this critique of a priori research was the emergence of a new research programme for financial reporting, a programme whose models and assumptions derived from Chicago School finance theories of valuation and the influence of positive economics (Brown 1989: 203; MacKenzie 2006). Though the 'new' research retained connections with neoclassical economics, it was a new type of association. Rather than focusing upon the economic foundations for the selection of accounting practices, attention was shifted towards a more general kind of cross-disciplinary relationship based upon the premise that financial accounting information is an economic commodity whose supply and demand relationships could be modelled in ways essentially similar to other information commodities. Information economics approaches in accounting research no longer asserted any kind of 'special' relationship between accounting and economics. Although economics (market-) based research still retains a dominant position in the hierarchy of accounting research paradigms, especially in the United States, accounting reports are recognized merely as 'information goods' that might serve capital markets. As

commentaries such as Dopuch and Shyam (1980) specified, most neoclassicists in accounting no longer held to the ideals of the importance of an analytical Conceptual Framework—and indeed seemed to be opposed to it (Ball and Brown 1968: 160).

A priori research fell out of favour in the United States—though not without some resistance (Brown 1989). Researchers, and clearly accounting regulators such as the Financial Accounting Standard Board (FASB), continued to pursue economic income-accounting profit research (Whittington 1983; Tweedie and Whittington 1984; Solomons 1986); however, the absence of any widespread or even partial agreement within the debate, and the apparent lack of direct or determining impact of such work on the development of accounting policy and practice, in conjunction with other developments, gradually conditioned a shift from this type of research towards ostensibly 'empirical' concerns such as accounting policy alternatives and stock market 'information' effects and the usefulness to share-market investors of accounting numbers (Ball and Brown 1968). Such developments were in turn not only an effect of developments in finance theory at Chicago and elsewhere, but also reflected the development of computer processing power, the establishment of stock price databases (such as the Center for Research in Securtiy Prices [CRSP] at Chicago) and developments in mathematical modelling (Brown 1989; Watts and Zimmerman 1990; Mackenzie 2006).

While academic accounting research underwent, in Beaver's phrase, a conceptual, decision-oriented 'revolution' during the 1960s (Beaver 1981), the formal regulation of financial reporting in both the United Kingdom and United States intensified (Zeff 1972). Although in the United Kingdom the accepted model of financial reporting regulation allowed the profession to adjudge many issues of accounting valuation within the framework of the 1948 Companies Act, by the end of the 1960s accountancy bodies such as the Institute of Chartered Accountants in England and Wales (ICAEW) had experienced a period of sustained criticism arising from perceived accounting failures (Leach 1969; Stamp 1969; Robson 1991). With the formation of the Accounting Standards Steering Committee in the United Kingdom, the regulatory role of the professional bodies slowly completed its perceived shift from the exercise of professional judgement to non-binding professional recommendations to professional binding standards. During the mid-1960s, in the United States perceived failures of professional regulation and SEC criticisms gave the Accounting Principles Board (APB) its 'years of trial' (Zeff 1972). By 1973 the controversies surrounding the APB led to its dissolution and the establishment of a private sector regulatory agency outside of the profession, the FASB.

The development of US GAAP and UK Statements of Standard Accounting Practice (SSAP) had a further effect. By the 1970s a strand of empirically driven research reacting to regulatory controversies had begun to problem-atize the effects of financial reporting in terms of the 'economic consequences' of financial reporting policies (Horngren 1973; Zeff 1973; Wyatt 1977; Rap-paport 1977; Brown 1979). If, as was suggested, different accounting policies lead to different distributional consequences, then the act of regulating financial reporting could be conceived as political in the sense that regulation was an interested endeavour. Thus following on from Zeff's claim that economic consequences had now arisen out of accounting regulation, accounting academics of the 'old [a priori] school' lamented the politicization of financial reporting (Solomons 1978, 1983; Chambers 1980).

But while senior academics committed to the income theory paradigm continued to the appropriate basis for selecting accounting methods, new research perspectives began to explore the 'standards setting process'. Taking a cue from Gerboth's (1973) research declaration that, without a political mandate, accountants had no authority to adjudicate policies with distribu-tional consequences, academic research started to model accounting regula-tion and the activities of the FASB as political agencies, subject to influences, power, and lobbying. Whether or not accounting policy decisions had in the past been subject to 'vested interests' (and Merino and Neimark's [1982] paper was later to suggest that they had), academic research took seriously the idea that they now were, and researchers commenced an exploration of theories that might explain or predict policy preferences and lobbying behaviours.

As accounting came to be considered more explicitly in terms of its relationship to its environment and the constituents of that environment, extant notions of an unvarying accounting truth were challenged by attempts to reveal accounting as an instrument of the powerful. For example, a number of studies attempted to apply concepts from political science to the study of the financial reporting policy-making process. Hope and Gray's (1982) article on the development of SSAP 13 mobilized Lukes' work on the three dimen-sions of power, although their analysis confined itself to the first dimension (who gets their way?). Noting that the development of SSAP 13 on Account-ing for Research and Development moved from the exposure draft proposals to expense all R&D to one in which, in certain circumstances, development expenditures could be capitalized, Hope and Gray inferred from this that the structure of UK government defence contracts would disfavour aerospace contractors who had to invest in R&D before contracts were finalized. Hence, they concluded:

the specific outcome of the decision-making process (the formulation of an R&D policy) was determined by the aerospace industry. (Hope and Gray 1982: 551)

Studies of this type concerning financial reporting policy formation and 'vested interests' continued briskly through the 1970s and 1980s (Selto and Newmann 1981). Studies inquired into the relationships between the views of the Big Eight accounting firms and the production of accounting standards (Puro 1984). Hussein and Ketz (1980) questioned whether the Big Eight constituted a dominating elite over accounting policy. Other analyses sought to identify other groups whose influence on policy formation could be shown to have been determining (Aranya 1979; Sutton 1984). Prakash and Rappaport (1976, 1977) and Wilner (1982) attempted to explore possible information inductance effects, wherein management attempts to shape accounting policies according to their perceived effects upon the decisions of others.

One of the more thoroughgoing, and also controversial, examinations of accounting policy-making came with Watts and Zimmerman's formulation of a Positive Theory of accounting policy-making (1978). Putting management lobbying at the centre of the policy-making process, Watts and Zimmerman sketched a model of three possible economic incentives management have to influence financial reporting standards: debt covenant contracts, performance-related bonuses, and organization/industry political risks. Watts and Zimmerman's studies (see also 1979) were distinctive in that their view of political motivations was aligned to specific economic calculations, and, in its way, Positive Theory continued a new line from the Chicago School influence of finance theory and Friedman's Positive Economics (Friedman 1953) in highlighting market practices. Although Watts and Zimmerman's models and underlying epistemological claims to value-free research, and allegiances to Friedman's positive theory generated substantial controversy (Christenson 1982; Lowe et al. 1983; Revsine 1991; Tinker and Puxty 1994), much of this reaction also possibly reflected the hypothesis that academic research was a 'market for excuses' for management (Watts and Zimmerman 1979). Yet as an empirical study of accounting standards-setting Watts and Zimmerman's work was all of a piece with the shift from accounting valuation approaches towards the examinations of accounting practices that emerged during the 1970s and 1980s. The key strength of their work, however, might be the focus upon a calculative type of motivations, albeit one whose rationality was firmly rooted in individualist, marginalist economic theorizing (Lowe et al. 1983). Nevertheless, such studies of financial accounting regulation had moved financial accounting's research agenda from the normative prescriptions of income theory studies towards more empirical examinations of the work of professionals, regulators, and management in constructing financial statements and reporting standards.

ANALYSING FINANCIAL ACCOUNTING CHANGE: THE VALUE ADDED STATEMENT IN ITS SOCIAL CONTEXT

The focus of the more 'political' studies of financial reporting and standard-setting process remained for many years fixed upon regulatory agencies and those who sought to influence their deliberations. Many papers including Hussein and Ketz (1978) and Hope and Gray (1982) studied voting patterns and analysed submissions on exposure drafts and other forms of communication with the regulatory agency responsible for establishing reporting requirements and standards. These studies employed concepts of power that emphasized 'who votes' and 'who gets their way' (Dahl 1961; Lukes 1974; Hindess 1988), and addressed research questions concerning the role of vested interests in influencing regulations. Actors' self-interests were assumed to be discernible from their written submissions. Further, whenever specific outcomes could be tied to the interests of specific groups or individuals then power was assumed to reside with them.

Such perspectives, however, revealed little about the construction of accounting problems including why particular topics emerged as issues of concern at specific times. They also did not explain the circumstances in which specific policies come to be regarded as issues requiring regulatory action. The social examination of accounting change became, in our view, a research issue with the publication of Burchell et al.'s study of the Value Added (VA) Statement in the United Kingdom (Burchell et al. 1985).

The authors sought to shed 'descriptive and analytical light on the processes of accounting change' employing the case of VA, an active subject for accounting regulators and professionals during the 1970s. The case helped to highlight several conceptual difficulties that marked earlier efforts at forging connections between accounting and society. Previous work presumed rather than described such connections and regarded environmental changes as signals of the need for accounting practices to change and maintain accounting's purported reflective abilities (1985: 383). Although social change was presumed to create an imperative for accounting change, this perspective offered little help in explaining why attention turned towards a particular set of accounting practices such as VA. In other words, the VA event could not be explained by reference to VA's assumed roles as 'there [did] not exist any unanimous agreement over what the roles of value added are in the first place' (1985: 389). Instead, Burchell et al. analysed the network of social relations in three arenas—macroeconomic policy, industrial relations, and accounting standards—'...in order to facilitate an investigation of how issues such as economic performance and calculation were brought into relation with those of the status of employees and trade unions rather than presuming an *a priori* necessity for this to happen' (p. 391).

Each arena shared an overlapping concern with the calculation of VA, though in relation to different aims and ideals. For example, in the macro-economic policy arena, VA incentive payment schemes were constructed as model schemes to maintain 'a continuous link between performance and rewards' (p. 395) that would in turn encourage the productivity growth considered key to UK economic success. In the industrial relations arena, the VA statement was regarded as a means to establish sound relations. Here, the statement was envisioned as a 'co-operative' representation of the pro-ductive activities of the firm and a supplement to financial statements whose construction favoured the perspectives of owners and shareholders. For a time the statement was imbued with the promise of expressing a new form of economic visibility around the corporation and acting as 'a means of achiev-ing a felicitous combination of participation, if not democracy and efficiency' (p. 399). As discussions of VA occurred in these other arenas, the formation of the UK government's Sandilands Committee contributed to the sense of professional crisis within the accounting profession (Robson 1994*a*). Antici-pating this committee's report, the profession formed its own committee '...to re-examine 'the scope and aims of published financial reports in the light of modern needs and conditions' (p. 393). Their report adopted a stakeholder model of financial reporting in which each stakeholder including the employee group was deemed entitled to information about the reporting entity. VA entered accounting discourse as an alternative performance meas-ure to assess managerial efficiency.

Burchell et al.'s study offered a radically different mode of analysis for the study of accounting change and, as we argue in the next section, had a significant impact upon the ways that 'accounting change' could be con-ceived. The mode of inquiry offered in our view three key elements that previous studies had either neglected or drastically understated.

Accounting Problematization in Space and Time. The VA study did much to reveal the work involved in constructing an accounting problem prior to its emergence on a regulatory agenda. The emergence of the VA statement as an accounting 'problem' owed much to a temporal conjunction of political and social discourses about accounting representations and their role in enabling macroeconomic stability and industrial democracy. By tracing the genealogy of VA, '...the space which [it] occupied is seen to be comprised of a very particular field of relations which existed between certain institutions, eco-nomic and administrative processes, bodies of knowledge, systems of norms and measurement, and classification techniques' (1985: 400)—an accounting constellation. The event was historically contingent and 'under different conditions debating the potential uses and advantages of value added might well be quite irrelevant' (p. 392). This contingency further suggested that accounting problematizations may unravel or shift towards another accounting topic as political and social discourses change. While the authors stressed the specificity of the VA constellation and its conditions of possibility, they argued such specificity did not limit the significance of their analytical method but served to explicitly '. . . recognize the diverse and changing factors that can intermingle with the processes of accounting change' (p. 401). With this recognition, Burchell et al. reinstated the importance of attending to the historical dimension when analysing accounting policy-making, standard-setting or, indeed, any other kind of accounting change.

Accounting and Social Interests. The VA paper helped to acquaint a generation of researchers with trends in social theory and promote a more thoroughgoing deployment of a sociological analysis. The paper was one of the earliest attempts to consider the implications of Foucault's work for the study of accounting practices. It also adopted a more sophisticated approach to the analysis of accounting change and the social, not least in the assumptions made about the concepts of self-interest and 'vested interests'.

In prior work the 'interests' brought to bear upon accounting policies, standards, etc. were usually adopted from conventional descriptions of social or economic groupings. Categories such as 'management' or 'shareholder' were deemed to have essential, stable, and enduring self-interests in accounting matters that would inform and structure their lobbying efforts and the positions taken on accounting issues. This is not to say that 'management' and those who speak on behalf of management may not articulate stable conceptions of accounting's role and their own interests, but the analysis of VA was 'concerned to discover how self-interests or particular policy positions are in fact established—including the role which specific economic calculations and accountings . . . play in the process' (p. 409). Interests moved outside of self-evident categories of occupational position towards a more fluid conception of actors' knowledgeability and the production of interests. This form of analysis became strongly associated with ideas about the constitutive role of accounting.

In turn the VA paper embraced broader notions of the economic and social actors whose 'interests' in accounting issues may be generated at certain points (Robson 1993). Thus 'interests' in VA encompassed the involvement of specific state agencies and their associated functions in its history and covered a contingent constellation of union representatives, academics, and governmental agencies, as well as the usual groupings of management, employer representatives, and accounting regulators. The authors stressed the purposive rather than purposeful nature of accounting action noting that the accounting constellation was '... produced as a consequence of the inter-section of a great many events... Most of these were produced by people with clear views of what they were doing... and no thought at all for an accounting constellation' (1985: 401). In other words, multiple actors, often with con-flicting purposes, may advocate similar accounting practices but whether these practices will serve an intended purpose cannot be assumed but 'is a matter for detailed and careful investigations across the diverse arenas in which specific accountings can become intertwined' (p. 402).

The Power of Accounting: Accounting Knowledge as Representation and Intervention. Perhaps most understated of all, but also finally one of the more influential elements of Burchell et al.'s analysis was the connection to ideas of power, knowledge, and to some extent the ambiguity of accounting numbers. In their discussion of the VA arenas, Burchell et al. pointed towards the multiple rationalities that actors might hold in their promotion of the VA statement. For some the concept of VA was, as we noted above, tied to the appeal of its representational form: an account that partitions the distribution of the value generated to labour, capital, and the state in a more or less even-handed way. In so doing the VA Statement offered a vision of tripartite cooperation.

Additionally, however, Burchell et al. make it clear that some actors con-ceived of the VA statement as a vehicle for influencing or even determining industrial relations harmony—not simply representing it—and implement-ing income policy. This 'interventionary' conception of the statement helped to illustrate a dual capacity for accounting numbers and statements—to both 'represent' and give visibility to certain relations between social and economic actors as well as to potentially influence those relations in particular ways. Burchell et al. (1985: 402) maintain that 'accounting can be found providing the conditions of existence of certain social relations... [and] is intimately implicated in the construction and facilitation of the contexts in which it operates'. This meeting of accounting information (knowledge) and potential power effects represented one of the earliest explorations of a view of account-ing (Power/Knowledge—Foucault 1979) owing much to a Foucauldian the-oretical perspective that was to influence social and organizational studies of accounting for the rest of the 1980s and much of the 1990s.

Plainly, different groupings in different arenas envisioned the purposes of the VAS in different and, at times, conflicting ways, but this confluence of ideas attached to a highly ambiguous accounting statement. This collision of social, political, and economic discourses with an accounting statement constituted the VA event of the 1970s. And while the VA statement has since declined in cultural significance, the theorization of the event had, in our view, a lasting impact upon the study of financial accounting regulation and change. In the next section we review those impacts and suggest areas where research might still follow.

PROBLEMATIZING ACCOUNTING, SHAPING THE ENVIRONMENT, AND UNPACKING ASSUMPTIONS

Compared with our insights into the economic theory of income calculation and the economic determinants and consequences of modes of corporate financial reporting, our knowledge of how forms of financial accounting emerge from, sustain and modify wider institutional and social structures is modest. (Hopwood 2000: 763).

Although this comment remains relevant today, following the publication of Burchell et al. researchers have worked to redress this gap in our understanding. In so doing, research has expanded upon the key elements explicated within Burchell et al. outlined in the previous section. In the sections that follow, we review this literature, particularly that appearing in *Accounting, Organizations and Society*. The selected studies focus upon financial accounting choice or change, broadly defined, and our review is organized into three categories: (*a*) studies of accounting problematization including the definition of accounting problems and the effects of non-accounting discourses on this process; (*b*) studies of accounting knowledge as representation and intervention—how accounting choice helps to shape the environment through its effects on other fields of action; and (*c*) studies that examine various institutions associated with accounting change and help to unpack taken-for-granted assumptions and concepts.

Accounting Problematization

Economic regulation, whether conducted by political and legal authorities or enacted through market operations, is both informed by and justified through financial accounting measures and disclosures. By altering the content of financial reports, accounting change/choice is said to impact the effectiveness and efficiency of economic regulation. Given these purported impacts, accounting choice has been typically described as a technical matter—a technical solution to some problem of representing or capturing particular transactions and events within the financial statements provided to external readers. This characterization facilitates regarding accounting problems as pre-given situations that have forced their way into a particular regulatory arena. It suggests an obviousness for such problems that ignores how some issues and not others come to be constructed as *accounting* problems. In so doing attention is diverted away from examining how an environment that has been partially constituted by and through the use of specific accounting practices later contributes to changes in those very practices. However, by recognizing the significance of an accounting dialectic and by elaborating on themes found in Burchell et al. (1985), researchers have redirected attention towards the various ways that particular contexts help to construct an accounting choice situation including the elements that contribute to defining a particular issue or situation as an accounting problem (Robson 1993; Young 1994) or requiring a new accounting agency (Robson 1991).

Young (1994) specifically focused upon the construction of accounting problems that were included on the FASB's agenda. She noted that while diversity in practice was invoked to justify the inclusion of agenda items, this condition was also present for accounting issues excluded from the standard-setting agenda. Using the concepts of regulatory space and logic of appropriateness Young examined how various actors worked to define this condition as one that warranted standard-setting attention.[1] Robson (1994*a*) explored policy debates in the United Kingdom concerning industry competitiveness and investment in R&D to explore how the emergent problematization of R&D accounting and 'disclosure' was linked to government programmes to act 'at a distance' upon private sector R&D expenditures. Through translation, industrial policy discourses suggested new roles for existing accounting practices and helped to formulate new problems and priorities to which such practices may be attached.

Action at a distance also informed Robson (1992) who explains the preference for accounting quantification by arguing that accounting numbers provide seemingly mobile, stable, and combinable inscriptions that are claimed to permit control from afar by re-presenting the entity to a distant centre. Young (1995) employed this concept to examine demands to get the accounting 'right' within the US savings and loan industry. The shifting definition of a 'right' accounting and the concomitant use of particular practices shifted throughout the 1980s as environmental conditions and regulatory requirements changed. By turns, accounting was asked to reveal, conceal, and then reveal once more the financial condition of savings and loan organizations, and thereby justify regulatory action or inaction. Despite the varying and conflicting demands placed upon accounting, the actors involved

---

[1] See Ryan (1998) for an alternative approach to exploring the regulatory agenda.

in its construction did not question whether the accounting could be made 'right' through different accounting choices by regulators.

Each of these studies examined instances of accounting change/choice by regulators or other policy actors.[2] While these actors may require the adoption of an accounting standard, corporations, nonprofit organizations, and governmental entities choose how to implement these standards and select which accounting method to use when alternatives are permissible.[3] Frequently, these choices are explained by reference to utility, profit, or some other maximization variable embedded within a neoclassical economic model. However, as frequently observed, such models ignore the social, historical, and institutional contexts in which accounting choices occur. Drawing on insights provided by institutional theory, the work of Mezias and Carpenter and Feroz help to address this omission. Studying accounting choice in the context of the US investment tax credit, Mezias (1990: 455) illustrated the usefulness of this theory in enriching our understanding of the ways that institutional environments 'contextualize and shape the rational pursuit of profit by organizations' and influence accounting choice by individual firms. Carpenter and Feroz (1992, 2001) present a rich case study of accounting choice by US state governments that illustrates the contribution of institutional theory in understanding the decision to adopt generally accepted accounting principles for external reporting. The authors argue that this theory integrates complementary theoretical perspectives and explains the 'complex motives, conditions, processes and constraints that influence accounting choice' (1992: 638).

Accounting Knowledge as Representation and Intervention

The studies outlined above focused on the contribution of the environment in shaping situations constructed as requiring accounting choice as well as shaping our understanding of the choices made by regulators and entities. With this emphasis, the constitutive potential for accounting was temporarily set aside. We now examine this constitutive potential more explicitly and discuss studies that emphasize the social functioning of accounting, and how accounting

---

[2] In contrast, Young (1996) uses the case of financial instruments to explore the limits of accounting change. She describes the conceptual framework as institutional thinking that limits what are defined as accounting problems as well as the solutions deemed appropriate to such problems.

[3] See Hopwood (1987) for an examination of the interconnections between accounting and organizational change. Also see Elbannan and McKinley (2006) who offer several propositions to explain corporate resistance to mandated accounting change.

practices and accounting discourses articulate with other fields of action.[4] These studies help us to understand how seemingly technical debates surrounding accounting concepts such as profit measurement, liability recognition, etc. as well as the emergence of different accounting practices spill over into and alter other fields including investment analysis or employee relations.

At times, accounting practices and/or theories widen existing debates and contribute to the expansion of concerns. Thompson (1987) uses the case of UK inflation accounting to study how this accounting debate intersected with other arenas and contributed to the emergence of various normative questions such as who should make investment decisions, where should investment funds be placed, etc. In a related study, Robson (1994*b*) used the case of inflation accounting to explore the processes through which accounting representations attempt to reconstruct their environment. He argued that accounting change can be understood as a process in which accounting techniques, calculations, and practices are subjected to translation by various social, economic, and political discourses that are frequently seen as unrelated (or indeed antagonistic) to the technical discourse of accounting. In the United Kingdom, four different policy arenas relied upon various calculative practices to intervene upon and promote policy choices concerning investment decisions, taxation, and wage bargaining. These calculations were based on accounting numbers and inflation was seen to threaten the usefulness of such numbers. Although the various techniques proposed to address inflationary effects differed in their details, each facilitated *action at a distance* and thereby enabled governmental action without direct regulatory intervention.

At other times, accounting practices and theories contribute to the reproduction and legitimation of unequal distributions of wealth (Merino 1993; Tinker and Ghicas 1993; Arnold and Oakes 1998). Tinker and Ghicas (1993) explored the distributional consequences of FAS 36, pension disclosures. They argue that by overstating the amount of pension excess disclosed by corporations this standard exacerbated the problems arising from corporate takeovers aimed at appropriating these 'excess' amounts. The formulation of accounting principles for post-retirement benefits played a role in altering employer–employee relationships in the United States as well as in reducing and/or eliminating promised future benefits. Arnold and Oakes (1998) document how debates that occurred during the crafting of SFAS 106, accounting for other post-retirement benefits, focused attention upon the potential magnitude of these future benefits and the threats they posed to the ongoing

---

[4] Also see Hines (1988, 1991), Shapiro (1997, 1998), Macintosh et al. (2000), McSweeney (2000), and Mouck (2004), who draw upon differing philosophical perspectives to explore the constitutive potential of financial accounting.

financial health of corporate enterprises. This focus diverted attention away from questions about whether these benefits should be regarded as moral obligations owed to employees for past services and thereby facilitated benefit reductions. Merino (1993) maintains that the adoption of proprietary theory in financial reporting with its emphasis on the calculation of profits available for distribution worked to reinforce the acceptance of shareholder ownership rights to corporate profits. By claiming that profits belonged to shareholders, however far removed they were from active participation in the corporate enterprise, this theory helped to negate the claims of labour and consumers to collectively produced profits.[5]

Symbolic as well as redistributive consequences may accompany accounting choices. Espeland and Hirsch (1990) argue that accounting practices helped to facilitate and legitimate the 1960s conglomerate movement and thereby contributed to establishing the superiority of financial capitalism. During this episode, accounting concepts such as earnings, profits, and debt were employed to 'project a "rational" image' of new corporate structures and conceptual schema that regarded firms as bundles of assets that could be profitably assembled and disassembled (1990: 80). Conglomerators used accounting creatively so as to increase and sustain earnings in an effort to convince investors that their companies were capable of maintaining these increases over time. Merger and acquisition accounting is also the focus of Arnold (1991) who documents the distributive and organizational consequences of this accounting upon the US hospital industry. Under US GAAP, companies were only permitted to revalue existing assets upwards after an acquisition. Arnold argues that such revaluations were 'desirable' as they allowed companies to obtain larger reimbursements from the Medicare insurance system. Consequently, increased Medicare spending coupled with accounting policies that encouraged merger and acquisition activity changed the healthcare organizational field and contributed to the rise of '....a peculiarly US phenomenon—the large investor-owned hospital corporation' (1991: 129).

Institutions and Accounting Choice—Unpacking the Taken-for-Granted

From the perspective of economic-based theories such as agency theory and transaction cost economics, accounting standards arise from the self-interested

[5] Also see Takatera and Sawabe (2000). These authors also emphasize the importance of accounting practices in mediating relationships between an enterprise and various stakeholders and the relevance of institutional analysis in understanding how accounting helps to mediate such relationships and build institutions.

actions of various actors and are therefore unnecessary, if not, counterproductive to the efficient operation of markets or explicit contractual arrangements.[6] Just as Burchell et al. (1985) regarded the category of interests as fluid and constructed, subsequent interdisciplinary accounting research has unpacked the taken-for-granted assumptions and values contained within neoclassical economics perspectives on accounting regulation and accounting change. For example, Hunt and Hogler (1993) do not assume that accounting regulation must serve only an economic purpose. Drawing on institutional theory, they argue that accounting standards may help '... to produce a more stable field for corporate activity' (1993: 356). Drawing directly on the work of Burchell et al., Robson (1993) unpacks and criticizes the simplistic use of interests employed by these economic theories. Rather than monolithic and pre-given, Robson illustrates the contextuality and contingency of interests including how discourse contributes to their constitution as well as their rhetorical significance in 'enrolling' others in efforts to achieve particular aims.

Questions about the legitimacy of mandated accounting change are frequently raised in both practice and research. However, in contrast to the mainstream financial literature with its focus on market efficiency, interdisciplinary work raises questions about the adequacy of procedures used to establish accounting rules and/or the acceptability of the assumptions embedded within the frameworks and discourses that inform this change. Hunt et al. (1996) address the representational adequacy of established voice mechanisms (e.g. comment letters and public presentations) used to obtain external input during the process of developing accounting standards. They found that corporations frequently used these mechanisms to express their preferences in the development of SFAS 106 but that the views of workers, retirees, or their representatives were, at best, poorly represented. Hunt and Hogler (1993) argue that this discrepancy raises troubling questions about the adequacy of existing due process procedures employed to enact accounting standards, particularly those standards that may have significant redistributive consequences. While these procedures are frequently invoked to suggest the legitimacy of mandated accounting change, these authors maintain that the 'apparent voice mechanisms are often either ineffective or are, in fact, ways of excluding participation and

---

[6] Given concerns about the legitimacy of accounting regulation, some researchers have argued that the contractual arrangements and/or common law processes offer acceptable alternatives to contemporary standard-setting organizations in selecting appropriate accounting practices (e.g. Watts and Zimmerman, 1978; Johnson, 1987). However, Mills (1993) raises significant questions about whether the courts or explicit contracting methods provide a 'proven institutional alternative' for establishing accounting standards.

influence' (1996: 424).[7] The standard-setting process is frequently described in terms suggestive of a neutral, rational process. Based on their study of the Emerging Issues Task Force, Mezias and Scarselletta (1994) present evidence that the regulatory processes for accounting change resemble the garbage can model more than an orderly rational choice process in which problems are identified and solutions subsequently developed. Indeed, they argue that their study supports the '...hypothesis that flows of problems, solutions, choice situations, and participants are independent'.

During the latter half of the twentieth century, the decision usefulness criterion has emerged as the primary justification for the products of the standard-setting process. This criterion maintains that investors and creditors are the primary users of financial statements and their information 'needs' should be considered paramount when establishing accounting standards to change financial accounting practices and reports. Macintosh (1999) argues that anxieties about the impacts of an increasing separation of ownership and control in large corporations during the depression years of the 1930s contributed to intensified concerns about the informativeness of external financial reports. Such anxieties and concerns underpinned the debate on corporate accountability between Berle and Dodd, two prominent American theorists. Although they disagreed about the proper scope of corporate accountability, Berle and Dodd did agree that corporate disclosure could be an effective means of ensuring corporate accountability. Macintosh claims that this point of agreement contributed to the subsequent transition in external financial reporting from an emphasis upon stewardship reporting to that of decision usefulness. Williams (1987) adopts a more critical perspective towards the decision usefulness criterion and highlights its conceptual inadequacies in guiding standard-setting efforts. He argues that this principle inappropriately excludes concerns with fairness and impairs our ability to meaningfully discuss and debate the consequences that are appropriate or permissible for accounting standards. Rather than examining decision usefulness directly, Young (2006) considers the significance of the emergence of the financial statement user as the primary focus of standard-setting attention. Remarkably, the emphasis upon the information needs of the financial statement user has occurred in the absence of much empirical insight into such needs. Young unpacks this taken-for-granted criterion by considering how the category of user has been both constructed within standard-setting practice as well as used to justify particular accounting disclosures and practices.

[7] The concern with legitimacy also contrasts sharply with studies interested in describing the ways in which financial statement users (i.e. analysts and institutional investors) participate in the standard-setting process. See, for example, Durocher et al. (2007).

FUTURE RESEARCH DIRECTIONS: FOLLOWING FINANCIAL REPORTING STANDARDS

In this closing section we offer suggestions as to where future research in financial accounting may be headed. To date interdisciplinary literature on financial accounting change has focused on the constitutive potential of financial accounting and its regulatory processes. While this focus has taken seriously the role of calculations and calculative devices as social actors, in a Latourian sense, it has thus far had little to say about the daily practices and mundane decisions that underpin the production of accounting reports (see, e.g., MacKenzie 2003). Moreover, most studies have disregarded processes of implementing regulations—the interpretation, and integration of new accounting standards and disclosures into corporate financial statements (Cooper and Robson 2006). Yet studies of implementation practices offer the opportunity to examine how, if at all, the accounting constellation (or assemblage) may shift during these processes, including the ensembles of actors, expertises, calculations, algorithms, and technologies that are pulled together to facilitate implementation.

To illustrate, consider SFAS 123R, *Share-Based Payment*, a standard requiring companies to recognize expense for share-based compensation to employees. To recognize expense, employee options must be valued—a process that may require consultations with valuation experts, the purchase of valuation softwares, the application of finance equations, discussions with other companies to assess the 'validity' of required estimates, etc. Company auditors appear in multiple implementation sites as they assess the validity of valuation processes, evaluate the reasonableness of accompanying disclosures, and publish implementation guidance. Implementation questions may be submitted to various regulatory staff who may, in turn, issue implementation guidance that must itself then be implemented. Each of these mediators has the opportunity to alter the achieved aims of the accounting and disclosure requirements. Indeed, accounting standards and regulations might be viewed as public experiments (or laboratories) in valuation practices and market mechanisms, experiments whose 'results' are negotiated and constantly under review (Fourcade 2007; Muniesa 2007). In our view such approaches are highly consonant with the research agenda initiated by Burchell et al. (1985).

As Cooper and Robson (2006) suggested actor network theory (ANT) offers one useful approach to this type of investigation, and, indeed, further research in this area may benefit from drawing on other methodologies engaged by sociological studies of science and technology. Social studies of finance, for example, have emerged lately as an important field of sociological study (e.g. MacKenzie and Millo 2003; Knorr Cetina and Preda 2005; MacKenzie 2006). This work has studied the production of financial markets including the 'roles of finance theory in constructing those markets, the relevance of networks of social and socio-technical interaction in them, their cognitive and cultural underpinnings and the effects of financial markets on the workings of corporations' (Uzzi 1999; Vollmer et al. 2008).

Social studies of finance (SSF) and their methods offer an opportunity to examine issues such as the changing constitution of accounting expertise as finance models penetrate accounting practices and methods, the emergence and acceptance of particular accounting calculations, the transformation of accounting numbers as they move from corporate reports into earnings and other financial releases reported in various media outlets, analyst models and regulatory capital calculations, and many other second-order measurements. Similarly, while the influence of corporate actors upon the standardization of financial reporting has been a central concern of many studies, few have considered how financial reporting standards have shaped organizations and co-produced organizational expertise. Zorn (2004; Zorn et al. 2005) in contrast, has shown how the rise of the chief financial officer in American firms is intimately related to regulatory changes in accounting rules from 1979 onwards. As accounting regulations have proliferated finance officers' role has been transformed from 'beancounters to spin doctors' as corporations seek new ways to implement rules to their advantage. Accounting standards and regulations, most particularly those connected to matters of financial accounting disclosure (Robson 1994*b*), also have the potential to pass into the organization and restructure management accounting and control practices. As accounting standards have been developed to cover the valuation of esoteric financial derivatives so these standards have helped construct and further develop financial markets in these products by according them stability and regulatory legitimacy (Yound 1996). Rather than viewing financial accounting regulations as outcomes of an established or pre-given market, there is scope to explore financial accounting standardization as implicated in market making (Fourcade 2007).

The methods of SSF may also provide a useful and overlapping frame to investigate the daily practice of accounting (see, e.g., MacKenzie 2006) as well as the shifting interconnections between academic accountants and accounting research and practice. As MacKenzie and Milo (2003) showed for the Black–Scholes–Merton stock options pricing model, studies of the performativity (Callon 1998; MacKenzie et al. 2007) of new standards and accounting calculations may help develop further insights into the construction and reconstruction of accounting and economic agency. How, for example, have academic theories of the entity, for example, contributed to matters such as alterations in the formulations of accounting problems, shifts in the content of accounting discourse and in descriptions of accounting's purpose(s), and changing conceptions of accounting's boundaries and objects?

In this chapter we have explored the emerging interest in the study of financial accounting regulation with particular reference to the shift from purely 'economic' towards socio-political and cultural accounts of accounting, a process that in our view was propelled significantly by the publication of the Burchell et al. (1985) study of VA. Since then, studies of the constructive and constitutive roles of financial accounting proliferated in the 1980s and 1990s. Nevertheless, much work remains to be done in examining the many aspects of accounting change in the financial reporting arena.

REFERENCES

Aranya, N. (1979). The influence of pressure groups on financial statements in Britain. In T.A. Lee and R.H. Parker (eds.), *The Evolution of Corporate Financial Reporting*. Sunbury-on-Thames: Nelson.

Arnold, P. (1991). Accounting and the State: Consequences of merger and acquisition accounting the U.S. hospital industry. *Accounting, Organizations and Society,* 16(2), 121–40.

—— and Oakes, L. (1998). Accounting as discursive construction: The relationship between Statement of Financial Accounting Standards No. 106 and the dismantling of retiree health benefits. *Accounting, Organizations and Society,* 23, 129–53.

Ball, R., and Brown, P. (1968). An empirical evaluation of accounting income numbers. *Journal of Accounting Research,* 159–77.

Baxter, W.T. (ed.) (1950). Studies in Accounting. London: Sweet & Maxwell.

Beaver, W.H. (1981). *Financial Reporting: An Accounting Revolution*. Englewood Cliffs, N.J.: Pearson Higher Education.

Brown, V.H. (1979). The economic impact of financial accounting standards. *Financial Executive,* September, 36–54.

Brown, P. (1989). Current studies on the information content of accounting earnings. *Journal of Accounting Research,* 27, 202—17.

—— and Ball, R. (1989). Current studies on the information content of accounting earnings. *Journal of Accounting Research,* 27, 202–17.

Burchell, S., Clubb, C., and Hopwood, A.G. (1985). Accounting in its social context towards a history of value added. *Accounting, Organizations and Society,* 10(4), 381–414.

Callon, M. (1998). *The Laws of the Markets*. Oxford: Blackwell.

Canning, J.B. (1929a). Some divergences of accounting theory from economic theory. *The Accounting Review,* March, 4, 1–8.

Canning, J.B. (1929*b*). *The Economics of Accountancy: A Critical Analysis of Accounting Theory*. New York: The Ronald Press Company.

Carpenter, V.L., and Feroz, E.H. (1992). GAAP as a symbol of legitimacy: New York State's decision to adopt generally accepted accounting principles. *Accounting, Organizations and Society*, 17(7), 613–43.

—— —— (2001). Institutional theory and accounting rule choice: an analysis of four US state governments' decisions to adopt generally accepted accounting principles. *Accounting, Organizations and Society*, 26, 7–8, 565–96.

Chambers, R.J. (1966). *Accounting, Evaluation and Economic Behavior*. Englewood Cliffs, N.J.: Prentice-Hall.

Chambers, R.J. (1980). The myths and the science of accounting. *Accounting, Organizations and Society*, 5(1), 167–90.

Christenson, C. (1983). The methodology of positive accounting. *The Accounting Review*, 58(1), 1–22.

Cooper, D., and Robson, K. (2006). Accounting, professions and regulation: Locating the sites of professionalization. *Accounting, Organizations and Society*, 31(4–5), 415–44.

Dahl, R.A. (1961). *Who Governs? Democracy and Power in an American City*. New Haven: Yale University Press.

Dopuch, N., and Shyam, S. (1980). FASB's statement on objectives and elements of financial reporting: A review. *The Accounting Review*, 55(1), 1–22. Reprinted in T. Keller and S. Zeff (eds.) (1985). *Financial Accounting Theory: Issues and Controversies*, 3rd edn. New York: McGraw-Hill. Also reprinted in A. Bloom and P.T. Elgers (eds.) (1986). *Accounting Theory and Policy: A Reader*, 2nd edn. New York: Harcourt, 66–88.

Durocher, S., Fortin, A., and Cote, L. (2007). Users' participation in the accounting standard-setting process: A theory building study. *Accounting, Organizations and Society*, 32(1–2), 29–59.

Edwards, E.O., and Bell, P.W. (1961). *The Theory and Measurement of Business Income*. California: University of California Press.

Elbannan, M., and McKinley, W. (2006). A theory of the corporate decision to resist FASB standards: An organization theory perspective. *Accounting, Organizations and Society*, 31(7), 601–22.

Espeland, W., and Hirsch, P. (1990). Ownership changes, accounting practice and the redefinition of the corporation. *Accounting, Organizations and Society*, 15(1–2), 77–96.

Fisher, I. (1906). *The Nature of Capital and Income*. New York: Macmillan.

Foucault, M. (1979). *Discipline and Punish*. Harmondsworth: Penquin.

Fourcade, M. (2007). Theories of markets and theories of society. *American Behavioral Scientist*, 50, 1015–34.

Friedman, M. (1953). *The Methodology of Positive Economics*. Chicago: University of Chicago Press.

Gerboth, D.L. (1973). Research, intuition and politics in accounting inquiry. *The Accounting Review*, 3, 475–82.

Gould, J.R. (1974). Opportunity cost: The London tradition. In H.C. Edey and B. S. Yamey (eds.), *Debits, Credits, Finance and Profits*. London: Sweet and Maxwell.

Hatfield, H.R. (1924). A historical defense of bookkeeping. *The Journal of Accountancy*, April, 37(4), 241–53.

Hindess, B. (1988). *Choice, Rationality and Social Theory*. London: Routledge.

Hines, R.D. (1988). Financial accounting: In communicating reality, we construct reality. *Accounting, Organizations and Society*, 13, 251–61.

—— (1991). The FASB's conceptual framework, financial accounting and the maintenance of the social world. *Accounting, Organizations and Society*, 16(4), 313–31.

Hope, A., and Gray, R. (1982). Power and policy making: The making of an R&D standard. *Journal of Finance and Accounting*, 9, 531–58.

Hopwood, A. (1987). The archaeology of accounting systems. *Accounting, Organizations and Society*, 207–34.

—— (2000). Understanding financial accounting practice. *Accounting, Organizations and Society*, 28(8), 763–6.

Horngren, C.T. (1973). The marketing of accounting standards. *The Journal of Accountancy*, October, 137(4), 61–6.

Hunt, H., and Hogler, R. (1993). An institutional analysis of accounting growth and regulation in the United States. *Accounting, Organizations and Society*, 18, 341–60.

—— —— and Wilson, P.A. (1996). Accounting standards, health care, and retired American workers: An institutional critique. *Accounting, Organizations and Society*, 21, 423–39.

Hussein, M., and Ketz, J.E. (1980). Ruling elites of the FASB: A study of the Big Eight. *Journal of Accounting, Auditing and Finance*, 3(4), 354–67.

Johnson, O. (1987). Common law accounting: The case of goodwill. *Research in Accounting Regulation*, 1, 131—51.

Klamer, A., and McCloskey, D. (1992). Accounting as the master metaphor of economics. *European Accounting Review*, 1(1), 145–60.

Knorr Cetina, K., and Preda, A. (2005). *The Sociology of Financial Markets*. Oxford: OUP.

Leach, R. (1969). Letter. *The Times*, September, Reprinted in R. Leach and E. Stamp (1981). *British Accounting Standards: The First Ten Years*. Cambridge: Woodhead Faulkner. 22.

Lowe, E.A., Puxty, A.G., and Laughlin, R.C. (1983). Simple theories for complex processes: Accounting policy and the market for myopia. *Journal of Accounting and Public Policy*, 2(1), 19–42.

Lukes, S. (1974). *Power: A Radical View*. London: Macmillan.

Macintosh, J.C.C. (1999). The issues, effects and consequences of the Berle–Dodd debate, 1931–1932. *Accounting, Organizations and Society*, 24(2), 139–53.

Macintosh, N.B., Shearer, T., Thornton, D.B., and Welker, M. (2000). Accounting as simulacrum and hyperreality: A Poststructuralist perspective. *Accounting, Organizations and Society*, 25(1), 13–50.

MacKenzie, D. (2003). Ethnoaccountancy: Empty cookie jar, *London Review of Books*, 25(10).

—— (2006). *An Engine, Not a Camera: How Financial Models Shape Markets*. Cambridge, Mass.: The MIT Press.

MacKenzie, D. (2008). Producing accounts: Finitism, technology and rule following in knowledge as social order. In M. Mazzoti (ed.), *Rethinking the Sociology of Barry Barnes*. Aldershot: Ashgate.

—— and Milo, Y. (2003). Constructing a market, performing theory: The historical sociology of a financial derivatives exchange. *American Journal of Sociology*, 109(1), 107–45.

—— Muniesa, F., and Siu, L. (2007). *Performing Economics*. Princeton: Princeton University Press.

McCloskey, D. (1986). *The Rhetoric of Economics*. Brighton: Harvester Wheatsheaf.

McSweeney, B. (2000). Looking forward to the past. *Accounting, Organizations and Society*, 28(8), 767–86.

Merino, B.D. (1993). An analysis of the development of accounting knowledge: A pragmatic approach. *Accounting, Organizations and Society*, 18(2/3), 163–85.

—— and Neimark, M. (1982). Disclosure regulation and public policy: A socio-historical reappraisal. *Journal of Accounting and Public Policy*, 1(1), 33–57.

Mezias, S. (1990). An institutional model of organizational practice: Financial reporting at the Fortune 200. *Administrative Science Quarterly*, 35, 431–57.

—— and Scarselletta, M. (1994). Resolving financial reporting problems: An institutional analysis of the process. *Administrative Science Quarterly*, 39(4), 654–78.

Mills, P. (1993). The courts, accounting evolution and freedom of contract: A comment on the case law research. *Accounting, Organizations and Society*, 18, 765–81.

Mouck, T. (1989). The irony of the 'Golden Age' of accounting methodology. *The Accounting Historians Journal*, 16, 85–106.

—— (2004). Institutional reality, financial reporting and the rules of the game. *Accounting, Organizations and Society*, 29, 525–41.

Muniesa, F. (2007). Market technologies and the pragmatics of prices. *Economy and Society*, 36, 3, 377–95.

Napier (1994). The intellectual and professional influence of economics on accounting in the United Kingdom: 1850–1950. Paper Presented at the Seventeenth Annual Congress of the European Accounting Association, Venice, 7 April.

—— (1996a). Academic disdain? Economic and accounting in Britain 1850–1950. *Accounting Business and Finance History*, 6(3), 427–50.

—— (1996b). Accounting and the absence of a business economics tradition in the UK. *European Accounting Review*, 5(3), 449–81.

Nelson, C. (1973). A priori research in accounting. In N. Dopuch and L. Revsine (eds.), *Accounting Research 1960–1970: A Critical Evaluation*. Urbana, Ill.: Center for International Education and Research in Accounting.

Paton, W.A., and Littleton, A.C. (1940). *An Introduction to Corporate Accounting Standards*. Washington, D.C.: American Accounting Association.

Prakash, P., and Rappaport, A. (1976). The feedback effects of accounting. *Business Week*, 12, January, 12.

—— —— (1977). Information inductance and its significance for accounting. *Accounting, Organisations and Society*, 2(1), 29–38.

Puro, M. (1984). Audit firm lobbying before the Financial Accounting Standards Board: An empirical study. *Journal of Accounting Research*, 22(2), 624–66.

Rappaport, A. (1977). Economic impact of accounting standards—Implications for the FASB. *The Journal of Accountancy*, May, 143, 89–99.

Revsine, L. (1991). The selective financial misrepresentation hypothesis. *Accounting Horizons*, December, 5, 16–27.

Robson, K. (1991). On the arenas of accounting change: The process of translation. *Accounting, Organizations & Society*, 16(5/6), 547–70.

——(1992). Accounting numbers as 'inscription': Action at a distance and the development of accounting. *Accounting, Organizations & Society*, 17(7), 685–708.

——(1993). Accounting policy making and 'interests': Accounting for research and development. *Critical Perspectives on Accounting*, 3, 1–27.

——(1994a). Connecting science to the economic: Accounting calculation and the visibility of research and development. *Science in Context*, 7(3), 497–514.

——(1994b). Inflation accounting and action at a distance: The Sandilands Episode. *Accounting, Organizations and Society*, 19, 45–82.

Ross, D. (1991). *The Origins of American Social Science*. Cambridge: Cambridge University Press.

Ryan, C. (1998). The introduction of accrual reporting policy in the Australian public sector: An agenda setting explanation. *Accounting, Auditing and Accountability Journal*, 11(5), 518–39.

Selto, F.H., and Neumann, B.R. (1981). A further guide to research on the economic consequences of accounting information. *Accounting and Business Research*, 11(3), 317–22.

Shapiro, B. (1997). Objectivity, relativism, and truth in external financial reporting: What's really at stake in the disputes? *Accounting, Organizations and Society*, 22, 165–85.

——(1998). Toward a normative model of rational argumentation for critical accounting discussion. *Accounting, Organizations and Society*, 23(7), 641–63.

Solomons, D. (1961). Economic and accounting concepts of income. *The Accounting Review*, July, 36(1), 56–70.

——(1978). The politicization of accounting. *Accounting Review*, November, 146 (11), 65–72.

——(1983). The political implications of accounting and accounting standard setting. *Accounting and Business Research*, 13, 50, 107–18.

——(1986). *Making Accounting Policy*. Oxford: OUP.

Stamp, E. (1969). The public accountant and the public interest. *Journal of Business Finance*, 1(1), 3–10.

Sutton, T.G. (1984). Lobbying of accounting standard-setting bodies in the UK and the USA: A Downsian analysis. *Accounting, Organisations and Society*, 9(1), 81–95.

Takatera, S., and Sawabe, N. (2000). Time and space in income accounting. *Accounting, Organizations and Society*, 28(8), 787–98.

Thompson, G. (1987). Inflation accounting in a theory of calculation. *Accounting Organizations and Society*, 12, 523–43.

Tinker, A., and Ghicas, D. (1993). Dishonored contracts: Accounting and the expropriation of employee pension wealth. *Accounting, Organizations and Society,* 18, 361–80.

——and Puxty, A., (eds.) (1994). *Policing Accounting Knowledge The Market for Excuses Affair.* Princeton: Marcus Weiner Publishers.

Tweedie, D., and Whittington, G. (1984). *The Debate on Inflation Accounting.* Cambridge: Cambridge University Press.

Uzzi, B. (1999). Embeddedness in the making of financial capital: How social relations and networks benefit firms seeking financing. *American Sociological Review,* August, 64(4), 481–505.

Vollmer, H., Mennicken, A., and Preda, A. (2008). Tracking the numbers: Across accounting, finance, organizations and markets. Working Paper.

Watts, R., and Zimmerman, J. (1978). Towards a positive theory of the determination of accounting standards. *The Accounting Review,* 112–34.

—— —— (1979). The demand for and supply of accounting theories: The market for excuses. *Accounting Review* April, 54(3), 273–305.

—— —— (1990). Positive accounting theory: A ten year perspective. *The Accounting Review,* 65(2), 131–56.

Whittington, G. (1983). *Inflation Accounting: An Introduction to the Debate.* Cambridge: Cambridge University Press.

Williams, P. (1987). The legitimate concern with fairness. *Accounting, Organizations and Society,* 12(2), 169–89.

Wilner, N.A. (1982). SFAS 8 and information inductance: An experiment. *Accounting, Organizations and Society,* 7(1), 43–52.

Wyatt, A. (1977). Economic impact of accounting standards. *The Journal of Accountancy,* October, 144: 92–9.

Young, J. (1994). Outlining regulatory space: The FASB and agenda issues. *Accounting, Organizations and Society,* 19(1), 83–109.

——(1995). Getting the accounting right: Accounting and the savings and loan crisis. *Accounting, Organizations and Society,* 20(1), 55–80.

——(1996). Institutional thinking: The case of financial instruments. *Accounting, Organizations and Society,* 21(5), 487–512.

——(2006). Making up users. *Accounting, Organizations and Society,* 31(6), 579–600.

Zeff, S. (1972). *Forging Accounting Principles in Five Countries.* Illinois: Stipes Publishing Company, xvii, 382.

——(1973). The rise of economic consequences. *The Journal of Accountancy,* 56–63.

Zorn, D. (2004). Here a chief, there a chief: The rise of the CFO in the American firm. *American Sociological Review,* 69(3), 345–64.

——Dobbin, F., Dierkes, J., and M. Kwok (2005). Managing investors: How financial markets reshaped the American firm. In K. Knorr-Cetina and A. Breda (eds.), *The Sociology of Financial Markets.* Oxford: Oxford University Press.

17

On the Eclipse of Professionalism in Accounting: An Essay

Sajay Samuel, Mark A. Covaleski, Mark W. Dirsmith

Dark clouds are once again gathering over the accounting profession. Barely dried off from the backwash of the dotcom bust, it is now caught up in the storm set off by the collapse of the US housing bubble. By the middle of 2008, billions of dollars have been written off by financial institutions, including banks, investments houses, and such government sponsored enterprises as Fannie Mae and Freddie Mac. As the markets for 'mark to market' assets evaporate, many billions more are 'marked' for extinction. To fend off a wider crisis in the capital and financial markets the Federal Reserve System has had to prop up private enterprises (JPMorgan Chase and Bear Stearns), while others (Citibank and Bank of America) have had to solicit monies from foreign sovereign wealth funds to shore up their depleted balance sheets (*Washington Post* 2008).

If the estimates of such organizations as Goldman Sachs and the International Monetary Fund (IMF) are to be believed, the losses from the credit markets are likely to exceed $1 trillion, which suggests the fallout from this most recent boom-bust cycle of finance capital will spread far and wide. Almost inevitably that will lead to a hunt for those responsible. Unscrupulous lenders, foolish borrowers, lax regulators, complicit credit rating agencies, free-market ideologies, computerized trading systems, 'exotic' financial instruments like collateralized debt obligations (CDOs), improper or ineffective incentives for brokers and CEOs, are all likely to be fingered. And if the future is like the past, then the accountants will not be spared from the 'blame game'.

Specifically, the rules regarding the proper valuation of financial assets are likely to come under intense scrutiny. Academic commentators have begun to

We (Sajay Samuel and Mark W. Dirsmith) thank the Smeal College of Business at Pennsylvania State University for research support.

suggest that the current crisis in credit markets is in no small measure due to the inadequate disclosure of the value and ownership of the exotic financial instruments (Ketz 2008; Roubini 2008). Recall that following the rules of FAS157, unmarketable financial instruments can be called and listed as 'level 3 *assets*'. It is precisely the merits of such accounting exactitude that has Wall Street mavens like the CEOs of JPMorgan Chase (James Dimon) and the Blackstone Group (Stephen Schwarzman) furiously debating the pros and cons of ostensibly 'fair-value accounting' (Sorkin 2008). Not be left out, even a US presidential candidate has promised to 'convene a meeting of the nations' accounting professionals to discuss mark-to-market accounting' (McCain 2008).

As the spotlight slowly turns on the accounting profession, the recent past could well be repeated. Calls to 'renew professionalism' in accounting are routinely heard after a crisis, and the last scandal was not exceptional in this respect. What the fiasco surrounding Enron, WorldCom, and the collapse of Arthur Andersen revealed was the space of discursive practice within which the accounting profession operates: external regulation and self-regulated professionalism. On the one hand, the accounting profession grudgingly confessed the inability to police itself and accepted regulations aimed partly at enforcing its self-proclaimed ideals of unbiased public service. On the other hand, to shore up its dimming prestige and dubious credibility, the profession denounced its own fall from professionalism—from the disinterested and objective practice of its craft. Indeed, all who were affected—practitioners, academics, regulators, politicians, and the public—reaffirmed the need for professionalism among accountants. Thus, even if the current crisis does not trigger further external regulation of accounting practices, it is very likely to stimulate avowals of professionalism by accountants. Like physicians, accountants provide a consequential service whose qualities are nevertheless unobservable. In the end, what accountants and accounting fosters is the trust that participants need to trade in the marketplace. Yet, trust in what accountants produce depends on the degree of trust in their person, and it is the professionalism of their conduct that engenders such trust. As a social type, the 'professional' is one who can be trusted. Though usually implicit and sometimes forgotten, moments of crisis expose the fact that the credibility of accounting and auditors depends on the believability in his/her professionalism.

In three movements, this essay explores the significance of the idea of 'professionalism' in accounting. In the first section, after recording the frequent reliance on this idea in and around the profession, we selectively review the accounting and related scholarship on the professions. Within this literature, the idea of 'professionalism' is fundamentally suspected as either a ruse of self-interested behavior or as a technique of self-presentation, of staging identity. Accordingly, at the limit, professionalism is understood as a more or less successful exercise in persuasion. In the second section, we take a historical detour to unpack the notion of the 'professional ideal'. We do this to emphasize 'professions' as a historically informed idea whose invocations since the late nineteenth century have entailed specific contours of practice. These historically formed contours, of selfless service, collegial self-regulation, and learned expertise, delimit the meaning and practice of 'professionalism'. What has a beginning can also come to an end, and we accordingly entertain the possibility that 'professionalism' is an idea whose time has passed. We note the shift of semantic emphasis in the 'profession', which is increasingly applied to a myriad occupations. Moreover, the rising faith in governance through numbers as a replacement for trust in persons has further contributed to the eclipse of the professional ideal. However, insofar as numbers are not self-certifying and imply trusting those who produce them, the recent explosion of accounting and auditing paradoxically exacerbates the calls for professionalism in accountants. Last, we point to a disquieting political question surrounding the issue of professionalism. Technologically advanced societies call for the rule by experts, exemplified by the boom of professionals at the end of the nineteenth century. From then until the mid-twentieth century, it was the learned disinterestedness of experts—their professionalism—that underwrote the legitimacy of their rule. Occupying the middle position between the self-interest of private enterprise and the public rule of state control, it was professionalism that legitimized the rule of experts who make private judgments of public consequence. We identify and leave open the question of what happens to the political legitimacy of public accountants if and when the accounting profession becomes an industry.

SCIENTISTS OF SUSPICION

At the American Accounting Association annual meeting in 2003, Arthur R. Wyatt gave a speech titled *Accounting Professionalism—They Just Don't Get It.* The profession was still smarting from the passage of the Sarbanes-Oxley Act (SOX) and the mood of critical self-examination had not passed. Wyatt's comments were not unusual given the circumstances, and his diagnosis of the state of the accounting profession was widely shared by academics and regulators (e.g. Kaplan 1987; Levitt 2000; Zeff 2003*b*; Beresford 2005). Nevertheless, his remarks are a useful exemplar of how the accounting profession reacts in times of crisis. Moreover, his decades-long tenure as a professional at the now defunct Arthur Andersen, before which he was an academic, gives his remarks historical pungency. Central to his diagnosis of the failings of the accounting profession is the claim that, as a whole, the profession has lost its sense of professionalism. He points to a number of enabling causes including: the unwieldy size of the big accounting firms; the transformation of the American Institute of Certified Public Accountants (AICPA) from a professional to a trade association; the increased proportion of non-accountants hired by accounting firms; the tremendous pressures to increase audit-related revenues generated by the boom in consulting services; and the far too close relations big accounting firms cultivated with their clients.

Though he nowhere defines 'professionalism', the sense of the term can be inferred from his remarks. For one, he notes that greed and envy of clients so intoxicated accounting professionals that the 'core values of the professional firm were undermined by primarily commercial interests'. Second, the pursuit of money through consulting services also meant hiring experts in areas relatively unrelated to auditing, and therefore those not schooled into the professional values and ethics of the accountant. The growing presence of non-accountants implied that an accounting education was increasingly irrelevant to delivering the lucrative non-accounting services offered by accounting firms. In the broadening menu of services, auditing was no longer the main course. What was once the principal service of the accounting profession came to be officially seen as a commodity or undifferentiated product (AICPA 2000). As consulting services began to beggar auditing and tax work by comparison, auditors shifted focus. Instead of ensuring that their service met the highest standards of quality, they were encouraged to maxi-mize the profit potential of their commodities, even to the extent of treating them as 'loss-leaders'. Producing commodities certainly calls for skills, but not necessarily for a professional education, and understanding auditing as a commodity reinforced the declining relevance of the formal learning and certification to accounting firms. Third, collegial self-regulation within the firms was distorted by the increasing influence of non-accountants in decid-ing the strategic shape and direction of accounting firms (Smith 1990). As accounting firms mutated into 'multi-disciplinary service firms', the account-ing professional was increasingly asked to think and behave as an entrepre-neur first and then as a professional. Thus, accounting standards and standards of professional conduct—the ideals of independence and profes-sional ethics—became objects to be purposefully manipulated in the service of profit-maximization rather than serve as normative guidelines for practice (Elliot 1999). Moreover, the ability of the profession as a whole to regulate itself was also distorted by the conflicting demands of commercialism on the profession. For instance, both accounting firms and the AICPA 'stonewalled all efforts by the Securities and Exchange Commission (SEC)' to limit the range of services offered by the firms.

Thus, service, learning, and autonomy seem to comprise what Wyatt means by professionalism. Professionalism of accountants entails the attitude and stance adopted by those who: serve the public or are not primarily driven by monetary consideration; possess learned expertise and are trained into professional values and ethics; and can exercise effective self-regulation. The failures of the accounting professional appear in the rearview mirror of this perspective: commercialism that distorts the service orientation of professionals; commodification that weakens the need for formal learning and training into professional values; and organizational transformation into multi-disciplinary service firms that compromises the collegial self-regulation characteristic of the professions.

However, this understanding of professionalism as expressed by a professional, even if in self-critical mode, does not accord with the academic literature on the professions. The sociology of professions more generally, and studies of the accounting profession specifically, are broadly consistent with Wyatt on the constituent elements of professionalism. Where it is in discord with Wyatt is on their interpretation. The literature on the professions is deeply suspicious of the very professionalism that Wyatt holds out as a regulative ideal, now lost and urgently needing of recovery.

The sociological study of the professions has reached a curious impasse. While studies of the professions continue to multiply, the focal subject of these studies has increasingly escaped from view. Recently, a noted historian of higher education offered a definition of professions. 'I propose to define professions as nothing more than a series of rather random occupations that have historically been called that in our culture' (Veysey 1988: 17). If one were to adhere to such a definition, then at least in the United States, accountants, mercenaries, and dog-walkers would all count as professionals. That the definition of this key term is indefinite in both content and form and therefore almost vacuous is not peculiar to Veysey. His is a judgment shared by most contemporary students of the professions. For example, in a recent volume on debating the organizational structures of work in professional service firms, the contributors seem to use the term 'profession' to refer to any occupation, such as of business consultancy, that calls itself one (Greenwood and Suddaby 2006). Similarly, whereas Abbott (1988: 8–9) is somewhat circumspect in admitting his definition of 'professions' as an artefact of his theoretical interests, Freidson (1984: 15) is more forthright when he says '... I think it fair to say that scholarship concerned with the professions is in an intellectual shambles'.

This intellectual disarray is somewhat paradoxical since it comes during a particularly fecund period of academic study of the professions. Since the post-war years, the professions have been the subject of far-ranging examination, prosecuted by diverse disciplinary segments of the academy, including sociologists, economists, psychologists, political scientists, and lately, even accountants (Moore and Rosenblum 1970). By the 1960s, the study of the professions began to reflect self-awareness, moving away from attempts to define the category 'profession' by enunciating its essential traits, towards analyzing the processes by which some occupations came to be professionalized (Goode 1961; Freidson 1986). The earlier 'trait model' of the professions was judged sterile and inadequate. Attempts to abstract a common set of characteristics or attributes that were both necessary and sufficient to define the professions multiplied, but bore little fruit. For instance, by the mid-1960s, not one of the 23 different essential characteristics of the professions identified collectively by 21 authors, was agreed to by all (Millerson 1964). The inadequacy of the trait approach to the study of the professions was closely allied to criticisms of the functionalist modes of explanation for which they were used. Functionalist theories took-for-granted the necessity of the professions in technologically complex societies. The expert skills of professionals founded on formal knowledge was considered indispensible to both the scientific management of social problems and the promotion of the public interest. Professions, it was argued, serve certain 'functions' or 'needs', whether of the client or society at large. Accordingly, professional claims to self-regulation were justified by functionalist scholarship precisely on the grounds that the hard won knowledge of professional was both necessary and not easy to penetrate (Carr-Saunders and Wilson 1933; Parsons 1968). Thus, rooted in the search for their essential traits within a framework of functionalist explanations, the first phase of the study of the professions recapitulated the very self-description held by the professions.

It was by distancing itself from its subject that the scholarship of the professions achieved self-awareness. This new mode of studying the professions disavowed functionalist explanations for uncritically repeating and therefore justifying the very claims by which the professions obtained differential social and economic rewards for themselves. As suggested by Freidson, this second phase in the study of the profession can be understood as one focusing on *power*, in contrast to the earlier functional emphasis on the necessity of formalized complex knowledge (Freidson 1984: 4–5). Specifically, the point of departure for this critical scholarship was to interpret professions primarily as economic entities. Accordingly, professions were thought of as occupations, within the generic terms of a consumer–producer relation. From this starting point, the ability of some occupations to control the conditions of their work; to fend off control by the state; to define or influence client and customer needs; and to regulate the entry and behavior of the members of that occupation, were studied as consequences of the contested exercise of power for monopoly rents (Johnson 1972). This attention, in an economic key, to the processes by which some occupations were able to construct themselves as professions, required that professional claims be viewed with scepticism, if not, suspicion.

Thus for instance, the professional insistence on formal learning was interpreted as attempts to erect educational barriers in order to create scarce resources—knowledge and skills—that could then be traded in for greater economic rewards (Larson 1977; see also, Collins 1979; Hall 1984). The propriety of professional self-regulation, once justified by claims of the mystery of professional work and knowledge, was now seen as the outcome of jurisdictional battles to obtain monopolistic control of a skill or service (Abbott 1988; Dingwall 2008). As for the professional claims to serve the public interest, these were met with a range of reactions from 'mild skepticism to curt dismissal', including the charge that 'professionals are wolves in sheep's clothing, monopolists who live by the rule of caveat emptor, but lack the integrity to admit it' (Haskell 1984: 181; see also, Derber et al. 1990).

The literature on the accounting profession over the last two decades shares a similar suspicion of professional claims (Tinker 1985; Willmott 1986; Hines 1989; Reed 1996). In one sense, the passage of the Securities Act of 1933 and 1934 are justly considered foundational events for the accounting profession. The legal requirement that all publicly held corporations publish audited financial statements, not only established a market for accountants but also sheltered them from potential competitors. Accordingly, the notion that a profession regulates itself is modulated by the recognition that it does so by establishing a recognized monopoly or oligopoly of control over setting standards for auditing and accounting practice (McEnroe and Pitman 2003). Moreover, even such foundational legislations as the Securities Acts, not to mention the numerous other congressional hearings and legislations including SOX, are understood equally as symbolic displays to pacify public worries concerning the state of capital markets and capitalism in general (Bealing et al. 1996). The SEC as the nominal enforcement agency did not actively pursue regulation in the 1930s, and in fact seemed to be captured by accounting profession (Merino and Mayper 2001). Though charged with the functions of a guard dog, the accounting profession disavowed the responsibility of detecting fraud by helping ensure that it was management who bore final responsibility for the integrity of financial statements (Felker 2003). The establishment of accounting standards, ostensibly to produce a uniformly high quality in accounting statements, function in practice as strategic instruments used by the profession to stave off more onerous government regulation (Byington and Sutton 1991). Peer evaluation, made general only by the 1980s, is less a tool to discipline wayward auditors than it is a mechanism for big accounting firms to minimize external scrutiny of their audit failures and to raise the cost of doing business on smaller firms (Fogarty 1996). Similarly, licensing laws to control the use of the CPA designation are used opportunistically by one cadre of accountants to the detriment of other equally capable accountants (Mills and Young 1999). Indeed, the overall claim to professional self-regulation has been argued as deliberately conflating the regulation *of* the profession with regulation *by* the profession (Robson et al. 1994). While the accounting profession lobbies Congress in the effort to influence legislation to its advantage (Thornburg and Roberts 2008), the global accounting firms enjoy an increased influence over shaping such legislation (Cooper and Robson 2006). State Boards of Accounting have systematically ignored and suppressed evidence of extraordinary levels of audit failures among the very accounting firms they are supposed to monitor (Fogarty et al. 1997). Indeed, these authors have suggested that contrary to the belief that self-regulation protects the public from substandard performance, it is more likely that self-regulation is 'systematically flawed, self-serving, and designed to create false assurances that practice conforms to the public interest' (p. 167).

Similarly, when scholars peer into the inner workings of accounting and auditing practice, that usually impenetrable core of formalized expertise and learning, they find the claims to professional mystery overblown (Power 1996, 2003). Bedard (1989) notes 'the evidence accumulated from behavioral studies [which] indicates that expert auditors do not behave differently from novice auditors' (p. 121). Apparently, neither formal education nor on-the-job training, nor indeed the years of auditing experience seems to make a difference to the judgement of auditors. Similarly, every phase of the auditing craft, from audit planning and internal control assessment, to evidence gathering and audit reporting, are less the disinterested expert tasks they are professionally portrayed to be, and more socially mediated processes of legitimation. Audit plans are used to legitimize what auditors do to constituents both inside and outside the firms (Humphrey and Mozier 1990). Audit policy manuals are not mere templates for action, but rather encode the cultural orientation of the accounting firm that prepares them (Carpenter et al. 1994). Similarly, the information and criteria used to evaluate client internal controls are hardly the stuff of rational and impartial decision-making, but reflect the differing perceptual grids shaping accounting firms (Dirsmith and Haskins 1991, 2007). Statistical sampling was primarily introduced and disseminated into audit practice not merely because it is used rationally, but to propagate the *appearance* of quantified rationality (Power 1992; Carpenter and Dirsmith 1993). Working papers documenting what auditors do are rituals that 'comfort' auditors and serve as ammunition when they are questioned (Pentland 1993). More recently, as accounting firms migrate towards what has come to be called business risk audits (BRA), scholars have documented how new techniques must be accepted as legitimate before they can be used to generate efficiencies (Fischer 1996) and are used to mediate the conflicting interests and struggles for power among different groups within accounting firms (Fischer and Dirsmith 1995).

Moreover, the propagation of new audit methodologies such as BRA goes hand in hand with propagating new ways of being a professional (Robson et al. 2007). Professionals are not fully born as such. Instead, they are schooled, trained, and socialized into behaving in specific ways that accord with and contribute to the ideals of professional behavior that, in turn, are resources capable of producing social and economic rewards (Fogarty 1992; Grey 1998). The production of accountant subjectivities has numerous sites, including the movies (Beard 1994; Hopwood 1994). The stereotypical accountant with green eyeshades, was the product of carefully orchestrated conduct and appearance that was suitably non-threatening, for owners to share control over their purse-strings (Bougen 1994; see also Freidman and Lyne 2001). The now defunct 'global knowledge expert' and the emerging form of the accountant as an 'entrepreneurial professional' are more or less successful efforts at reforming the stereotype to fit more contemporary economic imperatives (Covaleski et al. 2003). Firms are experimenting with impression management to convince the young that accounting is exciting, interesting, and fun (Jeacle 2007). Prudence only nominally refers to a cardinal virtue and the stance of a 'conservative accountant'. Its principal function in accounting is to display conformity with and acquiescence to the interests of management and investors against those of speculators (Maltby 2000). Such accounting procedures as Management by Objectives (MBO) is applied within firms to first produce and then reinforce the difference between workaday auditors on the one hand, and firm administrators on the other (Dirsmith et al. 1997). Elaborate social practices of mentoring are deployed to cultivate the kinds of values and attitudes suitable to successful accountants (Covaleski et al. 1998). The general conclusion of studies of the processes of socialization into the accounting profession is hard to miss: people are formed and re-formed as accountants at great expense and with much attention, as suggested by the title of a recent book, *Making Up Accountants* (Anderson-Gough et al. 2000).

In revealing the complex and contested processes by which occupations are socially constituted as professions, accounting scholars have cast doubt on the self-evidence professional claims. Whether of the formal knowledge that informs expert skills and judgement, or of the necessity for professional self-regulation or indeed of the comportment suitable for a professional, accounting and sociological studies does not accord with the self-understanding of the accounting profession. Scientific studies of the professions fundamentally suspects professional claims as either a ruse of self-interested behaviour, or as a technique of self-presentation or staging identity to achieve social status and monopolistic rents. Yet both the accounting profession and scholarship on it broadly agree on the terms that characterize the profession. Thus, despite the internal impasse within the scholarship on the profession on what constitutes one, born of doubting whether professions possessed essential traits, three characteristics nevertheless seem crucial to a profession: an orientation to service; the institutional architecture of self-regulation; and, last, inputs of formal knowledge that exceed skills learned on-the-job. Without debating whether these are essential aspects of a profession, it is still pertinent to ask how and why they have dominated present day understandings of the profession. In the next section, we suggest that the focus by both the professionals and their academic counterpart on these three dimensions is not accidental, but precisely the contours of discursive practice shaped by the history of the professions in the United States.

PROFESSIONALISM: A HISTORICAL LOOK

Around 1793, James Caulfield penned a book titled: *Blackguardia: Or, a Dictionary of Rogues, Bawds, Pimps, Whores, Pickpockets, Shoplifters… The Most Remarkable Professors of Villainy.* Less surprising than his language is his seemingly unusual use of the word 'professors'. Unlike us, he evidently did not refer to residents in the ivory towers, nor do his subjects carry the social status or privilege of 'professionals' today. Yet, such surprise only reflects that incomplete understanding induced by ignorance of the semantic history of 'professions'. Or so argues Bruce Kimball (1995) in a remarkable and largely overlooked essay on the US history of the professions. Kimball suggests *six moments* that constitute the history of our idea of 'profession'.[1] Attending to this history lends precision to the range of discursive practices made possible by invocations of 'professionalism'. Furthermore, such precision offers a

[1] Though our discussion here focuses on the semantics and idea of the 'profession', Kimball's own study is not 'idealist'. He considers the economic, social, and political dimensions correlative with this semantic history. Space constraints prevent a fuller engagement with his text here.

benchmark and point of departure from which to evaluate whether and to what extent contemporary avowals of professionalism represent a continuity or discontinuity in the history of professions.

For Cicero of late antiquity, '*professio*' meant an oath, vow, or declaration, a meaning that was carried into the high Middle Ages. Until the sixteenth century, it was used in a predominantly religious setting to signify the public vows of faith made by monks and clergy. In English, the noun 'profession' was extended from the act of avowal to also mean the 'group of those who made the vow'. This semantic ambiguity, between verb and noun, implied that one could 'make a profession' and also 'join a profession'. Furthermore, under the impetus of the Protestant Reformation, making a profession was not limited to the monastic orders, but covered the laity and secular clergy. By the seventeenth century, parish priests no less than monks could profess a creed or faith. According to Kimball, this two-fold extension of the word is the *first* constitutive moment in the formation of the twentieth century sense of 'profession' and 'professionalism'.

However, this early history reveals more than mere etymological nuance. The dual meaning of profession as at once avowal of creed and a group of the faithful also gave the word a predominantly theological cast. As Weber remarks of Luther, it was the latter who, in translating the Greek *klesis* with the German word *beruf*, expanded the meaning of 'calling' to refer to both spiritual vocations and worldly occupations. However, according to Kimball, it is the rhetorical development of the word 'profession' that semantically linked the purely religious sense of 'calling' to a secular occupation. Already, in classical and medieval Latin, '*professio*' was used, though sparingly, to denote an occupation. This sense of profession as occupation did pass into English, witnessed not only by the title of Caulfield. Yet, over the seventeenth and eighteenth centuries, the more typical synonyms for 'occupation' were 'employments', 'trades', 'callings', 'manufactures', or 'arts'. It was only by the early nineteenth century that profession came to be widely identified with any occupation, whether priestly or secular.

As the term 'profession' began to signify worldly occupations, it infused the sense of a spiritual calling into secular occupations, ennobling and dignifying the latter. This movement of theological roots nourishing the term 'profession', which so enriched, then confers esteem and worth to worldly occupations, Kimball considers the *second* constitutive moment in the history of the modern professions. Obviously, however, shoplifters and bawds are hardly the members of a dignified occupation. The conferring of esteem to worldly employments went hand in hand with a narrowing in the scope of the meaning of profession. From the early nineteenth century, 'profession' began to be largely restricted to those employments to which theology was linked in the medieval universities: law and medicine. Neither cooks nor rogues were thought of any longer as professors or belonging to a profession. Instead, as the adjectives 'learned' and 'liberal' when applied to 'profession' suggest, the social status of the professions is won by narrowing its range of reference. Moreover, insofar as the learned professions benefited from a liberal education, and liberality connoted generosity, freedom, and leisure, the association between education, wealth, and social status was cemented by restricting the range of professions to the learned and liberal. Thus, professions referred to those few occupations whose members were well-off, of high social standing, and of a liberal character.

The formation of this *third* constitutive moment of professionalism was indebted to theology in yet another and perhaps more consequential way. The theological source for 'profession' also ennobled the learned professions by conferring to them its ethic of selfless service. Service to others for their benefit, as a servant would, is a staple of Christian theology. What is less well understood is the inherent tension in this stance of selfless service. The Christian engages in selfless service in order to serve God and be saved. It is a kind of service that not only helps the served, but also raises the status and recognition of the servant. This dialectical unity can be construed as a ruse of the clerics as Nietzsche suspiciously charged, or as the clear-eyed recognition of the ineradicable gap between profession and action. Yet, it is precisely this theologically informed gap that indelibly marks the modern professions. On the one hand, it is what fuels their claim to serve the public interest, the common good, the client, or society at large. On the other hand, it is also what permits both professionals and their critics to be doubtful of this claim.

If theology gave the professions their ethic of selfless service, then it was the law that gave legitimacy to the notion of professional service and form to the architecture of professional associations. By the middle of the eighteenth century, the question of the formation of a polity had taken center stage. In the tracks of the momentous shift from a religious to a constitutional polity, perhaps best captured by the disestablishment of state churches, law displaced the significance and prominence of theology. The American Revolution was understood to mark the legal constitution of a commercial republic that enshrined liberalism in both senses of free-markets and free-thinking. Law was integral to establishing a polity rooted in the 'rule of law' and crucial to giving form to a commercial republic founded on the free trade of ideas and property. This displacement towards constitutional polities found semantic expression in the shifts of meaning and reference of 'profession', 'professed', and 'professional'. Though 'profession' was still being used in the sense of a religious vow, it referred less and less to the clergy. Instead, in religious contexts, 'confession' and 'denomination' had begun replaced the 'profession', which as we noted above, referred to secular employments as well. Moreover, the adjective 'professional' was originally used in a religious context to mean avowed, as still heard in the 'professional beliefs' spoken of by Thomas Paine in his *Rights of Man*. However, by the middle of the nineteenth century, it too underwent a change of reference and meaning in that 'professional' replaced 'professed' as the adjective referring to occupations.

But as Kimball argues, the *fourth* moment in the history of the professions is constituted by the contributions of law that give the notions of 'professional service', 'professional association', and 'professional' its contemporary ring. Lawyers were not only prominent as architects of the polity, but also most visibly enamored by the adjective professional. 'Professional character', 'professional business', and 'professional man' were rife in legal periodicals during the first quarter of the nineteenth century. In contrast, very few other occupations had yet to use the word in this manner. If it was no longer usual to speak of the 'professed' baker, then it was even more unusual to speak of the 'professional' baker. If the lawyers gave fillip to the use of 'professional' as modifier to dignify an occupation, they also invoked and modified the theological ethic of selfless service.

Lawyers adopted the notion of serving the public good, but did so by offering 'professional services'. Early heralds of the recent discovery of 'professional service firms', lawyers in the mid-nineteenth century, defined 'professional service' as service for a fee. Between the Revolution and the Civil War, lawyers were perhaps better compensated than any other occupation in the United States. At first look, this should be surprising since lawyers were bound by publicly announced fee statutes to limit the amount they could charge for their work. In addition, American lawyers, like British barristers, were prohibited from suing for recovery of their fees. Yet, they were able to become relatively better paid than any other occupation by convincing their fellow lawyers who were jurists on the bench of the validity of their claims. Disregarding that well-known dictum according to which a 'man should not be the judge in his own cause', lawyers drew a distinction between fees for counsel and fees paid to sheriffs, clerks, and other court officers. Lawyers argued that their professional services should be recompensed by what it was worth to the buyer. This principle of free-market exchange was thus adduced to permit 'professional persons' to freely sell their services. Curiously, in crafting their arguments, lawyers not only underplayed the theme of selfless service they adopted from the clergy, but were not below debasing the claim to a dignified occupation by equating their services with 'any mechanical art'. Lawyers argued that just as a baker or merchant was paid what he/she was worth, so also the legal profession should be freed from moralistic restrictions on their income. Hence, as was ruled in the late nineteenth century, the attorney–client relation was understood asa predominantly contractual one. Yet, the contractual nature of the 'professional services' did not mute the theological resonances. Even if distant and somewhat muffled, 'service' still carried the ring of selfless help and aid to others. This resulting inherent tension between commercial gain and selfless service was introduced by the legal profession with the notion of 'professional services' and would dog all who followed in their path. Perhaps it was a lawyer that Baudelaire had in mind in his *Counterfeit Money*: the one who seeks to do well by doing good!

Despite well-known efforts to link the phenomenon of professional associations to medieval guilds, the latter are not of the same kind. For instance, the medieval world was composed of estates and orders, which were the precise subject of contention under liberal jurisprudence and political theory. This is not to say that the faculties of the medieval university did not serve as a model for professional self-regulation in a later time. It is rather that professional associations are better understood as voluntary associations of individuals. When individuals are considered the bedrock of society, then any corporate body is necessarily fictional or instrumental, in a way that was not true of medieval society. Scientific societies, orphanages, corporations, and mutual aid societies were all instances of the proliferation of voluntary associations so characteristic of US civil society during the mid-nineteenth century. Lawyers, in their standing as the preeminent profession, also formed their own associations, though these were many and diverse in number. As Tocqueville remarked, 'the legal profession is thus always a brotherhood, and in this respect a direct contrast from the medical profession'. As with the associational movement in general, and among lawyers specifically, the norm was one of collegial self-government or self-regulation. Albeit on a smaller scale, the associational mode of organization thus reflected and instantiated the idea of a polity of self-governing citizens. Individuals formed little polities, acted in concert, without or beneath the reach of state regulation. As in the instance of their freedom to contract for fees, lawyers were not beyond obtaining legal rulings to support their cause. Yet, this did not violate the associational model of self-regulation, since lawyers were indeed judges in their own cause. The model of associational self-government or self-regulation was thus given prominence by its adoption by the legal profession and would form a second contribution of lawyers to the present day meaning of professional and professionalism. Moreover, it was only in the light cast by this associational model of self-regulation bequeathed by lawyers that the non-legal professions would be understood as having to solicit or fend off state regulations. That is, the tension between state regulation and self-regulation would be strictly germane to only those professions that could not count lawyers as members.

If the displacement of the term 'professor' by the 'professional' was spurred by the legal profession, then the restriction of the meaning of 'professor' to educators was the consequence of the predominance of science and the university during the last quarter of the nineteenth century. According to Kimball, this *fifth* moment in the semantic history of the professions was linked to a *sixth* moment, whereby educators lent the conceit of their occupation to the meaning of a 'professional', namely, as a repository of formal learning.

Historians among others have amply documented the rise of natural and social sciences housed in universities during the last quarter of the nineteenth century in the United States. Whatever the contested reasons for this development, science was the preferred method to reform society. Not only were the natural sciences seen as necessary to improving the material conditions of existence, but so also social science was thought vital to bringing order to a society in the throes of industrial transformation (Wiebe 1967; Ross 1991). To pursue knowledge scientifically entailed the formation of specialized disciplines, and the formation of professional sects associated with each discipline (Veysey 1965). Thus, economists, astronomers, biologists, and psychologists, among others, began to find a place within the burgeoning university. University or formal learning was no longer restricted to the faculties of the medieval university, but expanded to cover an increasing range of useful knowledges. For instance, accounting and business no less than agriculture moved from vocational training schools into the university by the late nineteenth century (Previts and Merino 1979: 105). As incredible as it seems today after Kuhn, Feyerabend, and Foucault, in the late nineteenth century, science was understood to deal with objective facts untainted by human values. Its practitioners, scientists, were construed as objective and disinterested seekers of effectual truths. By derivation, the professional, cast in the image of the scientist, was shaped as an impartial expert whose service to society was founded on scientific knowledge. Accordingly, quantification, empiricism, and experimental verification became the grist for not only scientific knowledge, but also to professional expertise. The image of the professional as impartial expert, steeped in learning, and housed in the university, was perhaps best captured in a phrase from Robert LaFollette characterizing the University of Wisconsin at the turn of the last century: a 'university on tap but not on top'. This indirect dominance of science and scientific expertise implied the reflected dominance of educators and teachers since formal knowledge or learning was an essential component of science. The teaching profession not only colonized the term 'professor', but also contributed to decisively coloring the 'professional' with the patina of formal learning. Whether baker or doctor, practitioners would no longer be able to be professors of their trade. Instead, that term was reserved exclusively for those concerned with education. Moreover, since occupational boundaries within educational establishments were relatively porous in the latter half of the nineteenth century, the term professor was initially applied to both administrators and teachers. It would take a few years before 'professors' were identified as teachers.

The teaching profession had already worn the theologically informed cloak of selfless service. Further, they leveraged their history in the medieval universities to constitute self-governing associations, following the lead of lawyers. Thus, they cemented the affective bonds tying members of professional associations closer together than those among people sharing a common place of work. Yet, the pre-eminence of the teaching profession during this period also influenced semantic changes in the word 'profession'. The dominance of the science and the university as a necessary passage for those occupations seeking to become professions, made the word 'learned' in the phrase 'learned profession' inessential. All professions were learned to the extent that they had to partake of the fruits of formal learning proffered by the teaching profession. Moreover, the requirement of formal education as a criterion of a profession even in fields of practical knowledge, once called the useful or mechanical arts, implied the superfluity of the 'liberal' in 'liberal professions'. The formation of attitudes of liberality was no longer required from formal learning, which had taken on a utilitarian cast. Thus, a 'professional' signified an expert in an occupation, trade, or craft requiring formal learning, and 'professions' designated zones of functional expertise leavened by selfless service. It was on this foundation of educated expertise that professional associations sought out licensing laws to restrict the supply and regulate the quality of their members. The two criteria usually adduced to grant occupational licenses were the relative difficulty of the knowledge base and the contribution of that knowledge to the public good. Thus, for instance, when practitioners of horse-shoeing attempted to obtain an occupational license, they were turned down on the grounds that learning to shoe a horse did not require an advanced education, nor did it have significant consequences for the health and welfare of society at large. Some such as Freidson (1984) argue that professions are separated from other occupations by licensed credentials to reflect the necessarily complex knowledge needed to perform professional tasks. Others, such as Larson (1977), suggest that occupations use licensing laws and impose educational restrictions to catapult themselves into a lucrative profession enjoying monopolistic rents. Despite these marked differences in interpretation of the relation between formal educational and a profession, it was the dominance of science, the university, and the teaching profession that established this link.

Accordingly, Kimball argues that the discursive space of professionalism is formed by in the light cast by these six moments in the history of US professions as also reflected in the semantic shifts of meaning in 'professor', 'professional', and 'professions'. A professional is one who works for the client or for the public interest; who has imbibed university-based formal learning and has certificates to show for it; and, last, belongs to a self-regulating association of like-minded members. This 'true professional ideal' was established by the early twentieth century and is perhaps captured in the definition of a professional offered by Louis Brandies, famed legal scholar and jurist, who also was one of the early proponents of business as a profession: 'an occupation for which the necessary preliminary training is intellectual in character, involving knowledge and to some extent learning, as distinguished from mere skill; which is pursued largely for others, and not merely for one's own self; and in which the financial return is not the accepted measure of success' (in Marty 1988: 75). He leaves out professional autonomy or self-regulation, but then Brandies was a key architect in building the regulatory US state apparatus of the late nineteenth century.

Thus, the space constituted by formal learning, a service orientation, and self-regulation circumscribes the range of meaning and practices that are comprehended under the term 'professionalism'. The historical elaboration of the professions forms contours that circumscribe the discursive practices of professionals. Though the scholarly discussion is spirited, the weight of scholarly opinion suggests a fundamental suspicion towards the claims of professionals. What the accounting profession holds up as an ideal, the academic sees through as a ruse of self-interest. When the professional claims effectual self-regulation or the impenetrability of learned judgments, the academic sees actors on a stage. However, even these scholarly criticisms and suspicions are framed largely within the discursive space of 'profession' and 'professionalism' as they were historically constituted by the early twentieth century.

Yet, on all three fronts of the historical constitution of professionalism—formal training, selfless professional service, and self-regulating associations—it would seem that the accounting profession is undergoing a period of profound crisis. Some, if not all of the changes affecting the accounting profession, appear to be also affecting the other professions, notably law and medicine. Indeed, the question is whether or not the transformations in the professions represent the eclipse of professionalism, in general. In the next section, we offer a preliminary evaluation of this proposition and some of its political consequences.

PROFESSIONALISM ECLIPSED?
LEGITIMACY BEGGARED?

This semantic history of 'profession' suggests that the professions have an unstable relation to occupations. On the one hand, the professions are not identical to occupations because they are bounded by the discursive practices of a service orientation, formal knowledge, and associational self-regulation. On the other hand, precisely because the 'professions' are socially constructed, contested, and enforced over time to differ from mere 'occupations', the boundaries of differentiation are porous and shifting. Therefore, the cultural significance of the professions as such, is understood as a contingent consequence of socio-historical processes. And it is this possibility that has begun to summon the attention of some scholars. For instance, a well-known student of the professions has recently advanced the notion the professions have begun to lose their historical significance and political power (Krauss 1996). After comparing the fortunes of a number of professions, including medicine, law and teaching, across five countries, and over the sweep of the twentieth century, Krauss concludes that the professions have been captured and diminished by the impetus of globalized capitalist rationalization. Despite the significant differences between the political regimes of countries and the diverse configurations of professions, he sees a decisive weakening in what he calls the 'guild power' of the professions. Specifically, Krauss notes the variety of ways in which state bureaucrats and capitalist managers have encroached upon and modified four interrelated sources of professional or guild power: the nature and quality of professional associations; the control over professional work; the ability and power to define client and customer relations; and the ability to set the terms of the relation of the profession to the state (pp. 3–6).

Numerous other commentators are in broad agreement with the assessment that the professions are undergoing a deep-seated and fundamental transformation, largely under the joint impact of neo-liberal rationales of government and capitalist rationalization of the workplace (Perkins 1989; Brint 1994; Freidson 2001). To be sure, differing theoretical commitments, methods of study, professions studied, and countries, or time-periods examined, generate differences among scholars on the causes, consequences, and extent of change in the professions (e.g of such disputes concerning the accounting profession, see Dezalay 1995; Willmott and Sikka 1997; Walker 2000). Yet, these differences do not dispel the growing sense that the cultural significance of the professions has been dimmed. First, the notions of 'public interest' and 'common good' have been rendered almost meaningless by an overly economic understanding of the polity and society (Arrow 1951). Second, credentials or other attestations of learning are widely understood as signals to the job market, which have little to do with improving the ability or knowledge brought to the job (Spence 1973; Collins 1979). Third, the autonomy of professional at both the individual and collective levels has lost its sheen. The autonomy of professional judgement has been undermined by the discovery of the heuristics, biases, and irrationalities than afflict it no less than that of laypeople (Kahneman et al. 1982). The autonomy of collective self-regulation has been compromised by its failures. With all its claims so undermined, the professions appeared as little more than a monopolistic industry.

As noted above, academics have helped to propagate and cement this shift in cultural perception of the professional and the professions over the past half-century. Moreover, it is not only the perspective of academics that lends credence to the claim of an eclipse of professionalism in general, and of accounting professionalism in particular. Recently, professionals themselves have complained bitterly of the cultural diminishment of professionalism, including doctors (Eddy 1990), lawyers (Linowitz and Mayer 1996), and educators (Bok 2004). A common refrain in these complaints bemoans the increasing commercial ethos that has overshadowed the ideals of professionalism. In these accounts, which parallel that of Wyatt discussed earlier, the professionalism in question alludes to precisely the three historically shaped dimensions that constitute a profession: a service orientation, formal knowledge, and associational self-regulation. Such concerns with the fading distinctiveness of the professions do not seem to be overwrought. At the linguistic register, 'profession' is, once again, not distinct from 'occupation', whether of money-managers, hair-dressers, or doctors. The scholars' inability to specify criteria by which to define a profession partly reflects the indiscriminate use of the term to signify almost any kind of employment. Further, 'professional services' had already instituted a tension between selfless service and service for a fee. This continuing source of friction between an ideal of service and rank commercialism was played out in both the legal and the accounting professions (Previts and Merino 1979: 213–15). Crucially, the professions are no longer accorded the rare privilege in law, to erect barriers against competition. Since the last quarter of the twentieth century, the professions are increasingly treated as identical to trades or occupations under the law. Thus, for example, in *Goldfarb vs. Virginia State Bar* (1975) it was held that the legal profession should be subjected to the strictures of antitrust laws applicable to commercial entities. Where it was once sheltered from competition by the claim to serve the public interest, the legal profession can no longer fix prices to extract monopolistic rents. Under the shadow cast by that case, the old argument that the professional was one who was paid to work and did not work to be paid apparently held little sway with accountants who began to low-ball audits as loss leaders. Similarly, as suggested by the rulings of the Federal Trade Commission in 1990, the accounting profession was no longer disallowed from charging commissions and contingent fees for all their services. Moreover, accounting firms could carry trade names instead of the names of partners, in keeping with the notion that accounting was more of an 'industry' than a profession. Neither professional nor legal strictures prevented the accounting profession from advertising its wares, once debated as evidence of self-praise unbecoming a professional. In addition, the growing size and reach of professional firms with the inevitable bureaucratization of work that implies; the proliferation of services offered which fragments the identity of a profession; and the continuing multiplication and fracturing of professional associations into contending specializations, can all be also adduced in contributing to the eclipse of the accounting profession, and *a fortiori*, of professionalism in accounting.

One measure of the eclipse of professionalism by commercial and rationalizing imperatives is the spread of numerical regimes of government, a well-documented event of recent decades (Rose 1991; Hood 1995; Power 1999). To render human activity calculable is arguably the foundational logic of modern accounting (Hoskins and Macve 1986, 1988). The explosion of accounting and auditing procedures into diverse new arenas, including government and non-profit organizations, law firms, hospitals, and universities, has subjected these sites to an ongoing and increasing slew of performance, productivity, and efficiency metrics based on accounting data. In large part, the justification for such use of accounting numbers is to banish or minimize the subjectivity of personal opinion and rule. Historically, experts became professionals when construed as objective, not only because they wielded numbers or because they were disinterested, but also because their learned judgments were beyond the reach of numerical representation (Covaleski et al. 1995, 1997). This new intensity in the spread of calculative practices of management into zones of professionalism has nevertheless revealed a paradoxical core. On the one hand, encapsulating 'professional judgement' in the algebra of efficiency, whether that of doctors, lawyers, or indeed accountants themselves, tarnishes the image of the professional. Symbolically at least, subjecting professional judgment to an accounting calculus says that the professional work is no less calculable than that of a line worker. On the other hand, the spreading regime of accountability entails the centrality of the accounting profession (*Economist*, 2003). The credibility of a regime of numerical governance, administered by accountants, and verified by auditors, presupposes their objective and disinterested stance inasmuch as such governance is propagated to further impersonal modes of government. That is, the use of accounting and auditing techniques to commercialize and rationalize professional practice contributes to enfeebling professions into occupations. After all, the fabrication of trust in numbers is won at the expense of the distrust in persons (Porter 1995). But it does so, only on the presumption that accounting and auditing are themselves imbued by professionalism. Thus, the demand for professionalism in accounting, which is itself a vector of deprofessionalization, is paradoxical and, for the reasons discussed earlier, suspect.

Consequently, we interpret the explosion in accounting and auditing methods to professional practice as representing a *seventh* moment in the modern history of the profession. The 'profession' was once a synonym for 'trade', 'occupation', or 'employment'. Over the late eighteenth and increasingly through the nineteenth centuries, it was differentiated from these latter on the grounds of a service orientation, formal knowledge, and autonomous governance. However, as with any historical phenomenon that has a beginning, the professions can also come to an end. In their historical configuration, the end of the professions would be signaled by a de-differentiation along all of the three dimensions that have constituted them. There is growing evidence of such a development, as already suggested ealier. The spreading regime of numerical governance then appears as a correlate to the eclipse of professionalism. Accordingly, the continued spread of accounting and audit techniques could well reflect that moment in which the professions are once again identified with occupations, its historical project of differentiation having come to an end.

It is in the light of such an eclipse of professions that the recent calls to professionalism and its defense should perhaps be heard. There are many such voices in sociology, management, and accounting (Kaplan 1987; Brint 1994; Zeff 2003*a*; see also Khurana [2007] for a plea to the business school faculty to rekindle professionalism). Nevertheless, we focus on the writings of Elliot Freidson, the noted historian and sociologist of the medical profession, who in a recent book, places what he calls the 'professional logic' at the center of his analysis (Freidson 2001). Exercised by the declining 'status of professions in advanced industrial society', he attempts to defend the professions by contrasting them with unregulated markets on the one hand, and bureaucratic organizations on the other. What is noteworthy about his analysis is his new emphasis on the service ethic of the professions. He states that it is 'devotion to a transcendent value', as for example, 'Justice, Salvation, Beauty,

Truth, Health and Prosperity', and the right to serve these values without interference from patrons, clients, or the state, that properly bespeaks a profession (p. 122). In contrast, in his prior work he demarcates the professions by the characteristics of self-regulation, formal knowledge and credentials, the latter two of which serve to give professions an economic advantage by protecting them from free-market competition (Freidson 1984). In that previous account, he makes little mention of the professions' claim to serve the public interest. It is a measure of the extent of his present disquiet concerning the 'assault on professionalism' that he feels the need to speak of transcendent values in his most recent defense of the professions. Less dramatic are the observations of other such sociologists as Leicht and Lyman (2006) who, in supporting Freidson's professional logic while providing evidence against it, are reduced to hoping that it come to fruition (p. 40). Similarly, in the accounting literature, calls to renew professionalism have implicated the theological notion of 'covenant' (Peace 2006), and those of 'virtue' and 'gentlemanly conduct' (McMillan 2004; see also Levitt 2000). These invocations not only confirm the theological roots of the modern professions but also suggest that something more is at stake in the possible eclipse of professionalism. Indeed, it may be that the legitimacy of liberal-democratic regimes is tied to that of the professions.

Therefore, there is good reason for accounting researchers to explore the political consequences of the atrophy of professionalism and the professions. As historians have suggested, the rush to professionalization in the United States occurred during the last quarter of the nineteenth century, in no small measure due to the onset of industrial society (Weibe 1967; Hays 1995). It was in response to the social problem caused by rapid industrialization that prompted contemporary observers such as Tawney, Durkheim, and Dewey to advocate for the expert management of society and economy. For these commentators, the professions were necessary not only to manage the complexities of technological society, but also because they did so in an anti-capitalist and anti-statist key (Haskell 1984). The diagram of professional power, which contrasts the professions to the market and the state or bureaucracy, was precisely what was the subject of political reflection during the turn of the last century. To one side, stood the unregulated forces of free-markets where competitive spirits were harnessed to the pecuniary self-interest. To the other side, stood the State that could totalize the field of society through regulations in the public interest. Almost as a solution to a mathematical puzzle, the professions were thought of as the key to unlock the dilemma facing the US political ideology at the time: How to regulate market forces without instigating communism, socialism, or widespread government regulations? Professions located within the zone of civil society and making judgements of public import in order to promote the public interest was seen as a neat solution to that conundrum of political ideology. It was to serve as a conduit of regulating market forces without invoking the powers of the state that the production of professionalism was fostered on two registers: at the level of government through the professionalization of the civil service, and at the level of society, through the propagation of a variety of professions. This was the historical frame for what commentators have called the implicit 'social contract' between society and the professions (Haber 1991). The professions are granted shelter from competition and resulting monopoly rents, the authority and honor of elite status in society, and the right to self-regulation for the *quid pro quo* of serving the public interest. An occupation too closely intertwined with its clients or the state cannot credibly claim to represent the public interest (Chatov 1985; Coffee 2006). An occupation that does not serve the public interest, even if only in name, does not fit into the historical frame of what constitutes the professions.

We suspect that the calls to revive professionalism in the face of the eclipse of professionalism are rooted in the not yet fully expressed recognition of this political role of the professions in liberal democracies. Both critics such as Larson (1977) and Fischer (1990), or champions such as Freidson (2001) and Halmos (1970), accept the necessity of expert knowledge for the management and control of technological society. Precisely because they occupy a liminal space between the public and the private without being fully one or the other, the professions have served to legitimize the necessary rule of the experts. Inasmuch as industrial society demands the rule of experts and does so in a democratic key, the professions serve as a ballast that keeps liberal-democratic ideology afloat. Despite the many valuable studies of how the professions in general, and the accounting profession in particular, have been socially constructed, contested, and contingently established over time, there is little reflection as yet on how to square a seeming circle: What will be the source of political legitimacy for expert rule should professionalism be permanently eclipsed? What legitimizes the accountants once accounting becomes an industry?

REFERENCES

Abbott, A. (1988). *The System of Professions*. Chicago: University of Chicago Press.
AICPA. (2000). AICPA announces new information credential. *The CPA Letter*, 3 May.
Anderson-Gough, F., Grey, C., and Robson, K. (2000). *Making up Accountants: The Professional and Organizational Socialization of Trainee Chartered Accountants*. Aldershot: Ashgate.

Arrow, K. (1951). *Social Choice and Individual Values.* New Haven: Yale University Press.

Bealing, W., Dirsmith, M., and Fogarty, T. (1996). Early regulatory action by the SEC: An institutional theory perspective on the dramaturgy of exchange relations. *Accounting, Organizations and Society,* 21, 317–38.

Beard, V. (1994). Popular culture and professional identity: Accountants in the movies. *Accounting, Organizations and Society,* 19, 303–18.

Bedard, J. (1989). Expertise in auditing: myth or reality. *Accounting, Organizations and Society,* 14, 113–31.

Beresford, D. (2005). Accounting professionalism: Do we get it? Available online at http://www.trinity.edu/rjensen/theory/00overview/BeresfordAAAspeech2005.htm

Bok, Derek. (2004). *Universities in the Marketplace: The Commercialization of Higher Education.* Princeton: Princeton University Press.

Bougen, P. (1994). Joking apart: The serious side of the accountant stereotype. *Accounting, Organizations and Society,* 19, 319–35.

Brint, S. (1994). *In an Age of Experts.* Princeton: Princeton University Press.

Byington, J.R., and Sutton, S.G. (1991). The self-regulating profession: An analysis of the political monopoly of the audit profession. *Critical Perspectives on Accounting,* 2, 315–30.

Carpenter, B. and Dirsmith, M.W. (1993). Sampling and the abstraction of knowledge in the auditing profession: An extended institutional theory perspective. *Accounting, Organizations, and Society,* 18, 41–63

———— and Gupta, P. (1994). Materiality judgments and audit firm culture: Social-behavioral and political perspectives. *Accounting, Organizations, and Society,* 19, 355–80.

Carr-Saunders, A.M., and Wilson, P.A. (1933). *The Professions.* Oxford: The Clarendon Press.

Chatov, R. (1985). The possible new shape of accounting in the United States. *Journal of Accounting and Public Policy,* 4, 161–74.

Coffee, J. (2006). *Gatekeepers: The Professions and Corporate Governance.* Oxford: Oxford University Press.

Collins, R. (1979). *Credential Society: Historical sociology of Education and stratification,* NY: Academic Press.

Cooper, D. and Robson, K. (2006). Accounting, professions and regulation: Locating the sites of professionalization. *Accounting, Organizations, and Society,* 31, 415–44.

Covaleski, M., Dirsmith, M.W., and Samuel, S. (1995). The use of accounting information in governmental regulation and public administration: The impact of John R. Commons and early institutional economists. *Accounting Historians Journal,* 22, 1–33.

———— (1997). A strategic deconstruction of John. R. Commons' regulatory discourse. *Journal of Economic Issues,* 31, 1–28.

—— —— Heian, J., and Samuel, S. (1998). The calculated and the avowed: Techniques of discipline and struggles over identity in big 6 accounting firms. *Administrative Science Quarterly,* 43, 293–327.

———— and Rittenberg, L. (2003). Jurisdictional disputes over professional work. *Accounting, Organizations, and Society,* 28, 323–55.

Derber, C., Schwartz, W.A., and Magrass, Y. (1990). *Power in the Highest Degree: Professionals and the Rise of a New Mandarin Order.* Oxford: Oxford University Press.

Dezalay, Y. (1995). 'Turf battles' or 'class struggles': The internationalization of the market for expertise in the 'professional society. *Accounting, Organizations, and Society,* 20, 331–44.

Dingwall, R. (2008). *Essay on Professions.* Hampshire: Ashgate.

Dirsmith, M.W., and Haskins, M. (1991). Inherent risk assessment and audit firm technology: A contrast in world theories. *Accounting, Organizations, and Society,* 16, 61–92.

———— (2007). The linguistic relatively hypothesis applied to Big 5 (4) public accounting firms' assessments of client internal control. *Human Organization,* 66, 438–52.

——Heian, J.B., and Covaleski, M. (1997). Structure and agency in an institutional setting: The application and social transformation of control in the big six. *Accounting, Organization and Society,* 22, 1–27.

Economist. (2003). The future of accounts. *Economist,* 23 April.

Eddy, D.M. (1990). The challenge. *Journal of the American Medical Association,* 263, 287–90.

Elliot, R.K. (1999). Remarks of Robert K. Elliott incoming AICPA chair, Seattle. Available online at www.AICPA.org/news/elliot.htm2000 (as seen on 1 August 2002).

Felker, N. (2003). The origins of the SEC's position on auditor independence and management responsibility for financial reports. *Research in Accounting Regulation,* 16, 45–60.

Fischer, F. (1990). *Technocracy and the Politics of Expertise.* London: Sage.

Fischer, M. (1996). Real-izing the benefits of new technologies as a source of audit evidence: An interpretive field study. *Accounting Organizations and Society,* 21, 219–42.

——and Dirsmith, M.W. (1995). Strategy, technology, and social processes within professional cultures: A negotiated order, ethnographic perspective. *Symbolic Interaction,* 18, 381–412.

Fogarty, T. (1992). Organizational sociology in accounting firms: A theoretical framework and agenda for future research. *Accounting, Organizations and Society,* 17, 129–49.

—— (1996). The imagery and reality of peer review in the US: Insights from institutional theory. *Accounting, Organizations and Society,* 21, 243–67.

——Zucca, L., Meonske, N., and Kirch, D. (1997). Proactive practice review: A critical case study of accounting regulation that never was. *Critical Perspectives on Accounting,* 8, 167–87.

Freidman, A., and Lyne, S. (2001). The beancounter stereotype: Towards a general model of stereotype generation. *Critical Perspectives on Accounting,* 12, 423–51.

Freidson, E. (1984). Are professions necessary? In T.L. Haskell (ed.), *The Authority of Experts.* Bloomington: Indiana University Press, 3–27.

—— (1986). *Professional Powers: A Study of the Institutionalization of Formal Knowledge.* Chicago: University of Chicago Press.

—— (2001). *Professionalism: The Third Logic.* Chicago: University of Chicago Press.

Goode, W. (1961). The librarian: From occupation to profession? *The Library Quarterly*, 31, 306–18.

Greenwood, R., and Suddaby, R. (2006). Professional service firms. *Research in the Sociology of Organizations 24*. London: JAI Press.

Grey, C. (1998). On being a professional in a big six firm. *Accounting, Organization and Society*, 5, 479–97.

Haber, S. (1991). *The Quest for Authority and Honor in the American Professions, 1750–1900*. Chicago: Chicago University Press.

Hall, P.D. (1984). The social foundations of professional credibility: Linking the medical profession to higher education in Connecticut and Massachusetts, 1700–1830. In T.L. Haskell (ed.), *The Authority of Experts*. Bloomington: Indiana University Press, 107–41.

Halmos, P. (1970). *The Personal Service Society*. New York: Schocken Books.

Haskell, T.L. (1984). Professionalism versus capitalism: R.H. Tawney, Emile Durkheim, and C.S. Pierce on the disinterestedness of professional communities. In T.L. Haskell (ed.), *The Authority of Experts*. Bloomington: Indiana University Press, 180–225.

Hays, S. (1995). *The Response to Industrialism: 1885–1914*. Chicago: University of Chicago Press.

Hines, R. D. (1989). Financial accounting knowledge, conceptual framework projects, and the social construction of the accounting profession. *Accounting, Auditing and Accountability*, 2, 72–92.

Hood, C. (1995). The 'new public management' in the 1980s: variations on a theme. *Accounting, Organizations and Society*, 20, 93–109.

Hopwood, A. (1994). Accounting and everyday life: An introduction. *Accounting, Organizations and Society*, 19, 299–301.

Hoskins, K., and Macve, R. (1986). Accounting and the examination: A genealogy of disciplinary power. *Accounting, Organizations and Society*, 11, 105–36.

——— (1988). The genesis of accountability: The west point connection. *Accounting, Organizations and Society*, 13, 37–73.

Humphrey, C., and Moizer, P. (1990). From techniques to ideologies: an alternative perspective on the audit function. *Critical Perspectives on Accounting*, 1, 217–38.

Jeacle, I. (2007). Beyond the boring grey: The construction of the colorful accountant. *Critical Perspectives on Accounting*, doi:10.1016/j.cpa.2007.02.08.

Johnson, T.J. (1972). *Professions and Power*. London: MacMillan.

Kahneman, D., Slovic, P., and Tversky, A. (1982). *Judgment under Uncertainty: Heuristics and Biases*. Cambridge: Cambridge University Press.

Kaplan, R.L. (1987). Accountants' liability and audit failures: When the umpire strikes out. *Journal of Accounting and Public Policy*, 6, 1–8.

Ketz, E. (2008). Are derivatives too complex? Is it time to regulate their use? Available online at http://accounting.smartpros.com/x61241.xml (as seen on 17 July 2008).

Khurana, R. (2007). *From Higher Aims to Hired Hands: The Social Transformation of American Business Schools and the Unfulfilled Promise of Anagement as a Profession*. Princeton: Princeton University Press.

Kimball, B. (1995). *The 'True Professional Ideal' in America*. Maryland: Rowan and Littlefield.

Krauss, E. (1996). *Death of the Guilds: Professions, States, and the Advance of Capitalism, 1930 to the Present*. New Haven: Yale University Press.

Larson, M.S. (1977). *The Rise of Professionalism: A Sociological Analysis*. Berkeley: University of Berkeley Press.

—— and Lyman, E. (2006). Markets, institutions, and the crisis of professional practice. In R. Greenwood, and R. Suddaby (eds.), *Professional Service Firms: Research in the Sociology of Organizations, vol. 24*. New York: Elsevier Press, 17–44.

Levitt, A. (2000). Renewing the covenant with investors. Speech before the New York University Center for Law and Business, 10 May. Available online at www.sec.gov/news/speeches/spch370.htm

Linowitz, S., and Mayer, M. (1996). *The Betrayed Profession: Lawyering at the End of the 20th Century*. Baltimore: Johns Hopkins University Press.

Maltby, J. (2000). The origins of prudence in accounting. *Critical Perspectives on Accounting*, 11, 51–70.

Marty, E.M. (1988). The Clergy. In N.O. Hatch (ed.), *The Professions in American History*. Notre Dame: University of Notre Dame Press, 73–91.

McCain, J. (2008). Available online at http://www.johnmccain.com/Informing/News/Speeches/bea72b48–35ba-48cb-8cea-b3b68b9be7ee.htm (as seen on 1 August 2008).

McEnroe, J.E., and Pitman, M.K. (2003). An analysis of the accounting profession's oligarchy: The accounting standards board. *Research in Accounting Regulation*, 16, 29–44.

McMillan, K. (2004). Trust and the virtues: A solution to the accounting scandals. *Critical Perspectives on Accounting*, 15, 943–95.

Merino, B., and Mayper, A. (2001). Securities legislation and the accounting profession in the 1930s: The rhetoric and reality of the American dream. *Critical Perspectives on Accounting*, 12, 501–25.

Millerson, G. (1964). Dilemmas of professionalism. *New Society*, 4, 1–15.

Mills, P.A., and Young, J.J. (1999). From contract to speech: The courts and CPA licensing laws 1921–1996. *Accounting, Organizations, and Society*, 24, 243–62.

Moore, W.E., and Rosenblum, G.W. (1970). *The Professions: Roles and Rules*. New York: Russell Sage Foundation.

Parsons, T. (1968). Professions. *International Encyclopedia of the Social Sciences, vol. 12*. New York: Macmillan Press, 436–547.

Peace, R. (2006). Accountants and a religious covenant with the public. *Critical Perspectives on Accounting*, 17, 781–97.

Perkins, H. (1989). *The Rise of Professional Society: England since 1880*. London: Routledge.

Pentland, B.T. (1993). Getting comfortable with the numbers: auditing and micro-production of macro-order, *Accounting, Organizations and Society*, 18, 605–20.

Porter, T. (1995). *Trust in Numbers*. Princeton: Princeton University Press.

Power, M. (1992). From common-sense to expertise: Reflections on the prehistory of audit sampling. *Accounting, Organizations, and Society*, 17, 37–62.

——(1996). Making things auditable. *Accounting, Organizations, and Society*, 21, 289–315.

——(1999). *The Audit Society: Rituals of Verification*. Oxford: Oxford University Press.

Power, M. (2003). Auditing and the production of legitimacy. *Accounting, Organizations and Society*, 28, 379–94.

Previts, G.J. and Merino, B.D. (1979). *A History of Accounting in America: An Historical Interpretation of the Cultural Significance of Accounting*. New York: Ronald Press.

Reed, M. (1996). Expert power and control in late modernity: An empirical review and theoretical synthesis. *Organization Studies*, 17, 573–97.

Robson, K., Willmott, H., Cooper, D., and Puxty, T. (1994). The ideology of professional regulation and the markets for accounting labor: Three episodes in the recent history of the UK accountancy profession. *Accounting, Organizations and Society*, 19, 527–53.

——Humphrey, C., Khalifa, R., and Jones, J. (2007). Transforming audit technologies: Business risk audit methodologies and the audit field. *Accounting, Organizations, and Society*, 32, 409–38.

Rose, N. (1991). Governing by numbers: figuring out democracy. *Accounting, Organizations and Society*, 16, 673–92.

Ross, D. (1991). *The Origins of American Social Science*. Cambridge: Cambridge University Press.

Roubini, N. (2008). Ten fundamental issues in reforming financial regulations and supervision in a world of financial innovation and globalization. Avaliable online at http://media.rgemonitor.com/papers/0/Nouriel-RegulationSupervision-March08.pdf (as seen on 7 August 2008).

Smith, G.S. (1990). Privileged communications, independence, and client advocacy: A perspective on professionalism. *Journal of Accounting and Public Policy*, 9, 135–57.

Sorkin, A. (2008). Dimon vs Schwarzman: The great accounting debate. Avaliable online at http://dealbook.blogs.nytimes.com/2008/07/09/dimon-vs-schwarzman-the-great-accounting-debate/ (as seen on 1 August 2008).

Spence, M.A. (1973). Job market signaling. *Quarterly Journal of Economics*, 84, 355–74.

Thornburg, S., and Roberts, R. (2008). Money, politics, and the regulation of public accounting services: Evidence from the Sarbanes-Oxley Act of 2002. *Accounting, Organizations and Society*, 33, 229–48.

Tinker, A.M. (1985). *Paper Prophets*. New York: Praeger.

Veysey, L. (1965). *The Emergence of the American University*. Chicago: University of Chicago Press.

——(1988). Higher education as a profession: Changes and continuities. In N.O. Hatch (ed.), *The Professions in American History*. Indiana: University of Notre Dame Press, 15–32.

Walker, S. (2000). Benign sacerdotalist or pious assailant: The rise of the professional accountant in British management. *Accounting, Organizations, and Society*, 25, 313–23.

Washington Post. (2008). Credit crises triggers unprecedented response. Available online at http://www.washingtonpost.com/wp-dyn/content/article/2008/08/08/AR2008080803415.html?nav=rss_business (as seen on 9 August 2008).

Wiebe, R. (1967). *The Search for Order: 1977–1920.* New York: Hill and Wang.

Willmott, H. (1986). Organizing the profession: A theoretical and historical examination of the development of the major accountancy bodies in the UK *Accounting, Organizations and Society,* 11, 555–80.

—— and Sikka, P. (1997). On the commercialization of accountancy thesis: A review essay. *Accounting, Organizations, and Society,* 22, 831–42.

Wyatt, A. (2003). Accounting professionalism: They just don't get it! Available online at http://aaahq.org/AM2003/WyattSpeech.pdf (as seen on 1 May 2008).

Zeff, S.A. (2003*a*). How the US accounting profession got where it is today: Part I. *Accounting Horizons,* 17, 189–205.

—— (2003*b*). How the US accounting profession got where it is today: Part II. *Accounting Horizons,* 17, 267–86.

18

All Offshore: The Sprat, the Mackerel,
Accounting Firms, and the State in
Globalization

Prem Sikka and Hugh Willmott

... [The] accountancy profession in the United Kingdom was born in the
context of government regulation of an intervention in the economy, and
has continued to flourish in that context. Difficulties associated with the
administration of the bankruptcy laws of the State provided a powerful
incentive for the formation of a professional institute. Thereafter the
profession developed in the context of a market for audit services that
was to become legally required, and eventually gained a legal monopoly
in its provision.... So much of the work of professional accountants
resides within the interstices of State interventionist policies, not only
in areas such as taxation and corporate restructuring, but also in their
capacity as applied economic consultants, specialists in compilation of
economic data and intelligence.

Even though it is difficult to understand the contemporary significance of
the accountancy profession in the United Kingdom without appreciating
its mutual intertwining with the modern conception of the State, the
profession itself has adopted a most entrepreneurial stance. It has repeatedly done what it has not done before... (Hopwood 1985: 13–14)

The intertwined relationships between accounting, accountancy bodies,
accounting firms, and the state[1] have been an under-explored theme in the
accounting literature. Accounting calculations play a major part in levying
taxes, regulating property rights, managing wars, promoting financial discipline in the public sector, and even persuading private capital to provide a
particular kind of public accountability. The state has long used accounting

---

[1] The state is best understood as an ensemble of institutional structures that have co-evolved
with the contradictory pressures and demands of a capitalist economy. The government, courts,
the church, law enforcement agencies and professional associations are examples of such
institutional structures (Gramsci 1971).

calculations to manage and displace recurring crises of capitalism. It has even been suggested that 'how the concept of capitalism was invented is an example of the influence of accounting ideas...' (Chiapello 2007: 264). In short, accounting is central to capitalism as a mode of production that, in its advanced form, exists in a mutually dependent and antagonistic relationship to the state, as a medium and outcome of the formation and reproduction of capitalism.

There is a complex and contradictory relationship between the state and the accounting industry. In the UK context, accountants have successfully mobilized powers of the state to secure markets, niches, and monopolies to earn economic rents. Often the state has been instrumental in (re)formulating accounting and auditing regulation and preserving forms of self-regulation (Sikka et al. 1989). The state has used the services of accounting firms to restructure the public sector and privatize many industries. This seems to have coincided with a reluctance to expose major accounting firms to public scrutiny. For example, the state has suppressed critical reports and demonstrated unwillingness to investigate anti-social practices (Sikka and Willmott 1995; Mitchell et al. 1998). Exceptionally, when the activities of accounting firms have threatened tax revenues and with it the operations of the state's machinery, the state has occasionally investigated and prosecuted major accounting firms (Sikka 2008*a*).

Globalization has added new complexities to the relationship between the state and capital. Whilst the state is primarily confined to a defined geographical jurisdiction, capital is free to roam the world and shop for possibilities of lower costs, regulation, and liabilities. Major corporations have often been able to persuade smaller states to enact desirable legislation. In turn, corporations have used this as a lever to squeeze concessions from larger states and reconfigure the economic and regulatory environment (Hampton and Abbott 1999; Palan 2002). Such strategies are dependent upon the availability of political and financial resources and accounting firms seem to have considerable supply of both, especially as accounting firms are a significant fraction of capital and the UK state has on occasion sought competitive advantage for local firms by refusing to cooperate with regulators from other countries (Arnold and Sikka 2001).

How relationships between accounting and the state develop are, it seems, contingent upon the formation of specific economies and, increasingly, upon institutional standardization initiatives pursued by global accounting firms and advanced capitalist states. The world of auditing is dominated by just four big firms (PricewaterhouseCoopers, KPMG, Deloitte & Touche, and Ernst & Young) whose combined global income of $96 billion[2] is exceeded

---

[2] As per the most recent reviews on their respective websites; as seen on 7 November 2008.

by the gross domestic product of only 55 nations.[3] In common with other fractions of capital, they too roam the world in search of opportunities to reduce their costs, increase revenues and swell profits. One, increasingly significant and growing aspect of their business concerns the provision of assistance in exploiting opportunities for profit enhancement presented by micro states commonly known as tax havens or offshore financial centres (OFCs) which offer lighter regulation, low/no tax and confidentiality. In providing a haven for capital, OFCs have rapidly grown in importance to become a 'cornerstone of the process of globalization' (Palan et al. 1996: 180) and thereby introduce a new dimension and related complexities to theories of the state and dynamics of the state-accounting firm relationship.

This chapter explores some trajectories in the relationship between the state and accounting firms by examining an episode in the auditor liability debate that gained fresh momentum in the United Kingdom in the mid-1990s. When major firms considered the UK state to be insufficiently responsive to their lobbying for the limitation of their liability, they exerted pressures upon the UK government by privately arranging for the drafting of a Limited Liability Partnership (LLP) Bill with the intention of persuading the government of Jersey, a small offshore financial centre, to enact the law so as to create a favourable liability regime. This strategic manoeuvre, we suggest, is illustrative of the 'entrepreneurial stance' cited in Hopwood's quotation at the beginning of this chapter and accounting firms' preparedness to do what they have 'not done before' in pursuit of a desirable environment, in this case a more benign and financially beneficial regulatory environment. It is, however, just one example of the numerous occasions on which the state has been mobilized to grant, preserve or enhance a number of privileges, including liability concessions, to auditing firms.

The chapter is divided into three further sections. The following section offers a perspective on the state–capital relationship that takes account of the globalization of economic activity including the expansion of accounting services in the context of the emergence of OFCs. We then look at the state–firm relationship through the lens of debates about auditor liability. Attention is drawn to a number of liability concessions granted to auditing firms by the UK state before providing details of the way the firms mobilized Jersey in pursuit of a more advantageous regulatory regime. The final section discusses the significance of the case for the state–accounting firm relationship.

---

[3] As per World Bank (http://siteresources.worldbank.org/DATASTATISTICS/Resources/ GDP.pdf).

STATE, CAPITAL, AND GLOBALIZATION

There are wide-ranging debates about the nature and concept of the state (Dunleavy and O'Leary 1987; Jessop 1990, 2002). Here we follow the assessment that 'the meaning of the state has shifted dramatically over the last thirty years and that the main forcing agent in that shift has been something called "globalization" (whatever that may mean)' (Harvey 2006: xvii). Whilst the significance and extent of globalization is contested by scholars (for a discussion, see Hirst and Thompson 1996; Stiglitz 2002; Bhagwati 2004; Saul 2005), there is considerable agreement over its association with the accelerating mobility of goods, services, capital, commodities, information, and communications across national frontiers (Robinson 2004). Such mobility has been promoted by a particular, neoliberal hegemony that prioritizes market-driven competition as the preferred mechanism of resource generation and allocation while admitting a subsidiary role for the state in supporting an infrastructure geared to supporting this priority (Harvey 2000). A neoliberal order is not, then, one in which the state is entirely hollowed out (the aspiration of laissez faire liberalism). Rather, it is an order in which allocation through the market is systematically privileged, as manifest in forms of privatization and deregulation. The state is reconstructed, not dismantled, as an emphasis upon regulation to protect the vulnerable from risk is counterbalanced by its use to stimulate and facilitate private sector expansion. With this change of emphasis comes a greater preparedness to weaken regulations (e.g. credit restrictions) that protect the vulnerable when these regulations are assessed to impede or penalize profitable private sector growth (Klimecki and Willmott 2008).

As a consequence of demutualizations and privatizations, the contemporary neoliberal state is largely excluded from direct involvement in the productive economic sphere, although recent events have made the state a reluctant acquisitor of a very substantial part of the banking sector (Elliott and Atkinson 2008). In principle, its role is to provide a legal and social framework that sanctifies private property; to supply public goods using private sector sub-contractors where possible; and to secure public order by dispensing bourgeois justice. Maintaining this framework requires revenues raised through taxes on wages, savings, and profits as well as goods and services—revenues that depend upon the activities of private businesses as employers and also public confidence in their practices and social obligations.

The state's dependence on capital to stimulate economic activity has made capital's welfare—notably, in the form of supportive and permissive de/regulation—a central plank of domestic and foreign policies. As Hutton (1999) puts it, 'The City [of London] has not just been the citadel of free financial markets; it has been the prime beneficiary of the most determined industrial policy sustained continuously by the British state in any branch of economic activity. Law, taxation, regulation, and economic policy have been bent to suit its needs' (p. 61), with, it might be added, the recent socialization of its losses being the latest twist in this process (Elliott and Atkinson 2008). The activities of the neoliberal state are dedicated primarily to stabilizing, enhancing the politico-economic context of business activity through a variety of de/regulatory and, when required, salvationary mechanisms.

Such mechanisms do not rely, in the first instance, upon naked coercion but instead depend upon processes of moral and cultural leadership provided by the institutions of civil society (Gramsci 1971), notably education and the media and extending to the legitimating expertise provided by inter alia accounting firms. That is to say, the neoliberal project requires (popular) legitimation from below in the form of, for example, a rising material standard of living, a sense of increasing personal wealth or, most recently, an understanding that opposition to bailing out the banks with public funds would be most disadvantageous to the very people — the ordinary taxpayer — who will pay for the funding with higher taxes and/or a deterioration in public services. The project of neo-liberalism is however, endemically problematic as the state faces competing demands from constituent elements of civil society as well as from fractions of capital. Faced with numerous, contradictory pressures, responses are politically expedient rather than rationally consistent. So, on occasion, pressures from some fractions of capital (e.g. to allow markets to eliminate the weak and to avoid 'moral hazards') may be resisted in preference for policies aimed at increasing public confidence in capitalism (e.g. to place failed banks, such as Northern Rock, in public ownership).

We stressed earlier how nation states increasingly form part of an interdependent global system of states. Some commentators have argued that the contemporary neoliberal celebration of free trade, intensification of competition, lowering of trade barriers, removal of exchange controls, and the accompanying increase in flows of capital and density of corporate networks heralds a slow death of the nation state (Ohmae 1995). Yet, even in processes of globalization, states remain key actors. Attentive to the constraints of domestic politics and institutional structures, states cooperate politically and economically. Their coalition may reconstruct sovereignty but it is also intended to protect or increase their capacity to secure local capital and attract mobile capital. Forms of economic and political cooperation between

otherwise antagonistic states are designed to create an environment conducive to the welfare of capital and thereby to finance the continuing supply of
social order and basic public goods. Of course, these outcomes cannot be
guaranteed as corporations have 'no intrinsic commitment to product, to
place, to country, or to type of economic activity. The commitment is to the
accumulation of capital. Therefore, the capitalist will shift locus of economic
engagement (product, place, country, type of activity) as shifts occur in
the opportunities to maximize revenues from undertaking' (Wallerstein
1996: 89). Nonetheless, states collectively, as well as individually, are engaged
in securing and enhancing the conditions (e.g. permissive company law and
labour legislation) that improve the prospects of retaining or attracting
capital investment as a condition of possibility of sustaining the economic
activity that funds public goods.

One key way in which the mobility of capital is facilitated and accelerated is
through policies that enable business vehicles to enjoy a relative freedom of
incorporation. Such vehicles can originate in one country, but be used to
trade in others. Businesses can also own vehicles in other countries and
collaborate with local networks to develop profitable opportunities. This
enhanced capacity to exit, with the threat of economic turbulence that
accompanies it, gives corporations considerable direct and indirect influence
over government policies as the prospect of possible capital flight or strikes is
factored into the policy-making process. Of most relevance for the present
chapter, the increased mobility and associated leverage of capital on governments has been assisted by policies pursued by OFCs.

Offshore Financial Centres (OFCs)

By the late 1990s, OFCs were estimated to hold about 50 per cent of all cross-
border assets (International Monetary Fund 2000). Almost one-third of the
world's Gross Domestic Product (GDP) and half of global monetary stock
passed through them at some stage (Oxfam 2000). OFCs have often been
established in micro, often small islands, states occupying a peripheral
position in global markets. Lacking significant natural, human, diplomatic
or military resources to develop their economies, such micro states have
opted to specialize in developing a low-tax, lightly regulated jurisdictions
for *inter alia* registering companies and investing in offshore funds. Historically, these states have relied upon such industries as agriculture and tourism
but these sources of income are difficult to sustain in the face of competition
from low-wage developing countries. When low growth and incomes failed to
meet the economic aspirations of their citizens, the response by a number of

micro states has been to mobilize the asset of sovereignty with its law-making powers to charge rents for sheltering capital in a haven of anonymity, low taxes, and light regulation (Hampton and Abbott 1999; Donaghy and Clarke 2003).

Key to the success of OFCs has been the development of policies allowing non-residents to escape regulation. This has provoked the accusation that OFCs 'auction off their sovereignty to the highest bidder, reaping great rewards in the process...' (Drezner 2001: 76–7) and enact 'laws with the sole purpose of getting around the laws of other countries [and] sell their sovereignty and their law to the highest bidder' (*Guardian*, 2 May 2000). In larger, established states, the neoliberal pressures to erode or sell off sovereignty (e.g. deregulation) in an effort to entice or retain capital can be somewhat mitigated by civil pressures to incorporate consideration of other constituencies (e.g. trades unions, the consumers of public services). In contrast, in OFCs such countervailing pressures are often weak, even to the point that key beneficiaries of changes in the law are permitted to draft laws with little public scrutiny (Naylor 1987).

The legal facilities offered by OFCs are designed to be attractive to capital. In integrated world markets, businesses do not have to uproot and relocate their entire operations because most countries have accepted the principle that 'legal persons could reside concomitantly in a number of jurisdictions' (Palan 2002: 72). Once established, this principle has created 'the risk that they would go shopping for the best bundles of regulation they could find' (ibid.). Shopping for the best regulation deal is facilitated by networks of lawyers and business advisers who specialize in legally permissible ways of avoiding regulation (McCahery and Picciotto 1995). Many businesses have improved and extended their regulatory options by establishing or renting residences in OFCs so as to take advantage of the diverse legal choices on offer.

Needless to say, regulatory arbitrage has the capacity to undermine and destabilize the regulatory regimes developed by other states which find themselves under intensified pressures to offer regulatory concessions in order to retain capital within their jurisdiction. In the following section, we illustrate this phenomenon by reference to the politics of auditor liability arrangements. Accounting firms in the United Kingdom have historically relied upon the state to secure liability concessions. With the intensification of globalization and the opportunities that it presents, the possibility of transferring activities to an alternative jurisdiction, in the form of an OFC, has provided an additional, potent weapon in the arsenal of accounting firms seeking to minimize their liabilities.

STATE AND ACCOUNTING FIRMS

Our analysis of the pressure exerted upon UK state regulators by the attempt to secure limited liability in an OFC is appropriately situated in a history of patronage from the UK state which has enabled accountants to secure prestige, niches, markets and eventually a state guaranteed monopoly of the external audit function. Accountants, as auditors, have cemented their social privileges on the basis of claims that their expertise mediates uncertainty and limits risks—to investors and markets as well as to employees and citizens— by preparing independent and objective, true and fair, accounts of corporate financial affairs. Auditors' knowledge claims are, however, precarious, not least because measures of revenues, costs, assets, liabilities and profits are all contested technically as well as politically and because capitalist economies are inherently prone to crises (O'Connor 1987). As a consequence, claims to expertise are frequently punctured by unexpected corporate collapses, frauds, and failures. For example, Lehman Brothers, America's fourth largest investment bank, received an unqualified audit opinion on its annual accounts on 28 January 2008, followed by a clean bill of health on its quarterly accounts on 10 July 2008. However, by early August it was experiencing severe financial problems and filed for bankruptcy on 14 September 2008 (Sikka 2008*c*). Such events fuel the suspicion that auditors lack the requisite independence or the expertise to check on the 'truth' and 'fairness' of company accounts. The severest problem for accounting firms is that when auditing reports are seen to fail, auditors face financial claims from other fractions of capital—investors and creditors—on the grounds that their losses are, in part, attributable to auditor negligence or incompetence. If successful, such claims reduce surpluses payable to partners as they erode both the financial and symbolic capital invested in accounting firms. Rather than leaving the resolution of such disputes to market forces or private prosecutions for damages, firms have sought to mobilize elements of the state to de/regulate the form, organization and liability of auditing firms.

As our brief overview implies, the regulation of auditor liability is a complex and contested matter. Processes of regulation face competing pressures from fractions of capital and from sections of civil society. The picture is even more complex as, in the case of auditor liability, accounting firms and especially their partners, for whom the form of regulation has direct implications for the security and expansion of their wealth, their accountability and taxation, may take differing positions on the balance of anticipated benefits and disadvantages, symbolic as well as material. The content and dynamic of the regulatory regime is, accordingly, a product of financial and political as well as ideological resources that are institutionalized and mobilized by the various protagonists who have invested their roles in divergent discourses of regulation.

The UK state has a long history of sheltering capital through a variety of corporate, partnership and insolvency laws. The Limited Liability Act 1855 was a major development as it enabled entrepreneurs to limit their losses. During the Victorian era, accountants tended to operate as sole traders and partnerships (Brown 1905), either because they were too small or found these structures most amenable for projecting an image of integrity, respectability and reliability, as well as providing a favourable basis of taxation. In the early twentieth century, there were debates about auditor liability, but auditors generally remained content with their position (Napier 1997). The Companies Act 1948 formally completed the qualified accountants' monopoly of the external audit function. Section 161(2) prohibited company auditors from trading through limited liability entities by stating that 'None of the following persons shall be qualified for appointment as auditor of a company...(3) a body corporate...'. In many ways, the legislation confirmed the favoured means of trading by accountants. Many traded as partnerships and 'joint and several' liability was established as the norm where partners were liable for their own and each others' negligence and omissions. This settlement began to come under strain as a process of consolidation and concentration—that is, the advance of monopoly capital—resulted in client companies becoming larger and auditors fearing greater financial liability from exposure from audit failures.

Since the 1970s, major accounting firms have campaigned to dilute their audit liability to shareholders and other stakeholders (Cousins et al. 1999). In the mid-1980s, the state responded by granting a number of liability concessions. Section 310 of the Companies Act 1985, as amended by Section 137 of the Companies Act 1989, enabled companies to buy insurance for its Directors and Officers, which included auditors. The Companies Act 1989 granted auditing firms the right to limit their partners' liability by trading as limited liability companies. Auditing firms received a further boost to their claims for limiting liability from the UK House of Lords' judgement in *Caparo Industries plc vs. Dickman & Others [1990] 1 All ER HL 568*. This judgement established that, in general, auditors owed a 'duty of care' only to the company, as a legal person, and not to any individual shareholder or creditor. The UK government additionally enhanced the protection afforded to accountants and other advisors through the concept of 'contributory negligence' (UK Law Commission 1993). This enabled auditors to argue that the negligence of other parties (e.g. directors and bankers) contributed to the damages suffered by plaintiffs and therefore that the damages against them should be correspondingly reduced. Nevertheless, despite these concessions, major auditing firms wanted to minimize their responsibilities or 'exposure', and therefore campaigned for full proportional liability and a 'cap' (Likierman 1989; Big Eight 1994).

Accounting Firms, Globalization, and Offshore Financial Centres

By the early 1990s, some UK firms began considering the possibility of forming Limited Liability Partnerships (LLPs) to shield their partners from lawsuits (*Accountancy*, December 1994: 23). This was encouraged by developments in the United States where some states offered LLPs to accountants and other professionals in order to limit their liability (Alberta Law Review 1998). In the mid-1990s, a report commissioned by the UK government (UK Department of Trade and Industry 1996) was poised to reject some of the liability concessions demanded by accounting firms. At this time, Ernst & Young and Price Waterhouse (now part of PricewaterhouseCoopers) had, coincidentally enough, hired a London law firm, at a cost of nearly £1 million, to draft a Limited Liability Partnership (LLP) Bill that would shield partners from liability lawsuits. The government of Jersey (part of the Channel Islands) had been approached by these firms; and its leading politicians had promised to 'fast track' the law (*Financial Times*, 26 September 1996: 7). It was reported that those politicians had declared themselves to be 'fighting for the City of London's business, and we are doing this to prove we can enact legislation which is in the interest of fast-moving corporations' (*Accountant*, August 1996: 1).

Once the seriousness of the two accounting firms' intent had been clearly signalled, they moved to demand equivalent liability concessions from the UK government. Ratcheting up the pressure, they stated that if their demands were not met they would leave the United Kingdom[4] and trade through LLPs in Jersey (*Financial Times*, 24 July 2006: 9). Ernst & Young reportedly 'threatened to move its [UK] headquarters to Jersey' (*Guardian*, 8 November 1996: 21). This was perhaps the first time that accounting firms had enrolled the law-making powers of a smaller state (Jersey) to squeeze, or perhaps hammer, concessions from a larger state.

---

[4] The campaign was also supported by 25 other professional groups (*Financial Times*, 17 April 1996: 8).

Why Jersey?

The choice of Jersey, a UK Crown Dependency, is unsurprising for a number of reasons. Though geographically closer to France, Jersey's main official language is English. With a population of 89,000, it is only 100 miles (160 km) south of mainland Britain and has established connections with the City of London. Its currency, the Jersey pound, is tied to the value of sterling. Yet, Jersey is neither part of the United Kingdom nor a member of the European Community (EC). As part of its accession to the EC, the United Kingdom negotiated a special status (Protocol 3) which enables its Crown Dependencies to trade favourably with the EC, but without adopting any of its laws or obligations (Plender 1990). Under the evolved constitutional arrangements, the UK government is responsible for their defence and international relations and ultimately for their 'good government' (*Hansard*, House of Commons Debates, 3 June 1998: cols. 471 and 465; 27 January 1997: col. 33).

In common with other states, Jersey can use its lawmaking powers to protect or privilege the position of elite groups—powers that extend not only to sheltering capital but also to enacting legislation intended to shield accounting firms from liability lawsuits. Since the 1960s, policies have been pursued to establish Jersey as an OFC as a means of supplementing its traditional economy based on agriculture and tourism (Hampton 1996; Hampton and Abbott 1999). In common with other OFCs, Jersey has sought to attract business by offering low/no tax, light regulation and business confidentiality.[5] So light is its regulatory touch that it led the Organisation for Economic Co-operation and Development (2000) to describe Jersey as a 'harmful' tax haven. It had also been criticized by the UK government (UK Home Office 1998) for the absence of independent regulation of the financial sector, inadequate consumer protection laws and lack of complaints investigation procedures. Notably, limited liability entities registered in Jersey are not required to publish audited financial statements. The very success of such policies has made Jersey highly dependent on financial services and correspondently vulnerable to capital

---

[5] Its light regulation had drawn criticisms from international regulators. For example, the New York Assistant District Attorney investigating frauds at the Bank of Credit and Commerce International (United States' Senate Committee on Foreign Relations 1992; Arnold and Sikka 2001) complained that,

My experience with both Jersey and Guernsey has been that it has not been possible for US law enforcement to collect evidence and prosecute crime. In one case we tracked money from the Bahamas through Curacao, New York and London, but the paper trail stopped in Jersey and Guernsey.... It is unseemly that these British dependencies should be acting as havens for transactions that would not even be protected by Swiss bank secrecy laws. (*Observer*, 22 September 1996: 19)

flight. Perversely, if also predictably, Jersey has found itself exposed to the very forces that, as a tax haven, it has sought successfully to harness. Jersey has, in some circles, acquired a reputation for offering its 'legislature for hire' (Hampton and Christensen 1999). At any rate, it has sought to diversify its economy by offering LLP legislation with the hope that 'its implementation in due course would encourage leading accounting and solicitors firms to be registered in Jersey…' (*Accountant*, November 1996: 5).

Doing Business with an OFC

We have noted how the development of LLP legislation in Jersey was stimulated by the interest of UK-based accounting firms rather than from any firm located in Jersey. The proposed legislation had to be scrutinized by the Jersey parliament whose institutional structures present their own challenges. The 53 part-time members of Jersey's single chamber of parliament are directly elected by the public. Members of parliament meet for about 3–7 days a month and generally lack the organizational resources and political will to scrutinize the executive effectively. In the absence of political parties, it is extremely difficult to develop a coherent programme of reform let alone to subject the executive to close examination. The difficulties are compounded by weak local trade unions, a lack of pressure groups and a media that rarely questioned government policies. Indeed, until, the late 1990s, the Island's main newspaper, *Jersey Evening Post*, was owned by a leading politician. Before 2005,[6] Jersey did not have a formal cabinet, prime minister, chief minister, or president. The island was governed by series of Committees (e.g. education, health, housing, finance and economics, etc.), each chaired by a president, which performed the functions normally associated with government ministries. A report reviewing Jersey's machinery of government noted that 'many decisions are taken by a small number of Committee members, perhaps only the president, or by the chief officer under delegated powers, and that other members are passengers, perhaps voluntarily, or perhaps because they are starved of information necessary for them to make informed decisions, or perhaps because they are overwhelmed by the masses of paperwork prepared for their meetings' (States of Jersey 2000: para. 4.2.7). Prior to 2005, almost all the legislators were members of one or more committees and thus effectively members of the government. There were no equivalents of the US Senate hearings or the UK Parliamentary Select Committees to scrutinize legislation, government policy, or the executive. During the 1990s, there was

---

[6] For post-2005 reforms, see States of Jersey (2000, 2005).

not even an official written record of parliamentary debates on major Bills. There was, and is, no official opposition in the Jersey parliament; and it is exceptional for members of one committee to criticize another. In short, given the combination of physical location, economic dependence, and political disorganization, it is not difficult to appreciate why an OFC with Jersey's profile would be attractive to accounting firms seeking help in extracting limited liability concessions from the UK government.

Networks have been found to be central to facilitating the mobility of capital (McCahery and Picciotto 1995) and their role was not insignificant in the Jersey case. In pursuit of their strategies of enlisting the Jersey 'sprat' to catch the UK 'mackerel', Price Waterhouse and Ernst & Young hired Ian Greer Associates, a prominent political lobbying firm with considerable connections with Jersey policymakers (*Observer*, 6 October 1996: 1). As early as 6 June 1995, Mr. Ian James, a partner in the Jersey law firm of Mourant du Feu & Jeune, had met the Director of Jersey's Financial Services Department (JFSD) to discuss the proposals developed by a London law firm, Simmons & Simmons, acting on behalf of Price Waterhouse and Ernst & Young. The Director of JFSD subsequently discussed the proposal with senior politicians and law officers (Sikka 2008b). After further informal discussions, Messrs Mourant du Feu & Jeune formally wrote to the President of the Jersey's Finance & Economics Committee on 19 October 1995. The 5-page letter (for an extended extract see Cousins et al. 2004: 28–9) stated,

My firm has been working with the UK partnership of Price Waterhouse (PW) and English solicitors, Slaughter and May, to find a method of obtaining some limited liability protection for the partners' personal assets without completely restructuring PW's business . . . the most favoured solution would be the introduction of Special Limited Partnership Law in Jersey which would give the partners of a partnership registered under that law limited liability whilst permitting them to take part in the management of the Special Limited Partnership. . . . PW's objective therefore is to find a means by which its partnership can have limited liability whilst retaining the characteristics of a partnership. . . . *PW's executive are satisfied that Jersey has all the necessary characteristics which makes it a suitable jurisdiction in which to register their UK partnership if appropriate legislation was passed by the States within the course of the next year.* . . . We are therefore seeking support of your Committee for the introduction of a Special Limited Partnership Law in Jersey during 1996. We appreciate that this is a very short time scale and that there are many other legislative matters which have a high priority for the States of Jersey. We would therefore propose that, based on a draft law prepared by Mr. David Goldberg QC for PW, this firm in close co-ordination with the Financial Services Department, will work with PW and Slaughter and May in order to prepare a draft law for consideration by your Committee during December this year with a view to it being debated in the States in January/February 1996. We would also propose that we would prepare any necessary subordinate legislation required in connection with the Special Limited Partnership Law... my firm is also instructed by the UK partnership of Ernst & Young... if the Committee is willing to proceed with this proposal that the States of Jersey's PR firm, Shandwicks, are instructed to coordinate the publicity together with PW's own PR people. (emphasis added)

This letter formally set Jersey's legal processes in motion. On 11 December 1995, the States of Jersey announced that the Finance and Economics Committee was working to introduce LLP legislation. Price Waterhouse and Ernst & Young announced that they were cooperating with the Jersey authorities to draft a new partnership law (*Accountancy Age*, 14 December 1995: 1 and 3). The Jersey government was assured that the law drafting work would be undertaken entirely at the expense of Price Waterhouse and Ernst & Young (Sikka 2008*b*). The level of secrecy surrounding the draft law was reflected in the way that Jersey's Law Society, which traditionally comments on draft laws, was initially denied the opportunity to comment, though subsequently it was given a very short period to do so.

On 21 May 1996, Jersey finally published a much delayed 62-page draft Bill on LLPs (Limited Liability Partnerships [Jersey] Law 199). The Bill diluted the principle of 'joint and several' liability and individual partners would not be personally liable for the liabilities of the LLP unless they actually caused the loss in the course of their work. The key features of the LLP Bill were that it required LLPs to have only a registered office address in Jersey. In this way, they could benefit from the LLP legislation without an agent or a partner operating in Jersey. The LLPs only needed to file an annual return and there was no need to publish audited accounts. Firms registering as LLPs could conduct audit, insolvency, financial services (as regulated in the United Kingdom by the Companies Act 1985, Insolvency Act 1986, and the Financial Services Act 1986), and any other kind of business. In Jersey, there was no dedicated regulator and no policies or procedures for investigating the conduct of errant auditors. LLPs registered in Jersey were to be exempt from all corporate/income taxes. The Jersey government reportedly hoped to levy £10,000 for an initial LLP registration and £5,000 annually thereafter (*Accountant*, August 1996: 1).

In line with Jersey's normal legislative processes, senior politicians expected the Bill to be passed quickly and quietly. Unexpectedly, it encountered resistance and delay (see Cousins et al. [2004] and Sikka [2008*b*] for some details) and became 'one of the most turbulent political debates in living memory' (*Financial Times*, 26 September 1996: 7). A senior partner of Price Waterhouse expressed dismay at this turn of events,

Earlier in the year [1996], we were roundly assured that the draft law would go to the States of Jersey Parliament in March/April, be nodded through, spend the summer with the Privy Council and be back in Jersey in time to be implemented in the statute book by September. Well, here we are in September and the Jersey Parliament is still arguing over its details. (*Accountancy*, September 1996: 29)

The LLP law was eventually passed on 24 September 1996, followed by a further delay of nearly 2 years (in May 1998) before the insolvency provisions were enacted and an Ernst & Young senior partner announced that, 'Having worked closely with the States of Jersey and Price Waterhouse to bring about the LLP law, we are pleased to see it finally being enacted' (*Accountancy Age*, 29 May 1998: 1).

During the 3-year period (1995–8), Ernst & Young and Price Waterhouse continued to ratchet up the pressure on the UK government with threats to move their operations from the United Kingdom to Jersey (e.g., see, *Financial Times*, 8 December 1995: 1 and 15; *The Times*, 14 December 1995; *Financial Times*, 25 September 1996: 11; *Accountancy*, November 1996: 19; *Accountancy Age*, 4 July 1996: 1; 12 December 1996: 3, 23 April 1998: 3; *Accountancy Age*, 28 May 1998: 1; 4 June 1998: 9;). The impact of these threats was, however, dampened by doubts about the feasibility of their implementation. For it is unlikely that the firms could have relocated their operations from the United Kingdom without major ramifications for tax, employment, and contractual matters (Sikka 1996; Sikka 2008*b*). Nonetheless, the threats to move to Jersey were interpreted by commentators as 'a cosh with which to threaten the [UK] government if it fails to come up with a workable LLP law' (*Financial Times*, 11 June 1998: 11). Price Waterhouse and Ernst & Young 'argued behind the scenes that the move to Jersey was a stick to beat the then Tory government and Labour opposition into agreeing that a UK-wide LLP Law was necessary. If that failed, they were serious about a move...PW insiders say it still wants a UK LLP law and the threat of the Jersey move is still a good stick to beat them with' (*Accountancy Age*, 4 June 1998: 9).

Of particular note, the extended media exposure of the limited liability issue had the potential to damage claims that the UK state favoured business-friendly policies. It is probable that this served to concentrate the minds of politicians. At one stage, the UK government promised equivalent legislation 'within a week' (*Financial Times*, 28 June 1996: 22; 24 July 1996: 9) and then 'at the earliest opportunity' (*Hansard*, House of Commons Debates, 7 November 1996: col. 617). A consultation document on creating limited liability partnerships was issued (UK Department of Trade and Industry 1997) followed by a Bill (in 1998), parliamentary scrutiny (in 1999 and 2000) and an Act[7] (Limited Liability Partnerships Act 2000) which came into existence on 6 April 2001. The UK legislation[8] was 'warmly welcomed'

---

[7] The history of the UK LLP legislation is yet to be written.
[8] There are some differences between the Jersey and UK LLPs (for further details, see Sikka 2008*b*).

by Price Waterhouse (*Accountancy*, December 1998: 124) and an Ernst & Young senior partner claimed the credit for these developments:

It was the work that Ernst & Young and Price Waterhouse undertook with the Jersey government...that concentrated the mind of UK ministers on the structure of professional partnerships....The idea that two of the biggest accountancy firms plus, conceivably, legal, architectural and engineering and other partnerships, might take flight and register offshore looked like a real threat...I have no doubt whatsoever that ourselves and Price Waterhouse drove it onto the government's agenda because of the Jersey idea. (*Accountancy Age*, 29 March 2001: 22).

What, then, of the take-up of LLPs in Jersey? On 28 November 2000, the President of Jersey's Finance and Economics Committee told parliament that 'At the time the law was passed, there were reasonable grounds for supposing that the registration of LLPs could bring substantial benefit to Jersey. In the event, despite the passage of the legislation, no LLP has been registered' (*Jersey Evening Post*, 29 November 2000). The Jersey 'sprat' had served its purpose now that the UK 'mackerel' had been landed.

SUMMARY AND DISCUSSION

The state is at once a powerful sponsor and a prime target of the dynamic forces of capitalism and globalization. It underpins property rights, commands a monopoly of the means of violence and is at the centre of processes of contestation and settlement that are more or less conducive to capital retention, attraction, and accumulation. The relationship between (fractions of) capital and the (elements of) the state is complex and certainly not fixed. In the United Kingdom, accounting firms and accounting bodies have been adept at mobilizing the state to secure and expand markets for their services and to shield them from critical public scrutiny relating to allegations of audit failures and money laundering (Sikka and Willmott 1995; Mitchell et al. 1998). Not only are these firms and bodies formed 'in the context of government regulation' but, as our case study of auditor liability has shown, they have 'continued to flourish in that context' (Hopwood 1985: 13). Notably, accountants have repeatedly secured concessions by diluting the redress available to injured stakeholders without any equivalent *quid pro quo* (i.e. without increasing auditor obligations or widening the scope of company audits). Through a 'mutual intertwining with the modern conception of the State', accounting bodies and firms have helped cement the UK state's reputation for providing business-friendly policies, and these concessions have boosted accounting firm surpluses and shielded their partners from lawsuits.

In the case examined in this chapter, leading accounting firms seized upon a convenient OFC, in the form of Jersey, as a lever with which to exert pressure upon the UK government to yield liability concessions. This case indicates how the global regulatory landscape is being altered by the growing indirect, as well as direct, use of OFCs. More broadly, it illustrates how OFCs are significant nodes in the global economy where their unchecked expansion and accessibility exerts comparatively veiled as well as more overt effects upon the regulative capacities of larger states. A significant impact of OFCs is upon the ability of states to track and tax flows of capital which, in turn, reduces the revenues available for spending on public goods, such as health and education. Our case study has shown how the existence of a welcoming OFC enabled accounting firms, as a fraction of capital, to press the UK state for a favourable recalibration of the balance of the risks and rewards pertaining to liabilities arising from their audit business. Persistent lobbying, backed by a substantial (£1 million) investment in a threatened transfer of business out of the United Kingdom, has had the desired effect of preserving and enhancing the rewards flowing the accounting firms as liability risks previously privatized within partnerships have become socialized through their transfer to every taxpayer.

REFERENCES

Alberta Law Review. (1998). Limited liability partnerships and other hybrid business entities. *Alberta Law Review.* Edmonton: Alberta Law Reform Institute.

Arnold, P., and Sikka, P. (2001). Globalization and the state–profession relationship: The case of the Bank of Credit and commerce International. *Accounting, Organizations and Society,* 26(6), 475–99.

Bhagwati, J. (2004). *In Defense of Globalization.* Oxford: Oxford University Press.

Big Eight. (1994). *Reform of Auditor Liability.* London: Coopers & Lybrand.

Brown, R. (1905). *A History of Accounting and Accountants.* Edinburgh: T.C. and E.C. Jack.

Chiapello, E. (2007). Accounting and the birth of the notion of capitalism. *Critical Perspectives on Accounting,* 18(3), 263–96.

Cousins, J., Mitchell, A., and Sikka, P. (1999). Auditor liability: The other side of the debate. *Critical Perspectives on Accounting,* 10(3), 283–311.

——————(2004). *Race to the Bottom: The Case of the Accountancy Firms.* Basildon: Association for Accountancy & Business Affairs.

Donaghy, M., and Clarke, M. (2003). Are offshore financial centres the product of global markets? A sociological response. *Economy and Society,* 32(3), 381–409.

Drezner, D.W. (2001). Sovereignty for sale. *Foreign Policy,* September/October, 76–7.

Dunleavy, P., and O'Leary, B. (1987). *Theories of the State: The Politics of Liberal Democracy.* Macmillan: London.

Elliott, L., and Atkinson, D., (2008). *The Gods that Failed.* London: The Bodley Head.

Gramsci, A. (1971). *Selections from Prison Notebooks.* London: Lawrence and Wishart.

Hampton, M.P. (1996). *The Offshore Interface: Tax Havens and Offshore Finance Centres in the Global Economy.* Macmillan: Basingstoke.

—— and Abbott, J.P. (1999). *Offshore Finance Centres Tax Havens.* Macmillan: Basingstoke.

—— and Christensen, J. (1999). A legislature for hire: The capture of the State in Jersey's offshore finance centre. In M.P. Hampton, and J.P. Abbott (eds.), *Offshore Finance Centres and Tax Havens: The Rise of Global Capital.* Basingstoke: Macmillan.

Harvey, D. (2000). *An Introduction to Neo-liberalism.* Oxford: Oxford University Press.

—— (2006). *Limits to Capital.* London: Verso.

Hirst, P., and Thompson, G. (1996). *Globalization in Question: The International Economy and the Possibilities of Governance.* Cambridge: Polity Press.

Hopwood, A. (1985). Accounting and the domain of the public: Some observations on current developments, Pricewaterhouse public lecture on accounting. University of Leeds. Reprinted in A.G. Hopwood, *Accounting from the Outside.* London: Garland.

Hutton, W. (1999). *The Stakeholding Society.* Cambridge: Polity Press.

IMF(International Monetary Fund). (2000). *Offshore Financial Centres: IMF Background Paper.* Washington, D.C.: IMF.

Jessop, B. (1990). *State Theory: Putting the Capitalist State in its Place.* Cambridge: Polity.

—— (2002). *The Future of the Capitalist Sstate.* Cambridge: Polity.

Klimecki, R., and Willmott, H. (2008). From the demutualization to meltdown: A tale of two wannabe banks. *Working Paper, Cardiff University Business School.*

Likierman, A. (1989). *Professional Liability: Report of the Study Teams.* London: HMSO.

McCahery, J., and Picciotto, S. (1995). Creative lawyering and the dynamics of business regulation. In Y. Dezalay, and D. Sugarman (eds.), *Professional Competition and Professional Power: Lawyers, Accountants and the Social Construction of Markets.* London: Routledge, 238–74.

Mitchell, A., Sikka, P., and Willmott, H. (1998). Sweeping it under the carpet: The role of accountancy firms in moneylaundering. *Accounting, Organizations and Society,* 23(5/6), 589–607.

Napier, C.J. (1997). Intersections of law and accountancy: Unlimited auditor liability in the United Kingdom. *Accounting, Organizations and Society,* 22(8), 831–42.

Naylor, R.T. (1987). *Hot Money and the Politics of Debt.* London: Unwin Hyman.

O'Connor, J. (1987). *The Meaning of Crisis: A Theoretical Introduction.* Oxford: Basil Blackwell.

OECD (Organisation for Economic Co-operation and Development). (2000). *Towards Global Tax Co-operation: Progress in Identifying and Eliminating Harmful Tax practices.* Paris: OECD.

Ohmae, K. (1995). *The End of the Nation State: The Rise of Regional Economies.* New York: The Free Press.

Oxfam. (2000). *Tax Havens: Releasing The Hidden Billions for Poverty Eradication.* London: Oxfam.

Palan, R. (2002). Tax havens and the commercialization of state sovereignty. *International Organization*, 56(1), 151–76.

—— Abbott, J., and Deans, P. (1996). *State Strategies in the Global Political Economy*. London: Pinter Press.

Plender, R. (1990). The protocol, the Bailiwicks and the Jersey cow. In R. Plender (ed.), *Legal History and Comparative Law*. London: Frank Cass.

Robinson, W.I. (2004). *A Theory of Global Capitalism: Production, Class and State in a Transnational World*. Baltimore: John Hopkins Press.

Saul, J.R. (2005). *The Collapse of Globalism and the Reinvention of the World*. London: Atlantic Books.

Sikka, P. (1996). Auditors' rocky road to Jersey. *The Times*, 4 July, 30.

—— (2008a). Enterprise culture and accountancy firms: New masters of the universe. *Accounting, Auditing and Accountability Journal*, 21(2), 268–95.

—— (2008b). Globalization and its discontents: accounting firms buy limited liability partnership legislation in Jersey. *Accounting, Auditing and Accountability Journal*, 21(3), 398–426.

—— (2008c). Accounting for the auditors. *Guardian* (Comment is Free). Available online at http://www.guardian.co.uk/commentisfree/2008/sep/18/marketturmoil. economics (as seen on 18 September).

—— and Willmott, H. (1995). Illuminating the state–profession relationship: Accountants acting as Department of Trade and Industry investigators, *Critical Perspectives on Accounting*, 6(4), 341–69.

—— —— and Lowe, T. (1989). Guardians of knowledge and public interest: Evidence and issues of accountability in the UK accountancy profession. *Accounting, Auditing and Accountability*, 2(2), 47–71.

States of Jersey. (2000). *Report of the Review Panel on the Machinery of Government in Jersey (Clothier Committee Report)*. St. Helier: States of Jersey.

—— (2005). *A Guide to Ministerial Government in Jersey*. St. Helier: States of Jersey.

Stiglitz, J.E. (2002). *Globalization and Its Discontents*. London: Penguin.

UK Department of Trade and Industry. (1996). *Feasibility Investigation of Joint and Several Liability*. London: HMSO.

—— (1997). *Limited Liability Partnership: A New Form of Business Association for Professions*. London: HMSO.

UK Home Office. (1998). *Review of Financial Regulation in the Crown Dependencies* (The Edwards Report). London: The Stationery Office.

UK Law Commission. (1993). *Contributory Negligence as a Defence in Contract*. London: HMSO.

Wallerstein, I. (1996). The interstate structure of the modern world-system. In S. Smith, K. Booth, and M. Zalewski (eds.), *International Theory: Positivism and Beyond*. Cambridge: Cambridge University Press.

Bibliography of Anthony Hopwood's Writings

'The Relationship Between Accounting and Personnel Management—Past Conflicts and Future Potential', *Personnel Review* (1972).

'An Empirical Study of the Role of Accounting Data in Performance Evaluation', *Empirical Research in Accounting: Selected Studies* (1972, Supplement to *Journal of Accounting Research*).

'Management Control, Accounting and Accountants', Parts I and II, *Certified Accountant* (September and October 1972; co-authored).

An Accounting System and Managerial Behaviour (Saxon House (UK) and Lexington (USA), 1973).

'Problems with Using Accounting Information in Performance Evaluation', *Management International Review* (1973).

'Leadership Climate and the Use of Accounting Data in Performance Evaluation', *The Accounting Review* (July 1974).

'Corporate Finance and Management Accounting', in K.D.C. Vernon (ed.),*Use of Management and Business Literature* (Butterworth, 1975).

'Budgetary Control of Salaries and Wages', in T. Lupton and A. Bowey (eds.), *Handbook of Salary and Wage Systems*, (Gower Press, 1975; 2nd edn., 1982; 3rd edn., 1989).

Accounting and Human Behaviour (Accountancy Age Books (UK), 1974, and Prentice-Hall (USA), 1976).

'Behavioural Research on Accounting: An Overview of an Overview', *Accounting Journal* (1977).

'Information Systems for Matrix Organizations', in K. Knight (ed.), *Matrix Management* (Saxon House, 1977).

'Accounting and Organizational Behaviour' in B. V. Carsberg and A. Hope (eds.), *Current Issues in Accounting* (Philip Allan, 1977; 2nd edn, 1984).

'Towards an Organizational Perspective for the Study of Accounting and Information Systems', *Accounting, Organizations and Society* (1978).

'A Bibliography of the French Social Accounting Literature', *Accounting, Organizations and Society* (1978).

'*Social Accounting: The Way Ahead?*' *Social Accounting* (Chartered Institute of Public Finance and Accounting, 1978. Reprinted in *Foretage Sociala Ansvar Och Social Redovisning* (Stockholm), 1978).

'Criteria of Corporate Effectiveness', in M. Brodie and R. Bennett (eds.),*Managerial Effectiveness* (Thames Valley Regional Management Centre, 1979).

'Towards the Economic Assessment of New Forms of Work Organization', in C. L. Cooper and E. Mumford (eds.), *The Quality of Working Life in Western and Eastern Europe* (Associated Business Books, 1979).

'Economic Costs and Benefits of New Forms of Work Organization', *New Forms of Work Organization*, Vol. 2 (International Labour Office (Geneva), 1979).

'Towards Designing Management Accounting Systems for the Support of New Concepts on Enterprise Accountability', in N. Bjorn-Andersen (ed.), *The Human Side of Information Processing* (North Holland, 1980).

'The Organizational and Behavioural Aspects of Budgeting and Control', in J. Arnold, B. Carsberg, and R. Scapens (eds.), *Topics in Management Accounting* (Allen, 1980).

'Social Accounting', *Public Finance and Accountancy* (September 1980).

'A Discussion of Some Inner Contradictions in Management Information Systems and the Behavioural Implications of Planning and Control Systems', in H. Peter Holzer' (ed.), *Symposium on Management Accounting*, (The Center for International Education and Research in Accounting, 1980).

'The Roles of Accounting in Organizations and Society', *Accounting, Organizations and Society* (1980) (with 4 co-authors; reprinted in N. Macintosh and T. Hopper, *Accounting, The Social and The Political: Classics, Contemporary and Beyond*, Elsevier, 2005).

'The Development of Accounting in its International Context: Past Concerns and Emergent Issues', *A Historical and Contemporary Review of the Development of International Accounting* (Atlanta, 1980; with Stuart Burchell and Colin Clubb).

'Accounting Research: An Academic Perspective', *Proceedings of the Centenary Conference of the Institute of Chartered Accountants in England and Wales* (1980).

'From Management Information to Information Management', in H. Lucas (ed.), *The Information Systems Environment* (North Holland, 1981; with Michael Earl. Reprinted in B. Langfors, A. A. Verrijn-Stuart, and G. Bracchi editorss, *Trends in Information Systems*, North-Holland, 1986; also reprinted in E. K. Somogyi and R. D. Galliers, *Towards Strategic Information Systems*, Abacus Press, 1987).

"A Message from Mars"—and other Reminiscences from the Past', *Accountancy* (October 1981; with S. Burchell and C. Clubb).

Essays in British Accounting Research (Pitman, 1981; co-edited with Michael Bromwich).

'Commentary on "The Study of Accounting History"', in M. Bromwich and A. G. Hopwood (eds.), *Essays in British Accounting Research* (Pitman, 1981).

'La Contrabilidad Social en El Reino Unido', *El Balance Social de la Empresa Y Las Instituciones Financieras* (Banco de Bilbao, 1982; with S. Burchell).

'Value for Money: Practice in Other Countries', *Value for Money Audits* (Royal Institute of Public Administration, 1982).

'Chaired Report', *Economics and Working Conditions: Methodological Aspects* (European Foundation for the Improvement of Living and Working Conditions, 1982).

'Some Thoughts on Information and the Structural Organization of Companies', Proceedings of the 5th Annual Conference of the Association of Information Officers in the Pharmaceutical Industry (1982).

'Issues Facing Auditing Research in the UK', in A. G. Hopwood, M. Bromwich and J Shaw (eds.), *Auditing Research: Issues and Opportunities* (Pitman, 1982; with Michael Bromwich).

Auditing Research: Issues and Opportunities (Pitman, 1982; with Michael Bromwich and Jack Shaw).

Accounting Standard Setting: An International Perspective (Pitman, 1983; with Michael Bromwich).

'Some Issues in Accounting Standard Setting: An Introductory Essay', in M. Bromwich and A. G. Hopwood (eds.), *Accounting Standard Setting: An International Perspective* (Pitman, 1983; with Michael Bromwich).

'On Trying to Account for Accounting', in M. Bromwich and A. G. Hopwood (eds.), *Accounting Standard Setting an International Perspective* (Pitman, 1983).

'On Trying to Study Accounting in the Context in which it Operates', *Accounting, Organizations and Society* (1983).

'Evaluating the Real Benefits', in H. J. Otway and M. Peltu (eds.), *New Office Technology: Human and Organizational Aspects* (Francis Pinter, 1983).

European Contributions to Accounting Research (Free University of Amsterdam Press, 1984; with Hein Schreuder).

Issues in Public Sector Accounting (Philip Allan, 1984; with Cyril Tomkins).

'Accounting Research in the United Kingdom', in A. G. Hopwood and H. Schreuder (eds.), *European Contributions to Accounting Research* (Free University of Amsterdam Press, 1984; with Michael Bromwich).

'Accounting and the Pursuit of Efficiency', in A. G. Hopwood and C. Tomkins (eds.), *Issues in Public Sector Accounting* (Philip Allan, 1984. Reprinted in J. Guthrie, L. Parker, and D. Shand (eds.), *The Public Sector: Contemporary Readings in Accounting and Auditing* (Harcourt Brace Jovanovich, 1990; R. Hodges (ed.), *Governance and the Public Sector*, Edward Elgar, 2005).

'Emerging Patterns of Management Accounting Research', in R. Lister, D. Otley, and R Scapens (eds.), *Management Accounting, Organizational Theory and Capital Budgeting* (Macmillan, 1984; with Michael Bromwich).

'The Tale of a Committee that Never Reported: Disagreements on Intertwining Accounting with the Social', *Accounting, Organizations and Society* (1985).

'Accounting and the Economic Future', *Accountancy* (September 1985; with Michael Page).

'The Development of Worrying about Management Accounting', in K. B. Clark, R. H. Hayes, and C. Lorenz (eds.), *The Uneasy Alliance: Managing the Productivity—Technology Dilemma* (Harvard Business School Press, 1985).

'Accountancy and Social Development in the UK', *Accountancy* (November 1985; with Michael Page).

'Accounting in its Social Context: Towards a History of Value Added in the United Kingdom', *Accounting, Organizations and Society* (1985; with Stuart Burchell and Colin Clubb. Reprinted in R. H. Parker and B. S. Yamey (eds.), *Accounting History: Some British Contributions*, Clarendon Press, 1994).

Accounting and the Domain of the Public: Some Observations on Current Developments. The Price Waterhouse Public Lecture on Accounting, (University of Leeds, November 1985. Reprinted in J. Guthrie, L. Parker, and D. Shand (eds.), *The Public Sector: Coutemporary Readings in Accounting and Auditing*, Harcourt Brace Jovanovich, 1990).

'Planning for the Profession in the Longer Term', *Accountancy* (January 1986; with Michael Page).

'Financing Change', ACI for the Implementation of New Technologies course, (The Open University, 1986, audio cassette re-released 1995).

Research and Current Issues in Management Accounting (Pitman, 1986; with Michael Bromwich).

'Economics and the Regime of the Calculative', *Developing the Socially Useful Economy* (Centre for Alternative Industrial and Technological Systems, 1984. Largely reprinted in S. Bodington, M. George, and J. Michaelson, *Developing the Socially Useful Economy*, Macmillan, 1986).

'The Future of the Professional Firm', *Accountancy* (May 1986; with Michael Page).

'Management Accounting and Organisational Action: An Introduction', in M. Bromwich and A. G. Hopwood (eds.), *Research and Current Issues in Management Accounting* (Pitman, 1986).

'The Future of the Accountant in Industry', *Accountancy* (September 1986; with Michael Page).

'The Future of IT and the Accountant', *Accountancy* (January 1987; with Michael Page).

'Accounting and Gender: An Introduction', *Accounting, Organizations and Society* (1987).

'The Archaeology of Accounting Systems', *Accounting, Organizations and Society* (1987. Reprinted in N. Macintosh and T. Hopper (eds.), *Accounting, The Social and The Political: Classics, Contemporary and Beyond*, Elsevier, 2005).

'Accounting and Organizational Action', in B. E. Cushing (ed.), *Accounting and Culture* (American Accounting Association, 1987. An earlier draft was published in J. Kinnunen (ed.), *Proceedings of the International Symposium on Recent Developments in Business Management Research*, Helsinki School of Economics, 1986; translated into Chinese as Paper #7 of the Beijing Centre for Investment Order, 2003).

'Future Scenarios for the Profession', *Accountancy* (August 1987; with Stuart Turley).

'The Future of Accounting Standards', *Accountancy* (September 1987; with Michael Page).

'Accounting History's Claim to Legitimacy', *International Journal of Accounting Education and Research* (1987; with Tom Johnson).

'The Generality and the Specificity of the Accounting Craft: Some Observations on Grounding an Understanding of Accounting in the Contexts in which it Operates', in M. Domsch, F. Eisenfuhr, D. Ordelheide, and M. Perlitz (eds.), *Unternehmungserfolg: Planung, Ermittlung, Kontrolle* (Gabler, 1988).

'Changing Roles on the City Stage', *Accountancy* (June 1988; with Michael Page).

'Production and Finance: The Need for a Common Language', *New Manufacturing Imperatives* (Axiom, 1988).

Accounting from the Outside: The Collected Papers of Anthony G. Hopwood (Garland, 1988).

Accounting Research and Accounting Practice: The Ambiguous Relationship Between the Two, the Deloitte, Haskins & Sells Accounting Lecture (University College of Wales, Aberystwyth, 1988).

International Pressures for Accounting Change (Prentice-Hall, 1989).

'Accounting and the Pursuit of Social Interests', in W. F. Chua, E. A. Lowe, and A. G. Puxty (eds.), *Critical Perspectives in Management Control* (Macmillan, 1989).

'Behavioural Accounting in Retrospect and Prospect', *Behavioural Research in Accounting* (1989).

'Organisational Contingencies and Accounting Configurations' in B. Freidman and L. Ostman (eds.), *Accounting, Development—Some Perspectives* (Stockholm School of Economics, 1989).

Understanding Accounting in a Changing Environment (Prentice-Hall, 1990; with M. Page and S. Turley).

The Future of Accounting Harmonisation in the Community. Report prepared for the European Commission and presented to the Intergovernmental Conference on the Future of Harmonisation of Accounting Standards within the European Community (1990).

Public Sector: Contemporary Readings in Accounting and Auditing (Harcourt Brace Jovanovich, 1990).

'Ambiguity, Knowledge and Territorial Claims: Some Observations on the Doctrine of Substance Over Form', *British Accounting Review* (1990).

'Harmonisation of Accounting Standards within the EC: A Perspective for the Future', *The Future of Harmonisation of Accounting Standards within the European Communities* (Commission of the European Communities, 1990).

The Mutual Recognition of Financial Statements. A report prepared for the Working Group on Accounting Standards (OECD, 1991).

Accounting and the Law (Prentice-Hall, 1992; with Michael Bromwich).

'The Intertwining of Accounting and the Law', in M. Bromwich and A. G. Hopwood (eds.), *Accounting and the Law* (Prentice-Hall, 1992; with M. Bromwich).

'Accounting Calculation and the Shifting Sphere of the Economic', *European Accounting Review* (1992).

'Discussion', in J. Fingleton (ed.), *The Internationalisation of Capital Markets and the Regulatory Response* (Graham and Trotman, 1992).

Accounting as Social and Institutional Practice (Cambridge University Press, 1994; with Peter Miller; Japanese translation, 2004).

'Accounting and Everyday Life: An Introduction', *Accounting, Organizations and Society* (1994).

'Value Added Accounting and National Economic Policy', in A. G. Hopwood and P. Miller (eds.), *Accounting as Social and Institutional Practice* (Cambridge University Press, 1994; with S. Burchell and C. Clubb).

'Reflections on the Harmonization of Accounting in the European Union', *European Accounting Review* (1994).

'Making Visible and the Construction of Visibilities: Shifting Agendas in the Design of the Corporate Report', *Accounting, Organizations and Society* (1996).

'Looking Across Rather than Up and Down: On the Need to Explore the Lateral Processing of Information', *Accounting, Organizations and Society* (1996).

'Probing Further into Auditing and its Consequences: An Introduction', *Accounting, Organizations and Society* (1996).

'On Forging an Academic Accounting Community', in I. Lapsley (ed.), *Essays in Accounting Thought* (Institute of Chartered Accountants of Scotland, 1996).

'Opening Comments' and 'Closing Comments', in M. J. Mumford and M. J. Page (eds.), *Trying Again* (ACCA, 1999)

'The United Kingdom', in S. McLeay (ed.), *Accounting Regulation in Europe* (McMillan, 1999; with H. Vieten).

'Strategy and Information: Time to Look Out', *Mastering Management Review* (November 1999).

'Understanding Financial Accounting Practice', *Accounting, Organizations and Society* (Vol 25, No. 8, November 2000).

'Creating a Community: The Establishment and Development of the European Accounting Association', *European Accounting Review* (Vol 11, No. 1, 2002, pp. 33–41).

"If Only there Were Simple Solutions, But there Aren't": Some Reflections on Zimmerman's Critique of Ittner and Larcker', *European Accounting Review* (Vol 11, No. 4, 2002).

The Economics and Politics of Accounting: International Perspectives on Research Trends, Policy and Practice (Oxford University Press, 2004; with Christian Leuz and Dieter Pfaff; Paperback edition, 2005).

'Afterword', in P. Gagliardi and B. Czarniawska, *Management Education and Humanities* (Edward Elgar, 2006).

Handbook of Management Accounting Research (Vols 1 and 2 (Elsevier, 2007); Vol 3 (2008; with Chris Chapman and Michael Shields).

'Whither Accounting Research?' *The Accounting Review* (Vol 82, No. 5, October 2007, pp. 1365–74).

'Operating at the Interface Between the Local and the International: An Appreciation of the Contributions of Kari Lukka', in M. Granlund (ed.), *Total Quality in Academic Accounting; Essays in Honour of Kari Lukka* (Turku School of Economics, 2007, pp. 9–11).

'The Role of Business Schools in the Process of University Reform', in C. Mezza and P Quattrone (eds.), *European Universities in Transition: Issues, Models and Cases* (Edward Elgar, 2007).

'Changing Pressures on the Research Process: On Trying to Research in an Age When Curiosity is Not Enough', *European Accounting Review* (Vol 17, No 1, 2008, pp. 87–96).

'Taking the European Accounting Review Forward', *Newsletter of the European Accounting Association* (March 2008).

'Making the Environment Visible', *Newsletter of the European Accounting Association* (September 2008).

'A Conversation with Anthony Hopwood', *Economic Sociology* (Vol. 10, No. 1, November 2008, pp. 21–8).

'Management Accounting Research in a Changing World', *Journal of Management Accounting Research* (2008).

'The Rankings Game: Reflections on Devinney, Dowling and Perm-Ajchan, *European Management Review* (Vol 5, No. 4, Winter 2008, pp. 209–14).

'On Striving to Give a Critical Edge to Critical Management Studies', in M. Alvesson, T. Bridgman, and H. Willmott (eds.), *The Oxford Handbook of Critical Management Studies* (Oxford University Press, 2009).

Index

ABB, 78
Abbott, A., 55, 371, 373
Abbott, J. P., 397, 402, 406
Abernathy, W., 267
Accountancy Age journal 410
Accountancy journal, 410–11
Accountant journal, 405, 409
accounting: actor network theory (ANT) and, 17, 34–35, 44; anticipating change and, 35–38; associational governance and, 53–55; behavioural, 6–7 (*see also* behavioural accounting); budgets and, 6–7; characterizing accounting in action and, 68–73; classical conceptions of, 4–7; controller agency and, 233–55; derivative products and, 259–87; differing forms of, 68; eclipse of professionalism in, 367–89; ethnographies of, 16–17; everyday practices in, 30–45; experimental, 116–33; future issues and, 20–22; Generally Accepted Accounting Principles (GAAP) and, 206, 226–27, 303, 309, 337, 341, 345–46, 356; governing economic life and, 18–20; heterogeneity and, 71–72; importance of context and, 2, 30; increasing complexity and, 8–9; innovation and, 112–33; as institutional practice, 9–11 (*see also* institutions); instrumental rationality and, 5–6; intentionality and, 31–35, 44, 55; internal/external reporting and, 11–12; internationalization of, 48–62, 324–38 (*see also* globalization); as intervention, 351–52, 354–56; management vs. financial, 11–12 (*see also* management accounting); methodologies in studying, 11–12; myth structures and, 12–14; new international financial architecture (NIFA) and, 207–12, 216–24; non-state environment and, 324–38; obscure functions and, 38–41; offshoring and, 48, 396–412; as organizational practice, 9–11 (*see also* organizations); partnership practices and, 37–38; performance measurement and, 13–14; periodizing and, 9–11; practice theory and, 32–41 (*see also* practice theory); as representation, 351–52, 354–56; scientific quantification of,

315–22; as social phenomenon, 4–7, 10 (*see also* social theory); standards and, 341–61 (*see also* standards); tripartite schema of, 1–4
Accounting, Auditing and Accountability Journal, 1n1
Accounting, Organizations and Society journal: earnings management and, 292; founding of, 125–26, 130, 259; Hopwood and, 10, 30, 65–71, 125–30, 259, 321–22; influence of, 126; innovations of, 125–27; research conferences associated with, 127–29
Accounting Advisory Forum, 178
Accounting and Human Behaviour (Hopwood), 119, 122
accounting choice: behavioural accounting and, 290–311; definitions for, 291; distinguishing motives in, 306–8; earnings management and, 290–311; experiment role in, 293–94; financial reporting and, 290–311, 356–58; future research directions for, 308–11; Generally Accepted Accounting Principles (GAAP) and, 303; institutions and, 356–58; problematization and, 349–54; regulation and, 294–305; surveys and, 293–94
'Accounting in Its Organizational Context' (conference), 128
Accounting journal, 1n1
Accounting Professionalism-They Just Don't Get It (Wyatt), 369
Accounting Review, The, 122
Accounting Standards Steering Committee, 345
Activity Based Costing (ABC) system, 168–69, 234
actor network theory (ANT), 17; aesthetic spacing and, 152; controller agency and, 235–36, 238, 250; field concept and, 183–98; financial reporting and, 359–60; governance and, 199–200; Hopwood and, 124–25; management accounting and, 71–74; old vs. new, 193–94; practice theory and, 34–35, 44; regulatory activism and, 176–83; social space and, 152; standard-setting and, 359
Adler, P. S., 3n3
aesthetic spacing, 151–52

Haber, S., 389
Habermas, J., 16, 69
habitus, 39–40
Hackenbrack, K., 299
Hacking, 2
Hadmo, T., 177
Hahn, C. K., 90
Haire, M., 165n3
Hakansson, H., 89–90
Hale, T. N., 209
Hall, L., 165
Hall, P., 331, 373
Halmos, P., 389
Halskan, O., 90
Hampton, M. P., 397, 402, 406
Hancké, R., 331
Handfield, R. B., 89, 92
Hanlon, G., 16, 53
Hansen, A., 71
Hansen, M., 149
Hanson, J., 137
Harvey, D., 137, 335, 399
Haskell, T. L., 373, 388
Haskins, M., 374
Haslam, J., 206–7
Hassard, J., 34
Hatfield, H. R., 344
Hayden, Cori, 277n17
Hayes, D. C., 8
Hays, S., 388
Healy, P. M., 290, 293, 295, 308
Hechter, M., 327
Heckscher, C., 235
hedge funds, 260n1, 263, 280
Hedges, L. V., 236
Hedmo, T., 183, 194
Hegarty, J., 52
Held, D., 207
Helper, S. R., 89
help gap, 116
Hernes, T., 157
Hesfort, J., 126
Hillier, B., 137
Hilmer, F. G., 89
Hindess, B., 348
Hines, R. D., 355n4, 373
Hinings, C. R., 50
Hirsch, P. M., 14
Hirshleifer, D., 296n4, 309
Hirst, D. E., 296, 309
Hirst, P., 50, 399
Hoberman, S., 90
Hodgson, D., 235

Hoffman, Dick, 117
Hofstede, G. H., 7, 234
Hogler, R., 357
Hollingsworth, J. R., 50–51, 53
Hood, C., 178, 180, 386
Hope, A., 346, 348
Hopkins, P. E., 296
Hopper, T., 15, 36, 137, 233–34
Hopwood, Anthony, 11, 320; *Accounting, Organizations and Society* journal and, 10, 30, 65–71, 125–30, 259, 321–22; audits and, 205–9, 218–25; background of, 117; budgetary information and, 7; communication channels and, 118–24; context and, 71, 73; controller agency and, 233–35; derivation and, 259, 265, 284; everyday accounting and, 30–31, 34–35, 43, 45; experimental accounting and, 117–33; field-based research and, 121–22; financial accounting and, 324–28, 331–37; forms of accountings and, 68; globalization and, 48–49, 52, 56, 324, 328, 332, 335, 337–38, 396, 398, 411; governance issues and, 175, 177–78, 192, 205–9, 218–25; heterogeneity and, 71–72, 77–78; historic constellations and, 18; importance of context and, 2, 30; influence of, 61, 65–68, 121–22; as innovator, 112, 117–33; interpersonal network of, 124–25; manageable objects and, 157, 170; management accounting and, 71, 74, 76–77, 80–81, 112, 117–33; non-state accounting and, 324–28, 331–37; organization theory and, 117, 137; personal interaction and, 124–25; professionalism and, 375; regulation effects and, 290; research publications of, 118–24; social space and, 152–53; spread of costing and, 19; standard-setting and, 352, 354n3; University of Chicago and, 117
Horngren, C. T., 346
Hoskin, K. W., 14, 33, 386
hospitals, 17, 21, 122, 143, 356, 386
Houston, R., 300
human capital, 144–45
Human Resources Management, 164–67, 171–72
Humphrey, Christopher, 205–32, 329, 374
Hunt, H., 357
Hunton, J. E., 296–97, 299, 303–7, 310
Hussein, M., 347–48
Hutchby, I., 217n15
Hutton, W., 400

Public Company Accounting Oversight Board (PCAOB), 214, 219
Public Interest Oversight Board (PIOB), 215–16
Public Oversight Boards (POBs), 213–16
Puro, M., 347
Puxty, A. G., 14, 16, 149, 324, 347

Quack, S., audits and, 208; non-state environment and, 329, 332, 334, 336; transnational dynamics and, 176–77, 181, 192, 194, 196
Quattrone, P., 36, 137, 152, 233
Quinn, J. B., 89

Radcliffe, V. S., 33, 35
Rahman, Z., 210
Raman, A., 90
Ramboll, 78
Rappaport, A., 116n3, 137, 346–47
Rauterberg, M., 138
Rayport, J., 98
Reagan, Ronald, 59
Reed, M., 373
regulation: accounting choice and, 294–305; activism and, 176–83; asset valuation and, 367–68; audits and, 205–23; bubbles and, 182; consequential incrementalism and, 181–83; earnings management and, 290–311; environmental, 177–79, 194; fair-value accounting and, 367–68; field-concept and, 183–98; financial reporting and, 295–99; Financial Stability Forum (FSF) and, 211–12, 215, 224–25; Generally Accepted Accounting Principles (GAAP) and, 206, 226–27, 303, 309, 337, 341, 345–46, 356; globalization and, 324–38 (*see also* globalization); golden era of, 175; institutional dynamics and, 186–98; International Accounting Standards Board (IASB) and, 59, 177–78, 194, 206, 208, 221, 225–26, 326, 332–37; International Financial Reporting Standards (IFRS) and, 48, 177, 206, 212, 220–21, 226; *Lex Mercatoria* and, 326–27; multi-level dynamics and, 183–86; multipolarity and, 180–81; new international financial architecture (NIFA) and, 207–12, 216–24; offshoring and, 396–412; professionalism and, 367–89; public oversight boards (POBs) and, 213–14; Sarbanes-Oxley Act and, 180, 214, 219, 225, 300–5, 369; Securities and Exchange Commission

(SEC) and, 13, 177, 206, 213, 215, 227, 300–1, 329, 371, 373, 377; self-regulation and, 213–14, 219, 368–76, 380–85, 388; soft, 178–80; standards-surveillance-compliance system and, 60; stock market crash of 1929 and, 55; transnational dynamics and, 175–200; transparency and, 21, 49, 56, 60, 62, 168, 181–82, 189, 209–11, 225, 244, 270, 276, 296–98, 309, 316, 320; Washington Consensus and, 209–10, 212, 223
regulatory activism: consequential incrementalism and, 181–83; environmental issues and, 177–79; governance and, 176–83; soft regulation and, 178–80
Regulatory Liaison Group, 221
Regulatory Working Group, 220
Reiter, S. A., 149
Report of the Working Group on Transparency and Accountability, 210–11
Report on the Observance of Standards and Codes (ROSC) programme, 52–53, 212
research: accounting choice and, 290–311; armchair, 117; audits and, 205–9; challenge of engagement and, 65–81; citations and, 126, 129–30; communication channels and, 114–15, 118–24; conferences and, 127–29; controller agency and, 233–55; critique of, 73–76; derivative products and, 259–87; diffusion of innovation and, 112–33; earnings management and, 290–311; elitism and, 114; field-based, 121–22; financial reporting and, 342–47, 359–61; Golden Age of, 344; Hopwood's call for deeper, 10, 30, 65–71; income theory and, 342–47; journals and, 114–15; networking and, 124–25; personal interaction and, 124–25; professionalism and, 367–69; social theory and, 137 (*see also* social theory); U.S. case study in, 116–33
results gap, 116, 131
Revsine, L., 347
Reyniers, D., 90
Richardson, J., 89
Richelstein, 126
Ricol, René, 214
Ridgway, V., 6
Rights of Man (Paine), 379
Robe, J.-P., 337
Roberts, J., 17, 34–35
Roberts, R., 374
Robertson, R., 137